PACIFIC SYMPOSIUM ON BIOCOMPUTING 2023

PACIFIC SYMPOSIUM ON BIOCOMPUTING 2023

Kohala Coast, Hawaii, USA,
3 – 7 January 2023

Edited by

Russ B. Altman
Stanford University, USA

Lawrence Hunter
University of Colorado Health Sciences Center, USA

Marylyn D. Ritchie
University of Pennsylvania, USA

Tiffany Murray
Stanford University, USA

Teri E. Klein
Stanford University, USA

World Scientific

NEW JERSEY • LONDON • SINGAPORE • BEIJING • SHANGHAI • HONG KONG • TAIPEI • CHENNAI • TOKYO

Published by

World Scientific Publishing Co. Pte. Ltd.

5 Toh Tuck Link, Singapore 596224

USA office: 27 Warren Street, Suite 401-402, Hackensack, NJ 07601

UK office: 57 Shelton Street, Covent Garden, London WC2H 9HE

Online ISSN: 2335-6936
Print ISSN: 2335-6928

British Library Cataloguing-in-Publication Data
A catalogue record for this book is available from the British Library.

BIOCOMPUTING 2023
Proceedings of the Pacific Symposium

ISBN 978-981-127-061-1 (ebook)
ISBN 978-981-127-060-4 (print)

PRECISION MEDICINE: USING ARTIFICIAL INTELLIGENCE TO IMPROVE DIAGNOSTICS AND HEALTHCARE

WORKSHOPS

ERRATUM

PACIFIC SYMPOSIUM ON BIOCOMPUTING 2023

2023 marks the 28th Pacific Symposium on Biocomputing (PSB). We once again expect to be on the Big Island in person with a recognizably "normal" PSB. Our community depends on annual face-to-face interactions to revitalize our work and catalyze progress in the field. As we turn our attention to the ongoing challenges to biology, the environment and health, we continue to see exploding opportunities for computation. In the US, the President has established an ambitious and well-funded Advanced Research Project Administration for Health (ARPA-H) with a mission of speeding progress in research related to health. Other efforts are emerging in synthetic biology, neuroscience, sustained efforts against cancer (e.g. the Cancer Moonshot program), the federation of biobanks, future pandemic preparedness, and many other areas. Computation is central to the success of all these efforts—sometimes this is obvious to their leadership, but at other times our community must demonstrate the power and impact of our technologies and capabilities. PSB is one wonderful forum for assessing the ability of our field to respond to the major challenges facing our society.

In addition to being published by World Scientific and indexed in PubMed, the proceedings from all PSB meetings are available online at http://psb.stanford.edu/psb-online/. PSB has 1298 papers listed in PubMed (as of today). These papers are routinely cited in archival journal articles and often represent important early contributions in new subfields—many times before there is an established literature in more traditional journals; for this reason, many papers have garnered hundreds of citations.

The Twitter handle for PSB is @PacSymBiocomp and the hashtag for PSB 2023 is #PSB23.

The efforts of a dedicated group of session organizers have produced an outstanding program. The sessions of PSB 2023 and their hard-working organizers are as follows:

Digital health technology data in biocomputing: Research efforts and considerations for expanding access
Organizers: Michelle Holko, Chris Lunt, Jessilyn Dunn

Graph Representations and Algorithms in Biomedicine
Organizers: Brianna Chrisman, Cliff Joslyn, Maya Varma, Sepideh Maleki, Maria Brbic, Marinka Zitnik

Overcoming health disparities in precision medicine
Organizers: Kathleen Barnes, Carlos Bustamente, Francisco De La Vega, Chris Gignoux, Eimear Kenny, Rasika Mathias, Bogdan Pasaniuc

Precision Medicine: Using computation and artificial intelligence to improve healthcare and public health
Organizers: Steven E. Brenner, Jonathan Chen, Dana C. Crawford, Roxana Daneshjou, Łukasz Kidziński, David Ouyang, Michelle Whirl-Carrillo

SALUD: Scalable Applications of cLinical risk Utility and prediction
Organizers: Shefali S. Verma, Rachel L. Kember, Renae Judy, Marijana Vujkovic, Olivia J. Veatch, Yoson Park, Pankhuri Singhal, Yogasudha Veturi

Towards Ethical Biomedical Informatics
Organizers: Peter Y. Washington, Dennis P. Wall, Steven E. Brenner, Gamze Gürsoy, Nicholas P. Tatonetti

We are also pleased to present five workshops in which investigators with a common interest come together to exchange results and new ideas in a format that is more informal than the peer-reviewed sessions. For this year, the workshops and their organizers are:

Biomedical research in the Cloud: Options and factors for researchers and organizations considering moving to (or adding) cloud computing resources
Organizers: Michelle Holko, Nick Weber, Chris Lunt, Steven E. Brenner

Accessing clinical-grade genomic classification data through the ClinGen Data Platform
Organizers: Karen P. Dalton, Heidi L. Rehm, Matt W. Wright, Mark E. Mandell, Kilannin Krysiak, Lawrence Babb, Kevin Riehle, Tristan Nelson, Alex H. Wagner

High-Performance Computing Meets High-Performance Medicine
Organizers: Anurag Verma, Jennifer Huffman, Ali Torkamani, Ravi Madduri

Risk prediction: Methods, Challenges, and Opportunities
Organizers: Rui Duan, Lifang He, Ruowang Li, Jason H. Moore

Single Cell Spatial Biology for Precision Cancer Medicine
Organizers: Aaron Newman, Andrew Gentles

The PSB 2023 keynote speakers are Heidi Rehm (Science keynote) and Keolu Fox (Ethical, Legal and Social Implications keynote).

Tiffany Murray has managed the peer review process and assembly of the proceedings since 2001 and plays a key role in many aspects of the meeting. We are grateful for the support of the National Institutes of Health[1], ISCB, Cleveland Institute for Computational Biology, and Galatea Bio Inc. The Research Parasite Awards benefit from support from GigaScience, Jeff Stibel, Mr. and Mrs. Stephen Canon, and Drs. Casey and Anna Greene. The Research Symbiont Awards benefit from support from the Wellcome Trust and the DragonMaster Foundation.

We are particularly grateful to the PSB staff Al Conde, Paul Murray, Ryan Whaley, Mark Woon, BJ Morrison McKay, Cynthia Paulazzo, Kasey Miller, Michael Arsenault, Jackson Miller, Heather Miller, and Nicholas Murray for their assistance. We also acknowledge the many busy researchers who reviewed the submitted manuscripts on a very tight schedule. The partial list following this preface does not include many who wished to remain anonymous, and of course we apologize to any who may have been left out by mistake.

We look forward to a great meeting and to seeing you on the Big Island. Aloha!

Pacific Symposium on Biocomputing Co-Chairs,
October 13, 2022

Russ B. Altman
Departments of Bioengineering, Genetics, Medicine & Biomedical Data Science, Stanford University

Lawrence Hunter
Department of Pharmacology, University of Colorado Health Sciences Center

Marylyn D. Ritchie
Department of Genetics and Institute for Biomedical Informatics, University of Pennsylvania

Teri E. Klein
Departments of Biomedical Data Science & Medicine, Stanford University

Thanks to the Reviewers

We wish to thank the scores of reviewers. PSB aims for every paper in this volume to be reviewed by three independent referees. Since there is a large volume of submitted papers, paper reviews require a great deal of work from many people. We are grateful to all of you listed below and to anyone whose name we may have accidentally omitted or who wished to remain anonymous.

Monica Agrawal
Frank Wolfgang Albert
Raquel Aoki
Thibault Asselborn
Marzieh Ayati
Erman Ayday
Sergio Baranzini
Kathleen Barnes
Brittany Baur
Lew Berman
Tim Bigdelli
Miranda Bogen
Luca Bonomi
Philip Bourne
Maria Brbic
Douglas Brubak
Elizabeth Burton
William Bush
Tiffany Callahan
Daniel Cameron
Ruoyi Chai
Irene Chen
Yiqun Chen
Yong Chen
Brianna Chrisman
Sam Crowl
Peng Dai
Roxana Daneshjou
George Dasoulas
Francisco De La Vega
Alex Derry
Yi Ding
Rui Duan
Lee Eckhardt
Todd Edwards
Yasha Ektefaia
H. Robert Frost
Tian Ge
Judy Gichoya
Chris Gignoux
Jennifer Goldsack
Pelin Gundogdu
Greg Hampikian
Arif Harmanci
Bryan He
Huan He
Sharona Hoffman
Michelle Holko
Kangcheng Hou
Qiwen Hu
Kexin Huang
Xiayuan Huang
Yepeng Huang
Jennifer Huffman
Sean Irvine
Shantanu Jain
Azka Javaid
Alvin Jeffrey
Xiaoqian Jiang
Cliff Joslyn
Clara De Paolis Kaluza
Mingon Kang
Eric Kernfeld
Justin Kerr
Warren Kibbe
Lukasz Kidziński
Dokyoon Kim
Grace Kim
Harsha Kokel
Da (Kevin) Kuang
Tsung-Ting Kuo
William La Cava
Evgeniya Lagoda
Mike Lee
Binglan Li
Michelle Li
Ruowang Li
Yun Li
Mei Liu
Gaurav Luthria
Ann Manzardo
Raiska Mathias
Magdalena Matusiak
Melissa McCradden
Jason McDermott
Eric Meslin
Rachel Mester
Jason Miller
Hugh Mitchell
Shamim Mollah
Janitza Montalvo-Ortiz
Michael Moore
Victorine Muse
Yonghyun Nam
Minh Nguyen
Parsa Nowruzi
David Ouyang
Joe Park
Minolo Perera
Dragutin Petkovic
Matthew Pjecha
Davide Placido
Yannick Pouliot
Laralynne Przybyla
Ting Qi
Owen Queen
Laura Raffield
Elissa Redmiles
Brooke Rhead
Manuel Rivas
Frederick Roth
Sushmita Roy
Tanmoy Roychowdhury
Camilo Ruiz
Camilo Andres Ruiz
Katrin Sangkuhl
Laura Schultz

Matt Schwede
Yashoda Sharma
Arunan Skandarajah
Feng Song
Dan Sosa
Yu Sun
Eric Swirsky
Seth Temple
Kevin Thomas
Jeffrey Thompson
Jiayi Tong
Raul Torres
Alan Trinh
Vanessa Troiani
Artem Trotsyuk
Maya Varma
Amey Verdhula
Kailas Vodrohalli
Matt Walsh
Qingbo Wang
Junhao Wen
Michelle Whirl-Carrillo
Genevieve Wojcik
Kevin Wu
Ray Wu
Dong Xu
Duo Yu
Mert Yuksekgoul
Haoran Zhang
Kui Zhang
Xiang Zhang
Wenyu Zhou
Gen Zhu

[1]Funding for this conference was made possible (in part) by R13LM006766 from the National Library of Medicine. The views expressed in written conference materials or publications and by speakers and moderators do not necessarily reflect the official policies of the Department of Health and Human Services; nor does mention by trade names, commercial practices, or organizations imply endorsement by the U.S. Government.

Digital health technology data in biocomputing: Research efforts and considerations for expanding access

Michelle Holko

Google, Google Public Sector
Washington, DC 20001, USA
Email: michelleholko@google.com

Chris Lunt

National Institutes of Health
Bethesda, MD 20892, USA
Email: chris.lunt@nih.gov

Jessilyn Dunn

Biomedical Engineering, Duke University
Durham, NC 27708, USA
Email: jessilyn.dunn@duke.edu

Data from digital health technologies (DHT), including wearable sensors like Apple Watch, Whoop, Oura Ring, and Fitbit, are increasingly being used in biomedical research. Research and development of DHT-related devices, platforms, and applications is happening rapidly and with significant private-sector involvement with new biotech companies and large tech companies (e.g. Google, Apple, Amazon, Uber) investing heavily in technologies to improve human health. Many academic institutions are building capabilities related to DHT research, often in cross-sector collaboration with technology companies and other organizations with the goal of generating clinically meaningful evidence to improve patient care, to identify users at an earlier stage of disease presentation, and to support health preservation and disease prevention. Large research consortia, cross-sector partnerships, and individual research labs are all represented in the current corpus of published studies. Some of the large research studies, like NIH's *All of Us* Research Program, make data sets from wearable sensors available to the research community, while the vast majority of data from wearable sensors and other DHTs are held by private sector organizations and are not readily available to the research community. As data are unlocked from the private sector and made available to the academic research community, there is an opportunity to develop innovative analytics and methods through expanded access. This Session solicited research results leveraging digital health technologies, including wearable sensor data, describing novel analytical methods, and issues related to diversity, equity, inclusion (DEI) of both the underlying research data sets and the community of researchers working in this area. We particularly encouraged submissions describing opportunities for expanding and democratizing academic research using data from wearable sensors and related digital health technologies.

Keywords: digital health technologies; wearables; sensors; waveform data; time-series data; algorithms.

1. Background

Use of digital health devices has grown; in 2016, only 12% of Americans were estimated to regularly use a wearable digital health device, but by 2020, the estimation jumped to 21% [1]. Digital Health Technologies (DHTs), including wearable sensors like smart watches, have the potential to inform us about our health. But there are gaps in who has access to data and devices, who is performing the research, and therefore who the new technologies are poised to help. Reviews of the current landscape of DHT research studies in the National Center for Biotechnology Information (NCBI)'s Clinical Trials database (clinicaltrials.gov), and of studies published by the top-20 funded private sector DHT companies, highlight several patterns and limitations:

1. **Small sample size:** Aside from a few large studies, most of the published clinical trials utilizing DHT have been relatively small, and are largely under-powered. "Nearly half the studies - 829, or 46.5% - had less than 100 enrollees. Only 8% had more than 1,000 [2]."
2. **Narrow Health Focus:** The majority of published DHT studies focus on cardiometabolic health and mental health/wellness, while relatively little published research examines critical healthcare burden diseases like stroke, chronic obstructive pulmonary disease (COPD), and diabetes [2].
3. **Narrow Population Focus:** Of studies published by the top 20 funded DHT private-sector companies, the majority (72%) include only healthy volunteers, rather than high-risk populations with comorbid conditions [3]. The breadth and diversity of the study population(s), including socioeconomic, healthcare status, and racial diversity, may be the most critical component of building AI-based DHT algorithms. This diversity is lacking in current published research, likely leading to biased results [4]. The "bring your own device" model has been used by many research studies, but this design may result in biased selection of participants, and therefore biased results [5].
4. **Limited Outcome Assessments:** Only 15% of published DHT studies measured clinical effectiveness, and only in relation to the patient outcomes and did not evaluate healthcare cost or access to care [6]. As healthcare cost and access are two of the most pressing needs in healthcare, it is important to expand research to examine these outcomes.
5. **Insufficient Reporting and Data Publishing:** Importantly, not only is reporting in clinicaltrials.gov not required for observational DHT trials, there is also no public database for DHT data and algorithms. This complicates the ability to understand the full range of DHT "real world evidence" (RWE)-based research, and undermines research reproducibility and

validation. The lack of a consensus DHT database also means that DHT data curation, feature (e.g., digital biomarker) discovery, and algorithm development is limited to those who have data, which is largely the private sector DHT companies. One attempt to develop standardized pipelines and data repositories for digital health data, the Digital Health Data Repository as part of the Digital Biomarker Discovery Pipeline [7], developed by co-organizer Jessilyn Dunn's lab, is still not fully funded.

6. **Bridging the Regulatory Gap and Moving to Clinical Implementation:** Despite tremendous progress in DHT research and development, there is still a lot of work to be done along the research → regulatory → clinical implementation continuum. The *All of Us* Research Program is uniquely situated within NIH to interact with FDA colleagues and assist in developing regulatory standards for this new and uncharted territory. There is also a relatively new FDA Center for Digital Health Excellence, led by Bakul Patel. The Digital Medicine Society is a professional organization that has been working across sectors with the community to support innovation and standardization, in part via the Digital Health Measurement Collaborative Community (DATAcc) [8] and the Digital Health Playbook [9]. There is also a Digital Health Consortium, housed within the Office of the National Coordinator, for senior leaders within the federal government to convene across the digital health continuum.

The above limitations don't begin to address potential bias in algorithm development due to a limited pool of researchers interacting with these data. The purpose of this Session is to provide a forum for current research, address issues related to Diversity, Equity and Inclusion (DEI) in terms of the types of research and the researchers engaged, and ultimately to energize non-commercial research in the area. Our motivating question is how can this community work together to create more equitable research in the digital health tech space to benefit the research community and resulting impact?

2. Relevance to biocomputing

Digital health technologies, including wearable sensors, lend themselves well to biomedical and computational biology research since they generate continuous or near-continuous data streams ripe for machine learning and artificial intelligence (ML/AI) research. Algorithms developed for detecting anomalies and other biomedically-related phenomena in wearable sensor data are increasingly being incorporated into research and moving into clinical practice and other health adjacent applications. In past years of this conference, there has been good representation of a variety of data types, including genomics, imaging and clinical data sets; there has been limited coverage of wearable sensors and digital health technologies research.

The topic is timely for PSB 2023 since not only is there a growing use of wearable sensors in research, but also because there are potential DEI issues for both research data sets and researchers working with these data. Searching PubMed for the keyword "wearable" (Figure 1) shows exponential growth in the number of publications, with 701 in 2021. "Digital health" shows a similar trend (graph not shown) with 1,306 publications in 2021. Some of the journals and conferences that generally cover DHT research include Nature Digital Medicine, Lancet Digital Health, AMIA, and IEEE Biomedical and Health Informatics (BHI). Many of the conferences are more focused on the clinical aspects and clinical trials, and not as much on the computational biology or biomedical research aspects of DHT data analysis and algorithm development. There have also been a few cross-sector seminars recently to explore regulatory and other issues related to digital health technologies research, including this one in early 2020:
https://fnih.org/our-programs/biomarkers-consortium/digitalmonitoring

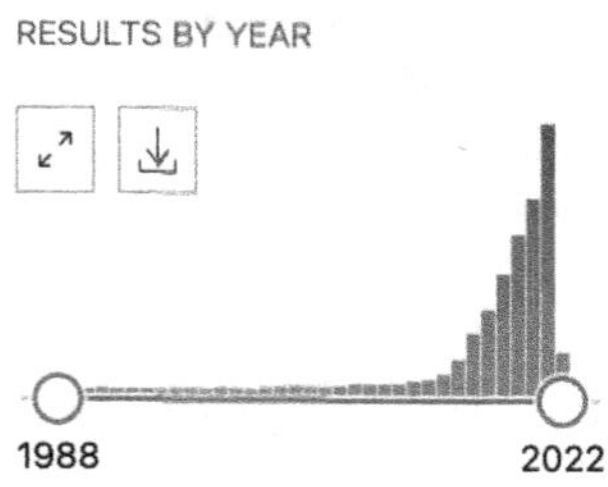

Fig. 1. Number of publications with "wearable" in PubMed from 1988-2021

This Session showcases recent research on digital health tech, DEI issues related to these data and research, and a discussion about what is needed to bridge these DEI gaps. The goal of this information sharing and discussion opportunity for participants and the community is to expand awareness and access to these data and tools, to enrich computational biology research, and bridge DEI gaps. The session also includes a range of voices from academia, government, and private sector. It's important to represent private sector voices in this discussion since much of the research is currently happening in tech companies developing digital health devices. Creating a forum for dialogue across sectors is important for bridging gaps in awareness and understanding, and encouraging more researchers to participate in developing computational methods and analysis of data from digital health tech.

The discussion will focus on key challenges facing the field, and participants are encouraged to contribute ideas to potential solutions and initiate lasting collaborations with researchers and communities in this area (e.g., the Digital Medicine Society). Further, participants will be exposed to cutting edge tools in this space with brief demos on how to use them, including the Digital Biomarker Discovery Pipeline (DBDP.org) [10], the Digital Health Data Repository, the *All of Us* Researcher Workbench, and others. The Session will also provide an opportunity to discuss as a community what is needed to truly enable cross-sector and expanded research for digital health technologies.

3. Session overview

The organizers will introduce the session, followed by a keynote from Eric Perakslis, the Chief Science and Digital Officer at the Duke Clinical Research Institute. He brings to the discussion his wide range of experience working on collaborative efforts in data science that spanned medicine, policy, engineering, computer science, information technology, and security, all from positions in academia, private sector, and the government.

There will then be a series of brief talks from the authors of the papers that were accepted for inclusion in the proceedings, and a panel discussion to include voices from industry and government. A moderated Q&A discussion will conclude the session. The talks are original research for publication, are widely varied, and include 1) comparing two wearable devices to augmenting prediction of mild cognitive decline using not only MRI but also language markers from speech, 2) a computational method for image segmentation of medical images, and 3) how fitbit data in the *All of Us* cohort can be used to improve upon current methods of predicting quality of life post-surgery.

The panel discussion will feature speakers from industry, including Ed Ramos and Julia Moore Vogel from Scripps Digital Trials Center and Care Evolution, Aaron Coleman, founder and CEO of Fitabase, Bakul Patel, currently at Google Health but the founding director of the FDA's Center for Digital Health Excellence, and Joshua Stein, Founder and Chief Growth Officer at Fitbit.

For the moderated Q&A discussion session all speakers, session organizers, and session attendees are welcomed to participate. The speakers and organizers represent a diverse set of perspectives across research efforts and related DEI issues. For both the talks and the panel, diversity and inclusion across gender, race and other factors are incorporated into the Session organization.

References

1. https://www.pewresearch.org/fact-tank/2020/01/09/about-one-in-five-americans-use-a-smart-watch-or-fitness-tracker/

2. https://jamanetwork.com/journals/jamainternalmedicine/article-abstract/2725079
3. https://www.healthaffairs.org/doi/full/10.1377/hlthaff.2018.05081
4. https://bmcmedicine.biomedcentral.com/articles/10.1186/s12916-019-1377-7
5. https://preprints.jmir.org/preprint/29510/accepted
6. https://www.healthaffairs.org/doi/full/10.1377/hlthaff.2018.05081
7. https://github.com/DigitalBiomarkerDiscoveryPipeline/Digital_Health_Data_Repository
8. https://datacc.dimesociety.org/
9. https://playbook.dimesociety.org/
10. https://pubmed.ncbi.nlm.nih.gov/33948242/

Detection of Mild Cognitive Impairment from Language Markers with Crossmodal Augmentation

Guangliang Liu[1], Zhiyu Xue[1], Liang Zhan[2], Hiroko H. Dodge[3], Jiayu Zhou[1,*]

[1]*Department of Computer Science and Engineering, Michigan State University, East Lansing, MI 48824, USA*

[2]*Department of Electrical & Computer Engineering, University of Pittsburgh, Pittsburgh, PA 15261, USA*

[3]*Department of Neurology, Massachusetts General Hospital, Harvard Medical School, Boston, MA 02129, USA*
Department of Neurology, Layton Aging and Alzheimer's Disease Center, Oregon Health & Science University, Portland, OR 97239, USA

[*] *Corresponding E-mail: jiayuz@msu.edu*

Mild cognitive impairment is the prodromal stage of Alzheimer's disease. Its detection has been a critical task for establishing cohort studies and developing therapeutic interventions for Alzheimer's. Various types of markers have been developed for detection. For example, imaging markers from neuroimaging have shown great sensitivity, while its cost is still prohibitive for large-scale screening of early dementia. Recent advances from digital biomarkers, such as language markers, have provided an accessible and affordable alternative. While imaging markers give anatomical descriptions of the brain, language markers capture the behavior characteristics of early dementia subjects. Such differences suggest the benefits of auxiliary information from the imaging modality to improve the predictive power of unimodal predictive models based on language markers alone. However, one significant barrier to the joint analysis is that in typical cohorts, there are only very limited subjects that have both imaging and language modalities. To tackle this challenge, in this paper, we develop a novel crossmodal augmentation tool, which leverages auxiliary imaging information to improve the feature space of language markers so that a subject with only language markers can benefit from imaging information through the augmentation. Our experimental results show that the multi-modal predictive model trained with language markers and auxiliary imaging information significantly outperforms unimodal predictive models.

Keywords: Mild Cognitive Impairment; Multi-modality Analysis; Crossmodal Augmentation

1. Introduction

Alzheimer's disease is the fifth-leading cause of death among individuals at age 65 and older.[1] A person with Alzheimer's will live through years of morbidity during the disease progression. Mild cognitive impairment (MCI) is the prodromal stage of Alzheimer's disease and serves as an important stage for early intervention and subject recruitment of cohort studies for understanding the disease and developing novel treatments.

There are extensive efforts on the identification of MCI and the associated markers. Because the progression of the disease is associated with structural changes in the brain,[2] the potential of detection from brain imaging of various types has been widely studied. Especially, magnetic resonance imaging (MRI) has provided a non-invasive way of examining the structure of the brain and tracking its changes. Studies have associated measurements from MRI with early-stage dementia.[3,4] The availability of a large amount of MRI data from Alzheimer's Disease Neuroimaging Initiative[5] largely facilitated the development of machine learning algorithms for detection.[6–8] Even though imaging markers from MRI are considered to be sensitive to early-stage MCI, the cost of MRI scans prevents them from being widely used for large-scale screening. The recent development of digital biomarkers, especially language markers, has shown promising sensitivity to detection of MCI.[9–14] For example, language markers can be used in conversational agents deployed on mobile devices or smart speakers to obtain a risk assessment of MCI.[9] However, the investigation of language markers is still in the early phase, where a critical issue is that the cohort sizes for studying language markers remain very limited,[15] demanding more data to unleash their power.

While imaging markers give anatomical descriptions of the brain, language markers capture the behavior characteristics of early dementia subjects. Such differences suggest the benefits of multi-modality analysis, where auxiliary information from the imaging modality can improve the power of accessible language markers further. However, one significant barrier to the multi-modality joint analysis is that in typical cohorts, there are only very limited subjects that have both imaging and language modalities. For example, in a cohort study from the I-CONECT clinical trial,[15] there are 40 subjects randomized for the experimental group for whom language makers (semi-structured conversations) are available. Yet among these subjects, there are only 16 subjects who have MRI scans available in the National Alzheimer's Coordinating Center (NACC) medical records. Typical multi-modality analysis approaches often require a substantial amount of data points that are shared or "aligned" across modalities to calibrate across different modalities and seek a common subspace,[16] and yet very few subjects in these cohorts can be used for existing multi-modality analysis. This results in a huge waste of collected data and often sub-optimal model performance due to insufficient sample size.

To tackle this challenge, in this paper, we developed a novel crossmodal augmentation tool, which leverages auxiliary imaging data to improve predictive modeling of language markers. Specifically, based on the language markers of a subject, the augmentation model constructs a feature embedding from the imaging domain by gauging its similarity with respect to other subjects and relating to the interconnection between two modalities. To achieve this, we introduced a model that learns to measure the consistency between any pair of language features and imaging features. The design of our model gives high sample efficiency, so that the learning can be done even when there are only a few subjects that have both modalities. During inference, the model assigns weights of existing imaging embedding for a given language embedding to construct the augmented features. We show in our empirical study that the proposed early MCI detection model, by augmenting language modality with constructed features from imaging information, significantly outperforms unimodal models and straightforward multi-modality models using aligned multi-modal data alone.

2. Related Works

Early Detection of MCI. Early detection of MCI is of great clinical importance and predictive models are built from a variety of data types, such as clinical information,[16] neuroimaging,[4,17] and, more recently, digital biomarkers.[12] Neuroimaging captures the structural information of the brain, and therefore imaging markers, especially from structural MRI,[17] have shown great sensitivity. Besides being non-intrusive, the cost of imaging markers is still prohibitive for large-scale screening of early dementia. Recent advances in digital biomarkers,[18] such as language markers, have provided an accessible and affordable alternative.[12] From the spontaneous speech, we can extract linguistic features (e.g., word preference, syntactic features, semantic features, data-driven word embedding) and acoustic information (e.g., MFCC).[11,12] It has been recently shown that combining acoustic features and linguistic features delivers an improved prediction performance.[12,13] The development of language markers is still in the very early phase, with limited data available for modeling. The analysis can benefit from more data from different data sources to deliver high predictive performance.
Multi-modality Learning. Multi-modality learning aims to characterize a concept (such as MCI) from different perspectives by using the complementary features from different modalities.[19] The paradigm has been widely used in biomedical and bioinformatics studies due to the ubiquitous need for joint analysis on multiple data modalities. Early fusion approaches fuse the features in the data/feature space and train a machine learning model based on the fused features. Late fusion approaches build independent models associated with an individual modality and produce the final classification score by combining the outcomes from each model. Most existing multi-modality approaches require the majority of data to be aligned across different modalities to learn the underlying connections among the modalities, which is the motivation of this work.
Feature Synthesis. Linear combination has been widely used in data analysis for synthesizing samples. SMOTE-based methods[20,21] alleviate the class imbalance problem by manually synthesizing new samples with linear combination in data space or feature space. Linear combination with Gaussian weights[22] is used to generate samples for biometrics tasks. More recently, MixUp-based methods[23,24] augment the training data using synthesized samples generated by linear combination, increasing performance and enhancing robustness.[25] Linearly synthesized T1 MRI features are shown to facilitate accurate attenuation correction maps.[26] We adopt linear combinations to construct features due to performance and computational efficiency.

3. Methods

3.1. *Data*

We use conversational data and imaging data from an ongoing clinical trial I-CONECT (Clinicaltrials.gov: NCT02871921)[a]. Briefly, this trial examines whether frequent conversational

[a]The data is available upon request at `https://www.i-conect.org/`.

engagement through video chats with standardized interviewers improves cognitive functions. Only the experimental group engages in frequent semi-structured conversations while the control group receives only 10 minutes of phone check-ins weekly. The recorded semi-structured conversation used among the experimental group (N=40) was utilized in the current analyses. Among these 40 subjects with available language markers, half of them are MCI, and the rest are cognitively normal (NL). For each subject, we randomly sample 15 individual conversational recordings and employ automatic speech recognition (ASR) to generate transcripts. Only the subjects' responses are used for analysis, the linguistic features are extracted over a whole transcript. Therefore there are 120 linguistic feature vectors as elaborated in the next subsection. For imaging data, we use the structural MRI data of 43 subjects from I-CONECT, where 26 of them are MCI, and 17 of them are cognitively normal. We extract variables from the T1-weighted (T1w) MRI data and diffusion MRI (dMRI) of each subject, and follow our previous work[17] to extract corresponding imaging features. Specifically, from T1w MRI we used the cortical volume and thickness measurements for 74 brain region-of-interests (ROIs) extracted by FreeSurfer. From dMRI we derived brain connectome network over 85 ROIs using Probtrackx tractography, following the protocol in Ref. 17. For each subject, we extracted the fiber counting feature among 85 ROIs. 16 subjects have both conversational recordings and MRI data, the others only have either imaging data or conversational data. And all subjects have clinical diagnoses (MCI or NL), which are determined according to the agreement of neurologists and neuropsychologists by referring to publicly available diagnostic criteria.[27]

3.2. *Language and Imaging Markers for Early Detection of MCI*

From raw speech data, we first translate the subjects' responses into text using Google ASR. From the text, we extract a comprehensive set of linguistic features from various levels of lexicon, syntax, and semantics. All features are extracted over the whole transcript. One example of lexical features is the average word length which measures the average number of letters to form a word. Syntactic features indicate how complex the syntactic structure of a sentence is. For example, the depth of syntactic tree counts the depth of a constituent syntax tree.[28] In terms of semantic features, we considered two kinds of features: local coherence and global coherence. Local coherence measures how the semantics of sentences change within the subject's responses to a question. We employ fasttext[29] to get the embedding representation of a sentence and calculate the cosine similarity between any two connective sentences. For the imaging data, we consider both T1w features and brain network features.[30] Mean/varaince statistics is available for all features, except those of LIWC word category and dMRI fiber count, are available. Because that the number of features is much larger than the sample size, which may easily lead to overfitting. We select features by stability selection,[17] 56 imaging features and 112 language features are reserved.

3.3. *Leverage Auxiliary Imaging Information in MCI Detection from Language Markers*

The goal of this paper is to augment the feature space of language markers utilizing complimentary information from the auxiliary imaging modality, and ultimately improve the predictive performance. In this way, all subjects with only accessible language markers in the future can benefit from performance improvements.

The early MCI detection from language data is formulated as a classification problem,[12] using language markers from a subject to predict the subject's clinical label. The proposed solution leverages the entire data available for training. The training data D_{train} includes a set of subjects that have language markers D_{lang} and another set of subjects that have imaging markers D_{img}. There are overlapped subjects that have both modalities, denoted by D_{align}, i.e., $D_{\text{train}} = \{D_{\text{lang}} \cup D_{\text{img}} \cup D_{\text{align}}\}$. A sample $(X_{\text{lang}}, X_{\text{img}}, Y) \in D_{\text{align}}$ has language markers X_{lang} and imaging markers X_{img}, and $Y \in \{0, 1\}$ is the clinical label such that 1 is MCI and 0 is cognitive normal (NL). We use the multi-modality training data D_{train} to learn a crossmodal augmentation model g_ω, parameterized by ω. Given any set of language markers $x_{\text{lang}} \in \mathbb{R}^{112}$, the model generates an augmented feature vector x_{aug} that has the same dimension as the imaging markers (56 in our study). We then train a classifier f, parameterized by θ, that takes the augmented features $[x_{\text{lang}}, x_{\text{aug}}]$ to predict the clinical label.

3.4. *Crossmodal Augmentation Model*

The key idea of the crossmodal augmentation model is to build a prediction model g_ω: given two modality vectors for a subject, one from imaging and one from language, the model g_ω predicts whether the two modality vectors are from the same subject. The foundation of the augmentation model has the same spirit as other multi-modality models, that is to capture the underlying connection between the pair modalities. During the inference, when the subject has only language modality (x_{lang}, y), the model g_ω is then used to assign weights to all available imaging feature vectors (from other subjects) to construct an augmented feature vector from $k-$highest predicted imaging features. The proposed crossmodal augmentation model can be extended to more than two modalities, and we leave the methodology extensions and their theoretical analysis to an extended version of this work.

The paired design allows us to construct a training dataset D'_{learning} for crossmodal augmentation model, which is the key to our sample efficiency. For each sample with both imaging and language features $(x_{\text{lang}}, x_{\text{img}}, y)$ in D_{align}, we randomly sample an image feature $d_{\text{img}} = (x'_{\text{img}}, y') \in D_{\text{img}}$ with the constraint that the label of D_{img} is different from that of d_{align}, to ensure that data modalities in manually created samples are not aligned. On the contrary, we create the aligned samples by randomly sampling imaging features with the same label to x_{lang}. The procedure creates two new samples $(x_{\text{lang}}, x_{\text{img}}, 1)$ and $(x_{\text{lang}}, x'_{\text{img}}, 0)$, where label 1 means aligned and 0 otherwise, to train the crossmodal augmentation model g_ω. Then a augmented training dataset D'_{aug} for classification model f_θ can be constructed by g_ω. Algorithm 1 summarizes the training procedure including the training the proposed crossmodal augmentation model g_ω and MCI detection model f_θ.

4. Experimental Results and Analysis

4.1. *Experimental settings*

In the experiment, we use the data of 83 subjects, where 40 of them have conversational recordings, 43 of them have imaging data, and only 16 subjects have both conversational

Algorithm 1 Learning of the Proposed Crossmodal Augmentation Model and MCI Detection Model

Input:

D_{align} - The training dataset for overlapped subjects that have both imaging data and language data; D_{img} - The training dataset for subjects that have imaging data; D_{lang} - The training dataset for subjects that have language data; k - The number of candidates considered for imaging feature synthesis.

Initialize:

$D'_{\text{learning}} = \varnothing$ - The training dataset for learning the crossmodal augmentation model; $D'_{\text{aug}} = \varnothing$ - The training dataset for learning the MCI detection model; g_ω - crossmodal augmentation model; f_θ - MCI detection model.

Procedure:

```
//Construct D'_learning
for (x_lang, x_img, y) ∈ D_align do
    randomly sample (x'_img, y') from D_img where y' = 1 − y
    append (x_lang, x_img, 1) and (x_lang, x'_img, 0) to D'_learning
//Learning ω
train g_ω with D'_learning
//Construct D'_aug
for (x_lang, y) ∈ D_lang ∪ D_align do
    initialize imaging feature synthesis dictionary D_syn = ∅
    for (x'_img, y') ∈ D_img do
        if p(y = 1|g_ω(x_lang, x'_img)) > 0.5 do
            update D_syn with {x'_img, p(y = 1|g_ω(x_lang, x'_img))}
    pick up samples with k largest values from D_syn as D_k
    get x_aug by weighted linear interpolation over D_k
    append (x_lang, x_aug, y) to D'_aug
//Learning θ
train f_θ on D'_aug
```

Output: f_θ.

recordings and imaging data. For each subject with conversational recordings, there are 15 transcripts used for data efficiency. For each experiment, we randomly sample 4 MCI subjects and 4 NL subjects from the 16 subjects with both data modalities as test data. We consider 100 different random train-test splits for each model and report the mean Area under the ROC curve (AUC), Accuracy, and F1 score on the test data. We adopt the elastic net regularized logistic regression[31] as our MCI detection model and employ a gradient-boosting decision tree as the crossmodal alignment model, with both implemented by the Python library scikit-learn.[32] To mitigate the influence of incorrect prediction from the crossmodal alignment model, we pick up a large number of subjects, e.g. 15, for imaging feature synthesis.

Our main goal is to augment language markers using imaging information and therefore evaluate the predictive performance of models learned with the augmented marker space

Table 1. MCI detection performance. Our method employs both data modalities and outperforms baseline models trained with only one data modality.

Models	Train Data Size	AUC	Accuracy	F1
MCI-Lang	32 subjects	0.80 ± 0.01	0.73 ± 0.07	0.71 ± 0.01
MCI-Img	35 subjects	$0.969 \pm 1e^{-6}$	$0.846 \pm 1e^{-11}$	$0.872 \pm 1e^{-11}$
Ours-Lang-AugImg	32 subjects	0.973 ± 0.001	0.848 ± 0.008	0.873 ± 0.004
Ours-Img-AugLang	35 subjects	0.98 ± 0.002	0.87 ± 0.005	0.89 ± 0.005

(Ours-Lang-AugImg). We also investigate a less practical setting, i.e., augmenting imaging markers using language information (Ours-Img-AugLang). We implement baseline models trained with only one data modality, the MCI-Lang model adopts language data and the MCI-Img model is learned with imaging data. The source code and experiment scripts are available at `https://github.com/illidanlab/XModalAug`.

4.2. *MCI Detection using Crossmodal Augmentation*

The MCI detection performance of baseline unimodality approaches and two crossmodal augmentation approaches is shown in Table 1. a) We see that for unimodality prediction settings, MCI-Img delivered an exceptional performance of 0.97 AUC. This confirms the power of neuroimaging. b) MCI-Lang yields an average of 0.8 AUC, showing the promise of the accessible digital biomarker. c) With the augmented variables from auxiliary imaging information, Ours-Lang-AugImg receives a striking performance gain to an AUC of 0.97, significantly outperforming the MCI-Lang and slightly outperforming MCI-Img. d) The best performer is Ours-Img-AugLang which uses the imaging markers as the main predictor, treats language markers are auxiliary information, and uses them to create augmented variables. The model has less practical usage due to the lack of accessibility of imaging markers, but the results confirm the benefits of joint analysis of imaging and language markers.

4.3. *Straightforward Multi-modal Model using Aligned Multi-modal Data*

In this section, we validate straightforward multi-modal prediction methods based on the small amount of aligned multi-modal dataset to show that our crossmodal augmentation method can effectively utilize large-sized partially-aligned multi-modal data. To fully explore the predictive power of multi-modal data, we implemented various multi-modal fusion methods: *ConFusion* concatenates imaging feature vector and language feature vectors, then feed the concatenated feature vector to the MCI detection model. *VotingAvgFusion* generates the mean prediction score of two individual classification models trained with language data and imaging data, respectively. *InterFusion* implements outer product operations on the language feature vector and the imaging feature vector. *InterConFusion* is a mix of ConFusion and InterFusion by concatenating the outer product of two feature vectors and the original feature vectors.

Table 2. The straightforward multi-modal MCI prediction with different multi-modality fusion methods based on linguistic features and imaging features. The ConFusion method that does not apply any fusion strategy outperforms other multi-modal fusion methods.

Models	**Train Data Size**	**AUC**	**Accuracy**	**F1**
VotingAvgFusion	8 subjects	0.51 ± 0.17	0.52 ± 0.15	0.63 ± 0.07
InterFusion	8 subjects	0.62 ± 0.05	0.56 ± 0.09	0.64 ± 0.07
InterConFusion	8 subjects	0.82 ± 0.08	0.71 ± 0.09	0.74 ± 0.08
ConFusion	8 subjects	0.84 ± 0.015	0.77 ± 0.009	0.78 ± 0.005

The performance of multi-modality fusion methods is shown in Table 2. ConFusion is the best performer. A possible hypothesis behind the results is that, since language markers are weaker predictors than imaging markers, and non-linear fusion methods (VotingAvgFusion, InterFusion and InterConFusion) may introduce noise to the imaging markers.

4.4. *Top Language Markers and Imaging Markers in Predictive Models*

We investigate important language and imaging markers identified by the predictive model, and also how the augmentation impacts these top markers in the model. On the language marker side, we extract the coefficients of our best MCI detection model trained with language data and calculate the feature importance by the absolute value of coefficients. The top 10 important language markers are listed in the first sub-table of Table 3. MCI subjects prefer personal pronouns like "we", "you", "I", but NL subjects take words related to space. An interesting finding is that MCI subjects tend to use long phrases, but NL subjects often prefer long verb phrases. The syntactic feature "coexistence of adverb phrase, verb phrase, and noun phrase" has the highest importance, which means a single sentence contains at least one adverbial phrase, one verb phrase, and one noun phrase. Constructing a sentence with a complex syntactic structure can be more challenging for MCI subjects, which is also shown by previous study.[33] Moreover, the word length is effective in detecting MCI since MCI subjects are more likely to use words containing fewer letters. Also, MCI subjects' expressions are not as coherent as those of NL subjects. The middle section of Table 3 shows top imaging markers extracted from the MCI detection model trained with imaging data. The feature name column represents a particular attribute of a given brain region, and the function column highlights the specific function of that brain region. We see that top-ranked feature variables are exclusively from T1-weighted MRI.

After applying crossmodal augmentation, we now have a set of auxiliary variables available, in addition to the original language markers we input to the augmentation model. Note that the augmented variables have one-one correspondence to imaging markers, and yet they do not necessarily possess the meaning. In this section, we show how top-ranked feature variables changed in the predictive models after using the augmented feature space. The bottom section of Table 3 shows the top markers in the model using augmented language markers. We

Table 3. High-impact feature variables in predictive models. Note that the prefix AUG means augmented feature variables from the Ours-Lang-AugImg model, the names after AUG show the correspondent feature names in imaging marker but they are not actual imaging features. coeff represents the logistic regression coefficients, higher absolute value of coeff indicates the associated feature is more important.

Top-ranked features from predictive model using only language markers		
Feature name		**coeff**
coexistence of adverb phrase, verb phrase and noun phrase		-2.04
word length in letters		-1.05
LIWC word category of nonfluencies		-0.91
LIWC word category of we		0.85
LIWC word category of anger		-0.68
LIWC word category of space		-0.66
verb phrase span ratio		-0.64
average phrase span		0.59
LIWC word category of sexual		-0.55
global coherence		0.53
Top-ranked features from predictive model using only imaging markers		
Feature name	Function	**—coeff—**
thickness of left lateral orbito frontal	Emotion	0.50
cortical volume of left pars orbitailis	Language	0.42
thickness of left posterior cingulate cortex	Neural Communication	0.42
cortical volume of left inferior temporal	Vision	0.41
cortical volume of left supramarginal gyrus	Language	0.33
thickness of right peri calcarine	Vision	0.30
thickness of right cauda lmiddle frontal	Memory	0.29
thickness of left posterior cingulate cortex	Neural Communication	0.28
cortical volume of right inferior temporal	Vision	0.27
thickness of left fusiform	Neural Communication	0.26
Top-ranked features from Ours-Language-AugImg		
Feature name	Function	**—coeff—**
AUG: cortical volume of left pars orbitalis	Language	1.1
AUG: cortical volume of right supramarginal	Language	1.07
AUG: thickness of left lateral orbito frontal	Emotion	1.05
AUG: thickness of left posterior cingulate	Neural Communication	0.97
AUG: cortical volume of left inferior temporal	Vision	0.82
AUG: thickness of left posterior cingulate	Vision	0.78
AUG: thickness of left caudal middle frontal	Memory	0.68
AUG: dMRI: fiber count right bankssts	Language/Biological perception	0.68
AUG: dMRI: fiber count left caudal middle frontal	Memory	0.65
AUG: cortical volume of left isthmus cingulate	Emotion	0.62

see that 1) the top-ranked features are dominated by auxiliary variables from our crossmodal augmentation model, demonstrating the importance and effectiveness of the proposed augmentation scheme, even though these markers are in fact generated according to the guidance of language markers. 2) the top-ranked augmented features and top-ranked imaging markers in the middle section of Table 3 are not consistent. Since the augmentation tries to synthesize imaging markers from language markers, the inconsistency in ranking means that not all imaging markers can be well synthesized through the linear combination, under the guidance of language markers. Some of the imaging variables may be better augmented by language markers due to their implicit connections to language functionalities.[34] 3) there are two dMRI features in top-ranked augmented features, whereas the corresponding actual imaging markers do not stand out in the imaging unimodal learning. This directly shows the importance of diffusion MRI variables in the crossmodal analysis and their differential benefits in modeling MCI, as also suggested in our previous work.[17]

5. Discussion

In this study, we propose a crossmodal augmentation method to augment language markers with synthesized variables guided by auxiliary imaging data, for improved performance on MCI detection. Our augmentation model learns to efficiently associate language information and imaging information with only a limited number of subjects having both data modalities. The learned model will then use the language markers of a subject to construct auxiliary variables by a linear combination of imaging markers from those that possess imaging information. The augmented language markers significantly improve the AUC score of MCI prediction from 0.8 to 0.973. We also validate the generalization of our method by augmenting imaging markers with language features, which contributes to an AUC score of 0.98. Our method tackles the problem of joint analysis to multi-modal data with limited crossmodal alignment supervision.

Though the proposed crossmodal augmentation approach has shown exceptional performance improvements, there are future studies and further improvements remain. 1) First of all, the augmented variables are constructed by a linear combination of a set of given imaging markers or "anchor" imaging markers. Such dependency has motivated us to study the impact of the anchor makers later on, with the possibility of using refined anchor markers. 2) Second, due to the small sample size available for training, we used the restricted assumption that the feature space of imaging data is linear, which may be further improved by non-linear assumptions. 3) Our analysis has shown a deeply convoluted relationship between language markers and imaging markers, as suggested by the top-ranked features. Such a relationship and its implications need further analysis, the understanding of which can further guide our improvements on the augmentation. 4) Last but not least, we only validate the crossmodal augmentation over two modalities. With the high sample-efficiency design, we can directly extend the approach to more than two modalities, and we will investigate these scenarios in our future work.

The proposed method can be directly extended to various clinical applications. One example is to improve MCI detection performance given only dialogue data. Assume that only the easily acquired dialogue data and public MRI data[5] are available in the institution A. One can learn a crossmodal alignment model with a private and labeled dataset from the institution B, and this dataset includes aligned dialogue and MRI data. Then apply the crossmodal alignment model to the dataset of A through considering the domain shift between two MRI datasets. Since the private MRI data from B is not released, we can achieve privacy-preserving prediction in the condition of missing modality. We leave this discussion to our future work.

6. Acknowledgement

This material is based in part upon work supported by the National Science Foundation under Grant IIS-2212174, IIS-1749940, Office of Naval Research N00014-20-1-2382, and National Institute on Aging (NIA) RF1AG072449, R01AG051628, and R01AG056102.

References

1. S. L. Murphy, K. D. Kochanek, J. Xu and E. Arias, Mortality in the united states, 2020 (2021).
2. C. R. Jack Jr, D. S. Knopman, W. J. Jagust, L. M. Shaw, P. S. Aisen, M. W. Weiner, R. C. Petersen and J. Q. Trojanowski, Hypothetical model of dynamic biomarkers of the alzheimer's pathological cascade, *The Lancet Neurology* **9**, 119 (2010).
3. C. R. Jack, R. C. Petersen, Y. C. Xu, P. C. O'Brien, G. E. Smith, R. J. Ivnik, B. F. Boeve, S. C. Waring, E. G. Tangalos and E. Kokmen, Prediction of ad with mri-based hippocampal volume in mild cognitive impairment, *Neurology* **52**, 1397 (1999).
4. R. S. Desikan, H. J. Cabral, C. P. Hess, W. P. Dillon, C. M. Glastonbury, M. W. Weiner, N. J. Schmansky, D. N. Greve, D. H. Salat, R. L. Buckner *et al.*, Automated mri measures identify individuals with mild cognitive impairment and alzheimer's disease, *Brain* **132**, 2048 (2009).
5. C. R. Jack Jr, M. A. Bernstein, N. C. Fox, P. Thompson, G. Alexander, D. Harvey, B. Borowski, P. J. Britson, J. L. Whitwell, C. Ward *et al.*, The alzheimer's disease neuroimaging initiative (adni): Mri methods, *Journal of Magnetic Resonance Imaging: An Official Journal of the International Society for Magnetic Resonance in Medicine* **27**, 685 (2008).
6. C. Hinrichs, V. Singh, G. Xu, S. C. Johnson, A. D. N. Initiative *et al.*, Predictive markers for ad in a multi-modality framework: an analysis of mci progression in the adni population, *Neuroimage* **55**, 574 (2011).
7. R. Cuingnet, E. Gerardin, J. Tessieras, G. Auzias, S. Lehéricy, M.-O. Habert, M. Chupin, H. Benali, O. Colliot, A. D. N. Initiative *et al.*, Automatic classification of patients with alzheimer's disease from structural mri: a comparison of ten methods using the adni database, *neuroimage* **56**, 766 (2011).
8. J. Zhou, J. Liu, V. A. Narayan, J. Ye, A. D. N. Initiative *et al.*, Modeling disease progression via multi-task learning, *NeuroImage* **78**, 233 (2013).
9. F. Tang, I. Uchendu, F. Wang, H. H. Dodge and J. Zhou, Scalable diagnostic screening of mild cognitive impairment using ai dialogue agent, *Scientific reports* **10**, 1 (2020).
10. J. Robin, M. Xu, L. D. Kaufman and W. Simpson, Using digital speech assessments to detect early signs of cognitive impairment, *Frontiers in digital health* **3**, p. 749758 (2021).
11. A. Balagopalan, B. Eyre, J. Robin, F. Rudzicz and J. Novikova, Comparing pre-trained and feature-based models for prediction of alzheimer's disease based on speech, *Frontiers in aging neuroscience* **13**, p. 635945 (2021).
12. F. Tang, J. Chen, H. H. Dodge and J. Zhou, The joint effects of acoustic and linguistic markers for early identification of mild cognitive impairment, *Frontiers in digital health* **3** (2021).
13. U. Petti, S. Baker and A. Korhonen, A systematic literature review of automatic alzheimer's disease detection from speech and language, *Journal of the American Medical Informatics Association* **27**, 1784 (2020).
14. K. D. Mueller, B. Hermann, J. Mecollari and L. S. Turkstra, Connected speech and language in mild cognitive impairment and alzheimer's disease: A review of picture description tasks, *Journal of clinical and experimental neuropsychology* **40**, 917 (2018).
15. K. Yu, K. Wild, K. Potempa, B. M. Hampstead, P. A. Lichtenberg, L. M. Struble, P. Pruitt, E. L. Alfaro, J. Lindsley, M. MacDonald *et al.*, The internet-based conversational engagement clinical trial (i-conect) in socially isolated adults 75+ years old: randomized controlled trial protocol and covid-19 related study modifications, *Frontiers in digital health* **3** (2021).
16. J. Venugopalan, L. Tong, H. R. Hassanzadeh and M. D. Wang, Multimodal deep learning models for early detection of alzheimer's disease stage, *Scientific reports* **11**, 1 (2021).
17. Q. Wang, L. Guo, P. M. Thompson, C. R. Jack Jr, H. Dodge, L. Zhan, J. Zhou, A. D. N. Initiative *et al.*, The added value of diffusion-weighted mri-derived structural connectome in evaluating mild cognitive impairment: A multi-cohort validation, *Journal of Alzheimer's Disease*

64, 149 (2018).

18. K. C. Fraser, K. Lundholm Fors, M. Eckerström, F. Öhman and D. Kokkinakis, Predicting mci status from multimodal language data using cascaded classifiers, *Frontiers in aging neuroscience* **11**, p. 205 (2019).
19. Y. Wang, Survey on deep multi-modal data analytics: Collaboration, rivalry, and fusion, *ACM Transactions on Multimedia Computing, Communications, and Applications (TOMM)* **17**, 1 (2021).
20. L. Torgo, R. P. Ribeiro, B. Pfahringer and P. Branco, Smote for regression, in *Portuguese conference on artificial intelligence*, (Springer, 2013).
21. N. V. Chawla, K. W. Bowyer, L. O. Hall and W. P. Kegelmeyer, Smote: synthetic minority over-sampling technique, *Journal of artificial intelligence research* **16**, 321 (2002).
22. M. Liu, W. Xie, X. Chen, Y. Ma, Y. Guo, J. Meng, Z. Yuan and Q. Qin, Heterogeneous face biometrics based on guassian weights and invariant features synthesis, in *2011 IEEE 2nd International Conference on Computing, Control and Industrial Engineering*, (IEEE, 2011).
23. H. Guo, Y. Mao and R. Zhang, Mixup as locally linear out-of-manifold regularization, in *Proceedings of the AAAI Conference on Artificial Intelligence*, (AAAI, April 2019).
24. H. Zhang, M. Cisse, Y. N. Dauphin and D. Lopez-Paz, mixup: Beyond empirical risk minimization, *arXiv preprint arXiv:1710.09412* (2017).
25. L. Zhang, Z. Deng, K. Kawaguchi, A. Ghorbani and J. Zou, How does mixup help with robustness and generalization?, *arXiv preprint arXiv:2010.04819* (2020).
26. A. Torrado-Carvajal, J. L. Herraiz, E. Alcain, A. S. Montemayor, L. Garcia-Canamaque, J. A. Hernandez-Tamames, Y. Rozenholc and N. Malpica, Fast patch-based pseudo-ct synthesis from t1-weighted mr images for pet/mr attenuation correction in brain studies, *Journal of Nuclear Medicine* **57**, 136 (2016).
27. M. S. Albert, S. T. DeKosky, D. Dickson, B. Dubois, H. H. Feldman, N. C. Fox, A. Gamst, D. M. Holtzman, W. J. Jagust, R. C. Petersen *et al.*, The diagnosis of mild cognitive impairment due to alzheimer's disease: recommendations from the national institute on aging-alzheimer's association workgroups on diagnostic guidelines for alzheimer's disease, *Alzheimer's & dementia* **7**, 270 (2011).
28. M. J. Pickering and R. P. Van Gompel, Syntactic parsing, in *Handbook of psycholinguistics*, (Elsevier, 2006) pp. 455–503.
29. A. Joulin, E. Grave, P. Bojanowski and T. Mikolov, Bag of tricks for efficient text classification, in *Proceedings of the 15th Conference of the European Chapter of the Association for Computational Linguistics: Volume 2, Short Papers*, (Association for Computational Linguistics, April 2017).
30. L. Zhan, J. Zhou, Y. Wang, Y. Jin, N. Jahanshad, G. Prasad, T. M. Nir, C. D. Leonardo, J. Ye, P. M. Thompson *et al.*, Comparison of nine tractography algorithms for detecting abnormal structural brain networks in alzheimer's disease, *Frontiers in aging neuroscience* **7**, p. 48 (2015).
31. H. Zou and T. Hastie, Regularization and variable selection via the elastic net, *Journal of the royal statistical society: series B (statistical methodology)* **67**, 301 (2005).
32. F. Pedregosa, G. Varoquaux, A. Gramfort, V. Michel, B. Thirion, O. Grisel, M. Blondel, P. Prettenhofer, R. Weiss, V. Dubourg, J. Vanderplas, A. Passos, D. Cournapeau, M. Brucher, M. Perrot and E. Duchesnay, Scikit-learn: Machine learning in Python, *Journal of Machine Learning Research* **12**, 2825 (2011).
33. J. E. Sung, S. Choi, B. Eom, J. K. Yoo and J. H. Jeong, Syntactic complexity as a linguistic marker to differentiate mild cognitive impairment from normal aging, *Journal of Speech, Language, and Hearing Research* **63**, 1416 (2020).
34. B. B. Biswal, M. Mennes, X.-N. Zuo, S. Gohel, C. Kelly, S. M. Smith, C. F. Beckmann, J. S. Adelstein, R. L. Buckner, S. Colcombe *et al.*, Toward discovery science of human brain function, *Proceedings of the National Academy of Sciences* **107**, 4734 (2010).

How Fitbit data are being made available to registered researchers in *All of Us* Research Program

Hiral Master, Aymone Kouame, Kayla Marginean, Melissa Basford, Paul Harris
Vanderbilt University Medical Center
Nashville TN, USA
Email: hiral.master@vumc.org, aymone.kouame@vumc.org, kayla.marginean@vumc.org, melissa.basford@vumc.org, paul.a.harris@vumc.org

Michelle Holko
Google Public Sector
Washington DC, USA
Email: michelle.holko@gmail.com

The National Institutes of Health's (NIH) *All of Us* Research Program aims to enroll at least one million US participants from diverse backgrounds; collect electronic health record (EHR) data, survey data, physical measurements, biospecimens for genomics and other assays, and digital health data; and create a researcher database and tools to enable precision medicine research [1]. Since inception, digital health technologies (DHT) have been envisioned as essential to achieving the goals of the program [2]. A "bring your own device" (BYOD) study for collecting Fitbit data from participants' devices was developed with integration of additional DHTs planned in the future [3]. Here we describe how participants can consent to share their digital health technology data, how the data are collected, how the data set is parsed, and how researchers can access the data.

Keywords: Wearables, Digital health technologies, Precision medicine

1. *Introduction*

In 2016, the U.S. Congress, via the 21st Century Cures Act, authorized a total of $1.5 billion over ten years to fund the *All of Us* Research Program at the National Institutes of Health (NIH). This program is publicly funded, with resources appropriated each year by the U.S. Congress. The program was borne out of the Precision Medicine Initiative, and strives to nurture relationships with participants, build a robust ecosystem of communities and researchers, and strives to deliver the largest and most diverse biomedical dataset. The program is accumulating multiple streams of health-related information such as electronic health records (EHRs), genomics, physical measures, participant surveys and wearables (such as Fitbit) from 1,000,000 or more Americans, with a focus on populations usually under-represented in biomedical research to date [1, 2].

In addition to EHR, genomics, physical measures and surveys, the program has an interest in incorporating digital health data, e.g., data from wearable devices like fitness trackers, to promote research in this space by diverse academic researchers on a diverse data set. The program currently invites participants to donate Fitbit and Apple HealthKit data in a "bring your own device" (BYOD) model [3, 4]. As of June 2022, Fitbit data for 12,844 *All of Us* Research Program participants were provided to registered researchers on the secure, cloud-basedResearcher Workbench platform. This report is focused on the back-end process by which participants can link their own Fitbit device, and what happens to this Fitbit data once they are shared with the program. We will discuss the current processes that are being employed to provide these data to the research community, and how researchers can access these data via *All of Us* Researcher Workbench platform.

In this report, we provide a high-level overview of the Fitbit data process from data ingestion to delivery. This report also provides a high-level overview on demographic characteristics, such as ethnicity, race, sex at birth, age, income, and employment of participants who contributed any Fitbit data in the *All of Us* Research Program. Additional digital health technology data streams are planned for the longer term of this study. Lastly, the report also highlights some unique opportunities on how digital health data from *All of Us* Research Program can be leveraged by registered researchers to advance healthcare for all.

2. *Methods*

2.1. *How are participants consented to be part of AoU and share Fitbit data?*

Participants may log on to the *All of Us* participant portal at https://participant.joinallofus.org to participate in the program. Participants need to provide primary consent to be part of the *All of Us* program, which aims to collect at least 10 years of data from participants. Given it is a long-term research program, participants remain in touch with the program via phone, email, and/or app. They may also connect their family members, in case participants cannot be reached. They might also use social media or public databases to help keep participant's contact information up to date. If participants have a fitness tracker, they may be asked to share data from it. **Figure 1** shows the *All of Us* Research Program participant facing portal where participants can elect to share Fitbit data with the program. Participants can withdraw from *All of Us* any time. Consent to share electronic health record (EHR) data is mandatory before participants can start sharing digital data. Once the consent to EHR is completed, participants can share their digital health data.

Data sharing process on participant portal (https://participant.joinallofus.org) lists the steps for deciding whether or not to share or not share data from their own Fitbit devices:

1. First, participants are provided with the program's working definitions for wearables. "Mobile apps and wearable devices can collect data outside of a hospital or clinic."
2. Participants are then shown the steps for securely sharing digital health data.
3. After confirming that they would like to share their data, participants are prompted to log into their Fitbit account to pair their device with their *All of Us* account.
4. Once a participant selects "approved", they are then redirected to the participant portal and are shown a success message.

Donation of digital health data is optional for participants. Participants may withdraw from participation or stop contributing data via the Connector at any time by revoking access for each individual data record type, or all data record types related to *All of Us* Research Program as a data sharing endpoint via the appropriate application. Participants may choose to re-enable their data sharing at any time, for each individual data record type, or all data record types. Data previously contributed by participants will remain with the *All of Us* Research Program after a participant's program withdrawal and will not be retroactively scrubbed.

2.2. *What happens to participants' data?*

The Participant Technology Systems Center (PTSC) securely stores all the Fitbit data on the cloud platform. Files are delivered by the PTSC to the Data and Research Center (DRC) at Vanderbilt University Medical Center. Specifically, files are uploaded in the Raw Data Repository (RDR) daily. **Figure 2** shows the flow of participant digital health data from the PTSC to the DRC. These data are structured as json files. These data then undergo curation in BigQuery, and are made available to researchers on the *All of Us* Researcher Workbench, a cloud-based platform.

3. *Results*

3.1. *How are Fitbit data parsed (Schema development)?*

The DRC uses a hands-off approach to data processing and delivery to support a wide range of scientific research investigations. Specifically, Fitbit data are available in json format, which is considered raw data. The contents of the filename are mapped to a single field and contents within each file are mapped into another field. These file contents are then parsed into a series of tables for data types, including:

- Heart Rate (By Zone Summary)
- Heart Rate (Minute-Level)
- Activity (Daily Summary)
- Activity Intraday Steps (Minute-Level)

Files are then mapped from the bucket to a Postgres database in a secure FISMA VM. The final output is mapped on the BigQuery database, which undergoes curation pipeline. During this process, the data are de-identified and are then being made available on Researcher Workbench as supplemental (non-OMOP) tables.

3.2. *How can Fitbit data be accessed by researchers?*

The program's goal is to share data widely but wisely to ensure rigorous measures are taken to protect participants' privacy. Therefore, the Fitbit data is delivered to researchers in a tiered approach. Specifically, the summary level information regarding the data can be accessed publicly via the website (https://www.researchallofus.org/). Researchers can access row-level de-identified data via the *All of Us* Researcher workbench, which is a secured cloud-based platform. On Researcher Workbench, researchers can access de-identified Fitbit data in Registered and Controlled tiers. In the registered tier, Fitbit data are date-shifted by random number between 1 to 365 to ensure participant's privacy. No date-shifting is performed in the controlled tier.

In order to access the de-identified data on the secured, cloud based platform, researchers need to create a Researcher Workbench account. The researcher must be a part of an institution that has a data use agreement. Currently, the list of institutions that have agreements in place can be viewed publicly on the website (https://www.researchallofus.org/institutional-agreements/). If the researcher's organization does not currently have a data use agreement in place, they can initiate this process by submitting a form online. Upon submission of request, the contracting officer from Vanderbilt University Medical Center reaches out to contacting contact from the requestor's institution within a couple of business days. Timeline to complete this process and obtain agreement varies based on workflows around the contracting processes at the requestor's institution. Once the institutional agreement is in place, the individual researcher can create an account and go through the relevant questionnaires and ethics training to validate their account. At present, any US-based academic, nonprofit, or health care institution can obtain data use agreement and there is no process for researchers outside the United States, or for researchers in the private sector to access the Workbench. However, expanding access to these groups is a priority for the program and a goal for future development.

3.3. *What Fitbit data are currently being made available on the Researcher Workbench?*

Currently, 12,844 *All of Us* Research Program participants provide any Fitbit data, which can be accessed via Researcher Workbench (**Table 1**). Nearly 13% of participants who provided Fitbit data resided in California state at the time of enrollment in the program (**Figure 3**). Of the participants who provide any Fitbit data, 80% are white, 88% are Non-Hispanic or Latino, 67% are Female at birth and 52% report being employed for wages (**Figure 4**). The detailed cohort characterization report is now publicly available on User Support Hub article [5].

4. *Discussion*

4.1. *Research Utility*

Digital health data on Researcher Workbench represent the data that are parsed from json files to structured tables. Specifically, this Fitbit data is longitudinal in nature. Thus, these device-generated summary and high-resolution intraday data are robust in nature and allow a wide-range of research, including method development and longitudinal study design. Currently, registered users can subset their analytical sample by presence of any Fitbit data by using graphical interface tools (e.g. cohort and dataset builder). However, there is an opportunity to develop various tools that would further wearable research. For instance, researchers on the platform can work on innovative projects and share their work with other registered users on Researcher Workbench. A couple examples of tools and methods that would be helpful to incorporate into the platform are for feature detection, e.g. periods of exercise and user behavior for wearing a Fitbit device). Time-series based tools, and methods to deal with data missingness over time (e.g. when charging or generally when the device is not worn or not functioning) will also be useful. Thus, these data support the program's overarching mission of accelerating health research and medical breakthroughs by enabling researchers to conduct various types of studies, including cross-sectional and longitudinal research designs.

4.2. *Lessons Learned*

Our initial work has provided insight and lessons that may be generalizable and applicable for other programs aiming to collect and share BYOD digital health data. These include establishing the system to integrate digital health data in cloud platforms and making decisions on how to deliver this large digital health data in sustainable and accessible fashion. Currently, we provide the digital health data as separate structured data tables on the cloud platform. Since the digital health data is collected from participant's own devices, the data is collected right from the time their Fitbit account was created, which gives opportunity for researchers to conduct longitudinal study design research projects.

4.3. *Limitations of dataset*

The characterization for digital health data is limited to specific data types such as activity and heart rate. Today, the standardized fashion of managing digital health data is in its infancy state, therefore, these data are being made available as separate datatables on Researcher Workbench. We acknowledge that the majority of participants whose Fitbit data is being made available on Researcher Workbench is biased, i.e., majority of participants who provided Fitbit data reported being White and employed for wages. However, these data represent participants who had their own Fitbit devices and consented to share EHR data. The program is currently expanding the efforts by providing Fitbit devices to *All of Us* Research Program participants who do not own Fitbit devices so they can participate and share their data [6]. Lastly, we acknowledge that access to row-level deidentified data is currently available to researchers who are part of an institution in the United States that has an institutional data use agreement in place. However, the program has initiated efforts to expand access globally and foster public-private relationships, ensuring programs' goals and mission are met.

4.4. *Future plans*

We plan to expand the digital technology data offerings not only in terms of providing more participant's data but also adding more data types and includes data from devices (e.g., Apple HealthKit, Garmin, etc.) in addition to Fitbit. For instance, in future, we plan to provide sleep and device information from Fitbit, which will expand the research use cases.

5. *Conclusion*

Digital Health Technologies are increasingly being used for health-related applications. The *All of Us* Research Program has a unique opportunity to continue to drive research using these devices, to understand how these data can be used to support individuals in their health journeys. Integrating additional devices, and collecting and making additional data available to researchers, will help contribute to a robust ecosystem for researchers. In addition, tools to help researchers analyze these data are needed. These can be developed both by the program and by the researcher community. Finally, promoting diversity, not only in the data set but also in the researchers analyzing the data, is important for reducing bias and inequity of results.

5.1. *Table*

Fitbit data type	Count of participant ids
Any Fitbit data type	12,844
Activity summary	12,794
Heart summary	11,575
Step intraday	12,790
Heart rate intraday	11,575

Table 1. Counts of participants who provide Fitbit by data type as of data, which is available on Researcher Workbench, starting June 22, 2022 (N Fitbit Pid = 12,844)

5.2. *Figures/Illustrations*

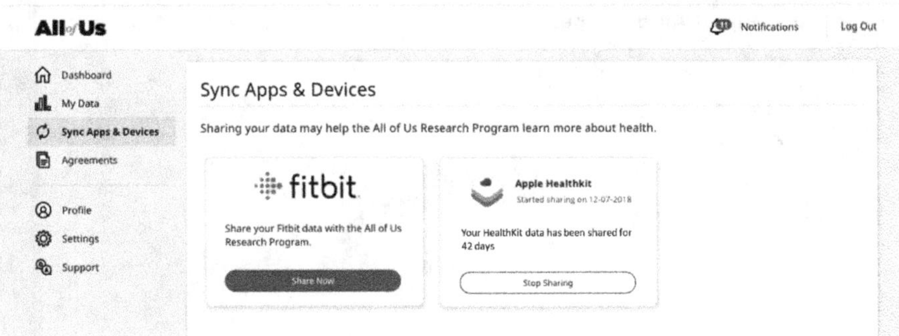

Fig. 1. *All of Us* Research Program participant facing portal where participants can share Fitbit data

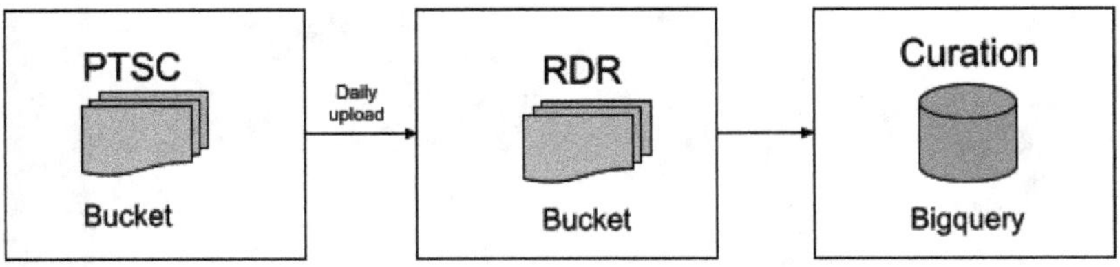

Fig. 2. *Flow of Fitbit data from the participant portal to the Data and Resource Center's raw data repository and curated data repository.*

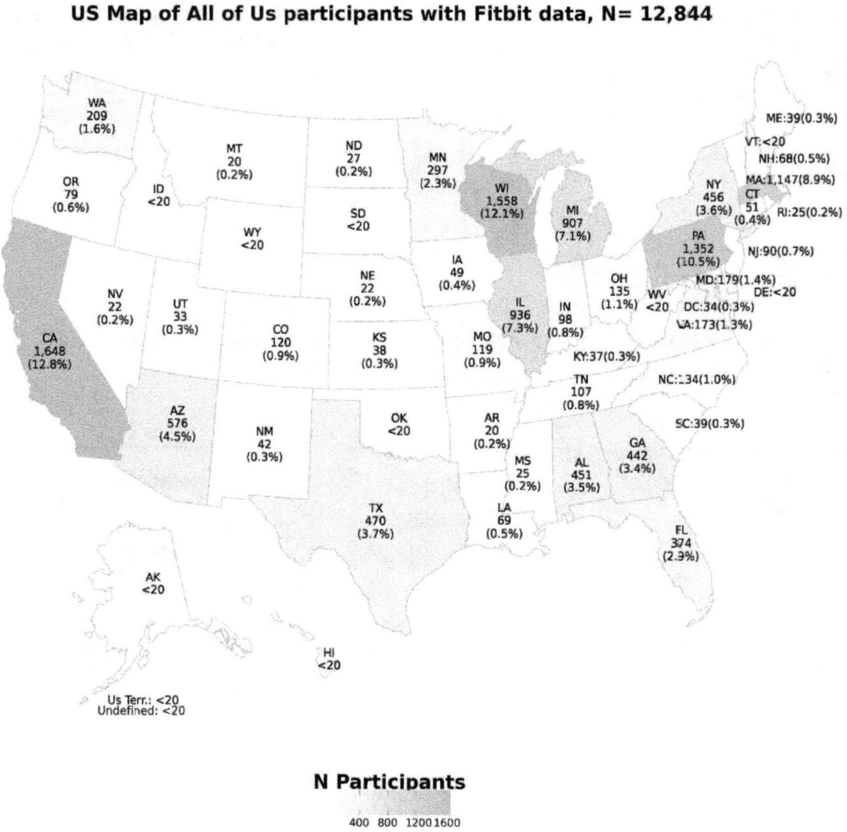

Fig. 3. State-wise distribution of participants who provided Fitbit data in the *All of Us* Research Program (N Fitbit Pid = 12,844).

a

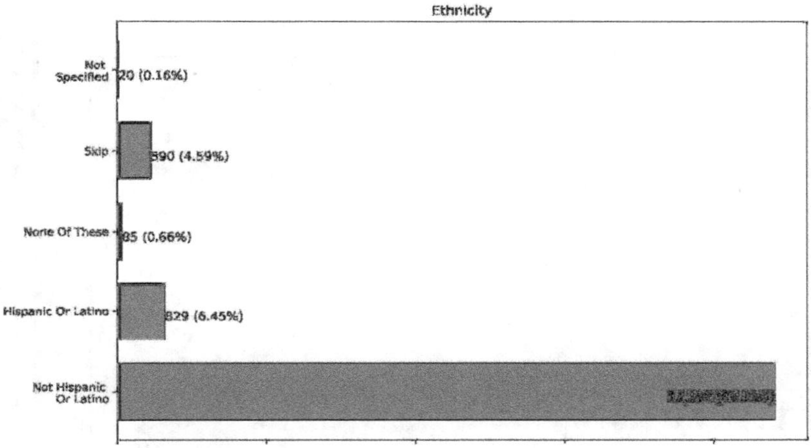
Ethnicity
Not Specified
20 (0.16%)
Skip
590 (4.59%)
None Of These
85 (0.66%)
Hispanic Or Latino
829 (6.45%)
Not Hispanic Or Latino

b

Race
Not Specified
569 (4.43%)
Skip
590 (4.59%)
None Of These
85 (0.66%)
More Than One Population
262 (2.04%)
Native Hawaiian & Other Pacific Islander
<20
Middle Eastern & North African
46 (0.36%)
Asian
394 (3.07%)
Black
618 (4.81%)
White
10,276 (80.01%)

c

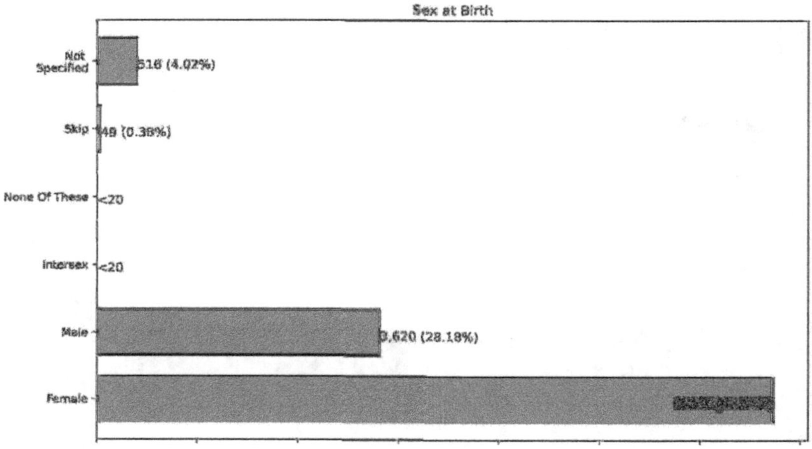
Sex at Birth
Not Specified
516 (4.02%)
Skip
49 (0.38%)
None Of These
<20
Intersex
<20
Male
3,620 (28.18%)
Female

d

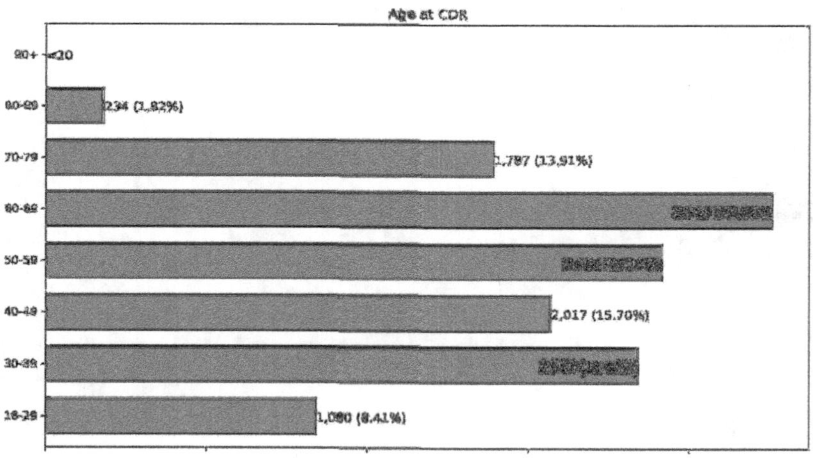
Age at CDR
90+
<20
80-89
234 (1.82%)
70-79
1,787 (13.91%)
60-69
50-59
40-49
2,017 (15.70%)
30-39
18-29
1,080 (8.41%)

e

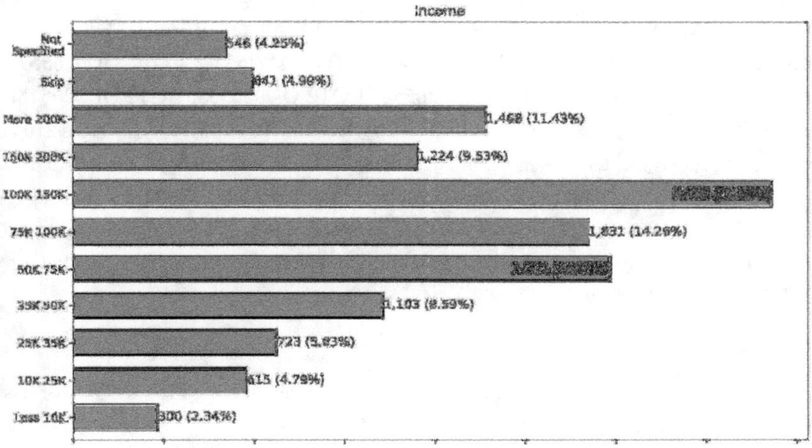

f

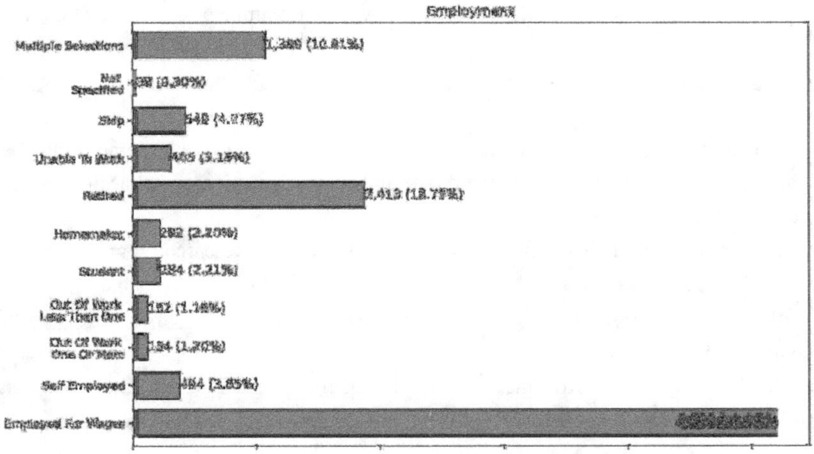

Fig. 4. Self-reported a) ethnicity, b) race, c) sex at birth, d) age e) income, and f) employment of participants with Fitbit data in June 2022 curated data repository, which can be accessed by registered users on Researcher Workbench (N Fitbit Pid = 12,844).

6. *Acknowledgments*

The *All of Us* Research Program would not be possible without the partnership of its participants. The *All of Us* Research Program is supported by the National Institutes of Health, Office of the Director: Regional Medical Centers: 1 OT2 OD026549; 1 OT2 OD026554; 1 OT2 OD026557; 1 OT2 OD026556; 1 OT2 OD026550; 1 OT2 OD 026552; 1 OT2 OD026553; 1 OT2 OD026548; 1 OT2 OD026551; 1 OT2 OD026555; IAA: AOD21037, AOD22003, AOD16037, AOD21041; Federally Qualified Health Centers: HHSN 263201600085U; Data and Research Center: 5 U2C OD023196; Biobank: 1 U24 OD023121; The Participant Center: U24 OD023176; Participant Technology Systems Center: 1 U24 OD023163; Communications and Engagement: 3 OT2 OD023205; 3 OT2 OD023206; and Community Partners: 1 OT2 OD025277; 3 OT2 OD025315; 1 OT2 OD025337; 1 OT2 OD025276.

References

1. *All of Us* Research Program Investigators, Denny JC, Rutter JL, et al. The "All of Us" Research Program. N Engl J Med. 2019;381(7):668-676.
2. Hudson K, Lifton R, Patrick-Lake B, and the Precision Medicine Initiative Working Group. The Precision Medicine Initiative Cohort Program: Building a Research Foundation for 21st Century Medicine. Working Group Report to the Advisory Committee to the Director, NIH. 2015. Available from: https://www.nih.gov/sites/default/files/research-training/initiatives/pmi/pmi-working-group-report-20150917-2.pdf
3. Holko, M., Litwin, T.R., Munoz, F. et al. Wearable fitness tracker use in federally qualified health center patients: strategies to improve the health of all of us using digital health devices. npj Digit. Med. 2022;5, 53.
4. *All of Us* Research Program News and Events [Internet]. *All of Us* Research Program Expands Data Collection Efforts with Fitbit. 2019. Available from: https://allofus.nih.gov/news-events-and-media/announcements/all-us-research-program-expands-data-collection-efforts-fitbit
5. Master, H., Labrecque, S., Kouame, A., et al [Internet]. 2022. 2022Q2R2 v6 Data Characterization Report: Overall *All of Us* Cohort Demographics. All of Us Research Program. Available from https://aousupporthelp.zendesk.com/hc/en-us/articles/7906441956244-2022Q2R2-v6-Data-Characterization-Report-Overall-All-of-Us-Cohort-Demographics
6. Scripps Research [Internet]. Through '*All of Us*' program, Scripps Research launches wearable technology study to accelerate precision medicine. 2021. Available from: https://www.scripps.edu/news-and-events/press-room/2021/20210224-aou-fitbit-study.html

Risk for Poor Post-Operative Quality of Life Among Wearable Use Subgroups in an All of Us Research Cohort

Nidhi Soley[1], Shanshan Song[1,3,4], Natalie Flaks-Manov[1], Casey Overby Taylor[1,2,3,4]

[1]Institute for Computational Medicine, Whiting School of Engineering, Johns Hopkins University, Baltimore, Maryland, USA, [2]Department of Biomedical Engineering, Johns Hopkins University, Baltimore, Maryland, USA, [3]Division of General Internal Medicine, Department of Medicine, Johns Hopkins University School of Medicine, Baltimore, Maryland, USA, and [4]Biomedical Informatics & Data Science Section, The Johns Hopkins University School of Medicine, Baltimore, Maryland

The objective of this research was to build and assess the performance of a prediction model for post-operative recovery status measured by quality of life among individuals experiencing a variety of surgery types. In addition, we assessed the performance of the model for two subgroups (high and moderately consistent wearable device users). Study variables were derived from the electronic health records, questionnaires, and wearable devices of a cohort of individuals with one of 8 surgery types and that were part of the NIH *All of Us* research program. Through multivariable analysis, high frailty index (OR 1.69, 95% 1.05-7.22, p<0.006), and older age (OR 1.76, 95% 1.55-4.08, p<0.024) were found to be the driving risk factors of poor recovery post-surgery. Our logistic regression model included 15 variables, 5 of which included wearable device data. In wearable use subgroups, the model had better accuracy for high wearable users (81%). Findings demonstrate the potential for models that use wearable measures to assess frailty to inform clinicians of patients at risk for poor surgical outcomes. Our model performed with high accuracy across multiple surgery types and were robust to variable consistency in wearable use.

Keywords: digital health technologies, wearables, predictive modeling, risk factors

Corresponding Author: Nidhi Soley, MS, Institute for Computational Medicine (ICM) Johns Hopkins Whiting School of Engineering 3101 Wyman Park Drive, Hackerman 318, Baltimore, MD 21218, USA; nsoley1@jh.edu

Introduction

Surgical procedures are becoming more common over the world, with one out of every 10 individuals getting one each year in high-income nations. After discharge, patients have the main responsibility for their recovery, and variance in adherence to this can result in varying outcomes [1].More than 10% of patients over the age of 45 encounter a significant postoperative complication, which is apparent in a variety of surgical groups [1]. Thus, there is a need to better identify patients that are at risk for such poor surgical outcomes with applicability to multiple surgical types.

Methods for accurately predicting the probability of post-surgical complications have been studied widely in the past. For predicting surgical morbidity, Copeland proposed the POSSUM (Physiological and Operative Severity Score for the enUmeration of Mortality and Morbidity) model in 1991. [2]. Since then, various post-operative morbidity prediction models have been suggested, including the E-POSSUM, Estimation of Physiologic Ability and Surgical Stress (E-PASS) [3], and Barwon Health (BH) 2009 models [4]. However, the predictive capacity of these models beyond the population used to create the model may be limited. Given there are no published models to predict poor post-surgical recovery for different types of surgeries, this work aimed to build a prediction model that uses data types that are accessible across a broad range of surgical patients.

One data type of particular interest was physical activity data from wearables. Recent studies have shown that utilizing the data from wearables to construct predictive models can help identify surgical complications earlier, improve recovery, and provide safe follow-up. Furthermore, wearables can help patients engage, assist, and care for themselves by bridging the gap between clinical services and their homes [5]. Despite the emergence of numerous digital initiatives in surgery, there has been little or no discussion of wearable use factors on the performance of the prediction models.

To build a model that predicts post-operative outcomes based on the preoperative wearable data, we used candidate risk factors taken from electronic health records (EHR) and a commercial wearable device (Fitbit). In addition, we assessed the impact of wearable usage on model performance. To do this, we assessed the accuracy of the model in cohort stratified by wearable use (high vs moderate/low pre-operative wearable use). We hypothesized that model performance is better for high users when compared to patients with moderate/low wearable usage.

Method

This is a retrospective cohort study based on data collected by the *All of Us* Research Program Dataset v5 (Registered & Controlled Tier) from May 6, 2018, to April 1, 2021 [6]. The cohort includes patients who had gone through one of eight surgeries: general, gynecology, orthopedics, plastic, neuro, vascular, urology, thoracic surgery, shared Fitbit data and completed the survey within 5 weeks since the surgery. Figure 1 (a) shows the flowchart for inclusion and exclusion criteria. 247 participants fulfilled the study criteria. The time range of data (Figure 1 (b)) was defined for a period of 5 weeks, all the variables were averaged for this period before the surgery date. For the study, we required EQ-5D score for Quality of Life (QoL), a self-reported outcome measure for recovery taken within 5 weeks after surgery. For the patients who did not meet this criterion, we adjusted their QoL values by adding the difference of the average QoL post and pre-surgery (0.02) to the pre indices and obtained the post QoL indices for all 247 patients.

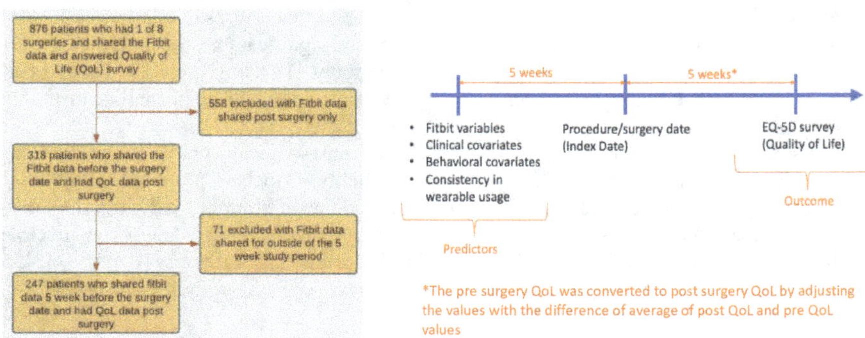

a b

Figure 1. a) Inclusion and exclusion criteria flow chart. b) Timeline of the study.

Data Source and Preprocessing

Primary Outcome

The EuroQOL instrument (EQ-5D-5L) was utilized to evaluate QoL. EQ-5D index has been used in several studies to assess the effect of surgery and the difference in the QoL pre- and post-surgery [7][8][9][10]. This is a standardized, proven QoL measurement tool. Mobility, Self-Care, Usual Activities, Pain/Discomfort, and Anxiety/Depression are the five dimensions included in the EQ-5D survey. We included two questions from each category. The responses to the questions were divided into 5 levels, 1 denotes an excellent state of health, and 5 is worse. The 5L profile, the 5-digit number, is generated based on the average of two questions in the five categories, for instance, if you have an excellent state of health your profile would be "11111". To estimate a single index value depending on the response to this categorization, a broad population-based algorithm was used for US population [11]. The index value is normally distributed and reflects how good or bad the health state is according to the preferences of the general population of a country. The index value for our dataset lies in the range of 0 (worse) to 1(good) [12]. Since we had patients who underwent different kinds of surgeries, we converted the continuous QoL to a status of good and poor recovery using the average QoL of the population as a threshold [9][10][13].

Variables

Fifteen clinicopathological and demographic variables that might affect the postoperative outcome were included. The demographic covariates were age, gender, race, and ethnicity. The clinical covariates included average hemoglobin level in blood (g/dL), average albumin level in blood (g/dL), and average BMI ratio. The values of all variables were observed in the time frame of 5 weeks before the surgery. The behavioral covariates included smoking habits and alcohol consumption habits prior to the surgery. The Fitbit activity data was available in a longitudinal form for each patient. The data from the Fitbit device was in a summarized format for a day and had variables like average calories burned, mean light active minutes, mean of very active minutes, mean of sedentary minutes, and mean of steps count in a day. The characteristics description of the entire cohort is summarized in Table 1.

Frailty is a well-validated predictor of poor postoperative outcomes [14]. We created a frailty index using a standard procedure described by Samuel at el. to assess the impact of frailty on the recovery status post-surgery [15]. The frailty index is frequently stated as a percentage of actual deficits to all deficits considered [15]. For instance, if a person had 10 of the 30 deficiencies that were considered, their frailty index would be 10/30, or 0.33. To create this index, we included 19 variables measured within 5 weeks before the surgery. Function, cognition, co-morbidity, health attitudes and behaviors, and physical performance metrics were all included in the database. The variables included activity data from Fitbit, clinical data, and various comorbid conditions chosen from Charles Comorbid Index's ICD9 and ICD10 codes for dementia, heart attack, malignancy, and diabetes. Health attitude variables included survey questions that assessed the person's general health like disability in walking/climbing, disability in dressing/bathing, and difficulty in reading/writing. For binary variables "0" denoted the absence of the deficit and "1" the presence of the deficit. To grade survey questions, we used Excellent as 0, Very Good as 0.25, Good as 0.5, Fair as 0.75, and Poor as 1. Similarly, for continuous variables, such as Fitbit activity data [19][20], hemoglobin level [22], known cut-points were applied. An individual's deficit scores were aggregated to create an index, with 0 denoting no deficit and 1 denoting the presence of all 19 deficits. To assess and validate the variable the slope of a best-fit log of the frailty index in proportion to age was plotted and the association between age and frailty was analyzed.

Quantifying Wearable Usage

To quantify wearable use, we calculated the consistency of using the Fitbit device. During the period of 5 weeks prior to the surgery, usage of the Fitbit device varied among the patients and was calculated using equation 1. Consistency and duration of Fitbit usage were used to divide the entire cohort into two subgroups (low/moderate wearable users and high wearable users).

$$\text{Consistency} = \frac{\text{Number of days the patient data was logged}}{\text{Number of days between first date and last date of use (duration)}} \tag{1}$$

Patients with 100% consistency and duration of usage of 5 weeks were classified as high wearable users. The patients with a consistency of less than 1 and a duration of Fitbit usage of fewer than 5 weeks were considered moderate/low users of a wearable device.

Statistical Analysis

Univariate Analysis

To determine the effect of individual risk factors on the binary outcome (good or poor recovery), we applied univariate analysis by chi-square test for categorical variables. For the risk factors like race, ethnicity, and alcohol consumption the small proportion categories were combined to make it a binary variable. Age was divided into three categories 18-49 years, 50-64 years, and 65 years and above. The frailty index was also divided into two categories based on the mean value of the population as non-frail (0-0.54) and frail (0.55-1). A P value of less than 0.05 was considered significant. The statistical approach was applied separately to each risk factor to obtain the odds, odds ratio (OR), and significance of predicting the poor outcome post-surgery. We also implemented these analyses for wearable device use subgroups (see "Quantifying Wearable Usage").

Multivariable Analysis

To obtain the driving risk factors of poor outcome post recovery, we implemented a multivariable logistic regression model on the entire cohort, on high wearable users, on moderate/low wearable user's dataset individually. All 15 variables were initially used for the analysis in this model. For collinearity diagnostics, variables with Variance Inflation Factor (VIF) above 5 were regarded as multicollinear. To exclude variables with multi-collinearity, multiple stepwise regression was used to iteratively build regression models that automatically chose independent variables. After removing three collinear variables, the stats model library's logistic regression model was applied to the remaining twelve independent variables and the binary outcome, recovery status. The statsmodel gives the OR, 95% confidence interval (CI), and p values for each risk factor.

Predictive Modeling

To build a predictive model of post-operative recovery status, we used a supervised machine learning algorithm. The logistic regression model was implemented individually for moderate/low wearable users, high wearable users, and the total population (baseline) datasets with 12 features that were identified non-collinear in multivariable analysis. To improve the model performance, we hyper-tuned the model using the grid search cross-validation technique. Since the outcome, poor recovery, and good recovery classes were imbalanced, we used the stratified K fold cross validation technique in the grid search cross-validation splitting strategy. After preprocessing, we divided the data into train and test sets, fitted the model on the train set, and then assessed the performance of the model for three separate test datasets (baseline, moderate/low wearable users, high wearable users).

Assessment of Model Performance

To compare the performance of the three models, we used AUC (area under the curve) score, accuracy, sensitivity, and ROC plot. The model with the highest AUC score was considered a better-performing model. The AUC score of the two subgroups was also tested for significance using their confidence intervals (CI). AUC CI calculated using bootstrap sampling method was used to compare the AUCs of models. The comparison of AUC was done using DeLong method [16]. If there was a difference in the two CIs, we concluded that the AUCs were different, and result was significant [17][18].

RESULTS

Study Population

Among a cohort of 247 people, most were female (77%, n=190), White (84%, n=208), and non-Hispanic or Latino (92%, n=228). Ages ranged from 26 to 86 years with an average of 60 years. Before the surgery, 45 % of the cohort had consumed alcohol and the smoking history was largely unknown (95%, n=235). The Fitbit data obtained 5 weeks before the surgery suggested that this was a physically active cohort as per the physical activity standards defined by WHO and CDC [19][20]. The daily average for “light active minutes” in the cohort was 180 minutes which is considered a “healthy lifestyle” according to the WHO [16]. However, the cohort also had average sedentary minutes that was higher than suggested for a healthy lifestyle (948 minutes compared to the suggested 540 minutes) [19][20]. The clinical covariates for the cohort lie in the normal range [21][22]. The average hemoglobin level in blood was 13.03 g/dL and the albumin level in blood was 4.12 g/dL. However, the cohort had an average BMI ratio slightly higher than the normal range [23] with the maximum BMI ratio being 78.3, indicating the presence of highly obese individuals. The smoking habit variable was not included in the study because of its disproportionate division of unknown versus the other categories. The validity of the frailty index was accessed by calculating the slope of the best fit log of the frailty index in proportion to age, the rate of accumulation of deficits was found to be 0.06, prior estimate is 0.03 per year [15]. The pre-surgery QoL adjustment was done for 115 (47%) patients. Characteristics of the cohort are summarized in Table 1.

When the entire cohort was divided into moderate/low (n=109) and high users (n=138) the distribution of the population changed and is summarized in Table 1. The proportion of individuals represented in different demographic and social factor groups were similar among subgroups. The clinical covariates for the two cohorts were also similar and lie within the normal range of albumin and hemoglobin level in the blood for a healthy adult [21][22]. The average frailty index appears to be higher for moderate/low wearable users (0.570) with respect to the entire cohort (0.549). The average frailty index for high users (0.541) was slightly lower than the average of the entire cohort. The Fitbit activity data for the two populations suggests that people who used the device consistently were more active as compared to those who used the device moderately. The patients using the device regularly on average had 35 minutes more light active minutes than the population using the device irregularly, and on an average burned 150 calories more than the moderate wearable users.

Table 1: Characteristics of study participants

		Total		Moderate/Low users		High users	
		N	%	N	%	N	%
Number of patients		247		109		138	
Categorical Variables							
Gender	Female	190	77%	83	76%	108	78%
	Male	57	23%	26	24%	30	22%
Race	White	208	84%	90	83%	117	85%
	Black or African American	13	5%	6	6%	7	5%
	Asian	5	2%	1	1%	5	4%
	None of these	21	9%	8	7%	9	7%
Ethnicity	Not Hispanic or Latino	228	92%	99	91%	129	93%
	Hispanic or Latino	14	6%	8	7%	6	4%
	None Of These	5	2%	2	2%	3	2%
Smoking Habit	Unknown	235	95%	105	96%	130	94%
	Past or Current Smoker	5	2%	3	3%	4	3%
	Never Smoked	7	3%	1	1%	4	3%
Alcohol consumer	Yes	112	45%	49	45%	61	44%
	No	3	1%	2	2%	3	2%
	Unknown	117	47%	58	53%	74	54%
Recovery (measured by QoL)	Good	153	62%	67	62%	94	68%
	Poor	94	38%	42	38%	43	32%
Continuous Variables	**Mean [SD]**	**Min**	**Max**	**Mean [SD]**		**Mean [SD]**	
Age *(years)*	60 [13.45]	26	86	57 [13.23]		62 [13.3]	
Frailty index*	0.5493 [0.082]	0.29	0.86	0.571 [0.07]		0.541 [0.08]	
Mean calories burnt in a day	802.19 [403.05]	573.87	2608.29	715.35 [389.80]		869.8[406.04]	
Mean light active minutes in a day	180.31 [73.59]	143.76	379.71	159.24 [77.62]		195.66 [67.41]	
Mean sedentary minutes in a day	947.97 [241.28]	329.29	1440	1044.08[249.9]		874.14[210.24]	
Mean very active minutes in a day	14.49 [17.96]	2.08	125.86	11.44 [13.92]		16.85 [20.29]	
Mean steps count in a day	6440 [3360.60]	4230	17543	5624 [3298]		7066 [3288]	
Albumin level	4.12 [0.361]	9.91	78.3	4.13 [0.45]		4.11 [0.26]	
Hemoglobin level	13.03 [1.280]	8.51	15.9	13.02[1.32]		13.04 [1.23]	
BMI ratio	32.4 [8.546]	9.91	78.3	33.8 [8.69]		31.3 [8.34]	

*Created using 19 variables including 5 wearable device variables.

Univariate Analysis

The primary risk factors of poor recovery from the univariate analysis for the entire population of 247 were gender, age, and frailty index. Findings from the univariate analysis of the entire cohort are summarized in Table 2. Females are at twice as high risk for having poor recovery post-surgery as compared to males (OR=2.22, $p<0.025$). People 65 years and over are at a threefold greater risk of having poor recovery after surgery (OR=3.11, $p<0.001$) as compared to people 18-49 years old. The frail population above an average frailty index (0.54) had a higher risk of having poor recovery as compared to the non-frail population (OR=2.72, $p<0.001$). Whites (OR= 1.68) and non-Hispanic or Latino (OR= 1.06) were not statistically significant.

On performing the univariate analysis (Table 2) for people who used the Fitbit device regularly, the significant risk factors were age and frailty index. High wearable users of Fitbit devices who are in the age range of 50-64 were associated with an increased risk for poor recovery post-surgery (OR 1.98, $p<0.048$) compared to young population (18-49 years). However, most of the elderly people (65 years and over) are in the category of good recovery post-surgery and have a lower risk of having poor recovery (OR 0.74, $p<0.048$).

Table 2: Univariate analysis of association between recovery status and risk factors.

		Total*							High usage of wearable*							Moderate/Low usage of wearable*						
		Good Recovery		Poor Recovery		Odds	OR	P value	Good Recovery		Poor Recovery		Odds	OR	P value	Good Recovery		Poor Recovery		Odds	OR	P value
		N	Rates per 100 patients	N	Rates per 100 patients				N	Rates per 100 patients	N	Rates per 100 patients				N	Rates per 100 patients	N	Rates per 100 patients			
Characteristics		153		94					95		43					70		39				
Gender	Female	110	57.9	80	42.1	0.73	2.22	0.025	72	67	36	33	0.50	1.62	0.410	49	59	34	41	0.70	2.92	0.074
	Male	43	75.4	14	24.6	0.33	1.00		23	77	7	23	0.31	1.00		21	81	5	19	0.24	1.00	
Race[#]	White	125	60.1	83	39.9	0.67	1.68	0.229	77	66	40	34	0.52	3.06	0.114	59	66	31	34	0.53	0.73	0.711
	Non-White	28	71.8	11	28.2	0.40	1.00		18	86	3	14	0.17	1.00		11	58	8	42	0.73	1.00	
Ethnicity[#]	Not Hispanic or Latino	141	61.8	87	38.2	0.62	1.06	1.000	88	68	41	32	0.47	1.63	0.821	65	66	34	34	0.53	0.53	0.523
	Other	12	63.2	7	36.8	0.59	1.00		7	78	2	22	0.29	1.00		5	50	5	50	1.00	1.00	
Alcohol consumer[#]	Yes	73	65.2	39	34.8	0.54	1.08	0.092	43	69	19	31	0.45	0.96	0.990	32	65	17	35	0.54	0.94	0.989
	Other	80	66.7	40	33.3	0.50	1.00		52	68	24	32	0.47	1.00		38	63	22	37	0.58	1.00	
Age	18-49	31	57.0	23	43.0	0.75	1.00		16	73	6	27	0.38	1.00		20	63	12	38	0.60	1.00	
	50-64	42	53.0	38	48.0	0.91	1.22	0.001	24	57	18	43	0.75	1.98	0.048	24	62	15	38	0.63	1.05	0.010
	65 years and over	34	30.0	79	70.0	2.33	3.11		58	78	16	22	0.28	0.74		12	32	26	68	2.17	3.62	
Frailty	0-0.54	90	71.0	36	29.0	0.40	1.00	0.001	58	78	16	22	0.28	1.00	0.015	30	75	10	25	0.34	1.00	0.114
	0.55-1	58	48.0	63	52.0	1.09	2.72		37	58	27	42	0.73	2.61		40	58	29	42	0.73	2.15	

*The division for good or poor recovery was done based on the average QoL of the population, for the entire cohort mean QoL is 0.663, for high wearable users the mean QoL is 0.67, for moderate/low wearable users the mean QoL is 0.65

[#]Combined all small proportion categories as other.

In moderate/low users of Fitbit, age was the only significant risk factor (Table 2). People who are 65 years and over are threefold higher risk of poor recovery post-surgery (OR 3.62, $p<0.010$) compared to young people (18-49 years).

Multivariable Analysis

Findings from the multivariable analysis of the entire cohort are summarized in Table 3. Among 247 patients, three covariates were observed to be significant risk factors of poor recovery status. Among sociodemographic variables, age and race were significant risk factors. The elderly population is more likely to have a poor recovery as compared to the population below that age group (OR 1.76, 95% 1.55-4.08, $p<0.024$). The frailty index was also a statistically significant risk factor. Population with a higher frailty index was at increased risk of poor recovery as compared to individuals whose frailty index was lower than 0.54 (OR 1.69, 95% 1.05-7.22, $p<0.006$).

The multivariable analysis on high wearable users shows that people with frailty index over 0.54 (frail) have higher risk of having poor recovery (OR 1.73, 95%CI 1.08-9.62, $p<0.007$). In moderate wearable users' frailty index is not a statistically significant risk factor (Table 3).

Table 3: Multivariable analysis for quality of life (QoL).

Risk Factors	**All users (N=247)**		**Moderate/Low wearable users (N=109)**		**High wearable users (N=138)**	
	OR (95% CI)	P value	OR (95% CI)	P value	OR (95% CI)	P value
Gender (Female, ref. Male)	2.67 (0.98-6.08)	0.055	3.05 (1.66-7.89)	0.012	1.31(0.26-5.43)	0.680
Race (White, ref. Non-White)	1.65 (1.25-4.05)	0.024	0.89 (0.27-6.99)	0.702	2.32 (0.26-8.09)	0.191
Ethnicity (Non-Hispanics, ref. others)	1.06 (0.27-8.88)	0.477	0.16 (0.36-2.58)	0.103	1.28(0.50-17.77)	0.660
Alcohol Consumer (Yes, ref. others)	0.68 (0.55-4.97)	0.838	0.08 (0.01-1.10)	0.056	0.98(0.15-5.39)	0.984
Age (over 65, ref. less than 65)	1.76 (1.55-4.08)	0.024	1.98 (0.29-2.24)	0.783	1.09(0.12-5.67)	0.089
Frailty Index (over 0.54, ref. less than 0.54)	1.69 (1.05-7.22)	0.006	2.08 (0.01-7.75)	0.071	1.73(1.08-9.62)	0.007
Mean light active minutes in a day	1.00 (0.99-1.05)	0.923	1.00 (1.00-1.01)	0.410	1.00(0.99-1.87)	0.560
Mean sedentary minutes in a day	1.00 (0.99-1.00)	0.691	0.99 (0.98-1.01)	0.078	1.00(1.00-1.02)	0.056
Mean very active minutes in a day	1.02 (0.99-1.03)	0.166	1.00(0.99-1.04)	0.720	1.08(0.89-1.09)	0.895

Albumin level	1.96 (0.95-5.56)	0.310	2.12 (1.96-6.98)	0.003	1.44(0.44-1.47)	0.542
BMI ratio	0.94 (0.92-.1.00)	0.051	0.98 (0.90-1.05)	0.520	0.95(0.89-1.20)	0.172
Hemoglobin level	0.89 (0.67-1.35)	0.507	0.82 (0.54-1.44)	0.224	0.96(0.61-1.69)	0.870
Model evaluation metrics						
Accuracy	0.79		0.73		0.81	
Misclassification	0.21		0.27		0.19	
Sensitivity	0.92		0.93		0.95	
Specificity	0.77		0.5		0.62	
AUC score (95%CI)	0.759 (0.652-0.772)		0.721 (0.610-0.733)		0.792 (0.741-0.879)	

Logistic Regression Model performance and wearable usage

The comparison of the Logistic Regression model performance on three datasets is summarized in Table 3. The model performance for all the participants in the baseline dataset (247) was intermediate between the subgroup datasets with high wearable and moderate wearable users. When we focused on the participants with consistent wearable usage, the accuracy of the model increased by 2% from the baseline dataset. The misclassification rate also reduced. The AUC score was highest for high wearable users (0.792, 95%CI 0.741-0.879) as compared to the other two datasets. The model performance decreased when we focused on a population that was moderate in using the device prior to surgery, the accuracy of the model dropped to 0.73 from the baseline 0.79, and the AUC score (0.721, 95%CI 0.610-0.733) was also reduced by 3 units. The ROC (Receiver Operating Characteristics) curve for the comparison between the models for the two-subgroup population is shown in Figure 2. The CI for the AUC score for high wearable users is different from the CI of moderate/low wearable users AUC score which suggests the difference between the scores obtained from the two datasets is significant.

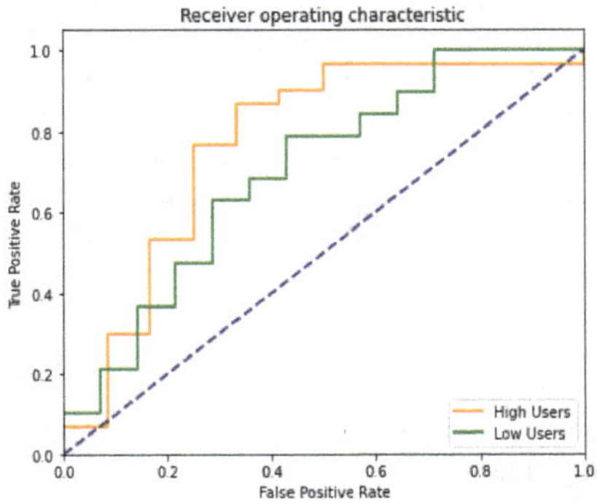

Figure 2. ROC curve for high vs moderate users of wearable device.

Discussion

In this retrospective study of AoU study participants who underwent 1 of 8 types of surgeries, we created a logistic regression model to predict poor QoL after surgery. We identified 15 risk factors to predict the recovery status post-surgery in terms of QoL. Out of which 5 risk factors were obtained from a wearable device. We examined the association between individual risk factors and QoL post-surgery using the chi-square test and multivariable logistic regression. In addition to analyzing the full cohort, we also conducted a separate analysis for the patients who were consistent in using the wearable device and patients who were moderately consistent in using the device. The model built with high wearable usage dataset had the best performance, outperforming the model implemented on the baseline dataset (see Table 3).

The findings from univariate and multivariable analyses of the entire cohort suggests that high frailty index, older age, and female gender are the driving risk factors of poor recovery post-surgery. The frailty index was the most significant risk factor which is a composition of data obtained from wearable device, survey questions and clinicopathological measures. Numerous studies have suggested that measurements from wearable sensors are related to clinical outcomes, such as complications, length of hospital stay, and readmission [24]. Adding to this evidence, we found that frailty (a measure created using the activity data obtained from the wearable device) was the most significant risk factor of poor recovery post-surgery across different datasets. Previous research also showed that patients with frailty had worse postoperative results across surgical specialties, including a greater incidence of morbidity, death, and ICU admission [25][26][27][28]. In our study, we also found a significant difference between the non-frail and frail patients in their risk associated with poor post-operative recovery. However, for the subgroup that used the device inconsistently and for a lower duration, there was no significant difference between frail and non-frail patients (Table 2 and 3). We believe that this could be because frailty is associated with older age and the population distribution in the moderate wearable users was uniform hence there is no difference in the frail and non-frail groups (Table 2). However, we did not find the 5 physical activity variables measured from wearable device to be a significant risk factor when considered independently in the univariate or multivariate analysis.

The logistic regression model with 12 features used to classify patients into poor or good recovery status gives the highest accuracy on high wearable use subgroup (provided Fitbit data continuously for 5 weeks prior to surgery) (Table 3). The good performance could be associated with the completeness, correctness, and homogeneity of the activity data obtained from the Fitbit device. Since we had observations for each day the average values of the variables for 5 weeks were non-null. The wearable usage measure defines the adherence to the device and our findings suggest that if the patient used the device more frequently to monitor themselves before the surgery, then it is more likely to accurately predict their recovery status post-surgery and readiness for the surgery.

Our findings from the logistic regression model comply with the findings of others that suggest that people at higher risk of poor recovery post-surgery could benefit the most from continuous preoperative monitoring using a wearable device [29]. In our study, the performance of the model is best on the high user dataset that includes more than half elderly population (over 65 years) and have a lower risk of poor postoperative recovery (Table 2) which could be associated with good pre-operative monitoring done through the wearable device.

The prospect of using wearable device technology for postoperative monitoring in both the hospital and the home will increase patient safety and promote continuity of care. Wearable technologies may ease early discharge and thereby minimize the length of hospital stay by continuously monitoring several health parameters [29]. Postoperative monitoring using wearable devices can also be extended before surgery to give baselines for comparison and as part of a prehabilitation approach, improving perioperative care holistically. From our findings, there is an opportunity for better guidance on wearable use to improve perioperative care. Additionally, there could be potential to integrate wearable activity data with other EHR measures. Frailty index was a good example and was one of most important risk factors for poor post operative recovery status that we identified. Another way to improve perioperative care could be to promote proper use of wearable device to monitor the patient including their vitals, and then using that data to predict the recovery status. If the patient is at high risk of poor recovery, then the surgery might be postponed, or the physician could take preventive measures to ensure better outcomes.

The major shortcoming of our work is the small sample size and QoL as the single post-operative outcome to study across multiple surgery types. Even so, the accuracy and other metrics of our model performance were good. Future work seeks to validate findings in larger datasets derived from a variety of hospital settings.

Acknowledgment

We thank Dr. Ryan Roemmich for discussion of experimental techniques and advice on experimental design and statistical interpretation. N.S., S.S., C.T. were supported by NIH NHGRI R35 HG010714.

References

1.Knight, Stephen R et al. "Mobile devices and wearable technology for measuring patient outcomes after surgery: a systematic review." NPJ digital medicine vol. 4,1 157. 12 Nov. 2021, doi:10.1038/s41746-021-00525-1

2. Copeland, G P et al. "POSSUM: a scoring system for surgical audit." *The British journal of surgery* vol. 78,3 (1991): 355-60.

3. Haga, Y et al. "Estimation of Physiologic Ability and Surgical Stress (E-PASS) as a new prediction scoring system for postoperative morbidity and mortality following elective gastrointestinal surgery." *Surgery today* vol. 29,3 (1999): 219-25.

4. Kong, Cherng H et al. "Recalibration and validation of a preoperative risk prediction model for mortality in major colorectal surgery." *Diseases of the colon and rectum* vol. 56,7 (2013): 844-9.

5. Cho, Sylvia, et al. "Factors Affecting the Quality of Person-Generated Wearable Device Data and Associated Challenges: Rapid Systematic Review." *JMIR mHealth and uHealth* vol. 9,3 e20738. 19 Mar. 2021.

6. The All of Us Research Program is supported by the National Institutes of Health, Office of the Director: Regional Medical Centers: 1 OT2 OD026549; 1 OT2 OD026554; 1 OT2 OD026557; 1 OT2 OD026556; 1 OT2 OD026550; 1 OT2 OD 026552; 1 OT2 OD026553; 1 OT2 OD026548; 1 OT2 OD026551; 1 OT2 OD026555; IAA #: AOD 16037; Federally Qualified Health Centers: HHSN 263201600085U; Data and Research Center: 5 U2C OD023196; Biobank: 1 U24 OD023121; The Participant Center: U24 OD023176; Participant Technology Systems Center: 1 U24 OD023163; Communications and Engagement: 3 OT2 OD023205; 3 OT2 OD023206; and Community Partners: 1 OT2 OD025277; 3 OT2 OD025315; 1 OT2 OD025337; 1 OT2 OD025276. In addition, the All of Us Research Program would not be possible without the partnership of its participants.

7. Jansson, Karl-Åke, et al. "Health-related quality of life (EQ-5D) before and after orthopedic surgery." *Acta orthopaedica* vol. 82,1 (2011): 82-9. doi:10.3109/17453674.2010.548026

8. Fermont, Jilles M et al. "The EQ-5D-5L is a valid approach to measure health related quality of life in patients undergoing bariatric surgery." *PloS one* vol. 12,12 e0189190. 18 Dec. 2017, doi:10.1371/journal.pone.0189190

9. Noyez, Luc. "Is quality of life post cardiac surgery overestimated?." *Health and quality of life outcomes* vol. 12 62. 29 Apr. 2014, doi:10.1186/1477-7525-12-62

10. Brooks R: EuroQoL: the current state of play. Health Policy 1996, 37: 53–72. 10.1016/0168-8510(96)00822-6
11. Dolan P: Modeling valuations for EuroQol health states. Med Care 1997, 35: 1094–1108
12. *EQ-5D-5L User Guide - University of Nebraska Medical Center.* (https://www.unmc.edu/centric/_documents/EQ-5D-5L.pdf)
13. Koide, Ryo et al. "Quality assessment using EQ-5D-5L after lung surgery for non-small cell lung cancer (NSCLC) patients." *General thoracic and cardiovascular surgery* vol. 67,12 (2019): 1056-1061. doi:10.1007/s11748-019-01136-0
14. Panayi, A C et al. "Impact of frailty on outcomes in surgical patients: A systematic review and meta-analysis." American journal of surgery vol. 218,2 (2019): 393-400. doi:10.1016/j.amjsurg.2018.11.020.
15. Searle, Samuel D et al. "A standard procedure for creating a frailty index." *BMC geriatrics* vol. 8 24. 30 Sep. 2008, doi:10.1186/1471-2318-8-24
16. DeLong, E R et al. "Comparing the areas under two or more correlated receiver operating characteristic curves: a nonparametric approach." Biometrics vol. 44,3 (1988): 837-45
17. Tian, Lili et al. "Confidence interval estimation of the difference between paired AUCs based on combined biomarkers." Journal of statistical planning and inference vol. 139,10 (2009): 3725-3732. doi:10.1016/j.jspi.2009.05.001
18. Comparing Two ROC Curves – Independent Groups Design. Retrieved from https://ncss-wpengine.netdna-ssl.com/wp-content/themes/ncss/pdf/Procedures/NCSS/Comparing_Two_ROC_Curves-Independent_Groups_Design.pdf
19. "Physical Activity." *World Health Organization*, World Health Organization, https://www.who.int/news-room/fact-sheets/detail/physical-activity.
20. "How Much Physical Activity Do Adults Need?" *Centers for Disease Control and Prevention*, Centers for Disease Control and Prevention, 2 June 2022, https://www.cdc.gov/physicalactivity/basics/adults/index.htm.
21. *BioPro: I Met Creatinine - Centers for Disease Control and Prevention.* https://wwwn.cdc.gov/nchs/data/nhanes/2015-2016/labmethods/BIOPRO_I_MET_CREATININE_DXC800.pdf.
22. "Myalgic Encephalomyelitis/Chronic Fatigue Syndrome (ME/CFS)." *Centers for Disease Control and Prevention*, Centers for Disease Control and Prevention, 1 June 2022, https://www.cdc.gov/me-cfs/pdfs/wichita-data-access/lab-tests-code.pdf
23. "Defining Adult Overweight & Obesity." *Centers for Disease Control and Prevention*, Centers for Disease Control and Prevention, 3 June 2022, https://www.cdc.gov/obesity/basics/adult-defining.html#:~:text=If%20your%20BMI%20is%2018.5,falls%20within%20the%20obesity%20range.
24. Wells, Cameron I et al. "Wearable devices to monitor recovery after abdominal surgery: scoping review." *BJS open* vol. 6,2 (2022): zrac031. doi:10.1093/bjsopen/zrac031
25. McIsaac, Daniel I et al. "Frailty as a Predictor of Death or New Disability After Surgery: A Prospective Cohort Study." *Annals of surgery* vol. 271,2 (2020): 283-289. doi:10.1097/SLA.0000000000002967
26. Shen, Yanjiao et al. "The impact of frailty and sarcopenia on postoperative outcomes in older patients undergoing gastrectomy surgery: a systematic review and meta-analysis." *BMC geriatrics* vol. 17,1 188. 21 Aug. 2017, doi:10.1186/s12877-017-0569-2
27. Panayi, A C et al. "Impact of frailty on outcomes in surgical patients: A systematic review and meta-analysis." American journal of surgery vol. 218,2 (2019): 393-400. doi:10.1016/j.amjsurg.2018.11.020.
28. Saxton A, Velanovich V. Preoperative frailty and quality of life as predictors of postoperative complications. Ann Surg. 2011;253(6):1223–9.
29. Amin, Tajrian et al. "Wearable devices for patient monitoring in the early postoperative period: a literature review." *mHealth* vol. 7 50. 20 Jul. 2021, doi:10.21037/mhealth-20-13

Feasibility of Using an Armband Optical Heart Rate Sensor in Naturalistic Environment

Hang Yu[†], Michael Kotlyar, Sheena Dufresne, Paul Thuras, Serguei Pakhomov

University of Minnesota,
Minneapolis, MN 55108, USA
[†]*E-mail: yu000408@umn.edu*

Consumer-grade heart rate (HR) sensors including chest straps, wrist-worn watches and rings have become very popular in recent years for tracking individual physiological state, training for sports and even measuring stress levels and emotional changes. While the majority of these consumer sensors are not medical devices, they can still offer insights for consumers and researchers if used correctly taking into account their limitations. Multiple previous studies have been done using a large variety of consumer sensors including Polar® devices, Apple® watches, and Fitbit® wrist bands. The vast majority of prior studies have been done in laboratory settings where collecting data is relatively straightforward. However, using consumer sensors in naturalistic settings that present significant challenges, including noise artefacts and missing data, has not been as extensively investigated. Additionally, the majority of prior studies focused on wrist-worn optical HR sensors. Arm-worn sensors have not been extensively investigated either. In the present study, we validate HR measurements obtained with an arm-worn optical sensor (Polar OH1) against those obtained with a chest-strap electrical sensor (Polar H10) from 16 participants over a 2-week study period in naturalistic settings. We also investigated the impact of physical activity measured with 3-D accelerometers embedded in the H10 chest strap and OH1 armband sensors on the agreement between the two sensors. Overall, we find that the arm-worn optical Polar OH1 sensor provides a good estimate of HR (Pearson $r = 0.90$, $p < 0.01$). Filtering the signal that corresponds to physical activity further improves the HR estimates but only slightly (Pearson $r = 0.91$, $p < 0.01$). Based on these preliminary findings, we conclude that the arm-worn Polar OH1 sensor provides usable HR measurements in daily living conditions, with some caveats discussed in the paper.

Keywords: Heart Rate, Photoplethysmography, Electrocardiography, Wearable Sensors

1. Introduction

Consumer wearable sensors can help people monitor their overall health and provide valuable information for prevention of severe diseases and injuries.[1–3] Cardiovascular parameters such as heart rate (HR) and heart rate variability (HRV) are among the most common physiological measures that people track with their wearable sensors. The HR and HRV measurements captured by the sensors not only provide information about physical health, they can also help track mental stress which has secondary deleterious effects on health, including mental health.[4–7] The most commonly used sensors for cardiovascular measurements are wrist-worn smart watches; however, chest strap sensors are also widely used, especially in the context of sports. More recently, a class of devices that are designed to be worn on the upper arm or the forearm have become commercially available. The wrist-worn and arm-worn sensors rely on photoplethysmography (PPG: optical sensing) and chest strap sensors rely on electrocardiography (ECG). The latter tend to be more accurate than the former.[3,4,8–11] While there has been extensive prior work validating wrist-worn heart rate sensors, most of this work has been done in laboratory conditions.[1,4,12] Less work has been done to examine the validity of optical HR sensors in completely unconstrained and uncontrolled naturalistic settings. For example, a recent meta-review of 44 studies that reported on validity of wrist-worn optical sensors found only 7 studies that included daily living activities outside of a lab setting.[13] Furthermore, the results of this work have been mixed with respect to the ability of optical sensors to accurately measure heart rate in these unconstrained conditions.[2,14–17] Even fewer studies have examined arm-worn devices as an alternative to wrist-worn sensors.[18–21] These studies focused mainly on the use of these devices in the context of sports activities and demonstrated that armband devices are robust to even very strenuous physical activity. For this reason, we selected the Polar OH1 armband as an alternative to wrist-worn devices. Our current study aims to add to this prior literature a preliminary investigation of an armband optical heart activity sensor worn for an extended period of time in everyday life settings. We use the Polar OH1 armband sensor together with the Polar H10 chest strap sensor as a reference device to collect PPG, ECG and accelerometer data and explore the feasibility and accuracy of using Polar OH1 armband's PPG measurements obtained in the naturalistic environment with Polar H10 chest strap's ECG measurements as the reference standard. Additionally, we aimed to examine the impact of motion on the accuracy of HR estimates.

2. Study Design

This preliminary study is part of a larger study of cigarette smokers. The larger study is ongoing and is aimed at predicting smoking events in order to develop or use therapeutic interventions (e.g., nicotine lozenge) that can be administered just-in-time. In this study, participants are asked to wear several sensors including the Polar H10 and OH1 for approximately 14 consecutive days (2 weeks). During both weeks, the participants are asked to use a smartphone app specifically designed for this study (PhysiAware®) that uses Bluetooth Low Energy (BLE) interface to connect to the study devices, collect the real-time measurements and transmit them to a study server several times a day. The participants are also asked to use the app to indicate when they smoke each cigarette and the reasons for smoking the cigarette. The current analysis includes only Polar H10 and OH1 heart activity trace and accelerometer data from the first 16 participants from the larger study.

3. Data Collection and Processing

This study was approved by the University of Minnesota Institutional Review Board and is currently ongoing.

3.1. *Data Collection*

The data collected from the armband and chest strap sensors are temporarily stored by the PhysiAware® app on the smartphone of each participant until the participants upload the data to a University of Minnesota server. The PhysiAware® app was developed specifically for this project as a native app on iOS and Android platforms. Figure 1 illustrates both versions and shows the main screen that the participants would see after logging in with their study credentials (a randomly generated study ID).

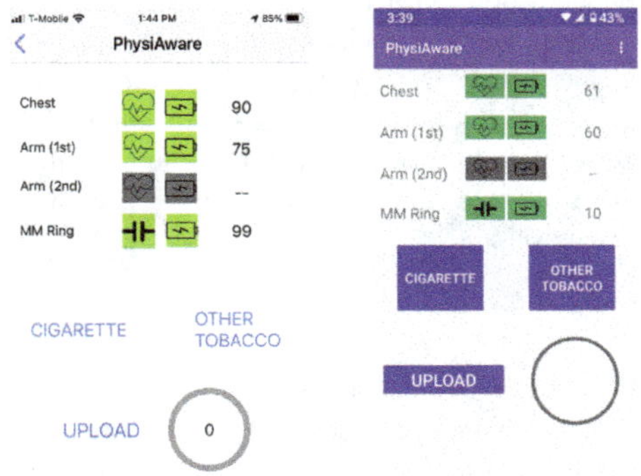

(a) (b)

Fig. 1: The iOS and Android versions of the PhysiAware app. a) iOS. b) Android.
* MM Ring is a ring sensor (MoodMetric®) used in the study for monitoring electrodermal activity - not relevant to the current analysis.

The iOS and Android apps implemented the standard Polar BLE application programming interface for collecting raw data from the sensors. Both the H10 chest strap and the OH1 armband sensors are capable of storing limited data in their onboard memory; however, this capability is not open to third-party developers when the OH1 armband sensor is operated in the "PPI" mode (i.e., the mode that calculates and reports inter-beat interval durations needed for heart rate variability measurements). For our study, we wanted to leverage the "PPI" mode specifically along with collecting raw blood volume pulse data. Thus, all sensor data were streamed "live" over the BLE interface rather than stored locally and transferred in batches. The streaming data were aggregated on the smartphone and the participants were prompted every 3-4 hours to upload their data to the study server. The motivation for not doing automated uploads stems from the fact that some of the participants may have limited or costly cellular data plans. Therefore, we designed the app to detect the presence of Wi-Fi connectivity and alert the participants only when a Wi-Fi network (vs. a cellular data network) was available to upload the data. We also wanted to provide the participants with the ability to manually control the uploads as they take a significant amount of bandwidth and can be disruptive to the participant's other activities on their smartphone. These design considerations were adopted in order to make the app as accessible as possible to a broad range of participants from a variety of socioeconomic backgrounds.

Due to the remote and naturalistic nature of the study, we encountered several other challenging issues that affected data collection. For example, Polar OH1 arm sensor battery life is approximately only 8 hours, which precludes continuous monitoring. To compensate for this challenge, each participant was provided with two OH1 sensors that they could use interchangeably while the other sensor was being charged. While all participants participated in a remote training session via Zoom with the study coordinator on how to wear and use the study devices, situations arose where participants unintentionally corrupted the data. This included wearing the sensors incorrectly, or forgetting to wear them at all. These challenges are inherent to remote naturalistic settings and result in lower volume of usable data than what can be obtained in laboratory conditions or with extensive hands-on training. The collected data still may present further challenges due to noise from the variability of the environments and participants' daily life activities.[22]

3.2. *Data Processing*

For the current study, we selected the signals available simultaneously from both the H10 chest strap and OH1 armband to time-align the two signals as illustrated in Figure 2. Some of the more frequent noise artifacts included short gaps with missing samples. The majority of these gaps were under 60 seconds in duration and were likely attributable to interruptions in BLE connectivity between the smartphone and the sensors. The missing data corresponding to these short gaps that are under 60 seconds comprises on average 0.52% of the total data volume for ECG and 0.94% for PPG. Our current approach for dealing with these short gaps is to back- and forward-fill them by taking half of the values needed to fill the gap from the preceding signal, and the other half from the subsequent signal. This approach is motivated by the thought that the HR signal does not typically change dramatically over a short period of time; however, if such a change does occur during the 60 second gap (e.g. the participant begins strenuous activity during the gap) by forward-filling the first half of the gap and back-filling the second half we expect to represent the start time of the increase in HR more accurately. Less frequent gaps longer than 60 seconds were left as missing data and excluded from analysis.

We collected the high frequency time indexed ECG data and 3-D acceleration data from Polar H10 chest strap sensor at a sampling rate of 130Hz and 200Hz, respectively. The time indexed PPG and 3-D acceleration data from the Polar OH1 armband were sampled at 135Hz and 50Hz, respectively. To detect peaks in the ECG and PPG signals and calculate instantaneous HR we used Kubios[23] software package (version 3.5.0) which also performs additional noise filtering and generates HR estimates in the output. Other computational approaches were considered such as band pass filtering, detrending methods for removing noise, and manually calculating HR with code. However, we opted to use the Kubios for preprocessing so that our results are more easily reproducible and applicable to a wider research audience. Kubios processes ECG and PPG data by using an automatic beat detection algorithm and HR calculation from inter-beat intervals. Additionally, Kubios applied a detrending approach on the

ECG and PPG data based on smoothness priors regularization. The detrending method removes the slow non-stationary component of the signals.[24] Peak detection and time-alignment between PPG and ECG signals are shown in Figure 2. Less frequent gaps longer than 60s were filled with zeros prior to Kubios processing to maintain the time-alignment between the ECG and PPG data. Kubios generates 'NaN' values for heart rate variability features for the zero-filled sections resulting in excluding these sections from analysis.

After handling missing data as described above, we imported the data into Kubios to generate HR estimates over 1-minute frames overlapping by 10 seconds. The resulting time series were used to calculate the Pearson correlation coefficients between ECG and PPG HR estimates. Due to the large size of the high frequency time series ECG and PPG data (e.g., up to 120 million rows for 11 days of ECG data per participant), we segmented the data into smaller chunks ranging from a few hours to one day (24 hours) before importing into Kubios.

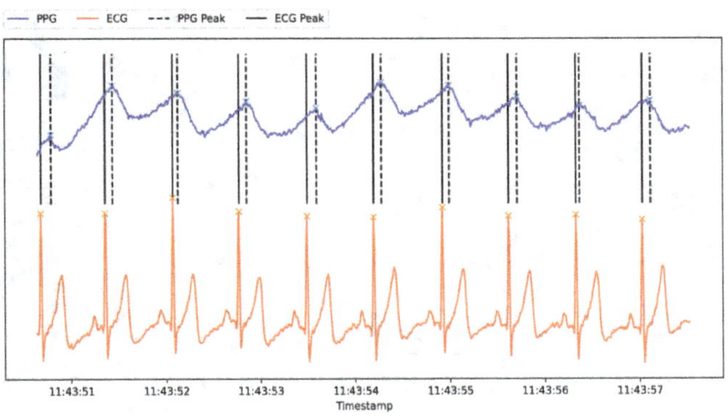

Fig. 2: Illustration of peak alignment between ECG (lower) and PPG (upper) signals.

3.3. *Filtering*

To investigate the impact of noise introduced by physical activity in daily life, we experimented with several physical activity filters based on 3-D accelerometer data from accelerometers embedded in the H10 chest-strap and OH1 armband devices. Since the H10 is attached to the person's torso and OH1 is attached to the upper forearm, we expect that these sensors will capture different and potentially complementary types of activity. All physical activity filters use the magnitude of acceleration along the x, y, z axes from a given 3-D accelerometer. The calculation of the magnitude of overall acceleration is as follows:

$$G = sqrt(x^2 + y^2 + z^2) \tag{1}$$

where G represents the magnitude of acceleration and x, y, z represents acceleration along each of the 3 axes. In the rest of the paper we refer to this overall magnitude of acceleration as

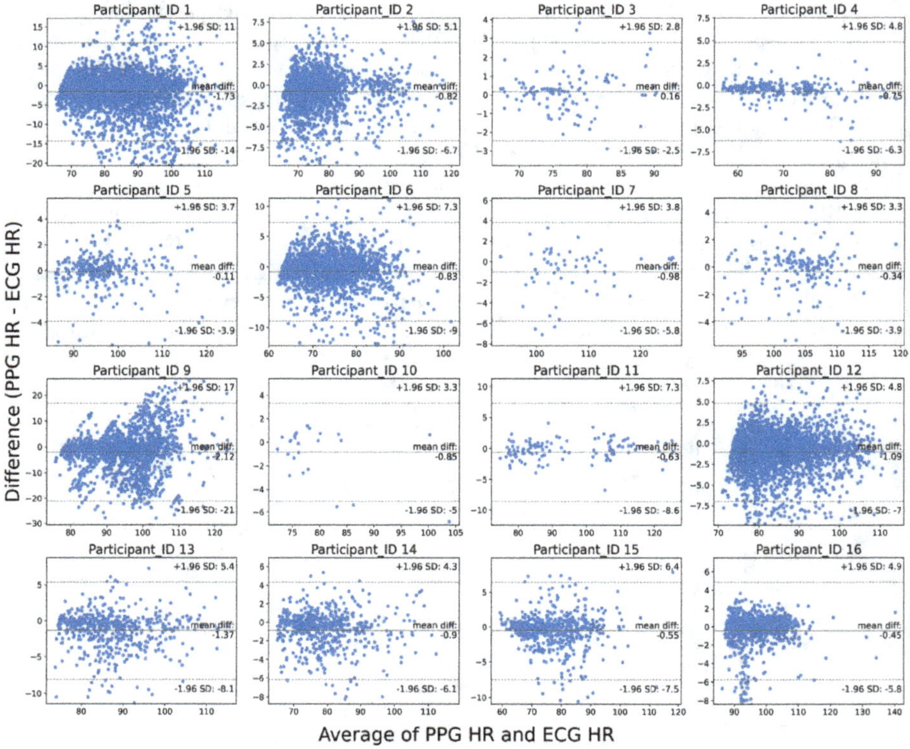

Fig. 3: Bland-Altman Plot of the differences in PPG and ECG estimates of HR without any filtering physical activity.

G-value. This measure is used to filter out the data that contain high levels of physical activity defined as above the 75th percentile of all G-values for a given sensor. We then defined three filters based on the G-values calculated from a) H10 chest strap, b) OH1 armband, and c) from the union of both H10 and OH1 G-values (i.e., when either the chest-strap or the armband device indicated excessive motion). Each of the three filters also removes samples that result in HR greater than 200 beats per minute (based on maximum heart rate calculated as 211 - (0.64*age)[25]) or lower than the empirically determined 3rd percentile. Activity filters were used in this study to assess if the correlation between the measures reported by the PPG and ECG sensors are adversely impacted by including periods of physical activity so as to assess the quality of the data collected by the arm-band sensor during times of physical activity.

Table 1: Participant Characteristics

D	Age	Sex	Race	Arm	HR (OH1) Mean (SD)	HR (H10) Mean (SD)	G-val (OH1) Mean (SD)	G-val (H10) Mean (SD)
	<40	m	non-white	left	83.56 (10.0)	85.29 (11.0)	1007 (23)	973 (14)
	<40	f	white	left	76.28 (9.0)	77.11 (9.0)	1021 (12)	1007 (17)
	40-50	f	white	left	77.43 (6.0)	77.27 (6.0)	968 (137)	1015 (7)
	<40	m	non-white	left	69.17 (8.0)	69.92 (9.0)	999 (15)	994 (11)
	40-50	f	white	left	96.73 (7.0)	96.84 (7.0)	1002 (9)	988 (29)
	>50	f	white	left	74.55 (7.0)	75.38 (7.0)	1001 (12)	995 (13)
	<40	m	white	left	106.9 (8.0)	107.88 (8.0)	1023 (11)	999 (28)
	<40	f	white	left	103.45 (5.0)	103.85 (5.0)	1012 (13)	993 (10)
	<40	m	white	left	94.02 (10.0)	96.14 (10.0)	1002 (18)	1019 (11)
0	40-50	f	white	left	79.88 (9.0)	80.73 (9.0)	1017 (6)	979 (17)
1	<40	m	white	left	94.22 (14.0)	94.85 (14.0)	1024 (22)	1019 (11)
2	40-50	m	white	left	84.0 (8.0)	85.09 (8.0)	1008 (12)	1006 (12)
3	>50	m	white	right	86.65 (8.0)	88.02 (9.0)	1019 (66)	1009 (10)
4	<40	f	white	left	78.8 (9.0)	79.71 (9.0)	1024 (14)	976 (16)
5	<40	f	white	left	76.19 (9.0)	76.75 (9.0)	1017 (16)	997 (20)
6	40-50	f	white	left	96.56 (6.0)	97.02 (6.0)	1013 (8)	991 (10)
Mean	42	–	–	–	86.14 (8.3)	87.0 (8.5)	1009.8(25)	997.5 (15)

4. Results

The basic demographic and physiological characteristics of participants are presented in Table 1. The participant characteristics presented in Table 1 demonstrate the variability present in HR measurements across study participants.

4.1. *Agreement between PPG and ECG HR Estimates*

We used the HR values generated by Kubios for both PPG and ECG signals and calculated Pearson correlation of the two sets of HR values. The Pearson correlation measures the strength of the linear relationship between two variables. As shown in Table 2, the HR calculated from PPG data is positively correlated with the HR calculated from ECG data with correlation coefficients higher than 0.80 except for one participant's data likely due to excessive motion or the chest strap not being tight enough. The results summarized in Table 2 show that the majority of participants' correlation coefficients increased only modestly after using physical activity filters. All correlations in Table 2 are statistically significant (p-value <0.01).

The average HR correlation before any physical activity filtering is 0.90. Using either or both the OH1 armband or H10 chest strap physical activity filter to remove data with high G-values increases the average HR correlation to 0.91. Since different participants have different numbers of samples, we also report correlations weighted by the number of samples resulting in slightly lower estimates but still remaining above 0.80 (see Table 2).

Correlations between PPG and ECG heart rate estimates by age and sex of the participants are illustrated in Figure 4 and suggest that these participant characteristics did not substantially affect the results.

Fig. 4: Differences in correlations between PPG and ECG HR by age & sex of the participants.

5. Discussion

The results of our preliminary study indicate that it is feasible to obtain HR estimates from the Polar OH1 armband that are in agreement with reference ECG estimates. These findings are encouraging for studies that involve observation of cardiac activity in naturalistic settings.

Several previous studies[26–28] that examined the agreement between PPG and ECG signals reported correlations between 0.91 and 0.98 which is comparable to the correlations we found in the present study; however, some previous studies noted somewhat variable performance of wrist-worn PPG sensors with some devices having correlation with ECG in the 0.83-0.84 range[16] or even lower.[17] Furthermore, while the ecological study by Nelson et al.[26] demonstrated overall low error rates for wrist-worn (Apple Watch 3 and Fitbit Charge 2) devices under sleeping, sitting, walking, and running conditions over a 24 hour period, they also found relatively high error rates during activities of daily living and as movement became more erratic during various conditions. These decreases in accuracy are likely due to the fact that wrist-worn devices by design tend to fit relatively loosely around the wrist. An overly tight fit would make the device uncomfortable to wear for long periods of time. The Polar OH1 armband used in our study seeks to overcome this problem by placing the sensor higher up the forearm which tends to experience lower amplitude motion than the wrist during activity and allows for tighter fit with an elastic strap that also minimizes the amount of motion. Another key difference in our study is the length of the observation period. In our study, participants wore the sensors as continuously as they were comfortable with over an approximately two-week period. We are not aware of other studies in which participants wore a chest strap and an armband for such an extended period of time. The extended nature of the observation period enables us to examine the performance of the armband sensor in a greater variety of naturalistic conditions and activities of daily living. The fact that we find the armband to provide accuracy on par with other devices used in laboratory conditions is particularly encouraging as they show that this type of PPG sensor can be comfortably worn over a long period of time and provides reliable measurements.

Table 2: Correlation between ECG and PPG estimates of HR and number of samples remaining after applying various physical activity filters based on accelerometers embedded in devices.

ID	Physical Activity Filters							
	No filter		**OH1 armband**		**H10 chest strap**		**OH1+H10**	
	Corr.	**N***	**Corr.**	**N**	**Corr.**	**N**	**Corr.**	**N**
1	0.82	4021	0.82	3146	0.85	3274	0.86	2600
2	0.95	2195	0.95	1950	0.94	1649	0.94	1466
3	0.97	124	0.97	101	0.98	92	0.98	79
4	0.95	280	0.94	216	0.98	245	0.98	198
5	0.96	326	0.96	291	0.96	275	0.96	252
6	0.83	2025	0.84	1762	0.85	1768	0.86	1544
7	0.95	64	0.96	60	0.77	44	0.76	42
8	0.93	177	0.93	148	0.92	139	0.92	120
9	0.53	2312	0.55	2026	0.58	1506	0.58	1298
10	0.98	26	0.98	25	0.97	25	0.98	24
11	0.96	114	0.99	80	0.99	76	0.99	63
12	0.93	3219	0.93	2395	0.92	2813	0.92	2102
13	0.92	569	0.94	536	0.95	292	0.95	269
14	0.96	613	0.97	514	0.96	559	0.97	479
15	0.93	677	0.93	615	0.95	530	0.95	489
16	0.90	1455	0.93	1264	0.90	1378	0.94	1196
Unweighted Mean	0.90	1137.3	0.91	945.5	0.90	916.6	0.91	763.8
Weighted Mean	0.85	1137.3	0.85	945.5	0.87	916.6	0.87	763.8

* number of samples (HR estimates) used to calculate the correlations. Each sample corresponds to HR calculated over a 1-minute frame and, thus, N also approximates the number of minutes of data included in the correlation analysis, not counting the overlaps between frames.

We also find some individual variation across participants as illustrated by the correlations reported in Table 2. Additionally, the Bland-Altman plots in Figure 3 show there's also some variability in the distribution of the differences between ECG and PPG HR estimates across the participants. However, the mean differences of all participants are close to zero and majority of the data is within the 95% confidence intervals of limits of agreement. The distribution of the points outside of the 95% confidence intervals does not suggest a clear pattern of association between the differences and the magnitude of the heart rate measurements.

Visual examination of the differences between groups by age and sex, shown in Figure 4, suggests no substantial differences between these groups. Due to the small number of participants, we did not perform a formal statistical subgroup analysis. The data shown in Figure 4 suggests that the male subgroup contains a possible outlier (participant 9 in Table 2).

Several prior studies examined the impact of skin tone on optical green wavelength heart rate sensor accuracy and found that these sensors were reasonably accurate across various skin tones but slightly less accurate for darker skin tones varying by devices and conditions.[13,29,30] While our study so far included only 2 participants with non-white skin tone, our results are consistent with this prior work in that we found that the optical OH1 armband was only slightly less in agreement with the ECG estimates of heart rate than the group average for one of the two non-white participants ($r = 0.82$ vs $r = 0.90$ - see Table 2, participant 1 in "No filter" column) and slightly higher than the group average for the other non-white participant ($r = 0.95$ vs $r = 0.90$ - see Table 2, participant 4 in "No filter" column). Clearly, we cannot draw any definitive conclusions from these results due to the small number of participants overall and non-white participants in particular.

Another important finding is that removing heart data that corresponds to physical activity based on the accelerometer values did not have a major impact on the agreement between ECG and PPG estimates of heart rate. This is an encouraging finding because it indicates that the armband sensor provides robust heart rate estimates in the presence of physical activity.

6. Limitations and Challenges

The results should be interpreted in light of several limitations. First, our sample size is small as this is a preliminary pilot study. Second, we use only the standard accelerometer-based filtering techniques. More advanced filtering techniques exist that may be able to further reduce noise, potentially increasing the correlation. Finally, the participants included in this study are smokers, whose physiological characteristics may differ from the general population.

In addition to the limitations listed above, we also want to highlight several valuable lessons that we learned in the process of doing this study that can be applied in our future work or by others who intend to perform similar studies. On the technical side, we found that some of the participants had some trouble with maintaining the connectivity between the wearable sensors and the smartphone. The Bluetooth devices used in this study have a relatively short range (10-30 meters); therefore, the "live" streaming mode for data transfer is vulnerable to the participants walking away from their smartphones beyond the Bluetooth range. Clearly, this results in undesirable data loss which may be prevented by recording data locally on the sensor devices in addition to streaming.

We also found significant differences in terms of the technical challenges in app development for the two platforms: iOS and Android. While developing for the Android platform was logistically easier than for iOS mostly due to complicated security controls on iOS apps, it was also much more challenging to use Android apps in the study due to large variability in how various Android smartphone manufacturers handle battery management. In order to maintain the streaming of data from devices to the smartphones, the battery management mode had to be manually turned off by the participants and was achieved with variable success depending on which smartphone the participant owned. This issue is more difficult to resolve without resorting to recruiting only participants who own Apple smartphones, which would make recruitment more difficult and may introduce unintended selection bias into the study. In the current study, we addressed this issue by monitoring incoming data on a regular basis for signs of significant data loss and had the study coordinator follow up with those participants that were identified this way.

7. Acknowledgments

Funded by NIH NIDA award DA049446 and supported by the University of Minnesota CTSI (UL1-TR002494). The content of this article is solely the responsibility of the authors and does not necessarily represent the official views of the NIH.

References

1. D. Castaneda, A. Esparza, M. Ghamari, C. Soltanpur and H. Nazeran, A review on wearable photoplethysmography sensors and their potential future applications in health care, *International journal of biosensors & bioelectronics* **4**, p. 195 (2018).
2. S. V. Pakhomov, P. D. Thuras, R. Finzel, J. Eppel and M. Kotlyar, Using consumer-wearable technology for remote assessment of physiological response to stress in the naturalistic environment, *Plos one* **15**, p. e0229942 (2020).
3. K. E. Speer, S. Semple, N. Naumovski and A. J. McKune, Measuring heart rate variability using commercially available devices in healthy children: A validity and reliability study, *European Journal of Investigation in Health, Psychology and Education* **10**, 390 (2020).
4. S. Heo, S. Kwon and J. Lee, Stress detection with single ppg sensor by orchestrating multiple denoising and peak-detecting methods, *IEEE Access* **9**, 47777 (2021).
5. S. Datar, L. Ferland, E. Foo, M. Kotlyar, B. Holschuh, M. Gini, M. Michalowski and S. Pakhomov, Measuring physiological markers of stress during conversational agent interactions, in *International Workshop on Health Intelligence*, 2021.
6. C.-Y. Chuang, W.-R. Han and S.-T. Young, Heart rate variability response to stressful event in healthy subjects, in *13th International Conference on Biomedical Engineering*, 2009.
7. V.-T. Ninh, S. Smyth, M.-T. Tran and C. Gurrin, Analysing the performance of stress detection models on consumer-grade wearable devices, *arXiv preprint arXiv:2203.09669* (2022).
8. K. Hinde, G. White and N. Armstrong, Wearable devices suitable for monitoring twenty four hour heart rate variability in military populations, *Sensors* **21**, p. 1061 (2021).
9. R. Gilgen-Ammann, T. Schweizer and T. Wyss, Rr interval signal quality of a heart rate monitor and an ecg holter at rest and during exercise, *European journal of applied physiology* **119**, 1525 (2019).
10. S. Ollander, C. Godin, A. Campagne and S. Charbonnier, A comparison of wearable and stationary sensors for stress detection, in *2016 IEEE International Conference on systems, man, and Cybernetics (SMC)*, 2016.
11. M. Umair, N. Chalabianloo, C. Sas and C. Ersoy, A comparison of wearable heart rate sensors for hrv biofeedback in the wild: An ethnographic study, in *25th annual international CyberPsychology, CyberTherapy & Social Networking Conference*, 2020.
12. A. Bellante, L. Bergamasco, A. Bogdanovic, N. Gozzi, L. Gecchelin, M. Khamlich, A. Lauditi, E. D'Arnese and M. D. Santambrogio, Emocy: Towards physiological signals-based stress detection, in *2021 IEEE EMBS International Conference on Biomedical and Health Informatics (BHI)*, 2021.

13. Y. Zhang, R. G. Weaver, B. Armstrong, S. Burkart, S. Zhang and M. W. Beets, Validity of wrist-worn photoplethysmography devices to measure heart rate: A systematic review and meta-analysis, *Journal of Sports Sciences* **38**, 2021 (2020), PMID: 32552580.
14. Y. S. Can, N. Chalabianloo, D. Ekiz, J. Fernandez-Alvarez, C. Repetto, G. Riva, H. Iles-Smith and C. Ersoy, Real-life stress level monitoring using smart bands in the light of contextual information, *IEEE Sensors Journal* **20**, 8721 (2020).
15. K. Hovsepian, M. Al'Absi, E. Ertin, T. Kamarck, M. Nakajima and S. Kumar, cstress: towards a gold standard for continuous stress assessment in the mobile environment, in *Proceedings of the 2015 ACM international joint conference on pervasive and ubiquitous computing*, 2015.
16. R. Wang, G. Blackburn, M. Desai, D. Phelan, L. Gillinov, P. Houghtaling and M. Gillinov, Accuracy of Wrist-Worn Heart Rate Monitors, *JAMA Cardiology* **2**, 104 (01 2017).
17. S. Gillinov, M. Etiwy, R. Wang, G. Blackburn, D. Phelan, A. Gillinov, P. Houghtaling, H. Javadikasgari and M. Desai, Variable accuracy of wearable heart rate monitors during aerobic exercise, *Medicine Science in Sports Exercise* **49**, p. 1 (03 2017).
18. M. Schubert, A. Clark and A. Rosa, The polar® oh1 optical heart rate sensor is valid during moderate-vigorous exercise, *Sports Medicine International Open* **02**, E67 (03 2018).
19. D. Muggeridge, K. Hickson, A. Davies, O. Giggins, I. Megson, T. Gorely and D. Crabtree, Measurement of heart rate using the polar oh1 and fitbit charge 3 wearable devices in healthy adults during light, moderate, vigorous, and sprint-based exercise: Validation study (preprint) (10 2020).
20. E. Hermand, J. Cassirame, G. Ennequin and O. Hue, Validation of a photoplethysmographic heart rate monitor: Polar oh1, *International Journal of Sports Medicine* **40**, 462 (07 2019).
21. I. Hettiarachchi, S. Hanoun, D. Nahavandi and S. Nahavandi, Validation of polar oh1 optical heart rate sensor for moderate and high intensity physical activities, *PLOS ONE* **14**, p. e0217288 (05 2019).
22. M. Gjoreski, H. Gjoreski, M. Luštrek and M. Gams, Continuous stress detection using a wrist device: in laboratory and real life, in *proceedings of the 2016 ACM international joint conference on pervasive and ubiquitous computing: Adjunct*, 2016.
23. M. P. Tarvainen, J.-P. Niskanen, J. A. Lipponen, P. O. Ranta-Aho and P. A. Karjalainen, Kubios hrv–heart rate variability analysis software, *Computer methods and programs in biomedicine* **113**, 210 (2014).
24. M. P. Tarvainen, P. O. Ranta-Aho and P. A. Karjalainen, An advanced detrending method with application to hrv analysis, *IEEE transactions on biomedical engineering* **49**, 172 (2002).
25. B. M. Nes, I. Janszky, U. Wisløff, A. Støylen and T. Karlsen, Age-predicted maximal heart rate in healthy subjects: The hunt fitness study, *Scandinavian Journal of Medicine & Science in Sports* **23**, 697 (2013).
26. B. W. Nelson and N. B. Allen, Accuracy of consumer wearable heart rate measurement during an ecologically valid 24-hour period: intraindividual validation study, *JMIR mHealth and uHealth* **7**, p. e10828 (2019).
27. A. Kumar, R. Komaragiri, M. Kumar *et al.*, A review on computation methods used in photoplethysmography signal analysis for heart rate estimation, *Archives of Computational Methods in Engineering* , 1 (2021).
28. S. E. Stahl, H.-S. An, D. M. Dinkel, J. M. Noble and J.-M. Lee, How accurate are the wrist-based heart rate monitors during walking and running activities? are they accurate enough?, *BMJ Open Sport & Exercise Medicine* **2** (2016).
29. B. Fallow, T. Tarumi and H. Tanaka, Influence of skin type and wavelength on light wave reflectance, *Journal of clinical monitoring and computing* **27** (02 2013).
30. B. Bent, B. A. Goldstein, W. Kibbe and J. P. Dunn, Investigating sources of inaccuracy in wearable optical heart rate sensors, *NPJ Digital Medicine* **3** (2020).

Graph Representations and Algorithms in Biomedicine

Brianna Chrisman[1], Maya Varma[1], Sepideh Maleki[2], Maria Brbic[3], Cliff Joslyn[4], Marinka Zitnik[5]
[1]Stanford University, [2]UT Austin, [3]EPFL, [4]Pacific Northwest National Labs,[5]Harvard University

1. Introduction

Connectivity is a fundamental property of biological systems: on the cellular level, proteins interact with each other to form protein-protein interaction networks (PPIs); on the organism level, neurons are arranged in a network; and on a community-level, species can have complex relationships with one another that drive the development and balance of an ecosystem. Graphs, representations of systems consisting of entities as vertices and their connections as edges, are a useful structure to characterize many such systems. Such models can be used to understand biological systems that naturally have a network structure, including PPIs, biological neurons, and ecosystems. In today's information age, graph representations and algorithms (often in combination with machine learning techniques) are used to organize massive amounts of related data, much of which may be heterogeneous or unstructured, and identify patterns that represent novel biological insights. PSB's 2023 session ``Graph Representations and Algorithms in Biomedicine," encompasses modern developments in graph theory and its applications to various fields of biomedicine. This session includes a wide range of research - knowledge graphs built from text-mined health data, heterogeneous networks using multi-omic databases, and graphs refined to represent uncertainty or improve memory usage.

Recent developments around graphs in biomedicine have primarily revolved around methods of constructing, comparing, and making predictions from graphs using massive datasets that have become commonplace in biomedical computation. Even more challenging, or perhaps more opportune, is that many problems in biomedicine involve multiple different data types. A specific challenge is how to integrate heterogeneous, sometimes unstructured data, to make network-based insights. The proceedings for this session tackle several different challenges: understanding and predicting protein networks (Eyuboglu et al., Ayati et al.), improving feature representations of various types of graphs (Chen et al., Soman et al., Luo et al.), making use of family structure via graph approaches (Shemirani et al., Mossel et al.), creatively applying traditional algorithms to novel tasks (Magnano et al.), and representing uncertainty in network structures (Liu et al., Krishnan et al.).

2. Understanding and Predicting Molecular Networks

Predicting the structure, function, and associated phenotypes of molecular networks has emerged as a grand challenge that is very amenable to graph-based approaches. One past related strategy for protein-protein interaction network prediction has been to quantify protein similarly in terms of protein sequence similarity, or their distance to one another in the network. However, Eyuboglu et al., Ayati et al., illustrate that there are other factors we can consider when trying to predict protein or molecule similarities, phenotypes, and networks. In their paper, "Mutual Interactors as a Principle for the Discovery of Phenotypes in Molecular Networks", Eyuboglu et al. suggest that molecular similarity is not dictated by molecule-molecule distances in graph space, but is better described using representations of a molecule's mutual interactors. They show that this principle - that molecules with similar sets of mutual interactors have similar phenotypes - holds for protein-protein, signaling, and genetic networks. To further showcase the application of this theory in practice, they build a machine learning model using a simple mutual interactor feature space, and illustrate that they can predict drug targets, disease proteins, and molecular functions better than complex algorithms and feature spaces.

Interestingly, Ayati et al. take a comparatively opposite approach. They argue that while many past strategies to predict kinase-substrate associations have used sequences alone, there is a wealth of publically available information on protein structure and function that could vastly improve kinase-substrate predictions. The authors use sequence similarity, shared molecular pathways, and co-evolution, co-occurrence, and co-phosphorylation patterns to construct a phosphosite-phosphosite association network, and protein-protein interactions, mutual biological pathways, and kinase family membership to construct kinase-kinase networks. Using these networks to represent kinase and substrates' node embeddings, they train a machine learning model that outperforms the state-of-the-art methods for predicting kinase-substrate interactions. Ayati et al.'s complex node embeddings using heterogenous information sources, and Eyuboglu et al.'s simple and interpretable representations of molecular similarities illustrate two different and creative approaches for improving the feature space that we use to understand and make predictions on molecular networks.

3. Understanding and Predicting Molecular Networks

Key contributions in both Ayati et al and Eyuboglu et al were improved representations of the feature space of molecular networks. Improving network feature representations - reducing memory or runtime requirements, boosting interpretability, or increasing accuracy in downstream machine learning pipelines - is a general goal of research in biomedical networks. "Contrastive learning of protein representations with graph neural networks for structural and functional annotations" by Luo et al., “A Graph Coarsening Algorithm for Compressing Representations of Single-Cell Data with Clinical or Experimental Attributes" by Chen et al., and "Time-aware Embeddings of Clinical Data using a Knowledge Graph" by Soman et al. all tackle this challenge in various ways.

In "Contrastive learning of protein representations with graph neural networks for structural and functional annotations", like Ayati et al and Eyuboglu et al, Luo et al. focus their efforts on the protein space. Rather than trying to use functional and structural information to predict protein-protein interactions, they use the ladder to predict functional and structural annotations. Their algorithm, "PenLight" uses a graph neural network (GNN) that integrates three dimensional protein structure, and sequence representation using a language model. They use contrastive earning to train the GNN to learn protein representations that reflect similarities encompassing not only similarities in the linear sequence space, but semantic similarities and similarities in the function or sequence space. They benchmark their algorithm on predicting EC (Enzyme Commission) numbers and CATH (class, architecture, topology, homologous superfamily) classifications, functional and structural annotations respectively available on the Protein Databank, demonstrating its superior performance.

In "A Graph Coarsening Algorithm for Compressing Representations of Single-Cell Data with Clinical or Experimental Attributes", Chen et al. introduce a novel approaching for compressing graphs of single-cell data. In single-cell experiments, measurements from tens or hundreds of thousands of cells are often visualized and analyzed by looking at a dimensionality-reduced representation of the cells. This dimensionality reduced representation of the cells can also be described in a graph, where cells or groups of cells with similar features in the latent space are connected to each other on the graph. Chen et al. develop a method for performing graph coarsening on this network, which can save memory, remove noise, and help distinguish biologically relevant patterns in downstream pipelines. Importantly, their algorithm “cytocoarsening”} not only uses not only cell-cell similarity in the single-cell measurements (in their case they were using mass cytometry data), but also clinical, experimental, and phenotypical attributes of the cells. Using single cell mass cytometry datasets from cohorts from studies of preeclampsia, COVID-19, and cytomegalovirus, the authors demonstrate that their algorithm has comparable runtime to state-of-the-art graph coarsening packages, and improved performance when it comes building coarsened graphs that depict biologically relevant patterns.

Finally, in "Time-aware Embeddings of Clinical Data using a Knowledge Graph", Soman et al. construct biomedical knowledge graphs from electronic health records to create machine readable representations of patient health data. They map a patient EHR data onto nodes of a popular biomedical knowledge network and use a random walk to create node embeddings with features corresponding to nodes in the knowledge network graph. To capture to temporal dynamics of the EHR data, they build embedding vectors unique to each yearly interval time frame. Such embeddings yield a highly interpretable two-dimensional array, with rows representing time and columns representing SPOKE nodes. Using these embeddings as feature representations for patients from a group of Parkinson's and non-Parkinson's phenotypes, they build a machine learning model that can predict Parkinson's using data from one year or earlier before a patient's diagnosis. Feature representations without the temporal representation were not as predictive, illustrating that the dynamic nature of electronic health records is an important aspect to capture when creating feature representations of EHR data.

4. Making Use of Family Structure

While molecular networks are an obvious candidate for graph representations and algorithms, another candidate is genetic data from related individuals. A classic family tree is a graph, and graphs can also depict more complicated genetic relationships from individuals. In "Selecting clustering algorithms for Identity-by-descent mapping" by Shemirani et al. and "Efficient Reconstruction of Stochastic Pedigrees: Some Steps from Theory to Practice" by Mossel et al., both authors use graphs to understand and quantify the genetic relatedness of individuals.

In "Selecting clustering algorithms for Identity-by-descent mapping" Shemirani et al. develop a metric for benchmarking identity-by-descent clustering algorithms. They introduce a novel approach for finding groups of individuals that share short segments of their genome inherited from a recent common ancestor (a concept known as "identical-by-descent"). They designed a clustering benchmark and used it to compare the performance of several popular IBD clustering algorithms. They found that Infomap and Markov clustering community detection methods had the highest statistical power in finding communities with shared IBD. Notably, they show that traditional clustering metrics, such as modularity and purity, do not necessarily provide the highest statistical power to IBD clustering applications, necessitating the development of improved IBD clustering benchmarking strategies.

In "Efficient Reconstruction of Stochastic Pedigrees: Some Steps from Theory to Practice", Mossel et al. build on their previous work where they reconstructed a pedigree from genetic data under a number of simplifying assumptions. In this newer work, the authors walk us through the process by which they made simplifications to improve the runtime of their algorithm, observe scenarios in which the faster algorithm has decreased performance, identified the theoretical issues and limiting cases with their new approach, and correct accordingly. Specifically, they found that the faster version of their algorithm performs with pedigrees that are beyond 2 generations. They claim that this is due to inbreeding nearly always present in large pedigrees, and show that the algorithm improves when inbreeding is limited in their simulation. Finally, they introduce a belief propagation heuristic that helps account for possible inbreeding, allowing for both fast and accurate pedigree reconstruction.

5. Applying Traditional Graph Algorithms to Novel Tasks

Molecular networks and pedigrees are natural structures by which graph strategies can be applies, but Magnano et al. show that traditional graph-based approaches can show promise for novel tasks. In "Graph algorithms for predicting subcellular localization at the pathway level", Magnano et al predict subcellular protein localization using an edge labeling task. Using biological pathway networks, the authors develop graph algorithms in order to predict the location within a cell that an interaction is taking place. They pose this challenge as an edge-labeling task and compare the performance of a variety of several models including GNNs, probabilistic models, and discriminative classifiers. Notably they found that directly using data from protein localization databases was not sufficient to accurately predict pathway level localization and topology or some other form of structural information is needed to predict localization in context. Finally, they use their findings to predict interaction localizations in a human cytomegalovirus infection.

6. Representing Uncertainty in Networks

A major weak point that often goes unaddressed in biomedical graph-related networks is that networks derived from publicly available data have noise and potential inaccuracies in their structures and topologies. Often this goes unaddressed, but accounting for such inaccuracies or better understanding their effects may allow us to build more graph-based feature representation and models of biological phenomenon. In "Improving target-disease association prediction through a graph neural network with credibility information", by Liu et al. and "Integrated Graph Propagation and Optimization with Biological Applications" by Krishnan et al., the authors tackle the challenge of representing uncertainty in such biological networks.

"Improving target-disease association prediction through a graph neural network with credibility information" Liu et al., hope to improve target-disease association (TDA) predictions using biological networks and text mined data from the literature. They develop creatTDA - a deep learning based framework that learned latent feature representations of targets and diseases. Uniquely, they propose a new way to encode credibility information obtained from literature in their mode. They do this by learning credibility encodings for different known target-disease associations, using their co-occurrences in the literature as a label. CreaTDA was able to predict known TDAs with higher sensitivity and specificity, as well as novel TDAs including an association between bronchiolitis and the epidermal growth factor receptor and viral diseases and vascular endothelial growth factor.

In "Integrated Graph Propagation and Optimization with Biological Applications," Krishnan et al. seek to understand how uncertainty effects graphs representing biological network dynamics. In mathematical models of biological systems, rate constants are often unknown and network propagation has emerged as a suitable method for understanding how changes in nodes effect one another, without the need for parameter estimation. Krishnan et al extend some of the ideas in network propagation theory to develop a system of identifying which specific perturbation patterns may drive networks into desired states. Their method Integrated Graph Propagation and Optimization (IGPON) embeds propagation into an objective function and uses optimization strategies to minimize the difference between a target and observed state. They illustrate the value of their algorithm on predicting gene expression patterns using various sets of knockout data.

7. Conclusion

This session of papers addresses a wide variety of biological challenges: predicting molecular interactions, deriving insights from unstructured EHR data, quantifying genetic relationships between related individuals, and understanding the relationships between drug, disease, and phenotype. Excitingly, these works tackle these challenges using a diverse collection of graph-based approaches. We hope the common language of graphs will make apparent the intersections and differences in the problems addressed and the strategies taken, and readers and authors alike will be able to take additional inspiration from the ideas posed in this session.

References

Ayati, M., Yilmaz, S., Lopes, F., Chance, M., Koyuturk, M. "Prediction of Kinase-Substrate Associations Using The Functional Landscape of Kinases and Phosphorylation Sites". Proceedings of the Pacific Symposium for Biocomputing 2022.

Chen, C., Crawford, E., Stanley, N. 1 "A Graph Coarsening Algorithm for Compressing Representations of Single-Cell Data with Clinical or Experimental Attributes". Proceedings of the Pacific Symposium for Biocomputing 2022.

Eyuboglu, S., Zitnik, M., Leskovec, J. "Mutual interactors as a principle for phenotype discovery in molecular interaction networks". Proceedings of the Pacific Symposium for Biocomputing 2022.

Krishnan, K., Shi, T. "Integrated Graph Propagation and Optimization with Biological Applications". Proceedings of the Pacific Symposium for Biocomputing 2022.

Liu, C., Yu, C., Lei, Y., Lyu, K., Tian, T., Li, Q., Zhao, D., Zhou, F., Zeng, J. "Improving target-disease association prediction through a graph neural network with credibility information". Proceedings of the Pacific Symposium for Biocomputing 2022.

Luo, J., Luo, Y. "Contrastive learning of protein representations with graph neural networks for structural and functional annotations". Proceedings of the Pacific Symposium for Biocomputing 2022.

Magnano, C.S., Gitter, A. "Graph algorithms for predicting subcellular localization at the pathway level". Proceedings of the Pacific Symposium for Biocomputing 2022.

Mossel, E., Vulakh, D. "Efficient Reconstruction of Stochastic Pedigrees: Some Steps From Theory to Practice". Proceedings of the Pacific Symposium for Biocomputing 2022.

Shemirani S. , Belbin G.M., Burghardt, K., Lerman, K., Avery, C.L., Kenny, E.E., Gignoux, C.R., Ambite, J. "Selecting Clustering Algorithms for Identity-By-Descent Mapping". Proceedings of the Pacific Symposium for Biocomputing 2022.

Soman, K., Nelson, C.A., Cerona, G., Baranzini, S.E. "Time-aware Embeddings of Clinal Data Using a Knowledge Graph". Proceedings of the Pacific Symposium for Biocomputing 2022.

Mutual interactors as a principle for phenotype discovery in molecular interaction networks

Sabri Eyuboglu,[1,*‡] Marinka Zitnik,[2,3,4,*] Jure Leskovec[1]

[1]*Department of Computer Science, Stanford University, Stanford, CA 94305*
[2]*Department of Biomedical Informatics, Harvard University, Boston, MA 02115*
[3]*Broad Institute of MIT and Harvard, Cambridge, MA 02142*
[4]*Harvard Data Science, Cambridge, MA 02138*

**Equal Contribution. ‡Corresponding author. Email: eyuboglu@stanford.edu*

Biological networks are powerful representations for the discovery of molecular phenotypes. Fundamental to network analysis is the principle—rooted in social networks—that nodes that interact in the network tend to have similar properties. While this long-standing principle underlies powerful methods in biology that associate molecules with phenotypes on the basis of network proximity, interacting molecules are not necessarily similar, and molecules with similar properties do not necessarily interact. Here, we show that molecules are more likely to have similar phenotypes, not if they directly interact in a molecular network, but if they interact with the same molecules. We call this the mutual interactor principle and show that it holds for several kinds of molecular networks, including protein-protein interaction, genetic interaction, and signaling networks. We then develop a machine learning framework for predicting molecular phenotypes on the basis of mutual interactors. Strikingly, the framework can predict drug targets, disease proteins, and protein functions in different species, and it performs better than much more complex algorithms. The framework is robust to incomplete biological data and is capable of generalizing to phenotypes it has not seen during training. Our work represents a network-based predictive platform for phenotypic characterization of biological molecules.

Keywords: Network medicine, Molecular phenotypes, Protein Interactions, Graph neural networks

1. Introduction

Molecules in and across living cells are constantly interacting, giving rise to complex biological networks. These networks serve as a powerful resource for the study of human disease, molecular function and drug-target interactions.[1,2] For instance, evidence from multiple sources suggests that causative genes from the same or similar diseases tend to reside in the same neighborhood of protein-protein interaction networks.[3–6] Similarly, proteins associated with the same molecular functions form highly-connected modules within protein-protein interaction networks.[7]

These observations have motivated the development of bioinformatics methods that use molecular networks to infer associations between proteins and molecular phenotypes, including diseases, molecular functions, and drug targets.[8–11] Many of these methods assume that molecular networks obey the organizing principle of homophily: the idea that similarity breeds connection (see Figure 1b).[12] However, while this principle has been well-documented in social networks of many types (*e.g.* friendship, work, co-membership), it is unclear whether it captures the dynamics of biological networks. If not, existing bioinformatics methods that assume homophily may not realize the full potential of biological networks for scientific discovery.

To better understand the place for homophily in bioinformatics, we consider groups of phenotypically similar molecules (*e.g.* molecules associated with the same disease, involved in the same function, or targeted by the same drug) and study their interactions in large-scale biological networks. We find that most molecules associated with similar phenotypes do not interact directly in molecular networks, a result which puts into question the assumption of homophily, an assumption that is taken for granted by so many bioinformatics methods.

In fact, a different principle better explains how phenotypic similarity relates to network structure in biology. On average, two molecules that interact directly with one another will have less in common than two molecules that share many *mutual interactors*, just as people in a social network may share mutual friends. We call this the mutual interactor principle and validate it empirically on a diverse set of biological networks (see Figure 1c).

Motivated by our findings, we develop a machine learning framework, *Mutual Interactors*, that can predict a molecule's phenotype based on the mutual interactors it shares with other molecules. We demonstrate the power, robustness, and scalability of *Mutual Interactors* on three key prediction tasks: disease protein prediction, drug target identification, and protein function prediction. With experiments across three different kinds of molecular networks (protein-protein interaction, signaling and genetic interaction) and four species (*H. sapiens, S. cerevisiae, A. thaliana, M. musculus*), we find that *Mutual Interactors* substantially outperforms existing methods, with gains in recall up to 61%. Additionally, we show that the weights learned by our method provide insight into the functional properties and druggability of mutual interactors.

Mutual Interactors is an approach based on a different network principle than existing bioinformatics methods. That it can outperform state-of-the-art approaches suggests a need to rethink the fundamental assumptions underlying machine learning methods for network biology.

2. Network connectivity of molecular phenotypes

One way we measure phenotypic similarity between two molecules is by comparing the set of phenotypes (e.g., diseases or functions) associated with each molecule and quantifying their similarity with the Jaccard index. We find that the average Jaccard index of the 62,084 molecule pairs that interact in the human reference interactome (HuRI) is significantly smaller than the average Jaccard index of the 62,084 molecule pairs with most degree-normalized mutual interactors ($p = 2.00 \times 10^{-59}$, dependent t-test).[13] We replicate this finding on three other large-scale interactomes: a PPI network derived from the BioGRID database[14] ($p = 3.56 \times 10^{-26}$) another derived from the STRING database[15] ($p = 1.29 \times 10^{-10}$) and the PPI network compiled by Menche *et al.* ($p = 1.02 \times 10^{-4}$).[16]

To further evaluate these two principles (i.e., homophily and Mutual Interactor), we collect 75,744 disease-protein associations[17] and analyze their interactions in the protein-protein interaction network (see Figure 1d-f and Figure D4). For each disease-protein association we compute the fraction of the protein's direct interactors that are also associated with the disease. In only 17.8% of disease-protein associations is this fraction statistically significant ($P < 0.05$, permutation test). Moreover, in 46.5% of disease-protein associations, the protein does not interact directly with any

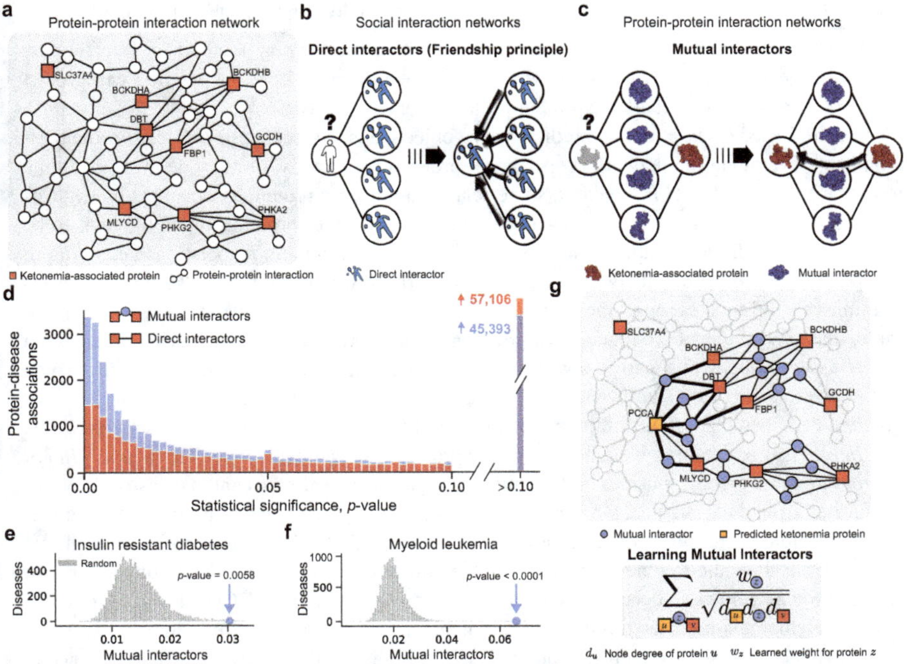

Fig. 1: **The mutual interactor principle. (a)** The human protein-protein interaction (PPI) network with proteins associated with ketonemia highlighted (in red). **(b)** Schematic illustration of the friendship principle (*i.e.*, network homophily[12]) in a social network of five individuals. **(c)** Schematic illustration of the mutual interactor principle in a PPI network. According to the *mutual interactor* principle, the grey protein is likely associated with ketonemia because it interacts with the same proteins as a known ketonemia protein (in red); the two proteins share four mutual interactors (in blue). **(d)** Comparison of mutual interactors and direct interactors as principles of disease protein connectivity in a human PPI network. For $75{,}744$ disease-protein associations, the statistical significance (p-value) of the mutual interactor score (in blue) and the direct interactor score (in red) is computed and plotted for comparison (see Section B.3). We calculate the average mutual interactor score of proteins associated with **(e)** insulin resistant diabetes and **(f)** myeloid leukemia (see Section B.3). **(e-f)** The observed mutual interactor scores (in blue) are significantly larger than random expectation (in grey).

other proteins associated with the same disease. For each disease-protein association, we also compute the degree-normalized count of mutual interactors between the protein and other proteins associated with the disease. We call this the association's *mutual interactor score* (see Section B.3). In 31.0% of disease-protein associations, this score is significant (permutation test, $P < 0.05$). For other molecular phenotypes, we get similar results: proteins targeted by the same drug have a significant direct interactor score 35.1% of the time and a significant mutual interactor score 67.5% of the time (see Figure 3b).[18] In only 31.0% of the protein-function associations in the Gene Ontology is the direct interactor score significant, compared with 56.7% for the mutual interactor score (see Figure D1a).[19] For biological processes in the Gene Ontology, these fractions are 26.7% and 46.3% for the direct and mutual interactor scores, respectively (see Figure D1b). These results suggest that, in biological networks, there is more empirical evidence for the Mutual Interactor principle than there is for the principle of homophily.

3. *Mutual Interactors* as a machine learning method for predicting molecular phenotypes

Based on the mutual interactor principle, we develop a machine learning method for inferring associations between molecules and phenotypes. Below, we describe how our method can predict disease-protein associations using the protein-protein interaction network.

In network-based disease protein prediction, the objective is to discover new disease-protein associations by leveraging the network properties of proteins we already know to be involved in the disease. Our method, *Mutual Interactors*, scores candidate disease-protein associations by evaluating the mutual interactors between the candidate protein and other proteins already known to be associated with the disease. Rather than score candidate disease-protein associations according to the raw count of these mutual interactors, our method learns to weight each mutual interactor differently. Intuitively, this makes sense: the significance of a mutual interactor depends on it's profile. For example, that two proteins both interact with the same hub-protein is probably less significant than two proteins both interacting with a low-degree signalling receptor. Rather than hard-code which mutual interactors we deem significant, through training on a large set of disease pathways, *Mutual Interactors* learns which proteins often interact with multiple proteins in the same disease pathway. *Mutual Interactors* maintains a weight w_z for every protein z in the interactome. This allows *Mutual Interactors* to down-weight spurious mutual interactors when evaluating a candidate association.

To further ground our method, we consider its application to a specific disease pathway. Ketonemia is a condition wherein the concentration of ketone bodies in the blood is abnormally high.[20,21] In Figure 1a, we show the Ketonemia pathway in the human protein-protein interaction network. In red are the proteins known to be associated with Ketonemia, including MLYCD and BCKDHA.[22,23] We see that Ketonemia-associated proteins rarely interact with one another. In Figure 1g, we show the same network and disease pathway, but now we've highlighted in blue the mutual interactors between Ketonemia-associated proteins. Of all 21,557 proteins in the human protein-protein interaction network, *Mutual Interactors* predicts that PCCA, shown in orange, is the most likely to be associated with Ketonemia. PCCA is a protein involved in the breakdown of fatty acids, a process which produces ketone bodies as a byproduct. PCCA shares mutual interactors with four proteins known to be associated with Ketonemia: BCKDHA, DBT, FBP1, and MLCYD. Further, two of these mutual interactors, MCEE and PCCB, are of very low degree (with 7 and 21 interactions respectively) and are weighted highly by *Mutual Interactors*.

3.1. *Problem Formulation*

Though *Mutual Interactors* was motivated by the molecular phenotype prediction problem, it is a general model that can be applied in any setting where we'd like to group nodes on a graph. Suppose we have a graph $G = \{V, E\}$ and a set of node sets $\mathbf{S} = \{S_1, S_2, ..., S_k\}$ where each set S_i is a subset of the full node set $S_i \subseteq V$. Note that the node sets need not be disjoint. For example, G could be a PPI network and each S_i could be the set of proteins associated with a different phenotype. We can split each node set S_i into a set of training nodes $\tilde{S}_i \subset S_i$ and a set of test nodes $S_i - \tilde{S}_i$. Given $\tilde{S}_i$ and the network G, we're interested in uncovering the full set of nodes S_i. Formally, this means computing a probability $Pr(u \in S|\tilde{S})$ for each node $u \in V$.

3.2. *The Mutual Interactors model*

The mutual interactors of two nodes u and v are given by the set $M_{u,v} = N(u) \cap N(v)$, where $N(u)$ is the set of u's one-hop neighbors. For each node $z \in V$, *Mutual Interactors* maintains a weight w_z. As we discussed above, these weights are meant to capture the degree to which each node in the graph acts as a mutual interactor in the node sets of $\mathbf{S}$. With a weight w_z for every possible mutual interactor in the network, we model the probability that a query node u is in a full node set S given the training set $\tilde{S} \subseteq S$ as

$$Pr(u \in S|\tilde{S}) = \sigma\left(a\left(\sum_{v\in\tilde{S}} \frac{1}{\sqrt{d_v d_u}} \sum_{z\in M_{v,u}} \frac{w_z}{\sqrt{d_z}}\right) + b\right) \tag{1}$$

where d_u is the degree of node u, $\sigma(x) = \frac{1}{1+e^{-x}}$ is the sigmoid function, a is a scale parameter, b is a bias parameter, and w_z is a learned weight for node z. With sparse matrix multiplication we can efficiently compute the probability for every node in the network with respect to a batch of k training sets $\{\tilde{S}_1, ..., \tilde{S}_k\}$. Let's encode training sets with a binary matrix $\mathbf{X} \in \{0,1\}^{k\times n}$, where $x_{ij} = 1$ if and only if $j \in \tilde{S}_i$. With $\mathbf{X}$, we can efficiently compute the probability matrix $\mathbf{P}$ where $P_{ij} = Pr(j \in S_i|\tilde{S}_i)$ with

$$\mathbf{P} = \sigma(a(\mathbf{X}\mathbf{D}^{-\frac{1}{2}}\mathbf{A}\mathbf{W}\mathbf{D}^{-\frac{1}{2}}\mathbf{A}\mathbf{D}^{-\frac{1}{2}}) + b) \tag{2}$$

where $\mathbf{A}$ is the adjacency matrix, $\mathbf{D}$ is the diagonal degree matrix and $\mathbf{W}$ is a diagonal matrix with the weights w_z on the diagonal. Note this formulation ignores any edge weights in the graph, future work should explore simple extensions of this formulation that incorporate edge weights.

3.3. *Training the Mutual Interactors model*

Given a meta-training set of k node sets $\mathbf{S} = \{S_1, ..., S_k\}$, we can learn the model's weights $\mathbf{W}$, a, and b that maximize the likelihood of observing the node sets in the meta-training set. During meta-training we simulate node set expansion by splitting each set S_i into a training set $\tilde{S}_i$ encoded by $\mathbf{X} \in \{0,1\}^{m\times n}$ and a target set $S_i - \tilde{S}_i$ encoded by $\mathbf{Y} \in \{0,1\}^{m\times n}$. For each epoch, we randomly sample 90% of associations for the training set and use the remaining 10% for the test set. The input associations $\mathbf{X}$ are fed through our model to produce association probabilities $\mathbf{P}$. We update model weights by minimizing weighted binary cross-entropy loss

$$\ell(\mathbf{X},\mathbf{Y}) = \sum_{i=1}^{m}\sum_{j=1}^{n} -[\alpha_p Y_{ij}\log P_{ij} + (1-Y_{ij})\log(1-P_{ij})] \tag{3}$$

where α_p is the weight given to positive examples. Since there are far more positive examples than negative examples, we set $\alpha_p = \frac{\#\text{ negative examples}}{\#\text{ positive examples}}$.

We can minimize the loss using a gradient-based optimizer. First, we compute the gradient of the loss with respect to model parameters via backpropagation. Then, we use ADAM with a learning rate of 1.0. We train *Mutual Interactors* with weight decay 10^{-5} and a batch size of 200.[24] We train for five epochs and use $\frac{1}{9}$ of the training labels as a validation set for early stopping.

4. Predicting disease-associated proteins with *Mutual Interactors*

We systematically evaluate our method by simulating disease protein discovery on 1,811 different disease pathways. In ten-fold cross-validation, we find that *Mutual Interactors* recovers a larger frac-

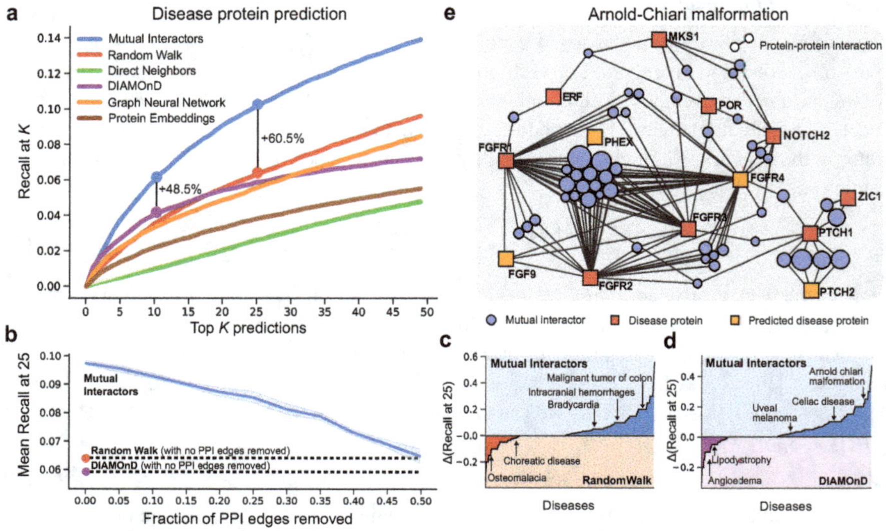

Fig. 2: **Uncovering disease proteins with the mutual interactor principle.** **(a)** Overall performance evaluation. The plot shows the fraction of disease proteins recovered within the top k predictions for $k = 1$ to $k = 50$ (recall-at-k). The dotted lines at $k = 10$ and $k = 25$ show the percent-increase in recall over the next best performing method. **(b)** Effect of data incompleteness on performance. Shown is Mutual Interactors' recall-at-25 as a function of the fraction of protein-protein interactions randomly removed from the network. Dotted lines indicate performance of random walks and DIAMOnD on a full PPI network with no PPIs removed. **(c-d)** Comparison of Mutual Interactors and baseline methods across diseases. For each disease in our dataset (x-axis), we plot the difference in recall-at-25 (y-axis) between Mutual Interactors and two baseline methods: **(c)** random walks, **(d)** DIAMOnD.[25] **(f)** Comparison of the degree-normalized Mutual Interactor weights of drug targets and non-targets. Shown is the distribution of degree-normalized Mutual Interactor weights for 2,212 drug targets[18] (in blue), and, for comparison, the distribution of degree-normalized Mutual interactor weights for 2,212 random proteins that are not targets of any drug (in grey). **(g)** Mutual Interactor neighborhood for Arnold-Chiari (AC) malformation. The neighborhood includes known disease proteins (red squares), Mutual Interactors' top predictions (orange squares), and the mutual interactors between them (blue circles). Mutual interactors are sized proportional to their learned Mutual Interactor weight, w_z.

tion of held-out proteins than do existing disease protein discovery methods. Specifically, for 10.2% of disease-protein associations our method ranks the held-out protein within the first 25 proteins in the network (recall-at-25 = 0.102). *Mutual Interactors*'s performance represents an improvement of 60.9% in recall-at-25 over the next best performing method, random walks. Other network-based methods of disease protein discovery including DIAMOnD[10] (recall-at-25= 0.059), random walks[26] (recall-at-25 = 0.063), and graph convolutional neural networks[25] (recall-at-25 = 0.057) recover considerably fewer disease-protein associations (see Figure 2a,c-d). Moreover, *Mutual Interactors* maintains its advantage over existing methods across disease categories: in all seventeen that we considered *Mutual Interactors*'s mean recall-at-100 exceeds random walks' (see Section C.3 and Figure C3). We also study whether *Mutual Interactors* can generalize to a new disease that is unrelated to the diseases it was trained on. To do so, we train *Mutual Interactors* in the more challenging setting where similar diseases are kept from straddling the train-test divide (see Section C.2 and Figure C2). In this setting, *Mutual Interactors* achieves a recall-at-25 of 0.096, a 50.7% increase in performance over the next best method, random walks. *Mutual Interactors* can naturally be extended to incorporate other sources of protein data.[27] In Section C.4, we describe a parametric *Mutual Interactors* model that incorporates functional profiles from the Gene Ontology when evaluating mutual interactors. Instead of learning a weight w_z for every protein z, this model learns one scalar-valued function mapping gene ontology embeddings to mutual interactor weights. We show that parametric *Mutual Interactors* performs on par with the original *Mutual Interactors* model, outperforming baseline methods by 45.5% in recall-at-25 (see Figure C4).

The experimental data we use to construct molecular interaction networks is often incomplete or noisy: it is estimated that state-of-the-art interactomes are missing 80% of all the interactions in human cells.[16] In light of this, we test if our method is tolerant of data incomplete networks. We find that *Mutual Interactors* exhibits stable performance up to the removal of 50% of known PPI interactions. *Mutual Interactors*'s performance with only half of all known interactions exceeds the performance of existing methods that use all known interactions (Figure 2b).

We perform an ablation study to assess the benefits of meta-learning mutual interactor weights w_z (see Figure D8). In the study, we compare our model with *Constant Mutual Interactors* where $w_z = 1 \; \forall z$. On tasks for which we have a large dataset of phenotypes (*i.e.* disease protein prediction and molecular function prediction in humans), meta-learning w_z improves performance by up to 16.6% in recall-at-25. However, on tasks for which data is scarce (i.e. drug-target prediction and non-human molecular function prediction) learning w_z does not provide a significant benefit. For these tasks, we report performance on *constant Mutual Interactors* where $w_z = 1 \; \forall z$.

Learned weights provide insight into the function and druggability of mutual interactors. Next we analyze the mutual interactor weights learned by our method. Recall that *Mutual Interactors* learns a weight w_z for every protein z in the interactome. This allows *Mutual Interactors* to down-weight spurious mutual interactors when evaluating a candidate disease-protein association. Here, we study what insights into biological mechanisms these weights reveal. We find that normalized *Mutual Interactors* weight $\frac{w_z}{\sqrt{d_z}}$ is correlated with neither degree ($r = 0.0359$) nor triangle clustering coefficient ($r = 0.0127$) (see Figure D9). However, we do find that proteins with high weight are often involved in cell-cell signaling. We perform a functional enrichment analysis on the 75 proteins with the highest normalized weight $\frac{w_z}{\sqrt{d_z}}$. Of the fifteen functional classes most enriched in these proteins, ten including *signaling receptor activity* and *cell surface receptor signaling pathway* are directly related to transmembrane signaling and the other five including *plasma membrane part* are tangentially related to signaling (see Figure D6). Further, we find that highly-weighted proteins are often targeted by drugs. Among the 500 proteins with the highest degree-normalized weight, 33.6% are targeted by a drug in the DrugBank database.[18] By contrast only 10.9% of proteins in the wider protein-protein interaction network are targeted by those drugs. This represents a significant increase ($p \leq 6.43 \times 10^{-24}$, Kolmogorov-Smirnov test). Although no drug-target interaction data was used, training our method to predict disease proteins gives us insights into which proteins are druggable.

5. Identifying drug targets with *Mutual Interactors*

The development of methods that can identify drug targets is an important area of research,[30–33] in this section we show how our method can also be used for this task. Recall that mutual interactors between proteins targeted by the same drug are statistically overrepresented in the protein-protein interaction network (see Figure 3a). Like with disease-protein associations, *Mutual Interactors* can score candidate drug-target interactions by evaluating the mutual interactors between the candidate target protein and other proteins already known to be targeted by the drug (see Section 3.1 for a technical description of the approach). When we simulate drug-target identification with ten-fold cross

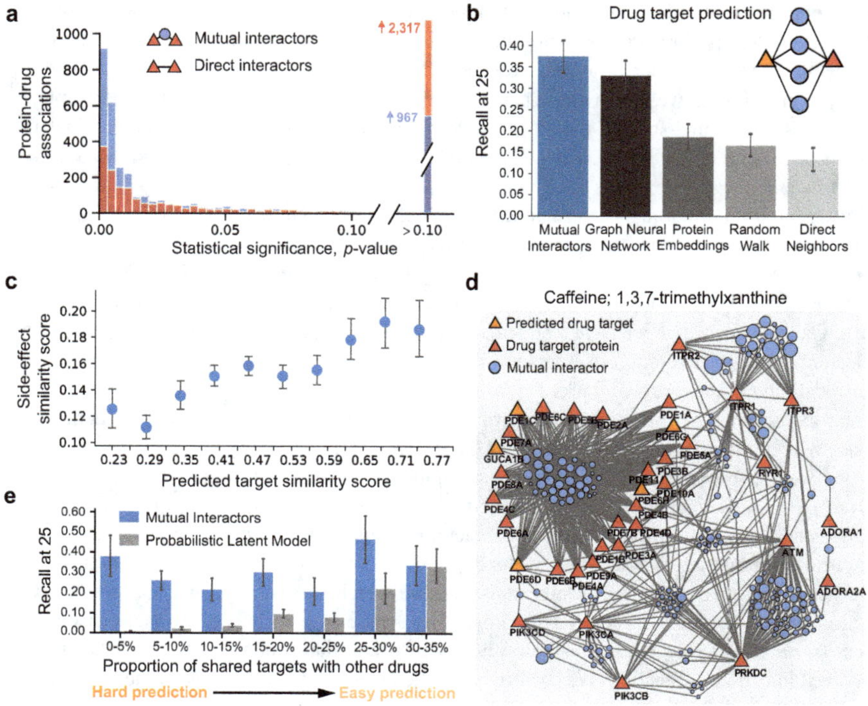

Fig. 3: **Identifying drug targets using the principle of mutual interactors.** Comparison of Mutual Interactors (in blue) and direct interactors (in red) as principles of drug-target connectivity in a human PPI network. For 4,403 drug-target associations,[28] the statistical significance (p-value) of the mutual interactor score (in blue) and the direct interactor score (in red) is computed and plotted for comparison (see Section B.3). **(a)** **(b)** Drug target identification. Shown is mean recall-at-25 across 190 drugs. **(c)** The side-effect similarity of drugs[29] (y-axis) is linearly related to the similarity of Mutual Interactors' predictions for those drugs (x-axis). **(d)** Mutual Interactors neighborhood for proteins targeted by Caffeine. The neighborhood includes caffeine-targeted proteins (red triangles), Mutual Interactors' top predictions for novel caffeine targets (orange triangles), and the mutual interactors between them (blue circles). Mutual interactors are sized proportional to their learned Mutual Interactors weight, w_z (see 3.1). **(e)** The fraction of a drug's targets recovered within the top 25 predictions (recall-at-25) vs. the maximum Jaccard similarity between the drug's targets and targets of other drugs in the training set used for machine learning. Bars indicate average recall-at-25 in each bucket.

validation on the drugs and targets in the DrugBank database,[18] we find that our method outperforms existing network-based methods of drug-target identification (recall-at-25=0.374), including graph neural networks (recall-at-25=0.329) and random walks (recall-at-25=0.166). We also compare *Mutual Interactors* with probabilistic non-negative matrix factorization (NMF).[30–32] On aggregate, our method's performance is comparable to NMF's. However, on the hardest examples, drugs that share few targets with the drugs in the training set, our method (recall-at-25=0.381) significantly outperforms NMF (recall-at-25=0.006) (see Figure 3e). Further, our method provides insight into the side-effects caused by off-target binding. For each drug in DrugBank, we use *Mutual Interactors* to identify potential protein targets that are not already known targets of the drug. Pairs of drugs for which our method makes similar target predictions tend to have similar side effects[34–37] (Figure 3c).

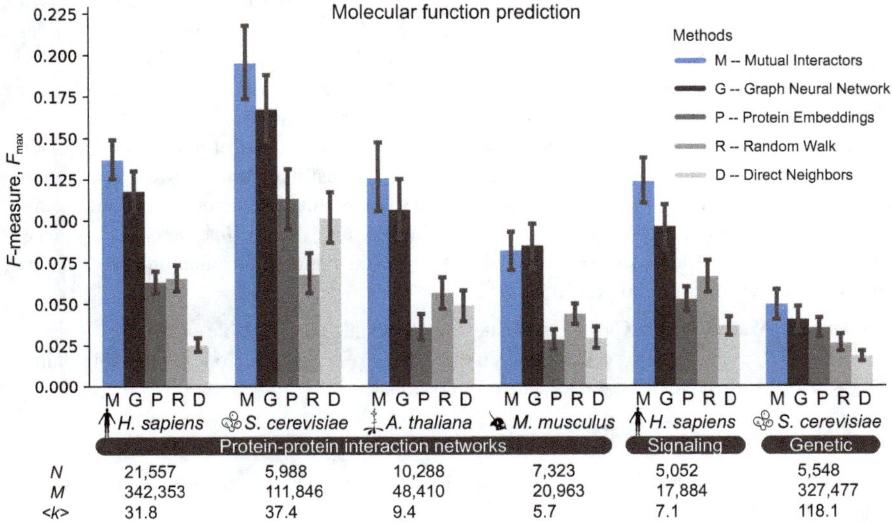

Fig. 4: **Predicting protein functions across species and molecular networks using mutual interactors.** Overall protein function prediction performance across four species and six molecular networks. We predict Molecular Function Ontology[38] terms using PPI, signaling, and genetic interaction networks for human, yeast *S. cerevisiae*, mouse *M. musculus*, and thale cress *A. thaliana*. We show average maximum F-measure.[39] A perfect predictor would be characterized by $F_{max} = 1$. Confidence intervals (95%) were determined using bootstrapping with $n = 1{,}000$ iterations. N – number of nodes, M – number of edges, $<k>$ – average node degree.

6. Predicting molecular function across species and molecular networks

Molecules associated with the same molecular function (e.g., RNA polymerase I activity) or involved in the same biological process (e.g., nucleosome mobilization) tend to share mutual interactors in molecular networks of various type and species (see Figure D1a-b). For example, the eleven proteins involved in the formation of the secondary messenger cAMP (cyclase activity, GO:0009975) do not interact directly with one another in the protein-protein interaction network, but almost all of them interact with the same group of twenty-five mutual interactors (see Figure D3). Using the Mutual Interactor principle, we can predict the molecular functions and biological processes of molecules. Via ten-fold cross validation, we compare *Mutual Interactors* to existing methods of molecular function prediction, including Graph Neural Networks[40] and Random Walks.[26] Across all four species and in three different molecular networks (protein-protein interaction, signaling, and genetic interaction), we find that *Mutual Interactors* is the strongest predictor of both molecular function (see Figure 4) and biological process (see Figure D2).

7. Conclusion

This work demonstrates the importance of rooting biomedical network science methods in principles that are empirically validated in biological data, rather than borrowed from other domains. This need for more domain-specific methodology in biomedical network science is also demonstrated by Kovács *et al.*, who find that social network principles do not apply for link prediction in PPI networks.[41] This study complements these findings: with experiments across three different kinds of molecular networks (protein-protein interaction, signaling and genetic interaction), and four species (*H. sapiens, S. cerevisiae, A. thaliana, M. musculus*) we show that a method designed specifically for biological data can better predict disease-protein associations, drug-target interactions and molecular function than can general methods of greater complexity. The power of *Mutual Interactors* to predict molecular phenotypes lies not in it's algorithmic complexity—it outperforms far more involved methods—but rather in the simple, yet fundamental, principle that underpins it. Motivated by our findings that molecules with similar phenotypes tend to share mutual interactors, we formalize the Mutual Interactor principle mathematically with machine learning. *Mutual Interactors* is fast, easy to implement, and robust to incomplete network data—its foundational formulation makes it ripe for extension to new domains and problems.

Supplementary Material and Code. Supplementary materials are available online at: `https://cs.stanford.edu/people/sabrieyuboglu/psb-mi.pdf`. Code is available online at: `https://github.com/seyuboglu/milieu`.

References

1. E. E. Schadt, Molecular networks as sensors and drivers of common human diseases, *Nature* **461**, 218 (September 2009).
2. P. Bork *et al.*, Protein interaction networks from yeast to human, *Current Opinion in Structural Biology* **14**, 292 (June 2004).
3. K. Lage *et al.*, A human phenome-interactome network of protein complexes implicated in genetic disorders, *Nature Biotechnology* **25**, p. 309 (2007).
4. A.-L. Barabási *et al.*, Network medicine: A network-based approach to human disease, *Nature Reviews Genetics* **12**, 56 (January 2011).
5. L. D. Wood *et al.*, The genomic landscapes of human breast and colorectal cancers, *Science* **318**, 1108 (2007).
6. J. Lim *et al.*, A protein–protein interaction network for human inherited ataxias and disorders of purkinje cell degeneration, *Cell* **125**, 801 (2006).
7. J. Chen *et al.*, Detecting functional modules in the yeast protein–protein interaction network, *Bioinformatics* **22**, 2283 (September 2006).
8. X. Wu *et al.*, Network-based global inference of human disease genes, *Molecular Systems Biology* **4**, p. 189 (2008).
9. W. Peng *et al.*, Improving protein function prediction using domain and protein complexes in PPI networks, *BMC Systems Biology* **8**, p. 35 (March 2014).
10. S. D. Ghiassian *et al.*, A DIseAse MOdule Detection (DIAMOnD) algorithm derived from a systematic analysis of connectivity patterns of disease proteins in the human interactome, *PLoS Computational Biology* **11**, p. e1004120 (2015).
11. M. Agrawal *et al.*, Large-scale analysis of disease pathways in the human interactome, *Pacific Symposium on Bicomomputing* **1**, 111 (2018).
12. M. McPherson *et al.*, Birds of a feather: Homophily in social networks, *Annual Review of Sociology* **27**, 415 (2001).
13. K. Luck *et al.*, A reference map of the human binary protein interactome, *Nature* **580**, 402 (April 2020).
14. R. Oughtred *et al.*, The BioGRID database: A comprehensive biomedical resource of curated protein, genetic, and chemical interactions, *Protein Science* **30**, 187 (2021).
15. D. Szklarczyk *et al.*, The string database in 2021: customizable protein–protein networks, and functional characterization of user-uploaded gene/measurement sets, *Nucleic Acids Research* **49**, D605 (2021).

16. J. Menche *et al.*, Uncovering disease-disease relationships through the incomplete interactome, *Science* **347**, p. 1257601 (February 2015).
17. J. Piñero *et al.*, The disgenet knowledge platform for disease genomics: 2019 update, *Nucleic acids research* **48**, D845 (2020).
18. D. S. Wishart *et al.*, DrugBank 5.0: a major update to the DrugBank database for 2018, *Nucleic Acids Research* **46**, D1074 (January 2018).
19. T. G. Ontology, The Gene Ontology Resource: 20 years and still GOing strong, *Nucleic Acids Research* **47**, D330 (January 2019).
20. K. Ennis *et al.*, Hyperglycemia accentuates and ketonemia attenuates hypoglycemia-induced neuronal injury in the developing rat brain, *Pediatric Research* **77**, 84 (2015).
21. O. Arisaka *et al.*, Iron, ketone bodies, and brain development, *The Journal of Pediatrics* **222**, 262 (2020).
22. X. Li *et al.*, Eleven novel mutations of the BCKDHA, BCKDHB and DBT genes associated with maple syrup urine disease in the Chinese population: report on eight cases, *European Journal of Medical Genetics* **58**, 617 (2015).
23. S. H. Lee *et al.*, A Korean child diagnosed with malonic aciduria harboring a novel start codon mutation following presentation with dilated cardiomyopathy, *Molecular Genetics & Genomic Medicine* **8**, p. e1379 (2020).
24. D. P. Kingma *et al.*, Adam: A Method for Stochastic Optimization, *arXiv:1412.6980 [cs]* (December 2014), arXiv: 1412.6980.
25. T. N. Kipf *et al.*, Semi-supervised classification with graph convolutional networks, *International Conference on Learning Representations* (2017).
26. *Analysis of protein-protein interaction networks using random walks* 2005.
27. M. Zitnik *et al.*, Machine learning for integrating data in biology and medicine: Principles, practice, and opportunities, *Information Fusion* **50**, 71 (2019).
28. D. S. Wishart *et al.*, Drugbank 5.0: a major update to the drugbank database for 2018, *Nucleic Acids Research* **46**, D1074 (2017).
29. N. P. Tatonetti *et al.*, Data-driven prediction of drug effects and interactions, *Science Translational Medicine* **4**, 125ra31 (2012).
30. *Probabilistic matrix factorization* 2008.
31. D. D. Lee *et al.*, Learning the parts of objects by non-negative matrix factorization, *Nature* **401**, 788 (October 1999).
32. *Structured non-negative matrix factorization with sparsity patterns* October 2008.
33. M. J. Keiser, B. L. Roth, B. N. Armbruster, P. Ernsberger, J. J. Irwin and B. K. Shoichet, Relating protein pharmacology by ligand chemistry, *Nature biotechnology* **25**, 197 (2007).
34. M. Campillos *et al.*, Drug Target Identification Using Side-Effect Similarity, *Science* **321**, 263 (July 2008).
35. R. Santos *et al.*, A comprehensive map of molecular drug targets, *Nature Reviews Drug Discovery* **16**, 19 (2017).
36. L. H. Calabrese *et al.*, Rheumatic immune-related adverse events from cancer immunotherapy, *Nature Reviews Rheumatology* **14**, 569 (2018).
37. F. Cheng *et al.*, Network-based prediction of drug combinations, *Nature Communications* **10**, 1 (2019).
38. M. Ashburner *et al.*, Gene Ontology: tool for the unification of biology, *Nature Genetics* **25**, p. 25 (2000).
39. P. Radivojac *et al.*, A large-scale evaluation of computational protein function prediction, *Nature Methods* **10**, p. 221 (2013).
40. T. N. Kipf *et al.*, Semi-Supervised Classification with Graph Convolutional Networks (September 2016).
41. I. A. Kovács *et al.*, Network-based prediction of protein interactions, *Nature communications* **10**, 1 (2019).
42. V. Matys *et al.*, TRANSFAC ® : transcriptional regulation, from patterns to profiles, *Nucleic Acids Research* **31**, 374 (January 2003).

43. A. Ceol *et al.*, MINT, the molecular interaction database: 2009 update, *Nucleic Acids Research* **38**, D532 (January 2010).
44. B. Aranda *et al.*, The IntAct molecular interaction database in 2010, *Nucleic Acids Research* **38**, D525 (January 2010).
45. M. Giurgiu *et al.*, Corum: the comprehensive resource of mammalian protein complexes—2019, *Nucleic acids research* **47**, D559 (2019).
46. M. Costanzo *et al.*, The Genetic Landscape of a Cell, *Science* **327**, 425 (January 2010).
47. M. Costanzo *et al.*, A global genetic interaction network maps a wiring diagram of cellular function, *Science* **353**, p. aaf1420 (September 2016).
48. D. Türei *et al.*, OmniPath: guidelines and gateway for literature-curated signaling pathway resources, *Nature Methods* **13**, 966 (December 2016).
49. S. Choobdar *et al.*, Assessment of network module identification across complex diseases, *Nature Methods* **16**, 843 (2019).
50. J. Piñero *et al.*, DisGeNET: a discovery platform for the dynamical exploration of human diseases and their genes., *Database : the journal of biological databases and curation* **2015**, bav028 (2015).
51. A. P. Davis *et al.*, The Comparative Toxicogenomics Database: update 2013, *Nucleic Acids Research* **41**, D1104 (January 2013).
52. UniProt Consortium, Activities at the Universal Protein Resource (UniProt), *Nucleic Acids Research* **42**, D191 (January 2014).
53. W. A. Kibbe *et al.*, Disease Ontology 2015 update: an expanded and updated database of human diseases for linking biomedical knowledge through disease data., *Nucleic acids research* **43**, D1071 (January 2015).
54. S. Navlakha *et al.*, The power of protein interaction networks for associating genes with diseases, *Bioinformatics* **26**, 1057 (2010).
55. S. Kohler *et al.*, Walking the Interactome for Prioritization of Candidate Disease Genes, *The American Journal of Human Genetics* **82**, 949 (April 2008).
56. A. Grover *et al.*, node2vec: Scalable Feature Learning for Networks (July 2016).
57. J. Tang, M. Qu, M. Wang, M. Zhang, J. Yan and Q. Mei, Line: Large-scale information network embedding, in *Proceedings of the 24th international conference on world wide web*, 2015.
58. B. Perozzi, R. Al-Rfou and S. Skiena, Deepwalk: Online learning of social representations, in *Proceedings of the 20th ACM SIGKDD international conference on Knowledge discovery and data mining*, 2014.
59. S. D. Ghiassian *et al.*, A DIseAse MOdule Detection (DIAMOnD) Algorithm Derived from a Systematic Analysis of Connectivity Patterns of Disease Proteins in the Human Interactome, *PLOS Computational Biology* **11**, e1004120 (April 2015).
60. M. Zitnik *et al.*, NIMFA: A Python Library for Nonnegative Matrix Factorization, *Journal of Machine Learning Research* , p. 5 (2012).
61. E. Guney *et al.*, Network-based in silico drug efficacy screening, *Nature Communications* **7**, 10331 (February 2016).
62. D. V. Klopfenstein *et al.*, GOATOOLS: A Python library for Gene Ontology analyses, *Scientific Reports* **8**, p. 10872 (July 2018).
63. A. Chatr-Aryamontri *et al.*, The BioGRID interaction database: 2015 update., *Nucleic acids research* **43**, D470 (January 2015).
64. D. Szklarczyk *et al.*, STRING v10: protein-protein interaction networks, integrated over the tree of life., *Nucleic acids research* **43**, D447 (January 2015).
65. L. Cowen *et al.*, Network propagation: a universal amplifier of genetic associations, *Nature Reviews Genetics* **18**, p. 551 (2017).
66. A.-L. Barabási *et al.*, Network medicine: a network-based approach to human disease., *Nature reviews. Genetics* **12**, 56 (January 2011).

Prediction of Kinase-Substrate Associations Using The Functional Landscape of Kinases and Phosphorylation Sites

Marzieh Ayati[1,†], Serhan Yilmaz[2], Filipa Blasco Tavares Pereira Lopes[3,4], Mark Chance[3,4,5], Mehmet Koyuturk[2,4,5]

[1]*Department of Computer Science, University of Texas Rio Grande Valley,Edinburg, TX*
[2]*Department of Computer and Data Sciences,* [3]*Department of Nutrition,* [4]*Center for Proteomics and Bioinformatics,* [5]*Case Comprehensive Cancer Center, Case Western Reserve University, Cleveland, OH*
†*E-mail: marzieh.ayati@utrgv.edu*

Protein phosphorylation is a key post-translational modification that plays a central role in many cellular processes. With recent advances in biotechnology, thousands of phosphorylated sites can be identified and quantified in a given sample, enabling proteome-wide screening of cellular signaling. However, for most ($> 90\%$) of the phosphorylation sites that are identified in these experiments, the kinase(s) that target these sites are unknown. To broadly utilize available structural, functional, evolutionary, and contextual information in predicting kinase-substrate associations (KSAs), we develop a network-based machine learning framework. Our framework integrates a multitude of data sources to characterize the landscape of functional relationships and associations among phosphosites and kinases. To construct a phosphosite-phosphosite association network, we use sequence similarity, shared biological pathways, co-evolution, co-occurrence, and co-phosphorylation of phosphosites across different biological states. To construct a kinase-kinase association network, we integrate protein-protein interactions, shared biological pathways, and membership in common kinase families. We use node embeddings computed from these heterogeneous networks to train machine learning models for predicting kinase-substrate associations. Our systematic computational experiments using the PhosphositePLUS database shows that the resulting algorithm, NetKSA, outperforms two state-of-the-art algorithms, including KinomeXplorer and LinkPhinder, in overall KSA prediction. By stratifying the ranking of kinases, NetKSA also enables annotation of phosphosites that are targeted by relatively less-studied kinases.
Availability: The code and data are available at compbio.case.edu/NetKSA/.

Keywords: Phosphoproteomics, Kinase-substrate association, Network embedding

1. Introduction

Protein phosphorylation is one of the most important post-translational modifications that play an important role in cellular signaling. Phosphorylation involves phospho-proteins whose activity can be altered by the phosphorylation of their specific sites (a.k.a substrate), kinases that phosphorylate the phospho-proteins at specific sites, and phosphatases that dephospho-

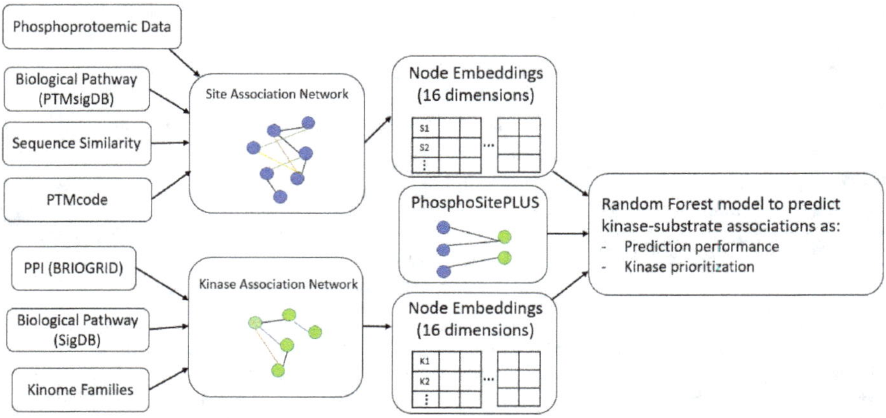

Fig. 1. **Workflow of NetKSA.** We first construct two networks to represent the functional relationships and associations among phosphosites and kinases. After construction of networks, we use node embedding algorithms on each network to compute a low-dimensional representation for each node. We then use the kinase-substrate associations (KSAs) obtained from PhosphoSitePLUS to train machine learning models for predicting KSAs.

rylate these proteins. Dysregulation of the kinase-substrate associations are regularly observed in complex diseases, including cancer. Therefore, kinases have emerged as an important class of drug targets for many diseases.[1]

Recent advances in mass spectrometry (MS) based technologies drastically enhanced the accuracy and coverage of phosphosite identification and quantification. However, most identified phosphosites do not have kinase annotations, and large scale and reliable prediction of which kinase can phosphorylate which phosphosites remains challenging. In the last decade, several computational methods are developed to predict kinase-substrate associations (KSAs). The earlier KSA prediction methods focus mainly on sequence motifs recognized by the active sites of kinases..[2–4] Later methods integrate other contextual information such as protein structure and physical interactions to improve the accuracy of prediction methods.[5–8] Recently, we developed CophosK,[9] the first kinase-substrate prediction algorithm that utilizes large-scale mass spectrometry based phospho-proteomic data to incorporate contextual information. While these tools improve the kinase-substrate associations prediction, the knowledge about the substrates of kinases is still unequally distributed, where 87% of phosphosites are assigned to 20% of well-studied kinases.[10]

In parallel, machine learning algorithms that utilize network models gain significant traction in computational biology.[11,12] Inspired by these developments, we here develop a comprehensive framework for integrating broad functional information on kinases and phosphoproteins to build machine learning models for predicting kinase-substrate associations. Our framework uses heterogeneous network models to represent the functional relationships between phosphorylation sites, as well as kinases. Namely, we integrate structural, evolutionary, functional, and contextual information to characterize the landscape of functional relationships and associations among phosphosites and kinases. Since MS-based phosphoproteomic data can present a relatively unbiased view of signaling states, we also incorporate co-occurrence and co-phosphorylation across multiple MS-based phosphoproteomic studies into network construction. After constructing phosphosite association and kinase association networks, we use node embedding algorithms to derive low-dimensional vector representations for phosphosites and kinases, which are in turn used to train machine learning models.

We systematically investigate the predictive performance of reliability of the proposed framework, NETKSA, using established kinase-substrate associations from PhosphositePLUS. Using a cross-validation framework in two problem settings (link prediction and prioritization), we investigate the effect of the network embedding algorithms, the contribution of different types of networks, the value added by network topology, and compare the performance of NETKSA against state-of-the-art algorithms. In order to mitigate the bias toward well-studied kinases in the KSA prediction,[13] we propose a kinase stratification strategy based on the number of known substrates. Our results show that NETKSA, outperforms state-of-the-art methods in overall prediction performance. Finally, we observe that the performance of NETKSA is robust to the choice of network embedding algorithms, while each type of network contributes valuable information that is complementary to the information provided by other networks.

2. Materials and Methods

The workflow of the proposed framework for kinase-substrate association prediction is shown in Figure 1. As seen in the figure, we first construct two networks, one to model the functional relationship between phosphorylation sites and the other to model the functional relationship between kinases. Subsequently, for each phosphosite and for each kinase, we compute low-dimensional embeddings using a node embedding algorithm on the respective network. Finally, we use these embedding as feature vectors and kinase-substrate associations obtained from PhosphoSitePLUS as training examples to train models for predicting kinase-substrate associations.

2.1. *PhosphoSite Association Network*

We define a PhosphoSite Association Network as a network $G_s(V_s, E_s)$that represents *potential* functional relationships between pairs of phosphosites. In this network, V_s denotes the set of nodes in the network, each of which represents a phosphorylation site. The edge set E_s denotes the set of pairwise functional relationships between phosphosites, where an edge $s_i s_j \in E$ between phosphosites $s_i, s_j \in V$ may represent one of the following relationships:

- **Functional, Evolutionary, and Structural Association.** PTMCode is a database of known and predicted functional associations between phosphorylation and other post-translational modification sites.[14] The associations included in PTMCode are curated from the literature, inferred from residue co-evolution, or are based on the structural distances between phosphosites. We utilize PTMcode as a direct source of functional, evolutionary, and structural associations between phosphorylation sites.

- **Sequence Similarity**. We download the sequences within ±7 residues around each site in the protein sequence from PhosphositePLUS, and perform sequence alignment using BLOSUM62 scoring method. There is an edge between two sites s_i and s_j if their distance is less than 3 standard deviation below average across all pairs of sites.
- **Shared Pathways**. We use PTMsigDB as a reference database of site-specific phosphorylation signatures of kinases, perturbations, and signaling pathways.[15] While PTMSigDB provides data on all post-translational modifications, we here use the subset that corresponds to phosphorylation. There are 2398 phosphosites that are associated with 388 different perturbations and signaling pathways. We represent these associations as a binary network of signaling-pathway associations among phosphosites, in which an edge between two phosphosites indicates that the phosphorylation of the two sites is involved in the same pathway.
- **Co-Occurrence**. Li et al.[16] show that phosphorylation sites that are modified together tend to participate in similar biological process. Based on this observation, they construct a binary occurrence profile for each phosphosite, where a 1 indicates that the site is identified in a given study, They then assess the co-occurrence of pairs of sites in terms of the mutual information between the respective occurrence profiles. Here, following Li et al.,[16] we use high-throughput MS analyses across 88 different studies from phosphoSitePLUS[17] to assess the co-occurrence of phosphorylation site. These studies include data from 16 human tissue as well as 28 cultural cell lines and 44 disease cells. We include an edge between two sites s_i and s_j if the p-value of their co-occurrence is less than 0.005.
- **Co-Phosphorylation**. Co-phosphorylation (Co-P) refers to correlated phosphorylation of two phosphosites across samples withing a given study.[18] While co-occurrence captures the relationship between pairs of sites that tend to appear in similar contexts at a broader scale, Co-P captures finer-scale correlations between the dynamic ranges of the phosphorylation levels of site pairs. To incorporate Co-P in the site association network, we use data from 9 mass spectrometry-based phosphoproteomic studied that represent a broad range of biological states and provide sufficient number of samples to enable reliable assessment of Co-P.[9] These datasets include data from three breast cancer studies,[19–21] two ovarian cancer studies,[20,22] one colorectal cancer,[23] one lung cancer,[24] one Alzheimer's disease[25] and one retinal pigmented eputhelium data.[26]

  Using each pair of sites that are identified in each dataset, we compute as $c_D(i,j)$ the co-P between site i and site j as measured by Biweight-midcorrelation of their phosphorylation profiles in dataset D. We then compute R^2 values for each pair of sites in each dataset by adjusting for the number of samples n_D in dataset D:

$$R^2_D(i,j) = 1 - \frac{n_D - 1}{n_D - 2}(1 - c_D(i,j)^2) \tag{1}$$

Finally, we integrate these individual co-P scores as follows:

$$c_{integrated}(i,j) = 1 - \prod_{D \in \mathcal{D}_{ij}} (1 - R^2_D(i,j)) \tag{2}$$

where $\mathcal{D}_{ij}$ denotes the set of datasets in which sites i and j are both identified. In

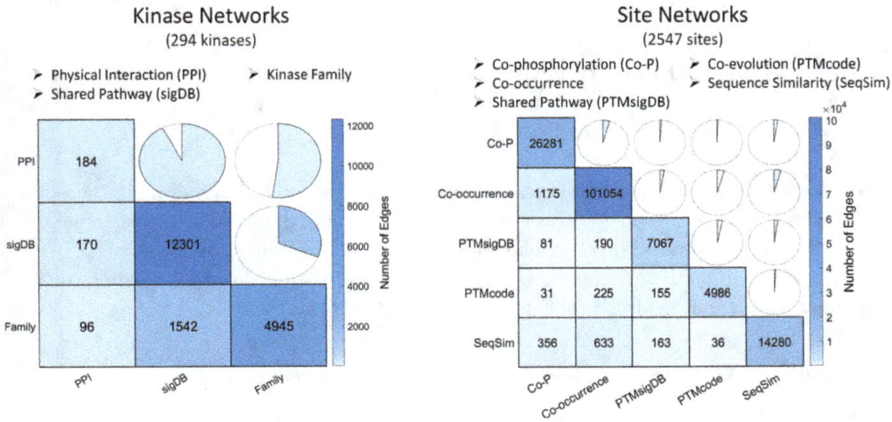

Fig. 2. **Kinase-kinase and phosphosite-phosphosite association networks used in this study.** Plots show the edge overlap between different types of networks. Kinase networks are shown on the left, phosphosite networks are shown on the right. The number of edges in each network are given in the diagonals. In each subplot, the pie charts in the top right side indicate the overlap coefficients (size of intersection divided by the smaller of the size of two sets) between any two networks.

the integrated Co-P network, we include an edge between two sites s_i and s_j if the absolute value of their co-phosphorylation is larger than 2 standard deviation of the average across all pairs of sites.

Note that the integrated phosphosite association network is a heterogeneous multiplex network, where the nodes are from a common space (phosphorylation sites) and edges in each network have different semantics. In recent years, many algorithms have been developed for computing embeddings for multiplex networks, which also account for the heterogeneity of the edges.[27–29] However, these algorithms are usually based on the inherent assumption that the overlap between the nodes of the networks is considerably large,[30] which is not the case in our application. For this reason, we here focus on assessing the value of the overall network model, as opposed to the algorithm used for integrating the networks or computing multiplex embeddings. With this motivation, we represent each network as a binary network by applying conservative edge inclusion criteria separately for each network, as described above. Subsequently, we integrate these networks into a single network by including an edge between two sites if there is an edge between them in at least one of the networks.

2.2. *Kinase Association Network*

We define a Kinase Association Network as a network $G_k(V_k, E_k)$ that represents functional relationship between pairs of kinases. In this network, V_k denotes the set of nodes each of which represents a kinase. The edge set E_k denotes the set of pairwise functional relationships between kinases. There is an edge $k_\ell k_r \in E_k$ between kinases $k_\ell, k_r \in V_k$ if the two kinases have one of the following relationships:

- **Protein-Protein Interaction (PPI)**. If two kinases k_ℓ and k_r physically interact, then there is an edge between k_ℓ and k_r. In our experiments, we use the PPIs that are annotated as "physical" in the BIOGRID PPI database[31] to infer the PPI edges in the network.
- **Biological Pathways**. If two kinases k_ℓ and k_r are reported to have a role in the same pathway, then there is an edge between k_ℓ and k_r. In our experiments, we use mSigDB, which provides a collection of canonical pathways and experimental signatures.[32]
- **Kinase Families**. If two kinases k_ℓ and k_r belong to the same family according to the Human Kinome database,[33] then there is an edge between them.

2.3. *Computing Network Profiles for Sites and Kinases*

To obtain a network profile for each phosphosite and each kinase, we use node embedding. Given a graph G, a node embedding is a mapping $f : v_i \rightarrow y_i \in R^d$ such that $d \ll |V|$ and the function f preserves some proximity measure defined on graph G.[34] In other words, a node embedding maps each node to a low-dimensional feature vector, aiming to preserve the network proximity between nodes. Many node embedding algorithms have been developed in recent years, and the performance of these algorithms depends on the application, the nature of the learning problem, and the topology of the network. For this reason, in our experiments, we use four different node embedding algorithms[34–37] to comprehensively evaluate the value of the information provided by the networks we utilize, independent of the node embedding algorithm that is used. For each site s_i in G_s, we compute node embedding $x_i \in \mathbb{R}^d$ and for each kinase k_ℓ in G_k we compute node embedding $y_\ell \in \mathbb{R}^d$. We do this separately for each network embedding algorithm, using the default parameters in each algorithm, and using different values of d.

2.4. *Predicting Kinase-Substrate Associations*

We use the sets of known KSAs obtained from PhosphoSitePLUS (PSP)[17] as a positive reference for training and testing our models. We generate negative training sets of equal size by selecting, uniformly at random, kinase-substrate pairs that are not reported to be associated in PSP. To train the models, we concatenate the network profiles of site-kinase pairs to obtain a $2d$-dimensional feature vector for the pair: $f(s_i, k_\ell) = x_i \,\|\, y_\ell = (x_i^{(1)}, \ldots, x_i^{(d)}, y_\ell^{(1)}, \ldots, y_\ell^{(d)})$. We consider two variants of KSA prediction:

(I) Link Prediction. We formulate the KSA prediction problem as a binary classification problem for a given kinase-site pair, i.e., given a list of established kinase-site associations, site-site association and kinase-kinase association networks G_s and G_k, and a kinase-site pair (s_i, k_l), our objective is to assess the likelihood that s_i is a target site for k_l. For this purpose, we train a Random Forest model by using the concatenated embeddings as features. Using 5-fold cross validation, we assess the overall performance of the method using area of the ROC curve (AUC).

(II) Prioritization of Kinases for Phosphosites. In practice, the kinase-substrate association prediction often manifests itself as a prioritization problem. The scientist discovers a new phosphorylation site that is associated with a certain process and phenotype and would like to know which kinase is responsible for the phosphorylation of that site. This problem is formulated as follows: Given a list of established kinase-site associations, site-site association and kinase-kinase association networks G_s and G_k, and a site s_i, rank kinases based on their likelihood of being associated with s_i. For this task, we use a Random Forest model using concatenated embeddings as well, but we use leave-one-out cross-validation to assess the performance of the resulting models. In this case, we use hit@k accuracy as the performance criterion. Namely, using each site as a test site, we report the fraction of times in which the actual kinase responsible for phosphorylating the site is ranked in the top k for that site, where $k \in \{1, 5, 10, 20\}$.

2.5. *Elucidating and Mitigating Bias in KSA Prediction*

In order to study the bias in the KSA predictions toward the more well-studied kinases,[13] we stratify the kinases based on the number of their known substrates which are in the phosphosite association network. Letting δ_ℓ denote the number of known substrates of kinase k_ℓ, we partition the kinases into three categories: (i) The poor kinases where $\delta_\ell < 5$, (ii) the average kinases, where $5 \leq \delta_\ell < 20$, and (iii) The rich kinases where $\delta_\ell \geq 20$. We then train separate models for each kinase category, by using kinases that belong to a specific category while training the respective model. Subsequently, when prioritizing the kinases for each phosphosite, we rank the kinases within their own category.

The premise of this approach is that the kinases in each category should compete with the kinases in the same category as themselves, and scientists should be able to separately investigate the rankings in each category. This will potentially enable discovery and experimental validation of relatively less-studied kinases. We evaluate the performance of the all the methods by considering this stratified analysis, as well as by ranking all kinases. This approach provides insights into the bias associated with each approach, i.e., how much a method improves its chances of making an accurate prediction by preferring well-studied kinases.

3. Results and Discussion

We use PhosphoSitePLUS as a reference dataset for kinase-substrate associations (KSAs).[17] Considering the phosphosites and kinases in our networks, we use 2083 KSAs from PhosphositePLUS in our computational experiments. To evaluate the performance of the kinase-substrate association prediction method, we limit the site network to the known substrates obtained from PhosphoSitePLUS. We remove the individual nodes that are not connected to any other nodes from both of the networks. The number of sites and edges in the final kinase-kinase and phosphosite-phosphosite association networks and their types are shown in Figure 2(a). The overlaps between different types of association networks are shown in Figure 2(b). The low overlap between different phosphosite-phosphosite association networks suggests that all different types of networks provide information that are potentially complementary with each other.

3.1. *Kinase-Substrate Association as Link Prediction*

We first use different embedding methods, and 5-fold cross validation to evaluate the performance of NetKSA in predicting KSAs formulated as link prediction. In our computational experiments, we consider different numbers of embedding dimensions and its effect on the performance. We find out that $d = 16$ is optimal for all algorithms considered, thus we perform all remaining experiments using 16 dimensions for the embedding vectors.

The link prediction performance of NetKSA using different embedding algorithms is presented in Figure 3(a). We evaluate the performance for all the KSAs, as well as KSAs that its kinase belongs to different category (i.e. poor, average, rich) separately. In this analysis, there are 103 kinases in the poor category ($\delta < 5$), 64 kinases in the average category ($5 \leq \delta < 20$), and 21 kinases in the rich category ($\delta \geq 20$) (the rest of kinases in the kinase-kinase association network do not have any target sites that are present in the site-site association network). These kinases corresponds to 218 KSAs in poor category, 613 KSAs in the average category and 1252 KSAs in the rich category. The negative set for the training of the model is randomly generated while keeping the proportion of KSA categories. The bar plots show the average across 10 runs. As seen in the figure, the prediction performance highly depends on the the kinase category and the AUC observed by considering all kinases together closely follows the prediction performance for rich kinases. This observation demonstrates the importance of performing stratified analyses to accurately characterize the performance of KSA prediction as a function of what is already known about the kinase and characterize the bias in algorithms.

As seen in Figure 3(a), the prediction performance of NetKSA is robust to the choice of network embedding algorithms. We select DNGR for further analyses due to its slightly better overall performance that is also most balanced across different kinase categories.

To evaluate the value added by the network to the prediction, we randomly permute site association and kinase association networks while preserving the degree distribution and apply NetKSA by using the permuted networks in place of the actual networks. The results of this analysis are presented in Figure 3(b). As seen in the figure, the prediction performance using original networks is one or more standard deviation(d) above the prediction performance of the method when using permuted networks. This result shows the networks contribute valuable information for KSA prediction. Importantly, randomization of the prediction performance declines more when the phosphosite network is permuted, suggesting that the functional information on the phosphosites provides significant and specific information on the kinase(s) that target(s) the phosphosites.

It is also interesting that the poor kinase category benefits the most in comparison with other categories when the original networks are used. This shows that the information provided by functional associations among sites and kinases reduce the gap between under-studied and well-studied kinases. Note that the models that are based on permuted networks perform better than what would be expected at random, suggesting that these models can learn bias in the benchmarking data to appear as if they are learning what they are designed to learn. However, the performance of the model that is trained on both permuted networks is equal to what would be expected at random for poor kinases, demonstrating that the validation strategy we employ here (stratification of kinases and comparison against permuted networks) provides

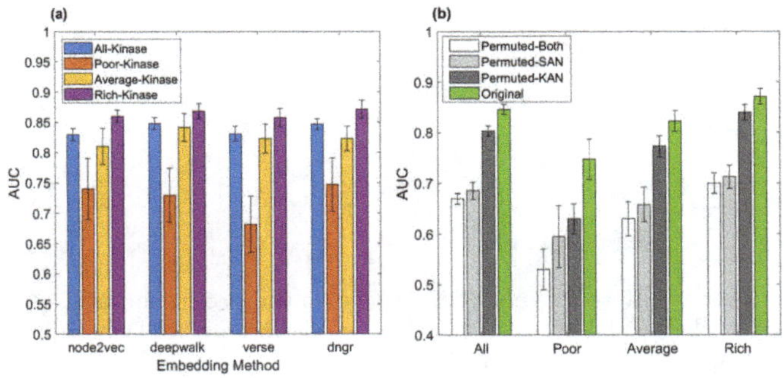

Fig. 3. **The contribution of embedding algorithms and functional networks on KSA prediction performance.** (a) The AUC of the predictions of NetKSA using four different node embedding algorithms. For each embedding algorithm, the AUC is shown for all KSAs (blue bar), the KSAs where the kinase belongs to the poor category (red), the average category (gold), and rich category (purple). (b) The prediction performance of NetKSA using DNGR for node embedding using real vs. randomized networks. AUC on the real kinase-kinase and phosphosite-phosphosite association networks (green bar), when only the kinase association network is randomly permuted by preserving node degrees (dark grey), when only the site association network is permuted by preserving node degrees (light grey), when both networks are permuted (white). Each bar shows the average AUC across 10 runs and the error bar shows standard deviation.

significant insights into what these models actually learn.

3.2. *Contribution of Different Networks on Prediction Performance*

In order to evaluate the contribution of different types of networks in capturing the landscape of functional association among phosphosites and kinases, we evaluate the performance of KSA predictions using different networks. For this analysis, we perform KSA prediction using 5-fold cross validation, by adding one network at a time to the integrated network of kinase-kinase and phosphosite-phosphosite associations, while keeping the other network fully integrated. The results of this analysis are shown in Figure 4. As seen in the figure, as we add different types of functional information for the sites and kinases, the prediction performance improves. We also evaluate the KSA coverage as the proportion of existing KSAs for which prediction can be made. The new networks add information about the the individual sites and kinases and connect them to other nodes, and consequently increase the KSA coverage. Finally, we observe that the information contributed by different phosphosite networks is more complementary to each other as compared to the kinase networks, which is not surprising as the overlap between these networks is also considerably low.

3.3. *Prioritization of Kinases for Phosphorylation Sites*

To test the effectiveness of our method, we use leave-one-out cross validation. Namely, for each phosphosite, we hide the association between phosphosite and its known kinase (called

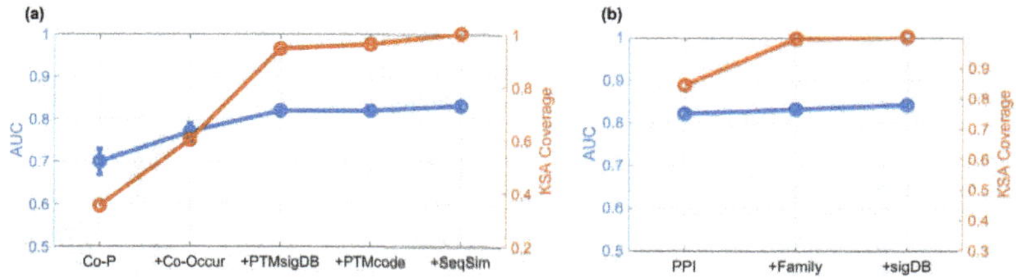

Fig. 4. **Contribution of different types of networks on the prediction of KSAs**. The cumulative effect of each (a) phosphosite-phosphosite association network and (b) kinase-kinase association network on the AUC of predictions (left y axis; blue), and the coverage of kinase-substrate associations (right y axis; red) - the fraction of KSAs for which both the kinase and the site are present in the integrated network so that a prediction can be made.

the target kinase), and we use other reported KSAs to rank the likely kinases for that phosphosite. For this analysis, we use dngr as the embedding method and random forest with 100 classification trees as the score prediction model. For each phosphosite, we rank all kinases based on the calculated score and determine the rank of the target kinase across all kinases. If the target kinase is within the top $k \in \{1, 5, 10, 20\}$, it is considered a the true positive. We compare our method with two other state-of-the-art methods, KinomeXplorer and LinkPhinder, that also use the network for KSA prediction. KinomeXplorer[5] utilizes the sequences match scoring and network proximity of kinases and substrates to predict KSAs. It is an improved version of NetworKIN[4] and NetPhorest.[38] LinkPhinder[39] is also another predictive model that utilizes the motif characteristics to create a knowledge graph and uses statistical relational learning and node embedding to predict KSAs. The result of this analysis is presented in Figure 5. As seen in the figure, the proposed method with kinase stratification outperform all methods in overall prediction performance, and also average and rich categories. For the poor kinases, the LinkPhinder presents a better result for top 1 and top 5 ranking. We believe integration of different data sources in NetKSA help extracting the relationship among sites and kinases which leads to a better overall performance.

3.3.1. *Kinase Stratification*

In the kinase prioritization, we rank the kinases in each category (i.e poor, average, rich) separately, and determine if the target kinase is ranked in top k of its category. The premise of this approach is that the kinase that are understudied does not to compete with the well-studies kinases. Using kinase stratification, the hypothesis is that it is more likely that the target kinase wins the competition in ranking compare to the kinases in its own category. We apply this strategy on NetKSAand also KinomeXplorer and LinkPhinder. The result of this analysis is presented in Figure 5. For each bar in the figure, the dark section is the performance without kinase stratification, and the light-color section is the improvement of the performance using the kinase stratification.

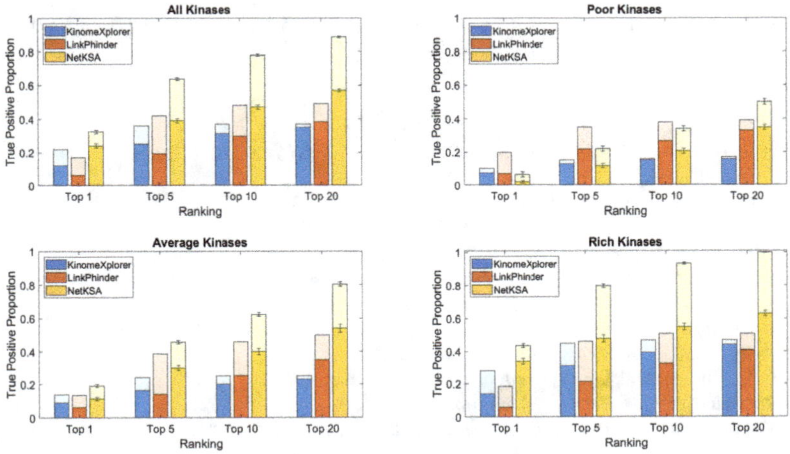

Fig. 5. **Performance of NetKSA, KinomeXplorer and LinkPhinder in prioritizing kinases for a given phosphosite.** For each phosphosite, we perform leave-one-out cross validation by hiding the association between the phosphosite and one of its associated kinases (target kinase) to rank the likely kinases for the phosphosite using KinomeXplorer(blue), LinkPhinder(red), and proposed method using constructed networks (gold). We report the fraction of phosphosites for which the target kinase is ranked in the top 1, top 5, top 10 and top 20 predicted kinases by each method. For each bar, the dark section presents the result when all the kinases are ranked together, and the light section presents the improvement of performance when the target kinase is ranked within its category (with stratification). Each panel presents the performance on each category of kinases: poor ($\delta < 5$), average($5 \leq \delta < 20$), and rich ($\delta \geq 20$) kinases (as indicated in each panel).

4. Conclusion

In this paper, we integrated a multitude of data sources to characterize the landscape of functional relationships and associations among phosphosites and kinases. As a result, we construct two heterogeneous networks presenting functional association among phosphosites and kinases. These networks incorporating static and dynamic data and present an extraordinary value in prediction of kinase-substrate association, and have great potential for analysis of phosphoproteomics data and identification of drug targets. Generalizing the method to include all the identified phosphosites is a challenging task which may point to an interesting research avenue to be addressed by future studies. Moreover, the kinase stratification approach to mitigate the bias toward well-studied kinases provides a great opportunity to researchers to investigate and study kinases in different categories separately.

Acknowledgments

This work was supported by National Institutes of Health grant R01-LM012980 from the National Library of Medicine.

References

1. F. M. Ferguson et al. *Nature reviews Drug discovery*, 17(5):353–377, 2018.
2. P. Durek, et al. *BMC bioinformatics*, 10(1):1–17, 2009.
3. J. C. Obenauer, et al. *Nucleic acids research*, 31(13):3635–3641, 2003.
4. R. Linding, et al. *Cell*, 129(7):1415–1426, 2007.
5. H. Horn, et al. *Nature methods*, 11(6):603–604, 2014.
6. M. Hjerrild, et al. *Journal of proteome research*, 3(3):426–433, 2004.
7. C. Song, et al. *Molecular & Cellular Proteomics*, 11(10):1070–1083, 2012.
8. E. M. Hobert et al. *Journal of the American Chemical Society*, 134(9):3976–3978, 2012.
9. M. Ayati, et al. *PLOS computational biology*, 2019.
10. E. J. Needham, et al. *Science signaling*, 12(565):eaau8645, 2019.
11. T. Gaudelet, et al. *Briefings in bioinformatics*, 22(6):bbab159, 2021.
12. G. Muzio, et al. *Briefings in bioinformatics*, 22(2):1515–1530, 2021.
13. I. Deznabi, et al. *Bioinformatics*, 36(12):3652–3661, 2020.
14. P. Minguez, et al. *Nucleic acids research*, 43(D1):D494–D502, 2014.
15. K. Krug, et al. *Molecular & cellular proteomics*, 18(3):576–593, 2019.
16. Y. Li, et al. *PLoS computational biology*, 13(5):e1005502, 2017.
17. P. V. Hornbeck, et al. *Nucleic acids research*, 43(D1):D512–D520, 2014.
18. M. Ayati, et al. *Bioinformatics*, 2022.
19. K.-l. Huang, et al. *Nature communications*, 8:14864, 2017.
20. P. Mertins, et al. *Molecular & cellular proteomics*, 2014.
21. P. Mertins, et al. *Nature*, 534(7605):55, 2016.
22. H. Zhang, et al. *Cell*, 166(3):755–765, 2016.
23. Y. Abe, et al. *Scientific reports*, 7(1):1–12, 2017.
24. D. Wiredja. PhD thesis, Case Western Reserve University, 2018.
25. E. B. Dammer, et al. *Proteomics*, 15(2-3):508–519, 2015.
26. C. Chiang, et al. *Journal of Biological Chemistry*, 292(48):19826–19839, 2017.
27. H. Cho, et al. *Cell systems*, 3(6):540–548, 2016.
28. A. Valdeolivas, et al. *Bioinformatics*, 35(3):497–505, 2019.
29. X. Zeng, et al. *Bioinformatics*, 35(24):5191–5198, 2019.
30. M. Li et al. In *International Conference on Complex Networks and Their Applications*, pages 39–52. Springer, 2020.
31. A. Chatr-Aryamontri, et al. *Nucleic acids research*, 45(D1):D369–D379, 2017.
32. A. Liberzon, et al. *Bioinformatics*, 27(12):1739–1740, 2011.
33. G. Manning, et al. *Science*, 298(5600):1912–1934, 2002.
34. A. Grover et al. In *Proceedings of the 22nd ACM SIGKDD international conference on Knowledge discovery and data mining*, pages 855–864, 2016.
35. B. Perozzi, et al. In *Proceedings of the 20th ACM SIGKDD international conference on Knowledge discovery and data mining*, pages 701–710, 2014.
36. S. Cao, et al. In *Proceedings of the AAAI Conference on Artificial Intelligence*, volume 30, 2016.
37. A. Tsitsulin, et al. In *Proceedings of the 2018 world wide web conference*, pages 539–548, 2018.
38. M. L. Miller, et al. *Science signaling*, 1(35):ra2–ra2, 2008.
39. V. Nováček, et al. *PLoS computational biology*, 16(12):e1007578, 2020.

A Graph Coarsening Algorithm for Compressing Representations of Single-Cell Data with Clinical or Experimental Attributes

Chi-Jane Chen[†], Emma Crawford[⅄], and Natalie Stanley[‡]
Department of Computer Science and Computational Medicine Program
The University of North Carolina at Chapel Hill,
Chapel Hill, NC, 27599, USA
{[†]*chijane@cs.unc.edu*,[⅄] *emmabc@email.unc.edu*,[‡] *natalies@cs.unc.edu*}

Graph-based algorithms have become essential in the analysis of single-cell data for numerous tasks, such as automated cell-phenotyping and identifying cellular correlates of experimental perturbations or disease states. In large multi-patient, multi-sample single-cell datasets, the analysis of cell-cell similarity graphs representations of these data becomes computationally prohibitive. Here, we introduce *cytocoarsening*, a novel graph-coarsening algorithm that significantly reduces the size of single-cell graph representations, which can then be used as input to downstream bioinformatics algorithms for improved computational efficiency. Uniquely, cytocoarsening considers both phenotypical similarity of cells and similarity of cells' associated clinical or experimental attributes in order to more readily identify condition-specific cell populations. The resulting coarse graph representations were evaluated based on both their structural correctness and the capacity of downstream algorithms to uncover the same biological conclusions as if the full graph had been used. Cytocoarsening is provided as open source code at `https://github.com/ChenCookie/cytocoarsening`.

Keywords: Graph Coarsening; Single-Cell Bioinformatics; Cytometry

1. Introduction

Advancements in a range of single-cell technologies, such as flow and mass cytometry and single-cell RNA sequencing, have become essential in uncovering and understanding cellular heterogeneity in a range of translational applications.[1–3] These immune profiling techniques have proven to be particularly essential in unraveling immunological heterogeneity through the simultaneous measurement of 20-45 protein markers in each cell.[4] This simultaneous measurement enables both phenotypic (e.g. cellular identity) and functional characterization of cells.[5] Despite effective identification and characterization of immune cell-types, a current challenge is to accurately link these immune cells to external *attributes* of interest, such as clinical labels or experimental perturbations.[6–9] For example, it is common in translational applications to profile blood samples from patients *across* clinical phenotypes or disease states in order to identify the driving, stratifying cell-types.[6,10] Blood samples are also often perturbed through stimulation,[11] and cellular correlates are identified by observing functional responses to the stimulation. Moreover, to efficiently link cellular heterogeneity to clinical or experimental attributes, automated bioinformatics methods have become critical in analysis.

Many of the bioinformatics algorithms for such tasks operate on a graph representation of the single-cell data.[7–9] In these graphs, nodes are cells, and edges between a pair of cells imply that they are sufficiently similar across measured features (for example, the aforementioned protein markers). The task at hand is to use the graph structure to identify cells that are prototypical of particular external attributes, such as clinical or experimental labels. MELD[7] accomplishes this by modeling the external attributes as a signal on the graph and computing a score for each cell reflecting its probability of association with each condition. To exemplify another approach, Milo[8] and CNA[9] seek to identify critical *cellular neighborhoods*, or groups of phenotypically-similar cells enriched across attributes.

Practically, it is challenging to apply these bioinformatics algorithms to the extremely large graph representations of multi-patient, multi-sample cohorts with millions of cells. Although the large graph size would make computations on it prohibitive, the graph inherently involves redundant information, since we have multiple cellular instances from a single population encoding the same biological information. To reduce the graph size, then, we merge redundant cells into *coarse nodes* or *super nodes*, leveraging existing graph-coarsening strategies[12,13] and adapting them to consider biologically relevant external attributes. The rich literature of existing graph-coarsening methods[13–18] tend to optimize for merges of nodes that maintain critical structural and spectral properties for the original graph, but do not consider these node attributes.

Baselines. As an example of a graph-coarsening approach, Loukas *et al.* proposed a family of *local variation* algorithms to simplify and reduce the size of the original graph.[14] These algorithms begin with a family of *coarsening candidate sets*: subsets of nodes that are known to be highly related based on the graph structure. The two main approaches discussed are edge-based variation (LV-E) or node-based variation (LV-N). Using LV-E, the candidate sets are exactly the edge pairs of the graph. In contrast, the candidate sets in LV-N are formed by grouping each node with its immediate neighborhood. In Ref.14, Loukas *et al.* compared these variation-based methods to other graph coarsening methods, including heavy-edge matching (HEM),[15] algebraic distance (AD),[16] and affinity (AFF).[17] The local variation methods outperformed these methods in spectral approximation, and all of the methods (with the exception of AFF, which is slower) scale quasi-linearly in the number of edges in the graph. Briefly, HEM seeks to coarsen the graph such that the principal eigenvalues and eigenspaces of the coarsened graph Laplacian are close to those of the original graph Laplacian. Instead of considering spectral properties, the AD and AFF methods identify nodes to merge by considering the connectedness of both individual nodes and node neighborhoods.

With existing coarsening approaches focusing primarily on preserving overall graph structure or underlying spectral properties, we seek to adapt the methods to additionally take into account external attributes of the cells, such as clinical state or experimental perturbation status. Our method will therefore merge individual nodes (representing cells) into coarse nodes according to both cellular phenotype and associated attributes (see overview figure, Fig 1). This gives us a graph of reduced size to use as input for downstream bioinformatics algorithms, and it facilitates simpler identification of cells that are related both in phenotype and in clinical or experimental attribute.

2. Methods

Notation and problem formulation. We consider a multi-sample single-cell dataset with p profiled samples, denoted as $\{\mathbf{X}_i\}_{i=1}^{p}$. Here, each $\mathbf{X}_i \in \mathbb{R}^{n_i \times d}$ represents the d protein or gene expression measurements for each of the n_i cells measured in sample i. We also assume that each cell has an *attribute label* (such as experimental label or disease state), encoded in the vector $\mathbf{x}$. A graph representation of all of these cells would render further computation expensive and time-consuming. Thus, we seek a graph representation of the $N = \sum_{i=1}^{p} n_i$ cells that has $N' << N$ nodes while still representing the biologically relevant information that would be present in the full graph. To accomplish this, we introduce the *cytocoarsening* algorithm. In this section, we outline the general steps of the algorithm; pseudocode is provided in Algorithm 1.

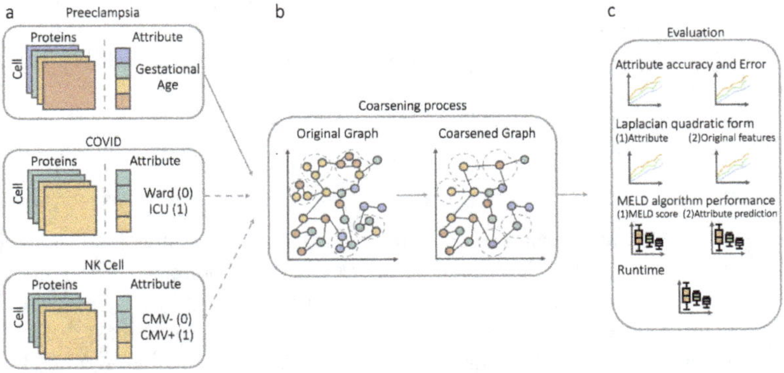

Fig. 1. **Overview.** Given a multi-sample single-cell dataset with clinical attributes (**a**), the cytocoarsening algorithm creates a *coarse* graph representation of all cells (**b**). The coarse graph representation takes into account phenotypic similarity of cells (edges) and the clinical attributes (colors). (**c**) Quantitative evaluation metrics were developed to assess the quality of the coarse graph representation and its effectiveness as input to downstream graph-based bioinformatics algorithms.

Graph representation of single-cell data. The algorithm begins by constructing a joint graph representation $\mathcal{G}$ of all profiled cells across samples. Given a data matrix of cells $\times$ measured features defined as $\mathbf{X} = [\mathbf{X}_1|\mathbf{X}_2|\cdots|\mathbf{X}_p]$ (where $|$ denotes vertical concatenation), each cell is connected to its K nearest neighbors according to Euclidean distance in the measured feature space via scikit-learn's `kneighbors_graph` function[19] (`KNN()` in Algorithm 1). To actually carry out computations with this graph, we will use the adjacency matrix $\mathbf{A}$, which has all the edge weights of the graph encoded in its off-diagonal entries and zeros on the diagonal. We will also use the graph Laplacian $\mathbf{L}$, which is exactly the negative of this matrix but with a diagonal instead defined as $L_{i,i} = \sum_{j=1}^{N} A_{i,j}$.

Algorithm 1 Cytocoarsening

Inputs: feature matrix $\mathbf{X}$, attribute vector $\mathbf{x}$, number of passes P, number of KNN neighbors K, cutoff parameter α
Output: coarsened graph $\mathcal{G}'$
for $1:P$ **do** ▷ P coarsening passes
  $\mathcal{G}$=`KNN`$(\mathbf{X}, K)$ ▷ Creates K-nearest neighbor graph from feature matrix
  C =`Get.K.Neighborhoods`$(\mathcal{G})$ ▷ Identifies coarsening candidates
  I^C = `Get.Index.Sets`(C) ▷ Gets indices of nodes in each candidate set
  $T = |C|/4$ ▷ Defines max number of coarse nodes
  for $C_j \in C$ **do**
    $c_j^d = \max_{j,k\in I_i^C} \{||\mathbf{X}_{j,:} - \mathbf{X}_{k,:}||_2\}$ ▷ Calculates distance cost
    $c_j^q = {\mathbf{x}_{C_i}'}^T \mathbf{L}_{C_i} {\mathbf{x}_{C_i}}'$ ▷ Calculates attribute cost
  end for
  $\{T^q, T^d\}$ = `Set.Thresholds`$(\mathbf{c}^q, \mathbf{c}^d, \alpha)$ ▷ Finds α^{th} percentile of each cost vector
  C^L =`Nodes.To.Coarsen`$(C,\mathbf{c}^q,\mathbf{c}^d)$ ▷ Finds lowest-cost coarsening candidates
  $\{S, I^S\}$ = `Form.Super.Nodes`$(C^L, V(\mathcal{G}))$ ▷ Creates coarse graph node list
  for $i = 1, \ldots, |C^L|$ **do**
    $\tilde{S}_i$ = `Find.Representative`(C_i^L) ▷ Locates optimal super node representative
  end for
  $\mathcal{G}'$ = `Make.Graph`(S) ▷ Creates coarse graph with node set S
  $\{\mathbf{X}, \mathbf{x}\}$ = `Update.Xs`$(\mathbf{X}, \mathbf{x}, I^S)$ ▷ Updates for next pass
end for

Establishing and ranking coarsening candidates. The KNN graph is used to define the *coarsening candidate node sets* as each node and its K nearest neighbors; the candidate sets are stored in the list C with corresponding index set list I^C, i.e. $I_j^C = \{i|v_i \in C_j\}$ (KNN enumeration → `get.K.Neighborhoods()`, indices of nodes within coarsening candidate → `get.Index.Sets()` in Algorithm 1). To decide which candidate sets to coarsen, we define two different cost functions: distance in feature space ($\mathbf{c}^d$) and graph-level attribute variation ($\mathbf{c}^q$).

Distance cost ($\mathbf{c}^d$). The distance cost reflects the overall phenotypical similarity between cells in a coarsening candidate to ensure that highly similar nodes are likely to be aggregated. We define c_i^d, the distance cost of the ith coarsening candidate, as the maximum euclidean distance of all cells within a coarsening candidate:

$$c_i^d = \max_{j,k\in I_i^C} \{||\mathbf{X}_{j,:} - \mathbf{X}_{k,:}||_2\} \,. \tag{1}$$

Attribute cost ($\mathbf{c}^q$). The attribute cost measures the overall variation of the attributes of cells within a coarsening candidate, so that we can prioritize merges of cells with similar attributes. Given a coarsening candidate, C_i, we can extract its sub-adjacency matrix, $\mathbf{A}_{C_i}$ via $\mathbf{A}_{C_i} = \mathbf{A}(I_i^C, I_i^C)$ and compute its corresponding Laplacian matrix, $\mathbf{L}_{C_i}$. We further let $\mathbf{x}_{C_i} = \mathbf{x}(I_i^C)$ be the corresponding subvector of attributes for the coarsening candidate set.

Then the attribute cost c_i^q for coarsening candidate C_i is computed as

$$c_i^q = \mathbf{x}_{C_i}^T \mathbf{L}_{C_i} \mathbf{x}_{C_i} \tag{2}$$

Joint cost (r). We use a joint ranking criteria to rank coarsening candidates according to their phenotypic between-cell similarity ($\mathbf{c}^d$) and attribute consistency ($\mathbf{c}^q$) by simply taking the log of their geometric mean:

$$r_i = 1/2(\log_2 c_i^q + \log_2 c_i^d). \tag{3}$$

The 30 coarsening candidates with the lowest joint cost are then considered for further evaluation.

Evaluating coarsening candidates. A coarsening candidate C will be added to the coarsening list C^L (i.e. selected to be aggregated) if all of the following are true: 1) less than T coarsening candidates have been chosen, 2) both costs $\mathbf{c}^q$ and $\mathbf{c}^d$ are below some percentile thresholds T^q and T^d (see `Set.Thresholds()` in Algorithm 1) to make sure both two costs are sufficiently low, 3) none of the nodes in C are already represented in the coarsening list. Our method will stop trying to find more coarsening candidates to merge if all coarsening candidates remaining have a cost larger than c_{max}, a global constant. If some nodes in the candidate are already present in C^L, then those nodes are removed from the set and the costs are recomputed for this smaller candidate set. In the cases where only one node remains or there are no edges between the remaining candidate nodes, we assign both costs the value of c_{max} in order to remove that set from consideration (see function `Nodes.To.Coarsen()` in Algorithm 1). Once the coarse node sets have been decided, we form the node set for the coarse graph S (with corresponding index set I^S) by taking the union of the coarse nodes with all the individual nodes from the original graph (see function `Form.Super.Nodes()` in Algorithm 1).

Defining super node representatives. Once we know which sets of nodes to merge, we find the original node in each set that is most representative of the group by considering two factors: phenotypical similarity and attribute similarity. Consider the ith super node in the following discussion. For phenotypical similarity, we find the mean point of the nodes in feature space $\mu_i = \frac{1}{|S_i|}\sum_{j \in I_i^S} \mathbf{X}_{j,:}$, and then we calculate the euclidean distance from μ_i to each node in the set. Weights are assigned so that nodes closer to μ_i are more highly weighted. For attribute similarity, we sort the attribute labels by the number of their occurrences in S_i and weight the nodes so that nodes with frequently-occurring attribute values are more highly weighted. To combine these two weights, we normalize them individually and add them together. The representative node is then chosen as the one with the maximum aggregate weight. We will denote the representative node for the ith super node as $\tilde{S}_i$, with original graph index $I^{\tilde{S}_i}$ (see function `Find.Representative()` in Algorithm 1).

Updating edge list. An edge is defined between a pair of nodes S_i and S_j in the coarse graph if, in the original graph, there was at least one edge between any of the nodes in S_i and S_j. (`Make.Graph()` function in Algorithm 1).

The above outlines one pass of the algorithm. To coarsen further, we update the feature matrix $\mathbf{X}_{new} = \mathbf{X}(I^{\tilde{S}}, I^{\tilde{S}})$ and the attribute vector $\mathbf{x}_{new} = \mathbf{x}(I^{\tilde{S}})$ (see function `Update.Xs()` in Algorithm 1).

3. Results

To explore the effects of graph coarsening on biological information, we applied our cytocoarsening algorithm to three publicly available mass cytometry (e.g. CyTOF) datasets. First, the *preeclampsia dataset*[20] profiles blood samples collected 9.7 millions cells from 45 women throughout their pregnancies (33 features measured per cell). The clinical attribute of interest for this dataset was cell gestational age, which ranged from 8 to 28 weeks. Next, the *covid dataset*[21] contains 6.5 million cells collected from 49 total patients (23 features measured per cell). The patients ranged in severity with 6 healthy patients, 23 patients having mild cases of COVID, and 20 experiencing severe responses and were under ICU care. Due to the imbalance in the number of patients for each severity level, we only considered cells from 22 mild patients (one sample had less than 1,000 cells and was thus not considered) and 20 patients that had severe (ICU) COVID. The attribute of interest was disease severity (mild or severe). Finally, the *NK-cell dataset*[22] contains 261 thousand cells collected from 20 total patients (29 measured features per cell). Cytomegalovirus (CMV) status was the attribute of interest, with nine patients being positive for Cytomegalovirus (CMV) and 11 being negative for CMV.

We performed several experiments (Fig. 1c, additional experiments in Supplementary Information [a]) on cytocoarsening and existing coarsening methods (LV-E, LV-N, HEM, AD, and AFF[14]) to quantify their effectiveness in preserving structural and attribute information and in acting as input to downstream graph-based bioinformatics tasks. All experiments were repeated 30 times, sampling a new subset of cells from each sample. Cytocoarsening was run on all datasets with $P = 10$ passes, thresholds $T^d = 26$ and $T^q = 26$, and the max number of coarse nodes as $T = \frac{1}{4}|C|$, where $|C|$ denotes the number of elements (coarsening candidates) of C.

Accuracy and error of attributes in coarse nodes We defined accuracy and error metrics (Fig. 2a and 2b) to evaluate the consistency of attribute values for cells assigned to a coarse node. For all of the "non super node" cells within a coarse node (e.g. those cells that were not chosen to be the representative), we predicted their attributes to be the same as that of the super node representative. The error and accuracy metrics between the true and inferred attribute labels of cells are defined as

$$\text{Error} = \frac{1}{N}\left(\sum_{i=1}^{N'}\sum_{j\in I_i^S} |x_j - x_i'|\right) \quad (4)$$

$$\text{Accuracy} = \frac{1}{N}\left(\sum_{i=1}^{N'}\sum_{j\in I_i^S} \rho(x_j, x_i')\right) \quad (5)$$

---

[a] `https://github.com/ChenCookie/cytocoarsening/blob/main/Supplemental_Material.pdf`

where $\rho(x, y)$ returns 1 if x and y are equal and 0 otherwise.

Across datasets and coarsening ratios, Cytocoarsening exhibited superior performance, followed most closely by the variation neighborhood method. We note that the continuous attribute labels of cells in the preeclampsia dataset make the task more challenging than predicting binary attributes.

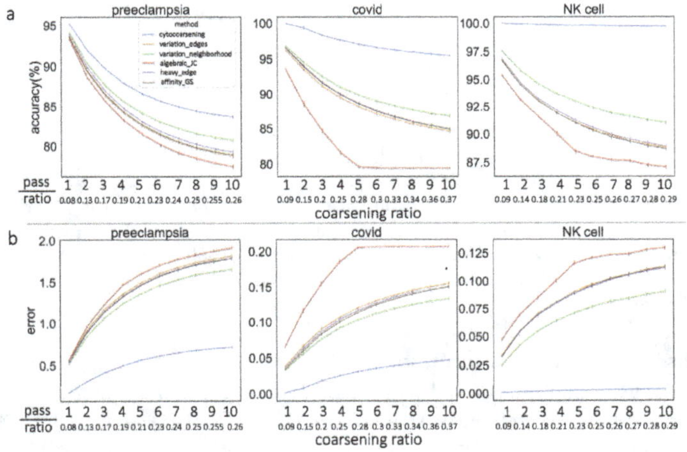

Fig. 2. **Attribute Consistency of Coarse Nodes.** Accuracy (**a**) and error (**b**) metrics were used to evaluate the similarity of attributes within each coarse node. Cytocoarsening (blue) excels in accuracy and error at maintaining consistent attributes within coarse nodes across datasets. For details about baselines, refer to "**Baselines**" in the introduction.

Quantifying attribute and original feature variation across the coarse graph Given the graph Laplacian $\mathbf{L}' = \mathbf{L}(I^{\tilde{S}}, I^{\tilde{S}})$ corresponding to the coarse graph $\mathcal{G}'$ and the coarse attribute vector $\mathbf{x}' = \mathbf{x}(I^{\tilde{S}})$, the normalized Laplacian quadratic form $\frac{1}{N'}\mathbf{x}'^T\mathbf{L}'\mathbf{x}'$ (where N' is the number of coarse graph nodes) summarizes the alignment between structure and attributes. Since the Laplacian quadratic form is small for vectors where neighboring nodes have similar vector entries, the quadratic form will be small if alignment is good (Fig. 3a). Similarly, we can quantify the overall variation in the features over $\mathcal{G}'$ (Fig. 3b) as $\frac{1}{N'}\text{trace}(\mathbf{X}'^T\mathbf{L}'\mathbf{X}')$, where $\mathbf{X}' = \mathbf{X}(:, I^{\tilde{S}})$ is the coarsened feature matrix.

A good coarsening strategy would produce low values for the Laplacian quadratic forms for both attributes and in the features used to construct the original graph, implying those vary smoothly over the graph. Results across the three datasets in Fig. 3 reveals cytocoarsening produces the lowest values for both attributes (a) and original features (b) for all coarsening ratios, suggesting the cytocoarsening faithfully encodes such information.

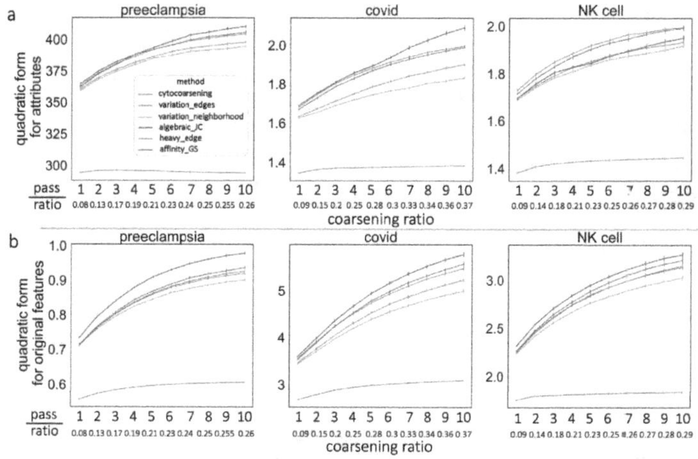

Fig. 3. **Evaluating Variation of Attributes and Original Features on $\mathcal{G}'$.** We used the Laplacian quadratic form on the coarse graph $\mathcal{G}'$ to quantify the variation of the attributes (**a**) and the original features (**b**) over $\mathcal{G}'$ as a function of the extent of graph coarsening (horizontal axis). Cytocoarsening (blue) achieves by far the lowest values for both attributes (**a**) and original features (**b**) across coarsening ratios.

Coarse graphs can be used as input to MELD. To see that we would reach the same biological conclusions by analyzing $\mathcal{G}$ and $\mathcal{G}'$, we used both of these graphs as inputs to MELD[7] and compared the results. Given binary attribute values $\{0, 1\}$, MELD returns a list M, where M_j is the probability that node v_j has an attribute value of 1. We therefore binarized the returned MELD score for a node as 1 if the for node j, $M_j > 0.5$ and assigned it a 0 otherwise. Let $\mathbf{m}^{coarse}$ denote the vector of coarse graph MELD scores. We assigned all nodes within a super node S_j to have the same MELD score as the super node representative. Notationally, then, we have $m_i^{\text{coarse}} = M_j$ whenever node v_i is in the jth super node. Let $\mathbf{m}^{\text{orig}}$ denote the vector of MELD scores of the original graph. We then defined two measures to quantify the similarity and correctness of the MELD results obtained for $\mathcal{G}$ and $\mathcal{G}'$: first, Acc_{MELD} for accuracy. The accuracy metric quantifies the correctness of the MELD score in the coarse graph, defined as

$$Acc_{\text{MELD}} = \frac{1}{N}\left(\sum_{i=1}^{N} \rho(m_i^{\text{orig}}, m_i^{\text{coarse}})\right). \tag{6}$$

Here, $\rho(x, y)$ returns 1 if x and y are equal and 0 otherwise. The results shown in Fig. 4b show that cytocoarsening has the highest MELD score correctness in the coarse graph when setting the smoothness parameter to the default of $\beta = 1$. We note that the attributes for preeclampsia dataset were dichotimized into early and late pregnancy. Although the other methods achieved accuracies above 0.9, cytocoarsening consistently achieved the highest results across datasets with both discrete and continuous attributes. Next, we computed $Corr_{\text{MELD}}$, which is the

Pearson correlation [b] between MELD scores of the coarsened graph and those of the original graph (Fig. 4a).

A high correlation implies high concordance between the MELD scores using $\mathcal{G}'$ as input and those obtained using $\mathcal{G}$, i.e. no critical biologically-meaningful information was lost by reducing the size of the graph. All coarsening methods achieved a reasonable $Corr_{\text{MELD}}$ in all three datasets (Fig. 4a), with cytocoarsening excelling and followed most closely by LV-N.

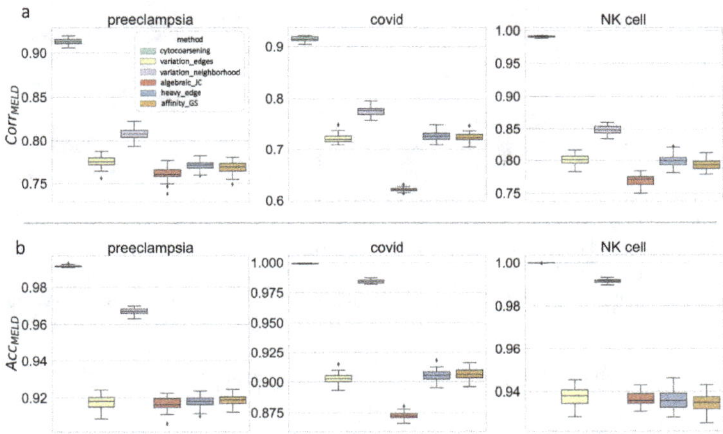

Fig. 4. **Quality of MELD Using $\mathcal{G}'$ as Input.** We computed metrics to evaluate the correlation (**a**) and the overall accuracy (**b**) between MELD results obtained on $\mathcal{G}$ and $\mathcal{G}'$ for six different coarsening methods and three datasets. Results suggest that cytocoarsening, followed by LV-N, produce coarse graph representations that are adequate inputs to MELD.

Sensitivity of MELD parameters in coarse graph representations. MELD has a critical parameter, β, which controls the smoothness or consistency of MELD scores across the graph. To study performance as a function of β, we varied β when computing MELD scores on both the original graph $\mathcal{G}$ and the coarse graph $\mathcal{G}'$ (we denote the parameter in each case as denoted β and β', respectively). We note that due to MELD's expensive runtime, all experiments used only 200 cells per sample. The resulting $Corr_{\text{MELD}}$ scores (averaged over 30 trials) are visualized in the heatmap in Fig. 5. Cytocoarsening achieved the highest scores (denoted by stars) across datasets and combinations of β and β' in 29 of the 48 comparisons (e.g. heatmap grids). The LV-N and LV-E methods are second and third in performance with a total of 12 and 11 best scores, respectively, and they perform more optimally for high values of β and β'.

[b]https://docs.scipy.org/doc/scipy-0.14.0/reference/generated/scipy.stats.pearsonr.html

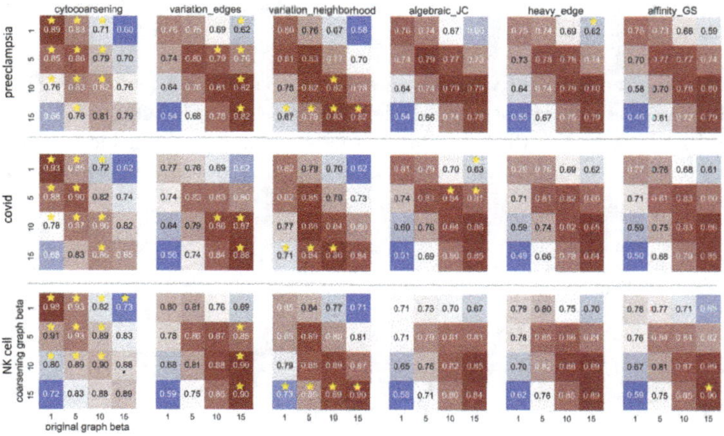

Fig. 5. **Sensitivity of MELD Results to β Parameter.** We evaluated the effect of various combinations for values of MELD's smoothing parameter, β across datasets coarsening methods. Each heatmap grid reflects the $Corr_{\text{MELD}}$ obtained using $\mathcal{G}$ (horizontal axis) and $\mathcal{G}'$ (vertical axis) for a particular dataset, coarsening algorithm and combination of β parameters. A starred grid entry implies that, for that particular combination of β, β', and dataset, the starred algorithm achieved the highest $Corr_{\text{MELD}}$ score; this is frequently achieved by cytocoarsening.

Runtime and scalability. We compared the scalability of cytocoarsening to all other coarsening methods[c] using 1000 subselected cells from each sample. (Fig. 6). To objectively compare our multipass cytocoarsening method to existing coarsening methods, which are only one pass, we also ran cytocoarsening with a single pass. Our results show that AFF has by far the longest runtime across three datasets. Although cytocoarsening is not the fastest method, the runtime only differs slightly from the other four methods. The preeclampsia dataset is the largest in terms of patient samples and measured features and hence took the most time. In contrast, the NK cell dataset is significantly smaller and took half the time (Fig. 6).

4. Discussion

The cytocoarsening algorithm compresses graphs of single-cells by adapting standard graph coarsening approaches to accommodate the associated clinical or experimental cellular attributes. While existing graph coarsening approaches are optimized to create a compressed graph representation with strong *structural* similarity to the original graph, our approach uses new cost functions and a joint ranking strategy to incorporate biologically meaningful cellular information into the coarsening process. We defined several quantitative evaluation strategies to evaluate cytocoarsening and the other existing coarsening approaches on their capacity to preserve more than just structural properties of the original graph. Using three

[c]https://github.com/loukasa/graph-coarsening

CyTOF datasets, we showed that, in comparison to other methods, the cytocoarsening method excels in grouping together cells that are both related in phenotype and in disease state or experimental condition.

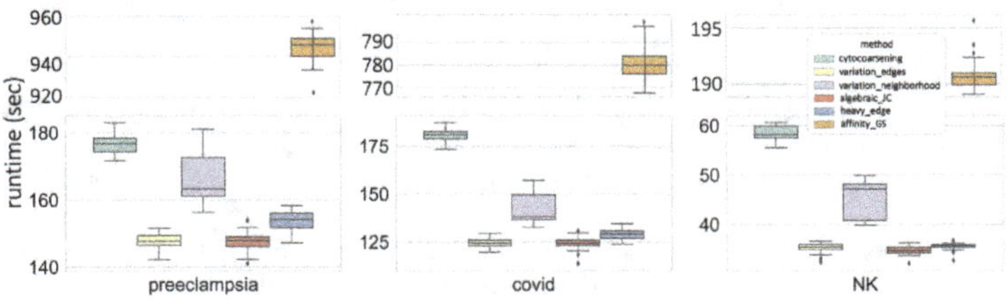

Fig. 6. **Run-Time Evaluations.** Evaluating run-time of all coarsening approaches across datasets, using 1000 cells per profiled sample. Cytocoarsening has similar run-times to the other coarsening strategies, while offering increased performance in encoding attribute information.

Cytocoarsening is a methodological innovation towards adapting primarily structure-preserving coarsening algorithms to single-cell data with associated clinical or experimental attributes, with the aim to compress the input graph for downstream graph-based bioinformatics algorithms. However, to further increase the utility of cytocoarsening in analyzing modern multi-sample flow and mass cytometry datasets, we can modify the initial graph-construction phase for improved scalability. An area of future work is to build coarse graph representations for each sample in *parallel*, and then merge there graphs in a principled manner. Further, additional work can explore how to optimize the coarsening ratio for a particular graph. In summary, Cytocoarsening facilitates more rapid identification of phenotypically-similar cells that are likely associated with a clinical or experimental condition.

References

1. E. A. Ganio, N. Stanley, V. Lindberg-Larsen, J. Einhaus, A. S. Tsai, F. Verdonk, A. Culos, S. Ghaemi, K. K. Rumer, I. A. Stelzer *et al.*, Preferential inhibition of adaptive immune system dynamics by glucocorticoids in patients after acute surgical trauma, *Nature communications* **11**, 1 (2020).
2. A. S. Tsai, K. Berry, M. M. Beneyto, D. Gaudilliere, E. A. Ganio, A. Culos, M. S. Ghaemi, B. Choisy, K. Djebali, J. F. Einhaus *et al.*, A year-long immune profile of the systemic response in acute stroke survivors, *Brain* **142**, 978 (2019).
3. V. L. Tawfik, N. A. Huck, Q. J. Baca, E. A. Ganio, E. S. Haight, A. Culos, S. Ghaemi, T. Phongpreecha, M. S. Angst, J. D. Clark *et al.*, Systematic immunophenotyping reveals sex-specific responses after painful injury in mice, *Frontiers in immunology* **11**, p. 1652 (2020).
4. T. Liechti, L. M. Weber, T. M. Ashhurst, N. Stanley, M. Prlic, S. Van Gassen and F. Mair, An updated guide for the perplexed: cytometry in the high-dimensional era, *Nature Immunology* **22**, 1190 (2021).
5. M. H. Spitzer and G. P. Nolan, Mass cytometry: single cells, many features, *Cell* **165**, 780 (2016).
6. N. Stanley, I. A. Stelzer, A. S. Tsai, R. Fallahzadeh, E. Ganio, M. Becker, T. Phongpreecha,

H. Nassar, S. Ghaemi, I. Maric *et al.*, Vopo leverages cellular heterogeneity for predictive modeling of single-cell data, *Nature communications* **11**, 1 (2020).

7. D. B. Burkhardt, J. S. Stanley, A. Tong, A. L. Perdigoto, S. A. Gigante, K. C. Herold, G. Wolf, A. J. Giraldez, D. van Dijk and S. Krishnaswamy, Quantifying the effect of experimental perturbations at single-cell resolution, *Nature biotechnology* **39**, 619 (2021).
8. E. Dann, N. C. Henderson, S. A. Teichmann, M. D. Morgan and J. C. Marioni, Differential abundance testing on single-cell data using k-nearest neighbor graphs, *Nature Biotechnology* **40**, 245 (2022).
9. Y. A. Reshef, L. Rumker, J. B. Kang, A. Nathan, I. Korsunsky, S. Asgari, M. B. Murray, D. Moody and S. Raychaudhuri, Co-varying neighborhood analysis identifies cell populations associated with phenotypes of interest from single-cell transcriptomics, *Nature Biotechnology* **40**, 355 (2022).
10. E. Dann, N. C. Henderson, S. A. Teichmann, M. D. Morgan and J. C. Marioni, Differential abundance testing on single-cell data using k-nearest neighbor graphs, *Nature Biotechnology* **40**, 245 (2022).
11. Z. B. Bjornson-Hooper, G. K. Fragiadakis, M. H. Spitzer, H. Chen, D. Madhireddy, K. Hu, K. Lundsten, D. R. McIlwain and G. P. Nolan, A comprehensive atlas of immunological differences between humans, mice, and non-human primates, *Frontiers in immunology* **13** (2022).
12. Y. Jin, A. Loukas and J. JaJa, Graph coarsening with preserved spectral properties, in *International Conference on Artificial Intelligence and Statistics*, 2020.
13. N. Stanley, R. Kwitt, M. Niethammer and P. J. Mucha, Compressing networks with super nodes, *Scientific reports* **8**, 1 (2018).
14. A. Loukas, Graph reduction with spectral and cut guarantees, *Journal of Machine Learning Research* **20**, 1 (2019).
15. A. Loukas and P. Vandergheynst, Spectrally approximating large graphs with smaller graphs, in *International Conference on Machine Learning*, 2018.
16. D. Ron, I. Safro and A. Brandt, Relaxation-based coarsening and multiscale graph organization, *Multiscale Modeling & Simulation* **9**, 407 (2011).
17. O. E. Livne and A. Brandt, Lean algebraic multigrid (lamg): Fast graph laplacian linear solver, *SIAM Journal on Scientific Computing* **34**, B499 (2012).
18. Y. Jin, A. Loukas and J. JaJa, Graph coarsening with preserved spectral properties, in *International Conference on Artificial Intelligence and Statistics*, 2020.
19. F. Pedregosa, G. Varoquaux, A. Gramfort, V. Michel, B. Thirion, O. Grisel, M. Blondel, P. Prettenhofer, R. Weiss, V. Dubourg, J. Vanderplas, A. Passos, D. Cournapeau, M. Brucher, M. Perrot and E. Duchesnay, Scikit-learn: Machine learning in Python, *Journal of Machine Learning Research* **12**, 2825 (2011).
20. X. Han, M. S. Ghaemi, K. Ando, L. S. Peterson, E. A. Ganio, A. S. Tsai, D. K. Gaudilliere, I. A. Stelzer, J. Einhaus, B. Bertrand *et al.*, Differential dynamics of the maternal immune system in healthy pregnancy and preeclampsia, *Frontiers in immunology* , p. 1305 (2019).
21. L. Vanderbeke, P. Van Mol, Y. Van Herck, F. De Smet, S. Humblet-Baron, K. Martinod, A. Antoranz, I. Arijs, B. Boeckx, F. Bosisio *et al.*, Monocyte-driven atypical cytokine storm and aberrant neutrophil activation as key mediators of covid-19 disease severity, *Nature communications* **12**, 1 (2021).
22. E. Arvaniti and M. Claassen, Sensitive detection of rare disease-associated cell subsets via representation learning, *Nature communications* **8**, 1 (2017).

Time-aware Embeddings of Clinical Data using a Knowledge Graph

Karthik Soman, Charlotte A. Nelson, Gabriel Cerono and Sergio E. Baranzini*
Weill Institute for Neuroscience, Department of Neurology, University of California San Francisco, San Francisco, California, United States of America
**Email: sergio.baranzini@ucsf.edu*

Meaningful representations of clinical data using embedding vectors is a pivotal step to invoke any machine learning (ML) algorithm for data inference. In this article, we propose a time-aware embedding approach of electronic health records onto a biomedical knowledge graph for creating machine readable patient representations. This approach not only captures the temporal dynamics of patient clinical trajectories, but also enriches it with additional biological information from the knowledge graph. To gauge the predictivity of this approach, we propose an ML pipeline called *TANDEM* (Temporal and Non-temporal Dynamics Embedded Model) and apply it on the early detection of Parkinson's disease. TANDEM results in a classification AUC score of 0.85 on unseen test dataset. These predictions are further explained by providing a biological insight using the knowledge graph. Taken together, we show that temporal embeddings of clinical data could be a meaningful predictive representation for downstream ML pipelines in clinical decision-making.

Keywords: temporal embedding; knowledge graph; electronic health record; machine learning.

1. Introduction

Clinical data comes from multiple modalities and encompasses heterogeneous information related to patient health. Electronic health records (EHR), a structured clinical data, encompasses different health variables of a patient such as diagnosis, medications, lab tests, clinical visit encounters, etc. Machine learning (ML) algorithms, owing to their ability to decipher patterns in large scale heterogeneous data, could be used to tap the invaluable information embedded in the EHR data for insightful clinical predictions[1]. There have been previous efforts along this line such as clinical concept embeddings, disease phenotyping/diagnosis and EHR de-identification[2,3].

Patient representation learning is an important aspect for running ML pipelines. Such representations are generally lower-dimensional latent vectors with predictive value for patient's health status[3]. This predictive value is further capitalized for downstream clinical predictive modeling. There have been predictive analyses that utilized the longitudinal aspect of EHR data such as measurements of lab tests[4], temporal history of diagnosis, medication and procedure codes[5] and long term temporal dependencies in patient medical records[6]. These modeling approaches utilized sequence models like Recurrent Neural Network (RNN) to capture the temporal dynamics in the longitudinal EHR data and embed patients' health state trajectories as internal latent representation[2]. Although such approaches have proven to be useful in predictive medicine, the abstract nature of patient representation affects their clinical interpretability.

There have been interpretable modeling approaches using knowledge networks for clinically relevant problems[7–9]. The major aspect of such an approach is the existence of biologically relevant edges in a knowledge network that could connect entities from molecular to phenotypic level[10]. Such a network level approach helps to understand the relationship between disease and underlying molecular/genetic pathways, thereby providing an insightful knowledge that transcends multiple levels of biology. There have been recent efforts to integrate EHR data with knowledge networks for a network level concept embedding and disease prediction[11,12], but without considering the longitudinal aspect of clinical data.

In this paper, we try to achieve the best of both worlds, i.e. embedding longitudinal EHR data on a biomedical knowledge graph to capture the temporal dynamics of patient clinical trajectory at a network level. We hypothesize that such an embedding approach could represent the health status of a patient with enriched biological information at a higher temporal resolution which could ultimately improve the predictability of disease diagnosis. With this objective, we introduce the concept of knowledge graph based temporal embeddings, and use them in an explainable modeling approach called *TANDEM* for the diagnosis of chronic diseases, in this study - Parkinson's Disease (PD).

2. Methods

2.1. *Scalable Precision medicine Open Knowledge Engine (SPOKE)*

SPOKE is a heterogeneous biomedical knowledge network with more than 3 million nodes of 16 types (such as genes, proteins, disease, symptoms etc.) and more than 16 million edges of 32 types between those nodes[11]. SPOKE integrates over 40 publicly available databases that are biologically relevant (such as GWAS, DOID, Uniprot, ChEMBL, DrugBank, SIDER, MESH). Graphical user interface of SPOKE network is made publicly available (https://spoke.rbvi.ucsf.edu/). In this study, we utilized the biological associations present in this large scale network to create meaningful patient representations for downstream ML analysis.

2.2. *Creating temporal embeddings of patients*

In the previous study[11], SPOKE knowledge graph was connected to EHR data using Observational Medical Outcomes Partnership (OMOP) common data model and Unified Medical Language System's (UMLS) Metathesaurus mappings. Then an embedding vector, called Propagate SPOKE Entry Vectors (PSEVs), for a clinical concept was created by using a modified version of topic-sensitive PageRank[11,13]. PSEVs can be created for any code in the EHR that has been recorded for a cohort of patients (e.g. Parkinson's Disease). A PSEV vector of a clinical concept stores how important each node in SPOKE is for that particular concept, which hence gives a network level representation of an EHR concept.

In this study, to produce temporal embeddings for an individual patient, PSEVs corresponding to the EHR codes (taken from the de-identified EHR database of UCSF medical center) from a specified time range (frame width = 1 year) in a patient's timeline were aggregated and normalized to create a patient specific embedding vector (Figure 1A). Stacking such embedding vectors from each time frame gave rise to a two-dimensional array whose rows represented time and columns represented SPOKE nodes (Figure 1A). We named this as temporal SPOKEsig since it holds the temporal dynamics of SPOKE nodes as a function of a patient's clinical data. We also created non-temporal SPOKEsig i.e. patient embedding without considering the temporal order of EHR concepts, hence generating a one-dimensional array of vector (i.e. no time axis, Figure 1A).

In this study we created embeddings for two patient cohorts (i.e. PD and non-PD). Patients were included in the PD cohorts if a PD diagnosis code was present in their EHR *diagnosis* table. We selected only those patients with enough temporal history (i.e. having clinical data in more than one year of time frame in their timeline). In the interest of analyzing disease dynamics and classifying patients into PD or non-PD classes before the clinical diagnosis, we created embeddings starting from one year before their actual clinical diagnosis and going further back in time (i.e. early detection of PD, Figure 1A). We created two sets of such embedding vectors for each cohort where one set was used for feature selection and training the downstream ML model and the other set was used to evaluate the performance of the model.

Considering M number of nodes in SPOKE, a patient cohort with N patients can be represented by a two-dimensional array of size NxM using the non-temporal approach (Figure 1B). The same patient cohort can be represented by a three-dimensional array of size NxTxM using the temporal approach, where T denotes the time axis of the embedding vector (Figure 1B). T corresponds to the largest visiting time of a patient in the cohort of interest, in this study the PD cohort.

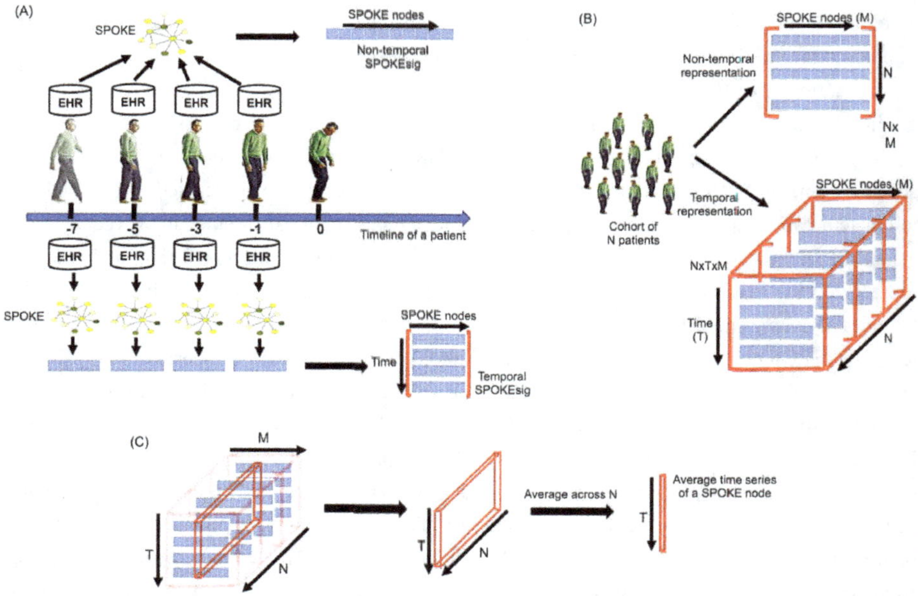

Fig. 1. (A) shows the schematic for the generation of temporal and non-temporal patient embeddings. The middle arrow shows the patient timeline where 0 represents the time when the diagnosis was made for the first time. -1 represents one year before the clinical diagnosis and a similar explanation holds for other tick labels shown on the timeline. (B) shows the way in which a patient cohort can be represented using non-temporal and temporal SPOKEsig approaches. (C) Schematic for the computation of the average time series of a SPOKE node. Starting from the left, it shows the time series of a SPOKE node as a strip in the three-dimensional array of temporal SPOKEsig. Averaging that strip across the depth (i.e. number of patient samples *N*) gives the average time series of that SPOKE node.

2.3. *Knowledge graph time series and feature selection*

For any useful data inference using an ML algorithm, the first step is to select predictive features from the embedding vectors that are used as training data for downstream ML pipeline. In a three-dimensional temporal SPOKEsig, each feature is a time series corresponding to nodes in the SPOKE knowledge graph. To evaluate how these nodes evolve in time with respect to disease progression, we first computed the average time series of each SPOKE node across all patients in the training data of each cohort (Figure 1C).

We then applied a non-parametric statistical test (*Mann-Kendall Trend Test, MKTT*[14]) on each average time series to identify a trend[15]. Trend can be treated as a feature that gives a measure of how time series evolve. MKTT only tests for linear monotonic trends in a time series[15]. Hence, a time-series can be classified as an increasing, decreasing or no trend. In addition to the trend type, the test also returns a trend value (slope) present in the time series and a p-value associated with it. Since we are looking at a classification problem, we wanted to retain predictive temporal features that show disparate temporal dynamics between the cohorts. Hence, we selected those features that satisfied at least one of the following three criteria:

1. A node has a trend in one cohort and no trend in the other cohort
2. A node has opposite trends in two cohorts
3. A node has the same trend in two cohorts, then select only if its slope in one cohort is more than double than in the other.

2.4. *Transformation of temporal embeddings of a patient cohort*

After feature selection, the next step is to train an ML classifier to identify if a patient has PD or not (two-class problem). Since temporal embeddings are sequential data (because of the time dimension), state-of-the-art models to learn such data are recurrent neural networks (RNN) like Long short-term memory (LSTM) networks[16], Gated recurrent unit (GRU) networks[17]. However, the patient cohort size used in this study was not large enough to train such deep neural networks with trainable parameters in the order of millions. This situation (less data and more parameters) could lead to data overfitting and that could affect the generalizability of the trained model. In such situations, previous studies have chosen models like random forest (RF) owing to their ensemble architecture [18–20] and we chose the same in our case.

To train a RF classifier, we transformed the temporal SPOKEsig from a three-dimensional array (NxTxM') to a two-dimensional array (NxM') where N corresponds to total number of patients in a cohort, T represents time and M' represents the selected features from an initial M features (after feature selection, $M' < M$). To retain the embedded temporal information in the transformed two-dimensional representation, we performed a linear approximation of temporal SPOKEsig by computing the trend value present in each time series of SPOKE nodes across all patients. Figure 2 shows the steps involved in this transformation process.

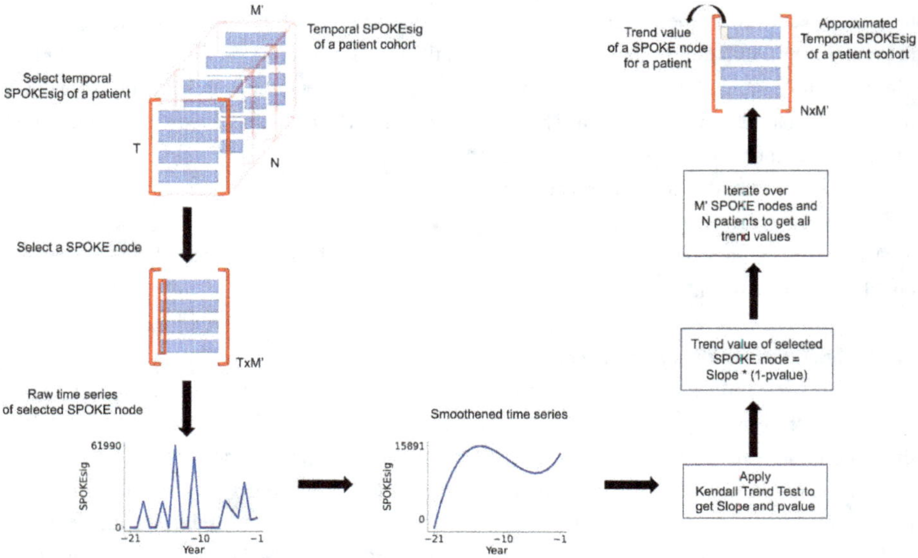

Fig. 2. Steps involved in the linear approximation of three-dimensional temporal SPOKEsig. Following the direction of arrows, it starts with selecting a temporal SPOKEsig of a patient, followed by selecting a time series of a SPOKE node. To prevent any false trend value estimates (because of the zero elements in the series coming from the sporadic hospital visits made by the patient), the raw time series was smoothened using Savitzky-Golay filter (window size = 21 and polynomial order = 3). We then applied Kendall trend test on the smoothed time series to get the trend (slope) and p-value. Final trend value was considered as the estimated slope multiplied by the probability for the presence of trend in that time series (which is 1-p-value). These steps were iterated for all SPOKE nodes across all patients in a cohort to get the approximated temporal SPOKEsig of a patient cohort which is a two-dimensional array.

To compensate for this linear approximation transformation, a second feature selection was done on the transformed two-dimensional array (of training data) such that we selected only those features whose absolute difference in their average slope values between PD and non-PD cohort is greater than a threshold value of 406 (chosen empirically).

2.5. *Temporal and non-temporal dynamics embedded model (TANDEM) for disease classification*

TANDEM includes both temporal and non-temporal embeddings of patients for disease classification. Specifically, we trained two separate RF models, one using approximated temporal SPOKEsig and the other one using non-temporal SPOKEsig. One model evaluated the linear trend and the other model evaluated the area swept by the time series of SPOKE nodes. Hence, both classifiers looked at two fundamentally different aspects of the time series data. Each model was trained using their respective training data. Since there existed less PD samples than non-PD samples in the data, training data was imbalanced. Hence, while training the classifiers, proper weights were assigned to patient samples in the training data based on their class distribution (hence more weightage was given to PD samples while training). Individual prediction scores of these two models were further normalized by their percentile scores. Finally, a logistic classifier was trained (using binary cross-entropy as the loss function) using the normalized prediction scores from temporal and non-temporal RF models to compute the final disease prediction score.

Classification performance was evaluated using an unseen test dataset. Model performance was quantified by computing the Area Under the Curve (AUC) of Receiver Operator Characteristic (ROC) curve. Bootstrap analysis was done by randomly sampling prediction scores (corresponding to both classes) with replacement and then computing AUC score for that sample. This process was repeated for 1000 times which generated a distribution of AUC scores for the model. In addition to AUC, we also computed F1 score and Average Precision score of each model for comparison.

3. Results

3.1. *Patient temporal embedding*

We selected a total of 283 PD and 74,059 non-PD patients respectively as training dataset. We had a separate test dataset (for model evaluation) with 1994 patients (17 PD and 1977 non-PD). EHR history of both cohorts spanned a maximum of 21 years from one year prior to the clinical diagnosis. There were a total of 389,297 SPOKE nodes in the embedding vector (i.e. dimension of the vector).

3.2. *Feature selection and PCA visualization*

Following the feature selection method using the MKT test (mentioned in the Methods section), we were able to reduce the features of temporal SPOKEsig from 389,297 to 109,256 (28.1% of initial features). Next, temporal dynamics of the selected and non-selected features were visualized by projecting them onto the first three principal components (Figure 3). A second feature selection on the linear approximated temporal SPOKEsigs (see Methods) reduced features from 109256 to 42012 (38.5% of initial features).

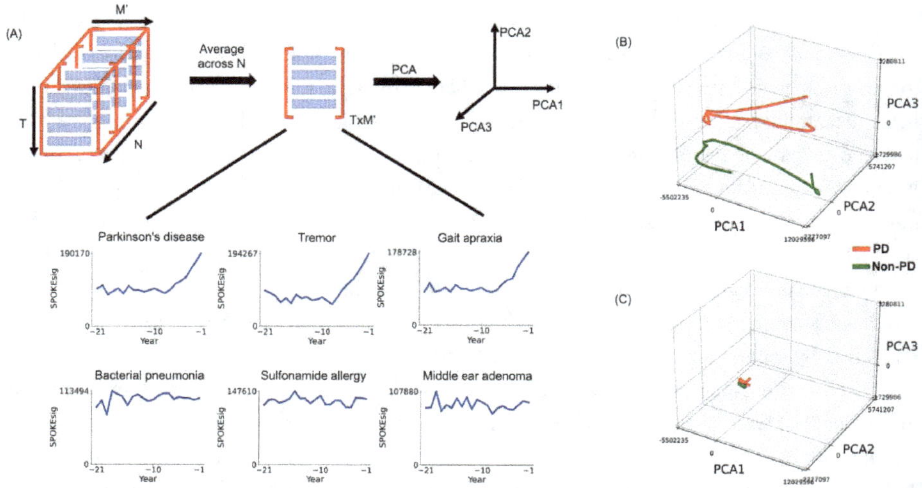

Fig. 3. (A) shows the steps in applying PCA on feature selected temporal SPOKEsig. The insight shows six examples of SPOKE node time series corresponding to PD cohort (averaged across patient samples). Upper row corresponds to SPOKE nodes that are closely related to PD and lower row corresponds to nodes that are less related to PD. (B) Temporal trajectory of selected features in PCA space. Two distinct trajectories are evident in the PCA space and the color code is shown in the legend. (C) Temporal trajectory of non-selected features in PCA space. For the sake of visual comparison, we included only those non-selected features that showed no trend in both PD and non-PD cohorts and had a p value > 0.5.

3.3. *Disease classification using TANDEM architecture*

AUC bootstrap analysis on the test data showed that temporal model showed higher performance than the non-temporal model (Figure 4A, Table 1, p-value=$4.5*10^{-52}$, N=1000, Mann Whitney U test). However, TANDEM architecture outperformed these two models significantly (Figure 4A, Table 1). We also compared these models using their F1-score and average precision score on the test data and it showed that in both cases TANDEM model held the highest score (Figure 4B-C).

For the explainability of TANDEM predictions from a biological perspective, we estimated the temporal slope (rate of growth) of PD related gene nodes' time series (i.e. gene nodes connected to PD node in SPOKE) for all patients that were correctly predicted by the TANDEM model. 13 PD (out of 17) and 1659 non-PD (out of 1977) test patients were correctly predicted by the TANDEM model. PD genes showed higher rate of temporal evolution in these PD patient group than the non-PD group (p-value = $1.4*10^{-06}$, N = 141, Mann Whitney U test, Figure 4D). We also showed the temporal evolution of PD-gene network for a single patient across three discrete time points in a patient's timeline (Figure 4E for PD patient and Figure 4F for non-PD patient).

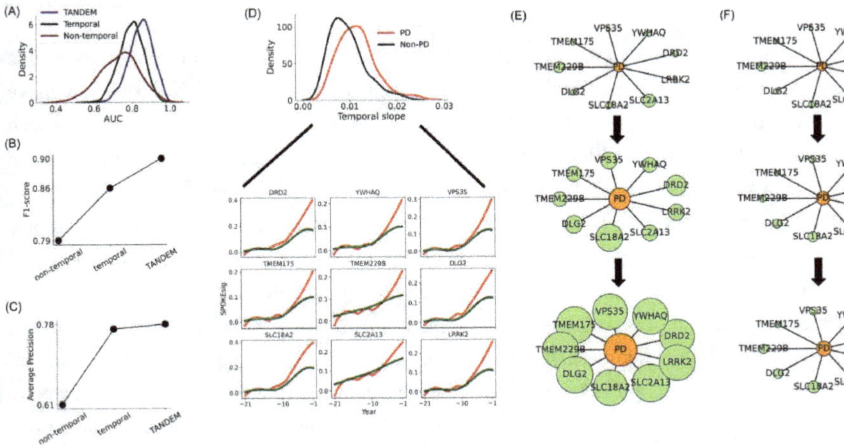

Fig. 4. (A) AUC distributions of three models in PD classification. (B)-(C) F1-score and Average Precision score of three models respectively (D) Distribution of temporal slope of PD related genes averaged across test patients correctly predicted by TANDEM. Insight shows the average time series of 9 PD related genes for PD (red) and non-PD (green) cohorts from the above distribution. (E)-(F) show the temporal evolution of PD-gene network for a PD patient (E) and a non-PD patient (F) across -15 (top), -4 (middle) and -1 year (bottom) before their clinical diagnosis. Green color nodes represent genes and the orange color node represents disease (PD). Size of a node at a specific time is proportional to the relevance of that node for an individual patient in that time.

Table 1. Comparison of model performances

Model	AUC ($\mu \pm \sigma$)	95% CI	Comparison with TANDEM (p-value, Mann Whitney U test, N = 1000)
Temporal	0.8± 0.06	(0.67, 0.91)	$3.1*10^{-64}$
Non-temporal	0.73±0.1	(0.52, 0.92)	$4.5*10^{-145}$
TANDEM	0.85±0.06	(0.71, 0.96)	-

4. Discussion

If we consider clinical events of a patient in the order in which they occurred, they naturally form a time series. By embedding this longitudinal EHR data on a knowledge network, we tried to achieve a network level interpretation of the temporal dynamics of disease (in this case PD). This approach could possibly bridge the two EHR modeling approaches i.e. knowledge network approach[10] and longitudinal data approach[2].

TANDEM model underlines the complementary nature of temporal and non-temporal features of clinical data in disease diagnosis. These two aspects of TANDEM worked in tandem and enhanced the overall prediction performance. Since the temporal SPOKEsig enriches a patient's clinical trajectory with additional biological information, this approach could give a biological perspective to the model predictions and thereby making it an explainable approach. For example, there was an increased temporal slope associated with the gene LRRK2 among PD patients correctly predicted by the model. There have been previous studies that pointed out the criticality of mutations in the LRRK2 gene and PD pathogenesis, thus making it a predominant genetic risk factor for PD[21,22]. This followed by the visualization of temporal evolution of PD-gene network at individual patient level brings an intuitive biological insight into the model's prediction. As a future work, we plan to apply this modeling architecture to other complex diseases to test its generalizability.

A major challenge in this study was the mapping of clinical data to SPOKE graph for creating embedding vectors. Not all EHR variables map to SPOKE nodes and hence that transformation was lossy. However, additional biological information from SPOKE knowledge graph could be considered as a compensatory factor for this loss. Another challenge is the limitation of patient data. Since this study relied on the temporal history of EHR data, we had to drop patients with fewer temporal information to analyze (~20% patients were dropped). This could be a bottleneck for a data driven pipeline. Lastly, linear approximation of temporal SPOKEsig could have compromised its predictive power. Hence, as a future work, we plan to use the three-dimensional temporal SPOKEsig in its entirety for disease prediction using deep learning sequence models.

Availability of Code and Data

We have made available patient graph representations and the python code for TANDEM in the github repository (https://github.com/BaranziniLab/TANDEM).

Acknowledgments

The development of SPOKE and its applications are being funded by grants from the National Science Foundation (NSF_2033569), NIH/NCATS (NIH_NOA_1OT2TR003450), and the UCSF Marcus Program in Precision Medicine Innovation. SEB holds the Heidrich Family and Friends Endowed Chair of Neurology at UCSF. SEB holds the Distinguished Professorship in Neurology I at UCSF.

References

1. Deep EHR: A Survey of Recent Advances in Deep Learning Techniques for Electronic Health Record (EHR) Analysis. https://doi.org/10.1109/JBHI.2017.2767063.

2. Xiao, C., Choi, E. & Sun, J. Opportunities and challenges in developing deep learning models using electronic health records data: a systematic review. *Journal of the American Medical Informatics Association* vol. 25 1419–1428 Preprint at https://doi.org/10.1093/jamia/ocy068 (2018).

3. Miotto, R., Li, L., Kidd, B. A. & Dudley, J. T. Deep Patient: An Unsupervised Representation to Predict the Future of Patients from the Electronic Health Records. *Sci. Rep.* **6**, 26094 (2016).

4. Razavian, N., Marcus, J. & Sontag, D. Multi-task Prediction of Disease Onsets from Longitudinal Lab Tests. (2016) doi:10.48550/arXiv.1608.00647.

5. Choi, E., Bahadori, M. T., Schuetz, A., Stewart, W. F. & Sun, J. Doctor AI: Predicting Clinical Events via Recurrent Neural Networks. (2015) doi:10.48550/arXiv.1511.05942.

6. Pham, T., Tran, T., Phung, D. & Venkatesh, S. DeepCare: A Deep Dynamic Memory Model for Predictive Medicine. (2016) doi:10.48550/arXiv.1602.00357.

7. Bean, D. M. *et al.* Knowledge graph prediction of unknown adverse drug reactions and validation in electronic health records. *Sci. Rep.* **7**, 1–11 (2017).

8. Himmelstein, D. S. & Baranzini, S. E. Heterogeneous Network Edge Prediction: A Data Integration Approach to Prioritize Disease-Associated Genes. *PLoS Comput. Biol.* **11**, e1004259 (2015).

9. Himmelstein, D. S. *et al.* Systematic integration of biomedical knowledge prioritizes drugs for repurposing. (2017) doi:10.7554/eLife.26726.

10. Barabási, A.-L., Gulbahce, N. & Loscalzo, J. Network medicine: a network-based approach to human disease. *Nat. Rev. Genet.* **12**, 56–68 (2010).

11. Nelson, C. A., Butte, A. J. & Baranzini, S. E. Integrating biomedical research and electronic health records to create knowledge-based biologically meaningful machine-readable embeddings. *Nat. Commun.* **10**, 1–10 (2019).

12. Nelson, C. A., Bove, R., Butte, A. J. & Baranzini, S. E. Embedding electronic health records onto a knowledge network recognizes prodromal features of multiple sclerosis and predicts diagnosis. *J. Am. Med. Inform. Assoc.* **29**, 424–434 (2021).

13. Haveliwala, T. H. Topic-sensitive PageRank. *Proceedings of the eleventh international conference on World Wide Web - WWW '02* Preprint at https://doi.org/10.1145/511446.511513 (2002).

14. Mann, H. B. Nonparametric Tests Against Trend. *Econometrica* vol. 13 245 Preprint at https://doi.org/10.2307/1907187 (1945).

15. Wang, F. *et al.* Re-evaluation of the Power of the Mann-Kendall Test for Detecting Monotonic Trends in Hydrometeorological Time Series. *Front. Earth Sci.* **0**, (2020).

16. Hochreiter, S. & Schmidhuber, J. Long Short-Term Memory. *Neural Comput.* **9**, 1735–1780 (1997).

17. Chung, J., Gulcehre, C., Cho, K. & Bengio, Y. Empirical Evaluation of Gated Recurrent Neural Networks on Sequence Modeling. (2014) doi:10.48550/arXiv.1412.3555.

18. Dietterich, T. G. Ensemble Methods in Machine Learning. in *Multiple Classifier Systems* 1–15 (Springer Berlin Heidelberg, 2000).

19. Breiman, L. Random Forests. *Mach. Learn.* **45**, 5–32 (2001).

20. Díaz-Uriarte, R. & Alvarez de Andrés, S. Gene selection and classification of microarray data using random forest. *BMC Bioinformatics* **7**, 1–13 (2006).

21. Tolosa, E., Vila, M., Klein, C. & Rascol, O. LRRK2 in Parkinson disease: challenges of clinical trials. *Nat. Rev. Neurol.* **16**, 97–107 (2020).

22. Dächsel, J. C. & Farrer, M. J. LRRK2 and Parkinson Disease. *Arch. Neurol.* **67**, 542–547 (2010).

Contrastive learning of protein representations with graph neural networks for structural and functional annotations

Jiaqi Luo[1], Yunan Luo[2,*]

[1] *Institute for Interdisciplinary Information Sciences, Tsinghua University*
[2] *School of Computational Science and Engineering, Georgia Institute of Technology*
**Corresponding author:* `yunan@gatech.edu`

Although protein sequence data is growing at an ever-increasing rate, the protein universe is still sparsely annotated with functional and structural annotations. Computational approaches have become efficient solutions to infer annotations for unlabeled proteins by transferring knowledge from proteins with experimental annotations. Despite the increasing availability of protein structure data and the high coverage of high-quality predicted structures, e.g., by AlphaFold, many existing computational tools still only rely on sequence data to predict structural or functional annotations, including alignment algorithms such as BLAST and several sequence-based deep learning models. Here, we develop PenLight, a general deep learning framework for protein structural and functional annotations. PenLight uses a graph neural network (GNN) to integrate 3D protein structure data and protein language model representations. In addition, PenLight applies a contrastive learning strategy to train the GNN for learning protein representations that reflect similarities beyond sequence identity, such as semantic similarities in the function or structure space. We benchmarked PenLight on a structural classification task and a functional annotation task, where PenLight achieved higher prediction accuracy and coverage than state-of-the-art methods.

Keywords: Protein annotation; Protein structure and function; Deep learning; Graph neural network; Contrastive learning; Representation learning

1. Introduction

With the decrease in the cost of sequencing technology, protein sequence data have been accumulated to an ever-increasing amount. How to characterize those amino acid sequences with structural and functional annotations is a long-standing and challenging problem in bioinformatics. The community has long been interested in developing computational tools to infer protein functions from their sequences, ranging from BLAST,[1] profile hidden Markov models (pHMM),[2] and several other popular methods.[3–6] Despite the success of these tools in inferring protein functional annotations, such as the Gene Ontology (GO) terms and Enzyme Commission (EC) numbers, the whole protein universe is still sparsely annotated. For example, in Pfam, a popular protein family database, it was reported that one-third of bacterial proteins cannot be annotated by alignment approaches.[7]

Recently, deep learning (DL) has emerged as a promising approach to complement traditional tools to expand protein annotations and has gained impressive success. For instance,

Bileschi et al. develop a deep neural network to predict protein functional labels, which was adopted by the Pfam database to expand its coverage by > 9.5%.[8] Other successful applications of DL in protein annotation include structure fold recognition,[9] GO term prediction[10] and EC number predictions.[11] Another notable trend along this line is protein language models (PLMs), which learn rich representations that encode intrinsic biophysical, evolutionary, and structural properties of proteins from large-scale unlabeled protein sequence data. PLMs have been found to substantially improve prediction accuracy for many protein structure and function prediction problems.[12]

It is believed that protein sequence determines protein structure, which dictates function. Knowing the three-dimensional (3D) information of protein structures can be useful for protein function prediction because structures are more conserved than sequences and more directly related to functions such as protein binding. However, due to the limited availability of solved protein structure data, most existing methods for functional annotations are trying to directly predict functions from sequences, assuming that proteins sharing high sequence similarity will have the same set of functions. This assumption may not always hold, as it has been found that proteins with similar structures can have seemly random sequence similarity. Fortunately, with advances in biotechnology such as cryo-EM,[13] the number of solved protein structures is constantly increasing.[14] The structure coverage is further improved by the high-quality structures predicted by DL models such as AlphaFold.[15] Remarkably, in August 2022, DeepMind released 200M AlphaFold's predicted structures, covering nearly every known protein on the planet. In parallel, the machine learning community has made great advancements in developing graph neural networks (GNNs) for modeling graph data, which have resulted in successful applications such as AlphaFold.[15] Despite the new opportunity offered by the largely available solved and predicted structures and the advancements in GNNs, integrating structure data and graph DL has not been widely exploited for protein functional and structural annotations.

The supervised learning paradigm has been a popular choice in previous deep learning methods for predicting protein functions, in which the protein sequence is directly mapped to the class output. This paradigm faces the challenge of class imbalance. For example, many Pfam families contain relatively few sequences, which makes it difficult for supervised models to predict because the training objective is dominated by the major Pfam classes. Another paradigm called contrastive learning has recently gained interest in the machine learning community.[16] Instead of directly mapping sequences to functions, contrastive learning optimizes a latent embedding space where sequences with similar functions are pulled together, while sequences of different functions are pushed away. The ProtTucker model developed by Heinzinger et al.[17] was among the first attempts of using contrastive learning for protein annotation, but the model only predicts protein structural annotations from protein sequence information. Extending contrastive learning to integrate structure data has not been explored for protein structural and functional annotations.

Here, we present PenLight (Protein contrastive learning with graph neural network for annotation), a contrastive deep learning model for protein structural and functional annotations. PenLight models protein 3D structure as a graph and uses a GNN to learn structure-aware representations for the input protein. A major innovation of our work is using contrastive learning for refining the learned protein representations so that the semantic similarity of protein structures or functions can be reflected in the embedding space. We demonstrate PenLight's applicability using a structure classification task (fold classification) and a functional annotation task (EC number prediction). On both tasks, PenLight outperformed existing methods, including alignment algorithms such as BLAST and previous deep learning approaches. We observed that PenLight was able to achieve high prediction accuracy as well as high coverage. We expect PenLight to be used as a general deep learning framework for protein annotations.

2. Materials and Methods

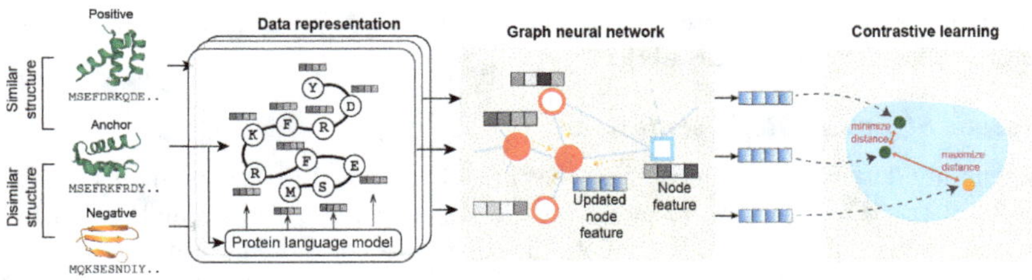

Fig. 1. **Schematic illustration of PenLight.**

Overview of PenLight. In this work, we develop PenLight, a graph neural network trained with contrastive learning, for predicting protein structural and functional annotations. As an overview (Fig. 1), PenLight receives the three-dimensional structure of a protein as input and represents it as a graph, where the graph's nodes are protein residues, and the edges encode the spatial proximity of residues. Protein language model embeddings and a set of geometric features (e.g., distance and orientation) derived from the input structure are used to initialize the node and edge features. PenLight then employs a contrastive learning scheme to learn a vector representation for each protein, such that the representations of structurally/functional similar proteins are pulled together while dissimilar proteins are pushed apart. PenLight then transfers the known annotations of a protein to an unlabeled protein if their representation distance is below a threshold. The source code of PenLight is available at `https://github.com/luo-group/PenLight`.

2.1. *Tasks and Datasets*

We showcase the applicability of PenLight using a structure classification task and a functional annotation task. Specifically, we train separate PenLight models to predict the structure classification code in the CATH database and the enzyme class (EC number) of a protein. Both CATH codes and EC numbers are four-level classification systems that characterize different levels of similarities of proteins, as described below.

Structure classification. We utilize the CATH dataset,[18] an expert-curated database that classifies 3D protein structures from the Protein Data Bank (PDB) database[14] into a hierarchical classification system. We downloaded and processed the structures from CATH following Heinzinger et al..[17] Each protein structure is assigned with a label (CATH code) at the Class (C), Architecture (A), Topology (T), and Homologous superfamily (H) levels, respectively. Intuitively, higher levels (H>T>A>C) contain proteins that are more similar in their 3D structure.

Functional annotation. We choose the Enzyme Commission number (EC number) prediction as an example of functional annotation tasks. Similar to CATH, EC number is also a four-level numerical classification scheme for enzymes, which assigns each enzyme with a label based on the chemical reactions it catalyzes. We downloaded structures annotated with EC numbers in the PDB database following a previous study.[19] While there exist promiscuous enzymes that are labeled with more than one EC number, most enzymes are labeled with only a single EC number. Therefore, we only consider the top-1 predictions when evaluating different prediction methods in this work.

2.2. *Protein Structure Representations*

The structure data of a protein contains the three-dimensional (3D) coordinates of atoms of the protein structure. Here, we focus on the C_α atoms of the backbone and use them to represent the residues of a protein. We denote the coordinates of those C_α atoms as $\mathcal{C} = \{\boldsymbol{c}_i \in \mathbb{R}^3\}_{i=1}^N$, where N is the number of residues. We represent the structure as a graph $\mathcal{G} = \{\mathcal{V}, \mathcal{E}\}$, where the node set $\mathcal{V}$ contains the residues and the edger set $\mathcal{E}$ indicates the residue contacts, which is defined by a distance cutoff of 8Å between pairwise C_α atoms.

To improve the expressiveness of the structure representation, we also associated features to each node and edge in the graph $\mathcal{G}$. We built a series of features that are invariant to rotations and translations following a previous study.[20] For the node feature $\boldsymbol{v}_i$ of residue i, we used the per-residue embeddings generated by ESM-1b[12] or ProtT5,[21] protein language models (PLM) that are trained on millions of protein sequences using unsupervised representation learning. It has been shown that PLM can boost the prediction accuracy for protein function and structure predictions.[12,22] We used ProtT5 embeddings for the structure classification task following Heinzinger et al.[17] and ESM-1b for the functional annotation task, as we found in nested cross-validation that this resulted in a better performance. For the edge between residues i and j, we concatenated multiple features $\boldsymbol{e}_{ij} = [(\boldsymbol{c}_j - \boldsymbol{c}_i)/\|\boldsymbol{c}_j - \boldsymbol{c}_i\|_2; \mathrm{RBF}(\|\boldsymbol{c}_j - \boldsymbol{c}_i\|_2); E_{pos}(\boldsymbol{c}_j - \boldsymbol{c}_i)]$, where the first term is the unit direction vector, the second term is the pairwise distance lifted into radial basis functions (RBFs), and the third term is the sinusoidal encoding of the relative distance and direction between the two residues.

2.3. *Graph Neural Network*

Now we introduced the GNN architecture used in PenLight. We used a modified version of graph attention network (GAT)[23,24] as our backbone model. Given the structure graph $\mathcal{G} = \{\mathcal{V}, \mathcal{E}\}$ of the input protein, GAT applies L layers of graph convolution operations that transform $\mathcal{G}$ to an embedding $\boldsymbol{z} \in \mathbb{R}^d$. The ℓ-th layer transforms residue i's embedding $\boldsymbol{h}_i^{(\ell)}$ to an updated embedding $\boldsymbol{h}_i^{(\ell+1)}$ by aggregating the information from residue i and its neighbor residues: $\boldsymbol{h}_i^{(\ell+1)} = \alpha_{i,i}\boldsymbol{W}^{(\ell)}\boldsymbol{h}_i^{(\ell)} + \sum_{j\in\mathcal{N}(i)} \alpha_{i,j}\boldsymbol{W}^{(\ell)}\boldsymbol{h}_j^{(\ell)}$, where $\mathcal{N}(i)$ is the set of neighbor nodes of node i, $\boldsymbol{W}$ are learnable weights of the GNN, and α_{ij}'s are attention weights used to adaptively aggregate embeddings from node i's neighbors. The embedding $\boldsymbol{h}_i^{(\ell)}$ is initialized using the node feature $\boldsymbol{v}_i$ for $\ell = 0$. The attention weights are computed as (the superscript of layer index ℓ is omitted for simplicity):

$$\alpha_{i,j} = \frac{\exp\left(\mathbf{a}^\top \sigma\left(\boldsymbol{\Theta}[\mathbf{h}_i \,\|\, \mathbf{h}_j \,\|\, \mathbf{e}_{i,j}]\right)\right)}{\sum_{k \in \mathcal{N}(i) \cup \{i\}} \exp\left(\mathbf{a}^\top \sigma\left(\boldsymbol{\Theta}[\mathbf{h}_i \,\|\, \mathbf{h}_k \,\|\, \mathbf{e}_{i,k}]\right)\right)}, \tag{1}$$

where $\boldsymbol{a}$ and $\boldsymbol{\Theta}$ are learnable weights, $\|$ is vector concatenation, and $\sigma(\cdot)$ is the Leaky ReLU activation function. PenLight used two stacked GAT layers with ReLU activation to transform the initial node features into 512-dimensional vectors $\boldsymbol{h}_i^L$ for each amino acid. A global mean pooling layer was used after the GNN to aggregate the embeddings of all amino acids into embeddings into a single embedding $\boldsymbol{z} \in \mathbb{R}^{128}$, representing the input protein.

2.4. *Contrastive Learning*

We applied contrastive learning to optimize the GNN model in PenLight, which directly optimizes an embedding space such that proteins with the same structural or functional category are located together in the embedding space. The GNN model receives a triplet of proteins (represented as graphs) as input each time, i.e., an anchor protein x_a, a positive protein x_p that is structurally/functionally similar to x_a, and a negative protein x_n that is structurally/functionally dissimilar to x_a. The objective of contrastive learning is to learn an embedding function (parameterized by the GNN) $f : \mathcal{G} \mapsto \mathbb{R}^d$ such that the distance between the positive pair is smaller than that of the negative pair: $d(f(x_a), f(x_p)) < d(f(x_a), f(x_n))$, where $d(\cdot,\cdot)$ is a distance function (e.g., Euclidean distance) defined on the embedding space.

Triplet sampling. How to sample the triplets is the key to learning a well-organized embedding space. Since both CATH codes and EC numbers are organized in hierarchical tree structures with four levels, and each label is represented as a four-digit number from coarse to fine (e.g., EC: 3.2.1.2), we adopted a hierarchical sampling strategy[17] to randomly sample the triplets (x_a, x_p, x_n) for both tasks. More specifically, during training, we sampled each protein in the training set as the anchor protein x_a. For each anchor protein we first randomly chose a similarity level $\gamma \in \{1, 2, 3, 4\}$. Then a different protein with the same label up to the γ-th digit was sampled as the positive protein x_p, and another protein with a different digit at the γ-th level but the same digit at the $(\gamma - 1)$-th level was sampled as the negative protein x_n. For example, if we sampled an anchor protein with CATH label 2.20.25.20 and we randomly chose the similarity level $\gamma = 2$ (the Architecture level), the positive protein should be randomly sampled from proteins with CATH label of type 2.20.*.* (i.e., having the same first two digits) and the negative should be randomly sampled from those with CATH label 2.a.*.* where a is not 20 (share the same Class code but different Architecture code).

Hard negatives/positives mining. Previous studies[25] have shown that another key to successful contrastive learning is the balance between the triviality and the hardness of the sampled triplets. Here, we further enhance the triplet samples by mining hard negatives and positives to improve the performance of contrastive learning, as did in Heinzinger et al..[17] During training, we utilized the batch-hard[25] technique inside each mini-batch. After getting a mini-batch of hierarchical sampled triplets, we shuffled all the anchor, positive and negative proteins in the mini-batch and applied hierarchical sampling in these proteins but with one more criterion that the positive had the maximum Euclidean embedding distance with the anchor among all the positive candidates selected under hierarchical sampling while the negative had the minimum distance with the anchor.

Training. During the model training, PenLight receives the sampled triplet as input and uses the GAT model to transform them into d-dimensional embeddings (the three GATs for anchor, positive and negative shared the same set of parameters). Based on inner-loop cross-validation results, the embedding size was set to 128 in the CATH classification task and 256 in the EC number prediction task. We used the soft margin loss as the objective to train PenLight: $\mathcal{L}(x_a^{(i)}, x_p^{(i)}, x_n^{(i)}) = \frac{1}{m}\sum_{i=1}^{m} \log\left(1 + \exp(d(x_a^{(i)}, x_p^{(i)}) - d(x_a^{(i)}, x_n^{(i)}))\right)$, where m is the dimension of the output embeddings, $d(\cdot,\cdot)$ is the Euclidean distance between embeddings. Adam with an initial learning rate 1e-4 and a weight decay of 1e-4 was used as the optimizer. Early stopping was also applied to avoid overfitting. We set the batch size to 256.

2.5. *Inference and Evaluation*

Since contrastive learning yielded a vector embedding instead of a direct label for each input protein, the final inference would be performed in a query-lookup manner. Given a lookup set $\mathcal{O}$, which contains proteins with known (structural or functional) labels, and a query (unlabeled) protein q that we would like to infer labels for, PenLight projects all proteins in $\mathcal{O}$ and q into the same embedding space. We call a protein $t \in \mathcal{O}$ a "hit" for the query protein q if their Euclidean embedding distance is below some threshold δ. We can then infer the annotations for the query q by transferring the annotations of all hit proteins, i.e., $\{t \in \mathcal{O} : d(f(t), f(q)) < \delta\}$, to the query q. The inference for individual query protein is very efficient since it only requires a single forward pass of the graph neural network and a distance comparison, both of which are matrix or vector operations that can be accelerated on GPUs. In practice, we found that the average inference time per protein was 0.68 seconds for CATH classification and 0.04 seconds for EC number prediction. We also observed that the prediction accuracy can be improved by an ensemble approach, i.e., two replicas of PenLight were trained on the same data, and the average distance given by them was used to find the hit proteins.

To evaluate the performance of PenLight and other baseline methods, we computed the accuracy, precision, recall, and F1 scores for each class (CATH code and EC number) and then average the metrics over all classes (i.e., macro-averaged metrics). Some baseline methods use a confidence threshold to decide whether to predict the annotations for a query protein (e.g, the E-value in BLAST). For those methods, we count it as a wrong prediction if the model does not predict any annotation for a query protein, unless otherwise specified.

3. Results

3.1. *Performance on Structure Classification*

We downloaded the CATH-S100 dataset (123k proteins, clustered based on identity 100%) from the CATH database (v4.3),[18] including both the structure data and their CATH code labels. We followed the study by Heinzinger et al.[17] to split the dataset into four splits, namely, the training set (~71k proteins), validation set (196 proteins), lookup set (~74k proteins), and test set (208 proteins). The median number of samples per CATH class is 2. The splits were created using the clusters generated by MMseqs2[6] such that any sequence in the training set does not share > 20% sequence identity to any protein in the validation or test set. To directly test PenLight's ability to transfer structural annotations from labeled proteins to unlabeled proteins, an independent lookup set that contains ~74k proteins was also created. Redundant sequences shared by the test set and lookup set were also removed. We compared PenLight with different types of baseline methods for structure classification, including sequence alignment algorithm (BLASTp[1]), unsupervised PLMs (ESM-1b[12] and ProtT5[21]), and the state-of-the-art contrastive learning method for structural annotation (ProtTucker[17]). For PLM baselines, we predicted the annotations for test proteins by applying an unsupervised k-nearest neighbor classifier with $k = 1$ or a supervised multi-class classifier (ProtT5-sup) on PLM representations.

Table 1. **Performance on CATH structure classification.**

Method	Supervised?	Type	Input	Accuracy	Precision	Recall	F1
BLASTp	unsupervised	Aln	seq	0.236	0.148	0.152	0.149
ESM-1b	unsupervised	PLM	seq	0.389	0.247	0.253	0.249
ProtT5	unsupervised	PLM	seq	0.442	0.288	0.304	0.293
ProtTucker	supervised	CL	seq	0.514	0.354	0.365	0.358
ProtT5-sup	supervised	no CL	seq	0.486	0.326	0.351	0.333
PenLight	supervised	CL	struct+seq	**0.524**	**0.363**	**0.377**	**0.367**

Performance shown for the finest level (superfamily) of CATH classification. The highest value of each metric was shown in bold. For supervised methods, the mean metric score of three independent runs was reported; standard deviations were < 0.01 but not listed in the table due to limited space. CL: contrastive learning; no CL: direct predict labels using a multi-class output layer, instead of using CL; PLM: protein language model; Aln: alignment; Struct: structure; Seq: sequence; sup: supervised.

We observed that PenLight consistently outperformed other methods when evaluated using several metrics (Table 1). First, we noticed that the information-rich features used in PenLight are extremely useful for predicting the CATH code. For example, PenLight achieved substantial improvements (+120% in accuracy and +146% in F1) compared to BLASTp, which only uses the raw amino acid sequences to perform sequence comparison. Second, our results also suggested the benefits of contrastive learning (CL) in PenLight. The PLM embeddings, used as the initial features in PenLight, were trained purely on sequence data and may not explicitly capture structure properties. However, the contrastive learning used in PenLight is able to refine the PLM embeddings to be discriminative and structure-aware by utilizing the CATH hierarchy. This is demonstrated in the clear distribution separation of structurally similar and dissimilar proteins in the embedding space (Fig. 2a). The well organized embedding space also translated into performance improvement, where PenLight boosted PLM's F1 score from 0.25+ (for ESM1-1b and ProtT5) to 0.37 (Table 1). These improvements suggested that contrastive learning is effective in learning representations that reflect the semantic similarities in the label space (e.g., the CATH classification here). Finally, we observed that PenLight also outperformed the state-of-the-art method ProtTucker that only considered sequence data as input, suggesting that incorporating the 3D structure information as input is useful for predicting the CATH classification of proteins. Overall, these results demonstrated PenLight's improved prediction performance in predicting the structural annotations of proteins.

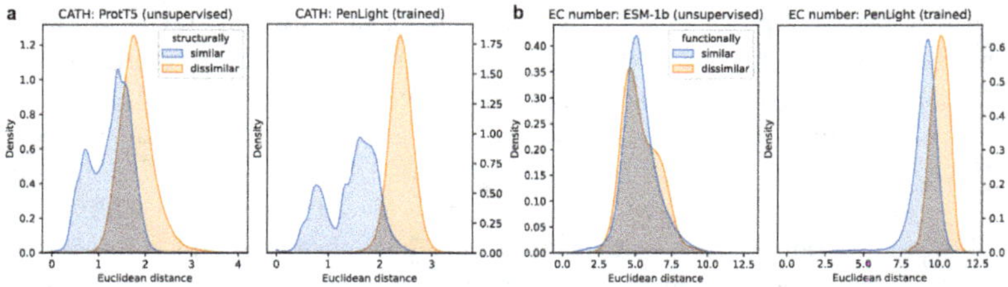

Fig. 2. **PenLight separated structural or functional similar proteins from dissimilar ones in the embedding space**. We consider two proteins are *structurally* similar if they are assigned with the same third-level but different fourth-level CATH codes, and two proteins are *functionally* similar if they are assigned with the same second-level but different fourth-level EC numbers. Euclidean embedding distances learned by PenLight and two PLMs were visualized for similar and dissimilar proteins in the training sequences of (a) the CATH dataset and (b) the EC number dataset.

3.2. *Performance on Functional Annotations*

After benchmarking PenLight on structure classification, we proceeded to evaluate PenLight's ability to predict functional annotations. We used the structure dataset collected in Gligorijevic et al.,[19] which contains 10,245 chains from the PDB database that have EC number annotations. The most specific (4th) level of EC numbers was used as the functional annotations to train and evaluate the models. The median number of samples per EC number is 12. The dataset was split into train, validation, and test sets with an approximate ratio 8:1:1, and the test set has no sequence sharing > 40% sequence identity to the training sequences.

Similar to the results of CATH classification, we also found that PenLight has learned embeddings that are discriminative between EC numbers (Fig. 2b). We compared PenLight with four state-of-the-art deep learning methods and found that PenLight achieved substantially higher performance (Table 2). PenLight first outperformed ProteInfer,[26] DeepEC,[11] and ProtTucker, three models that only take the amino acid sequence as input. PenLight also outperformed DeepFRI[19] by a large margin, which is a GNN model that considers both the sequence and structure of the input protein but was trained using a supervised multi-class scheme. An ablation evaluation of PenLight showed that contrastive learning has led to better performance than the multi-class classification paradigm (PenLight(-) in Table 2).

Notably, ProteInfer, DeepEC, and DeepFRI all have a coverage (defined as the fraction of test proteins for which the method made predictions) lower than PenLight because they only predict EC numbers for a query protein when the predicted score passes a predefined confidence threshold (we say it is a "called protein" hereafter). In contrast, PenLight always predicts for the query protein by transferring the known EC numbers from the top-1 closet lookup protein, thus having a prediction coverage of 1.0. To make a fair comparison, we also

Table 2. **Performance on EC number prediction.**

Method	Type	Input	Cov	Accuracy	Precision	Recall	F1	F1@Called
DeepEC	CNN	seq	0.34	0.287	0.466	0.326	0.361	0.737
DeepFRI	GNN	str+seq	0.60	0.442	0.451	0.353	0.380	0.432
ProteInfer	CNN	seq	0.42	0.367	0.538	0.414	0.448	**0.758**
ProtTucker	CL	seq	1.00	0.768	0.709	0.719	0.695	0.695
PenLight(-)	no CL	str+seq	1.00	0.676	0.604	0.609	0.585	0.585
PenLight	CL	str+seq	1.00	**0.777**	**0.720**	**0.736**	**0.711**	0.711

Performance shown for level 4 (most specific level) of EC number. The highest value of each metric was shown in bold. Coverage (Cov) is the fraction of test proteins for which a method makes a prediction. Proteins for which a method did not make a prediction (not called) will be counted as an incorrect prediction for metrics accuracy, precision, recall, and F1, but not for the F1@Called metric, which was calculated on called proteins of a method. The mean metric score of three independent runs was reported. Standard deviations were < 0.01 but not listed in the table due to limited space. CL: contrastive learning; Str: structure; Seq: sequence. no CL: direct predict labels using a multi-class output layer, instead of using CL.

restricted the evaluation on called proteins for those baselines, i.e., not counting non-called proteins as wrong predictions. We found that in this case PenLight still had a higher F1 score than DeepFRI ('F1@Called' column in Table 2). DeepEC and ProteInfer achieved a slightly higher F1 than PenLight but at an expense of much lower (< 0.5) coverage. Despite PenLight always predicting for every protein by transferring from the top-1 closest lookup protein, it is also possible to introduce a confidence threshold for PenLight, similar to those in our baseline methods, which will be demonstrated in the next section. Overall, the performance improvements achieved by PenLight in this task again demonstrated the advantages of integrating structure data and contrastive learning for protein function prediction.

3.3. *Analyses of PenLight's high coverage and high accurate predictions*

Here, we further dissect the relationship between PenLight's prediction accuracy and coverage. We first performed a detailed stratified comparison of prediction accuracy on the EC number prediction task. Specifically, we plotted the proportion of correct, incorrect and not called predictions of PenLight, ProteInfer, and DeepFRI at each EC number level (Figures 3a-c). ProteInfer had quite stable prediction accuracies ($\sim$0.4) across the four levels but failed to predict the EC numbers for approximately 57% of proteins. For DeepFRI, as the EC number levels become more specific (from level 1 to 4), both its prediction accuracy and coverage dropped, likely due to proteins being more similar in sequence at higher EC number levels, and it is more challenging to distinguish their differences in function. In contrast, PenLight had an accuracy > 0.75 for all four levels while maintaining a 100% coverage. The major reason for the high accuracy and high coverage of PenLight is the contrastive learning and the lookup strategy for making predictions. Methods like ProteInfer formulated the CATH code or EC number classification as a supervised multi-class classification problem and predict the class probabilities for thousands of classes using the single final layer in the neural network. This strategy inevitably suffers from the class size imbalance in the training data, and the ambiguity in the output layer is easily scaled up with the number of classes (e.g., thousands of EC

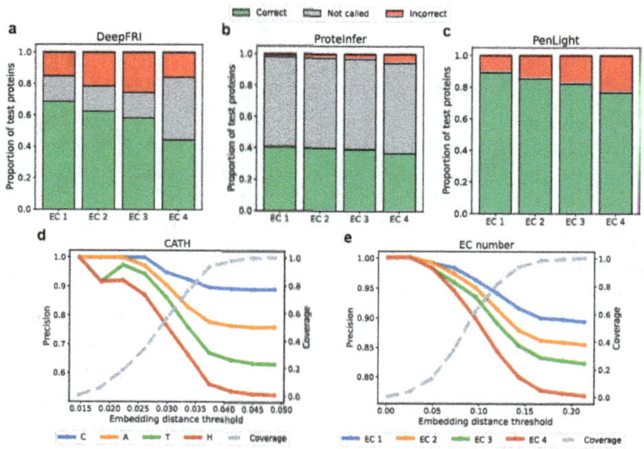

Fig. 3. **PenLight achieved prediction coverage and accuracy.** (a-c) Stacked bar plots of DeepFRI, ProteInfer and PenLight that visualized the fractions of correct, incorrect, and not called predictions at the four levels of EC numbers. (d-e) PenLight's prediction coverage and precision as a function of the embedding distance threshold. Here PenLight predicts the CATH code (d) or EC number (e) for a protein if its closest embedding distance to the lookup set protein is below a given threshold (called a hit). Coverage is defined as the fraction of hit in all test proteins, and precision is defined as the fraction of correct predictions for the hit proteins.

numbers or CATH codes). On the contrary, PenLight first applied contrastive learning to learn discriminative embeddings with respect to the functional or structural annotations, reducing the ambiguity between positive and negative data points (Fig. 2). PenLight then enumerated all proteins in the lookup set and identified the protein with the closest distance to the query protein. This similarity search process treats the distance to every lookup protein equally, without down-weighting any under-represented classes. Therefore, PenLight was able to accurately predict the labels even for under-represented EC numbers, where supervised-learning approaches often have large uncertainties. In our tests, we observed that when predicting for EC numbers that have only < 10 proteins in the training set, PenLight achieved an accuracy of 0.8 while ProteInfer, DeepEC, and DeepFRI only had an accuracy of ~ 0.6.

We next explore the possibility of introducing a confidence threshold into PenLight, similar to the E-value cutoff used in BLAST. A natural choice is to impose a cutoff on the Euclidean embedding distance, i.e., making predictions only when the query protein's closest distance to lookup proteins is below the cutoff. We thus varied the distance cutoff and evaluated how the prediction precision and coverage would change as the cutoff was changing. As expected, we observed that PenLight had a high prediction precision for the CATH task when the cutoff was very stringent (smaller values) since the model was confident in this regime of cutoff values (Fig. 3d). On the other hand, when the cutoff became more tolerant (larger values), the precision started to drop but the prediction coverage gradually increase. Similar trends were observed for EC task as well (Fig. 3e). Overall, this analysis validated that PenLight's embedding distance was correlated with prediction accuracy, and a cutoff can be used to tradeoff the prediction precision and coverage, depending on the practical use case (e.g., accurate annotations or data explorations).

Finally, we performed a t-SNE visualization to see whether PenLight has learned meaningful representations in terms of structural and functional similarity. We observed that, on the CATH task, the embedding space learned by PenLight was a more consistent with the CATH hierarchy, where the ProtT5's embeddings did not capture the structural similarities of CATH classes (Figs. 4a) while PenLight's embeddings showed separated grouping structures consistent with the first level of CATH classification (Fig. 4b). Similarly, on the EC number task, we found that PenLight's embedding space showed clustering patterns more consistent with six major enzyme groups than the ESM-1b model (Figs. 4c-d).

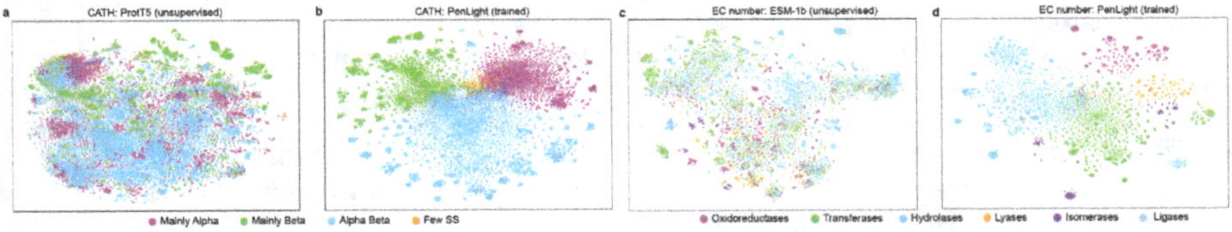

Fig. 4. **t-SNE visualizations.** Embedding space learned by PLMs and PenLight on (a) the CATH dataset and (b) the EC number dataset. Two PLMs (ProtT5 for CATH and ESM-1b for EC) were shown for comparison. One point represents a protein. Points were colored according to their assigned label at the first level of CATH class or EC number.

4. Conclusions

We described PenLight, a general deep learning framework that predicts protein structural and functional annotations. PenLight integrates 3D protein structures and protein language model embeddings with a structure-aware graph neural network (GNN). To learn protein representations that capture meaningful structural or functional similarities, PenLight used a contrastive learning strategy to train the GNN. We showcase PenLight's applicability using both structural and functional annotation tasks, and the experiment results suggested that PenLight outperformed several state-of-the-art methods in predicting the CATH structure hierarchy and enzyme class of proteins. As a general framework, PenLight can be extended to other protein annotation tasks as well, such as gene ontology classification. Recent progress in the graph deep learning community, including equivariant graph neural network,[27] can also be integrated with PenLight to enable better structure-based protein annotation.

Acknowledgements: This work was supported by the 2022 Seed Grant Program of the Molecule Maker Lab Institute, an NSF AI Institute (grant no. 2019897).

References

1. S. F. Altschul, W. Gish, W. Miller, E. W. Myers and D. J. Lipman, Basic local alignment search tool, *Journal of molecular biology* **215**, 403 (1990).

2. S. R. Eddy, Profile hidden markov models., *Bioinformatics (Oxford, England)* **14**, 755 (1998).
3. S. F. Altschul *et al.*, Gapped blast and psi-blast: a new generation of protein database search programs, *Nucleic acids research* **25**, 3389 (1997).
4. J. Söding, Protein homology detection by hmm–hmm comparison, *Bioinformatics* **21**, 951 (2005).
5. M. Remmert, A. Biegert, A. Hauser and J. Söding, Hhblits: lightning-fast iterative protein sequence searching by hmm-hmm alignment, *Nature methods* **9**, 173 (2012).
6. M. Steinegger and J. Söding, Mmseqs2 enables sensitive protein sequence searching for the analysis of massive data sets, *Nature biotechnology* **35**, 1026 (2017).
7. M. N. Price *et al.*, Mutant phenotypes for thousands of bacterial genes of unknown function, *Nature* **557**, 503 (2018).
8. M. L. Bileschi, D. Belanger, D. H. Bryant, T. Sanderson, B. Carter, D. Sculley, A. Bateman, M. A. DePristo and L. J. Colwell, Using deep learning to annotate the protein universe, *Nature Biotechnology* , 1 (2022).
9. J. Hou, B. Adhikari and J. Cheng, Deepsf: deep convolutional neural network for mapping protein sequences to folds, *Bioinformatics* **34**, 1295 (2018).
10. M. Kulmanov, M. A. Khan and R. Hoehndorf, Deepgo: predicting protein functions from sequence and interactions using a deep ontology-aware classifier, *Bioinformatics* **34**, 660 (2018).
11. J. Y. Ryu *et al.*, Deep learning enables high-quality and high-throughput prediction of enzyme commission numbers, *Proceedings of the National Academy of Sciences* **116**, 13996 (2019).
12. A. Rives *et al.*, Biological structure and function emerge from scaling unsupervised learning to 250 million protein sequences, *PNAS* **118**, p. e2016239118 (2021).
13. Method of the year 2015, *Nature Methods* **13**, 1 (dec 2015).
14. S. K. Burley *et al.*, Rcsb protein data bank: powerful new tools for exploring 3d structures of biological macromolecules for basic and applied research and education in fundamental biology, biomedicine, biotechnology, bioengineering and energy sciences, **49**, D437 (2021).
15. J. Jumper *et al.*, Highly accurate protein structure prediction with alphafold, *Nature* **596**, 583 (2021).
16. T. Chen, S. Kornblith, M. Norouzi and G. Hinton, A simple framework for contrastive learning of visual representations, *International conference on machine learning* , 1597 (2020).
17. M. Heinzinger, M. Littmann, I. Sillitoe, N. Bordin, C. Orengo and B. Rost, Contrastive learning on protein embeddings enlightens midnight zone, *NAR Genomics and Bioinformatics* **4** (2022).
18. I. Sillitoe *et al.*, Cath: increased structural coverage of functional space, *NAR* **49**, D266 (2021).
19. V. Gligorijević *et al.*, Structure-based protein function prediction using graph convolutional networks, *Nature communications* **12**, 1 (2021).
20. B. Jing, S. Eismann, P. Suriana, R. J. L. Townshend and R. Dror, Learning from protein structure with geometric vector perceptrons, *International Conference on Learning Representations* (2020).
21. A. Elnaggar *et al.*, Prottrans: towards cracking the language of lifes code through self-supervised deep learning and high performance computing, *IEEE TPAMI* (2021).
22. Y. Luo *et al.*, Ecnet is an evolutionary context-integrated deep learning framework for protein engineering, *Nature communications* **12**, 1 (2021).
23. P. Velickovic, G. Cucurull, A. Casanova, A. Romero, P. Lio and Y. Bengio, Graph attention networks, *stat* **1050**, p. 20 (2017).
24. S. Brody, U. Alon and E. Yahav, How attentive are graph attention networks?, *International Conference on Learning Representations* (2021).
25. A. Hermans, L. Beyer and B. Leibe, In defense of the triplet loss for person re-identification, *arXiv preprint arXiv:1703.07737* (2017).
26. T. Sanderson *et al.*, Proteinfer: deep networks for protein functional inference, *bioRxiv* (2021).
27. V. G. Satorras, E. Hoogeboom and M. Welling, E(n) equivariant graph neural networks, *International conference on machine learning* , 9323 (2021).

Pacific Symposium on Biocomputing 2023

Selecting Clustering Algorithms for Identity-By-Descent Mapping

Ruhollah Shemirani †[1], Gillian M Belbin[1], Keith Burghardt[2], Kristina Lerman[2], Christy L Avery[3], Eimear E Kenny[1], Christopher R Gignoux[4], José Luis Ambite[2]

[1] *Institute for Genomic Health, Icahn School of Medicine at Mount Sinai, New York, NY , USA*

[2] *Information Sciences Institute, University of Southern California, Marina Del Rey, CA, USA*

[3] *Department of Epidemiology, University of North Carolina, Chapel Hill, NC, USA*

[4] *Colorado Center for Personalized Medicine, University of Colorado Anschutz Medical Campus, Aurora, CO , USA*

† *E-mail: ruhollah.shemirani@mssm.edu*

Groups of distantly related individuals who share a short segment of their genome identical-by-descent (IBD) can provide insights about rare traits and diseases in massive biobanks using IBD mapping. Clustering algorithms play an important role in finding these groups accurately and at scale. We set out to analyze the fitness of commonly used, fast and scalable clustering algorithms for IBD mapping applications. We designed a realistic benchmark for local IBD graphs and utilized it to compare the statistical power of clustering algorithms via simulating 2.3 million clusters across 850 experiments. We found Infomap and Markov Clustering (MCL) community detection methods to have high statistical power in most of the scenarios. They yield a 30% increase in power compared to the current state-of-art approach, with a 3 orders of magnitude lower runtime. We also found that standard clustering metrics, such as modularity, cannot predict statistical power of algorithms in IBD mapping applications. We extend our findings to real datasets by analyzing the Population Architecture using Genomics and Epidemiology (PAGE) Study dataset with 51,000 samples and 2 million shared segments on Chromosome 1, resulting in the extraction of 39 million local IBD clusters. We demonstrate the power of our approach by recovering signals of rare genetic variation in the Whole-Exome Sequence data of 200,000 individuals in the UK Biobank. We provide an efficient implementation to enable clustering at scale for IBD mapping for various populations and scenarios.

Supplementary Information: The code, along with supplementary methods and figures are available at https://github.com/roohy/localIBDClustering

Keywords: Clustering; Community Detection; Identity-By-Descent; Comparative Analysis; Genome-wide Association Studies; Benchmark; Clustering Metrics.

1. Background

Finding structure in networks, known as community detection, or clustering, has a wide range of biomedical applications.[1–3] Recently, clustering algorithms have been applied in the context of Identity-By-Descent (IBD) mapping[4,5] as an alternative approach for rare variant association testing that leverages genotype data in the absence of directly observed variation for genomic discovery. This method relies on shared haplotypes along the genome co-inherited identically from a recent common ancestor and utilizes them as the basis for association testing, under the assumption that the haplotypes may co-harbour recently arisen rare variation not directly captured on genotyping arrays. In this process, as illustrated in Figure 1, the chromosome is first divided into consecutive windows. For each window, a graph of IBD sharing is generated, which we refer to as a local IBD graph. In these graphs, samples are represented as nodes and IBD sharing is represented by edges connecting the respective nodes carrying the shared haplotype. False-positive and false-negative edges, artifacts of errors in genotyping, phasing, and IBD estimation, add noise to these graphs. Clustering algorithm are used to refine them and consecutively the IBD information they represent. IBD sharing groups can then be tested for phenotype enrichment. In a study of individuals from the United Kingdom, Gusev et al.[4] found that, empirically, IBD mapping can yield up to forty times more statistical power than standard genome-wide association analyses (GWAS) in tagging rare genetic variation through recovering known and novel associations with binary phenotypes, especially in founder populations. Browning et al.[6] also replicated the results of a GWAS study via IBD mapping. Kenny et al.[7] used IBD mapping to fine-map known associations with plasma plant sterol levels in an isolated founder island population in Kosrae. Finally, Belbin et al.[8] identified the source of a common collagen disease in the Puerto Rican population of BioMe biobank.

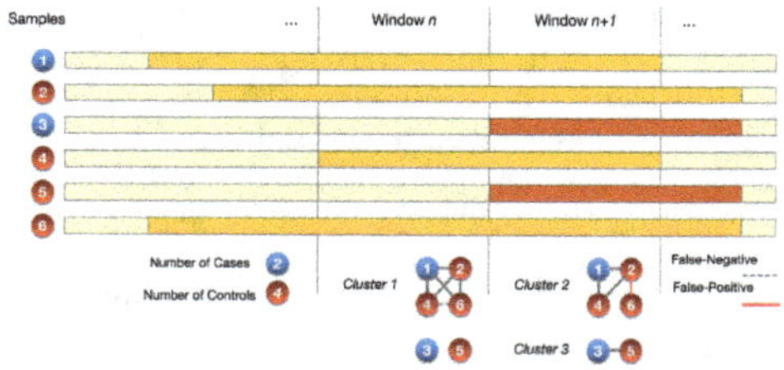

Fig. 1. A general schema of the IBD mapping process that can help identify shared haplotypes carrying rare causal variants. Haplotypes of the same color are inherited from the same ancestor.

There has been a plethora of innovations in clustering techniques, due to their increased importance.[9–13] New clustering methods have been proposed to address the size of social networks and internet hosts, which have grown to many millions of nodes in the past decade;[14–16] or to find new community structures that reflect the underlying data more accurately.[17,18] The emergence of large biobanks necessitates the employment of such new clustering techniques in the context of IBD-mapping. Yet, it remains unclear how advancements in community detection methods translate to this process, where the unique structural properties of local IBD graphs does not resemble that of common graphs analyzed in other fields of study. In this manuscript, we address this problem in three main aspects. First, we conduct a thorough analysis of the characteristics of local IBD graphs, and design a novel benchmark that realistically represents them. Second, we conduct a translational study of clustering metrics to IBD mapping related metrics to investigate their efficacy. Third, and most importantly, we evaluate both the power and scalability of common clustering algorithms in large datasets using both our benchmark and real data. By combining these aspects, we propose a methodical approach to find the most powerful algorithm for any datasets.

2. Methods

2.1. *Characterization of the Local IBD Graphs*

Common benchmark graphs such as those introduced by Lancichinetti et al.,[19] and Girvan and Newman,[18] are used to evaluate clustering methods in a variety of fields.[20] However, they should not be used to simulate local IBD graphs, mainly due to the properties of the local IBD relationships that generates these graphs. The topology of a graph that represents a relation between entities of a set is dictated by the properties of the relation. Local IBD relation is transitive. Thus, under ideal conditions, the local IBD relation can be represented as disjointed sets or cliques. In practice, false-positive and false-negative edges obfuscate these cliques, necessitating a graph representation. The goal in the clustering of local IBD graphs is to recover these well-defined cliques.

Noisy transitivity of local IBD relations results in uncommon graph properties. We look at the "small-world" property as an example.[21,22] This property cannot be calculated for local IBD graphs since, even before clustering, they are highly disconnected. For example, the local IBD graphs of chromosome 1 in the "Population Architecture using Genomics and Epidemiology" (PAGE) dataset[23] each have 13,961 connected components on average across 7952 local IBD graphs tested on chromosome 1, with an average of 3.74 nodes per connected component. In contrast, common benchmarking algorithms often generate a single connected component.[19]

Cluster size distribution is another area of difference between local IBD graphs and others. The LFR benchmark[19] only supports cluster size distributions that follow the power law. Estimating the local IBD cluster sizes using power law results in unrealistically low numbers of small clusters. A fitted power law distribution[24] underestimated the number of cluster sizes for clusters with less than thirteen members in PAGE dataset by a factor of ten (χ^2 p-value $= 3 \times 10^{-14}$). Cluster size distribution affects the statistical power of Louvain and Leiden clustering algorithms.[25] Thus, using power law distributions (as is common in graph benchmarking[19]) for our simulations would result in an erroneous evaluation of the fitness of clustering algorithms to recover local IBD communities.In the supplementary methods section 2.1, we describe our clique-centric benchmark that takes the specific properties of local IBD clusters into account and simulates phenotype for power analysis.

2.2. *Metrics*

Clustering metrics help analyze various properties of the recovered clusters that are either related to the inherent features of the clusters, such as the density of connections in the clusters, or their concordance with the true structure of the graph, such as the number of nodes that are in the same clusters as they are in the ground truth. We call the first group feature-based metrics in this manuscript to distinguish them from metrics that are based on ground truth. For local IBD clustering, it is important to calculate how much the results reflect the true structure of the cliques underneath the noise and errors. We studied 4 metrics based on ground truth, along with 6 feature-based metrics, since ground truth is often not available for real datasets. A full list and description of metrics is available in supplementary methods section 2.2.

2.3. *Clustering Methods*

We analyze five algorithms in three categories based on their methodology: Highly Connected Subgraphs(HCS)–the clustering algorithm used by DASH,[4] Louvain,[26] Leiden,[27] Infomap,[28] and Markov Clustering Algorithm (MCL).[29] Detailed description of these algorithms is available in supplementary method section 2.3. Every tested algorithm, except for HCS, is scalable to large datasets,[30] and can analyze our largest simulated dataset with 11,000 clusters in less than 5 minutes on average on our workstation running CentOS Linux release 7.4.1708 with 128 GB of memory and Intel® Xeon® Processors E5-2695 v2 (2.4 GHz) on a single thread.

3. Results

3.1. *Performance on Simulated Data*

Using our benchmark algorithm, we generated 750 graphs with a range of cluster counts, false-positive, false-negative rates, and phenotype prevalences, described in Supplementary Methods section 2.1.1, that added up to a total of 2,274,500 clusters with more than 6 million nodes across all simulated experiments. Our results show that this benchmark simulates the disjointedness of local IBD graphs, unlike the LFR algorithm (Supplementary Figure 2).

3.1.1. *Clustering Metrics*

We ran the clustering algorithms on the simulated datasets. We then calculated the scores achieved by every method for each metric. We calculated the Pearson correlation coefficients and R^2 scores[31] between metrics to see whether, and to what degree, each clustering metric is associated with statistical power. The results are displayed in Figure 2 and Supplementary Figure 1.

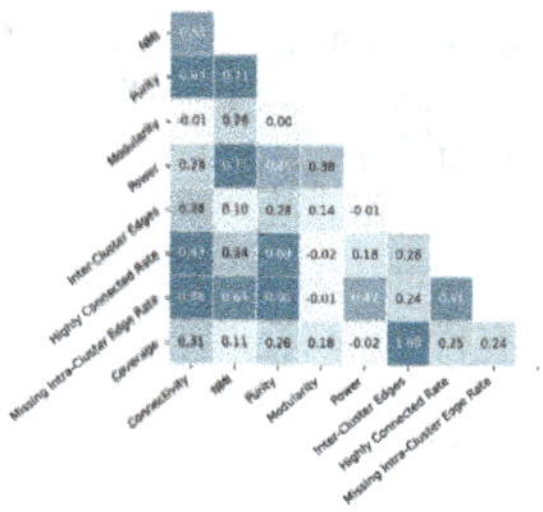

Fig. 2. R^2 scores among clustering metrics across all simulations.

Among all metrics, AMI has the highest concordance with statistical power, explaining 79% of the variation of the power score. Among the feature-based metrics, missing intra-cluster edge rate has the highest R^2 score of 29% with statistical power, while highly connected rate had the lowest score. While generating denser subgraphs with less missing edges is important to gain power, focusing solely on the density and ignoring coverage will counter those effects, resulting in lower power. Modularity showed a weak association with statistical power ($R^2 = 0.14$) compared to missing intra-cluster edge rate. This suggest that partitioning a graph into highly modular subgraphs (through optimizing modularity) does not necessarily result in clusters that represent the true IBD communities in the underlying population. While optimizing modularity is advantageous in finding large non-clique-like communities,[32] local IBD graphs are both clique-like and often smaller in scale. This high percentage of small cliques results in a discordance between modularity and power scores. If instead of a realistic cluster size distribution, we use a uniform distribution (resulting in a higher number of large clusters), the R^2 score for modularity and statistical power rises to 0.34 (from 0.15) and the gap between modularity/power and AMI/power R^2 scores decreases from 0.63 with realistic distribution, to 0.49 with the uniform distribution. At the same time AMI/power R^2 score increases only slightly to 0.83, compared to the 100% increase in modularity/power R^2 score.

The observed discordance between modularity and power in our experiments can also be explained through the concept of "resolution-limit" in modularity optimization, i.e., the inability of modularity optimizing methods in detecting fine-grained clusters. Fortunato and Barthelemy found that the modularity score for a clustering is not only dependant on the structure of the graph, but also on the expected maximum possible modularity of any random graph with the same number of edges, as modularity optimization fails to capture clusters that have an order of magnitude fewer edges compared to the total number of edges in the graph.[25] This results in smaller clusters getting collapsed into other clusters via the optimization process. Small, clique-like structure of local IBD graphs intensifies the effects of this phenomenon on the performance of modularity metrics and methods optimizing it.

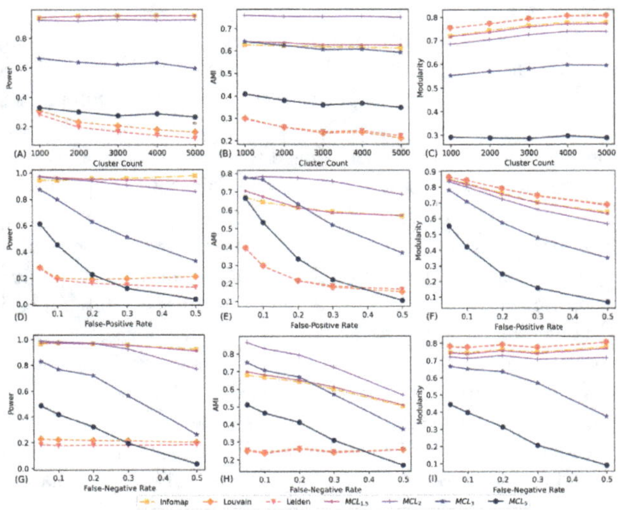

Fig. 3. The effects of number of simulated clusters, false-positives, and false-negatives edges on the performance of algorithms in terms of (A) power, (B) AMI, and (C) modularity.

Our results show that purity is unfit for our IBD clustering purposes. Regardless of the true underlying structure, a more granular clustering always yields a higher purity score. MCL_5, a clustering approach that has the fifth best performance in statistical power (Figure 3A) repeatedly gains the highest purity score, due to over-clustering, suggesting that purity score in the absence of others can be misleading and uninformative.

While AMI score is the best indicator of statistical power among the metrics we tested, due to the effects of smaller clusters (with less than 10 nodes), its concordance with statistical power is imperfect. As further demonstrated by the performances of MCL_2 and MCL_3 in Figure 3, compared to statistical power (Figure 3A), the gap between MCL_3 and top performing methods is less pronounced for the AMI scores (Figure 3B). Moreover, MCL_2 performance increases and surpasses the performance of Infomap and $MCL_{1.5}$ in terms of AMI score compared to the statistical power. The same issue, together with a high baseline, severely affects the performance of NMI as well. Compared to AMI scores, the gap in the NMI scores of MCL algorithms and Infomap is even less pronounced (Supplementary Figure 6).

Another disadvantage of the AMI metric is its reliance on the existence of ground truth data. However, in the absence of the true clustering information, our experiments show that none of feature-based metrics can be used to accurately predict statistical power. We look at missing intra-cluster edge rate as an example due to its higher R^2 score. Methods that yield the highest and lowest score in this metric (Leiden and MCL_5) both perform poorly in terms of statistical power, suggesting a lack of rank preservation in these metrics.

3.1.2. *Clustering Algorithms*

Table 1 shows the average score of clustering algorithms for every metric across all of the simulated datasets. Infomap received the highest average statistical power score, followed closely by MCL, while Louvain and Leiden got the lowest score (See Supplementary Figures 3,4, and 5).

As expected, Louvain and Leiden algorithms yield the most modular clustering results; followed by Infomap. In terms of conforming to the ground truth (purity, power, and AMI/NMI scores), however, Louvain and Leiden achieve a much lower score than MCL and Infomap; further corroborating our analysis of resolution limit in the previous section. As a result of resolution limit, Louvain and Leiden were unable to find smaller communities in our simulations. Greedy modularity optimization tends to merge lightly connected subgraphs into clusters. Although clusters of any size can be affected, those with fewer internal edges than $\sqrt{2E}$, with E as the total number of edges in the graph get merged frequently.[25] For example, the average number of edges for a graph with 2,000 clusters in our experiments is 62,007, which means any pairs of clusters that have a combined edge count smaller than $\sqrt{2 \times 62,007} = 352$ have a high chance of being merged by Louvain and Leiden if they are connected by a single edge, as it increases the modularity score. The vast majority of IBD clusters have less than 352 individuals.

This threshold for resolution limit grows at a faster rate compared to the number of large clusters (Supplementary Figure 9A). In other words, the average number of subgraphs that are larger than this threshold decreases as the total number of clusters increases. The approximate threshold for resolution limit grew from 227 to 744 as cluster count was increased from 1,000 to 10,000 clusters. At the same time, the percentage of clusters larger than the resolution limit threshold decreased from 23.4% to 0.8%. This effect also causes the modularity optimizing algorithms to have an improved modularity score as the number of clusters grows while their statistical power decreases.

We further analyze the distribution of connectivity scores achieved by the algorithms across all of our simulations in Supplementary Figure 7. The average percentage of nodes that were connected to at least half of the other members of their cluster, extracted by Louvain and Leiden, was 13% and 12%, respectively. The same average for MCL_2 was 78%, indicating that Louvain and Leiden merge more cliques together compared to other methods.

Resolution limit has another disadvantage; the dependence of accuracy on the overall edge count and not on the individual clusters[25] causes implications for local IBD clustering; where a variety of cluster size distributions exist for the same total edge count. For example, in the PAGE study dataset, the average number of edges per cluster for local IBD graphs that only include samples from Puerto Rican and African American populations is 96.8±12.7 and 1.6±0.1 respectively. Thus, the statistical power of Louvain and Leiden is subject to change between the two populations, even in the same dataset. The average number of nodes per cluster in the ground truth was 3.6 (std=0.2), the average number of nodes per clusters found by Louvain and MCL_5 were 197.7 (std=212.5) and 3.0 (std=1.7), respectively (See Supplementart Figure 10).

The Effects Of False-Positive Edges

Our experiments show that the supremacy of the Infomap, $MCL_{1.5}$, and MCL_2 performances over other methods is stable for false-positive rates ranging from 5% to 50% of the total num-

Table 1. Average scores (with standard error) of clustering algorithms across our experiments. Overall, MCL_2, Infomap, and $MCL_{1.5}$ yielded the best performances. Modularity optimizing methods had a much lower power.

Metrics		Infomap	Louvain	Leiden	$MCL_{1.5}$	MCL_2	MCL_3	MCL_5
Connectivity	Mean	41.52%	13.03%	12.28%	49.34%	78.78%	90.58%	**94.03%**
	Error	14.20	8.79	9.07	15.63	13.31	8.31	5.32
AMI	Mean	61.77%	24.81%	25.18%	63.05%	**75.60%**	61.36%	37.26%
	Error	8.62	12.04	11.65	9.51	12.69	22.12	26.02
Purity	Mean	63.24%	23.58%	23.03%	67.58%	86.85%	92.57%	**94.41%**
	Error	7.62	11.84	12.12	8.77	6.76	6.51	6.01
Modularity	Mean	75.52%	**78.64%**	78.48%	75.02%	71.76%	57.98%	29.07%
	Error	13.52	11.99	12.17	13.19	14.32	21.14	24.39
Power	Mean	**95.49%**	21.54%	17.98%	95.47%	92.61%	62.85%	29.05%
	Error	5.84	10.36	10.98	3.69	12.19	31.64	30.97
ICE*	Mean	14.26%	**8.70%**	9.10%	14.64%	17.91%	32.66%	66.35%
	Error	10.61	6.77	7.45	9.80	11.66	21.84	27.19
HCR**	Mean	27.40%	19.53%	15.95%	33.80%	82.50%	**95.15%**	91.67%
	Error	12.27	19.35	16.42	17.11	19.47	9.56	23.31
MICER***	Mean	37.92%	94.33%	94.09%	36.44%	25.51%	22.17%	**14.65%**
	Error	13.93	6.24	6.12	14.64	16.20	13.84	8.04
Coverage	Mean	85.74%	**91.30%**	90.90%	85.36%	82.09%	67.34%	33.65%
	Error	10.61	6.77	7.45	9.80	11.66	21.84	27.19
NMI	Mean	91.72%	58.89%	59.65%	92.02%	**95.26%**	94.10%	91.70%
	Error	3.58	19.47	19.19	2.90	2.89	3.36	3.58

*: Inter-Cluster Edges **:Highly Connected Rate ***: Missing Intra-Cluster Edges Rate

ber of edges. Figure 3 illustrates the effects of false-positives on the performance of algorithms in three metrics. High rates of false-positive edges were simulated to simplify detection and comparison of performance patterns. They do not happen in our real data experiments regularly since iLASH, our IBD estimation algorithm, has a low false-positive rate.[33] The statistical power of Infomap and $MCL_{1.5}$ stays stable as the number of false-positives grows (Figure 3 D). The power of MCL_2 slightly decreases as the rate of false-positives is increased above 30%. However, it stays above 0.9. This suggests that these methods do not: (1) break the clusters into smaller ones, and (2) mix them together as a results of their false-positive connections to each other. This is not true for other clustering methods as their power seemingly converges to a minimum value that is determined by the large clusters that are less structurally affected by the higher rates of false-positive edges. In case of modularity optimizing methods, the lower bound is also affected by the resolution limit. Increasing the number of edges in the graph (by adding false-positive edges), thus has a twofold effect on Louvain and Leiden merging pairs of loosely connected clusters.

AMI score trends slightly differ from power, primarily due to a more pronounced effect of smaller clusters. $MCL_{1.5}$ and Infomap yield less stable results. While MCL_3 and MCL_5 have a similar performance to the top performing methods with a false-positive rate of 5%, their performance declines with higher intensity, resulting in the same pattern as their power score.

False-Negatives Edges

As shown in Figure 3G, the effects of false-negative edges on the power of the algorithms is less pronounced than that of the false-positives edges. While false-negative edges have an adverse effect on the power of MCL and Infomap, they do not affect the power of Louvain and Leiden significantly. Resolution limit works slightly in favor of Louvain and Leiden here. Still, even the lowest power scores of $MCL_{1.5}$, MCL_2, and Infomap, at a false-negative rate of 50%, is 70% higher than the scores of Louvain and Leiden. The effects of false-negative edges on modularity of the graph are also eviden in the modularity score. While their power score decreased, the top performing algorithms gained higher modularity scores. This is the opposite of what happened when the number of false-positives edges grew; causing modularity to have a higher correlation with power and AMI.

Runtimes

Supplementary Figure 11 displays the average amount of time (in seconds) each method took in our experiments to analyze a dataset as the number of clusters in the dataset grew. The runtime for all methods seem to grow quadratically with respect to the number of simulated clusters. Louvain and Leiden were the fastest methods, analyzing datasets with 5,000 clusters in 0.9 and 0.6 of a second, respectively. Infomap, took 191 seconds on average for the same number of clusters, while $MCL_{1.5}$ and MCL_2, took 30 and 15 seconds on average, respectively.

Highly Connected Subgraphs

The DASH algorithm has been a standard tool for IBD mapping in recent years.[4] DASH requires the fine-tunning of two parameters based on the IBD inference performance. This raises a challenge as we do not always have such information *a priori*. Moreover, as the oldest clustering method that we analyzed, it does not scale to the size of our experiments. We ran

HCS, and the other four algorithms, on a set of 750 small graphs, with cluster counts ranging from 100 to 500. While other algorithms took less than half a second on average to analyze graphs with 100 clusters, HCS took 81.6. This number grew quadratically to 5595 seconds to analyze graphs with 500 clusters (Supplementary Figure 11). For the same number of clusters, MCL_2 analysis took only 1 second on average. Our simulations of smaller datasets showed that HCS has a lower statistical power compared to that of Infomap and MCL. The average statistical power of HCS algorithm in these experiments was 0.23 while the top performing algorithm, Infomap had an average score of 0.92.

Performance on Real Data

We next used the PAGE study dataset to compare the algorithms wth real data. First, we ran iLASH over the chromosome 1 genotype data to estimate IBD and generated local IBD graphs using the output. Out of the resulting 8,447 local IBD graphs, we randomly chose 800 ($\sim$ 10%) to cluster using every algorithm. We then calculated the feature-based metric scores of the results. The real dataset results further demonstrate the effects of the resolution limit on Louvain and Leiden. In every population, the two algorithms returned the lowest percentages of node connectivity and highly-connected subgraphs, not able to detect false-positive edges. An inflated percentage of missing intra-cluster edges further proves this. Their total clustering of the PAGE data on chromosome 1 requires 43% additional edges in order to turn all the clusters to cliques, compared to $MCL_{1.5}$ (top performing method in the simulations) which requires 10% less edges. MCL_5 requires only 19.7% additional edges to achieve the same task, 24% less than Louvain and Leiden.

The score gap between Infomap, $MCL_{1.5}$, and MCL_2 on feature-based clustering metrics decreases in the real datasets compared to the simulated ones. This can be partly explained by a lower false-positive rate demonstrated in the high coverage scores achieved by all the methods. To verify this, we trained a linear regressor based on the feature-based metric scores in our simulations to predict false-positive and false-negative rates of the graphs. The linear regressor could predict false-positive and false-negative rates in our simulated graphs with an average error of 2% (std=1%) and 1%(std=2%), respectively. We employed cross validation leaving 20% of the data for testing each round. Using the linear regression model, we estimated that, in our PAGE dataset, the false-positive rate is 2% (std$<$ 1%), and the false-negative rate is 24% (std=3%). Focusing exclusively on the simulated graphs with false-positive and false-negative rates close to the ones estimated for the PAGE study dataset shows a clear superiority for MCL_2 in terms of statistical power. We simulated 100 graphs, each containing 11,000 clusters (the average number of clusters in a PAGE study dataset local IBD graph) and with realistic false-positive/false-negative rates we estimated. In these simulations, MCL_2 yielded the highest average statistical power score of 98.8%, followed by $MCL_{1.5}$ (98.6%), MCL_3 (97.6%) and Infomap (95.5%). Louvain and Leiden had the lowest score at 35%, considerably lower than the MCL methods (See Supplementary Figure 8).

We also calculated the ability of local IBD clusters in recovering rare variants in the Whole-Exome Sequence data obtained from 200,000 participants of UK Biobank and compared it to a set of randomly generated clusters of the same sizes. After extracting local IBD clusters in UK Biobank using our approach, for every rare variant, we tried to find a cluster covering its region that includes the highest number of the carriers of that variant and looked at the fractions of the number of carriers per allele counts. The results are shown in Figure 4. Local IBD clusters outperformed the random clusters by fully recovering 35% of doubletons and tripletons, while randomized clusters fully recovered only 0.01%. For variants with minor allele frequencies between 10-20, real clusters had an average recovery rate of 42% against 7% for the randomized clusters.

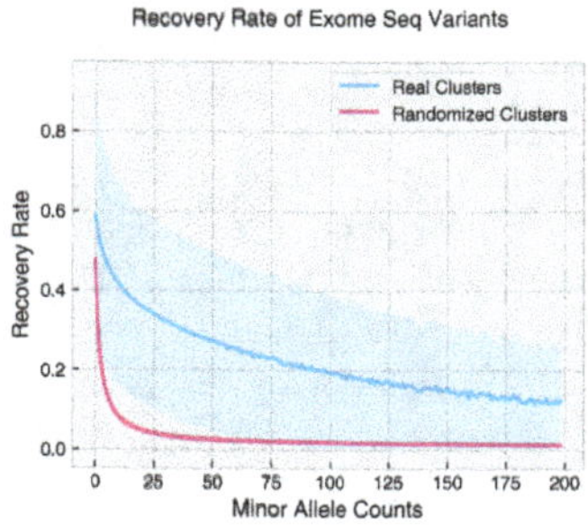

Fig. 4. The recovery rate of local IBD graphs when tagging rare genetic variants captured by whole-exome sequencing data in the UK Biobank compared to a null model with randomized clusters.

Discussion

We proposed a realistic approach to simulate local IBD graphs that addresses distinctive properties of such graphs. It provided us with a ground truth for analyzing a group of scalable clustering algorithms and common clustering metrics for the purpose of local IBD clustering for the first time. We demonstrated that available analyses on clustering algorithms and clustering metrics do not apply to local IBD graphs, further stressing the importance of our analysis. Common clustering metrics cannot be considered sufficient substitutes for power in IBD mapping.

As suggested by Emmons et al,[20] the definition and structure of communities under study should derive the decision on what clustering methods to use. Our real dataset analysis shows various populations may require specific clustering approaches. MCL_2 generally performed better than the other methods in our realistic experiments. However, various datasets and IBD estimation algorithms necessitate dataset specific simulations in order to find the fittest clustering algorithm. We found novel utility for feature-based clustering metrics by using them to enable realistic dataset-specific simulations of local IBD graphs. The simulations determine the fittest clustering algorithm in terms of statistical power.

We showed that both the cluster size distribution of IBD graphs, which is heavily skewed towards smaller clusters, and the size of the dataset could lead some clustering algorithms to aggregate groups of small clusters, specially methods that are based on greedy modularity optimization. Moreover, we found further evidence that the performance of greedy modularity optimizing methods is dependent on the size of the graph being analyzed, making them unpredictable. While IBD mapping can help us understand the genetic origins of some traits, its potential is bound by the capabilities of its clustering approach. Even slight clustering errors can negatively affect the accuracy due to the small size of the local IBD communities.

We plan to utilize our approach to conduct a large IBD mapping analysis in the UK Biobank dataset. We believe distinctive properties of UK Biobank, such as its size, and health record availability, together with power of IBD mapping will help us find novel genetic associations. We plan to add two functionalities to our benchmark algorithm. First, we aim to design a realistic approach to simulate edges weights for the graphs that represent IBD segments length, augmenting local IBD graphs with segment lengths as edge weights can help clustering methods (that support weights) detect false-positives more accurately. The longer the segment, the lower the probability of it being a false-positive edge. Second, we plan to simulate overlapping local IBD graphs, where a group of IBD graphs are merged and processed together to save computing resources. In order to reduce the number local IBD graphs to process, we can aggregate them in groups via dividing the chromosome into windows of static length (for example 0.5 cM). We aim to evaluate clustering algorithms' power in detecting overlapping communities in our benchmark. Simulating these two phenomena requires a genetic coalescence simulation that was outside the scope of the current manuscript.

References

1. E. Hartuv, A. O. Schmitt, J. Lange, S. Meier-Ewert, H. Lehrach and R. Shamir, An algorithm for clustering cdna fingerprints, *Genomics* **66**, 249 (2000).
2. E. Han, P. Carbonetto, R. E. Curtis, Y. Wang, J. M. Granka, J. Byrnes, K. Noto, A. R. Kermany, N. M. Myres, M. J. Barber *et al.*, Clustering of 770,000 genomes reveals post-colonial population structure of north america, *Nature communications* **8**, p. 14238 (2017).
3. G. M. Belbin, S. Wenric, S. Cullina, B. S. Glicksberg, A. Moscati, G. L. Wojcik, R. Shemirani, N. D. Beckmann, A. Cohain, E. P. Sorokin *et al.*, Towards a fine-scale population health monitoring system, *bioRxiv* , p. 780668 (2019).
4. A. Gusev, E. E. Kenny, J. K. Lowe, J. Salit, R. Saxena, S. Kathiresan, D. M. Altshuler, J. M. Friedman, J. L. Breslow and I. Pe'er, Dash: a method for identical-by-descent haplotype mapping uncovers association with recent variation, *AJHG* **88**, 706 (2011).
5. Y. Qian, B. L. Browning and S. R. Browning, Efficient clustering of identity-by-descent between multiple individuals, *Bioinformatics* **30**, 915 (2014).
6. S. R. Browning and E. A. Thompson, Detecting rare variant associations by identity-by-descent mapping in case-control studies, *Genetics* **190**, 1521 (2012).
7. E. E. Kenny, A. Gusev, K. Riegel, D. Lütjohann, J. K. Lowe, J. Salit, J. B. Maller, M. Stoffel, M. J. Daly, D. M. Altshuler *et al.*, Systematic haplotype analysis resolves a complex plasma plant sterol locus on the micronesian island of kosrae, *Proceedings of the National Academy of Sciences* **106**, 13886 (2009).
8. G. M. Belbin, J. Odgis, E. P. Sorokin, M.-C. Yee, S. Kohli, B. S. Glicksberg, C. R. Gignoux, G. L. Wojcik, T. Van Vleck, J. M. Jeff *et al.*, Genetic identification of a common collagen disease in puerto ricans via identity-by-descent mapping in a health system, *Elife* **6**, p. e25060 (2017).
9. S. Papadopoulos, Y. Kompatsiaris, A. Vakali and P. Spyridonos, Community detection in social media, *Data Mining and Knowledge Discovery* **24**, 515 (2012).
10. J. Shi and J. Malik, Normalized cuts and image segmentation, *IEEE Transactions on pattern analysis and machine intelligence* **22**, 888 (2000).
11. Association for Computational Linguistics, *Chinese whispers: an efficient graph clustering algorithm and its application to natural language processing problems* Jan 2006.

12. F. Lamberti, A. Sanna and C. Demartini, A relation-based page rank algorithm for semantic web search engines, *IEEE Transactions on Knowledge and Data Engineering* **21**, 123 (2008).
13. Springer, *SIGNUM: A graph algorithm for terminology extraction* 2008.
14. *Metafac: community discovery via relational hypergraph factorization* 2009.
15. *Detecting strong ties using network motifs* 2017.
16. D. Camacho, A. Panizo-LLedot, G. Bello-Orgaz, A. Gonzalez-Pardo and E. Cambria, The four dimensions of social network analysis: An overview of research methods, applications, and software tools, *arXiv preprint arXiv:2002.09485* (2020).
17. G. Palla, I. Derényi, I. Farkas and T. Vicsek, Uncovering the overlapping community structure of complex networks in nature and society, *nature* **435**, 814 (2005).
18. M. Girvan and M. E. Newman, Community structure in social and biological networks, *Proceedings of the national academy of sciences* **99**, 7821 (2002).
19. A. Lancichinetti, S. Fortunato and F. Radicchi, Benchmark graphs for testing community detection algorithms, *Physical review E* **78**, p. 046110 (2008).
20. S. Emmons, S. Kobourov, M. Gallant and K. Börner, Analysis of network clustering algorithms and cluster quality metrics at scale, *PloS one* **11** (2016).
21. D. J. Watts and S. H. Strogatz, Collective dynamics of 'small-world'networks, *nature* **393**, p. 440 (1998).
22. A.-L. Barabási and R. Albert, Emergence of scaling in random networks, *science* **286**, 509 (1999).
23. G. L. Wojcik, M. Graff, K. K. Nishimura, R. Tao, J. Haessler, C. R. Gignoux, H. M. Highland, Y. M. Patel, E. P. Sorokin, C. L. Avery *et al.*, The page study: how genetic diversity improves our understanding of the architecture of complex traits, *bioRxiv* , p. 188094 (2018).
24. A. Clauset, C. R. Shalizi and M. E. Newman, Power-law distributions in empirical data, *SIAM review* **51**, 661 (2009).
25. S. Fortunato and M. Barthelemy, Resolution limit in community detection, *Proceedings of the national academy of sciences* **104**, 36 (2007).
26. V. D. Blondel, J.-L. Guillaume, R. Lambiotte and E. Lefebvre, Fast unfolding of communities in large networks, *Journal of statistical mechanics: theory and experiment* **2008**, p. P10008 (2008).
27. V. A. Traag, L. Waltman and N. J. van Eck, From louvain to leiden: guaranteeing well-connected communities, *Scientific reports* **9**, 1 (2019).
28. M. Rosvall and C. T. Bergstrom, Maps of random walks on complex networks reveal community structure, *Proceedings of the National Academy of Sciences* **105**, 1118 (2008).
29. S. V. Dongen, Graph clustering by flow simulation, PhD thesis, University of Utrecht Amsterdam, (Netherlands, 2000), pp. ix + 10.
30. A. Lancichinetti and S. Fortunato, Community detection algorithms: a comparative analysis, *Physical review E* **80**, p. 056117 (2009).
31. F. Pedregosa, G. Varoquaux, A. Gramfort, V. Michel, B. Thirion, O. Grisel, M. Blondel, P. Prettenhofer, R. Weiss, V. Dubourg, J. Vanderplas, A. Passos, D. Cournapeau, M. Brucher, M. Perrot and E. Duchesnay, Scikit-learn: Machine learning in Python, *Journal of Machine Learning Research* **12**, 2825 (2011).
32. M. T. Schaub, J.-C. Delvenne, S. N. Yaliraki and M. Barahona, Markov dynamics as a zooming lens for multiscale community detection: non clique-like communities and the field-of-view limit, *PloS one* **7** (2012).
33. R. Shemirani, G. M. Belbin, C. L. Avery, E. E. Kenny, C. R. Gignoux and J. L. Ambite, Rapid detection of identity-by-descent tracts for mega-scale datasets, *Nat Comms* **12**, 1 (2021).

Efficient Reconstruction of Stochastic Pedigrees: Some Steps From Theory to Practice

Elchanan Mossel and David Vulakh*

Department of Mathematics, Massachusetts Institute of Technology,
77 Massachusetts Ave, Cambridge, MA 02139, USA
**E-mail: dvulakh@mit.edu*

In an extant population, how much information do extant individuals provide on the pedigree of their ancestors? Recent work by Kim, Mossel, Ramnarayan and Turner (2020) studied this question under a number of simplifying assumptions, including random mating, fixed length inheritance blocks and sufficiently large founding population. They showed that under these conditions if the average number of offspring is a sufficiently large constant, then it is possible to recover a large fraction of the pedigree structure and genetic content by an algorithm they named REC-GEN.

We are interested in studying the performance of REC-GEN on simulated data generated according to the model. As a first step, we improve the running time of the algorithm. However, we observe that even the faster version of the algorithm does not do well in any simulations in recovering the pedigree beyond 2 generations. We claim that this is due to the inbreeding present in any setting where the algorithm can be run, even on simulated data. To support the claim we show that a main step of the algorithm, called ancestral reconstruction, performs accurately in an idealized setting with no inbreeding but performs poorly in random mating populations.

To overcome the poor behavior of REC-GEN we introduce a Belief-Propagation based heuristic that accounts for the inbreeding and performs much better in our simulations.

1. Introduction

We follow up on a recent work by Kim et al.,[1] the main motivation of which is to understand how much kinship information can be learned from DNA. More concretely, Kim et al. study the inference problem of recovering ancestral kinship relationships of a population of *extant* (present-day) individuals using only their genetic data for a mathematical generative model of pedigrees and DNA sequences on them based on the combinatorial framework of Steel and Hein[2] and Thatte and Steel,[3] who also proved a rigorous statement about recovery of idealized pedigree models. The goal is to use this extant genetic data to recover the *pedigree* of the extant population under this model.

To study this question, Ref. 1 introduces an idealized model for generating pedigree data. The population model they use is a standard random mating model, but the genetic inheritance model assumes that inheritance blocks are of fixed length. This removes the additional difficulty of "phasing" which allows for a rigorous analysis.

The main contribution of Ref. 1 is to show that under certain conditions, the algorithm proposed in the paper, named REC-GEN, approximately recovers the true, unknown pedigree as well as its genetic content. There is a huge body of work on pedigree reconstruction, see e.g. Ref. 4–11. In contrast to Ref. 1, most of this work does not provide theoretical guarantees. In this paper we take the theoretical analysis in Ref. 1 and study to what extent it can be applied in more realistic settings.

There is a tension between different aspects of the assumptions in Ref. 1. On one hand, they require a very big pedigree to avoid inbreeding. On the other, the algorithm Rec-Gen has cubic running time. While in the limit as the pedigree size goes to infinity, this tension disappears, we find that applying the algorithm on simulated data results either in poor accuracy or an infeasible running time.

Our main contributions in this paper are:

- We improve the algorithm runtime to essentially quadratic for model-generated data.
- We then observe that even the faster version of the algorithm does not do well in any simulations in recovering the pedigree beyond 2 generations.
- We claim that this is due to the inbreeding present in any setting where the algorithm can be run, even on simulated data.
- To support the claim we show that a main step of the algorithm, called ancestral reconstruction, performs accurately in a setting with no inbreeding but performs poorly in random mating populations.
- Finally, to overcome the poor behavior of REC-GEN we introduce a Belief-Propagation based heuristic that accounts for the inbreeding and performs much better in our simulations.

2. Model Description

We model populations as in Ref. 1. Here, we briefly restate the definition of a *coupled pedigree*, the structure manipulated by the REC-GEN algorithm and introduce notation relevant to the description of our modified algorithm.

A (N, B, T, ξ)-*uncoupled pedigree* $\mathcal{U}$ is a directed acyclic graph (V, E) in which vertices $v \in V$ represent individuals and edges $e = (u, v) \in E$ represent the relationship that u is a *parent* of v. The set of vertices V can be partitioned into $T + 1$ subsets $V_0, \ldots, V_T$ so that each $v \in V_i$, $0 \leq i < T$ has exactly two in-edges, both of which are from vertices in V_{i+1}. The sets V_i represent *generations*, where V_0 is the *extant population* and V_T is the *founding population*. The size of the founding population $|V_T|$ equals N. The vertices V also satisfy *monogamy* — within each generation V_i, $i > 0$, the vertices V_i can be partitioned into pairs (v_1, v_2) such that if u is a child of v_1 if and only if u is a child of v_2; such pairs are called *couples*. The number of children of each couple is randomly drawn from the distribution ξ.

Each vertex v has associated genetic information in the form of B *blocks*, each of which contains a symbol sampled from some alphabet Σ. The symbol at block b of the genome of vertex v is denoted $s_v(b)$.

The (N, B, T, ξ)-*coupled pedigree* $\mathcal{P}$ induced by an uncoupled pedigree $\mathcal{U}$ is formed by merging each couple into a single vertex — the resulting vertices are called *coupled nodes*. Now each v in a generation other than the extant represents a pair of individuals, and an edge from a coupled node u to a coupled node v represents that u is the parent of one of the individuals in couple u. All vertices in $\mathcal{P}$ have in-degree two, except vertices in the extant population, which remain uncoupled and have in-degree 1. The genetic information $s_v(b)$ of a coupled node v is the set of all symbols that are in block b for some individual in the couple represented by v.

When we say that some graph is a pedigree in this paper without specifying whether the pedigree is coupled or uncoupled, we are referencing coupled pedigrees.

3. Rec-Gen

The REC-GEN reconstruction algorithm presented in Ref. 1 proceeds in three main phases. In each generation, siblinghood detection reconstructs relationships in the current generation, outputting a siblinghood hypergraph in which triple u, v, w forms a hyperedge if they are likely to be siblings. Parent construction processes maximal cliques in the outputted hypergraph, populating the parent generation. Symbol collection reconstructs the genetic information of the parent generation.

3.1. *Runtime Analysis*

Naïve implementations of siblinghood detection and symbol collection both run in $\Omega(BN_0^3)$ time. The siblinghood test counts the number of shared blocks in all triples, which can require $\Omega(BN_0^3)$ in the worst case.

To naïvely find a triple of extant vertices sharing a gene in block b with u as their joint-LCA for some u in generation t of the pedigree for symbol collection it may be necessary to inspect all triples of extant descendants of u in each block b, which is also $\Omega(BN_0^3)$.

We wish to improve both of these processes to $O(BN_0^2)$, as described in Sections 3.2 and 3.3.

3.2. *Faster Siblinghood Detection*

The greatest bottleneck in the runtime of REC-GEN is the siblinghood detection step, which for each generation t is cubic in the size of that generation N_t. To reduce the runtime from $O\left(N_t^3 B\right)$ to $O\left(N_t^2 B\right)$, we begin by processing all pairs of vertices, marking pairs that share some threshold $\theta = 0.4$ of their blocks as *sibling candidates*. We then only consider triples of vertices formed from sibling candidates when generating the siblinghood hypergraph. Pseudocode of the alternate algorithm FAST-TEST-SIBLINGHOOD follows:

3.3. *Faster Symbol Collection*

To decrease the complexity of executing the REC-GEN symbol-collection phase on v, we avoid explicitly searching for extant triples that have v as their joint-LCA. Instead, we make the simplifying assumption that any three extant vertices x, y, z descended from distinct children of v have v as a joint-LCA. Now, we can use the following modified algorithm to achieve an effect equivalent to the original symbol collection of Ref. 1:

- Let $\hat{G}_u(b)$ for a child u of v and block b be the set of genes g such that there exists an extant descendant x of u such that $\hat{s}_u(b) = \{g\}$.

Algorithm 1 Perform statistical tests to detect siblinghood

procedure FAST-TEST-SIBLINGHOOD(depth $(k-1)$ pedigree $\hat{\mathcal{P}}$)
    $C \leftarrow \varnothing$
    $V \leftarrow$ vertices of $\hat{\mathcal{P}}$ at level $k-1$
    for all distinct pairs $\{u, v\} \in 2^V$ **do**
        if $\geq 0.4|B|$ blocks b such that $\hat{s}_u(b) \cap \hat{s}_v(b) \neq \varnothing$ **then**
            $C \leftarrow C \cup \{u, v\}$
    $E \leftarrow \varnothing$
    for all pairs $\{u, v\} \in C$ **do**
        for all $w \in V$ at level $k-1$ such that $w \neq u \wedge w \neq v$ **do**
            if $\geq 0.21|B|$ blocks b such that $\hat{s}_u(b) \cap \hat{s}_v(b) \cap \hat{s}_w(b) \neq \varnothing$ **then**
                $E \leftarrow E \cup \{u, v, w\}$
    $\hat{G} \leftarrow (V, E)$
    return $\hat{G}$

- Compute $\hat{G}_u(b)$ for all children u of v.
- Let $\hat{s}_v(b)$ be the two genes that are present in the greatest number of computed sets $\hat{G}_u(b)$.

Pseudocode of this modified process can be seen in Algorithm FAST COLLECT-SYMBOLS.

Ref. 1 prove that, conditioned on the nonoccurence of undesirable inbreeding events, the existence of a joint-LCA v for three nodes x, y, z entails that v is their unique LCA. Therefore, if most extant nodes have a joint-LCA, then the algorithm described above is equivalent to the initial description of symbol-collection. Empirically, very few ($< 1\%$ of) extant triples in simulated pedigrees are descended from unique children of a vertex that is not their joint-LCA.

Generating $\hat{G}_u$ requires time that is linear in the number of nodes in the descendants pedigree of u. Since $\alpha > 2$, this is on expectation bounded above by a linear function of the number of extant descendants of u. Each extant individual v has at most 2^t ancestors in generation t. Therefore, the sum of the number of extant descendants of u over all u in generation t is at most $2^t N_0$, where N_0 is the size of the extant population, so that the runtime of invoking Algorithm FAST COLLECT-SYMBOLS for all u at generation t is $O(B \cdot (2^t N_0 + |G|))$. Since $\alpha > 2$, $2^t \subseteq O(\alpha^t) \subseteq O(\mathbb{E}[N_t]/N_T)$, so that the total runtime of Algorithm FAST COLLECT-SYMBOLS is $O(B \cdot \mathbb{E}[N_t] N_0 / N_T) \subseteq O(BN_0^2)$.

4. Simulations

We assess the empirical accuracy of REC-GEN and other algorithms presented later in this work by running them on simulated pedigrees. We generate pedigrees satisfying the stochastic model, as described in section 4.1. The extant populations of the pedigrees can be used as input for our implementations of the reconstructive algorithms, and a grader program evaluates the accuracy of the result as described in section 4.2.

Algorithm 2 Empirically reconstruct the symbols of top-level node v in $\mathcal{P}$.

procedure FAST COLLECT-SYMBOLS($v, \hat{\mathcal{P}}$)
    for all blocks $b \in [B]$ **do**
        $c_g \leftarrow 0 \; \forall \, g$
        for all children u of v **do**
            $\hat{G}_u(b) \leftarrow \varnothing$
            for all extant x descended from u **do**
                $\hat{G}_u(b) \leftarrow \hat{G}_u(b) \cup \hat{s}_x(b)$
            for all $g \in \hat{G}_u(b)$ **do**
                $c_g \leftarrow c_g + 1$
        $\sigma_1 \leftarrow g$ with highest c_g
        $\sigma_2 \leftarrow g$ with second-highest c_g
        Record the symbols σ_1, σ_2 for block b in v.

4.1. *Generating Pedigrees*

For a given α, our pedigree generator program creates (N, B, T, ξ)-coupled pedigrees according to the breeding and inheritance behaviors described in Section 2, where ξ is either Poisson-distributed with parameter α or a constant distribution, $\xi = \alpha$.

4.2. *Assessing Reconstruction Accuracy*

Our grader program takes as input a parameter $\alpha \in [0, 1)$ and two pedigrees with identical extant populations and the same numbers of generations — an original pedigree $\mathcal{P}$ and its reconstruction $\mathcal{P}'$. It outputs a partial mapping between the coupled nodes of $\mathcal{P}$ and $\mathcal{P}'$, where a coupled node $v \in \mathcal{P}$ of the original pedigree is mapped to a coupled node $v' \in \mathcal{P}'$ of the reconstructed pedigree only if v' is an *α-successful* reconstruction of v. α-successful reconstructions are defined recursively in the following manner:

- In generation 0 (the extant population) a vertex $v' \in \mathcal{P}'$ is an α-successful reconstruction of $v \in \mathcal{P}$ if and only if v and v' are the same coupled node.
- In generation $t > 0$, let $c(v, v')$ for $v \in \mathcal{P}, v' \in \mathcal{P}'$ denote the number of pairs u and u' from generation $t-1$ of $\mathcal{P}$ and $\mathcal{P}'$, respectively, for which u is a child of v, u' is a child of v', and u' is an α-successful reconstruction of u. Also, let f be the number of children of v and f' be the number of children of v'. Then v' is an α-successful reconstruction of v if and only if $c(v, v') > \alpha f$ and $c(v, v') > \alpha f'$.

In the case that multiple vertices $v' \in \mathcal{P}'$ are an α-successful reconstruction of some $v \in \mathcal{P}$, the grader program maps v to the one that maximizes $c(v, v')$. If the program maps some v' to v, we consider v successfully reconstructed.

The grader also outputs the following statistics for each generation t:

- The number and percent of successfully reconstructed vertices
- The number and percent of successfully reconstructed edges (these are the sum of

$c(v, v')$ over reconstructed v and the ratio of that sum to the sum of f over all v in t)
- The number of reconstructed blocks, where a block g in position b of v is considered reconstructed if v' also has g in position b[a], as well as the percent of blocks reconstructed out of all blocks in generation t and out of blocks belonging to reconstructed nodes in generation t.

When using the grader to study the behavior of the reconstruction of symbols, we typically apply a generous $\alpha = 0.5$ threshold, so as not to exclude information about weakly reconstructed vertices. For the accuracy metrics presented throughout this paper, we usually use $\alpha = 0.75$ or $\alpha = 0.99$.

5. Simulation Results for Rec-Gen

5.1. *Results for* $T = 3$

Experiments using simulated data as described in Section 4.1 indicate that, even in pedigrees with relatively small founding populations ($N = 50$) and fertility rates ($\alpha = 6$), REC-GEN reliably reconstructs two generations above the extant (the 'parent' and 'grandparent' generations) in pedigrees with $T = 3$. However, performance at the third generation declines sharply, and in individual simulations with $T = 4$ (not included in the batched results in this section; see Section 5.2), REC-GEN fails to recover even a single vertex of the founding population. Figures 1 and 2 graph the average vertices and blocks reconstructed over α for three generation pedigrees with $N = 50$ and $B = 5000$ for two values of the reconstruction accuracy threshold: 0.75 and 0.99.

As one would expect, reconstruction accuracy generally improves as α increases (an exception is for the high accuracy threshold 0.99 in the case of constant fertilities — when there is a larger number of children, even an algorithm that reconstructs each with higher probability may reconstruct all of them with lower probability). Additionally, REC-GEN performs better for the case of constant fertilities than for the case of Poisson-distributed fertilities. Since REC-GEN performs poorly for vertices with low fertility (and is incapable of reconstructing vertices with fertility less than 3), we attribute the relatively poor performance of REC-GEN for the Poisson case as compared to the deterministic case to the incidence of low-fertility nodes.

5.2. *Decline at* $T = 4$

As demonstrated in Figure 3 (a), REC-GEN appears to encounter major difficulties by the fourth generation, failing to recover even a single founding node in our simulations. This failure seems to be precipitated by a rapid decline in accuracy of reconstructed blocks, as shown in Figure 4. Recall that symbol collection requires that triples share at least 21% of their blocks to be identified as siblings. In generations 0 and 1, the distribution of shared reconstructed

[a]In case that v has two identical genes in some position, they are both considered reconstructed only if v' also has two copies of that gene; otherwise, only one is considered reconstructed. Note, however, that this should not happen regularly, as it is an indication of inbreeding.

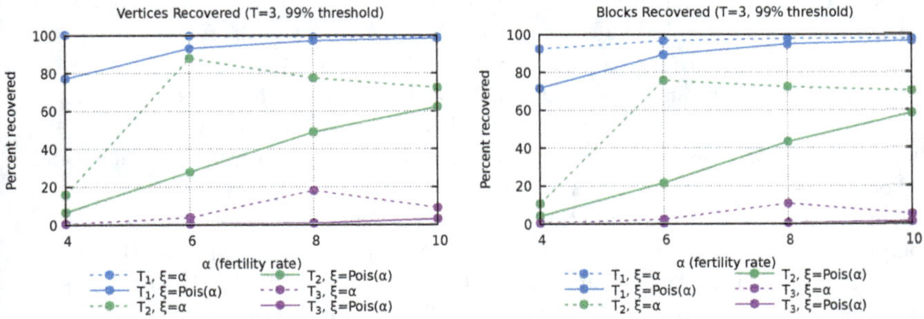

Fig. 1: Average percent vertices and blocks 0.99-successfully reconstructed in each generation

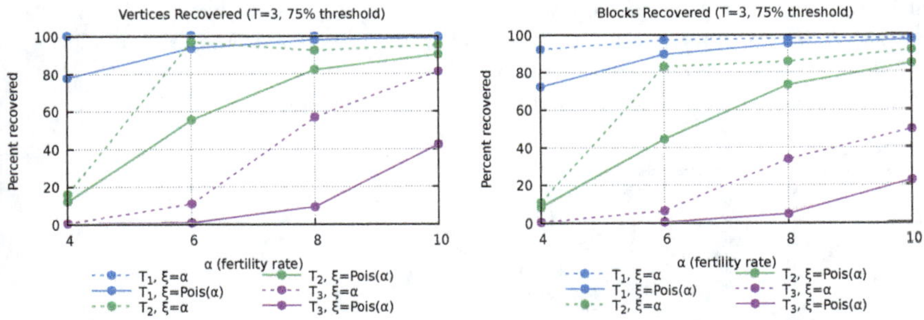

Fig. 2: Average percent vertices and blocks 0.75-successfully reconstructed in each generation

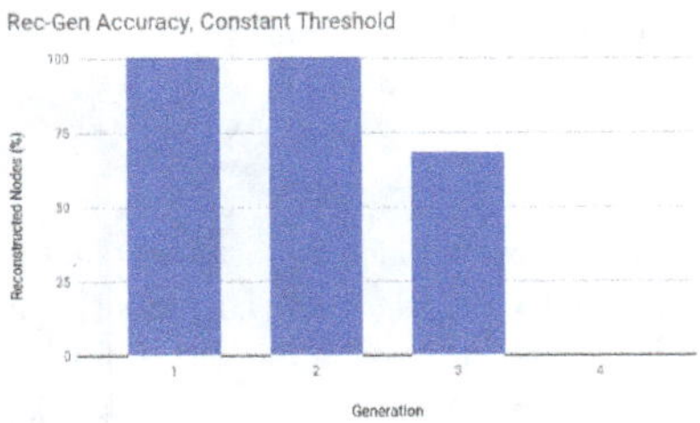

(a) Constant threshold

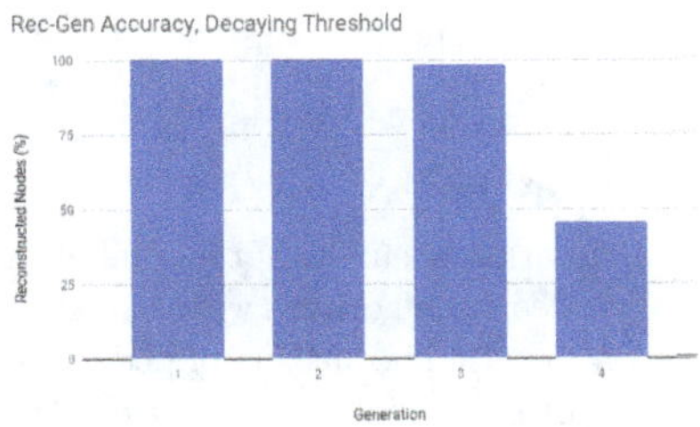

(b) Adjusted threshold

Fig. 3: Vertices 0.5-reconstructed by Rec-Gen for a $T = 4$ pedigree, with both the default 21% siblinghood threshold (a) and a manually optimized siblinghood threshold (b). Note that 0 nodes are reconstructed in generation 4 in (a).

blocks for sibling triples lies entirely above the 21% threshold. By generation 2, it shifts slightly to the left so that some siblings are not recognized (and, as a result, not all of the generation 3 is reconstructed). In generation 3, there are two clusters in the distribution of shared triples:

one at 0% and one around 10%. The cluster at 0% is the result of the members of generation 3 who were not reconstructed at all; the rest of the distribution consists of the remaining triples, which still share distinctly more blocks than non-sibling triples, but fewer than 21%.

When we manually set the siblinghood threshold to decay with each generation to match the accumulation of errors, we can extend the number of generations for which REC-GEN accurately reconstructs the topology. Figure 3 (b) demonstrates the improvements when using the siblinghood thresholds 21%, 21%, 17%, 4% for generations 0, 1, 2, and 3 respectively.

This experiment implies that the step that introduces the most error into REC-GEN is the symbol-collection step. In reality, we cannot easily manually adjust the siblinghood threshold, because the optimal threshold varies from pedigree to pedigree and may be difficult to determine without knowledge of the true pedigree topology. We can further assume that these errors are largely the result of failure of the combinatorial REC-GEN algorithm to correctly handle inbreeding. We confirm this assumption by running REC-GEN on a large pedigree constructed as though it were a section sampled from an infinitely wide pedigree — indeed, REC-GEN has almost perfect accuracy in this case, as expected (the only errors were the result of blocks that were not passed down to any descendants, which can happen with frequency $1/2^{\alpha}$). We therefore wish to improve the robustness of the symbol-collection step against inbreeding.

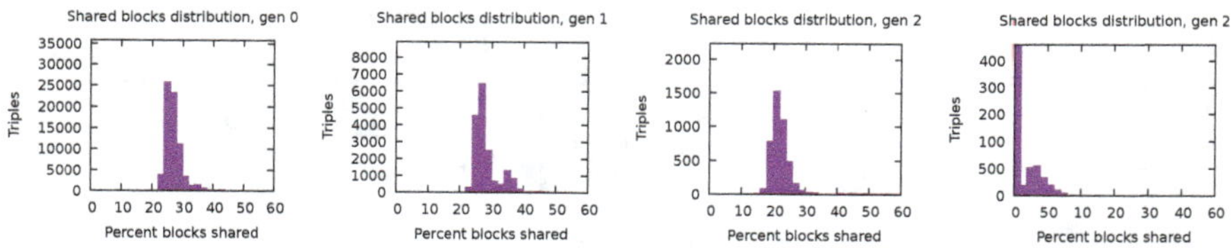

(a) Extant (b) Parents (c) Grandparents (d) Founder's children

Fig. 4: Distribution of percent reconstructed blocks shared in all triples for a $T = 4$ pedigree.

6. Belief Propagation

To improve the empirical accuracy of the symbol collection step, we replace the original combinatorial symbol collection algorithm with a single pass of a Belief-Propagation (BP) algorithm for recovering the genetic information of pedigrees. BP is a message-passing algorithm for inference that is most successful in locally tree-like models. Mezard and Montanari[12] give the BP equations in the following setting:

- $\mathbf{x}$ is a tuple of N variables $(x_1, \ldots, x_N)$ assuming values from the finite alphabet $\mathcal{X}$.
- There are M constraints in the form of the marginals $\psi_1, \ldots, \psi_M$ governing the distribution of values assumed by $\mathbf{x}$, so that the probability distribution of x satisfies

$$p(\mathbf{x}) \cong \prod_{a=1}^{M} \psi_a \left(\mathbf{x}_{\partial a}\right)$$

where $\mathbf{x}_{\partial a} = \{x_i : i \in \partial a\}$ and $\partial a \subseteq [N]$ is the set of variable indices constrained by ψ_a

(here, the notation $x \cong y$ denotes that the two functions $x, y : \mathcal{X} \to \mathbb{R}$ are equal down to a constant factor).

In this context, the relationships between variables can be modelled by a bipartite graph in which each vertex representing a variable x_i has an edge to each 'factor vertex' representing a constraint $\psi_a : i \in \partial a$; this graph is called the *factor graph*. The BP equations that permit approximation of the marginal distribution of each variable govern 'messages' sent over the edges of the factor graph at each time step $t+1$:

- Message from the jth variable to the ath factor:
$$\nu_{j \to a}^{(t+1)}(x_j) \cong \prod_{b \in \delta j \setminus a} \widehat{\nu}_{b \to j}^{(t)}(x_j)$$
- Message from the ath constraint to the jth variable:
$$\widehat{\nu}_{a \to j}^{(t)}(x_j) \cong \sum_{\mathbf{x}_{\partial a \setminus j}} \psi_a(\mathbf{x}_{\partial a}) \prod_{k \in \partial a \setminus j} \nu_{k \to a}^{(t)}(x_k)$$

The estimate for the marginal distribution of variable i at time t is
$$\nu_i^{(t)}(x_i) \cong \prod_{a \in \partial i} \widehat{\nu}_{a \to i}^{(t-1)}(x_i)$$

If the factor graph is a tree, then BP is known to be exact — that is, the values ν_i converge, and they converge precisely to the true marginals of the variables. Moreover, the exact marginals can be computed with BP in linear time in the tree case, as ν_i assume the values of the marginals of x_i after two passes through the tree, as described in Ref. 12.

For our modified symbol-collection step, we effectively complete one BP sweep (half of the tree algorithm) independently for each position in the genome. Let G be the set of all genes, $\mathbf{ch}(v)$ be the tuple of children of vertex v, $0 < \varepsilon < 1$ be some constant that represents the probability of an error in the topology of the reconstruction, $\mathbf{g}_v$ be the variable the value of which is the pair of genes in a given block of vertex v, and ν_v be a function from unordered pairs from G to the unit interval, the BP estimate of the marginal distribution of $\mathbf{g}_v$.

For each extant vertex v with gene g, we introduce a constraint
$$\psi \cong \mathbb{I}_{\mathbf{g}_v = (g,g)}$$

For each nonextant vertex v, we introduce a constraint indicating that a child of v is an anomaly in the topology (shares no genes with v) with probability ε:
$$\psi \cong \varepsilon^{|\{u \in \mathbf{ch}(v) : \mathbf{g}_v \cap \mathbf{g}_u = \varnothing\}|}$$

Then the computed values of ν_v are as follows. For extant couples v with gene g, we have
$$\nu_v(g_1, g_2) \cong \mathbb{I}_{g_1 = g_2 = g}$$

And for nonextant couples v
$$\nu_v(g_1, g_2) \cong \sum_{\mathbf{g} \in (G^2)^{|\mathbf{ch}(v)|}} \varepsilon^{|\{i \in [1, |\mathbf{ch}(v)|] : \{g_1, g_2\} \cap \mathbf{g}_i = \varnothing\}|} \prod_{i \in [1, |\mathbf{ch}(v)|]} \nu_{\mathbf{ch}(v)_i}(\mathbf{g}_u)$$

We record the gene pair with the highest probability according to ν_v as the genes reconstructed for couple v.

Computing ν_v directly would be computationally inefficient — worse than $O\left(|G|^{2\alpha}\right)$ on expectation, as $|\mathbf{ch}(v)|$ is Poisson-distributed with parameter α. We can substantially improve this runtime by computing the probability distribution by summing over the number of children indicating topology errors, rather than over all possible assignments of genes. To do this, we construct a DP table $\mathbf{DP}(g_1, g_2)_{i,j}$ that stores, for the first i children, the probability that j of them indicate topology errors. The recursive definition follows:

$$\mathbf{DP}(g_1, g_2)_{i,j} = \begin{cases} \mathbb{I}_{j=0} & i = 0 \\ \mathbf{DP}(g_1, g_2)_{i-1,j-1} \sum_{(h_1,h_2)\in G^2} \mathbb{I}_{\{h_1,h_2\}\cap\{g_1,g_2\}=\emptyset}\nu_{\mathbf{ch}(v)_i}(h_1, h_2) + & \\ + \mathbf{DP}(g_1, g_2)_{i-1,j} \sum_{(h_1,h_2)\in G^2} \mathbb{I}_{\{h_1,h_2\}\cap\{g_1,g_2\}\neq\emptyset}\nu_{\mathbf{ch}(v)_i}(h_1, h_2) & i > 0 \end{cases}$$

Once we have computed the values of this table for $i = |\mathbf{ch}(v)|$, we can compute ν_v:

$$\nu_v(g_1, g_2) \cong \sum_{j=0}^{|\mathbf{ch}(v)|} \varepsilon^j \cdot \mathbf{DP}(g_1, g_2)_{|\mathbf{ch}(v)|,j}$$

Constructing the DP table takes $O\left(\alpha|G|^4\right)$ time per block, which dominates the runtime of computing the marginals by this method. We can further reduce the runtime by directly maintaining the marginal probability that some single gene appears in each node (in addition to the probability estimate over pairs of genes ν_v):

$$S_v(g) = \sum_{g'\in G} \nu_v(g, g')$$

Then we can compute the DP as below:

$$\mathbf{DP}(g_1, g_2)_{i,j} = \begin{cases} \mathbb{I}_{j=0} & i = 0 \\ \mathbf{DP}(g_1, g_2)_{i-1,j} \left(S_v(g_1) + \mathbb{I}_{g_1\neq g_2}(S_v(g_2) - \nu_{\mathbf{ch}(v)_i}(g_1, g_2))\right) + & \\ + \mathbf{DP}(g_1, g_2)_{i-1,j-1} \left(1 - (S_v(g_1) + \mathbb{I}_{g_1\neq g_2}(S_v(g_2) - \nu_{\mathbf{ch}(v)_i}(g_1, g_2)))\right) & i > 0 \end{cases}$$

Computing the DP table in this manner requires only $O\left(\alpha|G|^2\right)$ time.

However, as presented, the BP sweep for symbol collection has a memory complexity of $O\left(|G|^2\right)$ per block per node, which in practice is prohibitive even for pedigrees with relatively small founding populations. To reduce the memory complexity by a factor of $|G|$, we make the simplifying assumption that the probability that some vertex v has at least one of a pair of genes g_1, g_2 approximately equals $S_v(g_1) + S_v(g_2)$; this permits us to store only the marginal probabilities over single genes, rather than the entire distribution over pairs of genes.

The DP values are then calculated as follows:

$$\mathbf{DP}(g_1, g_2)_{i,j} = \begin{cases} \mathbb{I}_{j=0} & i = 0 \\ \mathbf{DP}(g_1, g_2)_{i-1,j} \left(S_v(g_1) + \mathbb{I}_{g_1\neq g_2} S_v(g_2)\right) + & \\ + \mathbf{DP}(g_1, g_2)_{i-1,j-1} \left(1 - (S_v(g_1) + \mathbb{I}_{g_1\neq g_2} S_v(g_2)\right) & i > 0 \end{cases}$$

On small pedigrees, this assumption does not produce a decrease in reconstruction accuracy. We also show that simulations on large pedigrees, which are impractical with the $O\left(|G|^2\right)$ per-block memory complexity, perform well.

We also implement a relatively simple parsimony-based symbol collection step, which greedily takes the genes that entail the fewest topology errors.

7. Simulation Results for BP

Experiments using simulated data generated as described in Section 4.1 indicate that using BP or Parsimony instead of the combinatorial symbol-collection step of REC-GEN significantly improves accuracy and permits substantial recovery of the founding populations of $T = 4$ pedigrees without manual intervention in the siblinghood threshold. Figures 5 and 6 show the reconstruction accuracy of BP with two values of ϵ (0.01 and 0.001), parsimony, and the original REC-GEN symbol-collection step. Parsimony and both instances of BP have similar accuracy, which past the grandparent generation is significantly better than that of the original REC-GEN. BP with $\epsilon = 0.01$ tends to slightly outperform BP with $\epsilon = 0.001$ and parsimony. These results indicate that BP is more robust against inbreeding than the combinatorial REC-GEN. While parsimony is a simple approximation of BP, its reliability decreases when the distribution of fertilities is non-constant.

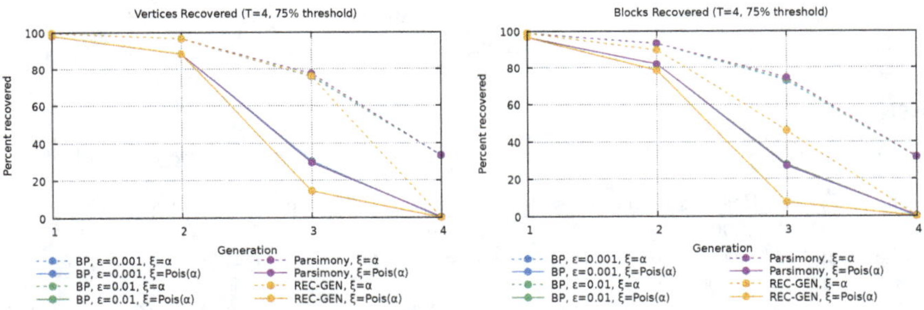

Fig. 5: Average percent vertices and blocks 0.75-successfully reconstructed using each of four different procedures for symbol collection in each generation of $T = 4$ pedigrees

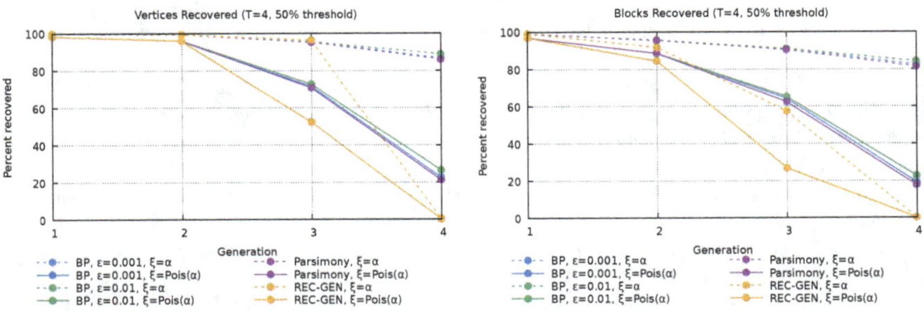

Fig. 6: Average percent vertices and blocks 0.50-successfully reconstructed using each of four different procedures for symbol collection in each generation of $T = 4$ pedigrees

8. Discussion

The changes to the Rec-Gen algorithm of Ref. 1 presented in this paper contribute significant improvements in practical efficiency and accuracy on simulated pedigree data without sacrificing many of the original algorithm's theoretical guarantees. We show how to reduce the complexity of the sibling-identification step from cubic in the size of the extant population to essentially quadratic while continuing to use triples as the basis for reconstructing sibling relations and replace the combinatorial genome reconstruction step with a significantly faster and more accurate Belief Propagation procedure; this Belief Propagation procedure is also more accurate than parsimony when the distribution of fertilities is not constant.

Adaptation of our ideas to real-world data is beyond the scope of this work as our model assumes well-defined generations, high fertilities, and no phasing. However, we believe that the presented contributions can be used in practical tools for reconstruction.

Source code and simulation data are available at `https://github.com/dvulakh/RecGen`

Acknowledgments

This work was partially supported by Vannevar Bush Faculty Fellowship ONR-N00014-20-1-2826, NSF award DMS-2031883, MIT UROP, and by a Simons Investigator award (622132).

The authors thank the reviewers for their thoughtful comments.

References

1. Y. Kim, E. Mossel, G. Ramnarayan and P. Turner, Efficient reconstruction of stochastic pedigrees (2020).
2. M. Steel and J. Hein, Reconstructing pedigrees: a combinatorial perspective, *Journal of theoretical biology* **240**, 360 (2006).
3. B. D. Thatte and M. Steel, Reconstructing pedigrees: a stochastic perspective, *Journal of theoretical biology* **251**, 440 (2008).
4. E. A. Thompson, Statistical inference from genetic data on pedigrees, *NSF-CBMS Regional Conference Series in Probability and Statistics* **6**, i (2000).
5. B. Kirkpatrick, S. C. Li, R. M. Karp and E. Halperin, Pedigree reconstruction using identity by descent, *Journal of Computational Biology* **18**, 1481 (2011).
6. D. He, Z. Wang, B. Han, L. Parida and E. Eskin, Iped: inheritance path-based pedigree reconstruction algorithm using genotype data, *Journal of Computational Biology* **20**, 780 (2013).
7. E. A. Thompson, Identity by descent: variation in meiosis, across genomes, and in populations, *Genetics* **194**, 301 (2013).
8. D. He, Z. Wang, L. Parida and E. Eskin, Iped2: Inheritance path based pedigree reconstruction algorithm for complicated pedigrees, in *Proceedings of the 5th ACM Conference on Bioinformatics, Computational Biology, and Health Informatics*, BCB '14 (Association for Computing Machinery, New York, NY, USA, 2014).
9. D. Shem-Tov and E. Halperin, Historical pedigree reconstruction from extant populations using partitioning of relatives (prepare), *PLoS computational biology* **10** (2014).
10. J. Huisman, Pedigree reconstruction from snp data: parentage assignment, sibship clustering and beyond, *Molecular ecology resources* **17**, 1009 (2017).
11. J. Wang, Pedigree reconstruction from poor quality genotype data, *Heredity* **122**, 719 (2019).
12. M. Mezard and A. Montanari, *Information, Physics, and Computation* (Oxford University Press, Inc., USA, 2009).

Graph algorithms for predicting subcellular localization at the pathway level

Chris S Magnano[1,2,3] and Anthony Gitter[1,2,4]
[1]*Department of Computer Sciences, University of Wisconsin-Madison, Madison, WI, USA*
[2]*Morgridge Institute for Research, Madison, WI, USA*
[3]*Center for Computational Biomedicine, Harvard Medical School, Boston, MA, USA*
[4]*Department of Biostatistics and Medical Informatics, University of Wisconsin-Madison, Madison, WI, USA*

Protein subcellular localization is an important factor in normal cellular processes and disease. While many protein localization resources treat it as static, protein localization is dynamic and heavily influenced by biological context. Biological pathways are graphs that represent a specific biological context and can be inferred from large-scale data. We develop graph algorithms to predict the localization of all interactions in a biological pathway as an edge-labeling task. We compare a variety of models including graph neural networks, probabilistic graphical models, and discriminative classifiers for predicting localization annotations from curated pathway databases. We also perform a case study where we construct biological pathways and predict localizations of human fibroblasts undergoing viral infection. Pathway localization prediction is a promising approach for integrating publicly available localization data into the analysis of large-scale biological data.

Keywords: Probabilistic graphical model, graph neural network, spatial proteomics

1. Introduction

Cellular state is dictated by a wide range of factors from chromatin accessibility to protein abundance to the physical location of proteins within the cell. Cells are compartmentalized into subcellular locations that provide the chemical environment around proteins. That local environment informs proteins' structure and available interaction partners. Protein localization not only dictates protein interactions in normal biological processes,[1] but also is an important factor that can contribute to abnormal cellular behavior. Alzheimer's disease, amyotrophic lateral sclerosis, Wilson disease, and multiple cancers involve abnormal protein localizations.[2]

Although protein localization is dynamic and context-specific,[3] many localization resources present a fixed, static view. Localization databases such as MatrixDB,[4] Organelle DB,[5] Compartments,[6] and ComPPI[7] track primary experimental data, computational predictions, or combinations of multiple information sources. Up to 50% of proteins localize to multiple cellular compartments.[8,9] Databases typically provide multiple possible localizations per protein, but that does not determine the conditions under which subsets of each protein's localiziations are relevant. Many tools can predict possible locations of a protein based on its sequence[10–12] using machine learning methods such as logistic regression[13] or deep neural networks.[14] Some methods incorporate additional information, such as gene expression,[15] Gene Ontology annotations,[16] and network information.[17–20] Methods using network information consider the localizations of neighboring proteins in protein-protein interaction databases to aid in localization prediction and do not attempt to represent any particular biological context. Some predictive methods consider tissue context,[21] but proteins vary in their subcellular localization even between single cells of the same tissue type.[1]

We present graph algorithms for estimating context-specific protein localizations by modeling them in biological pathways[a]. Biological pathways, graphs of biological entities such as proteins, can represent a particular biological process or context. Although traditionally thought of in terms of curated pathway databases, pathway reconstruction graph algorithms[22–24] can generate custom pathway representations of a specific process given a background protein interaction network and condition-specific data such as proteomic measurements as input. However, there is no straightforward way to contextualize and apply available protein localization data to this type of predicted biological pathway. In order to provide context-specific localization information for a particular biological dataset, we develop graph algorithms for the simultaneous prediction of a subcellular localization for all interactions in a reconstructed biological pathway. Computationally, this can be seen as an edge labeling task on an existing graph. This predictive step can be added to existing pathway reconstruction workflows. Estimating localization information at the pathway level enables examining where proteins or other biological entities are when they perform a biological function. Pathway-specific localization annotation can help interpret the predicted pathway and potentially provide additional information to guide followup experiments.

Our strategy to understand context-specific protein localization through graph-based annotations of reconstructed pathways offers advantages over alternative approaches. Some curated pathway databases provide localization information at the interaction level and include information about non-protein biological entities.[25,26] However, many pathway databases contain incomplete or no localization information. For instance, of the 8 pathway databases included in Pathway Commons,[27] 2 are fully labeled with localization information, 5 are partially labeled with localization information, and 1 contains no programmatically available localization information. Additionally, curated pathways often do not line up with experimental data[28–31] and a curated pathway may not be available for a particular biological condition of interest. While condition-specific localization information can be experimentally derived[1] using mass spectrometry or cellular imaging, these methods can be expensive, require experimental expertise, and have incomplete coverage. Predicting localization based on pathways is less precise than acquiring localization data experimentally, but the predictions provide an initial coarse estimate of all proteins' localizations without requiring new specialized data.

We develop and compare three categories of methods for predicting localization for interactions within the context of a biological pathway: graph neural networks, probabilistic graphical models, and classifiers that do not use graph topology. First, we quantitatively evaluate these strategies for pathway-based localization prediction by holding out annotated localizations

[a]Supplementary Information and code can be found at `https://github.com/gitter-lab/pathway-localization` and archived at `https://doi.org/10.5281/zenodo.7140733`.

from pathway databases. Then, we demonstrate how our approach can be used in practice with a case study involving human cytomegalovirus (HCMV) infection over time.[32] While there are disparities between localization information in pathway databases and experimentally-derived localization data, pathway-level localization prediction is a promising approach for combining publicly available localization data with the analysis of large-scale biological data.

2. Methods

2.1. *Pathway Localization Prediction Problem Definition*

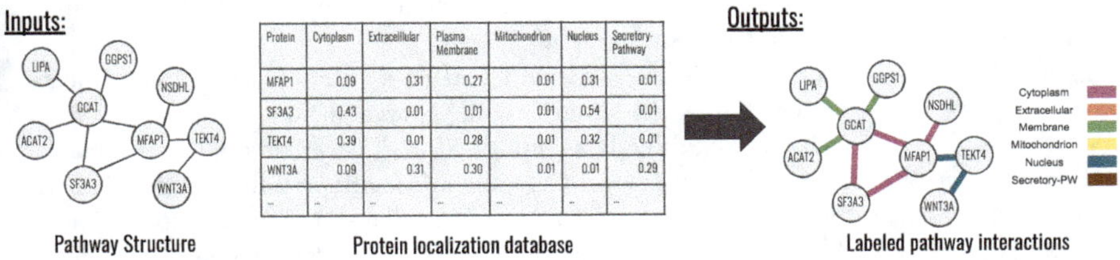

Protein	Cytoplasm	Extracellular	Plasma Membrane	Mitochondrion	Nucleus	Secretory-Pathway
MFAP1	0.09	0.31	0.27	0.01	0.31	0.01
SF3A3	0.43	0.01	0.01	0.01	0.54	0.01
TEKT4	0.39	0.01	0.28	0.01	0.32	0.01
WNT3A	0.09	0.31	0.30	0.01	0.01	0.29
...	...	...	...	...	...	...

Fig. 1. Overview of the pathway localization prediction experimental workflow.

Given a biological pathway represented as a graph, the goal is to predict one subcellular localization for each edge. The pathway represents some cellular function and can be constructed from large-scale biological datasets using pathway reconstruction.[33] We predict a localization for each edge in the pathway, which can be viewed as a class label assignment for each edge in the graph. Protein-level localization information is used as input to the prediction task as node features. Thus, the pathway-specific subcellular localization task can be defined as:

Input: (1) A context-specific pathway graph consisting of nodes and edges $G = (N, E)$, and (2) a distribution over possible localizations for each node in the graph. Output: A single localization assignment for each interaction $e \in E$. See Figure 1.

We chose to assign localizations to edges as opposed to nodes and to assign each interaction a single localization. Pathway databases such as Reactome[25] and popular pathway file formats such as BioPax[34,35] only allow proteins to be in a single subcellular location, creating multiple protein entries if they occur in multiple localizations and assigning them to interactions. While many proteins have multiple localizations, among all Reactome and PathBank pathways less than 5% of total interactions have multiple localizations within the same pathway.

2.2. *Experimental Setup*

2.2.1. *Pathway Database Localization Prediction*

We investigated how well protein localization databases can be used to predict context-specific localizations in pathway databases, both to examine the feasibility of pathway-specific localization prediction and to elucidate the relationship between node labels in protein localization databases and edge labels in pathway databases. Pathways with interaction localization labels from the Reactome[25] and PathBank[26] databases were each used as ground truth datasets.

The original pathways in both Reactome and PathBank are represented as hypergraphs, where reaction edges can contain more than two nodes. Pathway Commons converts these hypergraphs to graphs using a set of rules[b]. To represent a protein-complex that contains n proteins, the hypergraph conversions create an edge between every possible pair of nodes, resulting in n^2 edges. For instance, the 4 hyperedges that make up the PathBank pathway Protein Synthesis: Serine are converted to 3,318 edges, of which 3,315 are of type "in-complex-with". We collapsed protein complexes into single nodes where possible in all pathways. This was done by removing any nodes if all of its edges were redundant with the protein-complex's edges, leaving a single node for each complex. Though this loses some node information, collapsing protein complexes resulted in pathways that more more closely resembled the original hypergraph in edge distribution, topology, and class balance.

Three different node feature sets were used: the ComPPI database,[7] the Compartments database,[6] and UniProt keyword[36] features. ComPPI and Compartments contain localization scores for each protein, which are used directly as input features. We created a dimensionality reduction-based vectorization of UniProt keyword assignments for all proteins (Section S1.3.3). All 8 predictive models (Section 2.3) were tested on all feature sets with the exception of the NaivePGM model, which could not use the UniProt keyword features as it interprets input features directly as conditional probabilities. All pathways in the 2 pathway databases Reactome and PathBank, which contain interaction-level localization labels, were tested on resulting in a total of 46 runs. Models were trained using 5-fold cross validation, and model selection and hyperparameter selection were performed on a tuning set of the 53 Reactome pathways categorized as developmental and a randomly chosen 10% of all PathBank pathways. Tuning pathways were excluded from cross validation.

2.2.2. *Human Cytomegalovirus Case Study*

To examine how predicting context-specific localization at the pathway level could be used in a realistic setting, we performed a case study with bulk spatial mass spectrometry (MS) data from multi-organelle profiling on primary fibroblasts during HCMV infection.[32] In multi-organelle profiling, gradient centrifugation is used on a bulk sample to partially separate organelles. Protein levels in each subcellular fraction are then measured using tandem mass tags MS, and localization labels are determined by clustering proteins with similar fraction profiles. We investigated whether a predictive model can infer localizations in the context of viral infection, potentially bypassing the need to collect spatial proteomic data.

We performed pathway reconstruction[33] by combining a background protein-protein interaction network[28,37,38] with label-free MS data, which measured protein abundance across the entire fibroblast at 120 hours post infection (hpi) without regards to localization. Measured protein levels were used to create biological networks representing the cell state following infection. The combined top pathways chosen (Section S1.1) contained a total of 386 edges with localization information at 120hpi.

We then trained one of the best performing models from the pathway database prediction

[b]`http://www.pathwaycommons.org/pc2/formats`

task, the graph attention network, in three different scenarios. First, we trained a model using data from the PathBank database as described in Section 2.1. Second, we trained a model using a separate dataset that measured protein localization using a similar method on a different cell type and under a different biological condition, HeLa cells undergoing EGF stimulation.[39] Third, we trained a model on the same HCMV experiment at the 24hpi timepoint. This third scenario is unlikely to occur, as it would require a dataset to already exist for an identical cell type and condition, but gives a useful benchmark for best case predictive performance.

2.3. *Pathway Localization Prediction Models*

We evaluated three general categories of models (Section S1.2): general classifiers,[40] probabilistic graphical models, and graph neural networks (Figure 2). The fully-connected neural network (FullyConnectedNN), random forest (RF), and logisitic regression (Logit) served as baseline classifiers because they use no topological information from the pathway graph (Figure S1). These models instead concatenate the node features of each interaction's endpoints as their input. All other models use topological information from the pathway graph to encourage interactions near each other to have similar localizations.

Graph convolutional network (GCN): Graph convolutional networks[41] incorporate a series of message-passing convolutional layers before the final fully connected layers. The convolutional layers allow for information to be shared across the topology of the input network, providing a first-order approximation of spectral graph convolutions.[42] All neural network models were implemented using PyTorch Geometric.[43]

Graph attention network (GAT): Graph attention networks extend graph convolutional networks by allowing each node to choose which neighbors to pay attention to. As opposed to taking the average of its neighbors, each node computes a weighted average of its neighbors in graph convolutional layers.[44,45] The GAT is multi-headed, where multiple attention weights are computed in parallel for each node. The number of heads is a hyperparameter.

Graph isomorphism network (GIN): Graph isomorphism networks[46] take advantage of the similarity between neighbor aggregation in graph neural networks and the Weisfeiler-Lehman (WL) graph isomorphism test.[47] The WL graph isomorphism test is a heuristic algorithm for determining graph isomorphisms. The neighbor aggregation in each graph layer of a graph isomorphism network is formulated to be at least as powerful as the WL isomorphism test; the lth layer is guaranteed to generate different embeddings of two graphs if those graphs would be found to be non-isomorphic via the WL isomorphism test in l iterations.

Probabilistic graphical models: Given the nature of the label propagation inherent in the pathway level localization prediction task, and that many localization databases provide scores or even probabilities, probabilistic graphical models are a natural choice. However, these models only provide predictions on the nodes of the graph, while we are interested in localization labels on the edges. To convert the input pathway into an appropriate graphical model, each pathway is converted into a bipartite graph, where an additional node is added to that graph for each edge (Figure S2).

Probabilistic graphical models represent a set of N random variables $\mathbf{y}$ as nodes and dependencies between them as a set of edges E. We created two pairwise undirected probabilistic

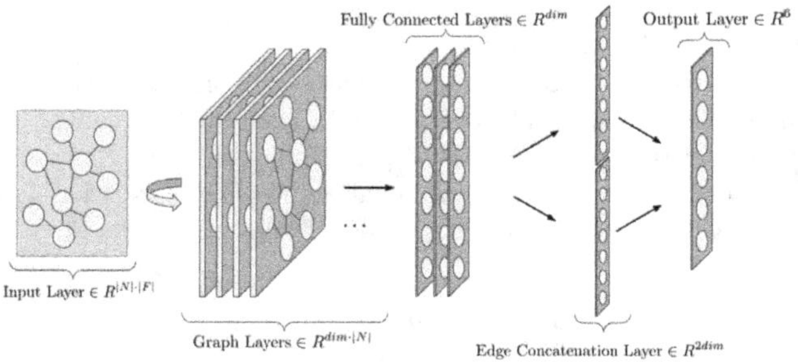

Fig. 2. Overview of neural network architecture for graph neural networks. The number of graph layers (convolutional depth) and number of fully connected layers (linear depth) are hyperparameters. $|N|$ is the number of nodes in the input pathway. $|F|$ is the number of input features for each node.

graphical models,[48] which we call NaivePGM and TrainedPGM. In these probabilistic graphical models the random variables obey a local Markov property, such that each random variable is conditionally independent of all others given its neighbors in the graph.

The NaivePGM is a Markov random field, where protein localization database data is used to create conditional probability tables. In the TrainedPGM, input features are treated as observations of additional variables to train potential functions on each node. These potential functions are represented by discriminative classifiers,[49] here random forests. This type of model is referred to as a discriminative random field.[50] This was chosen over a more traditional log linear parameterization due to better performance on the tuning data.

We performed 30 iterations of hyperparameter selection via Bayesian optimization[51] using Ax for neural network models and Scikit-optimize for classifier models[c] (Tables S1 and S2).

3. Results

3.1. *Comparing Pathway and Localization Databases*

To better understand the feasibility of predicting interaction localizations from protein-level localization data, we compared the edge localizations present in biological pathway databases to node localizations in protein localization databases. The Reactome and PathBank pathway databases significantly disagree with both protein localization databases. For instance, among all proteins with an edge localized to the membrane in Reactome, ComPPI scores more as being in the cytosol than in the membrane. In all cases there is a wide distribution when stratifying the ComPPI node scores used as features by the Reactome or PathBank edge localizations used as labels (Figures S3 and S4). Therefore, for any individual protein and interaction there is a significant chance that protein's most likely localization according to ComPPI or Compartments is not the localization Reactome or PathBank assigned it to.

Directly using data from protein localization databases is not sufficient to accurately pre-

[c] `https://ax.dev/` and `https://scikit-optimize.github.io/stable/`

dict pathway level localization. Many interactions have at least one contradictory interaction with an identical featurization but a different localization label, over 40% when using ComPPI and over 20% when using Compartments. In addition, many interaction localizations would be considered impossible when using a protein localization database alone. Almost 14% of interactions in Reactome are between proteins that have no protein localizations in common in ComPPI. Even without featurization, for 9.5% and 11.5% of total interactions in Reactome and PathBank, respectively, there exists another interaction between the same unique proteins in another pathway that has a different localization. This indicates that pathway topology or some other form of additional information beyond that of individual proteins is needed to correctly predict localization in context.

3.2. *Pathway Database Localization Prediction*

We used cross-validation to train our models on protein information and some labeled database pathways and evaluate their edge localization predictions for other database pathways given only protein information and graph structure as input. Overall, models were able to achieve better interaction localization prediction performance on PathBank pathways (Figure 3) than Reactome pathways (Figure 4). Generally, models' performance in predicting PathBank interaction localizations was more consistent across pathways. However, on both datasets all models' performance had high variance across pathways. Except for logistic regression, all models got at least some pathways completely correct and some pathways completely wrong across all databases and feature sets. The graph neural network models, GCN, GAT, and GIN, generally outperformed other models in all conditions. However, in Reactome no model was able to achieve a median multiclass F1 score (hereafter called 'F1 score') of over 0.5

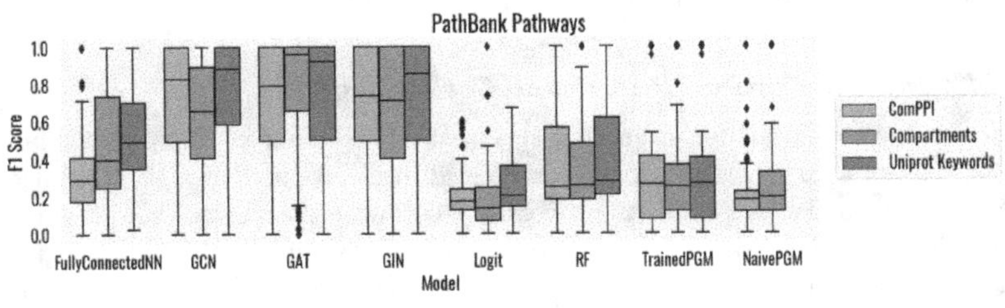

Fig. 3. Multiclass F1 score of predictive performance on PathBank localizations across all 427 considered PathBank pathways. Scores are calculated per pathway; the distribution of scores is shown for each model.

Probabilistic graphical models and models that used no pathway topology had generally comparable performance. The FullyConnectedNN model was able to outperform other models when predicting PathBank localizations using Compartments or UniProt keyword features. It should be noted, however, that when calculating performance by pathway as done in this setting, the size of each pathway is not taken into account. This means that edges in very small pathways can have an outsized effect on total performance.

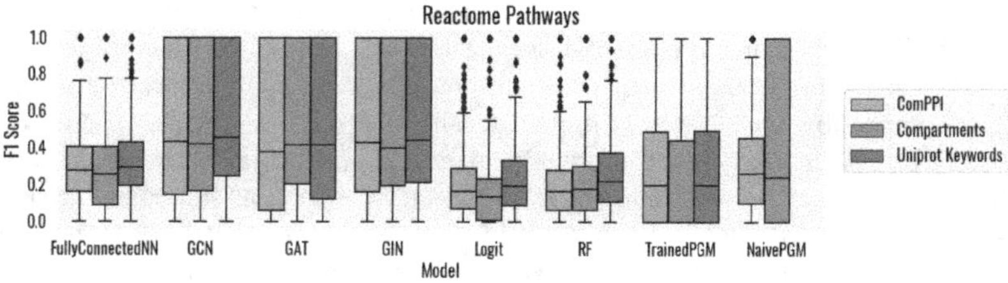

Fig. 4. Multiclass F1 score of predictive performance on Reactome localizations across all 918 considered Reactome pathways. Scores are calculated per pathway; the distribution of scores is shown for each model.

Alternatively, Figures S5 and S6 show F1 scores for each model aggregated from all pathways, where all edges are used for a single performance calculation. When aggregated in this way, all non-neural network models perform comparably. The probabilistic graphical models, and the TrainedPGM model in particular, struggled with small pathways.

The number of real and predicted unique localizations in each pathway also had a large effect on model performance. This can be thought of as the smoothness of the real or predicted localizations in a pathway, or how strong the tendency is for edges nearby in a pathway to have the same localization. Ideally, a model would be able to detect that a pathway exists entirely in a single localization and aggressively smooth its localization predictions over the pathway. Pathways with a single localization had the widest range of performance within each model. More extreme performances, at or nearly at 1.0 or 0.0 for these pathways, indicate that the model correctly predicted that the pathway had only a single localization. Figure S7 shows the distributions of the number of predicted unique localizations by the different models.

3.3. *HCMV Infection Spatial Proteomics Case Study*

We considered three scenarios for evaluating localization prediction in an experimental setting. Here, we examine if localizations can be inferred in the context of a HCMV infection (Section S1.1). We simulate an exploratory workflow by first constructing HCMV infection-specific biological pathways using pathway reconstruction[23] (example pathway topologies can be viewed in Figures S8 and S9). We then use the context provided by these pathways' topologies to predict interaction localizations with the best performing model from pathway database prediction, GAT, using node features from the Compartments database.

In all scenarios, we predict localizations for each interaction of pathways created from protein abundance measurements at 120hpi. Localization data from spatial MS taken at the same timepoint was used as ground truth. Each scenario differs in the labeled training data used: pathways from a pathway database, a different experiment using a different context and cell type, or data from the same experiment at a different timepoint. In all scenarios, all data from the 120hpi timepoint was held out until the final evaluation. We also consider a baseline model that always predicts the most frequent localization among all training set interactions.

While in all scenarios the model substantially outperformed the baseline, there was a large gap in performance between the model trained using pathway databases versus those trained on a different experiment (Figure 5). Both scenarios using experimental data achieved an F1 score of over 0.8. Although the GAT model predictions do not perfectly recapitulate the spatial proteomics localizations, it is encouraging that the GAT model trained in a plausible setting with data from an unrelated biological context is almost as accurate as the unrealistic, best case GAT model trained on another timepoint from the same HCMV infection experiment.

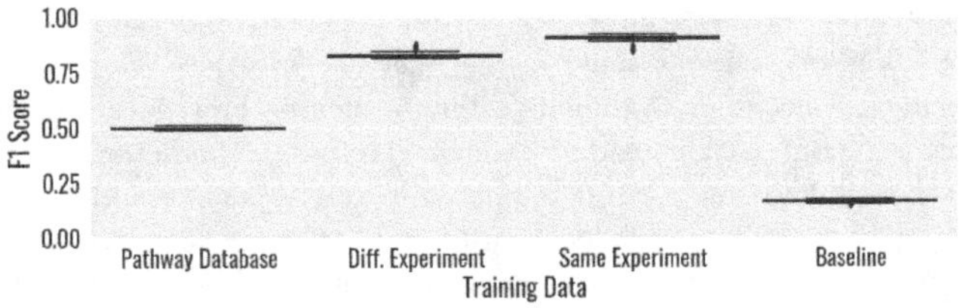

Fig. 5. Multiclass F1 score of the GAT model on spatial MS data of viral infection at 120hpi. Performance is shown in each scenario for the 50 top pathways created from a parameter sweep. The baseline model always predicts the most common localization in the training dataset.

4. Conclusions and Future Work

Although there is some correspondence between protein localization databases and localization data in pathway databases, these two types of localization data generally disagree. Graph neural network models were required to achieve high predictive performance on PathBank localizations, and all models performed poorly in predicting Reactome localizations.

There are a number of possible reasons for this misalignment between localization information in pathway databases and protein localization databases. While the best-performing models include topological information, implying that topology is needed to bring context to protein localization, it is possible that other types of data are needed. Protein features derived from UniProt keywords only slightly improved performance, and tissue- or cell-specific localization may be necessary to fully realize context-specific localization. That type of information may not be available for pathway databases, which are often provided independent of tissue type, but could be for reconstructed pathways. The protein localization databases may also be too noisy and general for context-specific localization prediction. While some signal does exist, the wide range of distributions for ComPPI and Compartments scores across different pathway localizations highlights the imprecise nature of the prediction problem.

While graph neural networks outperformed other methods in predicting pathway localizations, it is unclear how large a role pathway topology played in these methods' performance. It is possible that increased performance over other models comes solely from how graph convolutions share information between nodes, as opposed to the biological information inherent in each pathway's topology aiding localization prediction.

The conversion of pathways from hypergraphs to graphs greatly impacted the class distribution and topology of Reactome and PathBank pathways. Treatment of protein complexes can lead to orders of magnitude difference in the number of edges in the resultant pathways. We created protein complex nodes to represent complexes, which removes node information but better preserves the edge structure and balance in the pathway. An analysis task focused specifically on nodes may want a conversion that better preserves node information at the possible cost of edge information. Important future work would be to consider these conversions in a more systemic way and quantify the hypergraph properties they alter or keep invariant.

Pathway reconstruction has already proven to be a powerful strategy for interpreting transcriptomic, proteomic, or other data in a network context, and the ability to coarsely approximate interaction localizations could further increase its value. We observed the GAT model may have sufficient accuracy to roughly estimate such pathway localizations as long as it is trained on experimental data instead of pathway databases. Predictions using the model trained on HeLa cells still had an error rate of approximately 17% but could plausibly be used to obtain an estimate of context-specific localization predictions in the absence of other data. Further testing is required to assess how similar the training conditions and assay types must be to the test conditions and assays and what types of pathway reconstruction algorithms are compatible with our GAT localization prediction model.

There are additional biological contexts where localization prediction could prove valuable. Single-cell spatial proteomics experiments have previously found proteins to vary by as much as 16% in either expression or spatial distribution between cells undergoing the same process in the same tissues.[8] Predicted protein localizations for individual cells could add an additional layer of information in single-cell analyses. Additionally, targeted identification of abnormal protein localizations could provide insight in diseases where protein localization is known to play a role.[52] The current predictive method could be expanded to attempt to quantify a localization being unexpected given a constructed pathway representing some cellular state.

References

1. E. Lundberg and G. H. H. Borner. Spatial proteomics: A powerful discovery tool for cell biology. *Nature Reviews Molecular Cell Biology*, 20(5):285–302, May 2019.
2. M.-C. Hung and W. Link. Protein localization in disease and therapy. *Journal of Cell Science*, 124(20):3381, October 2011.
3. N. C. Bauer et al. Mechanisms regulating protein localization. *Traffic*, 16(10):1039–1061, 2015.
4. E. Chautard et al. MatrixDB, the extracellular matrix interaction database. *Nucleic Acids Research*, 39(suppl_1):D235–D240, September 2010.
5. N. Wiwatwattana and A. Kumar. Organelle DB: a cross-species database of protein localization and function. *Nucleic Acids Research*, 33(suppl_1):D598–D604, January 2005.
6. J. X. Binder et al. COMPARTMENTS: unification and visualization of protein subcellular localization evidence. *Database*, 2014(bau012), February 2014.
7. D. V. Veres et al. ComPPI: a cellular compartment-specific database for protein-protein interaction network analysis. *Nucleic acids research*, 43(Database issue):D485–D493, January 2015.
8. P. J. Thul et al. A subcellular map of the human proteome. *Science*, 356(6340):eaal3321, May 2017.
9. S. Zhang et al. DBMLoc: A Database of proteins with multiple subcellular localizations. *BMC Bioinformatics*, 9(1):127, February 2008.
10. J. L. Gardy and F. S. L. Brinkman. Methods for predicting bacterial protein subcellular localization. *Nature Reviews Microbiology*, 4(10):741–751, October 2006.

11. K. Imai and K. Nakai. Prediction of subcellular locations of proteins: Where to proceed? *PROTEOMICS*, 10(22):3970–3983, 2010.
12. A. Alaa et al. Protein Subcellular Localization Prediction Based on Internal Micro-similarities of Markov Chains. In *2019 41st Annual International Conference of the IEEE Engineering in Medicine and Biology Society (EMBC)*, pp. 1355–1358, July 2019.
13. S. Hua and Z. Sun. Support vector machine approach for protein subcellular localization prediction. *Bioinformatics*, 17(8):721–728, August 2001.
14. J. J. Almagro Armenteros et al. DeepLoc: prediction of protein subcellular localization using deep learning. *Bioinformatics*, 33(21):3387–3395, July 2017.
15. A. Drawid and M. Gerstein. A Bayesian system integrating expression data with sequence patterns for localizing proteins: comprehensive application to the yeast genome. *Journal of Molecular Biology*, 301(4):1059–1075, August 2000.
16. A. Fyshe et al. Improving subcellular localization prediction using text classification and the Gene Ontology. *Bioinformatics*, 24(21):2512–2517, August 2008.
17. M. M. Ananda and J. Hu. NetLoc: Network based protein localization prediction using protein-protein interaction and co-expression networks. In *2010 IEEE International Conference on Bioinformatics and Biomedicine (BIBM)*, pp. 142–148. IEEE, December 2010.
18. P. Du and L. Wang. Predicting Human Protein Subcellular Locations by the Ensemble of Multiple Predictors via Protein-Protein Interaction Network with Edge Clustering Coefficients. *PLOS ONE*, 9(1):e86879, January 2014.
19. H. S. Garapati et al. Predicting subcellular localization of proteins using protein-protein interaction data. *Genomics*, 112(3):2361–2368, May 2020.
20. A. Grover and L. Gatto. ProtFinder: finding subcellular locations of proteins using protein interaction networks. *bioRxiv*, 2022.
21. L. Zhu et al. Tissue-Specific Subcellular Localization Prediction Using Multi-Label Markov Random Fields. *IEEE/ACM Transactions on Computational Biology and Bioinformatics*, 16(5):1471–1482, September 2019.
22. A. Ritz et al. Pathways on demand: automated reconstruction of human signaling networks. *npj Systems Biology and Applications*, 2(1):1–9, March 2016.
23. N. Tuncbag et al. Network-Based Interpretation of Diverse High-Throughput Datasets through the Omics Integrator Software Package. *PLOS Computational Biology*, 12(4):e1004879, April 2016.
24. E. Cerami et al. Automated Network Analysis Identifies Core Pathways in Glioblastoma. *PLOS ONE*, 5(2):e8918, February 2010.
25. A. Fabregat et al. The Reactome Pathway Knowledgebase. *Nucleic Acids Research*, 46(D1):D649–D655, 2018.
26. D. S. Wishart et al. PathBank: a comprehensive pathway database for model organisms. *Nucleic Acids Research*, 48(D1):D470–D478, 10 2019.
27. I. Rodchenkov et al. Pathway Commons 2019 Update: integration, analysis and exploration of pathway data. *Nucleic Acids Research*, 48(D1):D489–D497, 10 2019.
28. A. S. Köksal et al. Synthesizing Signaling Pathways from Temporal Phosphoproteomic Data. *Cell Reports*, 24(13):3607–3618, September 2018.
29. L. Cao et al. Quantitative Phosphoproteomics Reveals SLP-76 Dependent Regulation of PAG and Src Family Kinases in T Cells. *PLOS ONE*, 7(10):e46725, October 2012.
30. S. J. Humphrey et al. High-throughput phosphoproteomics reveals in vivo insulin signaling dynamics. *Nature Biotechnology*, 33(9):990–995, September 2015.
31. R. C. J. D'Souza et al. Time-resolved dissection of early phosphoproteome and ensuing proteome changes in response to TGF-beta. *Science Signaling*, 7(335):rs5, 2014.
32. P. M. Jean Beltran et al. A Portrait of the Human Organelle Proteome In Space and Time during

Cytomegalovirus Infection. *Cell Systems*, 3(4):361–373.e6, October 2016.
33. C. S. Magnano and A. Gitter. Automating parameter selection to avoid implausible biological pathway models. *npj Systems Biology and Applications*, 7(1):1–12, 2021.
34. E. Demir et al. The BioPAX community standard for pathway data sharing. *Nature Biotechnology*, 28(9):935–942, September 2010.
35. B. M. Gyori and C. T. Hoyt. PyBioPAX: biological pathway exchange in Python. *Journal of Open Source Software*, 7(71):4136, March 2022.
36. The UniProt Consortium. UniProt: the universal protein knowledgebase in 2021. *Nucleic Acids Research*, 49(D1):D480–D489, 11 2020.
37. S. Razick et al. iRefIndex: A consolidated protein interaction database with provenance. *BMC Bioinformatics*, 9(1):405, September 2008.
38. P. V. Hornbeck et al. PhosphoSitePlus, 2014: mutations, PTMs and recalibrations. *Nucleic Acids Research*, 43(D1):D512–D520, December 2014.
39. D. N. Itzhak et al. Global, quantitative and dynamic mapping of protein subcellular localization. *eLife*, 5:e16950, June 2016.
40. F. Pedregosa et al. Scikit-learn: Machine learning in Python. *Journal of Machine Learning Research*, 12:2825–2830, 2011.
41. T. N. Kipf and M. Welling. Semi-supervised classification with graph convolutional networks. In *International Conference on Learning Representations (ICLR)*, 2017.
42. D. K. Hammond et al. Wavelets on graphs via spectral graph theory. *Applied and Computational Harmonic Analysis*, 30(2):129–150, 2011.
43. M. Fey and J. E. Lenssen. Fast graph representation learning with PyTorch Geometric. In *ICLR Workshop on Representation Learning on Graphs and Manifolds*, 2019.
44. P. Veličković et al. Graph Attention Networks. *International Conference on Learning Representations*, 2018.
45. S. Brody et al. How attentive are graph attention networks? *arXiv:2105.14491*, 2021.
46. K. Xu et al. How powerful are graph neural networks? In *International Conference on Learning Representations*, 2019.
47. B. Weisfeiler and A. Leman. The reduction of a graph to canonical form and the algebra which appears therein. *Nauchno-Technicheskaya Informatsia*, 2(9), 1968.
48. U. B. Gewali and S. T. Monteiro. A tutorial on modelling and inference in undirected graphical models for hyperspectral image analysis. *International Journal of Remote Sensing*, 39(20):7104–7143, 2018.
49. S. Kosov. *Multi-layer conditional random fields for revealing unobserved entities*. PhD thesis, Universität Siegen, 2018.
50. S. Kumar and M. Hebert. Discriminative random fields. *International Journal of Computer Vision*, 68(2):179–201, 2006.
51. M. Balandat et al. Botorch: A framework for efficient Monte-Carlo Bayesian optimization. In H. Larochelle et al., editors, *Advances in Neural Information Processing Systems*, volume 33, pp. 21524–21538. Curran Associates, Inc., 2020.
52. K. E. Blise et al. Single-cell spatial architectures associated with clinical outcome in head and neck squamous cell carcinoma. *npj Precision Oncology*, 6(1):1–14, February 2022.

5. Acknowledgements

This work was supported by NIH award T15LM007359, NSF award DBI 1553206, the Morgridge Institute for Research, and the University of Wisconsin–Madison Office of the Vice Chancellor for Research and Graduate Education with funding from the Wisconsin Alumni Research Foundation. We thank Sushmita Roy for her valuable feedback.

Improving target-disease association prediction through a graph neural network with credibility information

Chang Liu[1,†], Cuinan Yu[2,†], Yipin Lei[1,†],
Kangbo Lyu[1], Tingzhong Tian[1], Qianhao Li[3],
Dan Zhao[1,*], Fengfeng Zhou[2,*], and Jianyang Zeng[1,*]

[1]*Institute for Interdisciplinary Information Sciences, Tsinghua University, Beijing 100084, China*
**E-mail: zhaodan2018@tsinghua.edu.cn (D.Z.), zengjy321@tsinghua.edu.cn (J.Z.)*
[2]*Key Laboratory of Symbolic Computation and Knowledge Engineering of Ministry of Education, College of Computer Science and Technology, Jilin University, Changchun, Jilin 130012, China*
**E-mail: FengfengZhou@gmail.com (F.Z.)*
[3]*Silexon AI Technology Co., Ltd., Nanjing, Jiangsu Province, China*

Identifying effective target-disease associations (TDAs) can alleviate the tremendous cost incurred by clinical failures of drug development. Although many machine learning models have been proposed to predict potential novel TDAs rapidly, their credibility is not guaranteed, thus requiring extensive experimental validation. In addition, it is generally challenging for current models to predict meaningful associations for entities with less information, hence limiting the application potential of these models in guiding future research. Based on recent advances in utilizing graph neural networks to extract features from heterogeneous biological data, we develop CreaTDA, an end-to-end deep learning-based framework that effectively learns latent feature representations of targets and diseases to facilitate TDA prediction. We also propose a novel way of encoding credibility information obtained from literature to enhance the performance of TDA prediction and predict more novel TDAs with real evidence support from previous studies. Compared with state-of-the-art baseline methods, CreaTDA achieves substantially better prediction performance on the whole TDA network and its sparse sub-networks containing the proteins associated with few known diseases. Our results demonstrate that CreaTDA can provide a powerful and helpful tool for identifying novel target-disease associations, thereby facilitating drug discovery.

Keywords: target-disease association, graph neural network, credibility information, drug discovery.

1. Introduction

The development of a drug generally takes more than five years and costs more than \$4.5 billion,[27] with most of the resources sunk into clinical failures that happen at later stages of drug development.[11] To alleviate the massive cost of drug development, it is crucial to determine credible (i.e., to identify plausible drug targets for a specific disease) at the beginning of the drug development process.

Based on the latent feature representations and similarities between targets and diseases

† These authors contributed equally.

learned from sufficient data, machine learning (ML) models can "predict" potential target-disease associations (TDAs) useful for future studies. For example, a range of ML classifiers trained based on TDA data from the Open Targets platform have been used to predict novel TDAs.[12] A tensor factorization method has also been proposed to reconstruct a drug-target-disease network by integrating drug-drug, target-target, and disease-disease similarity matrices as multi-view auxiliary networks.[4] However, the underlying Tucker tensor model generally suffers from linearity and data sparsity,[5] thus undermining its prediction capacity.

Graph neural networks (GNNs) are nonlinear ML models that generalize convolutional neural networks (CNNs) to graph/network data,[10] combined with information passing and aggregation techniques.[13] Moreover, recent advances in generalizing GNNs to heterogeneous network (HN) data have brought considerable performance improvement.[15,28,32] Since the relation prediction tasks such as target-disease association (TDA) prediction can be viewed as link prediction on networks of biological data, GNNs can theoretically be utilized as high-capacity models for these tasks. Indeed, NeoDTI, a GNN that predicts DTIs from an HN, outperformed state-of-the-art DTI prediction models under several challenging and realistic scenarios.[30]

Nevertheless, these machine learning methods still have the following two shortcomings:

First, human labor is generally needed to verify the prediction results by searching for supporting evidence from literature or conducting wet-lab experiments. Without a gauge of the credibility of these predictions, the amount of human effort needed in these analyses would be daunting, undermining the level of autonomy of the prediction pipeline and thus failing to address the lengthiness and costliness problem of drug development.

Second, *exposure bias* may heavily influence model performance. Exposure bias is a phenomenon in recommendation systems where users are only exposed to a part of specific items so that the unobserved interactions do not always represent the negative preferences.[6] In such a scenario, models are inclined to predict more relations between entities with more available information. However, the failure to produce meaningful predictions for entities with less information restricts the application potential of the models in guiding future research. Moreover, it is generally more difficult for the models to learn the latent feature representations of entities with less information, hence undermining their overall prediction performance.

In this paper, we propose CreaTDA (CRedibility-Encoding grAph neural network for TDA prediction), an end-to-end deep learning-based framework, to perform TDA prediction. In addition to exploiting the structured heterogeneous data in the form of biological networks, CreaTDA fully takes advantage of unstructured data in the form of entity co-occurrence in the literature, which encodes the credibility of the interactions/associations between entities. We showed that CreaTDA (i) achieved superior performance over baseline models on the TDA prediction task and (ii) generated novel predictions with higher credibility and more literature support, and (iii) exhibited robustness to the effect of exposure bias. These results suggested that CreaTDA can provide a helpful tool for drug target identification and benefit the whole drug development process.

2. Methods

2.1. *The heteroneneous network data*

CreaTDA uses heterogeneous network (HN) data as input. We first give a formal definition of an HN:

Definition 1 (Heterogeneous Network) An HN is a directed/undirected graph $G = (V, E)$, where each node $v \in V$ is of a node type from a node type set O, and each edge $e \in E, E \subset V \times V \times R$ is of an edge type from an edge type set R.

The HN used in our framework is an undirected graph with the node type set O ={*drug*, *target (protein)*, *side effect*, *disease*} and the edge type set R ={*drug-drug-structure-similarity*, *protein-protein-sequence-similarity*, *drug-drug-interaction*, *drug-side-effect-association*, *drug-protein-interaction*, *drug-disease-association*, *protein-disease-association*, *protein-protein-interaction*}. Note that we will use the terms "protein" and "target" interchangeably in the remaining parts of this paper.

Here, our individual networks (defined by specific edge types) are adopted from Luo et al.,[20] including:

- A drug-protein interaction network and a drug-drug interaction network, derived from Drugbank Version 3.0;[17]
- A protein-protein interaction network, extracted from the HPRD database Release 9;[16]
- A drug-disease association network and a protein-disease association (TDA) network, derived from the Comparative Toxicogenomics Database;[8]
- A drug-side-effect association network, derived from the SIDER database Version 2;[18]
- A drug-drug-structure-similarity network, computed using RDKit (`rdkit.org`) according to the Dice similarity of the Morgan fingerprints with radius 2;[24]
- A protein-protein-sequence-similarity network, computed according to the Smith-Waterman scores.[29]

The *association* and *interaction* networks have 0/1 binary edge weights. The 1 values indicate that the entailed associations/interactions exist in the corresponding database. The 0 values indicate either (i) the entailed associations/interactions are established not to exist or (ii) evidence supporting the associations/interactions is lacking. The edges of the *similarity* networks are weighted with real values. With all the networks stored as adjacency matrices, the final HN hosts 12015 nodes, including 1512 targets, 5603 diseases, 708 drugs, and 4102 side effects.

2.2. *The CreaTDA pipeline*

CreaTDA first computes node embeddings that encode the topology of the HN, then uses these embeddings to reconstruct individual networks that encode credibility (Fig. 1), imputing the original 0 values. We describe these two components of CreaTDA below.

2.2.1. *Obtaining node embeddings*

In our framework (Fig. 1), node embeddings are computed via a GNN through two steps: (i) passing and aggregating information for each node through edge-type-specific neighbors and (ii) updating node embeddings. These steps are formally defined as follows:

Definition 2 (Neighborhood information passing and aggregation) Given an HN G, an initial

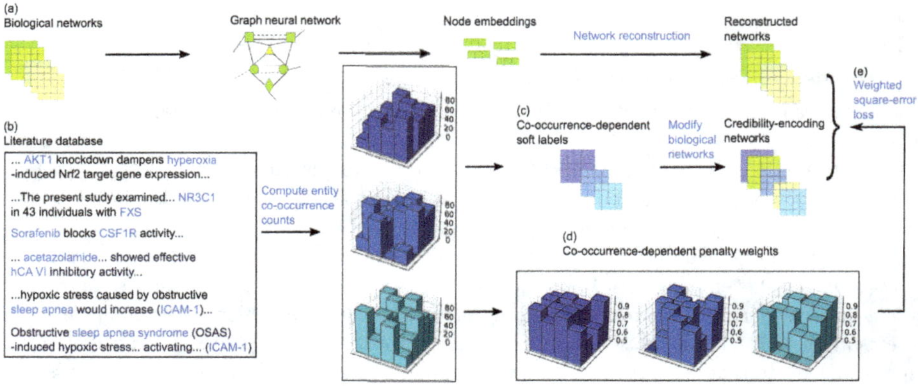

Fig. 1. Overview of CreaTDA. CreaTDA uses a graph neural network to **(a)** obtain node embeddings from individual biological networks that encode the network topology. CreaTDA further encodes credibility by **(b)** computing entity co-occurrence counts in the PubMed database and then transforming these raw counts into co-occurrence-dependent **(c)** soft labels (Eq. 3) and **(d)** penalty weights (Eq. 4). **(e)** CreaTDA reconstructs the credibility-encoding networks containing the soft labels by minimizing a weighted square-error loss derived based on the penalty weights (Eq. 5).

node embedding function $f^0 : V \rightarrow \mathbb{R}^d$ maps each node to an initial node embedding, and an edge embedding function $m : E \rightarrow \mathbb{R}$ maps each edge $e \in E$ to a corresponding value in the network, which can be represented as an adjacency matrix. The information a_v of node $v \in V$ is then aggregated from its neighborhood as follows:

$$a_v = \sum_{\substack{r \in R, u \in N_r(v) \\ e=(u,v,r) \in E}} \frac{m(e)}{Z_{v,r}} (W_r f^0(u) + b_r), \tag{1}$$

where $N_r(v) = \{u | u \in V, u \neq v, (u, v, r) \in E\}$ denotes the nodes connected to $v \in V$ via an edge of type $r \in R$, which are also defined as the "r-neighbors of v." $W_r \in \mathbb{R}^{d \times d}, b_r \in \mathbb{R}^d$ denote the model parameters depending only on the edge type, and $Z_{v,r} = \sum_{u \in N_r(v), e=(u,v,r)} m(e)$ denotes a normalization term. In CreaTDA, f^0 is initialized as a truncated normal sampler with mean 0, standard deviation 0.1, minimum cutoff value -0.2, and maximum cutoff value 0.2.

In other words, for each edge-type r, the embeddings of the $r-$neighbors of v are passed through a linear transformation and then weighed by the normalized edge weights $\frac{m(e)}{Z_{v,r}}$. After that, the results over all edge types are summed.

Definition 3 (Node embedding updating) Using a_v obtained from Eq. 1, the initial embeddings $f^0(v)$ are updated as follows:

$$f^1(v) = g(ReLU(W^1(f^0(v) \| a_v) + b^1)), \tag{2}$$

where "$\|$" denotes the concatenation operation, $ReLU(x) = \max\{0, x\}$, $g(\cdot)$ denotes the ℓ_2 normalization operation, and $W^1 \in \mathbb{R}^{d \times (2d)}$ and $b^1 \in \mathbb{R}^d$ denote global parameters shared by all nodes.

For each node v, its neighborhood information and initial embedding both contribute to its updated embedding, thus allowing the network topology information to be encoded.

2.2.2. *Reconstructing the credibility-encoding networks*

We seek to improve the credibility of the predicted TDAs, i.e., the reproducibility of the results indicating the TDAs, by encoding credibility information into the CreaTDA framework, such that credibility can be learned as part of the latent feature representations of nodes. While the credibility of an interaction/association is elusive to quantify, it can be reflected by the abundance of literature documenting this interaction/association, which can be approximated by the quantity of literature in which the two interacting/associated entities both appear.

We curated about three million papers in the PubMed database maintained by the United States National Library of Medicine (NLM).[23] The number of papers that a *drug-protein*, *protein-disease*, or *drug-disease* pair co-occurs in was computed by sub-string matching using the Trie hashing algorithm (see Supplementary Information for more details). These co-occurrence counts were then organized into co-occurrence matrices $C_r, r \in R_c = \{drug\text{-}protein, protein\text{-}disease, drug\text{-}disease\}$, where $C_r[i,j]$ represents the number of co-occurring papers for entities i and j associated with edge-type r. We assumed that $C_r[i,j]$ is positively correlated with the credibility of the interaction/association between entities i and j. Hence, by incorporating C_r into CreaTDA, the notion of credibility can be introduced.

Here, we formally describe a method of integrating C_r into the CreaTDA framework. We first give mathematical definitions of the key terms used:

Definition 4 (Co-occurrence-dependent soft label) For an edge $e = (i,j,r)$ of edge-type $r \in R_c$ between entities i and j, its soft label is defined as:

$$l(e) = \sigma(C_r[i,j] + \alpha) \cdot m(e) \tag{3}$$

where α stands for a hyperparameter, $\sigma(x) = \frac{1}{1+e^{-x}}$, and $m(e)$ represents the edge embedding function defined in Eq. 1.

Definition 5 (Co-occurrence-dependent penalty weight) For an edge $e = (i,j,r)$ of edge-type $r \in R_c$ between entities i and j, the penalty weight of the reconstruction loss of e is defined as:

$$w(e) = \sigma(C_r[i,j] + \beta) \cdot m(e) + (1 - m(e)) \tag{4}$$

where β stands for a hyperparameter and $m(e)$, $\sigma(x)$ are the same as defined in Eq. 3.

In the implementation of CreaTDA, α and β are set to $\ln 3$ and 0, respectively, as they yielded the best performance according to the cross-validation results (Section 3.1).

The information in C_r is then incorporated in the network reconstruction step to encode the credibility information of TDAs:

Definition 6 (Credibility-encoding network reconstruction) For the parameter set $\Theta = \{f^0, W_r, b_r, G_r, H_r, W^1, b^1\}$, the optimization objective of CreaTDA is:

$$\begin{aligned}\min_{\Theta} & \sum_{r \in R \setminus R_c} \sum_{\substack{u,v \in V \\ e=(u,v,r) \in E}} (m(e) - f^1(u)^T G_r H_r^T f^1(v))^2 \\ & + \sum_{r \in R_c} \sum_{\substack{u,v \in V \\ e=(u,v,r) \in E}} w(e)(l(e) - f^1(u)^T G_r H_r^T f^1(v))^2,\end{aligned} \tag{5}$$

where $m(e)$ denotes the edge embedding function (Eq. 1), $w(e)$ denotes the co-occurrence-dependent penalty weight (Eq. 4), $l(e)$ denotes the co-occurrence-dependent soft label (Eq.

3), and $G_r, H_r \in \mathbb{R}^{d \times k}$ denote the edge-type specific projection matrices. In the implementation of CreaTDA, the ℓ_2-regularization terms on f^0, W_r, G_r, H_r, and W^1 are also summed. In addition, if $r \in$ {*drug-drug-structure-similarity, protein-protein-sequence-similarity, drug-drug-interaction, protein-protein-interaction*}, where the corresponding adjacency matrix is symmetric, the constraint $G_r = H_r$ is imposed to enforce such a symmetry.

The network reconstruction step projects the node embeddings $f^1(\cdot)$ onto the edge-type-specific vector spaces such that the matrix products of the projected vectors best match the corresponding individual networks. Notably, the credibility information is *not* introduced for the negative interactions/associations in the HN, that is, when $m(e) = 0$, $l(e)$ and $w(e)$ are set to 0 and 1 (Eqs. 3 and 4), respectively, thus preventing the potential data leakage problem during the cross-validation process.

2.3. *Ablation studies*

To show that the integration of C_r into the CreaTDA framework is necessary for achieving better performance, we developed four models as the control in our ablation studies to nullify the credibility information encoded in the labels and/or weights: CreaTDA_og (no credibility encoded), CreaTDA_rl (random soft labels), CreaTDA_rw (random penalty weights), and CreaTDA_rlrw (both random soft labels and random penalty weights). More details about the mathematical definitions of these control models can be found in the Supplementary Information.

3. Results

3.1. *CreaTDA yields superior performance in predicting target-disease associations*

While the objective of CreaTDA is to reconstruct the HN, TDA prediction can be considered a binary classification task (i.e., whether an association exists or not). Though we used the modified labels for the optimization objective (Eq. 5), we still measured the prediction performance in terms of the area under the precision-recall curve (AUPR) and the area under the receiver operating characteristic curve (AUROC), using the *original* binary TDA labels as ground truth. We observed that the ratio between the numbers of "1"- and "0"-entries in the network is 0.232, suggesting data imbalance. As stated in previous works, AUPR generally presents a more informative metric than AUROC on the performance of models on those imbalanced datasets.[9,26]

Table 1. Cross-validation results, measured in terms of AUROC and AUPR, in the form of "mean ± standard deviation" over ten rounds of entry-wise cross-validation and cluster-wise cross-validation (Section 3.1), respectively. The results where CreaTDA outperformed all baseline methods are presented in boldface.

	GTN	RGCN	HGT	DTINet	CreaTDA
Entry-wise cross-validation					
AUROC	0.953 ± 0.002	0.974 ± 0.001	0.950 ± 0.002	0.859± 2e-5	**0.986 ± 2e-4**
AUPR	0.822 ± 0.017	0.915 ± 0.004	0.846 ± 0.006	0.658± 1e-5	**0.967 ± 5e-4**
Cluster-wise cross-validation					
AUROC	0.725 ± 0.003	0.738 ± 0.014	0.569 ± 0.012	0.815 ± 0.007	0.814 ± 0.007
AUPR	0.397 ± 0.004	0.332 ± 0.013	0.211 ± 0.006	0.503 ± 0.018	**0.516 ± 0.016**

We performed five-fold cross-validation, during which we conducted a random stratified splitting on the entries of the TDA matrix, which were divided into five folds, preserving the global positive-to-negative ratio as much as possible in each fold. For each of the five iterations, we sequentially chose one fold as test data and sampled 10% of the remaining four folds as validation data for hyperparameter tuning (the remaining 90% formed the training set). We refer to this cross-validation scheme as *entry-wise cross-validation.*

We computed the average AUROC and AUPR scores on the test sets of the five iterations as the performance statistics for one round of cross-validation. To account for the randomness effect, we performed ten rounds of five-fold cross-validation (with different random states) and recorded the means and standard deviations of the performance statistics (Table 1).

We compared the performance of CreaTDA to those of several baseline methods that have reached state-of-the-art performance on heterogeneous graph prediction tasks, including GTN,[32] RGCN,[28] HGT,[15] and DTINet[20] (see Supplementary Information for more details). We found that CreaTDA significantly outperformed all the baseline methods (Table 1), suggesting that CreaTDA can better learn the latent feature representations of the underlying network topology of the given HN.

However, with CreaTDA yielding near-perfect performance, the prediction task may be trivial. Indeed, "similar" TDAs may appear in both training and test sets, thus constituting "easy" predictions that inflated the performance of the models. To more accurately gauge the performance and generalization capacity of the models, we conducted additional tests by reducing the similarity between training and test data. Specifically, we first performed agglomerative clustering on the disease entities according to the Jaccard similarities between their association profiles, i.e., the corresponding columns in the *protein-disease-association* adjacency matrix. We then developed a new cross-validation scheme by partitioning the resulting *clusters* of columns into training, validation, and test sets. The ratios between the sizes of the three datasets and the ratio between positive and negative samples in each dataset were roughly the same as those in the previous entry-wise cross-validation procedure. We refer to this new cross-validation scheme as *cluster-wise cross-validation.*

Table 1 shows that all models had a significant drop in performance when switching from entry-wise to cluster-wise cross-validation. However, CreaTDA still took the lead in performance (though DTINet yielded a comparable AUROC score with CreaTDA, the former achieved a poorer AUPR score), further verifying the superior predictive power of CreaTDA.

We also found that all control models yielded performance inferior to CreaTDA on the cluster-wise cross-validation (Supplementary Table 1), suggesting that the encoded credibility information in both the designed labels and weights can effectively advance CreaTDA to accurately capture the latent feature representations of the underlying network topology.

3.2. *CreaTDA improves the credibility of TDA predictions*

To evaluate the credibility of the novel predictions of CreaTDA, we investigated their corresponding C_r values, which approximate the abundance of literature documenting the entailed TDAs (Section 2.2.2). Here, the "novel" predictions were obtained through the following process: (i) training CreaTDA on the whole HN using the hyperparameters that yielded the best performance in the cluster-wise cross-validation scheme (Section 3.1); (ii) selecting those "significant" predictions whose output values in the reconstructed TDA matrix were greater

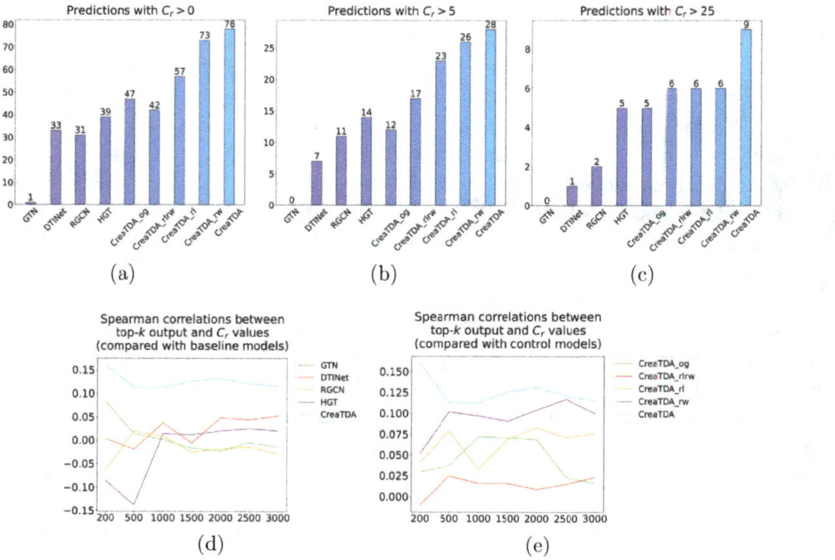

Fig. 2. Examining the credibility of model predictions. **(a)**, **(b)**, and **(c)** document the numbers of predictions among the top-200 novel predictions with $C_r > 0, 5, 25$, respectively. **(d)** and **(e)** plot the Spearman correlations between the output values of the top-k ($k = 200, 500, 1000, 1500, 2000, 2500, 3000$) predictions and their corresponding C_r values, with **(d)** comparing CreaTDA with the baseline models and **(e)** comparing CreaTDA with the four control models developed in our ablation study. The P-values of the correlations, calculated using the *sklearn* package,[22] can be found in Supplementary Table 2.

than $\mu + 2\sigma$, where μ and σ stand for the mean and the standard deviation of the predicted values of elements in each row, respectively; and (iii) choosing the "novel" predictions, which were assigned with the label "0" in the original TDA matrix (i.e., $m(e) = 0$), from the above "significant" predictions. Since these novel predictions had edge weights equal to 0, their corresponding C_r values were not encoded (Eqs. 3 and 4), hence precluding data leakage.

We first examined the C_r values of the novel predictions with the top-200 output values. We found that compared with all baseline and control models, among their corresponding top-200 novel predictions, CreaTDA predicted more novel TDAs with C_r values greater than 0, 5, and 25, respectively (Fig. 2a-2c). Such results showed that CreaTDA could produce novel predictions with more evidence support from PubMed, even though their credibility information was not encoded in CreaTDA during the prediction process.

We next examined the Spearman correlation between the output and the corresponding C_r values of the top-k predictions. We found that CreaTDA yielded a stronger correlation than all baseline (Fig. 2d) and control models (Fig. 2e). We also conducted a hypothesis test (two-sided t-test), in which the null hypothesis meant that the output and C_r values were uncorrelated. We found that CreaTDA yielded overall lower P-values than all baseline and control models (Supplementary Table 2). Here, a stronger correlation (with a lower P-value) indicated that the model predicted TDAs with higher credibility (i.e., larger C_r values). Such results illustrated that the novel TDAs predicted by CreaTDA were more likely to be valid.

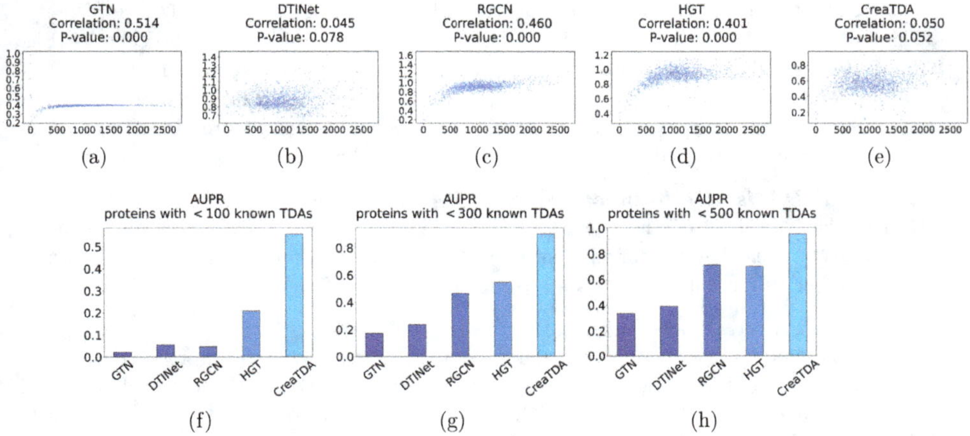

Fig. 3. Examining the robustness against the effect of exposure bias for different models. **(a)-(e)** plot the row-wise maximum values over the 0-labeled entries of the reconstructed TDA matrix (y-axis) against the row-wise sums of the original TDA matrix (x-axis) for the baseline models and CreaTDA. The Spearman correlations between these two vectors and their P-values, calculated using the *sklearn* package, are also reported. **(f)-(h)** present the AUPR scores on the sparse sub-networks of the whole TDA network containing proteins associated with few known TDAs.

3.3. *CreaTDA is robust to the effect of exposure bias*

In this section, we showed that CreaTDA was robust to the effect of exposure bias, a common phenomenon in recommendation systems where the unobserved interactions are often misrepresented as negative preferences.[6] This phenomenon also arises in our TDA prediction task, where those TDAs with 0-labels in the input data are not necessarily "negative" associations. Due to exposure bias, the models generally produce fewer meaningful TDA predictions for those proteins/diseases with few known TDAs and often have difficulty learning their latent feature representations. To investigate the robustness of the models against the effect of exposure bias, we computed the Spearman correlation between the row-wise maximum values over the 0-labeled entries of the reconstructed TDA matrix and the row-wise sums of the original TDA matrix (i.e., the number of diseases associated with the corresponding protein) for the baseline models and CreaTDA. We found that CreaTDA yielded a significantly lower correlation than GTN, RGCN, and HGT, only slightly exceeding the correlation yielded by DTINet (Fig. 3a-3e). Here, a strong correlation indicates two possible drawbacks: (i) the predicted values of TDAs depend heavily on the amount of known information, i.e., the number of diseases known to be associated with the involved protein; and (ii) the top predictions of the model are likely to leave out biologically significant TDAs for those proteins with less available information. Therefore, the above results indicated that with a significantly weaker correlation, CreaTDA suffered less from these two drawbacks.

We then examined the prediction performance (AUPR scores) on the sparse sub-networks of the original TDA network for different models trained on the whole HN. More specifically, we selected those rows of the original TDA matrix with a sum less than 100, 300, and 500, respectively, to simulate three sparse sub-networks. We found that CreaTDA consistently achieved higher AUPR scores than the baseline methods on these sparse sub-networks (Fig. 3f-3h). Here, a higher AUPR score indicated that for proteins with few known TDAs, CreaTDA could generate more accurate predictions and better learn their latent feature representations. These results suggested that CreaTDA is robust to the effect of exposure bias and thus can provide a helpful tool to predict novel TDAs, especially for those proteins with less information.

3.4. *CreaTDA is able to predict novel TDAs with literature support*

To show that CreaTDA can help scientists find reliable TDAs, we validated the top-200 novel predictions of CreaTDA by searching for literature support and presented several representative cases (see the complete list of the top-200 predictions in Supplementary Table 3).

3.4.1. *CreaTDA reveals potential targets with literature support*

Respiratory syncytial virus (RSV) is a major cause of severe lower respiratory tract illness in children, including bronchiolitis. CreaTDA predicted an association between bronchiolitis and the epidermal growth factor receptor (EGFR). Previous studies showed that EGFR interacts with the RSV 2-20 F protein in a strain-specific manner and is thus a potential target for RSV diseases,[7] which exactly supported our prediction result. We also extended to a general category of virus diseases as an example. CreaTDA predicted an association between virus diseases and vascular endothelial growth factor-A (VEGF-A, also known as VEGF), a principal pro-angiogenic factor. This association can also be supported by previous research,[1] which illustrated that viruses, e.g., the human papillomavirus[19] and herpes simplex virus-1[31] exploit cell signaling mechanisms to upregulate VEGF expression and thus benefit their pathogenesis. In addition, recent research on COVID-19 has shown that anti-VEGF medication may be a potential treatment for those critically ill patients.[25] These validation results showed that CreaTDA could successfully identify novel targets critically involved in specific diseases.

3.4.2. *CreaTDA provides new perspectives for understanding diseases*

CreaTDA predicted an association between the fragile X syndrome (FXS) and the glucocorticoid receptor gene NR3C1. This prediction can be supported by previous research, which showed that the G allele in the BclI polymorphism of NR3C1 has a protective effect among female individuals against FXS and is associated with altered patterns of the anxiety/fear network of the brain.[2] Hence, our prediction about NR3C1 may help understand the diverse clinical outcomes associated with FXS and thus inspire effective therapies for individuals with specific polymorphisms.

3.4.3. *CreaTDA discovers new biomarkers for disease studies*

CreaTDA detected an association between sleep apnea syndromes and the intercellular adhesion molecule 1 (ICAM-1). ICAM-1 has been known as a marker widely used in studies on obstructive sleep apnea syndrome (OSAS) to investigate inflammation.[3] In a previous study, scientists found that OSAS patients displayed a significant decrease in ICAM-1 level after nasal continuous positive airway pressure (nCPAP) therapy, suggesting that OSAS-induced hypoxia activates ICAM-1.[21] CreaTDA also predicted an association between retinopathy of prematurity (ROP) and myeloperoxidase (MPO). This finding was consistent with a previous result that MPO is one of the nine proteins with the potential to increase the ROP risk.[14] All these findings verified that CreaTDA could provide an effective tool to identify novel biomarkers useful in clinical studies.

4. Conclusion

In this paper, we presented CreaTDA, an end-to-end deep learning-based framework to predict novel TDAs. CreaTDA first learns the node embeddings that encode features of the network topology and then reconstructs the modified biological networks with the encoded credibility information of TDAs. We showed that compared with state-of-the-art baseline methods, CreaTDA achieved superior performance on both the standard TDA prediction task and a more challenging task with a low similarity between training and test data. Moreover, comprehensive tests demonstrated that CreaTDA could predict novel TDAs with improved credibility and more literature support. In addition, we discovered that CreaTDA was robust to the effect of exposure bias and maintained decent performance for those entities with less information. All these results suggest CreaTDA can provide a powerful and helpful tool to advance the drug discovery process.

Acknowledgements

This work was supported in part by the National Key Research and Development Program of China (2021YFF1201300), the National Natural Science Foundation of China (61872216, T2125007 to JZ, 31900862 to DZ), the Turing AI Institute of Nanjing, the Tsinghua-Toyota Joint Research Fund, the Senior and Junior Technological Innovation Team (20210509055RQ), and the Jilin Provincial Key Laboratory of Big Data Intelligent Computing (20180622002JC). The authors thank Dr. Fangping Wan for helpful discussions.

Availablility

The source code, data, and supplementary information of this study can be accessed at `https://github.com/Dr-Patient/CreaTDA`.

References

1. Alkharsah KR. Vegf upregulation in viral infections and its possible therapeutic implications. *International journal of molecular sciences*, 19(6):1642, 2018.
2. Bruno JL, et al. Glucocorticoid regulation and neuroanatomy in fragile x syndrome. *Journal of Psychiatric Research*, 134:81, 2021.
3. Carpagnano GE, et al. Systemic and airway inflammation in sleep apnea and obesity: the role of icam-1 and il-8. *Translational Research*, 155(1):35, 2010.
4. Chen H, et al. Modeling relational drug-target-disease interactions via tensor factorization with multiple web sources. In *The World Wide Web Conference*, 218–227. 2019.
5. —. Learning data-driven drug-target-disease interaction via neural tensor network. In *International Joint Conference on Artificial Intelligence (IJCAI)*. 2020.
6. Chen J, et al. Bias and debias in recommender system: A survey and future directions. *arXiv preprint arXiv:201003240*, 2020.
7. Currier MG, et al. Egfr interacts with the fusion protein of respiratory syncytial virus strain 2-20 and mediates infection and mucin expression. *PLoS pathogens*, 12(5):e1005622, 2016.
8. Davis AP, et al. The comparative toxicogenomics database: update 2017. *Nucleic acids research*, 45(D1):D972, 2017.
9. Davis J, et al. The relationship between precision-recall and roc curves. In *Proceedings of the 23rd international conference on Machine learning*, 233–240. 2006.

10. Defferrard M, et al. Convolutional neural networks on graphs with fast localized spectral filtering. *Advances in neural information processing systems*, 29, 2016.
11. Failli M, et al. Prioritizing target-disease associations with novel safety and efficacy scoring methods. *Scientific reports*, 9(1):1, 2019.
12. Ferrero E, et al. In silico prediction of novel therapeutic targets using gene–disease association data. *Journal of translational medicine*, 15(1):1, 2017.
13. Hamilton W, et al. Inductive representation learning on large graphs. *Advances in neural information processing systems*, 30, 2017.
14. Holm M, et al. Systemic inflammation-associated proteins and retinopathy of prematurity in infants born before the 28th week of gestation. *Investigative ophthalmology & visual science*, 58(14):6419, 2017.
15. Hu Z, et al. Heterogeneous graph transformer. In *Proceedings of The Web Conference 2020*, 2704–2710. 2020.
16. Keshava Prasad T, et al. Human protein reference database—2009 update. *Nucleic acids research*, 37(suppl_1):D767, 2009.
17. Knox C, et al. Drugbank 3.0: a comprehensive resource for 'omics' research on drugs. *Nucleic acids research*, 39(suppl_1):D1035, 2010.
18. Kuhn M, et al. A side effect resource to capture phenotypic effects of drugs. *Molecular systems biology*, 6(1):343, 2010.
19. Li G, et al. Overexpression of human papillomavirus (hpv) type 16 oncoproteins promotes angiogenesis via enhancing hif-1α and vegf expression in non-small cell lung cancer cells. *Cancer letters*, 311(2):160, 2011.
20. Luo Y, et al. A network integration approach for drug-target interaction prediction and computational drug repositioning from heterogeneous information. *Nature communications*, 8(1):1, 2017.
21. Ohga E, et al. Effects of obstructive sleep apnea on circulating icam-1, il-8, and mcp-1. *Journal of applied physiology*, 94(1):179, 2003.
22. Pedregosa F, et al. Scikit-learn: Machine learning in Python. *Journal of Machine Learning Research*, 12:2825, 2011.
23. Roberts RJ. Pubmed central: The genbank of the published literature, 2001.
24. Rogers D, et al. Extended-connectivity fingerprints. *Journal of chemical information and modeling*, 50(5):742, 2010.
25. Sahebnasagh A, et al. Anti-vegf agents: As appealing targets in the setting of covid-19 treatment in critically ill patients. *International Immunopharmacology*, 101:108257, 2021.
26. Saito T, et al. The precision-recall plot is more informative than the roc plot when evaluating binary classifiers on imbalanced datasets. *PloS one*, 10(3):e0118432, 2015.
27. Schlander M, et al. How much does it cost to research and develop a new drug? a systematic review and assessment. *PharmacoEconomics*, 39(11):1243, 2021.
28. Schlichtkrull M, et al. Modeling relational data with graph convolutional networks. In *European semantic web conference*, 593–607. Springer, 2018.
29. Smith TF, et al. Identification of common molecular subsequences. *Journal of molecular biology*, 147(1):195, 1981.
30. Wan F, et al. Neodti: neural integration of neighbor information from a heterogeneous network for discovering new drug–target interactions. *Bioinformatics*, 35(1):104, 2019.
31. Wuest TR, et al. Vegf-a expression by hsv-1–infected cells drives corneal lymphangiogenesis. *Journal of Experimental Medicine*, 207(1):101, 2010.
32. Yun S, et al. Graph transformer networks. *Advances in neural information processing systems*, 32, 2019.

Pacific Symposium on Biocomputing 2023

Integrated Graph Propagation and Optimization with Biological Applications

Krithika Krishnan[1], Tiange Shi[2]
[1]*Institute of Artificial Intelligence and Data Science*
[2]*Department of Biostatistics*
University at Buffalo
Buffalo, NY 14214, USA

Han Yu[3]
Department of Biostatistics and Bioinformatics
Roswell Park Comprehensive Cancer Center
Buffalo, NY 14263, USA

Rachael Hageman Blair[1,2,*]
**Corresponding Author*
[1]*Institute of Artificial Intelligence and Data Science*
[2]*Department of Biostatistics*
University at Buffalo
Buffalo, NY 14224, USA
E-mail: hageman@buffalo.edu

Mathematical models that utilize network representations have proven to be valuable tools for investigating biological systems. Often dynamic models are not feasible due to their complex functional forms that rely on unknown rate parameters. Network propagation has been shown to accurately capture the sensitivity of nodes to changes in other nodes; without the need for dynamic systems and parameter estimation. Node sensitivity measures rely solely on network structure and encode a sensitivity matrix that serves as a good approximation to the Jacobian matrix. The use of a propagation-based sensitivity matrix as a Jacobian has important implications for network optimization. This work develops Integrated Graph Propagation and OptimizatioN (IGPON), which aims to identify optimal perturbation patterns that can drive networks to desired target states. IGPON embeds propagation into an objective function that aims to minimize the distance between a current observed state and a target state. Optimization is performed using Broyden's method with the propagation-based sensitivity matrix as the Jacobian. IGPON is applied to simulated random networks, DREAM4 *in silico* networks, and over-represented pathways from STAT6 knockout data and YBX1 knockdown data. Results demonstrate that IGPON is an effective way to optimize directed and undirected networks that are robust to uncertainty in the network structure.

Keywords: Network, propagation, optimization, Broyden's method, iterative methods

1. Introduction

Network analysis remains a cornerstone of systems biology that has been widely used to examine gene regulation, protein-protein interaction and metabolic systems. Mathematical representations of biological systems often depend on complex nonlinear functions that are not fully understood and lack the dynamic data to fully parameterize. These systems can be examined at steady-state, which reduces the model to a linear system. In applications, a common objective is the inference of a network structure that captures the complex biological relationship between variables. Although structure provides insights into the direct and indirect relationships in a network, it represents a premature endpoint in an analysis.

Network propagation describes the process of absorbing information into a network and propagating it through the network to update node states. Propagation can be used to initiate information flow through a graph, and thus has the potential for prediction. In the field of systems biology, this can be viewed as an *in silico* experiment within a biological network. Although propagation has been broadly used in other fields, applications in systems biology are limited. The PRIoritizatioN and Complex Elucidation (PRINCE) algorithm[1] was one of the first studies to associate network modules with disease through network propagation. The PRINCE algorithm has been used to connect nodes in a graph representing biological variables, such as proteins or genes, with disease.[1] The iterative procedure generates prioritization scores for vertices related to various diseases of interest obtained through graph propagation.

Recently, DYNamics-Agnostic Network MOdels (DYNAMO)[2] was developed to connect the ideas of propagation to the problem of characterizing perturbation patterns in a biological system. The major finding was that a sensitivity matrix derived from propagation solely on the structure of the network effectively captured the Jacobian matrix of partial derivatives for biological systems. In other words, the sensitivity matrix captures the effects of small perturbations on individual nodes in the network. In most biological applications and databases, only the network structure is known, without analytical forms of the biochemical reactions or kinetic rate parameters. Thus, in practice, the Jacobian is difficult or impossible to obtain. The performance of DYNAMO was benchmarked on a database of 120 BioModels representing different biochemical networks and model organisms. Propagation also outperformed alternative approximations based on network measures such as distance and neighborhoods.

The ability to estimate a sensitivity matrix from propagation on the structure has important implications for network optimization, which to the authors' knowledge has not been explored. Coupling network optimization with a sensitivity matrix enables the identification of optimal perturbations that will drive a system to the desired state, providing insight into Biological Engineering and identifying optimal targets for drug therapy and interventions. This work develops the first optimization framework that leverages the sensitivity matrix to identify optimal perturbation patterns to drive a network to a target steady-state. A novel approach, Integrated Graph Propagation and OptimizatioN (IGPON), is developed, which casts the problem as an unconstrained optimization that minimizes the difference between a current network state and a desired target network state.

A distinguishing feature of this method is that the optimization relies on using two primary ingredients: a parameterized network structure and target node states. Thus, IGPON bypasses the need for complex forms of biochemical reactions and derivatives. In contrast, node states are defined iteratively through the PRINCE algorithm.[1] Optimization utilizes Broyden's method,[3] a quasi-Newton method that does not require functional forms of the objective function. It leverages a network-derived sensitivity matrix to represent the Jacobian. The output of IGPON is the prediction of an optimal perturbation that will drive the network to the desired state. IGPON is applied to simulated networks, DREAM4[4] *in silico* networks and over-represented pathways from STAT6 knockdown data and YBX1 knockdown data[5]. Results demonstrate IGPON as an effective way to optimize directed and undirected networks that are also robust to noise in the sensitivity matrix that reflects potential misspecification in the structure.

2. Methods

2.1. *Graph propagation*

A network (graph), G, is defined by a set of nodes (vertices), V, and edges, E, that connect them. Mathematically, undirected graphs can be represented by a symmetric binary adjacency matrix with entries $g_{i,j} = 1$ when there is an edge between vertices v_i and v_j. Directed graphs are binary matrices with $g_{i,j} = 1$ if there is a directed edge between v_i and v_j. This work utilizes propagation through graphs using the PRINCE algorithm,[2] which is used to obtain influence scores for each node.

Let, $F^t \in \mathbb{R}^n$, be the updated vector of n node scores at iteration t. Let $D \in \mathbb{R}^{n\times n}$ be a diagonal matrix with entries, $d(i,i)$, that correspond to the sum of the absolute values of the ith row of G. The normalized propagation weights are given as $G' = D^{-1/2}GD^{-1/2}$. The influence score at iteration t is given as $F^t := \alpha G' F^{t-1} + (1-\alpha)\cdot Y$, where α is a diffusion constant that score enforces smoothness over the network, and Y is an initial set of scores, F^0. We define the sensitivity matrix, $S \in \mathbb{R}^{n\times n}$, which captures a node's influence on other nodes in the network. The rows of the sensitivity matrix are computed by systematically setting each node to 1, and the other nodes to 0, and propagating through the network. Notably, this iterative approach to estimating the sensitivity matrix through propagation has been shown to converge to the closed form.[6] However, it has the added advantage of scalability to large networks. Whereas the closed form sensitivity calculation requires large matrix inversions, which can be infeasible or unstable.[2]

2.2. *Unconstrained optimization*

We define $F(x)$ as a system of m non-linear algebraic equations, $\{f_1(x), f_2(x), \ldots, f_m(x)\}$, in n variables, $x = \{x_1, x_2, \ldots x_n\}$. The objective is to solve the linear system: $F(x) = Ax - b = 0$, where A is the Jacobian matrix of $F(x)$. Broyden's method is an iterative quasi-Newton method for solving a nonlinear equation that can be used as an alternative to Newton's method when the Jacobian is expensive to compute, or unavailable.[3,7] In our case, quasi-Newton methods are required because both the Jacobian and the functional form of the system of nonlinear equations are not known. In contrast to a graph modeled by a well-defined system of nonlinear equations, our system is defined through graph structure and propagation. Let the initial Jacobian, $A_0 \in \mathbb{R}^{n\times n}$, be defined as the sensitivity matrix defined in Section 2.1. Let A_k be the Jacobian approximation at iteration k and let $s_k = x_{k+1} - x_k$. Then, the updated Jacobian approximation A_{k+1} must satisfy the secant equation: $A_{k+1}s_k = F(x_{k+1}) - F(x_k)$. Broyden's method generates subsequent matrices using the update formula:[3]

$$A_{k+1} = A_k + \frac{(y_k - A_k s_k)s_k^T}{s_k{}^T s_k},$$

where $y_k = F(x_{k+1}) - F(x_k)$. Broyden's method is described in Algorithm 2.2.

Initialize: $F : \mathbb{R}^n \to \mathbb{R}^n, x_0 \in \mathbb{R}^n, A_0 \in \mathbb{R}^{n \times n}$
for $k = 1, 2, \ldots \max$ **do**
  Solve $A_k s_k = -F(x_k)$ for s_k
  $x_{k+1} := x_k + s_k$
  $y_k := F(x_{k+1}) - F(x_k)$
  $A_{k+1} := A_k + \frac{(y_k - A_k s_k)s_k^T}{s_k{}^T s_k}$
end for
Output: x_k

2.3. *Integrated Graph Propagation and Optimization*

Integrated Graph Propagation and OptimizatioN (IGPON) is our approach to integrating propagation (Section 2.1) into optimization (Section 2.2) for the purpose of driving a graph to an optimal target state. A schematic describing IGPON is shown in Figure 1 for a simple ten node graph. The network structure, G, can be directed or undirected and contains n nodes. The structure is assumed to be known *a priori* as either inferred from data or specified by an expert or database (Figure 1A). We define the propagation function, $\Phi(\cdot)$, as the iterative PRINCE algorithm. The sensitivity matrix[2] plays the role of the initial Jacobian, A_0, and is estimated directly using graph propagation, $\Phi(G)$, as described in Section 2.1 (Figure 1B). Let $F^0 \in \mathbf{R}^{n\times 1}$ denote an observed network that we want to drive to a target state, $F^T \in \mathbf{R}^{n\times 1}$. The observed steady-state of the nodes F^0 is assumed to result from the propagation of an unobserved underlying state, x^0, through the network (Figure 1C). Our objective is to identify the underlying perturbation to this initial state, $F^0 + \Delta = x^T$, such that $\Phi\left(F^0 + \Delta\right) = \Phi\left(x^T\right) = F^T$ (Figure 1C). The unconstrained minimization problem is defined as:

$$\min_x \|\Phi(x) - F^T\|_2.$$

This objective can be embedded into an unconstrained optimization problem and solved with Broyden's method (Algorithm 1). However, in this setting, the objective function is not defined in functional form, but rather defines a set of states approximated at every iteration through propagation. Specifically, we define the state of the network through $\Phi(x) = F$. The details of IGPON are outlined in Algorithm 1.

2.4. *Applications to simulations and biological pathways*

Simulation: IGPON was applied to both simulated random graphs and data from the DREAM4 *in silico* challenge.[4] Random graphs were generated with 50 and 150 nodes us-

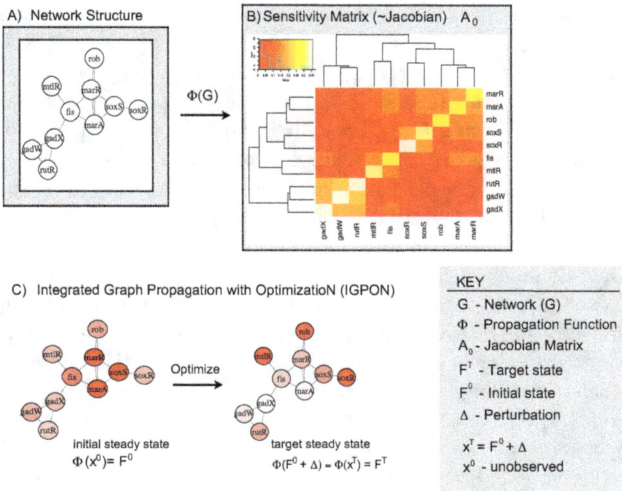

Fig. 1. A schematic of the integrated graph propagation and optimization with biological applications (IGPON) method. **(A)** The structure of the network (graph), G, is assumed to be given. **(B)** The sensitivity matrix derived through graph propagation, $\Phi(G)$, on the network structure, serves as the initial Jacobian, A_0. **(C)** IGPON drives an observed initial steady-state of the network, F^0, to a target steady-state, F^T, through the identification of an optimal perturbation, Δ, such that $\Phi(F^0 + \Delta) = F^T$.

Algorithm 1 Integrated Graph Propagation and Optimization (IGPON)

Initialize: $A_0 \in \mathbb{R}^{n\times n}, x_0 = F^0 \in \mathbb{R}^n, F^T \in \mathbb{R}^n$
for $k = 1, 2, \ldots \max$ **do**
  Solve $A_k s_k = -\Phi(x_k)$ for s_k
  $x_{k+1} := x_k + s_k$
  Propagate $F_{k+1} = \Phi(x_{k+1})$
  $y_k := F_{k+1} - F_k$
  $A_{k+1} := A_k + \frac{(y_k - A_k s_k)s_k^T}{{s_k}^T s_k}$
end for
Output: $\hat{x}^T = x_k$, $\hat{F}^T = F_k$

ing the Barabasi-Albert model[8] implemented in the `igraph` package.[9] The probability of an edge between two arbitrary vertices was set at $p = 0.10$. The DREAM4 data are derived from biological networks and are used as a benchmark in the community.[4] DREAM networks that are 10 nodes and 98 nodes were considered. The 98 node graph was derived from the DREAM4 100 node graph after the removal of two unconnected nodes.

The experimental setup was identical for simulated random graphs and the DREAM4 networks. For each graph, the values of target variable were drawn from a uniform distribution

$x^T \sim \mathbf{U}[0,1]$. This variable was propagated through the graph to obtain the target state, $\Phi(x^T) = F^T$. The values x^T and F^T are what we are seeking to estimate using IGPON (Figure 1). Initial estimates of the sensitivity matrix, A_0, were obtained as described in Section 2.1. A random initialization was generated, $x_0 \sim \mathbf{U}[0,1]$, and propagated to obtain $\Phi(x_0) = F_0$. IGPON was applied until convergence $||F^T - \hat{F}_k||_2 < 10^{-6}$ and $||x^T - \hat{x}_k||_2 < 10^{-6}$. Convergence of individual nodes, x_i, was also assessed using relative error: $F_{err}(i) = \frac{|F^T(i) - F_k(i)|}{F^T(i)}$. In order to examine how robust IGPON is to misspecification in the network structure, we systematically added white noise (10% – 50%) to the initial sensitivity matrix. A total of 100 graphs were generated for each experimental condition.

Biological Pathways: Gene expression data was utilized from the knockTF database for two different sets of experimental conditions.[5] Knockout data for transcription factor signal transducer and activator of transcription 6 (STAT6) was extracted from the database.[10] The knockout was reported to significantly alter pathways related to IL4/interleukin-4- and IL3/interleukin-3-mediated signaling, and apoptotic activity. The gene expression data contained wild-type controls ($N = 27$) and STAT6 knockout ($N = 27$).[10] The mean gene expression data used in this study was taken from the Gene Expression Omnibus[10,11] accession GSE17851, and our focus was the downstream IL-17 signaling pathway in KEGG,[12] which was reported as significant in the pathway enrichment analysis. Data related to the pro-oncogenic transcription factor YBX1 was also extracted from the database. Briefly, YBX1 is an RNA-binding protein involved in many important signaling pathways and associated with the occurrence and development of numerous cancers. Our focus was restricted to the Hedgehog (HH) pathway and P53 pathway from the KEGG database,[12] which were two downstream pathways over-represented in pathway enrichment analysis reported in the database. The HH signaling pathway is shown to be closely related to the development of tumor cells.[13] The P53 signaling pathway plays an important role in tumor suppression.[14] The data included several different breast cancer cell lines with both normal cell types ($N = 24$) and YBX1 knockdown ($N = 24$).[15]

KEGG identifiers from these pathways were mapped to the data and KEGGgraph[16] was used to construct the graphs in the R programming environment. The nodes that were unconnected were eliminated. The HH pathway contained 52 genes and 162 edges, the P53 signaling pathway contained 62 edges and 75 edges and the IL-17 pathway contained 53 genes and 147 edges. These subgraphs were used in connection with the IGPON algorithm. Both directed and undirected versions of the graph were utilized. The undirected graphs were derived using igraph[9] conversion tools.

Each of the subgraphs was parameterized with the gene expression data to create two graphs with the same structure, one for the treated (knockout/ knockdown), and one for the controls. The objective was to use the IGPON algorithm to drive the states of the graph, F^0, to the states of the target graph, F^T. Without loss of generality, we assume the target graph states correspond to the knockout or knockdown data, and the initially observed graph is parameterized by the controls. Note that the selection of initial and target was arbitrary and either set of states could play the role of the target. Sets of minimum driver node set (MDS)[17] were also estimated from the graph structures as one of the following; critical (if that node must always be controlled to control the system), redundant (never required for control), or ntermittent (if it is a driver node in some control configurations, but not in others).

3. Results

IGPON was tested on simulations of random graphs, DREAM4 networks[4] and using data from a knockout database.[5] In each simulation, the objective was to use IGPON to drive the network to a target state. The number of iterations for the optimization varied according to graph size, noise and complexity, but the number of iterations needed for the network propagation required for the objective function was kept constant at 500, which was sufficient for all cases considered. Overall, the results were found to be rather insensitive to the parameter α, which controls the relative importance of prior information in the graph, which supports previous findings.[1]

In the simulations of scale-free graphs and the DREAM4 networks, IGPON was able to drive all simulations to their target states (Figure 2). Note that since, $\hat{F}^T = \Phi(\hat{x}^T) = \Phi(F^0+\hat{\Delta})$, we expect these error profiles to be correlated, which indeed they are for all simulations. IGPON was also observed to be robust to up to 50% noise in the initial Jacobian (Figure 2). With no noise applied to the Jacobian, the graphs converge within only a few iterations (Figure 2 A-D) in Figure 2. On the other hand, as the percentage of white noise is increased from 10%, 25% to 50%, the iterations needed to bring the graph to the target state naturally increases. In addition to noise levels, convergence is also clearly a function of graph size (Figure 2). For example, nearly three times the number of iterations are needed to push a larger graph, such as the simulated $N = 150$ nodes, to its target state when the noise level was increased from 25% (Figure 2H) to 50% (Figure 2L).

Individual node convergence profiles were also examined. Figure 3 shows the relative difference between the target for a node $F^T(i)$ and its estimated state $\hat{F}^T(i)$ for our simulation with 50 nodes. The random initialization is relatively close to the target state by nature of the parameters used for the uniform distribution (Figure 3A). However, as IGPON proceeds, the nodes move further away from their targets (Figure 3B). Some nodes more actively move around and take longer to settle (Figure 3B-D). In fact, many nodes begin to converge to their target (Figure 3C) before again moving further away from the target (Figure 3D), and finally converging (Figure 3B-D). This demonstrates the push and pull of node state values gained through the propagation that are ultimately required to drive the graph to the target. There does not appear to be any clear association between the node trends and graph properties such as degree, and clustering coefficients (data not shown). Similar patterns and trends were observed for graphs of various sizes in the simulations.

IGPON was also used to drive expression profiles to targets in the HH, IL-17, and p53 pathways. In both directed and undirected representations, convergence was achieved across all noise levels (Table 1). As noise levels increased, more iterations were required to achieve convergence. It is also clear that the directed graphs achieve faster convergence across the board. Upon further investigation, there are substantial differences in the MDS node characterizations[17] in the directed and undirected representations. In the IL-17 directed pathway, 18 of the nodes were identified as critical, 10 were intermittent, and the remaining were redundant. In the undirected representation of the IL-17 pathway, only two nodes were identified

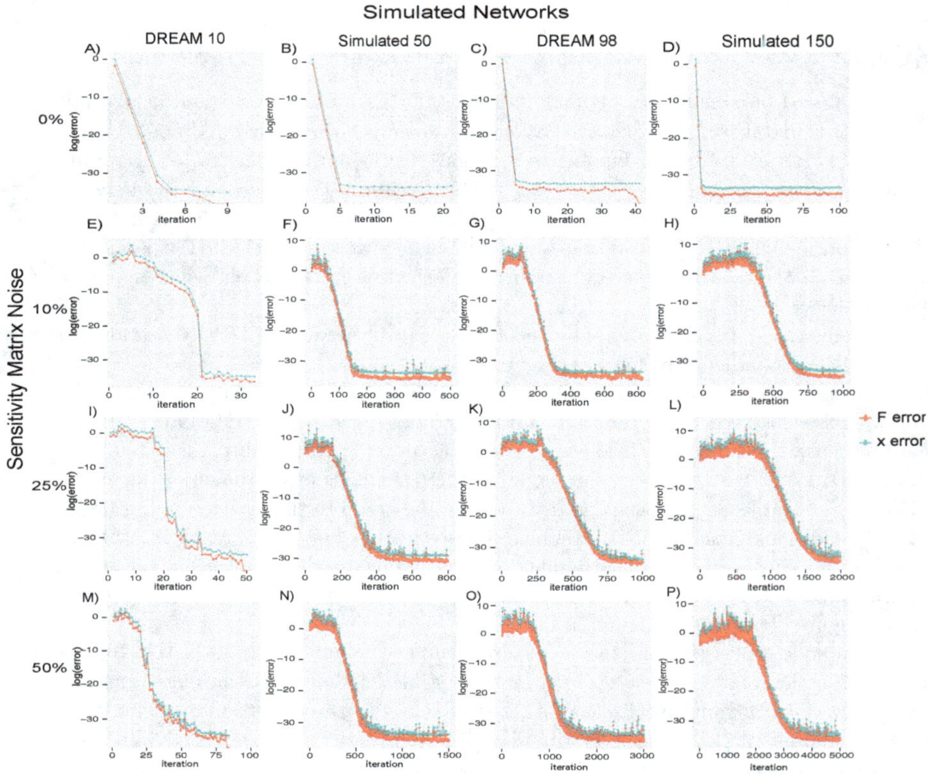

Fig. 2. Convergence profiles of the log(error) for F (coral) and x (blue). Simulated graphs are ordered according to size (columns): columns 1 ($N = 10$), column 2 ($N = 50$), column 3 ($N = 98$), and column 4 ($N = 150$). The rows represent the noise level added to the sensitivity matrix in the optimization. **(A-D)** No noise is added **(E-H)** 10%, **(I-L)** 25% and **(M-P)** 50%.

as critical, 31 were intermittent, and the remaining were redundant. This trend was observed for the other two pathways as well. In the HH pathway, in the directed representation 10 of the nodes were identified as critical (1 in the undirected) and 12 were intermittent (19 in the undirected). In the P53 pathway, in the directed representation 10 of the nodes were identified as critical (3 in the undirected) and 6 were intermittent (13 in the undirected). Taken together, there is a migration of nodes from critical to intermittent classifications when moving from directed to undirected representations. This may also influence the slower convergence observed in the undirected representations. These observations regarding the diffuse structure and weaker control in the undirected graphs are further supported by an examination of the

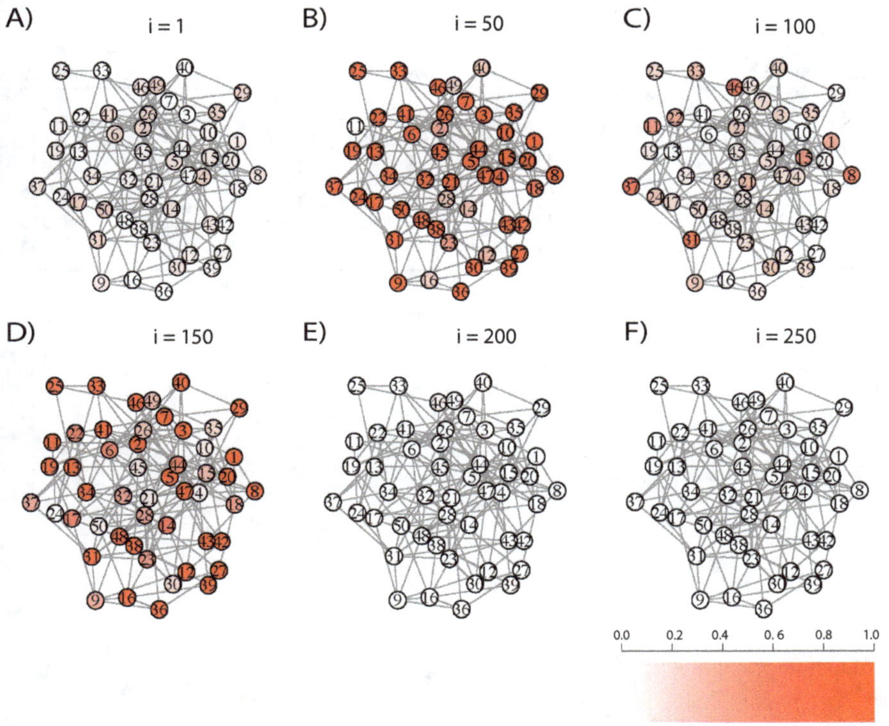

Fig. 3. Node convergence profiles for the simulated 50 network with 25% noise added to the Jacobian at select IGPON iterations k. The coloring of a node i corresponds to the relative error, $\frac{|F^T - F_k(i)|}{F^T}$ at iteration **(A)** $k = 1$, **(B)** $k = 50$, **(C)** $k = 100$, **(D)** $k = 150$, **(E)** $k = 200$ and **(F)** $k = 250$.

sensitivity matrices. Overall, sensitivity matrices for the undirected graphs were found to be of lower magnitude and exhibit weaker co-regulation patterns. In contrast, the sensitivity matrices for the directed graphs had a larger range of magnitudes and patterns of co-regulation. Sensitivity matrices for the IL-17 pathway directed and undirected representations are shown in Figure 4. The HH and p53 exhibited similar trends (data not shown).

4. Discussion

IGPON embeds propagation into an optimization that can be used to drive an undirected/ a directed graph to a desired steady-state. To the authors knowledge, this is the first approach of this type that aims to drive a network to the desired state by optimizing node perturbations. This novel approach harnesses connectivity patterns in the graph, and information propagation through the graph to guide the optimization. We demonstrate this approach to be successful in

Table1: Convergence of Biological Pathways to Target States

Pathway Name	KEGG Identifier	Nodes (genes) × Edges	Graph Type	Number of iterations			
				0% noise	10% noise	25% noise	50% noise
HH	04340	52 × 162	Directed	2	69	154	278
			Undirected	2	85	178	338
IL-17	04657	53 × 147	Directed	2	72	162	335
			Undirected	2	87	202	388
p53	04115	62 × 75	Directed	2	79	199	383
			Undirected	2	90	230	390

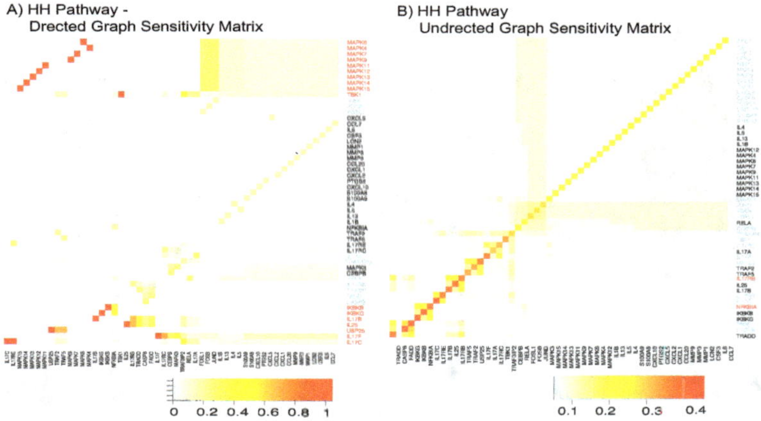

Fig. 4. Sensitivity matrices for the IL-17 pathway (**A**) directed and (**B**) undirected representations. The matrices are clustered to show patterns of co-regulation. Critical nodes (red), intermittent (blue) and redundant nods are indicated by text color.

real and simulated networks with different sizes, different architectures, and with knockdown and knockout data. IGPON is able to drive both directed and undirected graphs with up to a 0.5 signal-to-noise ratio that expresses the uncertainty in the structure of the network.

In the area of biological networks, examples of analysis of steady-state biological systems often center on flux estimation methods.[18] In these methods, the objective is flux rate estimation through the optimization of an objective function subject to physiological constraints. Flux rates are represented as the edges in the graph, which depict biochemical reaction rates or biochemical species uptake and release. IGPON can also be viewed as an optimization of a steady-state model. However, in contrast with flux analysis, the quantity of interest are the node values, not the flux rates.

This approach has many strengths. IGPON works with an assumed graph structure, but makes no parametric assumptions, and does not require parameter inference. Our experiments examine the addition of noise to the sensitivity matrix to demonstrate the robustness of our approach to structural uncertainty and misspecification in the edges. Even in severe cases, with noise levels as high as 50%, IGPON converged to the target state. This notion of misspecification is an important one because in many applications, e.g., in the biological or social sciences, the network structure may not be known exactly, or is assumed to have some structural uncertainty. A future direction of this work will be to extend this algorithm to address problems with structural uncertainty through summarizations over ensembles of graphs. There are also some limitations to our approach. The unconstrained optimization occurs over the full set of nodes in the network. However, it may not be desirable, or even feasible to fully perturb the entire network. A future direction of this work will be to couple IGPON with a feature selection method. Extensions of IGPON into a constrained optimization framework would enable feature selection and enable the use of bounds to enforce feasible values of nodes. This extension will broaden the applications of this approach to drug discovery and intervention predictions.

The Jacobian of a biological system conveys the sensitivity of individual nodes (e.g., biochemical species) to changes in parameters. However, when the functional form of the system is unknown, the specification of the Jacobian is not possible. This work builds from an important result from Santolini *et al.*,[2] which shows that the sensitivity matrix obtained through systematic propagation within the network is a good approximation of the true Jacobian of the underlying system. Although the Jacobian is updated at every iteration, the updated sensitivity matrix in Broyden's method was not considered an output of interest, although also found to converge. Results suggest that both propagation through the structure and the sensitivity matrix provide good approximations to the functional form of the system and its partial derivatives, respectively. Taken together, we conclude that optimization frameworks can be effectively bridged with propagation methodologies.

Network propagation is also used in connection with Probabilistic Graphical Models (PGMs).[19] In the PGM setting, evidence is incorporated into the graph and propagated through derived clique graphs to make queries of interest regarding changes in joint, conditional, and marginal probabilities. There are fundamental differences between PGM propagation[19] and the propagation described in PRINCE.[1] PGMs require parametric assumptions and parameter learning, whereas PRINCE relies on network structure only, but cannot be interpreted probabilistically. Moreover, in PGMs exact probabilistic reasoning can only be performed in directed acyclic graphs known as Bayesian Networks. PGMs that are directed or undirected graphs with cycles are not guaranteed to converge to exact posterior probabilities, making reasoning with them challenging. On the other hand, PRINCE can work with both directed and undirected network structures, with no restriction on cycles.

In conclusion, the use of graph structure and the integrated propagation to optimize has enabled us to drive any graph from an initial steady-state to another. IGPON works directly with a network structure and does not rely on any complex parameterizations. Predicting optimal perturbations to drive biological systems to a desired state is a promising area of research in biological and genetic engineering. This approach is implemented in the `igpon` package on GitHub and will be made available on CRAN upon publication.

References

1. O. Vanunu, O. Magger, E. Ruppin, T. Shlomi and R. Sharan, Associating genes and protein complexes with disease via network propagation, *PLoS Computational Biology* **6**, p. e1000641 (January 2010).
2. M. Santolini and A.-L. Barabási, Predicting perturbation patterns from the topology of biological networks, *Proceedings of the National Academy of Sciences* **115**, E6375 (2018).
3. C. G. Broyden, A class of methods for solving nonlinear simultaneous equations, *Mathematics of Computation* **19**, 577 (1965).
4. D. Marbach, T. Schaffter, C. Mattiussi and D. Floreano, Generating realistic in silico gene networks for performance assessment of reverse engineering methods, *Journal of Computational Biology* **16**, 229 (2009).
5. C. Feng, C. Song, Y. Liu, F. Qian, Y. Gao, Z. Ning, Q. Wang, Y. Jiang, Y. Li, M. Li, J. Chen, J. Zhang and C. Li, KnockTF: a comprehensive human gene expression profile database with knockdown/knockout of transcription factors, *Nucleic Acids Research* **48**, D93 (2020).
6. D. Zhou, O. Bousquet, T. N. Lal, J. Weston and B. Schölkopf, Learning with local and global consistency, in *Advances in Neural Information Processing Systems*, 2004.
7. J. E. Dennis Jr and R. B. Schnabel, *Numerical Methods for Unconstrained Optimization and Nonlinear Equations* (SIAM, 1996).
8. A.-L. Barabási and R. Albert, Emergence of scaling in random networks, *science* **286**, 509 (1999).
9. G. Csardi and T. Nepusz, The igraph software package for complex network research, *InterJournal, Complex Systems* **5**, p. 1695 (2006).
10. L. L. Elo, H. Järvenpää, S. Tuomela, S. Raghav, H. Ahlfors, K. Laurila, B. Gupta, R. J. Lund, J. Tahvanainen, R. D. Hawkins, M. Oresic, H. Lähdesmäki, O. Rasool, K. V. Rao, T. Aittokallio and R. Lahesmaa, Genome-wide profiling of interleukin-4 and STAT6 transcription factor regulation of human Th2 cell programming, *Immunity* **32**, 852 (2010).
11. E. Clough and T. Barrett, The gene expression omnibus database, in *Statistical Genomics*, (Springer, 2016) pp. 93–110.
12. M. Kanehisa and S. Goto, KEGG: Kyoto encyclopedia of genes and genomes, *Nucleic Acids Research* **28**, 27 (2000).
13. M. Evangelista, H. Tian and F. J. de Sauvage, The Hedgehog signaling pathway in cancer, *Clinical Cancer Research* **12**, 5924 (2006).
14. S. L. Harris and A. J. Levine, The p53 pathway: positive and negative feedback loops, *Oncogene* **24**, 2899 (2005).
15. H. Goodarzi, X. Liu, H. C. Nguyen, S. Zhang, L. Fish and S. F. Tavazoie, Endogenous tRNA-derived fragments suppress breast cancer progression via YBX1 displacement, *Cell* **161**, 790 (2015).
16. J. D. Zhang and S. Wiemann, KEGGgraph: a graph approach to KEGG pathyways in R and bioconductor, *Bioinformatics* **25**, 1470 (2009).
17. T. Jia and A.-L. Barabási, Control capacity and a random sampling method in exploring controlability of complex networks, *Scientific reports* **3**, p. 2354 (2013).
18. J. D. Orth, I. Thiele and B. Ø. Palsson, What is flux balance analysis?, *Nature Biotechnology* **28**, 245 (2010).
19. D. Koller and N. Friedman, *Probabilistic graphical models: principles and techniques* (The MIT Press, 2009).

Overcoming health disparities in precision medicine

Kathleen C. Barnes and Francisco M. De La Vega
Tempus Labs, Inc.
Chicago, IL 60654, USA
Email: kathleen.barnes@tempus.com; francisco.delavega@tempus.com

Carlos D. Bustamante
Galatea Bio, Inc.
Miami, FL, USA
Email: carlos.bustamante@galatea.bio

Chris R. Gignoux
University of Colorado Anschutz Medical Campus
Boulder, CO, USA
Email: hris.gignoux@cuanschutz.edu

Eimear Kenny
Ichan School of Medicine at Mount Sinai
New York, NY, USA
Email: eimear.kenny@mssm.edu

Rasika A. Mathias
Johns Hopkins School of Medicine
Baltimore, MD, USA
Email: rmathias@jhmi.edu

Bogdan Pasaniuc
University of California Los Angeles.
Los Angeles, CA, USA
Email: niuc@ucla.edu

1. Overview

Precision medicine and precision public health rely on the premise that determinants of disease incidence and differences in response to interventions can be identified and their biology understood well enough that applications to reduce risk of disease and improve treatment can be developed. However, there are well-documented racial and ethnic disparities throughout health care at the patient, provider, and healthcare system levels. These disparities are driven by a complex interplay among social, psychosocial, lifestyle, environmental, health system, and biological determinants of health (Freedman, et al. 2021).

Inequities in genome-informed precision medicine are driven by a Eurocentric bias in genetic studies: the vast majority (86%) of genomics studies have been conducted in individuals of European descent. Eurocentric biases in genetics studies are not only inequitable, but also result in major missed scientific opportunities (Fatumo et al. 2022). As underrepresented minority populations within the United States grow to record numbers, and precision medicine is beginning to be deployed worldwide, it is increasingly important to invest in efforts to characterize, understand, and end racial and ethnic disparities in healthcare.

2. Equitable risk prediction

Despite the significant advances in disease risk prediction derived from the analysis of the large-scale data available in the UK Biobank, the underrepresentation of participants from minority and disadvantaged groups has limited the use of this data in the development of prediction models that can be generalized to diverse populations. The paper of Gu et al. (2023) proposes a transfer learning framework based on random forest models (TransRF) that can incorporate risk prediction models trained in a source population to improve the prediction performance in a target underrepresented population with limited sample size.

Polygenic risk scores (PRS) are numerical indicators of risk based on multiple genetic markers associated with a disease or trait and are derived from data from genome-wide association studies (GWAS). Research in this field has recently accelerated, and scores are available for a wide array of traits and conditions, including for conditions such as coronary artery disease, type 2 diabetes, and common cancers. However, research has shown that their performance is lower and somewhat unpredictable in non-European populations. In this volume, Machado Reyes et al. (2023) present a method called FairPRS, which is based on domain-adaptation problems in machine learning such as Invariant Risk Minimization (IRM) to obtain an ancestry-invariant PRS estimates from pre-computed PRS or GWAS summary statistics. FairPRS provides risk estimates with negligible effect of ancestral groups of the subjects, while increasing phenotype prediction accuracy, in both simulated and real data sets and showcases how machine learning methods can be applied to improve the portability of PRS.

Regarding disparities in outcome prediction, Chu et al. (2023) employ association rule mining, a technique that infers probabilistic implications from data in transactional databases, to identify the most significant risk categories for adverse pregnancy outcomes (APOs) in a dataset of over 10,000 nulliparous women, that is representative of the US population. Using this method, they find that the effects of age and body mass index have major yet differential effects on the risk of APOs and the observed racial/ethnic disparities. This work shows that association rule mining could be a powerful method to explore inequities in clinical datasets.

3. Pharmacoequity

While the growing body of pharmacogenomics research has significant potential for guiding treatment decisions, the persistent heterogeneity of observed treatment responses in many clinical situations suggests that additional genetic and other biologic factors may contribute to the success or failure of a given treatment approach in individuals of different racial and ethnic backgrounds. Pharmacogenomic studies have long neglected to collect data from African Americans, Hispanics/Latinos and other ethnicities, preventing an understanding of the role of ancestry in pharmacoequity. Yang et al. (2023) make some progress in this subject by analyzing the role of both global and local ancestry on measures of response to clopidogrel therapy in a cohort of 167 African American patients. They find that local ancestry at the transcription start site of three relevant genes as well as ancestry-adjusted association with variants in another gene help to explain the variability in drug response seen in African Americans.

The widespread availability of antiretroviral therapies (ART) for HIV-1 have generated considerable interest in understanding the pharmacogenomics of ART. In some individuals, ART has been associated with excessive weight gain, which disproportionately affects women of African ancestry. The paper of Keat et al. (2023) explored whether a multi-ancestry PRS for body mass index (BMI) can achieve high cross-ancestry performance for predicting baseline BMI in diverse, prospective ART clinical trials. They show that the BMI PRS explained ~5%-7% of variability in baseline BMI, with high performance in both European and African genetic ancestry groups, but that this score was not associated with the change in BMI on ART. This study thus argues against a shared genetic predisposition for baseline BMI and ART-associated weight gain.

4. Race, genetic ancestry, and population structure

A challenge in precision medicine is the continued use of "race"— a categorization based on common physical characteristics — and "ethnicity" — a categorization based on shared cultural traits — in medicine, which has become a matter of intense debate. A key element of genome-informed precision medicine is the accurate assessment and utilization of ancestry to understand its impact on disease susceptibility and the outcomes of therapies. Genomics can capture ancestry in a more precise way, allowing genetic influences to be teased apart from the impact of social and environmental factors. Understanding shared genetic ancestry and defining genetically related subpopulations can help us better understand disease susceptibilities and health disparities. Along this topic, the work of Chaichoompu et al. (2023) presents improvements in an unsupervised method, IPCAPS, to identify population substructure guided by genetic similarity. This method could be particularly useful for populations in geographically confined regions, where IPCAPS was shown to detect meaningful subgroups, which are otherwise hard to detect with classic methods such as PCA or ADMIXTURE. These subgroups can be carried downstream in population or disease association analysis instead of race/ethnicity and could prove useful in precision medicine.

5. Conclusion

The heightened impact of COVID-19 on medically underserved populations and enhanced focus on social justice issues has highlighted the need to better address health disparities in a meaningful way. New computational and statistical methods are needed to assess, counteract, and overcome health disparities in healthcare. While there is much more work to be done, we believe the work presented in this session showcases advances that will be helpful to the goal of overcoming health disparities in precision medicine.

Acknowledgments

We thank the anonymous reviewers that helped in the peer review process of the submissions to this session.

References

Chaichoompu K., Wilantho A., Wangkumhang P., TongsimaS., Cavadas B., Pereira L., and Kristel Van Steen (2023) Fine-scale subpopulation detection via SNP-based unsupervised method: A case study on the 1000 Genomes Project Resources. In. Pacific Symposium on Biocomputing 2023.

Chu H., Ramola R., Jain S., Haas D.M., Natarajan S., and Radivojac P. (2023) Using Association Rules to Understand the Risk of Adverse Pregnancy Outcomes in a Diverse Population. In. Pacific Symposium on Biocomputing 2023.

Fatumo S., Chikowore T., Choudhury A., Ayub M., Martin A.R., Kuchenbaecker K. (2022) A roadmap to increase diversity in genomic studies. Nat Med. 2022 Feb;28(2):243-250.

Freedman J.A., Abo M.A., Allen T.A., Piwarski S.A., Wegermann K., and Patierno S.R. (2021) Biological Aspects of Cancer Health Disparities. Ann. Rev. Med. 72:229-241

Gu T., Han Y., and Duan R. (2023) A transfer learning approach based on random forest with application to breast cancer prediction in underrepresented populations. In. Pacific Symposium on Biocomputing 2023.

Keat K., Hui D., Xiao B., Bradford Y, Cindi Z., Daar E.S., Gulick R, Riddler S.A., Sinxadi P., Haas D.W., and Ritchie M.D. (2023) Leveraging Multi-Ancestry Polygenic Risk Scores for Body Mass Index to Predict Antiretroviral Therapy-Induced Weight Gain. In. Pacific Symposium on Biocomputing 2023.

Machado Reyes D., Bose A., Karavani E., and Parida L. (2023) FairPRS: a fairness framework for Polygenic Risk Scores. In. Pacific Symposium on Biocomputing 2023.

Yang G., Alarcon C, Friedman P., Gong L., Klein T., O'Brien T., Nutescu E.A., Tuck M., Meltzer D., Perera M.A. (2023) The Role of Global and Local Ancestry on Clopidogrel Response in African Americans. In. Pacific Symposium on Biocomputing 2023.

A transfer learning approach based on random forest with application to breast cancer prediction in underrepresented populations

Tian Gu[1], Yi Han[2] and Rui Duan[1,†]

[1] *Department of Biostatistics, Harvard T.H. Chan School of Public Health, Boston, MA 02115, USA*

[2] *School of Mathematical Sciences, Shanghai Jiaotong University, Shanghai, 200240, China*

[†]*E-mail: rduan@hsph.harvard.edu*

Despite the high-quality, data-rich samples collected by recent large-scale biobanks, the underrepresentation of participants from minority and disadvantaged groups has limited the use of biobank data for developing disease risk prediction models that can be generalized to diverse populations, which may exacerbate existing health disparities. This study addresses this critical challenge by proposing a transfer learning framework based on random forest models (TransRF). TransRF can incorporate risk prediction models trained in a source population to improve the prediction performance in a target underrepresented population with limited sample size. TransRF is based on an ensemble of multiple transfer learning approaches, each covering a particular type of similarity between the source and the target populations, which is shown to be robust and applicable in a broad spectrum of scenarios. Using extensive simulation studies, we demonstrate the superior performance of TransRF compared with several benchmark approaches across different data generating mechanisms. We illustrate the feasibility of TransRF by applying it to build breast cancer risk assessment models for African-ancestry women and South Asian women, respectively, with UK biobank data.

Keywords: Transfer Learning; Random Forest; Underrepresented Population; Breast Cancer.

1. Introduction

Risk prediction tools can guide disease prevention, early detection, and intervention. Some well-known examples include the Gail model for assessing breast cancer risks,[1] and the Bach model for lung cancer risk prediction,[2] which are helpful for both risk stratification and cancer screening recommendations. Over the past few decades, genome-wide association studies (GWAS) have identified significant genetic loci associated with many complex diseases, suggesting the great potential for combining genetic information with epidemiological, clinical, and other risk factors to further improve the performance of risk prediction models.[3] With the development of large-scale biobanks, such as the UK biobank (UKB),[4] the Mass General Brigham (MGB) biobank,[5] and the Million Veteran Program (MVP) mega-biobank,[6] clinical information obtained from electronic health records is linked with participants' genomic data, health survey data, and other health-related measures, providing unique opportunities to develop enhanced risk prediction tools that integrate different types of risk factors.[7]

However, a long-standing problem is the lack of participants from minority and disadvantaged groups in biomedical studies, which may lead to underperformance of risk prediction models in these underrepresented populations, and might exacerbate health disparities.[8,9] For example, most breast cancer risk prediction models have been developed based on data from White women, resulting in underestimated risk in Black women and inaccurate estimation for other racial groups such as American Indian or Alaska Native.[10] Many large-scale biobanks also have disproportionately fewer participants from non-European ancestry than the European ancestry populations. There are less than 6% participants of non-European ancestry in UKB, while the MGB biobank only contains 6% African Americans, 5% Hispanics, and 4% Asians. Such lack of representation has raised significant challenges for developing and evaluating risk assessment tools for underrepresented populations. More inclusive data collection strategies are needed to tackle these challenges, while methodological advancements are also essential to improve the use of existing resources.

Transfer learning methods have been successfully applied in many areas, including text recognition and imaging classification,[11] due to their capability of leveraging shared information from source populations with relatively sufficient data to build prediction models in a target population with limited data. Unlike many transfer learning methods that require individual-level data from both the source and target populations,[12,13] we consider the situation where we can only obtain fitted models from a source population instead of their individual-level data. This is a common situation in biomedical studies, where data are often protected by various regularities or rules to be made publicly available, while trained models can be shared through open-source platforms such as GitHub, or more protected environments such as the Phenotype Knowledgebase website (PheKB).[14] As increasing efforts have been devoted to building collaborative environments for evaluating and validating machine learning algorithms across different health care datasets, sharing fitted models is expected to become increasingly feasible.[15] Consequently, model-based transfer learning methods that can leverage existing fitted models are needed.

Existing model-based transfer learning methods mainly involve parametric models such as regression,[16,17] which may have limited predictive power when the model is misspecified. Network-based deep transfer learning methods mostly follow the idea of fine-tuning a pre-trained neural network,[18] which often lacks clear model interpretation, practical guidance, and theoretical justification.[19] Among many risk prediction models, tree-based methods such as random forest (RF) have been widely used in biomedical research, including risk prediction,[20,21] disease diagnosis,[22,23] and digital phenotyping.[24] Tree-based methods enjoy several advantages, including the ability to handle non-linear relationships, the property to learn feature importance, and good interpretability. Importantly, recent studies have laid the theoretical foundation of RF models,[25] which further helps researchers to understand how well these methods work under different scenarios.

The development of model-based transfer learning methods built upon RF models is still an open area due to the non-parametric nature of RF. Recently, a few strategies have been proposed based on using target data to either refine each source tree's structure or adjust the numeric threshold of each split.[26,27] Such structure-based transfer learning methods may not perform well in cases where the optimal tree structures in the two populations are highly different and each source tree performs relatively poorly in the target population. In addition, pruning and adjusting a large number of trees with limited target data may be inefficient. The lack of performance of the structure-based transfer learning methods are demonstrated in our data application.

In this paper, we propose a RF-based transfer learning framework termed TransRF. Our method is based on an ensemble of multiple transfer learning approaches covering various types of similarity between the source and target models. Unlike existing work that relies on tree structural similarities, our method is more robust and applicable to different scenarios. More importantly, with slight modifications, our approach can be extended to adapt a broader range of prediction models beyond RF. We evaluate our method using extensive simulation studies and apply it to predict breast cancer patients in African-ancestry (AFR) women and South Asian (SAS) women, respectively, using UKB data.

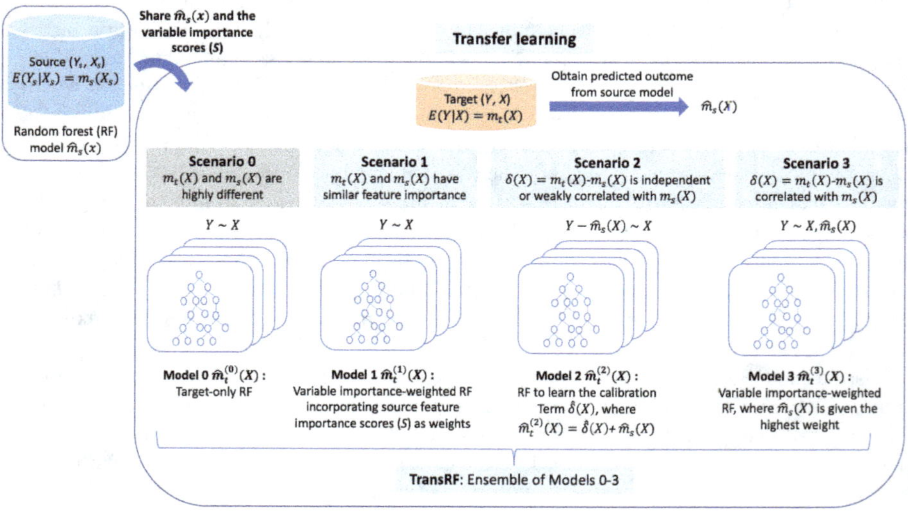

Fig. 1. The schematic illustration of TransRF, an ensemble of a forest trained using only the target data (scenario 0) and multiple forests that transferred information from a source forest (described by scenarios 1-3).

2. Method

2.1. *Overview and notation*

We start with an overview of the proposed framework. TransRF aims to improve the prediction performance in an underrepresented population with limited data by incorporating a RF model trained in a source population with relatively more sufficient data. To leverage the information contained in the source model, we develop transfer learning models that cover several practical scenarios, in which the source model shares certain similarities with the target population. An ensemble learning strategy is used to combine multiple transfer learning models to improve the method's robustness. A schematic illustration is presented in Fig. 1.

We denote (Y, X) as the target data, where $Y \in \mathbb{R}^n$ is the outcome variable and $X \in \mathbb{R}^{n \times p}$ is the p-dimensional feature variables. Correspondingly, we denote data from the source population as (Y_s, X_s). To improve the applicability of the method, we consider the case where only a fitted source model $\hat{m}_s(x)$ is available, which is an estimator of the true conditional mean function $m_s(x) = \mathbb{E}(Y_s|X_s = x)$. The distribution of the target data can be different from the source data, i.e., either the feature distribution or the conditional distribution $m_t(x) = \mathbb{E}(Y|X = x)$ could be different from the source. Our goal is to estimate $m_t(x)$, using target data (Y, X) and the fitted source model $\hat{m}_s(x)$.

2.2. *Three ways to incorporate the source model*

Leveraging feature importance. One potential similarity between the source and the target models is that they may have similar feature importance rankings (see **Scenario 1** in Fig. 1). When training a RF model with limited target data, we can use the variable importance scores obtained from the source model, which we denoted by $S = (s_1, \ldots, s_p)$. This is especially useful when the number of features is large. The importance scores can be normalized to weights to determine the probabilities of selecting the features in each tree.[28] We denote the fitted model as $\hat{m}_t^{(1)}(x)$, and refer it to *Model 1*. Intuitively, Model 1 is expected to perform well if the source and target share similar feature importance rankings, even if the underlying $m_t(x)$ and $m_s(x)$ are highly different. When $m_s(x)$ and $m_t(x)$ are close, Model 1 might be less effective as it does not directly use the predicted values from the source model. Thus, we introduce the following two scenarios.

Calibration of the source model by learning the discrepancy. Due to population heterogeneity, the predicted values $\hat{m}_s(X)$ may not be accurate when directly applying the source model to the target data. We propose to use the target data to calibrate the source model. Denote the discrepancy between the two underlying true models as $\delta(X) = m_t(X) - m_s(X)$. One possible situation is that $\delta(X)$ is independent or weakly correlated with $m_s(X)$ (see **Scenario 2** in Fig. 1), meaning that the discrepancy term captures complementary information of the source model. In such a case, instead of fitting a model using the original outcome Y, we propose to obtain the residual term, defined as $Y - \hat{m}_s(X)$, which is the difference between the observed outcomes and the predicted values. Treating the source model as an anchor, we fit a RF model using the residual term as the outcome and X as the features. When $\delta(X)$ has some sparse or low-dimensional structure, we can benefit from such sparsity by targeting the discrepancy term.[29] Finally, we obtain $\hat{m}_t^{(2)}(X) = \hat{\delta}(X) + \hat{m}_s(X)$, which we refer to as *Model 2* hereafter.

Calibration of the source model by adding a new feature. We now consider the case where the discrepancy term $\delta(X)$ is correlated with the source model $\hat{m}_s(X)$ so that the above Model 2 might not be able to learn $\delta(X)$ accurately. In other words, $\hat{m}_s(X)$ could be an important feature for predicting the discrepancy so as to predict Y. In this case, we propose to add $\hat{m}_s(X)$ as an additional feature for predicting Y (see **Scenario 3** in Fig. 1). Since $\hat{m}_s(X)$ is likely an important feature, we propose using weighted RF and assigning it a large weight. We can assign equal or different weights for other features, X, according to prior knowledge of whether certain features have different effects in two populations. We denote the fitted model as $m_t^{(3)}(x)$, and refer it to *Model 3*.

2.3. *Ensemble learning to boost the robustness and prevent negative transfer*

Each of the models described above relies on certain assumptions about the true underlying functions $m_t(x)$ and $m_s(x)$, where the validity of the assumptions is unverifiable in practice. As we will later show in the simulation studies, the performance of Models 1-3 varies under different settings. In addition, when the source population is highly different from the target population, the source model could not provide any useful information to the training of the target model, and the above models may even have lower performance compared to a RF model trained by using the target data alone (the *target-only model, or Model 0 shown in Fig.1*, denoted as $\hat{m}_t^{(0)}$). To prevent such "negative transfer" and to leverage the strength of each model, we propose to obtain an ensemble model which is a linear combination of $\hat{m}_t^{(0)}, \hat{m}_t^{(1)}, \hat{m}_t^{(2)}$ and $\hat{m}_t^{(3)}$. We denote the *TransRF model* as

$$\hat{m}_t(x) = \sum_{i=0}^{3} w_i \hat{m}_t^{(i)}(x)$$

where w_i is the weight of the i-th model. Many existing methods can be used to obtain the ensemble weights. For example, with a small validation dataset $(\tilde{X}, \tilde{Y})$, we can obtain the ensemble model by fitting a linear regression model treating $\hat{m}_t^{(0)}(\tilde{X}), \hat{m}_t^{(1)}(\tilde{X}), \hat{m}_t^{(2)}(\tilde{X})$ and $\hat{m}_t^{(3)}(\tilde{X})$ as features. Alternatively, we can use methods such as Q-aggregation[30] to learn the weights. The sample size of the validation dataset can be relatively small compared to the training data, and a cross-fitting strategy can be used to potentially achieve better accuracy.

As illustrated in Fig. 1, TransRF requires only the fitted RF model and the corresponding feature importance scores from the source population, especially preferable in settings where individual-level data is not shareable across sites. Our framework can be modified to incorporate other possible transfer learning models that might work better in scenarios not described above, such as the structure-based transfer learning models.[26]

3. Simulation studies

We conduct Monte Carlo simulations to assess TransRF and several comparisons under three settings. Due to space limitations, we outline the data generating procedures in this section and leave the detailed choices of parameters, transformation, and distribution functions in the online Supplementary Materials. In each setting, we generate X and X_s from a multivariate truncated normal distribution with different means to mimic the potential shifts in feature distributions. The dimension of features is set to $p = 20$. The mean function $m_s(x)$ and $m_t(x)$ are set to be some non-linear functions of X, which are different across settings. We then add random noise to the mean functions $m_s(x)$ and $m_t(x)$ to obtain the outcomes in the source and the target populations. For each simulated dataset, we generate target data of size $n = 200$ for the training purpose and an independent testing set with $n_{\text{test}} = 100$. A source sample of size $n_{\text{src}} = 1000$ is generated to fit the source model. We evaluate the model performance using the mean squared prediction error (MSE) of the testing set over 200 simulation replications. We now describe the three simulation settings:

(i) In Setting 1, we consider that the source and the target populations share a similar variable importance ranking, where the similarity between the two populations is measured by the correlation of their variable importance rankings. To generate $m_s(x)$ and $m_t(x)$, we apply some non-linear transformations on each feature in X and obtain the transformed features Z. We then combine the transformed features through a linear combination to obtain $m_s(x)$ and $m_t(x)$, i.e., $m_s(x) = Z\beta_s$ and $m_t(x) = Z\beta_t$, where β_s and β_t are p-dimensional vectors whose magnitude determines the feature importance. By changing the correlation between β_t and β_s, we vary the similarity degree of their feature importance.

(ii) In Setting 2, we consider that the discrepancy between $m_s(X)$ and $m_t(X)$ is independent or weakly correlated with $m_s(X)$. To achieve this, we first generate $m_s(x)$ in the same way described in Setting 1. We then generate $\delta(x)$, the function of a random subset of all the features, on which we apply different feature transformations and linear combinations compared to $m_s(x)$. We obtain $m_t(x) = m_s(x) + \delta(x)$. We vary the variance explained by the source model $m_s(x)$ to control the similarity between the source and the target populations.

(iii) In Setting 3, we consider that the discrepancy term is correlated with $m_s(X)$. We generate Y_s following the same data generating mechanism in Setting 2 except that we set $m_t(X) = Cm_s(X) + \delta(X)$, where C is a constant. In this case, the true discrepancy is $m_t(X) - m_s(X) = (C-1) * m_s(X) + \delta(X)$. With $C \neq 1$, $m_s(X)$ is correlated with the discrepancy, and we vary C to alter the strength of the correlation.

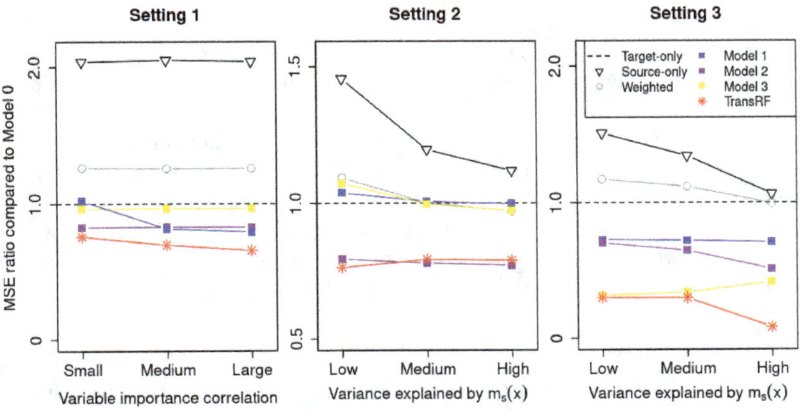

Fig. 2. MSE ratio compared to Model 0 (the target-only model) in simulation settings 1 (left), 2 (middle), and 3 (right).

In each setting, we use Model 0, i.e., the target-only model, as the reference and compare the performance of six models with it: (1) Source-only: $\hat{m}_s(x)$; (2) Weighted: a weighted average of predictions from source-only model and target-only model, using inverse MSE of validation data as weights; (3) Model 1: $\hat{m}_t^{(1)}(x)$; (4) Model 2: $\hat{m}_t^{(2)}(x)$; (5) Model 3: $\hat{m}_t^{(3)}(x)$; and (6) TransRF: the proposed method, combining Models 0-3. Note that for methods (2) and (6), a validation dataset is needed to train the weights, where we randomly split $n_{val} = 50$ samples from the training data. For each method (k), $k \in \{1, \ldots, 6\}$ described above, we report its MSE ratio compared to the reference, denoted as MSE_k/MSE_0, where a ratio larger than 1 represents worse performance than the reference. In contrast, a ratio smaller than 1 represents improved prediction compared to the reference. We build TransRF algorithm in R software[31] on the basis of *viRandomForests* package. Code to implement TransRF along with the example data, and Supplementary Materials are available at https://github.com/gutian-tiangu/TransRF.

3.1. *Simulation results*

Results of Setting 1 (the left panel of Fig. 2) show that the performance of Model 1 improves over the increasing correlation of feature importance. When the correlation is large, Model 1 outperforms most of the compared methods, while it performs slightly worse than Model 0 when the correlation is low. Interestingly, Model 2 performs well across all settings, which might be due to the discrepancy term $m_t(x) - m_s(x)$ under this setting is weakly correlated with the source mean structure when we alter the correlations between the feature importance. TransRF has the best performance over different correlation levels and the MSE ratios to Model 0 range from 0.66 to 0.76.

In Setting 2 (the middle panel of Fig. 2), we observe that when the performance of the source model increases, Model 2 outperforms all the compared methods. Since Model 2 has much better performance than Models 0, 1, and 3, TransRF has nearly identical performance as Model 2, with a MSE of 0.78 times that of Model 0.

In Setting 3 (the right panel of Fig. 2), we alter the parameter C in $m_t(X) = Cm_s(X) + \delta(X)$ from 10 to 1 corresponding to three levels shown in the x-axis. When C is getting closer to 1, the variance explained by the source model increases (from low to high), and so as the performance of the source-only model. When C is larger than 1, Model 3 performs better than other methods and similarly to TransRF. When $C = 1$, the performance of all the other methods improves, and therefore TransRF has better performance, where its MSE ratios to Model 0 range between 0.08 and 0.30.

In summary, the performance of each transfer learning model varies in different settings, where each model has the best performance in a specific scenario. TransRF that combines Models 0-3 often outperforms its underlying constituents and is robust against negative transfer.

4. Application using UKB data

We apply TransRF to UKB breast cancer data, treating European (EUR) women as the source population, and AFR women SAS women as the target population, respectively.

4.1. *Defining breast cancer case and control, ancestry, and other variables*

We identify breast cancer cases using the ICD-10 code (C50) following a recently released UKB disease phenotyping definition.[32] When using retrospective data like UKB to build risk prediction models, one should exclude the prevalent cases where observations already had breast cancer diagnosed before they entered the study, and only keep incident cases who developed breast cancer after entering the study. In our example, as the target sample size is minimal, we want to keep as many target samples as possible. We decide to include both incident and prevalent cases and only use time-invariant predictors (excluding variables that can potentially happen after the diagnosis). When selecting candidate controls, we identify women who have not been diagnosed with breast cancer or ovarian cancer (ICD-10 code, C56) as these cancers are closely related.[33] We select a subset of subjects to obtain controls with a case-control ratio approximately equal to 1:2.

To define the ancestry population for EUR, AFR and SAS, we use a mutual set of self-reported ancestry through UKB survey data and the principal component-based ancestry prediction proposed by Zhang, Dey, and Lee.[34] Only those whose self-claimed ancestry matched the ancestry prediction are included. We define the following clinical variables that are commonly known as breast cancer risk factors: ever smoking (yes or no), age at the start of menstruation in years, had a college degree (yes or no), ever had a live birth (yes or no).[35,36] For a small percentage of participants who had missing age at the start of menstruation (<3%), we impute the missingness with a mean age of 13. We identify 479 SAS samples (173 cases and 306 controls), 440 AFR samples (126 cases and 314 controls), and 43,576 EUR samples (14,240 cases and 29,336 controls) that contain complete data of outcomes and clinical variables. For each target population, we randomly split a validation set of size 50 (20 cases and 30 controls) and a testing set of size 90 (30 cases and 60 controls), whereas the remaining samples are used as training data (339 samples including 123 cases and 216 controls when using SAS as the target; and 300 samples including 76 cases and 224 controls when using AFR as the target).

4.2. *Genotyping, quality control and imputation*

Details on genotype calling and quality control for UKB data are described elsewhere.[4] We include 330 novel breast cancer susceptibility single-nucleotide polymorphisms (SNPs) identified in a GWAS study.[37] We perform standard quality control, including removing participants who have mismatched self-reported sex versus biological sex, those who failed UKB official genotype quality control, and all pairs of participants who are estimated to be genetically related. A total of 272 SNPs are found in the UKB data, used as genetic predictors, among which 151 contain a small percent of missingness (over 90% SNPs with missingness have a missing rate $< 5\%$). For each SNP with missingness, we impute the missingness using the value with the largest frequency.

4.3. *Results*

Fig. 3 shows the area under the operating characteristic curve (AUC) of different transfer learning methods after incorporating source model information for SAS as the target model in the left panel and AFR as the target model in the right panel. When using AFR as the target population, compared with Model 0 (dashed vertical line, AUC=0.61), Model 1 by directly sharing the variable importance score has the highest AUC, equal to 0.70. Model 2 that learns the discrepancy term has an AUC of 0.69, while Model 3 by including source predicted values as the most important feature does not show improved performance with AUC equal to 0.60.

TransRF by aggregating Models 0-3 shows an AUC of 0.70, a 10% improvement compared to the target-only model and a 5% improvement compared to the weighted model by naively aggregating Model 0 and the source-only predictions. On the contrary, the SER model by using the target data to fine-tune the source tree structure[26] shows the worst performance among others. This may result from insufficient target data to refine the tree or dissimilarity between the source and the target tree structure.

When comparing the results that each uses SAS and AFR as the target population, we observe that each transfer learning model performs differently, e.g., Model 3 has the worst performance in transferring EUR information to AFR while it has the best performance when leveraging EUR information to SAS. This might be due to different similarities of genetic architectures between EUR and AFR versus EUR and SAS.[38]

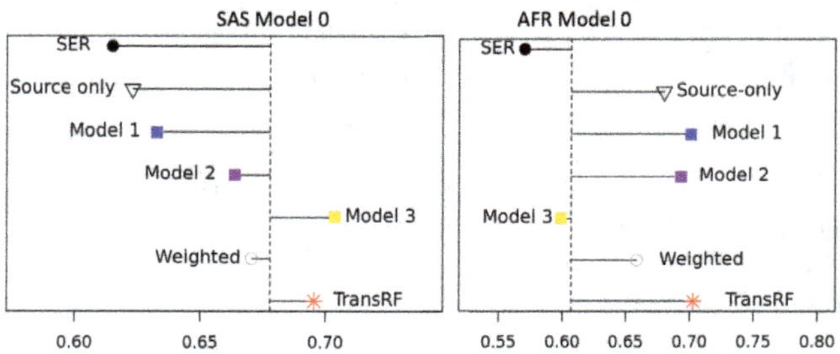

Fig. 3. AUC of transfer learning methods compared to Model 0 (the target-only model) for SAS (left) and AFR (right).

In Table 1, we present the top 20 important variables from the source and each target-only model, along with the corresponding variable importance scores. Age at the start of menarche is found in all three models, and it is the most important variable in both the EUR model and AFR Model 0. Two predictors, rs16886165 and "Ever had a college degree", overlap in EUR model and AFR Model 0, while the top one feature of SAS Model 0, rs4784227, is also found important in the EUR model. In addition, rs9315973 is identified with high importance in both AFR and SAS Model 0's, an intron variant belongs to gene EPSTI1 that is known to be associated with many traits and diseases, including breast cancer in European and East Asian.[39]

It is worth noting that rs16886165 is an intergenic variant identified as associated with breast cancer in European populations.[40,41] The known risk effect of rs4784227, an intron variant mapped to gene CASC16, associated with breast cancer has been validated in European[42,43] and East Asian ancestries.[44–46] Other than these two SNPs, the ranking of the rest of the top SNPs between the target and the source populations is not consistent, which might suggest underlying differences in genetic architectures across populations.[38] However, with a limited sample size in the target population, the estimated feature importance scores may have large variability.

5. Discussion

In this study, we propose TransRF, a RF-based transfer learning framework targeting risk prediction in underrepresented populations. By incorporating fitted models from a large source population, TransRF combines the strengths of several novel transfer learning models motivated by various practical situations. Our simulation studies reveal that the effectiveness of different

Table 1. Top 20 variables (importance score) from the fitted EUR model, Model 0 treating South Asian (SAS) as the target population, and Model 0 treating African Ancestry (AFR) as the target population. Variables identified from all three populations indicated in bold text. Variables shared by the EUR and SAS populations are indicated in blue. Variables shared by the EUR and AFR populations are indicated in red. Variables shared by the SAS and AFR populations are indicated in orange.

Rank	Fitted EUR model (score)	SAS Model 0 (score)	AFR Model 0 (score)
1	**Menarche age (0.056)**	rs4784227 (0.043)	**Menarche age** (0.148)
2	rs4442975 (0.021)	rs7848334 (0.04)	Had a college degree (0.048)
3	rs630965 (0.02)	rs12472404 (0.031)	rs2454399 (0.045)
4	rs10941679 (0.017)	rs12422552 (0.031)	rs144767203 (0.031)
5	rs16886165 (0.016)	rs332529 (0.03)	rs2181965 (0.028)
6	rs910416 (0.016)	**Menarche age (0.029)**	rs2403907 (0.02)
7	rs6913578 (0.016)	rs4866496 (0.028)	rs9693444 (0.019)
8	rs10096351 (0.015)	rs78540526 (0.027)	rs56387622 (0.018)
9	rs7072776 (0.014)	rs4868701 (0.026)	rs35542655 (0.018)
10	Had a college degree (0.014)	rs719338 (0.02)	rs7924772 (0.018)
11	rs9931038 (0.014)	rs7842619 (0.02)	rs16886165 (0.018)
12	rs35668161 (0.014)	rs3010266 (0.019)	rs3819405 (0.017)
13	rs552647 (0.014)	rs10832963 (0.019)	rs2356656 (0.016)
14	rs661204 (0.012)	rs9315973 (0.018)	rs9364472 (0.016)
15	rs4784227 (0.012)	rs55872725 (0.018)	rs9315973 (0.016)
16	rs17343002 (0.012)	rs7830152 (0.018)	rs11693806 (0.015)
17	rs11249433 (0.012)	rs28539243 (0.016)	rs7800548 (0.014)
18	rs10164323 (0.011)	rs335160 (0.015)	rs665889 (0.013)
19	rs10197246 (0.011)	rs9712235 (0.015)	rs889310 (0.012)
20	rs4602255 (0.011)	rs7121616 (0.014)	Ever had a live birth (0.012)

transfer learning models varies with the underlying relationship between the source and the target models. TransRF reaches comparable performance to the transfer learning method with the best performance across different scenarios, demonstrated by both simulation studies and the application to UKB data.

Our paper considers the practical situation where we can only obtain a fitted model from the source population, whereas the individual-level data are unavailable. A relevant problem is transfer learning in a federated setting, where summary-level statistics (not necessarily the trained model) can be shared across populations. In such a setting, Li et al.[47] proposed a federated transfer learning algorithm based on penalized generalized linear regression models, which requires sharing the gradients of likelihood functions iteratively across populations, and we refer to the relevant works discussed therein. This type of method is more applicable to research networks with specific infrastructures to facilitate timely information sharing and model updating. In contrast, the model-based transfer learning framework proposed in this paper can be helpful in a broader range of applications.

There are several limitations to this study. In the breast cancer example, both instant and prevalent cases are included. Due to the limited sample size in the target population, only including the breast cancer incidents will result in too few target samples. Although we only use time-invariant features or features that are most likely to happen before breast cancer diagnosis, such as education level and menarche age, there is still uncertainty in terms of their actual temporal relationships. We aim to use this data example to show the feasibility of TransRF. As a future direction, we will explore the potential of TransRF for disease risk prediction by incorporating more precise temporal information based on codified and unstructured information in biobank data.

Acknowledgements

This research was supported by the Harvard Data Science Initiative Postdoctoral Fellow Research Fund.

References

1. M. H. Gail *et al.*, Projecting individualized probabilities of developing breast cancer for white females who are being examined annually, *J. Natl. Cancer Inst.* **81**, 1879 (1989).
2. K. A. Cronin *et al.*, Validation of a model of lung cancer risk prediction among smokers, *J. Natl. Cancer Inst.* **98**, 637 (2006).
3. A. Lee *et al.*, Boadicea: a comprehensive breast cancer risk prediction model incorporating genetic and nongenetic risk factors, *Genetics in Medicine* **21**, 1708 (2019).
4. C. Bycroft *et al.*, The UK biobank resource with deep phenotyping and genomic data, *Nature* **562**, 203 (2018).
5. E. W. Karlson *et al.*, Building the partners healthcare biobank at partners personalized medicine: Informed consent, return of research results, recruitment lessons and operational considerations, *Journal of Personalized Medicine* **6** (2016).
6. J. M. Gaziano *et al.*, Million veteran program: A mega-biobank to study genetic influences on health and disease, *Journal of clinical epidemiology* **70**, 214 (2016).
7. C. J. O'Donnell, Opportunities, challenges and expectations management for translating biobank research to precision medicine, *European Journal of Epidemiology* **35**, 1 (2020).
8. P. Kim *et al.*, Minority participation in biobanks, *Biobanking* , 43 (2019).
9. W. L. Teagle *et al.*, Comorbidities and ethnic health disparities in the UK biobank, *JAMIA Open* **5**, p. ooac057 (2022).
10. A. W. Kurian *et al.*, Performance of the ibis/tyrer-cuzick model of breast cancer risk by race and ethnicity in the women's health initiative, *Cancer* **127**, 3742 (2021).
11. K. Weiss *et al.*, A survey of transfer learning, *Journal of Big data* **3**, 1 (2016).
12. Y. Yao *et al.*, Boosting for transfer learning with multiple sources, *CVPR* , 1855 (2010).
13. R. Chattopadhyay *et al.*, Multisource domain adaptation and its application to early detection of fatigue, *ACM Trans Knowl Discov Data* **6**, 1 (2012).
14. J. C. Kirby *et al.*, Phekb: a catalog and workflow for creating electronic phenotype algorithms for transportability, *JAMIA* **23**, 1046 (2016).
15. J. Shiffman *et al.*, The emergence and effectiveness of global health networks: findings and future research, health policy and planning, *Health Policy and Planning* **31** (2016).
16. T. Gu *et al.*, Commute: communication-efficient transfer learning for multi-site risk prediction, *MedRxiv* (2022).
17. P. Han, A discussion on "a selective review of statistical methods using calibration information from similar studies" by qin, liu and li, *Stat. Theory Relat. Fields* , 1 (2022).
18. C. Tan *et al.*, A survey on deep transfer learning, *ICANN* , 270 (2018).
19. J. R. Geis *et al.*, Ethics of artificial intelligence in radiology: summary of the joint european and north american multisociety statement, *CAR Journal* **70**, 329 (2019).

20. B. Dai *et al.*, Using random forest algorithm for breast cancer diagnosis, *International Symposium on Computer, Consumer and Control* , 449 (2018).
21. Q. Wang *et al.*, Random forest with self-paced bootstrap learning in lung cancer prognosis, *ACM TOMM* **16**, 1 (2020).
22. F. Yang *et al.*, Using random forest for reliable classification and cost-sensitive learning for medical diagnosis, *BMC bioinformatics* **10**, 1 (2009).
23. M. Zhu *et al.*, Class weights random forest algorithm for processing class imbalanced medical data, *IEEE Access* **6**, 4641 (2018).
24. J. Benoit *et al.*, Systematic review of digital phenotyping and machine learning in psychosis spectrum illnesses, *Harvard Review of Psychiatry* **28**, 296 (2020).
25. S. Athey *et al.*, Generalized random forests, *Ann. Stat.* **47**, 1148 (2019).
26. N. Segev *et al.*, Learn on source, refine on target: A model transfer learning framework with random forests, *IEEE Trans. Pattern Anal. Mach. Intell.* **39**, 1811 (2016).
27. W. Fang *et al.*, Adapted tree boosting for transfer learning, *IEEE* , 741 (2019).
28. Y. Liu *et al.*, Variable importance-weighted random forests, *Quant. Biology* **5**, 338 (2017).
29. J. Klusowski, Sparse learning with cart, *Advances in NeurIPS* **33**, 11612 (2020).
30. G. Lecué *et al.*, Optimal learning with q-aggregation, *Ann. Stat.* **42**, 211 (2014).
31. R. C. Team *et al.*, R: A language and environment for statistical computing (2021).
32. D. J. Thompson *et al.*, UK biobank release and systematic evaluation of optimised polygenic risk scores for 53 diseases and quantitative traits, *MedRxiv* (2022).
33. J. Schildkraut *et al.*, Evaluating genetic association among ovarian, breast, and endometrial cancer: evidence for a breast/ovarian cancer relationship., *Am. J. Hum. Genet.* **45**, p. 521 (1989).
34. D. Zhang *et al.*, Fast and robust ancestry prediction using principal component analysis, *Bioinformatics* **36** (2020).
35. K. Al-Ajmi *et al.*, Risk of breast cancer in the uk biobank female cohort and its relationship to anthropometric and reproductive factors, *PLoS One* **13**, p. e0201097 (2018).
36. S. K. Hussain *et al.*, Influence of education level on breast cancer risk and survival in sweden between 1990 and 2004, *International Journal of Cancer* **122**, 165 (2008).
37. H. Zhang *et al.*, Genome-wide association study identifies 32 novel breast cancer susceptibility loci from overall and subtype-specific analyses, *Nat. Genet* **52**, 572 (2020).
38. L. Shang *et al.*, Genetic architecture of gene expression in european and african americans: an eqtl mapping study in genoa, *Am. J. Hum. Genet.* **106**, 496 (2020).
39. K. Michailidou *et al.*, Association analysis identifies 65 new breast cancer risk loci, *Nature* **551**, 92 (2017).
40. G. Thomas *et al.*, A multistage genome-wide association study in breast cancer identifies two new risk alleles at 1p11.2 and 14q24.1 (rad51l1), *Nat. Genet* **41**, 579 (2009).
41. N. Brandes *et al.*, Genetic association studies of alterations in protein function expose recessive effects on cancer predisposition, *Scientific reports* **11**, 1 (2021).
42. J. Hu *et al.*, Supervariants identification for breast cancer, *Genetic epidemiology* **44**, 934 (2020).
43. F. J. Couch *et al.*, Identification of four novel susceptibility loci for oestrogen receptor negative breast cancer, *Nat. Commun.* **7**, 1 (2016).
44. K. Ishigaki *et al.*, Large-scale genome-wide association study in a japanese population identifies novel susceptibility loci across different diseases, *Nat. Genet* **52**, 669 (2020).
45. J. Long *et al.*, Identification of a functional genetic variant at 16q12. 1 for breast cancer risk: results from the asia breast cancer consortium, *PLoS genetics* **6**, p. e1001002 (2010).
46. S. Sakaue *et al.*, A cross-population atlas of genetic associations for 220 human phenotypes, *Nat. Genet* **53**, 1415 (2021).
47. S. Li *et al.*, Targeting underrepresented populations in precision medicine: A federated transfer learning approach, *ArXiv* (2021).

FairPRS: adjusting for admixed populations in polygenic risk scores using invariant risk minimization

Diego Machado Reyes[†,1], Aritra Bose[†,2], Ehud Karavani[3], and Laxmi Parida[‡,2]

[1]*Biomedical Engineering Department, Rensselaer Polytechnic Institute, Troy, NY, USA*

[2]*IBM T.J Watson Research Center, Yorktown Heights, NY, USA*

[3]*IBM Research, Israel*

† *Equal Contribution*

‡ *Email: parida@us.ibm.com*

Polygenic risk scores (PRS) are increasingly used to estimate the personal risk of a trait based on genetics. However, most genomic cohorts are of European populations, with a strong under-representation of non-European groups. Given that PRS poorly transport across racial groups, this has the potential to exacerbate health disparities if used in clinical care. Hence there is a need to generate PRS that perform comparably across ethnic groups. Borrowing from recent advancements in the domain adaption field of machine learning, we propose `FairPRS` - an Invariant Risk Minimization (IRM) approach for estimating fair PRS or debiasing a pre-computed PRS. We test our method on both a diverse set of synthetic data and real data from the UK Biobank. We show our method can create ancestry-invariant PRS distributions that are both racially unbiased and largely improve phenotype prediction. We hope that `FairPRS` will contribute to a fairer characterization of patients by genetics rather than by race.

Keywords: Polygenic Risk Scores; Fairness; Racial Disparity; Invariant Risk Minimization; Machine Learning; Precision medicine

1. Introduction

Genome wide association studies (GWAS) were developed for finding statistical associations between single nucleic polymorphisms (SNPs) and phenotype traits. Later, these associations were then aggregated into a score – a polygenic (risk, for diseases) score (PRS) – for predicting traits.[1] PRS became extremely popular due to its promise of harnessing one's genome to act as a biomarker for personalizing medical risk estimation. This capacity for personalization can also translate to heterogeneity on the population level with PRS helping to identify subpopulations that are at higher risk of disease.[2]

Unfortunately, PRSs are plagued by many issues. Primarily GWAS cohorts strongly suffer from a lack of sample diversity. For example, 79% of all participants in the NHGRI-EBI GWAS catalog[3] are of European descent despite being only 16% of the global population.[4] The under-representation of minority groups in cohorts leads to inferior PRS because PRS derived from European ancestry tend to perform poorly in genetically diverse populations and even within other admixed European populations.[5] As a simple example, polygenic scores for height predict all Africans to be shorter than Europeans, contrary to empirical evidence.[6] Thus, using PRS for precision medicine in its current form may exacerbate health disparities until the lack of representation is solved.[4]

Reducing racial bias in genomic prediction may contribute to more equitable healthcare for all. But to establish health equity in precision medicine we require better genetic cohorts whose multi-ethnic representation matches real life. This solution, however, is resource heavy and is long-term. Meanwhile, we can apply advances in machine intelligence to mitigate bias in trait prediction from PRS.

There is prior work on using computational frameworks for making PRS generalize better across subgroups. These include deconvoluting ancestry and partial PRS computation,[7] computing ancestry-specific PRS to showcase their utility as predictors across different populations,[8] or enabling more accurate effect size estimation by leveraging linkage disequilibrium diversity with GWAS summary statistics.[9] Advances in machine learning such as using transfer learning-based methods[10] and deep learning based methods have been applied to make PRS more portable across ancestries.[11] However, either some of these methods assume part of the background genome is still of European origin[7,10] or consider pre-computed associated markers as input to reduce search space which can contain significant bias or spurious associations.

In this work, we apply a domain-adaptation-based paradigm called Invariant Risk Minimization (IRM)[12] in the context of PRS. We consider the problem of generalizability of PRS as an *out of distribution* generalization problem, a common machine learning problem where models are developed in one domain but are deployed in another.[13] IRM's goal is to generate invariant predictors given multiple training domains. In our context, these different domains are adapted to be the different ancestry groups, therefore allowing for race-invariant phenotype prediction from PRS. Our goal is then to learn a generalizable PRS that contains as little ancestry information as possible, while still accurately predicting the phenotype of interest.

We present `FairPRS`, a framework for finding and mitigating bias in PRS which improves generalizability across populations and make it portable while increasing the prediction accuracy of the phenotype of interest. `FairPRS` is robust across both rigorous simulation studies involving arbitrary population structure and pre-computed PRS obtained from UK Biobank (UKB).[14]

2. Methods

`FairPRS` offers an entire pipeline from genetic data to trait prediction. It has three possible access points for input: genotypes, genotypes with summary statistics, or a pre-computed PRS. We will explain the `FairPRS` framework herein, followed by the autoencoder architecture, training, and evaluation phases of the pipeline. Thereafter, we will discuss the simulation and real data used in the study for evaluating `FairPRS` including computational details.

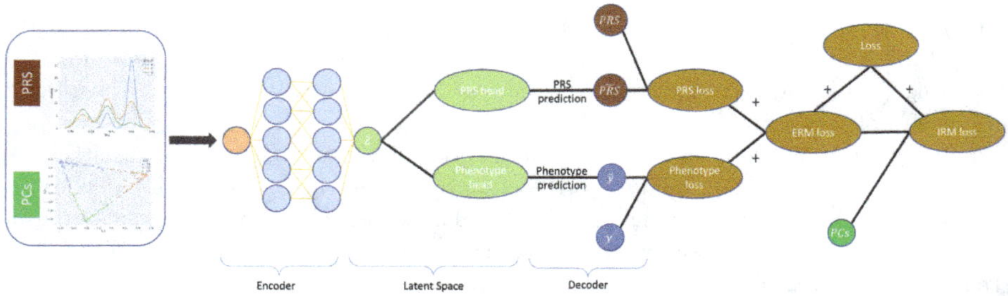

Fig. 1. Pipeline of **FairPRS** outlining the input variables: pre-computed PRS and genetic structure as represented by PCs from test data, the autoencoder used with IRM loss for learning the fair PRS output estimates with negligible ancestry influence.

2.1. *FairPRS framework*

The FairPRS pipeline is designed for ease and customization with multiple access points based on the user needs. Moreover, the pipeline can be run for a user-determined number of iterations for all or specific portions. The first stage focuses on processing the genotype data towards PRS computation. It allows to calculate the summary statistics, from GWAS, and principal components (PCs) of the genotype data. The PCs can be used as covariates for the GWAS and as input to the FairPRS model. The summary statistics are computed using `PLINK v2.0`[15] and the PCs are efficiently calculated for large scale data using `TeraPCA`.[16] Next, the pipeline allows starting at the PRS computation step if the user has previously calculated the summary statistics. The betas are extracted from the summary statistics and used for PRS computation through `PRSice2`[17] in the validation cohort.

Lastly, the third stage is the FairPRS model which uses the pipeline-computed or user-provided PRS and PCs as input, while the phenotype and the PRS will be used for the training supervision. The model is implemented as a dual task autoencoder and MLP as shown in Figure 1. Briefly, first, the data is encoded into a shared latent representation. The latent representation is then fed into two tasks in parallel: decoding the PRS input and predicting the phenotype. The losses are then combined with the ancestry information to obtain the IRM loss. The fair PRS estimates are obtained from the PRS decoder output. A key point in this step is the automatic multi-thread hyperparameter tuning per iteration with allows the pipeline to train high-performing models in an efficient manner. After the model training and evaluation, the average performance over the iterations is reported and a dictionary with all the results per iteration is saved for further analysis and reproducibility purposes.

2.1.1. *Implementation and Evaluation*

Detailed architecture The encoder is a single layer with ReLU activation, and latent space size determined as a hyperparameter. Both the PRS decoder and the phenotype prediction head perform a 10% dropout and then apply a single linear layer. The ERM loss is obtained by adding the two MSE losses with equal weight. The final loss is a weighted sum of the

ERM and IRM losses, with the weight being a hyperparameter. Adam method was used for optimization.[18] The framework is implemented using PyTorch 1.11.[19]

Training The proposed model allows using regression losses for the double task network and employs multiple environments corresponding to the number of populations present in the PRS data. An automatic hyper-parameter search with parallel trials is used while training to fine-tune the model in a more efficient manner. The random search of hyperparameters was done for the learning rate (log-uniform $[10^{-5}, 0.1]$), the dimension of the latent space (uniform from $2^i : i \in [2, 9]$), and the relative weight of the IRM loss (uniform $[0.5, 1.5]$). The search space was defined based on preliminary experiments allowing for a wide search without a prohibitively computationally expensive search space. Tuning was done using Ray Tune.[20] UK Biobank data was also randomly split to train (70%), validation (20%), and test (10%) sets. The best hyperparameter configuration was selected based on a validation set and was subsequently used for evaluation.

Evaluation To test the model against a baseline in a fair way, both the original PRS and those resulting from the model were regressed separately against the outcome using ordinary least squares. The covariate-adjusted coefficients of determination ($adjustedR^2$ scores) for both models are reported. Regression was done in Python using statsmodels.[21] Results per iteration are computed to finally report the mean performance across all iterations.

2.2. *Data*

`FairPRS` was evaluated on multiple simulated and real datasets. The simulated datasets included a wide array of configurations and were generated using the data simulator in a previous work.[22] Additionally, UK Biobank enhanced PRS (ePRS-UKB) for multiple phenotypes were used to further evaluate the model in real-world scenarios across different disease outcomes.

Simulated data Three models for simulating genetic datasets with arbitrary population structure: Balding-Nichols (BN), Prichard-Stephens-Donelly (PSD), and 1000 Genomes Project (TGP) with 3 variance proportion configurations for genetic, environment and noise, $\{v_{gen}, v_{env}, v_{noise}\}$, totaling in 9 different simulation scenarios were used to evaluate `FairPRS`. We used three populations for BN and PSD and ten populations for TGP. For each, model we generated 10 iterations resulting in 90 different datasets. The 3 proportions configurations used were $\{v_{gen} : v_{env} : v_{noise}\} = \{5 : 5 : 90,\ 10 : 20 : 70,\ 20 : 40 : 40\}$. The number of causal SNPs was set at 5% for all simulated datasets. Moreover, for all configurations the simulated datasets included 100,000 SNPs, 10,000 samples for GWAS, 1000 for PRS training and 400 for PRS testing.

Real data PRS and ancestry data were obtained from the UKB for further model validation.[23] ePRS-UKB for 6 different conditions across 104,231 multi-ethnic individuals were used in our analysis, these are height, body mass index (BMI), glycated hemoglobin (HBA1C), high-density lipoprotein cholesterol (HDL), and low-density lipoprotein cholesterol (LDL).

3. Results

3.1. *Simulated data*

FairPRS consistently achieved higher or comparable phenotype prediction accuracy with respect to the original PRS computed by PRSice2,[17] measured in terms of adjusted R^2 after correcting for top eight principal components (PCs) computed by TeraPCA[16] (Supplementary Figure 1). FairPRS achieved better results on all models across all simulation scenarios (Figure 2), each run with 10 iteration for reproducibility. Kolmogorov-Smirnov (KS)

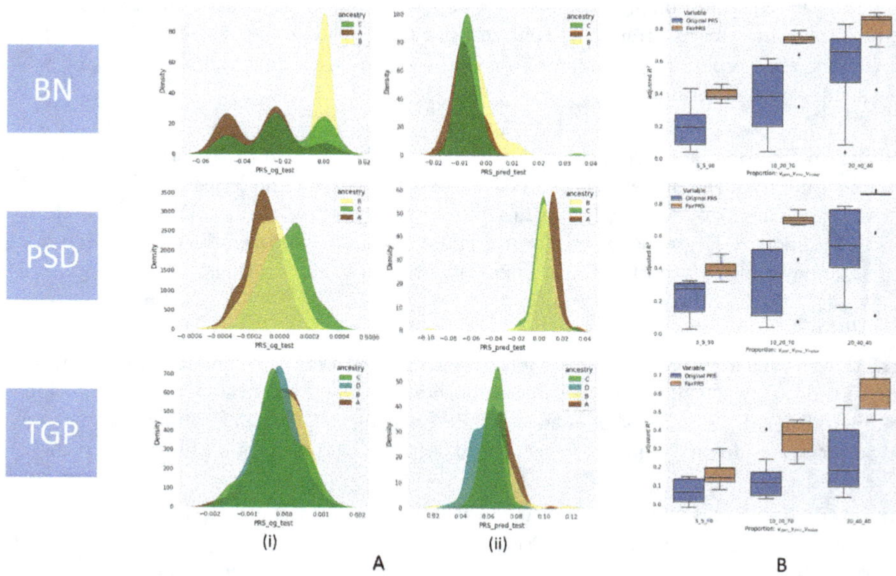

Fig. 2. Simulation study results for three simulation models, BN, PSD and TGP. **A.** Distributions of ancestry-specific PRS computed by (i) PRSice2 and (ii) FairPRS. **B.** Box-and-whisker plot of adjusted R^2 between the phenotype and PRS computed by PRSice2 and FairPRS across the variance proportions for $\{v_{gen} : v_{env} : v_{noise}\}$.

two-sample tests, a goodness of fit test of equality of the original vs. observed PRS distributions were done to test the null hypothesis of whether the two distributions were sampled from the same unknown distribution. This resulted in very low p-values ($p < 10^{-160}$) across all simulation scenarios which rejected the null hypothesis that the FairPRS distributions and the original PRS distribution were sampled from the same distribution (see Supplementary Table 1). The KS tests were done using SciPy package in python.

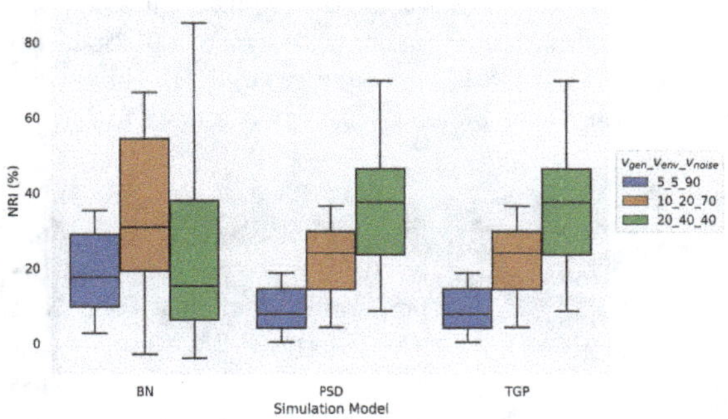

Fig. 3. Box-and-whisker plot of NRI (%) between the phenotype and PRS after using `FairPRS` from pre-computed PRS, across the variance proportions for $\{v_{gen} : v_{env} : v_{noise}\}$.

The Net Reclassification Index (NRI), a percentage score reflecting the directional change and the difference in adjusted R^2 by using `FairPRS` on top of pre-computed PRS using `PRSice2` shows that as the genetic variance (v_{gen}) increases in contribution to the phenotype, the NRI also increases (Figure 3). Hence, when a pre-computed PRS is augmented with `FairPRS` not only do we observe a higher R^2 across all the simulation scenarios, but we also obtain a relatively unbiased PRS estimate with negligible ancestry influence.

3.2. *Real data*

To demonstrate how `FairPRS` estimates real-world traits, we applied it on UKB-ePRS across six traits as mentioned above. `FairPRS` achieves considerably higher R^2 compared to the pre-computed ePRS-UKB for all traits analyzed (Figure 4).

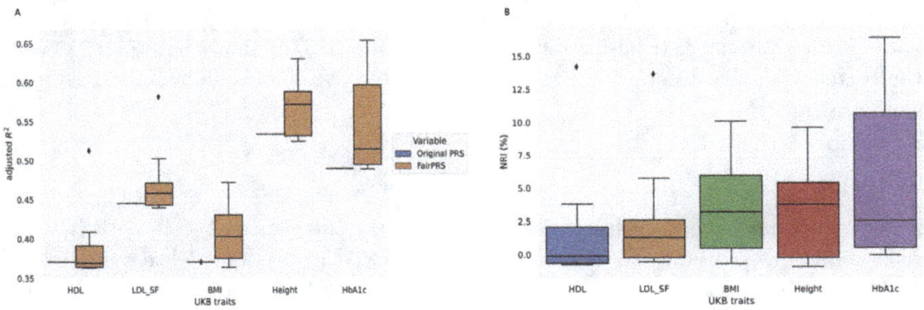

Fig. 4. Applying `FairPRS` on UKB-ePRS estimates. **A.** Box-and-whisker plot of adjusted R^2 between the UKB traits and PRS computed by `PRSice2` and `FairPRS`. **B.** Box-and-whisker plot of NRI (%) of adjusted R^2 between the phenotype and PRS after using `FairPRS` from pre-computed PRS.

We compared `FairPRS` with another recent transfer learning approach, TL-PRS[10] and found that on the demo data set made available by TL-PRS, `FairPRS` performed similarly in predicting the phenotype after correcting for covariates.

We further examined the variance explained within each ancestry group. Figure 5 shows that, for all traits, **FairPRS** achieves increased performances among white, mixed, black ancestry groups while performing marginally better in the Asian ancestry group. HDL cholesterol is decreased in black with marginal increase in other populations as it is known to have a protective effect on Black British.[24]

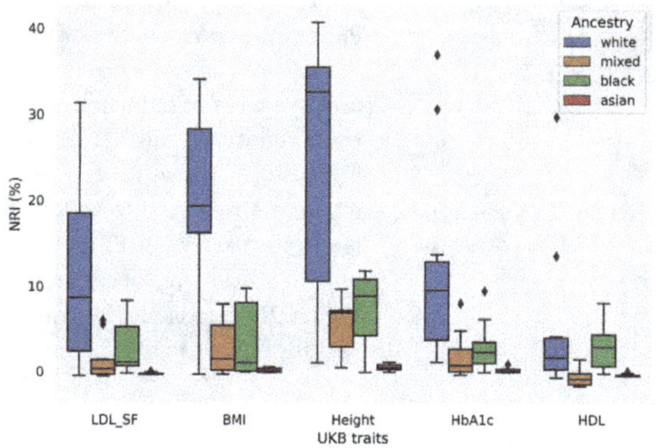

Fig. 5. Applying **FairPRS** on UKB-ePRS estimates. Box-and-whisker plot of NRI (%) of adjusted R^2 between the phenotype and PRS after using **FairPRS** from pre-computed PRS per ancestry group.

FairPRS was run 10 times for each ePRS-UKB trait analyzed for reproducibility and hyperparameter tuning. The NRI was computed by the percentage difference in R^2 when using **FairPRS** vs. pre-computed PRS. Maximum NRI was observed in glycated hemoglobin (HbA1c) which is a biomarker for Type 2 Diabetes and has been shown to have high predictive accuracy for PRS. This was followed by BMI and Height, respectively which are very well-studied in terms of phenotypic variance explained by PRS.[25] KS test for the two PRS distributions, **FairPRS** and pre-computed ePRS-UKB also resulted in the rejection of the null hypothesis (see Supplementary Table 2) and demonstrated that **FairPRS** learns a domain invariant distribution different from its input. This shows how **FairPRS** can result in better predictive accuracy in large biobanks such as UKB and can be integrated into precision medicine efforts.

4. Discussion

In this work, we combined notions from classical genetics: the polygenic risk scores (PRS), with notions from machine learning and domain adaptation. We developed a model that applies an Invariant Risk Minimization (IRM) approach to estimating PRS. Using both synthetic data and pre-computed PRS from the UK Biobank, we obtained PRS that are indistinguishable across races, while improving overall prediction accuracy in terms of *adjusted* R^2 and NRI.

Our results show that performance also improved within ancestry groups in the UK Biobank data. Predictive performance improved for all ancestry groups, except Asians (east and south), for whom the performance was equivalent to the ePRS.[23] The fact that improvement in accuracy did not come at the expense of either group is reassuring, suggesting **FairPRS** is safe in the sense it might not cause more harm than using regular PRS.

Despite their potential, GWAS are often plagued by the over-representation of European ancestry populations in their cohorts. If left uncorrected, this disproportional representation of population structure can lead to spurious associations and might only be able to explain a small fraction of heritability, among others issues.[26] As PRS are computed from GWAS summary statistics, PRS inherits many of these drawbacks which contribute to its poor generalizability and transferability across populations due to the underlying influence of LD structure and environmental factors.[2] Our method for finding fair estimates of PRS based on domain adaptation learns ancestry-invariant estimates which provide both qualitative and quantitative advantages.

Domain adaptation is a sub-field of machine learning focusing on model performance across multiple domains. The simplest driving example is when the distribution of data used for development, shifts during the deployment of the model. For example, using images of Swiss cows in the grassy Alps for training, while deploying the model to identify cows on the sandy beaches of Corsica.[12,27] By having training data from multiple such sources and by training in an environment-aware approach - as with IRM, we can reduce the number of spurious correlations our model learns, like the grassy Alpine background.

In this work, we extend the notion of "domains" to different population ancestries. We apply the IRM framework, a form of supervised domain adaptation, to adjust the pre-computed PRS scores to be ancestry ignorant. Intuitively, we try to learn the most phenotype-predictive PRS, while forcing ourselves to ignore (or "forget") any residual race information. Using IRM means we encourage the model to learn only information that is shared across ancestries. By constraining the PRS distribution of ancestries to coalesce, we ensure that when using the PRS for phenotype prediction, we get equal performance across ancestries. Thus, leading to a fairer PRS.

Different ancestries do exhibit disparities in health-related measures, and, therefore, different phenotypic distributions. However, these differences are rarely inherently biological. More often they are the result of how different ethnic subgroups interact with the healthcare system differently.[28,29] (More formally, race disparities are more of an acquisition shift, rather than population or prevalence shift[30]). Consequently, forcing to disentangle race information from genetic information will (at least partially) remove race bias and will lead to a fairer usage of genetic data when assessing genetic risk.

Nonetheless, IRM is not limitations-free. First, more generally, IRM includes a challenging bi-level optimization that can fail if test data are too dissimilar to the training data.[31] To counter that, more advanced flavors of IRM have been subsequently developed.[32] In this work, we used the original formulation since we observe all environments (ancestries) during training, guaranteeing that test-time environments are indeed similar to training-time ones. Secondly, We also encountered difficulties when modeling binary traits, probably due to combining a cross-entropy loss for the classification task with a mean squared error for the continuous PRS reconstruction, which operate on different scales, requiring an additional hyper-parameter to weigh between them and further complicating the training process. Substituting the cross-entropy loss with an MSE, which is equivalent to a Brier score[33] objective, lead to smoother training, but not necessarily better performance. We aim to fix this part of the model in future to obtain similar performance in binary traits as we observed in continuous traits. Thirdly, we saw a performance deterioration after increasing the number of expected environments and having not all of these present in the dataset, e.g., when having six expected ancestries in UKB experiments. However, in the real world we usually only have two to four ancestries that present relevant population structure, so while this was observed, it might be less of concern. An exciting future research direction is delving deeper into the interplay of `FairPRS` with local-ancestry based methods which highlights population sub-structure.

Limitations notwithstanding, `FairPRS` can be used as a tool to find unbiased estimates of pre-computed PRS or from GWAS summary statistics which would better predict the phenotype of interest. Unlike other methods which adjusts for admixed populations or LD interactions in computing PRS[9,10] and needs summary statistics, LD information, etc. `FairPRS` can work with pre-computed PRS as well as summary statistics, making it easier to work with.

`FairPRS` estimates can be used as a step forward to achieve equity in precision medicine and evaluating disease risk in large clinical cohorts. It can be extensively used for out-of-sample prediction with pre-computed PRS to obtain ancestry-robust PRS which transport better across ancestries and datasets. In future work, we want to compare the performance of PRS computed by state-of-the-art methods and ancestry-robust `FairPRS` and evaluate their portability to other ancestries.

As the use of PRS is being advocated in clinical care, `FairPRS` can be an important tool to achieve equity in healthcare as well as further our understanding of true genetic causes of disease risk. We hope that `FairPRS` will contribute to a fairer characterization of patients by genetics rather than by race.

Code Availability A Pytorch based implementation of `FairPRS`, along with scripts, descriptions and sample data to run experiments are available at `https://github.com/ComputationalGenomics/FairPRS`

Data Availability Simulated data is made available upon request. UKB-ePRS are available from UK Biobank.

Supplementary Material Supplementary material is hosted in the Supplementary directory in `https://github.com/ComputationalGenomics/FairPRS`

Acknowledgements This work was funded by IBM. We would like to thank Kenney Ng for helping with data access.

References

1. F. Dudbridge, Power and predictive accuracy of polygenic risk scores, *PLoS genetics* **9**, p. e1003348 (2013).
2. F. M. De La Vega and C. D. Bustamante, Polygenic risk scores: a biased prediction?, *Genome medicine* **10**, 1 (2018).
3. J. MacArthur, E. Bowler, M. Cerezo, L. Gil, P. Hall, E. Hastings, H. Junkins, A. McMahon, A. Milano, J. Morales *et al.*, The new nhgri-ebi catalog of published genome-wide association studies (gwas catalog), *Nucleic acids research* **45**, D896 (2017).
4. A. R. Martin, M. Kanai, Y. Kamatani, Y. Okada, B. M. Neale and M. J. Daly, Clinical use of

current polygenic risk scores may exacerbate health disparities, *Nature genetics* **51**, 584 (2019).
5. A. B. Kamiza, S. M. Toure, M. Vujkovic, T. Machipisa, O. S. Soremekun, C. Kintu, M. Corpas, F. Pirie, E. Young, D. Gill *et al.*, Transferability of genetic risk scores in african populations, *Nature Medicine* , 1 (2022).
6. A. R. Martin, C. R. Gignoux, R. K. Walters, G. L. Wojcik, B. M. Neale, S. Gravel, M. J. Daly, C. D. Bustamante and E. E. Kenny, Human demographic history impacts genetic risk prediction across diverse populations, *The American Journal of Human Genetics* **100**, 635 (2017).
7. D. Marnetto, K. Pärna, K. Läll, L. Molinaro, F. Montinaro, T. Haller, M. Metspalu, R. Mägi, K. Fischer and L. Pagani, Ancestry deconvolution and partial polygenic score can improve susceptibility predictions in recently admixed individuals, *Nature communications* **11**, 1 (2020).
8. L. G. Fritsche, Y. Ma, D. Zhang, M. Salvatore, S. Lee, X. Zhou and B. Mukherjee, On cross-ancestry cancer polygenic risk scores, *PLoS genetics* **17**, p. e1009670 (2021).
9. Y. Ruan, Y.-F. Lin, Y.-C. A. Feng, C.-Y. Chen, M. Lam, Z. Guo, L. He, A. Sawa, A. R. Martin, S. Qin *et al.*, Improving polygenic prediction in ancestrally diverse populations, *Nature Genetics* **54**, 573 (2022).
10. Z. Zhao, L. G. Fritsche, J. A. Smith, B. Mukherjee and S. Lee, The construction of multi-ethnic polygenic risk score using transfer learning, *medRxiv* (2022).
11. P. K. Gyawali, Y. L. Guen, X. Liu, H. Tang, J. Zou and Z. He, Improving genetic risk prediction across diverse population by disentangling ancestry representations, *arXiv preprint arXiv:2205.04673* (2022).
12. M. Arjovsky, L. Bottou, I. Gulrajani and D. Lopez-Paz, Invariant risk minimization, *arXiv preprint arXiv:1907.02893* (2019).
13. Z. Shen, J. Liu, Y. He, X. Zhang, R. Xu, H. Yu and P. Cui, Towards out-of-distribution generalization: A survey, *arXiv preprint arXiv:2108.13624* (2021).
14. C. Sudlow, J. Gallacher, N. Allen, V. Beral, P. Burton, J. Danesh, P. Downey, P. Elliott, J. Green, M. Landray *et al.*, Uk biobank: an open access resource for identifying the causes of a wide range of complex diseases of middle and old age, *PLoS medicine* **12**, p. e1001779 (2015).
15. C. C. Chang, C. C. Chow, L. C. Tellier, S. Vattikuti, S. M. Purcell and J. J. Lee, Second-generation PLINK: rising to the challenge of larger and richer datasets, *GigaScience* **4**, p. 7 (February 2015).
16. A. Bose, V. Kalantzis, E.-M. Kontopoulou, M. Elkady, P. Paschou and P. Drineas, Terapca: a fast and scalable software package to study genetic variation in tera-scale genotypes, *Bioinformatics* **35**, 3679 (2019).
17. S. W. Choi and P. F. O'Reilly, Prsice-2: Polygenic risk score software for biobank-scale data, *Gigascience* **8**, p. giz082 (2019).
18. D. P. Kingma and J. Ba, Adam: A method for stochastic optimization, *arXiv preprint arXiv:1412.6980* (2014).
19. A. Paszke, S. Gross, F. Massa, A. Lerer, J. Bradbury, G. Chanan, T. Killeen, Z. Lin, N. Gimelshein, L. Antiga, A. Desmaison, A. Kopf, E. Yang, Z. DeVito, M. Raison, A. Tejani, S. Chilamkurthy, B. Steiner, L. Fang, J. Bai and S. Chintala, Pytorch: An imperative style, high-performance deep learning library, in *Advances in Neural Information Processing Systems 32*, eds. H. Wallach, H. Larochelle, A. Beygelzimer, F. d'Alché-Buc, E. Fox and R. Garnett (Curran Associates, Inc., 2019) pp. 8024–8035.
20. R. Liaw, E. Liang, R. Nishihara, P. Moritz, J. E. Gonzalez and I. Stoica, Tune: A research platform for distributed model selection and training, *arXiv preprint arXiv:1807.05118* (2018).
21. S. Seabold and J. Perktold, Statsmodels: Econometric and statistical modeling with python, in *Proceedings of the 9th Python in Science Conference*, eds. Stéfan van der Walt and Jarrod Millman, (61) (n.p, 2010).
22. A. Bose, M. C. Burch, A. Chowdhury, P. Paschou and P. Drineas, Clustrat: a structure in-

formed clustering strategy for population stratification, in *International Conference on Research in Computational Molecular Biology*, (Springer, 2020).
23. D. J. Thompson, D. Wells, S. Selzam, I. Peneva, R. Moore, K. Sharp, W. A. Tarran, E. J. Beard, F. Riveros-Mckay, D. Palmer *et al.*, Uk biobank release and systematic evaluation of optimised polygenic risk scores for 53 diseases and quantitative traits, *medRxiv* (2022).
24. G. D. Batty, C. R. Gale, M. Kivimäki, I. J. Deary and S. Bell, Comparison of risk factor associations in uk biobank against representative, general population based studies with conventional response rates: prospective cohort study and individual participant meta-analysis, *bmj* **368** (2020).
25. A. V. Khera, M. Chaffin, K. H. Wade, S. Zahid, J. Brancale, R. Xia, M. Distefano, O. Senol-Cosar, M. E. Haas, A. Bick *et al.*, Polygenic prediction of weight and obesity trajectories from birth to adulthood, *Cell* **177**, 587 (2019).
26. R. J. Loos, 15 years of genome-wide association studies and no signs of slowing down, *Nature Communications* **11**, 1 (2020).
27. S. Beery, G. Van Horn and P. Perona, Recognition in terra incognita, in *Computer Vision – ECCV 2018*, eds. V. Ferrari, M. Hebert, C. Sminchisescu and Y. Weiss (Springer International Publishing, Cham, 2018).
28. J. S. Kaufman, L. Dolman, D. Rushani and R. S. Cooper, The contribution of genomic research to explaining racial disparities in cardiovascular disease: a systematic review, *American journal of epidemiology* **181**, 464 (2015).
29. Z. Obermeyer, B. Powers, C. Vogeli and S. Mullainathan, Dissecting racial bias in an algorithm used to manage the health of populations, *Science* **366**, 447 (2019).
30. D. C. Castro, I. Walker and B. Glocker, Causality matters in medical imaging, *Nature Communications* **11**, 1 (2020).
31. E. Rosenfeld, P. Ravikumar and A. Risteski, The risks of invariant risk minimization, *arXiv preprint arXiv:2010.05761* (2020).
32. K. Ahuja, K. Shanmugam, K. R. Varshney and A. Dhurandhar, Invariant risk minimization games, in *Proceedings of the 37th International Conference on Machine Learning*, ICML'20 (JMLR.org, 2020).
33. G. W. Brier *et al.*, Verification of forecasts expressed in terms of probability, *Monthly weather review* **78**, 1 (1950).

Using Association Rules to Understand the Risk of Adverse Pregnancy Outcomes in a Diverse Population

Hoyin Chu[1], Rashika Ramola[1], Shantanu Jain[1], David M. Haas[2],
Sriraam Natarajan[3], Predrag Radivojac[1]

[1]*Northeastern University,* [2]*Indiana University School of Medicine,* [3]*University of Texas at Dallas*

Racial and ethnic disparities in adverse pregnancy outcomes (APOs) have been well-documented in the United States, but the extent to which the disparities are present in high-risk subgroups have not been studied. To address this problem, we first applied association rule mining to the clinical data derived from the prospective nuMoM2b study cohort to identify subgroups at increased risk of developing four APOs (gestational diabetes, hypertension acquired during pregnancy, preeclampsia, and preterm birth). We then quantified racial/ethnic disparities within the cohort as well as within high-risk subgroups to assess potential effects of risk-reduction strategies. We identify significant differences in distributions of major risk factors across racial/ethnic groups and find surprising heterogeneity in APO prevalence across these populations, both in the cohort and in its high-risk subgroups. Our results suggest that risk-reducing strategies that simultaneously reduce disparities may require targeting of high-risk subgroups with considerations for the population context.

Keywords: Adverse pregnancy outcomes, risk assessment, health disparities

1. Introduction

The U.S. department of Health and Human Services defines health disparity as a particular kind of health difference that is closely linked with social, economic, and/or environmental disadvantage.[1] The American healthcare system has many examples of disparities between communities.[2–4] In 2016-2018, the all-cause mortality rate among Black populations was 24% higher than among White populations nationally.[5] Similarly, the Hispanic population in the USA has lesser access to health insurance than other racial/ethnic groups—before the implementation of the Affordable Care Act in 2014, 30% of Hispanic individuals reported no health insurance as compared to 11% of non-Hispanic White individuals.

In addition to the adverse consequences for the affected people and their communities, health disparities result in larger economic burden for the entire nation.[6,7] Eliminating health disparities could have reduced direct medical expenses by approximately $230 billion, and indirect productivity costs by more than $1 trillion for the years 2003-2006, with the most of the estimated cost reduction attributed to the generally poorer health outcomes of the Black and Hispanic communities.[6]

Adverse pregnancy outcomes (APOs) such as gestational diabetes mellitus (GDM), preeclampsia (PReEc), preterm birth (PTB) and new hypertension (NewHTN) are known to disproportionally affect racial/ethnic groups. As an example, a study of 5,562 women found the rate of GDM was the highest among Asian American women (16%), followed by non-Hispanic Black women (9%), Hispanic women (11%), and non-Hispanic White women (8%).[8] In another study, non-Hispanic Black women were found to be significantly more likely to experience preterm birth, hypertensive disease of pregnancy, and small-for-gestational-age birth than were non-Hispanic White women.[9] Understanding these disparities is critical to ensuring equitable health outcomes; however, due to the complex interaction between biological, social, and environmental factors, the mechanisms that lead to their formation are difficult to identify. It therefore remains challenging to design policies or intervention strategies that can reduce both APO risks and existing disparities.[10]

When designing this study, we had four different goals in mind. First, to identify subgroups at high risk for APOs from a large cohort pregnant women. Second, to quantitatively measure racial/ethnic disparities within these high-risk subgroups and compare them to the population-level disparities. Third, to identify potential intervention strategies that may lead to the greatest reduction in APO prevalence. And fourth, to measure the impact of such intervention strategies on existing disparities. To achieve this, we obtained data from the diverse nuMoM2b cohort which contained clinical data for 10,038 nulliparous women,[11] and used association rule mining to identify high-risk subgroups. By increasing the resolution of the disparity analysis from the population-level to high-risk subgroups, we gained additional insights into the interplay between the main risk factors and disproportionate health outcomes. In addition, by measuring the effects of potential intervention on disparity, we found that the largest risk-reducing intervention may not be the largest disparity-reducing intervention. This finding could have implications for the design of future clinical interventions, as risk factors may vary significantly across racial/ethnic groups.

2. Methods

2.1. *The nuMoM2b cohort*

The Nulliparous Pregnancy Outcomes Study: Monitoring Mothers-To-Be (nuMoM2b) cohort was recruited prospectively to identify factors that contribute to APOs.[11] The study enrolled 10,038 subjects from eight clinical centers in the US. Women were eligible for enrollment if they had a viable singleton gestation, had no previous pregnancy that lasted more than 20 weeks of gestation (i.e., nulliparous), and were between 6 0/7 and 13 6/7 weeks of gestation at enrollment, which was also the first study visit. Haas et al.[11] provide an overview of the biospecimen collection, clinical measurements, and standardized questionnaire instruments that were collected during each of the three study visits and at delivery. The cohort is racially and ethnically diverse, with more than 4,000 individuals reporting race other than White, and has a high concordance between self-reported race and inferred ancestry from genetic data.[12] Operationally, the cohort comprises of 1,509 subjects positive for at least one APO. Of those, 807 were positive for PTB, 568 for preeclampsia, 55 for fetal demise, 414 for GDM, and 406 experienced fetal growth restriction.

To capture an accurate representation of the participants prior to any clinical interventions, we used data from the first study visit only. For quality control, 10 individuals with high information missingness were excluded. To ensure our findings are based on sufficiently large sample sizes and to reduce possible confounding introduced by mixed cultural effects within groups, only self-reported races/ethnicities with more than 100 participants were included and participants who did not report race/ethnicity ($n = 639$) or reported more than one race ($n = 486$) were excluded. Participants were then assigned to one of four racial/ethnic groups based on their self-reported race and ethnicity: non-Hispanic Asian, non-Hispanic Black, non-Hispanic White, and Hispanic. In total, 8,903 participants were included in the final analysis.

Our study primarily relies on clinical variables and the features selected for analysis include basic demographic features and a curated set of features previously known to affect the likelihood of developing APOs.[13] These include age, body mass index (BMI), family history of diabetes mellitus (Family DM), polycystic ovary syndrome history (PCOS), Alternate Healthy Eating Index-2010 (AHEI2010) score, activity levels measured by the metabolic equivalent of tasks (METs),[14] and high blood pressure (High BP). The diet of a participant was considered "poor" if her AHEI2010 score was below the 25th percentile of all scores, "normal" if it was between 25th and 75th percentile, and "good" if it was above the 75th percentile. Consistent with previous studies, a participant's exercise level was considered "inactive" if her METs is below 450 and "active" otherwise.[14,15] Participants reporting age or BMI of zero were recoded as having missing age or BMI. For compatibility with downstream association rules analysis, age and BMI were discretized into intervals as defined by the nuMoM2b study.[11]

2.2. *Clinical data as a transactional database*

To find interesting and interpretable patterns in the nuMoM2b data, we converted it to a transactional database and performed association rule mining.[16] An association rule is a probabilistic implication discovered from a transactional database. For example, in the context of nuMoM2b, a high-confidence rule $\{\mathsf{Race} = \mathsf{Asian}, \mathsf{Age} > 40\} \Rightarrow \{\mathsf{GDM} = 1\}$ has the interpretation "Pregnant Asian women above the age of 40 are likely to be diagnosed with GDM".

A transactional database $\boldsymbol{D} = \{t_1, t_2, ..., t_m\}$ is a set of transactions, where each transaction is a subset of items from $\mathcal{I} = \{i_1, i_2, \ldots, i_n\}$. To represent a clinical database as a transactional dataset, we first convert the collected descriptors and clinical measurements into clinically relevant binary features such as $\{\mathsf{Race} = \mathsf{Asian}\}$, $\{\mathsf{Age} > 40\}$ and $\{\mathsf{GDM} = 1\}$. Then for each subject in the cohort, we create a transaction containing only those binary features (as items) that are true for the subject. For example, based on the three features above, an Asian participant above the age of 40 and diagnosed with GDM, would be represented as $\{\mathsf{Race} = \mathsf{Asian}, \mathsf{Age} > 40, \mathsf{GDM} = 1\}$. In total, 25 binary features were created from Age (5), BMI (5), Family DM (2), PCOS (2), High BP (2), Exercise (2), Diet (3) and APOs (4) in the nuMoM2b data.

2.3. *Association rules*

For a transactional database $\boldsymbol{D}$ defined on a set of items $\mathcal{I}$, an association rule is an implication of the form $A \Rightarrow B$, where A and B are disjoint subsets of $\mathcal{I}$ and are referred to as the antecedent and the consequent of the rule, respectively. Typically, the evidence of a rule in $\boldsymbol{D}$ is quantified in terms of the *confidence* defined as fraction of transactions containing all items in B out of the transactions that contain all items in A. In other words, it quantifies the conditional probability of seeing B in a transaction given that A has been already seen. Formally,

$$\text{Confidence}_{\boldsymbol{D}}(A \Rightarrow B) = \frac{\text{Support}_{\boldsymbol{D}}(A \cup B)}{\text{Support}_{\boldsymbol{D}}(A)},$$

where $\text{Support}_{\boldsymbol{D}}(A)$ is the fraction of transactions in $\boldsymbol{D}$ that contain A; i.e., $\text{Support}_{\boldsymbol{D}}(A) = |\boldsymbol{D}_A|/|\boldsymbol{D}|$, and $\boldsymbol{D}_A = \{t|A \subseteq t, t \in \boldsymbol{D}\}$ is the set of transactions containing A. Applying these definitions to the example above, $\text{Confidence}_{\boldsymbol{D}}(\{\mathsf{Race} = \mathsf{Asian}, \mathsf{Age} > 40\} \Rightarrow \{\mathsf{GDM} = 1\})$ is the fraction of women diagnosed with GDM out of all Asian women above the age of 40 in the cohort; i.e., the empirical probability that a pregnant Asian woman above the age of 40 has GDM. $\text{Support}_{\boldsymbol{D}}(\{\mathsf{Race} = \mathsf{Asian}, \mathsf{Age} > 40, \mathsf{GDM} = 1\})$ is the fraction of Asian women above the age of 40 diagnosed with GDM in our cohort.

Association rules can be efficiently discovered with the Apriori algorithm.[16] We apply Apriori to the transactional database created from the nuMoM2b data using the efficient-apriori Python package with the parameters min_support = 0.0005, min_confidence = 0.001, and max_length = 6. Afterwards, we extracted rules with APOs as the consequent; i.e., $\{\mathsf{GDM} = 1\}$, $\{\mathsf{NewHTN} = 1\}$, $\{\mathsf{PReEc} = 1\}$, and $\{\mathsf{PTB} = 1\}$.

2.3.1. *Measuring clinical significance of association rules*

While confidence is easily interpretable as a conditional probability, it fails to capture the relative improvement over the baseline probability of the consequent.[17] Any rule $A \Rightarrow B$, where B has low support, is likely to have low confidence, irrespective of the relative increase in the conditional probability over the baseline. Such rules are still important in clinical applications; e.g., finding causal attributes for rare diseases. To overcome the limitations of confidence, we use positive likelihood ratios (LR^+), a standard measure used in clinical settings.[18] Formally,

$$\text{LR}^+(A \Rightarrow B) = \frac{\text{Confidence}_{\boldsymbol{D}}(A \Rightarrow B)/(1 - \text{Confidence}_{\boldsymbol{D}}(A \Rightarrow B))}{\text{Support}_{\boldsymbol{D}}(B)/(1 - \text{Support}_{\boldsymbol{D}}(B))},$$

with asymmetric 95% confidence intervals determined by bootstrapping.[19] We additionally test the null hypothesis that the association between A and B occurs by chance, using Fisher's exact test, and compute the p-value.

2.4. *Quantitative measure of disparity*

Disparity of outcomes across different groups can be measured in several ways and there is not a single best quantitative measure for it.[20] We adopt the measure often used in the field of economics to study income inequalities, and define disparity as the Gini coefficient of APO prevalence rates among different populations.[21] More formally, let a binary outcome variable Y (e.g., GDM) take values $\mathcal{Y} = \{0, 1\}$, where 1 (0) indicates presence (absence) of an APO. Let X be a variable of interest (e.g., racial/ethnic group) taking values in $\mathcal{X}$, where different values of X characterize different subpopulations of interest. Let $p(x, y)$ be a joint distribution over variables X and Y. We define the disparity of Y with respect to (w.r.t.) X as the Gini coefficient of the conditional probabilities $p(Y = 1|X = x)$ over all values of $x \in \mathcal{X}$; i.e.,

$$\delta(Y|X) = \text{Gini}(\{p(Y = 1|X = x)\}_{x \in \mathcal{X}}), \text{ where Gini}(S) = \frac{\sum_{a \in S} \sum_{b \in S} |a - b|}{2|S| \sum_{a \in S} a}$$

computes the Gini coefficient of the set S. Note that Gini coefficient is scale independent, due to normalization by $\sum_{a\in S} a$, unlike measures such as standard deviation. This property makes it ideal to compare disparity between two populations (e.g., before and after removing high-risk individuals) with outcomes on different scales.

We study disparity of APOs w.r.t. racial/ethnic groups in the nuMoM2b dataset. Under the disparity formulation given above, an APO $\in$ {GDM, PReEc, PTB, NewHTN} serves as Y and racial/ethnic groups serve as X. Let $\boldsymbol{D}$ denote a cohort under study given as a transactional database defined on a set of items $\mathcal{I}$ (Section 2.2). In particular, $\mathcal{I}$ contains items $Y = 1$ and $X = x$ for $\forall x \in \mathcal{X}$. $\boldsymbol{D}$ defines an empirical distribution over X and Y given by

$$p_{\boldsymbol{D}}(x, y) = \begin{cases} \text{Support}_{\boldsymbol{D}}(X = x \ \cup \ Y = 1) & \text{when } y = 1, \\ \text{Support}_{\boldsymbol{D}}(X = x) - \text{Support}_{\boldsymbol{D}}(X = x \ \cup \ Y = 1) & \text{when } y = 0, \end{cases}$$

where $\text{Support}_{\boldsymbol{D}}(A)$ denotes the Support of an itemset $A \subseteq \mathcal{I}$ computed on $\boldsymbol{D}$. Furthermore, the conditional probability $p_{\boldsymbol{D}}(Y = 1|X = x)$ under $\boldsymbol{D}$ is given by

$$p_{\boldsymbol{D}}(Y = 1|X = x) = \text{Confidence}_{\boldsymbol{D}}(X = x \ \Rightarrow \ Y = 1),$$

where $\text{Confidence}_{\boldsymbol{D}}(A \Rightarrow B)$ denotes the confidence of the rule $A \Rightarrow B$ computed on $\boldsymbol{D}$. Thus the disparity of the APOs (Y) w.r.t. racial/ethnic groups (X) on $\boldsymbol{D}$ is given by

$$\delta_{\boldsymbol{D}}(Y|X) = \sigma(\{p_{\boldsymbol{D}}(Y = 1|X = x)\}_{x\in\mathcal{X}}), \text{ where } \sigma(S) = \text{Gini}(S).$$

We are interested in the contribution of the high-risk subgroups, defined in terms of the risk factors such as age and BMI, towards the overall prevalence and the disparities of each APO. To do so, we evaluate the relative difference in APO prevalence and disparity when the high-risk participants are omitted from the cohort. Let $R \subseteq \mathcal{I}$ be the attributes (not including APO or racial/ethnic groups) identifying the high-risk individuals. Let $\boldsymbol{D}_R = \{t|R \subseteq t, t \in \boldsymbol{D}\}$ denote the set of transactions (individuals) in $\boldsymbol{D}$ that contain R. Let $\overline{\boldsymbol{D}}_R = \boldsymbol{D} \setminus \boldsymbol{D}_R$ be the set of transactions in $\boldsymbol{D}$ that do not contain R. The disparity of the APOs (Y) w.r.t. racial/ethnic groups (X) on $\overline{\boldsymbol{D}}_R$ is given by,

$$\delta_{\overline{\boldsymbol{D}}_R}(Y|X) = \sigma\left(\left\{p_{\overline{\boldsymbol{D}}_R}(Y = 1|X = x)\right\}_{x\in\mathcal{X}}\right).$$

The relative change in disparity on removing the participants having all phenotypes/attributes in R is given by

$$\frac{\delta_{\overline{\boldsymbol{D}}_R}(Y|X) - \delta_{\boldsymbol{D}}(Y|X)}{\delta_{\boldsymbol{D}}(Y|X)}.$$

Similarly, for the subpopulation having $X = x$, the relative change in the APO prevalence rate on removing the participants having all phenotypes/attributes in R is given by

$$\frac{p_{\overline{\boldsymbol{D}}_R}(Y = 1|X = x) - p_{\boldsymbol{D}}(Y = 1|X = x)}{p_{\boldsymbol{D}}(Y = 1|X = x)}.$$

2.4.1. *Identifying high-risk subgroups*

To identify high-risk subgroups used in the disparity analysis, we started with the initial set of rules with the APOs in the consequent, that pass the support and confidence thresholds. The rules were further filtered based on the following inclusion criteria: LR^+ value above 1; does not contain the variable of interest (race/ethnicity) in the antecedent; and the size of the antecedent is no more than 3.

3. Results

3.1. *Association rules effectively identify high-risk subgroups*

A total of 1,627 rules satisfied filtering criteria, among which 726 were nominally significant ($p < 0.05$) and 527 (GDM: 188; NewHTN: 130; PReEc: 119; PTB: 90) were significant after adjusting for multiple hypothesis testing using the Benjamini-Hochberg procedure.[22] Among the statistically significant subgroups, 21 rules had one attribute in the antecedent, 146 rules had two attributes and 360 had three attributes. BMI and Age were the two most common attributes in the rules, where 339 rules (64.3%) contained a BMI attribute and 234 rules (44.4%) contained an Age attribute (Table S1).

The generated rules were able to capture many known risk factors that are common to all APOs. For example, obesity is a known risk factor for APOs and the subgroup $\{\text{BMI} \geq 35\}$ was generated as a high-risk subgroup with varying likelihood ratios in APOs (Table 1). In addition, the generated rules were also able to capture APO-specific high-risk subgroups. For example, older age is a risk factor for GDM[23] and NewHTN,[24] while younger age is a risk factor for PTB[25] and PReEc.[26] Consistently with prior findings, we observe the corresponding risk groups $\{\text{Age} = \text{35-39}\}$ and $\{\text{Age} < 18\}$ being generated in the association rules. The association between dietary choices and risk on PReEc was recently reported[27] and we similarly see an increased risk for PReEc for the subgroup that has poor diet.

Table 1. Examples of statistically significant association rules for the nuMoM2b cohort.

Antecedent	Consequent	Confidence	LR^+ [95% CI]	Adjusted p-value
$\{\text{Age} = \text{35-39}\}$	$\{\text{GDM} = 1\}$	9.6% (51/531)	2.5 [1.9, 3.2]	4.7×10^{-7}
$\{\text{Age} = \text{35-39}\}$	$\{\text{NewHTN} = 1\}$	21.1% (112/531)	1.4 [1.1, 1.7]	1.1×10^{-2}
$\{\text{Age} < 18\}$	$\{\text{PTB} = 1\}$	14.3% (70/489)	1.8 [1.4, 2.3]	1.7×10^{-4}
$\{\text{BMI} \geq 35\}$	$\{\text{GDM} = 1\}$	8.8% (78/882)	2.3 [1.8, 2.8]	5.8×10^{-9}
$\{\text{BMI} \geq 35\}$	$\{\text{PTB} = 1\}$	11.9% (105/882)	2.2 [1.8, 2.7]	7.2×10^{-4}
$\{\text{BMI} \geq 35\}$	$\{\text{NewHTN} = 1\}$	25.3% (223/882)	1.8 [1.5, 2.0]	1.1×10^{-10}
$\{\text{Diet} = \text{poor}\}$	$\{\text{PReEc} = 1\}$	7.9% (146/1853)	1.4 [1.2, 1.6]	3.0×10^{-4}
$\{\text{Exercise} = \text{inactive}, \text{High BP} = 1\}$	$\{\text{PTB} = 1\}$	21.4% (19/89)	2.9 [1.8, 4.8]	5.7×10^{-3}
$\{\text{Diet} = \text{poor}, \text{High BP} = 1\}$	$\{\text{PReEc} = 1\}$	22.2% (16/72)	4.7 [2.7, 8.1]	1.2×10^{-3}
$\{\text{Age} = \text{35-39}, \text{BMI} = \text{30-35}\}$	$\{\text{NewHTN} = 1\}$	33.3% (22/66)	2.6 [1.6, 4.3]	3.6×10^{-3}

Furthermore, association rules were able to identify high-risk subgroups from combinations of features where each feature individually may not necessarily be a strong risk factor. Such

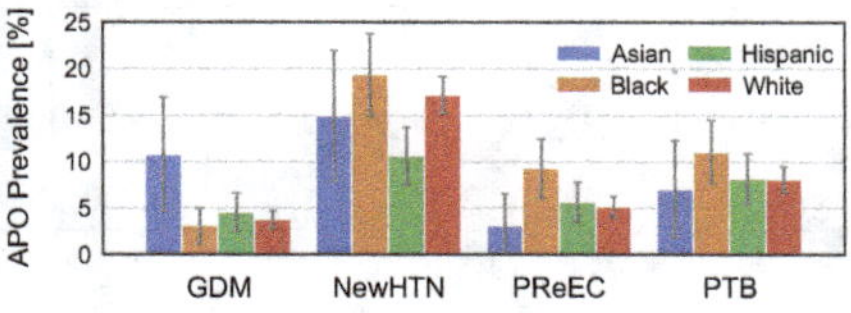

Fig. 1. The prevalence of each adverse pregnancy outcome (APO) with respect to self-reported race/ethnicity. GDM: gestational diabetes mellitus; NewHTN: new hypertension; PReEc: preeclampsia; PTB: preterm birth. A pairwise comparison of APO rates by race/ethnicity is available in Table S2.

combinations of features also allow for investigating the impact of a singular feature on an existing subgroup. All generated rules are listed in Supplementary Table S1, which is available online at the project github (`https://github.com/hoyinchu/PSB_2023_Supplement`).

3.2. *Disparity is highly heterogeneous within and across APOs*

We assessed the level of disparity over the entire cohort as well as in high-risk subgroups finding significant heterogeneity across APOs (Fig. 1, Table 2) and risk groups (Table S1). For example, Black participants have the lowest prevalence of GDM compared to other groups (3.1%), but the highest rates of all other APOs (9.3% in PReEc, 11.1% in PTB, 19.4% in NewHTN). Asian participants have the highest rate of GDM (10.8%), while also having the lowest rate of PReEc (3.2%). The rates of APOs in White participants are comparable to those in Hispanic, except for NewHTN (17.2% vs. 10.7%). Surprisingly, disparities in high-risk subgroups do not follow a regular pattern either. In GDM, for example, the disparity of the {Age = 35-39} subgroup ($LR^+ = 2.5$; $p = 4.7 \times 10^{-7}$) is reduced from 0.268 (population; Table 2) to 0.112 (high-risk subgroup; Table S1), whereas the disparity of the {BMI = 30-35} subgroup ($LR^+ = 1.9$; $p = 1.1 \times 10^{-6}$) is increased to 0.356 (Table S1). Similar patterns were observed in other APOs.

Table 2. Prevalence and count of APOs in each racial/ethnic group, their respective disparity measure and p-values from a chi-square (χ^2) test.

APO	Asian ($n = 381$)	Black ($n = 1291$)	Hispanic ($n = 1587$)	White ($n = 5644$)	Total	Gini	χ^2 p-value
GDM	41 (10.8%)	40 (3.1%)	72 (4.5%)	213 (3.8%)	366 (4.1%)	0.268	1.70×10^{-10}
NewHTN	57 (15.0%)	250 (19.4%)	169 (10.7%)	968 (17.2%)	1444 (16.2%)	0.114	9.32×10^{-11}
PReEc	12 (3.2%)	120 (9.3%)	90 (5.7%)	291 (5.2%)	513 (5.8%)	0.204	2.43×10^{-8}
PTB	27 (7.1%)	143 (11.1%)	130 (8.2%)	459 (8.1%)	759 (8.5%)	0.087	0.004

3.2.1. *Disparities in high-risk GDM subgroups*

For simplicity and interpretability, we focus our analysis mainly on single-attribute high-risk subgroups. In GDM, the {Age $\geq$ 40} subgroup has the highest LR^+ compared to other single-attribute subgroups, followed by the {Age = 35-39}, and {High BP = 1} subgroups; Fig. 2a. Among these subgroups, the one with the highest disparity measure was also the {Age $\geq$ 40}

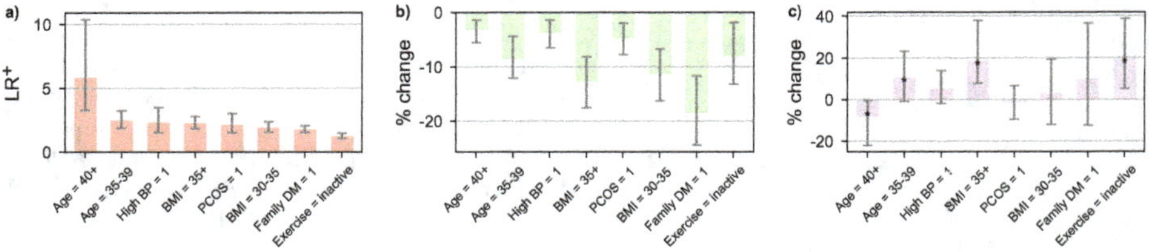

Fig. 2. The prevalence and disparities of GDM and high-risk subgroup relative contribution to the disparity. (a) The LR^+ associated with high-risk GDM subgroups. (b) The relative change in GDM prevalence if a subgroup is omitted from the cohort. (c) The relative change in Gini coefficient if a subgroup is omitted from cohort, with markings for statistically significant values. Exact values and prevalence by each racial/ethnic group are available in Supplementary Tables S3-S6.

subgroup, followed by the $\{\mathsf{BMI} = \text{30-35}\}$ and $\{\mathsf{High\ BP} = 1\}$ subgroups (Table S3). We then evaluated the proportion of GDM patients in each of these subgroups to understand how these risk-factors may differentially impact races/ethnicities. We found that across risk-factors, Asian participants have higher rates of GDM compared to other races/ethnicities within the same subgroup except in the $\{\mathsf{Age} = \text{35-39}\}$ subgroup (Table S4). In particular, the rate of GDM is considerably higher in the $\{\mathsf{Age} \geq 40\}$ subgroup, which is also the subgroup with the highest GDM disparity measure (Table S3).

We next investigated the contribution of GDM rates from each high-risk subgroup to the overall GDM rate in the cohort by calculating the relative difference between the rate of GDM before and after the subgroup is removed from the cohort; see Methods. We observe the largest decrease in GDM rate if the $\{\mathsf{Family\ DM} = 1\}$ subgroup is omitted, followed by $\{\mathsf{BMI} \geq 35\}$ and $\{\mathsf{BMI} = \text{30-35}\}$ subgroups; see Fig. 2b and Table S5. Subsequently, we calculated the relative change in disparity if these subgroups were to be omitted. We observe the greatest decrease in GDM disparity when the $\{\mathsf{Age} \geq 40\}$ subgroup is omitted (Fig. 2c), which is reflected in the large decrease in GDM rate in Asian participants (Table S6).

3.2.2. *Disparities in high-risk NewHTN subgroups*

In NewHTN, the top three single-attribute subgroups with the largest LR^+ are $\{\mathsf{BMI} \geq 35\}$, $\{\mathsf{BMI} = \text{30-35}\}$ and $\{\mathsf{Age} = \text{35-39}\}$ (Fig. 3a), where the disparity measure is the highest in the $\{\mathsf{BMI} = \text{25-30}\}$, $\{\mathsf{BMI} \geq 35\}$ and $\{\mathsf{Family\ DM} = 1\}$ subgroups (Table S3). The relative prevalence of NewHTN by race/ethnicity in each high-risk subgroup is highly heterogeneous: in high BMI groups such as $\{\mathsf{BMI} = \text{25-30}\}$ and $\{\mathsf{BMI} \geq 35\}$, Asian participants have the highest rate of NewHTN, whereas White participants have the highest NewHTN rate in the $\{\mathsf{Age} = \text{35-39}\}$ groups and Black participants have the highest NewHTN rate in the $\{\mathsf{Family\ DM} = 1\}$ group, as shown in Table S4.

When omitted from cohort, the top three single-attribute subgroups that result in the largest reduction in NewHTN rate were all BMI-related ($\{\mathsf{BMI} \geq 35\}$, $\{\mathsf{BMI} = \text{30-35}\}$, $\{\mathsf{BMI} = \text{25-30}\}$); see Fig. 3b. However, only the $\{\mathsf{BMI} \geq 35\}$ subgroup led to a decrease in disparity measure when omitted (Fig. 3c). The racial/ethnic group for which the reduction in

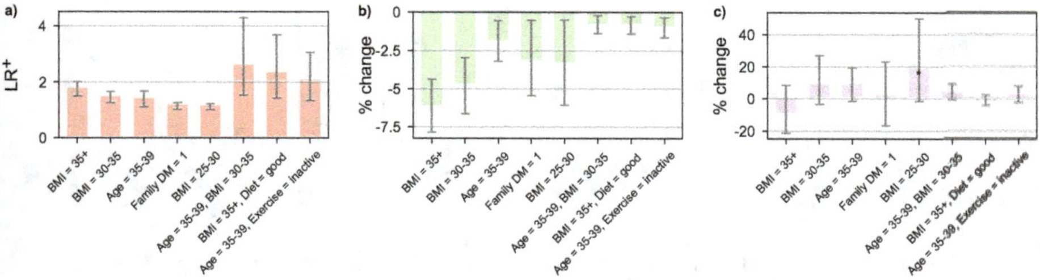

Fig. 3. The prevalence and disparities of NewHTN and high-risk subgroup relative contribution to the disparity. (a) The LR^+ associated with high-risk NewHTN subgroups. (b) The relative change in NewHTN prevalence if a subgroup is omitted from the cohort. (c) The relative change in Gini coefficient if a subgroup is omitted from cohort, with markings for statistically significant values. Exact values and prevalence by each racial/ethnic group are available in Supplementary Tables S3-S6.

NewHTN risk was the highest was also different for each BMI subgroup, where omitting the $\{\mathsf{BMI} \geq 35\}$ subgroup leads to the greatest reduction in NewHTN risk in Black participants, omitting the $\{\mathsf{BMI} = \text{30-35}\}$ subgroup leads to the greatest reduction in NewHTN risk in Hispanic participants, and omitting the $\{\mathsf{BMI} = \text{25-30}\}$ subgroup leads to the greatest reduction in NewHTN risk in Asian participants (Table S6).

3.2.3. *Disparities in high-risk PReEc subgroups*

The subgroup with the highest LR^+ for PReEc is the $\{\mathsf{High\ BP} = 1\}$ subgroup, followed by the $\{\mathsf{BMI} \geq 35\}$ and $\{\mathsf{BMI} = \text{30-35}\}$ subgroups (Fig. 4a, Table S3). The disparity measures for each of these subgroups are also similar, with $\{\mathsf{High\ BP} = 1\}$, $\{\mathsf{PCOS} = 1\}$ and $\{\mathsf{Age} < 18\}$ being the three subgroups with the highest disparity (Fig. 4b), two of which are also in the highest disparity subgroups for PTB. The rates of PReEc by race/ethnicity are comparable as well, with Black participants having higher rates of PReEc across similar risk factors (Table S4).

The top three best PReEc risk-reducing when omitted single-attribute subgroups are $\{\mathsf{BMI} \geq 35\}$, $\{\mathsf{Diet} = \mathsf{poor}\}$, and $\{\mathsf{BMI} = \text{30-35}\}$. Among these high-risk subgroups, the $\{\mathsf{Diet} = \mathsf{poor}\}$ subgroup is unique to PReEc and is not a high-risk subgroup found in other APOs in isolation (Table S5). The best disparity-reducing single-attribute subgroup when omitted is $\{\mathsf{High\ BP} = 1\}$, followed by $\{\mathsf{BMI} \geq 35\}$ and $\{\mathsf{Diet} = \mathsf{poor}\}$; see Table S5. The effect of omitting these subgroups on the overall rate of PReEc varied, where omitting the $\{\mathsf{High\ BP} = 1\}$ subgroup leads to the highest reduction in PReEc rate in Black participants, omitting $\{\mathsf{BMI} \geq 35\}$ leads to significant reduction in both White and Black participants, and omitting the $\{\mathsf{BMI} = \text{30-35}\}$ or $\{\mathsf{Family\ DM} = 1\}$ lead to the highest reduction in PReEc rate in Asian participants, although not statistically significant (Table S6).

3.2.4. *Disparities in high-risk PTB subgroups*

The landscape of disparity in PTB was vastly different from that in GDM. In PTB, the subgroup with the highest LR^+ is $\{\mathsf{High\ BP} = 1\}$, followed by $\{\mathsf{Age} < 18\}$ and $\{\mathsf{PCOS} = 1\}$; Fig. 5a.

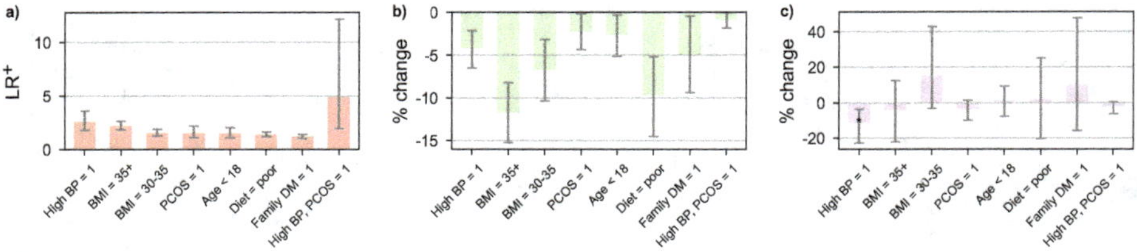

Fig. 4. The prevalence and disparities of PReEc and high-risk subgroup relative contribution to the disparity. (a) The LR^+ associated with high-risk PReEc subgroups. (b) The relative change in PReEc prevalence if a subgroup is omitted from the cohort. (c) The relative change in Gini coefficient if a subgroup is omitted from cohort, with markings for statistically significant values. Exact values and prevalence by each racial/ethnic group are available in Supplementary Tables S3-S6.

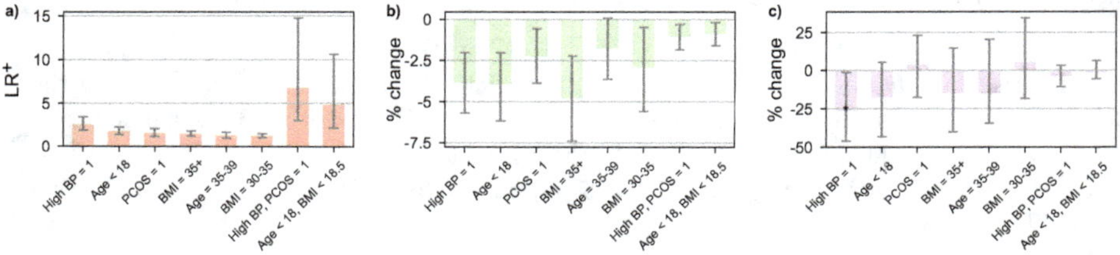

Fig. 5. The prevalence and disparities of PTB and high-risk subgroup relative contribution to the disparity. (a) The LR^+ associated with high-risk PTB subgroups. (b) The relative change in PTB prevalence if a subgroup is omitted from the cohort. (c) The relative change in Gini coefficient if a subgroup is omitted from cohort, with markings for statistically significant values. Exact values and prevalence by each racial/ethnic group are available in Supplementary Tables S3-S6.

For these high-risk subgroups, the disparity measure is the highest in $\{\textsf{Age} < 18\}$ followed by $\{\textsf{Age} = \textsf{35-39}\}$ and $\{\textsf{High BP} = 1\}$; see Table S3. The prevalence of PTB by racial/ethnic group also differed from that of GDM, with Black participants being the group with the highest PTB rate across high-risk subgroups except those in the $\{\textsf{Age} < 18\}$ subgroup, where the proportion of PTB patients are the highest among White participants (Table S4).

When omitting high-risk subgroups, we observe the greatest reduction in PTB rate is achieved when the $\{\textsf{BMI} \geq 35\}$ subgroup is omitted, followed by $\{\textsf{Age} < 18\}$ and $\{\textsf{High BP} = 1\}$ (Fig. 5b). Omitting the subgroup $\{\textsf{BMI} \geq 35\}$ led to highest reduction in disparity, followed by $\{\textsf{Age} < 18\}$ and $\{\textsf{High BP} = 1\}$; see Table S5. Upon investigating the effect of omitting subgroup on PTB rate by race/ethnicity, we found all three high-risk subgroups where reduction in PTB prevalence is the most significant ($\{\textsf{BMI} \geq 35\}$, $\{\textsf{Age} < 18\}$, $\{\textsf{High BP} = 1\}$) are also the groups that when omitted lead to the highest rate reduction in Black participants (Table S6).

3.3. *Major APO risk-factors are associated with population structure*

Given the frequent occurrence of Age and BMI as attributes in high-risk groups and the high variance in APO prevalence by race in these subgroups, we hypothesize that one of the

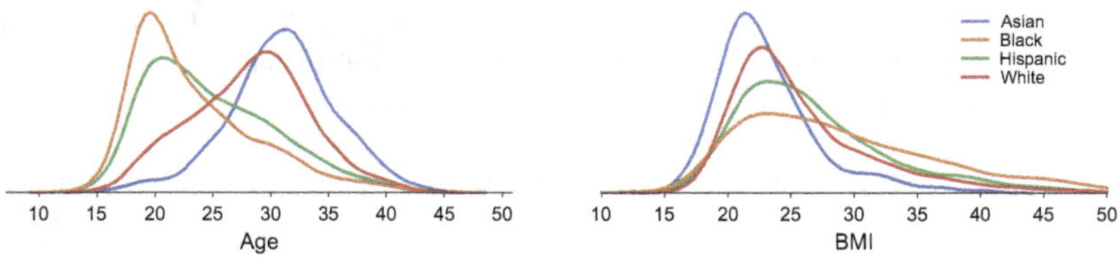

Fig. 6. Age and BMI distributions for each racial/ethnic group in the cohort visualized using the kdeplot function from the Python library Seaborn.

components for disparities in APO could be partially attributable to the differences in age and BMI distributions between races/ethnicities in our cohort. We then employed the Kruskal-Wallis H-test on the age and BMI distributions marginalized by race and found the difference in distributions to be highly significant (Age: $p = 8.7 \times 10^{-280}$, BMI: $p = 7.0 \times 10^{-268}$); see Fig. 6.

4. Discussion

Adverse pregnancy outcomes can affect a family long after the delivery, and the ability to identify sources of disparities is crucial for ensuring equitable access to resources needed to address these outcomes. In this study, we used association rule mining as a tool to detect subgroups that are at increased risk for experiencing APOs, and evaluated the racial/ethnic disparities within these subgroups. We discovered significant heterogeneity in APO prevalence across racial/ethnic groups, quantified the disparity in each high-risk subgroup, and evaluated each subgroup's contribution to the total risk and disparity through observing the relative rate change when the subgroup was omitted from the cohort. In addition, we identified significant differences in age and BMI distributions across racial/ethnic groups, which appear to play an important role in shaping the APO risk landscape. The simplicity and interpretable nature of association rules also enable the findings to be accessible to wide audiences including clinicians and policy makers. While the study does not model clinical intervention, our findings can be used to inform planning of policy interventions, such as influencing resource allocation in communities where disparities and health outcomes need to be addressed. For example, the high prevalence of GDM among Asian participants above the age of 40 could serve as evidence for prioritizing education on the potential impact of maternal age on the risk of gestational diabetes in Asian communities, while the high prevalence of PReEc among Black participants with high blood pressure could serve as evidence for prioritizing education on blood pressure management in Black communities.

As with any clinical data, some variables used in our study may be underreported or incorrectly recorded. Additionally, the modest sample size resulted in relatively large confidence intervals in some high-risk subgroups. The change in APO proportion if a subgroup is omitted also represents an idealized form of intervention with two strong assumptions; i.e., we assume that if an intervention on a risk factor is given, then (1) this risk factor is reduced to 0% in the population and (2) individuals who originally harbored these risk factors will proportionally distribute to other subgroups. These should not be taken as a realistic estimate of how much

APO prevalence might decrease if an intervention is placed on a specific risk factor but rather an estimate of the contribution of the risk factors to the overall prevalence of APOs. It is also worth mentioning that when a high-risk subgroup is omitted but the disparity measure increases, it does not necessarily mean that addressing such a subgroup should not be performed; instead, it shows that some groups may not receive equal benefits from addressing these risk factors.

This study can be extended to include higher-resolution groupings of risk factors as well as the possibilities that other factors (e.g., social, economic, cultural) could have larger impact on disparities than the features investigated herein. Of note, however, this work does not provide evidence for biological differences between races and ethnicities that may predispose one over another towards certain APOs. Overall, this study calls for the investigation of disparities beyond the population level, and brings to attention the importance of considering subgroup-level disparities, which may manifest differently from their population form.

Acknowledgements

The authors acknowledge the support by the NIH grant R01HD101246 to DMH, SN, and PR.

References

1. R. Aungst, *Perspect Audiol* **7**, 29 (2011).
2. Lasser *et al.*, *Am J Public Health* **96**, 1300 (2006).
3. Orsi *et al.*, *Am J Public Health* **100**, 349 (2010).
4. Lavizzo-Mourney *et al.*, *N Engl J Med* **384**, 1681 (2021).
5. Benjamins *et al.*, *JAMA Netw Open* **4**, e2032086 (2021).
6. T. Laveist and D. Gaskin, *Int J Health Serv* **41**, 231 (2011).
7. M. Engelgau *et al.*, *Ethn Dis* **29**, 103 (2019).
8. E. Petersen *et al.*, *Morb Mortal Wkly Rep* **68**, 762 (2019).
9. W. Grobman *et al.*, *Obstet Gynecol* **131**, 328 (2018).
10. D. Williams and T. Rucker, *Health Care Financ Rev* **21**, 75 (2000).
11. D. Haas *et al.*, *Am J Obstet Gynecol* **212**, 539.e1 (2015).
12. Guerrero *et al.*, Genetic polymorphisms associated with adverse pregnancy outcomes in nulliparas, *medRxiv 2022.02.28.22271641* (2022).
13. N. Artzi *et al.*, *Nat Med* **26**, 71 (2020).
14. W. Bao *et al.*, *JAMA Intern Med* **174**, 1047 (2014).
15. K. A. Pagel *et al.*, *JAMA Netw Open* **5**, e2229158 (2022).
16. R. Agrawal, T. Imieliński and A. Swami, *ACM SIGMOD Rec* **22**, 207 (1993).
17. P. N. Tan, M. Steinbach and V. Kumar, *Introduction to data mining* (Pearson, 2006).
18. A. S. Glas *et al.*, *J Clin Epidemiol* **56**, 1129 (2003).
19. B. Efron and R. Tibshirani, *Stat Sci* **1**, 54 (1986).
20. K. Keppel *et al.*, *Vital Health Stat 2* , 1 (2005).
21. F. G. De Maio, *J Epidemiol Community Health* **61**, 849 (2007).
22. Y. Benjamini and Y. Hochberg, *J R Stat Soc Series B* **57**, 289 (1995).
23. T. Lao *et al.*, *Diabetes Care* **29**, 948 (2006).
24. A. Dietl and J. Farthmann, *Lancet* **386**, 1627 (2015).
25. C. Ferré *et al.*, *Morb Mortal Wkly Rep* **65**, 1181 (2016).
26. J. Sheen *et al.*, *Am J Obstet Gynecol* **220**, S222 (2019).
27. N. Makarem *et al.*, *Circulation* **145**, A073 (2022).

The Role of Global and Local Ancestry on Clopidogrel Response in African Americans

Guang Yang[1], Cristina Alarcon[1], Paula Friedman[1], Li Gong[2], Teri Klein[3], Travis O'Brien[4], Edith A. Nutescu[5], Matthew Tuck[6], David Meltzer[7], Minoli A Perera[1]

1. *Department of Pharmacology, Center for Pharmacogenomics, Feinberg School of Medicine, Northwestern University, Chicago, IL.*
2. *Department of Biomedical Data Science, Stanford University, Stanford, CA.*
3. *Department of Biomedical Data Science and Department of Medicine, Stanford University, Stanford, CA.*
4. *Department of Pharmacology and Physiology, The George Washington University, School of Medicine and Health Sciences, Washington, DC*
5. *Department of Pharmacy Practice and Center for Pharmacoepidemiology and Pharmacoeconomic Research, University of Illinois Chicago, College of Pharmacy, Chicago, IL.*
6. *Washington DC VA Medical Center, Washington, DC and The George Washington University, Washington, DC*
7. *Section of Hospital Medicine, Department of Medicine, University of Chicago, Chicago, IL.*

Pharmacogenomics has long lacked dedicated studies in African Americans, resulting in a lack of in-depth data in this populations. The ACCOuNT consortium has collected a cohort of 167 African American patients on steady state clopidogrel with the goal of discovering population specific variation that may contribute to the response of this anti-platelet agent. Here we analyze the role of both global and local ancestry on the clinical phenotypes of P2Y12 reaction units (PRU) and high on-treatment platelet reactivity (HTPR) in this cohort. We found that local ancestry at the TSS of three genes, *IRS-1, ABCB1* and *KDR* were nominally associated with PRU, and local ancestry-adjusted SNP association identified variants in *ITGA2* associated to increased PRU. These finding help to explain the variability in drug response seen in African Americans, especially as few studies on genes outside of *CYP2C19* has been conducted in this population.

Keywords: African American, Pharmacogenomics, Clopidogrel, Ancestry.

1. Introduction

Clopidogrel is an anti-platelet agent used in coronary artery disease (CAD), acute coronary syndrome (ACS) in patients undergoing percutaneous coronary intervention (PCI), peripheral vascular disease (PVD) and stroke. Wide inter-individual variation in response, defined by either laboratory response (i.e., P_2Y_{12} reaction units [PRU]) or clinical response, has been documented.[1,2] High on therapy PRU (HTPR), defined as measures over 230, have been linked to greater risk of major cardiovascular events in clinical trials.[3] Variable response is, at least in part, heritable, with up to 70% of the variability observed in clopidogrel response attributed to genetic factors.[4,5]

Clopidogrel is an oral prodrug that requires the hepatic cytochrome P450 enzymes, *CYP2C19*, to be biologically active. Several pharmacogenomic studies have shown that both loss-of-function (LOF) and gain-of-function alleles in *CYP2C19* are associated with clopidogrel efficacy and risk of major adverse cardiac events. Specifically carriers of the *CYP2C19*2* and **3* alleles are at a significantly greater risk of myocardial infarction after stent placement than non-carriers.[6,7] Hence, the Food and Drug Administration (FDA) added a boxed warning recommending the reduction of clopidogrel in patient carrying LOF variants in *CYP2C19*.[8] Yet, African Americans (AAs) made up a small proportion of the initial pharmacogenomic discovery studies and clinical trials, and little is known about population-specific variation that may affect their response to clopidogrel.

Genetic admixture is the result of recent interbreeding between previously separated populations. In AAs, this has resulted in the addition of European DNA segments into the background of an African genome. The result is a genome which contains a mosaic of both populations. Genetic ancestry varies substantially between AAs, with the global proportion of African ancestry ranging from nearly 100% to as low as 20% in self-identified AAs.[9] However, at any specific loci the local genetic ancestry can vary drastically, even between individuals that have relatively similar global proportions of African ancestry. This more fine-scaled ancestry is dubbed local ancestry (LA). this may be especially important for gene regulation, which occurs in discrete nearby locations to the gene. We have already shown that LA is an important in eQTL mapping for admixed populations and that global ancestry proportions are significantly correlated to the expression of several hepatic gene.[10,11] Here we investigate the association of global or LA at candidate genes to clinical phenotypes related to clopidogrel response.

2. Methods

2.1. *Cohort*

One hundred and seventy AAs on clopidogrel were recruited from 5 hospital system in Chicago and Washington DC (University of Chicago Medical Center, University of Illinois and Northwestern Memorial Hospital, George Washington University Hospital and Medical Faculty Associates, and the Washington DC VA Medical Center) through the African American Cardiovascular Pharmacogenomics Consortium (ACCOuNT).[12] All subjects self-identified as AAs over the age of 18, were able to consent and provided at least two blood samples: one purple top tube for DNA extraction and one sodium citrate coagulation tube for PRU measurement. All subjects were on clopidogrel for at least 15 days at the time of recruitment and PRU measures. PRU measures were obtained from either the Northwestern Memorial Hospital or the VA medical Center clinical laboratories through the VerifyNow Assay (Accumetrics, San Diego, California). Clinical and demographic variables related to clopidogrel response were collected and included: age, sex, concomitant medications, platelet counts, and indication for therapy. HTPR was prespecified as PRU greater than or equal to 230 on clopidogrel therapy as previously described.[13]

2.2. *Genotyping and Quality Control*

The ACCOuNT clopidogrel cohort was genotyped with the Infinium Multi-Ethnic Genotyping Array (Illumina) at the University of Chicago Genomics Core. Quality control measures included: SNPs exclusion based on genotyping rate <95%, minor allele frequency (MAF) <5%, and failed

Hardy-Weinberg equilibrium tests p <0.00001. SNPs were also excluded if they were: A/T or C/G SNPs to eliminate flip-strand issues, SNPs on the X and Y chromosomes or mitochondrial SNPs. Genotype data was used to validate gender and identity-by-descent (IBD). Samples were also excluded due missingness >0.05, gender misspecification, or IBD >0.125. Additionally, principal components 1 and 2 were used to confirm ancestry of all individuals (**Sup. Figure**). Genotypes were phased using Eagle v2.4 and imputed using the TopMed Imputation server in NCBI build 38 (hg38) coordinates. Post imputation quality control involved exclusion of SNPs if the MAF was <0.05, imputation quality <0.8, and failed Hardy-Weinberg equilibrium tests p <0.00001. This resulted in 141 subjects retain in the analysis. Because of the small sample size of our cohort, we restricted the LA analysis (described below) to a set of candidate genes known to be associated with clopidogrel response, adverse events, or platelet function while on clopidogrel. Genes were chosen from a query of significant variants associated to clopidogrel phenotypes from PharmGKB (https://www.pharmgkb.org/chemical/PA449053/variantAnnotation). This resulted in 35 genes used the LA ancestry analyses (listed in **Appendix A**).

2.3. *Global Ancestry Association Analysis*

The genotypes of 141 subjects were merged with HapMap phase 3 reference data from four global populations: Yoruba in Ibadan, Nigeria (YRI); Utah residents with Northern and Western European ancestry (CEU); Han Chinese in Beijing, China (CHB); and Japanese in Tokyo, Japan (JPT). Population structure of the merged data was inferred by the Bayesian clustering algorithm STRUCTURE deployed within fastStructure v1.0 and performed without any prior population assignment.[14] We employed the admixture model, and the burn-in-period and number of Markov Chain Monte Carlo repetitions were set to 20,000 and 100,000, respectively. The number of parental populations (K) was set to 3. West African Ancestry (WAA) percentages of each subject were calculated and used for association to PRU and HTPR using a linear or logistic regression in R.

2.4. *Local Ancestry Association Analysis*

We estimated the local ancestry of each subject with RFMix version 2 using YRI and CEU samples from 1000 Genome phase 3 as the reference populations, using a window size of 0.2 Mb. [15] The LA at the gene transcriptional start site of each candidate gene was assigned as 2 African alleles (AFR/AFR), two European Alleles (EUR/EUR) of one of each (AFR/EUR) for association with mean PRU and HTPR. We used a general linear model (Gaussian method) in R for the association to PRU with LA and a general logistic binomial in R for the association of HTPR to LA. All analyses used age, sex, diabetes, hypertension and the first 2 genomics PCs as covariates. We prespecified a p<0.001 (0.05/35) as significant.

We conducted local ancestry-adjusted SNP association, restricted to SNPs within 1Kb of each candidate gene resulting in 10962 SNPs included in this analysis. We used the TRACTOR [16] deconvolved model to conduct the ancestry adjusted analysis in each ancestry separately. TRACTOR uses the following model:

$$Y = b_0 + b_1x_1 + b_2x_2 + b_3x_3 + b_4x_4 + b_5x_5 \ldots + b_kx_k$$

where x_1 is the number of haplotypes coming from the index ancestry, and x_2 and x_3 represent the risk alleles, and x_4-x_k are other covariates such as age, sex, genomics PCs. This analysis produces ancestry specific effect size estimates and p-values for each SNP in each ancestry. We prespecified a $p< 1x10^{-6}$ as significant. We then ran a meta-analysis on the deconvoluted AFR and EUR summary statistics using METAL.[17] All analyses used age, sex, diabetes, hypertension and the first 2 genomic PC as covariates. These results were compared to association without the inclusion of LA conducted in PLINK.

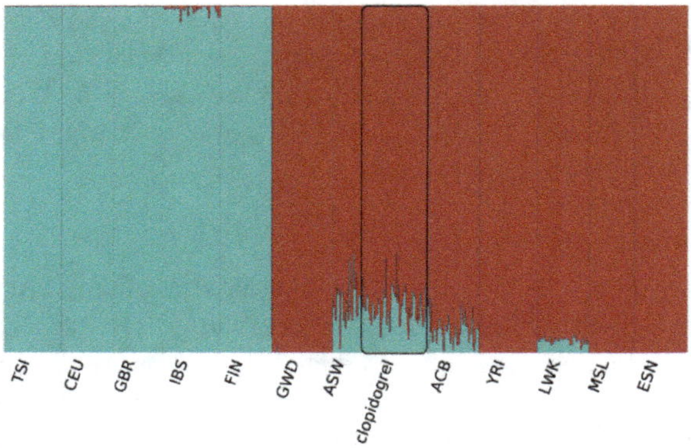

Figure 1: Ancestry proportions continental and admixed populations.
Admixture percentages inferred from fastSTRUCTURE in the EUR (TSI- Toscana in Italy, CEU – Utah residents with European ancestry, GBR – British, IBS – Iberian in Spain, FIN – Finns) and AFR (GWD – Gambians, ASW – African Americans, ACB, African Caribbeans, YRI - Yoruban, LWK – Luhya in Kenya, MSL - Mende in Sierra Leone, ESN – Esan in Nigeria) superpopulations in 1000 genomes and the ACCOuNT clopidogrel cohort (black box). fastSTRUCTURE was run with K= 3. Each column represents an individual within each population with the proportion of each population shown as the colored bars. The African proportion (shown as in red) was use in the global association analysis.

3. Results

We estimate WAA in our ACCOuNT clopidogrel cohort as well as in the 1000 genomes AFR and EUR superpopulations using fastSTUCTURE (**Fig. 1**). The average percentage of WAA in our cohort was 80.9% (range 53.9% - 95.8%).

We investigate the association of WAA on both PRU and HTPR. In this cohort of patients, the prevalence of high on-treatment platelet reactivity (HTPR), was 26%. There was no significant difference in any demographic or clinical covariates between cases with HTPR and controls (**Table 1**), though both Type 2 diabetes (T2D) and hypertension were more common in the cases (Percent difference 19.5%, p = 0.11, and 9.7%, p = 0.28 respectively) though not statistically different. Hypertension was associated to PRU (p<0.05) and was thus included in the downstream analysis. We included T2D as a covariate in all analyses as some of the candidate genes tested were specifically found in patient with diabetes while on clopidogrel. We then tested the association of both PRU and HTPR to WAA percentage. Neither of these phenotypes were associated with percentage of WAA ($p = 0.09$ and 0.14 respectively)

Table 1: Demographics of the ACCOuNT cohort.

Variable	Cases (PRU≥230) N=38	Controls (PRU<230) N = 103	P-value
Age (mean ± SD)	67.3 ± 11.4	64.6 ± 14.5	0.27
Sex (% Female)	14 (38.9%)	37 (41.6%)	0.94
BMI (mean ± SD)	28.96 ± 4.56	29.8 ± 6.7	0.41
Type 2 Diabetes (T2D)	24 (66.7%)	42 (47.2%)	0.11
Hypertension	33 (91.7%)	73 (82.0%)	0.28
Platelet count (mean ± SD)	237 ± 68.38	254.6 ± 81.78	0.15

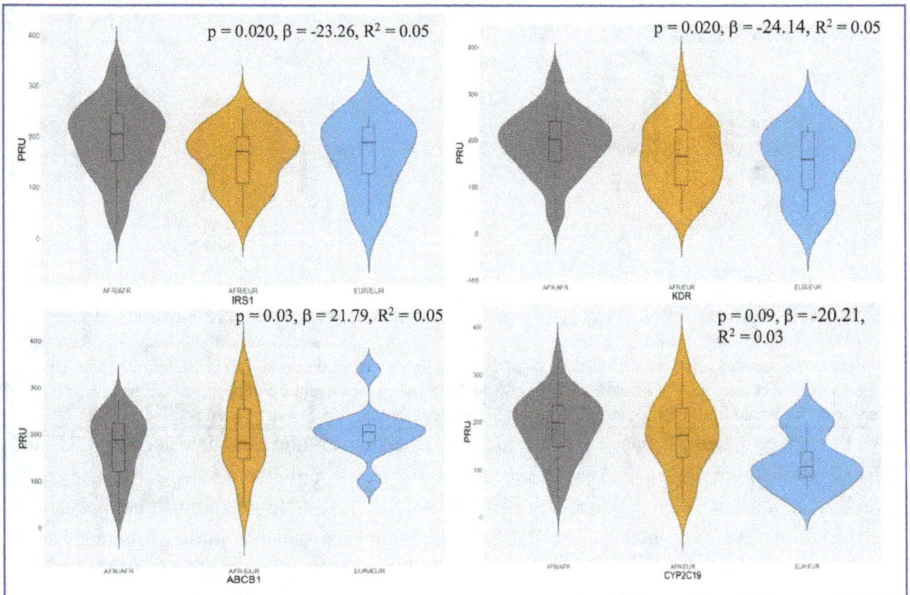

Figure 2: Violin plots showing the association of LA at the gene TSS of *IRS-1, KDR, ABCB1* and *CYP2C19*

Next, we tested if LA at the TSS of candidate genes was associated to either PRU or HTPR. We found no significant associations in either analysis, though three genes, *IRS-1* ($p = 0.02$), *KDR* ($p = 0.02$), and *ABCB1* ($p = 0.03$) reached nominal significance with PRU, and *IRS-1* reached nominal significance with HTPR ($p = 0.05$, lower HTPR in individuals with EUR ancestry). Additionally, *CYP2C19*, *CYP2C9,* and *ECS1* showed suggestive association ($p = 0.09$, 0.09 and 0.06 respectively) with PRU. Figure 2 shows that *IRS-1, KDR, and CYP2C19* had higher PRU in individuals with local AFR ancestry and *ABCB1* had lower PRU in individuals with local AFR ancestry.

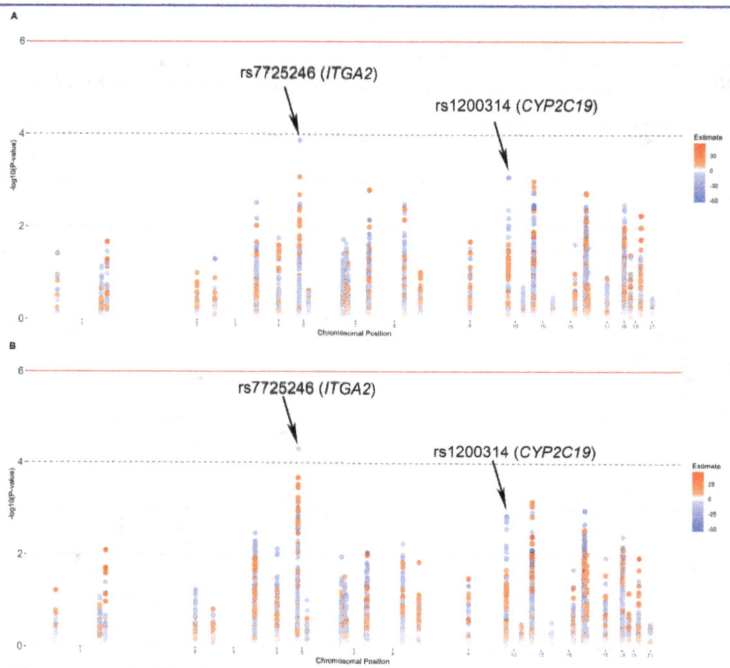

Figure 3: Ancestry-specific GWAS results
Manhattan plots of (A) AFR-specific and (B) Meta-analysis LA-adjusted SNP associations. Both analyses were corrected for age, sex, hypertension, diabetes and the first 2 PCs. The x-axis represents chromosomal location while the y-axis represents -log$_{10}$(p value). Each dot is a SNP tested for an association with PRU and the color of each dot represents the effect size of the association where blue and red colors are negative and positive effects, respectively. A significant threshold line is drawn at 1×10^{-6}. A suggestive threshold line is drawn at 1×10^{-4}

We then investigated the ancestry-adjusted SNP association around candidate genes to PRU and HTPR. Given the high degree of African ancestry in our cohort, only the AFR-specific analysis is reported, as only a few AAs had adequate EUR ancestry at these SNP positions to be included in the analysis. However, we included the EUR-specific summary statistics in the meta-analysis to adjust for both ancestries. We identify a new near significant association in Chr. 5 at *ITGA2* (lead SNP: rs7725246, $p = 4.75 \times10^{-5}$, $\beta = -25.48$) in the meta-analysis. This SNP also showed a suggestive association in the AFR-specific analysis (lead SNP: rs7725246, $p = 1.36 \times10^{-4}$, $\beta = -29.82$) (**Figure 3**). The most significant SNPs in the EUR analysis were also found on in Chr 5 (rs27618), but only reached a p-value at 0.003, as only 58 people were included in this analysis (**Table 2**). These SNPs are common across global populations. The most significant SNP at the *CYP2C19* locus (rs1200314) has a higher allele frequency in AFR populations, is associated with increased PRU and is not in LD with *CYP2C19*2* ($r^2 < 0.02$). Of note, the *CYP2C19*2* alleles were not significant ($p > 0.02$) in either the AFR-specific analysis or the meta-analysis. None of these SNPs were signficanat in in the standard association analysis using PC correction.

Table 2: Top SNPs from LA inferred (LAI) SNP association.

AFR-specific results					
Chr	**SNP**	**EAF**	**Effect**	**P**	
5	rs7725246	0.70	-29.82	1.36E-04	
10	rs1200314	0.87	33.54	8.51E-04	
15	rs7182019	0.47	28.82	1.05E-03	
Meta-analysis results					
Chr	**SNP**	**EAF**	**Effect**	**P (LAI)**	**P (Standard analysis)**
5	rs7725246	0.70	-25.48	4.75E-05	0.89
10	rs1200314	0.87	30.58	1.37E-03	0.03
15	rs4271565	0.21	29.61	7.01E-04	0.67

4. Discussion

Here we describe the association of both global ancestry and LA at candidate genes with clinically relevant association to clopidogrel response. Antiplatelet therapy with clopidogrel has been the mainstay for thromboprophylaxis of CVDs[18]. The American Heart Association and American College of Cardiology recommend clopidogrel as first-line antiplatelet therapy in patients suffering non-ST-elevation acute coronary syndrome.[19] Despite the clinical benefits, many patients have cardiovascular events after being prescribed clopidogrel and inter-individual variability in drug response affects both the efficacy and safety profile.[2] Little is known about the effect of population specific variants on clopidogrel response outside of East Asians and Europeans. Most GWAS studies of both PRU and adverse cardiovascular event after clopidogrel treatment have not included African Ancestry populations. Given the unique cohort of an admixed African population taking clopidogrel, we explored the association of both global and local ancestry on PRU (a clinical measure of clopidogrel efficacy) and HTPR (a clopidogrel outcomes measure).

We identified nominal associations with the candidate genes *IRS-1* (insulin receptor Substrate 1), *KDR (*Kinase Insert Domain Receptor, also called VEGFR2) and *ABCB1* (ATP Binding Cassette Subfamily B Member 1, also called *MDR1*) to PRU. *IRS-1*, a ligand of insulin receptor tyrosine kinase, is central to the insulin signal transduction pathway.[20] SNPs within this gene have previously been associated with HTPR (as defined as the 75th percentile of the ADP-induced platelet aggregation) and ADP and arachidonic acid induced platelet aggregation in diabetic patients on clopidogrel.[21,22] Notably, both studies were done in East Asian populations. Clinical trials have shown that diabetes mellites and high serum glucose are independently associated with clopidogrel nonresponse. In our study we did not see an association with HTPR and diabetes though we used T2D co-morbidity as a covariate in our analysis. As people with AFR ancestry at the locus had higher PRU, this suggests that *IRS-1* may be more highly expressed in those with local African ancestry at this locus and thus may result in great nonresponse to clopidogrel therapy. Further experimental validation is needed.

KDR has been associated to arthrosclerosis and coronary artery disease (CAD) as well as clopidogrel non-response.[23,24] KDR can bind to VEGF and cause angiogenesis. The dysregulation of this process is thought to contribute to a wide variety of diseases including atherosclerosis and CAD.[25-27] Two SNPs, rs7667298 and rs2305948, in this gene have been associated with increased risk of angina pectoris when treated with clopidogrel in people with CAD.[28] Both of these risk alleles are more common in African ancestry populations. The effect of these SNPs on *KDR* expression has been limited, with rs2305948 thought to affect the binding efficacy of VEGF to KDR and KDR serum levels.[29,30]

ABCB1 encodes an intestinal efflux transporter protein, P-glycoprotein, which modulate the absorption of clopidogrel. A LOF allele, rs1045642, in this gene has been association with major adverse cardiovascular event and death in patient on clopidogrel.[31,32] *ABCB1* gene expression has been shown to be higher in European as opposed to African Americans in peripheral blood.[33] Between different ethnic groups in Brazil, the allele frequency of rs1045642 differs by group affiliation, with those identifying as African having the lowest frequency.[34] In our study AFR ancestry at *ABCB1* was associated with decreased PRU, suggesting this gene may play a smaller role in clopidogrel adverse events in African ancestry populations as compared to Europeans.

While the association of LA at neither *CYP2C19* nor *CYP2C9* reached nominal significance, we presented our findings as these genes have been the most widely studies in relation to clopidogrel response. The *CYP2C19*2* allele explains about 12% of the variability in PRU in Europeans and 7% of variability in PRU in admixed Puerto Ricans (mean EUR and AFR ancestry of 70% and 19% respectively).[35,36] Our result show that AFR ancestry at the TSS of both genes trend toward higher PRU. In our previous work in African American primary hepatocytes, we found that *CYP2C19* was significantly associated with proportion of WAA (global ancestry) with lower expression of *CYP2C19* with increase WAA. This agrees with previous findings that African Americans as a group have higher major adverse myocardial event while on clopidogrel than other populations.[37] Notably, *CYP2C19*2* was not significantly associated to PRU or HTPR, suggesting other variants may play a role in response variability. Taken together these findings suggest additional population specific variation in these genes may contribute to clopidogrel response.

In our AFR specific GWAS and meta-analysis we identified SNPs within *ITGA2* with near significant associated with PRU. SNPs in this gene have been associated with residual platelet activity in the plasma of patient on clopidogrel and increase platelet aggregation.[38,39] *ITGA2* also positively correlated to platelet aggregation with collagen.[40] Our previous work on population difference in the platelet transcriptome did not identify *ITGA2* as differentially expressed.[41]

There are several limitations to this study. Our cohort size is small, especially for the HTPR analyses in which only 38 subjects were defined as cases. Thus, we are underpower to detect small to medium effects. Our LA-adjusted method is able to identify those alleles with large difference in allele frequency between populations but may have reduced power to find allele that have more similar allele frequencies between populations as previously reported.[42] We were not able to replicate the previous associations found in *CYP2C19* in the ancestry-adjusted SNP associations. Others have reported that the association to *CYP2C19*2* to mortality and myocardial infarction risk in AAs was not significant though these associations were robust in European subjects.[43] The lack of AA cohorts on clopidogrel with PRU data hampers our effort to replicate our findings. Even the most recent GWAS by the International Clopidogrel Pharmacogenomics Consortium, which included 2592 patients, was exclusively European.[44]

Our studies represent a unique analysis on an all AA clopidogrel cohort with PRU and HTPR phenotypes. This work highlights who variability in ancestry between African Americans may be useful in identifying potential genes and SNPs associated to pharmacogenomic phenotypes.

5. Acknowledgments

This work was supported by 1U54MD010723 and the participants in ACCOuNT studies along with the physicians, nurses and clinical recruiters that enabled the gathering of this data.

6. Appendix

Appendix A: Candidate Gene List

Gene	Effect on Clopidogrel
ABCB1	Metabolism, Efficacy, ADR
AGAP3	Efficacy (Asian only)
ATP10A	Efficacy (Asian only)
B4GALT2	Platelet Aggregation, PRU
CDH13	Efficacy
CDH15	Efficacy
CES1	Metabolism, Platelet Aggregation, Efficacy,
CES1P1	PRU (East Asian only)
CYP1A2	Survival and ADR (African Americans only)
CYP2B6	PRU (European only)
CYP2C19	PRU, HTPR, Platelet aggregation, Efficacy, Metabolism, ADR
CYP2C9	PRU, HTPR, Platelet Aggregation, Metabolism, Efficacy, ADR
CYP3A4	Platelet Aggregation (European only)
CYP3A5	Efficacy, Platelet Aggregation, ADR, PRU, Metabolism
CYP4F2	Efficacy, Platelet Aggregation,
ECHS1	Efficacy (East Asian only)
EFR3A	Efficacy (East Asian only)
F2R	PRU (East Asian only)
FMO3	HTPR (East Asian only)
IRS-1	PRU (East Asian only)
ITGA2	Platelet Aggregation, PRU,
ITGA3	Efficacy
KDR	Efficacy
MED12L	Platelet Aggregation, PRU
MYOM2	Efficacy (East Asian only)

Supplementary Figure: PC plot of Clopidogrel cohort.

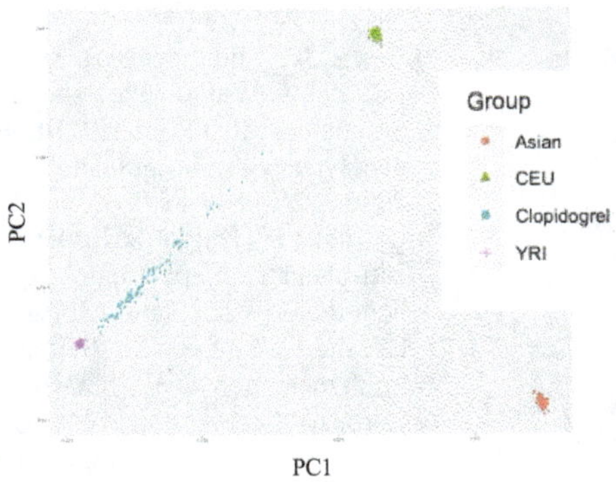

N6AMT1	Metabolism, Efficacy (East Asian only)
NECAB1	Efficacy (East Asian only)
NOS3	Efficacy
P2RY12	Efficacy, ADR, PRU, Platelet Aggregation
PEAR1	HTPR, PRU, Platelet Aggregation, Efficacy
PON1	Efficacy, PRU, Platelet Aggregation
PTGS1	Efficacy
SLC14A2	Efficacy (East Asian only)
WDR24	Efficacy (East Asian only)
ZDHHC3	Efficacy (East Asian only)

References

1. Nagareddy P, Smyth SS. Inflammation and thrombosis in cardiovascular disease. *Curr Opin Hematol.* 2013;20(5):457-463.
2. Nguyen TA, Diodati JG, Pharand C. Resistance to clopidogrel: a review of the evidence. *J Am Coll Cardiol.* 2005;45(8):1157-1164.
3. Sharifi H, Habibi V, Emami Zeydi A. Platelet reactivity unit (PRU) in patients undergoing elective PCI: Rethinking the optimal cut point. *Anatol J Cardiol.* 2017;18(2):164.
4. Lewis JP, Shuldiner AR. Clopidogrel pharmacogenetics: Beyond candidate genes and genome-wide association studies. *Clin Pharmacol Ther.* 2017;101(3):323-325.
5. Shuldiner AR, O'Connell JR, Bliden KP, et al. Association of cytochrome P450 2C19 genotype with the antiplatelet effect and clinical efficacy of clopidogrel therapy. *JAMA.* 2009;302(8):849-857.
6. Carlquist JF, Knight S, Horne BD, et al. Cardiovascular risk among patients on clopidogrel anti-platelet therapy after placement of drug-eluting stents is modified by genetic variants in both the CYP2C19 and ABCB1 genes. *Thromb Haemost.* 2013;109(4):744-754.
7. Cavallari LH, Lee CR, Beitelshees AL, et al. Multisite Investigation of Outcomes With Implementation of CYP2C19 Genotype-Guided Antiplatelet Therapy After Percutaneous Coronary Intervention. *JACC Cardiovasc Interv.* 2018;11(2):181-191.
8. Administration USFD. FDA Drug Safety Communication: Reduced effectiveness of Plavix (clopidogrel) in patients who are poor metabolizers of the drug. https://www.fda.gov/drugs/postmarket-drug-safety-information-patients-and-providers/fda-drug-safety-communication-reduced-effectiveness-plavix-clopidogrel-patients-who-are-poor. Published 08/03/2017. Updated 08/03/2017. Accessed February 26, 2021, 2021.
9. Bryc K, Durand EY, Macpherson JM, Reich D, Mountain JL. The genetic ancestry of African Americans, Latinos, and European Americans across the United States. *Am J Hum Genet.* 2015;96(1):37-53.
10. Zhong Y, De T, Alarcon C, Park CS, Lec B, Perera MA. Discovery of novel hepatocyte eQTLs in African Americans. *PLoS Genet.* 2020;16(4):e1008662.
11. Park CS, De T, Xu Y, et al. Hepatocyte gene expression and DNA methylation as ancestry-dependent mechanisms in African Americans. *NPJ Genom Med.* 2019;4:29.
12. Friedman PN, Shaazuddin M, Gong L, et al. The ACCOuNT Consortium: A Model for the Discovery, Translation, and Implementation of Precision Medicine in African Americans. *Clin Transl Sci.* 2019;12(3):209-217.

13. Garabedian T, Alam S. High residual platelet reactivity on clopidogrel: its significance and therapeutic challenges overcoming clopidogrel resistance. *Cardiovasc Diagn Ther.* 2013;3(1):23-37.
14. Raj A, Stephens M, Pritchard JK. fastSTRUCTURE: variational inference of population structure in large SNP data sets. *Genetics.* 2014;197(2):573-589.
15. Maples BK, Gravel S, Kenny EE, Bustamante CD. RFMix: a discriminative modeling approach for rapid and robust local-ancestry inference. *Am J Hum Genet.* 2013;93(2):278-288.
16. Atkinson EG, Maihofer AX, Kanai M, et al. Tractor uses local ancestry to enable the inclusion of admixed individuals in GWAS and to boost power. *Nat Genet.* 2021;53(2):195-204.
17. Willer CJ, Li Y, Abecasis GR. METAL: fast and efficient meta-analysis of genomewide association scans. *Bioinformatics.* 2010;26(17):2190-2191.
18. Ray S. Clopidogrel resistance: the way forward. *Indian Heart J.* 2014;66(5):530-534.
19. Amsterdam EA, Wenger NK, Brindis RG, et al. 2014 AHA/ACC guideline for the management of patients with non-ST-elevation acute coronary syndromes: executive summary: a report of the American College of Cardiology/American Heart Association Task Force on Practice Guidelines. *Circulation.* 2014;130(25):2354-2394.
20. Feng X, Tucker KL, Parnell LD, et al. Insulin receptor substrate 1 (IRS1) variants confer risk of diabetes in the Boston Puerto Rican Health Study. *Asia Pac J Clin Nutr.* 2013;22(1):150-159.
21. Zhang D, Zhang X, Liu D, et al. Association between insulin receptor substrate-1 polymorphisms and high platelet reactivity with clopidogrel therapy in coronary artery disease patients with type 2 diabetes mellitus. *Cardiovasc Diabetol.* 2016;15:50.
22. Angiolillo DJ, Bernardo E, Zanoni M, et al. Impact of insulin receptor substrate-1 genotypes on platelet reactivity and cardiovascular outcomes in patients with type 2 diabetes mellitus and coronary artery disease. *J Am Coll Cardiol.* 2011;58(1):30-39.
23. Liu D, Song J, Ji X, Liu Z, Cong M, Hu B. Association of Genetic Polymorphisms on VEGFA and VEGFR2 With Risk of Coronary Heart Disease. *Medicine (Baltimore).* 2016;95(19):e3413.
24. Al Awaida W, Ahmed AA, Hamza AA, et al. Association of KDR rs1870377 genotype with clopidogrel resistance in patients with post percutaneous coronary intervention. *Heliyon.* 2021;7(2):e06251.
25. Waltenberger J, Claesson-Welsh L, Siegbahn A, Shibuya M, Heldin CH. Different signal transduction properties of KDR and Flt1, two receptors for vascular endothelial growth factor. *J Biol Chem.* 1994;269(43):26988-26995.
26. Barger AC, Beeuwkes R, 3rd, Lainey LL, Silverman KJ. Hypothesis: vasa vasorum and neovascularization of human coronary arteries. A possible role in the pathophysiology of atherosclerosis. *N Engl J Med.* 1984;310(3):175-177.
27. Moulton KS. Plaque angiogenesis: its functions and regulation. *Cold Spring Harb Symp Quant Biol.* 2002;67:471-482.
28. Zhang LJ, Zhang YQ, Han X, Zhang ZT, Zhang ZQ. Association of VEGFR-2 Gene Polymorphisms With Clopidogrel Resistance in Patients With Coronary Heart Disease. *Am J Ther.* 2016;23(6):e1663-e1670.

29. Paradowska-Gorycka A, Stypinska B, Pawlik A, et al. KDR (VEGFR2) Genetic Variants and Serum Levels in Patients with Rheumatoid Arthritis. *Biomolecules.* 2019;9(8).
30. Wang Y, Zheng Y, Zhang W, et al. Polymorphisms of KDR gene are associated with coronary heart disease. *J Am Coll Cardiol.* 2007;50(8):760-767.
31. Su J, Xu J, Li X, et al. ABCB1 C3435T polymorphism and response to clopidogrel treatment in coronary artery disease (CAD) patients: a meta-analysis. *PLoS One.* 2012;7(10):e46366.
32. Mega JL, Close SL, Wiviott SD, et al. Genetic variants in ABCB1 and CYP2C19 and cardiovascular outcomes after treatment with clopidogrel and prasugrel in the TRITON-TIMI 38 trial: a pharmacogenetic analysis. *Lancet.* 2010;376(9749):1312-1319.
33. Tornatore KM, Brazeau D, Dole K, et al. Sex differences in cyclosporine pharmacokinetics and ABCB1 gene expression in mononuclear blood cells in African American and Caucasian renal transplant recipients. *J Clin Pharmacol.* 2013;53(10):1039-1047.
34. Santos PC, Soares RA, Santos DB, et al. CYP2C19 and ABCB1 gene polymorphisms are differently distributed according to ethnicity in the Brazilian general population. *BMC Med Genet.* 2011;12:13.
35. Duconge J, Santiago E, Hernandez-Suarez DF, et al. Pharmacogenomic polygenic risk score for clopidogrel responsiveness among Caribbean Hispanics: A candidate gene approach. *Clin Transl Sci.* 2021;14(6):2254-2266.
36. Peprah E, Xu H, Tekola-Ayele F, Royal CD. Genome-wide association studies in Africans and African Americans: expanding the framework of the genomics of human traits and disease. *Public Health Genomics.* 2015;18(1):40-51.
37. Pendyala LK, Torguson R, Loh JP, et al. Racial disparity with on-treatment platelet reactivity in patients undergoing percutaneous coronary intervention. *Am Heart J.* 2013;166(2):266-272.
38. Giusti B, Gori AM, Marcucci R, et al. Role of glycoprotein Ia gene polymorphisms in determining platelet function in myocardial infarction patients undergoing percutaneous coronary intervention on dual antiplatelet treatment. *Atherosclerosis.* 2008;196(1):341-348.
39. Angiolillo DJ, Fernandez-Ortiz A, Bernardo E, et al. 807 C/T Polymorphism of the glycoprotein Ia gene and pharmacogenetic modulation of platelet response to dual antiplatelet treatment. *Blood Coagul Fibrinolysis.* 2004;15(5):427-433.
40. Eicher JD, Wakabayashi Y, Vitseva O, et al. Characterization of the platelet transcriptome by RNA sequencing in patients with acute myocardial infarction. *Platelets.* 2016;27(3):230-239.
41. Garofano K, Park CS, Alarcon C, et al. Differences in the Platelet mRNA Landscape Portend Racial Disparities in Platelet Function and Suggest Novel Therapeutic Targets. *Clin Pharmacol Ther.* 2021;110(3):702-713.
42. Hou K, Bhattacharya A, Mester R, Burch KS, Pasaniuc B. On powerful GWAS in admixed populations. *Nat Genet.* 2021;53(12):1631-1633.
43. Cresci S, Depta JP, Lenzini PA, et al. Cytochrome p450 gene variants, race, and mortality among clopidogrel-treated patients after acute myocardial infarction. *Circ Cardiovasc Genet.* 2014;7(3):277-286.
44. Verma SS, Bergmeijer TO, Gong L, et al. Genomewide Association Study of Platelet Reactivity and Cardiovascular Response in Patients Treated With Clopidogrel: A Study by the International Clopidogrel Pharmacogenomics Consortium. *Clin Pharmacol Ther.* 2020;108(5):1067-1077.

Leveraging Multi-Ancestry Polygenic Risk Scores for Body Mass Index to Predict Antiretroviral Therapy-Induced Weight Gain*

Karl Keat[1], Daniel Hui[1], Brenda Xiao[1], Yuki Bradford[2], Zinhle Cindi[3], Eric S. Daar[4], Roy Gulick[5], Sharon A. Riddler[6], Phumla Sinxadi[3], David W. Haas[7,8], Marylyn D. Ritchie[2,9*]

[1]Genomics and Computational Biology Graduate Program, [2]Department of Genetics, University of Pennsylvania, Philadelphia, PA 19104, USA

[3]Division of Clinical Pharmacology, Department of Medicine University of Cape Town, Cape Town, South Africa

[4]Lundquist Institute at Harbor-UCLA Medical Center Torrance, CA 90502, USA

[5]Weill Cornell Medicine, New York, New York, NY 10065, USA

[6]University of Pittsburgh, Pittsburgh, PA 15260, USA

[7]Vanderbilt University Medical Center, Nashville, TN, USA

[8]Meharry Medical College, Nashville, TN, USA

[9]Institute for Biomedical Informatics University of Pennsylvania, Philadelphia, PA 19104, USA

**Email: marylyn@pennmedicine.upenn.edu*

Widespread availability of antiretroviral therapies (ART) for HIV-1 have generated considerable interest in understanding the pharmacogenomics of ART. In some individuals, ART has been associated with excessive weight gain, which disproportionately affects women of African ancestry. The underlying biology of ART-associated weight gain is poorly understood, but some genetic markers which modify weight gain risk have been suggested, with more genetic factors likely remaining undiscovered. To overcome limitations in available sample sizes for genome-wide association studies (GWAS) in people with HIV, we explored whether a multi-ancestry polygenic risk score (PRS) derived from large, publicly available non-HIV GWAS for body mass index (BMI) can achieve high cross-ancestry performance for predicting baseline BMI in diverse, prospective ART clinical trials datasets, and whether that PRS_{BMI} is also associated with change in BMI over 48 weeks on ART. We show that PRS_{BMI} explained ~5-7% of variability in baseline (pre-ART) BMI, with high performance in both European and African genetic ancestry groups, but that PRS_{BMI} was not associated with change in BMI on ART. This study argues against a shared genetic predisposition for baseline (pre-ART) BMI and ART-associated weight gain.

Keywords: HIV; AIDS; Polygenic Risk Scores; BMI; Pharmacogenomics.

1. Introduction

1.1. *Many antiretroviral therapies for HIV are associated with weight gain*

There are ~1.2 million individuals in the United States and ~38 million worldwide living with HIV-1.[1] With >30 FDA-approved antiviral agents for treating HIV-1, many available in combination co-formulated tablets, and with long-acting injectable agents now available, HIV is now a chronic treatable infection in most patients with access to contemporary antiretroviral therapy (ART). However, there remains considerable interindividual variability in HIV treatment responses including drug toxicity, immune recovery, and drug-drug interactions. Variable responses may be influenced by polymorphisms in drug absorption, distribution, metabolism, and elimination (ADME) genes and/or off-target genes. Beyond the need to develop novel therapies and optimize current therapies are newer priorities which include achieving functional or sterilizing cure of HIV and reducing HIV-associated inflammation and immune activation so as to prevent end-organ complications.

Weight gain following ART initiation is common with most modern ART regimens.[2] The greatest weight gain has been observed in individuals of African ancestry, especially among women of African ancestry. While environmental and social factors likely play a role, there is also the potential for an underlying genetic predisposition.[3] As a few examples among many, it has been shown that, among patients who switched from efavirenz- to integrase strand transfer inhibitor (INSTI)-based ART, *CYP2B6* genotype was associated with weight gain, possibly reflecting withdrawal of inhibitory effects of higher efavirenz levels.[4] Analyses using Phase 1 clinical trials data showed that *CYP2B6* slow metabolizers who switch from efavirenz to dolutegravir will have more prolonged subtherapeutic dolutegravir levels.[5] In ART-naïve AIDS Clinical Trial Group (ACTG) studies, *CYP2B6* slow metabolizers had less weight gain at week 48 in participants receiving efavirenz with tenofovir disoproxil fumarate (TDF) but not those receiving efavirenz with abacavir.[4] We previously discovered and replicated an association between *CYP2B6* 15582C→T (rs4803419) and efavirenz C_{min} in self-identified Black, Hispanic, and white individuals, showed that this single nucleotide polymorphism (SNP) improved prediction of efavirenz plasma exposure in individuals living with HIV in South Africa, and showed that this polymorphism is associated with decreased plasma nevirapine clearance in Asians.[6,7] While we and others have identified potential genetic associations with weight gain, a large proportion of variation remains unexplained. Given this discrepancy, it is plausible that susceptibility to ART-associated excessive weight gain will be affected by each individual's overall genetic predisposition at many genetic loci.

1.2. *Polygenic risk scores allow for prediction of complex traits such as body mass index*

Polygenic risk scores (PRS) are the cumulative, mathematical aggregation of risk derived from the contributions of many DNA variants across the genome. PRS are a powerful technology in the field of disease risk prediction and have been shown to be correlated with disease incidence in coronary artery disease, type 2 diabetes, atrial fibrillation, breast cancer, schizophrenia, and many other traits.[8–15] In recent years there have been advances in PRS methodology that incorporate diverse ancestry groups, quantitative and qualitative phenotypes, and consider different linkage disequilibrium (LD) reference panels.[16–19] In addition, PRS and SNP-based heritability estimation have been applied to body mass index (BMI) in large biobank populations and genome-wide significant SNPs have been shown to explain ~6% of trait interindividual variation in BMI (while considering all common SNPs, the estimate is greater than 20%).[20,21] When considering the underlying genetic predisposition to weight gain in response to ART, is it possible that the underlying genetic background for BMI in populations without HIV will also be predictive of weight gain in response to ART? In this paper, we explore whether susceptibility to ART-associated weight gain is influenced by each individual's overall genetic predisposition to higher BMI as reflected by PRS for BMI (PRS_{BMI}) derived from large datasets from populations without

HIV. Figure 1 shows an overview of our study design, which is described in more details in *Methods*.

2. Methods

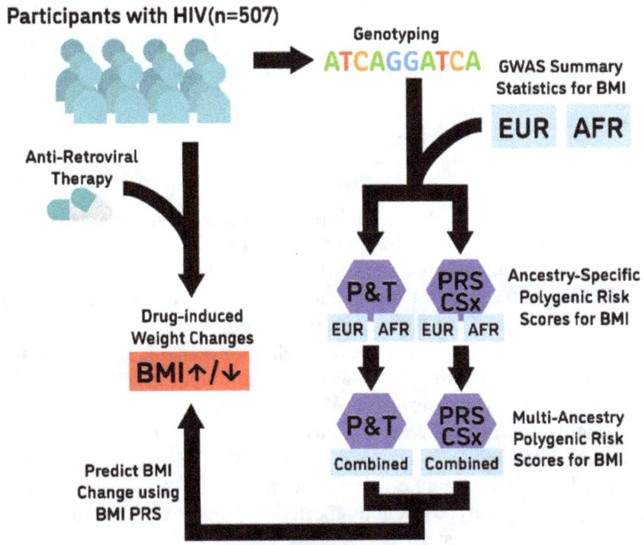

Fig. 1. Study Overview

2.1. *Data and Study Participants*

2.1.1. *GWAS Summary Statistics*

We used publicly available summary statistics from existing genome-wide association studies (GWAS) for BMI in European and African ancestry populations. The European ancestry summary statistics come from the GIANT consortium's meta-analysis of ~700,000 individuals of European ancestry which contained 2,336,269 SNPs.[21] The African ancestry summary statistics come from the African American Anthropometry Genetics Consortium's GWAS of 42,752 individuals which included ~18,000,000 variants.[22] Both sets of summary statistics were subset to the ~1.1 million HapMap3 SNPs included in the PRS-CSx LD reference for the PRS-CSx analysis.[18]

2.1.2. *AIDS Clinical Trials Group Data*

These study data are from a retrospective analysis of a clinical trials cohort from efavirenz-containing arms of prospective, randomized ACTG protocols. Data were from ART-naïve individuals who initiated efavirenz-containing regimens in ACTG studies A5095 (NCT00013520), A5142 (NCT00050895), and A5202 (NCT00118898) in the United States and consented to genetic testing.[23-27] All participants provided written informed consent for genetic research and provided DNA for analysis. Drug class components of regimens were randomly assigned (efavirenz-based versus comparator) except for nucleoside reverse transcriptase inhibitor (NRTI) choice in A5142. Eligible individuals met the following criteria: initial efavirenz-containing regimens included TDF or abacavir; available weight data at entry and week 48 (± 4 weeks); >100 CD4 T-cells/mm3 at baseline and week 48; HIV-1 RNA <400 copies/mL at week 48; and available *CYP2B6* genotypes. This cohort did not receive INSTIs. The participants' sex was 78.4% male (n = 413) and 21.6% female (n = 114). Data on participants' gender was not available.

2.2. *Quality Control*

2.2.1. *Genotypic Data*

DNA was extracted from whole blood collected from consenting participants, and DNA extracted. Samples were labelled with coded identifiers. Stored DNA was genotyped in seven different phases using different genotyping arrays. Phases 1, 2, and 3 were genotyped at the Broad Institute with HumanHap650Yv3_A for phases 1 and 2, and Human1M-Duov3_B for phase 3. For phases 4-7, genotyping was performed at the Vanderbilt Technologies for Advanced Genomics (VANTAGE) facility using the Human Core Exome chip for phase 4, HumanOmni2.5Exome-8-v1.1_A1 chip for phase 5, the HumanOmni25-8v1-2_A1 chip for phase 6, and the Illumina Infinium Multi-Ethnic Global BeadChip (MEGAEX) for phase 7.

Post-genotype quality control was performed by Vanderbilt Technologies for Advanced Genomics Analysis and Research Design (VANGARD). All quality control steps were performed using PLINK version 1.9.[28] Genotyping efficiency per participant was > 99% for all samples, and discordant samples between genotype sex and reported sex were removed from the datasets prior to imputation. After quality control steps, each genotyping phase was imputed separately using the TOPMed reference panel after transforming to genome build 38 using liftOver and stratification by chromosome to parallelize the imputation process.[29] The seven imputed datasets were merged using PLINK, and we excluded imputed polymorphisms with imputation R^2 scores < 0.3, genotyping call rates < 95%, or minor allele frequency (MAF) < 0.05.[28] Genotype data were transformed back to genome build 37 using liftOver to allow compatibility with the PRS-CSx LD reference panels. Genetic ancestry was inferred using principal component analysis with 1000 Genomes as the reference, to assign each participant to a superpopulation of African (AFR), Admixed American (AMR), East Asian (EAS), European (EUR), South Asian (SAS), or Other.

2.3. *Polygenic Risk Score Construction*

2.3.1. *Pruning and thresholding*

A PRS for baseline BMI (PRS_{BMI}) was created using PRSice 2.3.5 (2021-09-20) for LD clumping and p-value thresholding with default optimization parameters.[17] A multi-ancestry LD reference was generated using data from the 1000 Genomes Project.[30] Optimal p-value thresholds were estimated in a subset of the target data comprising 20% of the total target set (n=105/527) for both the European and African ancestry summary statistics. This threshold was then used to calculate an EUR-derived PRS_{BMI} and AFR-derived PRS_{BMI} for the remaining 80% of individuals. This approach was also used to separately optimize p-value thresholds for predicting BMI change on ART.

2.3.2. *PRS-CSx*

PRS-CSx (version July 29, 2021) was used to construct a multi-ancestry PRS_{BMI}, where both the European and African ancestry summary statistics were jointly adjusted by the model using default optimization parameters to learn the shrinkage factor.[18] The output was then converted to risk scores using the PLINK '--score' function as described in the PRS-CSx documentation.[28] The resulting PRSs were analyzed independently for their performance in each ancestry group and were also linearly combined to create a multi-ancestry PRS_{BMI}. A mixing parameter for the combined PRS_{BMI} was optimized in a subset of the target data comprising 20% of the total target set (n=105/527) and was optimized to minimize the difference in mean PRS_{BMI} between the AFR and EUR ancestry groups. The resulting PRS_{COMB} took the form of $PRS_{COMB} = PRS_{EUR} + \alpha * PRS_{AFR}$ where α is the mixing parameter.

2.4. *Computational and statistical analysis*

All data analyses were performed using python3, scipy, and pandas in a jupyter notebook.[31–33] The distribution of PRS_{BMI} scores was compared between ancestry groups to evaluate systematic ancestry-dependent trends and biases. Performance of each PRS_{BMI} was evaluated as the R^2 value of the PRS_{BMI} in the test set against the phenotype of interest (baseline BMI or change in BMI). Linear regression was used to calculate a p-value for each PRS_{BMI}. For the pre-ART BMI phenotype, we also adjusted for the first 10 principal components, age, sex, and baseline weight in our regression and calculated the incremental performance of our PRS_{BMI} by comparing the PRS_{BMI} + covariates R^2 to the covariates-only model and recorded the p-value for the PRS_{BMI} parameter in the PRS_{BMI} + covariates model. For BMI change, we also adjusted for the first 10 principal components, age and sex, as well as baseline BMI.

3. Results

3.1. *PRS-CSx produces a high-performing multi-ancestry PRS for baseline BMI*

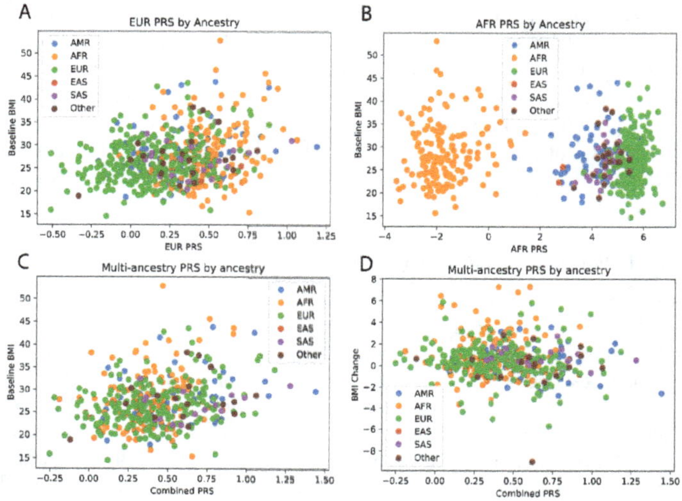

Fig. 2. Distribution of PRS$_{BMI}$ from PRS-CSx in each ancestry group. (A) European-derived PRS$_{BMI}$ vs baseline BMI. (B) African-derived PRS$_{AFR}$ vs baseline BMI. (C) Combined PRS$_{AFR}$ + PRS$_{EUR}$ vs baseline BMI. (D) Combined PRS$_{AFR}$ + PRS$_{EUR}$ vs BMI change from baseline to week 48 on ART.

3.1.1. *PRS$_{BMI}$ generated from European summary statistics systematically overestimate BMI in African ancestry individuals*

Consistent with other work applying PRS across ancestry groups, the EUR-derived PRS$_{BMI}$ (PRS$_{EUR}$) from PRSice and PRS-CSx both perform best in the EUR ancestry subset of our data and have significant performance decreases in other ancestry groups. Before covariate adjustment, PRS$_{EUR}$ from PRSice performs better at predicting baseline BMI in EUR than the PRS$_{EUR}$ from PRS-CSx, with an R^2 of 0.080 versus 0.070. However, the PRSice PRS$_{EUR}$ performs very poorly in AFR compared to the PRS-CSx PRS$_{EUR}$, with R^2 in AFR of 0.0032 and 0.055 respectively. Scatterplots of the PRS vs BMI show that the discrepancy in performance is accompanied by a systematic overestimation of AFR BMI in the PRSice PRS$_{EUR}$ (Supplementary Figure 1). This trend is also present in the PRS-CSx results (Figure 1A). Full PRS performance results are provided in Supplementary Table 1. Interestingly, the performance of the PRSice PRS$_{EUR}$ in AMR was high, with an R^2 of 0.110.

3.1.2 *PRS generated from African summary statistics produces a bimodal distribution*

Similar to the trend in PRS$_{EUR}$, the AFR-derived BMI PRS (PRS$_{AFR}$) performs better in the AFR ancestry subset of our data, with R^2 in AFR of 0.052 and 0.062 for PRSice and PRS-CSx respectively. However, the PRS_{AFR} from PRSice performs much worse in EUR than the PRS-CSx one does, with R^2 of 0.0063 and 0.034 respectively. In both the PRSice and PRS-CSx results, the distribution of PRS varies by ancestry, but the difference is particularly pronounced between AFR and EUR, where scores in the AFR population and EUR population from both PRSice and PRS-CSx are entirely disjoint, with the highest AFR score being lower than the lowest EUR score (Figure 1B, Supplementary Figure 1).

3.1.2. *Linear combination of the European and African PRS_{BMI} improves performance in both European and African ancestry populations*

Table 1. Multi-ancestry PRS-CSx PRS_{COMB} performance for BMI prediction in each ancestry group

Target Ancestry	R^2	p-value
EUR (n=206)	0.0725	9.1e-5
AFR (n=128)	0.0795	1.3e-3
AMR (n=43)	0.0674	0.060
Multi-ancestry (n=422)	0.0663	8.1e-8

Given that PRS_{EUR} overestimates BMI in AFR compared to EUR and that PRS_{AFR} underestimates BMI in EUR compared to AFR, we combined the two PRS additively, tuning a mixing parameter such that we minimized the difference in mean combined PRS (PRS_{COMB}) between the AFR and EUR test sets (Table 1). Beyond outperforming both PRS_{AFR} and PRS_{EUR} in AFR test set, the PRS_{COMB} also improves performance in the EUR set. The PRS_{COMB} also improves performance for admixed individuals (AMR) over the PRS-CSx PRS_{EUR} which achieved an R^2 0.056. For comparison purposes, we explored a similar linear combination of the PRSice scores, but to avoid further reducing the sample size, we opted to optimize the combination in the entire test set by also minimizing the difference in mean PRS. Despite the possibility of overfitting to the test data, we found that this approach resulted in drastically diminished performance in the AFR test set, with an R^2 of 0.0016. This seems to indicate that linear combination of PRS_{BMI} from pruning and thresholding is not as effective for creating an unbiased multi-ancestry PRS_{BMI}. Full PRS_{BMI} performance results for predicting BMI in each ancestry group are provided in Supplementary Table 1. Additionally, when we adjust our PRS_{BMI} for the first 10 principal components, age, sex, and height, the incremental performance of PRS-CSx PRS_{COMB} on the entire population is greater than the incremental performance of the PRSice PRS_{COMB} with R^2 increases of 0.053 and 0.038 respectively over the covariates alone. Furthermore, we see that the incremental performance of the PRS-CSx PRS_{COMB} is greater than the incremental performance of the single-ancestry PRS-CSx PRSs (Supplementary Table 2).

3.2. *PRS_{BMI} is not correlated with weight change on antiretroviral therapy*

Table 2. Multi-ancestry PRS_{BMI} performance for weight change prediction in each target ancestry group

Target Ancestry	R^2	p-value
EUR (n=206)	0.0085	0.186
AFR (n=128)	8.97e-07	0.992
AMR (n=43)	0.020	0.305
Multi-ancestry (n=422)	0.0073	0.080

With our high-performing multi-ancestry PRS_{BMI} from PRS-CSx, we then measured its performance in predicting BMI change from baseline to week 48 following initiation of ART. Across all ancestry groups, the PRS_{BMI} was not a significant predictor of weight change and had small R^2 values in all analyses (Table 2). The performance of the other PRSs for BMI change prediction can be found in Supplementary Table 3 with concurrent results. When we subsequently adjust for the first 10 principal components, age, sex, and baseline BMI, we see negligible change in prediction performance or statistical significance (Supplementary Table 4). This evidence further supports the conclusion that weight gain following ART shares little to no underlying genetic predisposition with baseline BMI.

4. Discussion

Our work carries interesting implications for the underlying biology of ART-associated weight gain and for the application of PRS derived from large population GWAS for predicting potentially related traits. First, we were able to successfully construct PRS for BMI (PRS_{BMI}) using large, publicly-available GWAS summary statistics for BMI in different ancestry groups. We showed that while pruning and thresholding produced higher performance in EUR using the EUR summary statistics, PRS-CSx produced a better multi-ancestry PRS, with the exception of the AMR population subset, where pruning and thresholding-based combined PRS performed higher than any other ancestry or PRS. A larger validation set of AMR individuals will be needed to see whether this performance holds, but this could be a consequence of the use of a multi-ancestry subset of the dataset to tune the p-value threshold. Notably, we also demonstrated that our PRS_{BMI} derived from summary statistics from a population without HIV is highly predictive of BMI pre-treatment in individuals with HIV. Through the use of PRS-CSx, we were subsequently able to create a multi-ancestry PRS_{BMI} that performed very well in both EUR and AFR populations. This followed from the peculiar observation that the PRS_{AFR} from both PRSice and PRS-CSx showed a disjoint bimodal distribution where PRS_{AFR} is drastically lower in the AFR subset of the population. Since PRS_{EUR} tends to overestimate BMI in the AFR subset, the PRS_{AFR} can be seen as a "correction factor" for the PRS_{EUR}, increasing scores for EUR and decreasing scores for AFR to mitigate the bias. Despite this trend appearing from both PRSice and PRS-CSx, PRSice did not produce a very effective multi-ancestry PRS.

Despite the strong correlation between our PRS_{BMI} and baseline BMI, the PRS_{BMI} was not well correlated with BMI change in response to ART, and we did not find statistically significant evidence that PRS_{BMI} is associated with BMI change in response to efavirenz-based therapy, even when adjusting for covariates including baseline BMI. Our results provide compelling evidence that an individual's genetic predisposition based on a common variant PRS for higher BMI may not contribute to greater ART-associated weight gain. It is still possible that other genetic models and/or low frequency variants not captured by PRS may play a role in ART-associated weight gain. Future research on the causes of ART-associated weight gain should explore distinct mechanisms beyond our canonical understanding of the genetics of obesity and BMI.

There are limitations to this work which may have influenced our results. First, our PRS_{BMI} testing sample size was limited to approximately 500 individuals, and when subdivided by ancestry the sample sizes become smaller, limiting our power to find associations between our PRS and target traits. As such, it remains a possibility that PRS_{BMI} could be associated with ART-associated weight gain, but at a smaller effect size than we could detect given our statistical power. Additionally, due to particularly small sample sizes of East Asian and South Asian individuals, we mostly focused on cross-ancestry performance in EUR, AFR, and AMR populations, as well as in the entire population. Finally, it is also worth noting that integrase inhibitor-associated weight gain is greater than efavirenz-associated weight gain and that integrase inhibitors are currently the preferred initial therapy for most people. The ACTG cohorts included in this study did not receive INSTIs; thus the effect sizes may be larger if this investigation was repeated in a cohort of individuals who experienced weight gain after receiving INSTIs.

Subsequent work in this area could investigate how other covariates may influence BMI change. In further exploration of the use of large sample-size GWAS to construct PRS for drug response traits, one could study other phenotypes, such as how GWAS for liver function tests (such as alanine transaminase (ALT) and aspartate transaminase (AST)) may be predictive of adverse liver events, or whether a PRS derived from GWAS for major depressive disorder is predictive of neurological effects of ART. These approaches have the potential to leverage large, publicly available datasets to generate new discoveries in smaller pharmacogenetic cohorts. As more associations or lack thereof are found, we continue to narrow down the likely biological causes of adverse drug reactions such as excessive weight gain, bringing us closer to the true etiology.

5. Acknowledgments

The authors are grateful to the many persons living with HIV who volunteered for ACTG protocols A5095, A5142 and A5202. In addition, they acknowledge the contributions of study teams and site staff for these protocols. We thank Paul J. McLaren, PhD (Public Health Agency of Canada, Winnipeg, Canada) for prior involvement and collaborations that used these genome-wide genotype data. Study drugs were provided by DuPont Pharmaceutical Company, Bristol-Myers Squibb, Inc., GlaxoWellcome, Inc., Gilead Sciences, Inc., GlaxoSmithKline, Inc.. The clinical trials were A5095 (NCT00013520), A5142 (NCT00050895), and A5202 (NCT00118898).

Research reported in this publication was supported by the National Institute of Allergy and Infectious Diseases of the National Institutes of Health under Award Number UM1 AI068634, UM1 AI068636 and UM1 AI106701. The content is solely the responsibility of the authors and does not necessarily represent the official views of the National Institutes of

Health, Supported in part by grants funded by the National Center for Research Resources and the National Center for Advancing Translational Sciences.

Grant support included TR000124 (to E.S.D.); AI110527, AI077505, TR000445, and AI069439 (to D.W.H.). This work was supported by the Tennessee Center for AIDS Research (P30) AI110527.

Clinical research sites that participated in ACTG protocols A5095, A5142 and/or A5202, and collected DNA under protocol A5128 were supported by the following grants from the National Institutes of Health (NIH): A1069412, A1069423, A1069424, A1069503, AI025859, AI025868, AI027658, AI027661, AI027666, AI027675, AI032782, AI034853, AI038858, AI045008, AI046370, AI046376, AI050409, AI050410, AI050410, AI058740, AI060354, AI068636, AI069412, AI069415, AI069418, AI069419, AI069423, AI069424, AI069428, AI069432, AI069432, AI069434, AI069439, AI069447, AI069450, AI069452, AI069465, AI069467, AI069470, AI069471, AI069472, AI069474, AI069477, AI069481, AI069484, AI069494, AI069495, AI069496, AI069501, AI069501, AI069502, AI069503, AI069511, AI069513, AI069532, AI069534, AI069556, AI072626, AI073961, RR000046, RR000425, RR023561, RR024156, RR024160, RR024996, RR025008, RR025747, RR025777, RR025780, TR000004, TR000058, TR000124, TR000170, TR000439, TR000445, TR000457, TR001079, TR001082, TR001111, and TR024160.

Supplementary Figures/Tables

Supplementary Figure 1. PRSice PRS for BMI plotted against baseline BMI
Supplementary Table 1. Performance of each PRS for predicting baseline BMI
Supplementary Table 2. Incremental performance of each PRS for predicting baseline BMI
Supplementary Table 3. Performance of each PRS for predicting BMI change
Supplementary Table 4. Incremental performance of each PRS for predicting BMI change

All supplemental data can be found at the links above or at: https://ritchielab.org/publications/supplementary-data/psb-2023/actg-bmi-prs.

References

1. HIV/AIDS. https://www.who.int/data/gho/data/themes/hiv-aids.
2. Lake, J. E. *et al.* Risk Factors for Weight Gain Following Switch to Integrase Inhibitor–Based Antiretroviral Therapy. *Clin. Infect. Dis.* **71**, e471–e477 (2020).
3. Erlandson, K. M. *et al.* Mitochondrial DNA haplogroups and weight gain following switch to integrase strand transfer inhibitor-based antiretroviral therapy. *AIDS* **35**, 439–445 (2021).
4. Leonard, M. A. *et al.* Efavirenz Pharmacogenetics and Weight Gain Following Switch to Integrase Inhibitor-Containing Regimens. *Clin. Infect. Dis. Off. Publ. Infect. Dis. Soc. Am.* **73**, e2153–e2163 (2021).
5. Haas, D. W. *et al.* Pharmacogenetic interactions of rifapentine plus isoniazid with efavirenz or nevirapine. *Pharmacogenet. Genomics* **31**, 17–27 (2021).
6. Holzinger, E. R. *et al.* Genome-wide association study of plasma efavirenz pharmacokinetics in AIDS Clinical Trials Group protocols implicates several CYP2B6 variants. *Pharmacogenet. Genomics* **22**, 858–867 (2012).
7. Bertrand, J. *et al.* Multiple genetic variants predict steady-state nevirapine clearance in HIV-infected Cambodians. *Pharmacogenet. Genomics* **22**, 868–876 (2012).

8. Rao, A. S. & Knowles, J. W. Polygenic risk scores in coronary artery disease. *Curr. Opin. Cardiol.* **34**, 435–440 (2019).
9. Khera, A. V. *et al.* Genome-wide polygenic scores for common diseases identify individuals with risk equivalent to monogenic mutations. *Nat. Genet.* **50**, 1219–1224 (2018).
10. McCarthy, M. I. & Mahajan, A. The value of genetic risk scores in precision medicine for diabetes. *Expert Rev. Precis. Med. Drug Dev.* **3**, 279–281 (2018).
11. Pulit, S. L. *et al.* Atrial fibrillation genetic risk differentiates cardioembolic stroke from other stroke subtypes. *Neurol. Genet.* **4**, (2018).
12. Mavaddat, N. *et al.* Polygenic Risk Scores for Prediction of Breast Cancer and Breast Cancer Subtypes. *Am. J. Hum. Genet.* **104**, 21–34 (2019).
13. Li, H. *et al.* Breast cancer risk prediction using a polygenic risk score in the familial setting: a prospective study from the Breast Cancer Family Registry and kConFab. *Genet. Med. Off. J. Am. Coll. Med. Genet.* **19**, 30–35 (2017).
14. Wimberley, T. *et al.* Polygenic Risk Score for Schizophrenia and Treatment-Resistant Schizophrenia. *Schizophr. Bull.* **43**, 1064–1069 (2017).
15. Miller, A. P. *et al.* Polygenic liability for schizophrenia predicts shifting-specific executive function deficits and tobacco use in a moderate drinking community sample. *Psychiatry Res.* **279**, 47–54 (2019).
16. Ni, G. *et al.* A Comparison of Ten Polygenic Score Methods for Psychiatric Disorders Applied Across Multiple Cohorts. *Biol. Psychiatry* **90**, 611–620 (2021).
17. Choi, S. W. & O'Reilly, P. F. PRSice-2: Polygenic Risk Score software for biobank-scale data. *GigaScience* **8**, giz082 (2019).
18. Ruan, Y. *et al.* Improving polygenic prediction in ancestrally diverse populations. *Nat. Genet.* **54**, 573–580 (2022).
19. Privé, F., Arbel, J. & Vilhjálmsson, B. J. LDpred2: better, faster, stronger. *Bioinformatics* **36**, 5424–5431 (2020).
20. Locke, A. E. *et al.* Genetic studies of body mass index yield new insights for obesity biology. *Nature* **518**, 197–206 (2015).
21. Yengo, L. *et al.* Meta-analysis of genome-wide association studies for height and body mass index in ~700000 individuals of European ancestry. *Hum. Mol. Genet.* **27**, 3641–3649 (2018).
22. Ng, M. C. Y. *et al.* Discovery and fine-mapping of adiposity loci using high density imputation of genome-wide association studies in individuals of African ancestry: African Ancestry Anthropometry Genetics Consortium. *PLOS Genet.* **13**, e1006719 (2017).
23. Gulick, R. M. *et al.* Triple-Nucleoside Regimens versus Efavirenz-Containing Regimens for the Initial Treatment of HIV-1 Infection. *N. Engl. J. Med.* **350**, 1850–1861 (2004).
24. Gulick, R. M. *et al.* Three- vs Four-Drug Antiretroviral Regimens for the Initial Treatment of HIV-1 InfectionA Randomized Controlled Trial. *JAMA* **296**, 769–781 (2006).
25. Riddler, S. A. *et al.* Class-Sparing Regimens for Initial Treatment of HIV-1 Infection. *N. Engl. J. Med.* **358**, 2095–2106 (2008).
26. Daar, E. S. *et al.* Atazanavir plus ritonavir or efavirenz as part of a 3-drug regimen for initial treatment of HIV-1. *Ann. Intern. Med.* **154**, 445–456 (2011).
27. Haas, D. W. *et al.* A multi-investigator/institutional DNA bank for AIDS-related human genetic studies: AACTG Protocol A5128. *HIV Clin. Trials* **4**, 287–300 (2003).
28. Chang, C. C. *et al.* Second-generation PLINK: rising to the challenge of larger and richer datasets. *GigaScience* **4**, 7 (2015).

29. Hinrichs, A. S. *et al.* The UCSC Genome Browser Database: update 2006. *Nucleic Acids Res.* **34**, D590-598 (2006).
30. Xiao, B. *et al.* Inference of causal relationships based on the genetics of cardiometabolic traits and conditions unique to females in >50,000 participants. 2022.02.02.22269844 Preprint at https://doi.org/10.1101/2022.02.02.22269844 (2022).
31. Virtanen, P. *et al.* SciPy 1.0: fundamental algorithms for scientific computing in Python. *Nat. Methods* **17**, 261–272 (2020).
32. Reback, J. *et al.* pandas-dev/pandas: Pandas 1.4.3. (2022) doi:10.5281/zenodo.6702671.
33. McKinney, W. Data Structures for Statistical Computing in Python. *Proc. 9th Python Sci. Conf.* 56–61 (2010) doi:10.25080/Majora-92bf1922-00a.

Fine-scale subpopulation detection via an SNP-based unsupervised method: A case study on the 1000 Genomes Project resources

Kridsadakorn Chaichoompu[1]
GIGA-R, BIO3, University of Liege, Avenue de l'Hôpital 11, 4000 Liège, Belgium

Alisa Wilantho, Pongsakorn Wangkumhang, and Sissades Tongsima[2]
National Biobank of Thailand, 111 Thailand Science Park, Phahonyothin Road, Khlong Neung, Khlong Luang, Pathum Thani, 12120, Thailand

Bruno Cavadas and Luísa Pereira[3]
Instituto de Investigação e Inovação em Saúde, Universidade do Porto, Rua Alfredo Allen, 208 | 4200-135 Porto, Portugal
Instituto de Patologia e Imunologia Molecular da Universidade do Porto, Rua Júlio Amaral de Carvalho, 45 | 4200-135 Porto, Portugal

Kristel Van Steen[1]
GIGA-R, BIO3, University of Liege, Avenue de l'Hôpital 11, 4000 Liège, Belgium
Email: kristel.vansteen@uliege.be[4]

SNP-based information is used in several existing clustering methods to detect shared genetic ancestry or to identify population substructure. Here, we present a methodology, called IPCAPS for unsupervised population analysis using iterative pruning. Our method, which can capture fine-level structure in populations, supports ordinal data, and thus can readily be applied to SNP data. Although haplotypes may be more informative than SNPs, especially in fine-level substructure detection contexts, the haplotype inference process often remains too computationally intensive. In this work, we investigate the scale of the structure we can detect in populations without knowledge about haplotypes; our simulated data do not assume the availability of haplotype information while comparing our method to existing tools for detecting fine-level population substructures. We demonstrate experimentally that IPCAPS can achieve high accuracy and can outperform existing tools in several simulated scenarios. The fine-level structure detected by IPCAPS on an application to the 1000 Genomes Project data underlines its subject heterogeneity.

Keywords: fine-level population structure; SNP-based population clustering; iterative clustering; 1000 Genome project.

[1] Supported by Fonds de la Recherche Scientifique (FNRS PDR T.0180.13)
[2] Supported by National Science and Technology Development Agency research grant (P18507439)
[3] Supported by European Regional Development Fund (COMPETE 2020 and Portugal 2020), and by Portuguese funds through Fundação para a Ciência e a Tecnologia (POCI-01-0145-FEDER-007274)
[4] Corresponding author

1. Introduction

Over time, evolutionary processes, for instance, natural selection, migration, and genetic drift, are the key factors that have contributed to the variations in genetic makeup and admixture of populations. Populations living in the same geographical area share a similar genetic background. Generally, genetic population substructure is analyzed using single nucleotide polymorphisms (SNPs) or haplotypes (derived from SNPs). Haplotype-based methods usually involve making haplotype inferences, which are computationally more cumbersome than direct allele frequency processing in SNP-based methods. Subpopulation detection has an important role in precision medicine and is beneficial for downstream analyses, especially for genome-wide association studies (*1*) and drug target identification for homogenized groups of individuals (*2*). Hence, the accuracy of population subtyping methods is crucial to generate sufficient power in these efforts.

Several SNP-based clustering algorithms exist, each leading to different clustering results and accuracy. Promising results in the context of SNP-based fine-scale population subtyping have been demonstrated for the following iterative algorithms. The iterative pruning Principal Component Analysis (ipPCA) method classifies individuals into groups without prior assumptions (*3*, *4*). The idea of iteratively creating latent Principal Component (PC) spaces can be applied to estimating the number of clusters. Spectral Hierarchical clustering for the Inference of Population Structure (SHIPS) is based on determining the number of clusters in the post-process (*5*). This method incorporates a divisive hierarchical clustering, which allows a progressive investigation of population structure. The SHIPS method estimates the number of clusters in a dataset via the gap statistic (*6*). The method produces a promising solution to infer fine-scale genetic patterns and has a low computational cost when applied to genome-wide SNP data. The graph-based method iNJclust is an alternative unsupervised clustering method (*7*). It operates iteratively on the Neighbor-Joining (NJ) tree. This framework uses the allele-sharing distance to build up the neighbor-joining tree. The behavior of the fixation index (F_{ST}) is utilized as a stopping criterion for this algorithm.

This paper presents detailed information on IPCAPS (implemented as R package (*8*)), including its underlying methodology, its performance via large-scale simulations, and a real-life application. IPCAPS is based on the ipPCA mechanism and relies on iterative PCA estimation from SNP data. However, all known limitations of ipPCA are addressed by IPCAPS. These include: resolving limitations of inflated type I errors caused by a 2-means algorithm, advancing on ipPCA's stopping criteria based on Tracy-Widom statistics (*3*) and the EigenDev heuristic (*4*), mowing away from a commercial implementation environment (MATLAB) toward a widely accessible environment (R environment (*9*)), and identifying outliers interfering with robust clustering. Most importantly, although ipPCA can capture general population structure, it cannot detect fine-level structure when F_{ST} is close to 0.001, such as is the case for Swedish-Norwegian samples (F_{ST}=0.001) or Polish-German samples (F_{ST}=0.0012) (*10*). A proof of concept for IPCAPS' ability to identify fine-scale structure was given before on a relatively small African dataset (*8*). In this paper, we not only showcase IPCAPS on 1000 Genomes data, using populations from African, American, European, East Asian, and South Asian ancestries, but we also demonstrate IPCAPS performance in a variety of theoretical scenarios via an extensive simulation study.

2. IPCAPS methodology for SNP-based subtyping

The current implementation of IPCAPS takes GWAS SNPs as input and iteratively creates PCA spaces to identify substructures in populations. Hence, prior to IPCAPS applications, Quality Control (QC) pre-processing steps largely coincide with standard practices to GWAS QC or SNP-based PCA analyses for population structure evaluations. In particular, data QC may include missing genotype filtering (missingness < 0.02), Hardy–Weinberg equilibrium (HWE) testing ($p<0.001$), and linkage disequilibrium (LD) pruning ($r^2<0.1$). Each missing genotype is replaced by the most common value (*11*); see also supplementary section S1. QC processing steps are followed by a data matrix construction for IPCAPS analysis: rows of this data matrix represent individuals, and the columns represent SNPs. SNPs are encoded as 0, 1, and 2, reflecting the number of minor alleles present at the corresponding loci. As a consequence, the encoded data matrix contains numeric values suitable for standard PCA. The data matrix is subsequently normalized by a zero-mean and unit variance procedure. In case all individuals contain only a single genotype at some loci, the normalized value is zero representing no variation. In practical applications, this issue frequently occurs for common alleles.

IPCAPS' core methodology can be broken down into the following steps (see Supplementary Figure S1 for a graphical workflow):

Step 1: In each iteration, select genotype data X according to the remaining individuals from the previous iteration; however, the whole data are used for the first iteration. The matrix X contains N rows and M columns representing a number of individuals and a number of SNPs, respectively. The SNP matrix is normalized using zero-mean and unit variance methods.

Step2: Construct a covariance matrix from matrix multiplication XX^T in order to reduce complexity for computation.

Step 3: Extract principal components (PCs) from the matrix XX^T as $XX^T = UDU^T$, where U represents eigenvectors and D is a diagonal matrix of positive eigenvalues of XX^T eigenvalues. A matrix of eigenvectors is used as PCs. For faster computation, PCs are calculated partially (*12*) according to the estimated high-impact number of PCs (P) in *Step 4* from the previous iteration. The matrix PCs contains N rows and P columns representing a number of individuals and a number of PCs, respectively.

Step 4: Calculate the EigenFit value from the matrix D (Step 3), defined as in Eq. (1):

$$EigenFit = max(D), \tag{1}$$

where D is a vector of differences defined as in Eq. (2)

$$D = (|L_1 - L_2|, |L_2 - L_3|, \dots, |L_{N-1} - L_N|) \ , \tag{2}$$

with L_i the eigenvector corresponding to the logarithm of eigenvector i ($i=1,\dots,N$). If the EigenFit is less than a user-specified threshold, then stop the iteration and define the current set of individuals as a subgroup. If not, continue to the next step. In this step, the P high-impact PCs is also estimated to be used in *Step 3* in the next iteration, where P is derived from P' as defined in Eq. (4) and (5):

$$P' = \sum_{i=1}^{N-1} I_{[i \leq m]} \tag{4}$$

$$I_{[i \leq m]} = \begin{cases} 1 & i \leq m \\ 0 & i > m \end{cases} \tag{5}$$

with $i = 1, 2, 3, ..., N$, and m is an order of EigenFit in vector D. To have at least a 3D PC space for clustering, if P' is less than or equal to 3, then $P = 3$, otherwise $P = P'$.

Step 5: Apply RubikClust (*13*) on P high-impact PCs. Higher-dimensional outlier detection via RubikClust is used to enhance the stability of IPCAPS clustering, which identified outliers are allocated to separate clusters.

Step 6: Check if the number of subgroups obtained from RubikClust equals 1. If so, submit PCs to MIXMOD clustering in *Step 7*. If not, skip to *Step 9*.

Step 7: Apply MIXMOD clustering on PCs via the function mixmodCluster in the R package Rmixmod (*14*) and the Bayesian information criterion (BIC) (*15*) to determine the optimal number of subtypes (clusters). Additional details are provided in supplementary section S2.

Step 8: Check if the number of subgroups obtained from MIXMOD clustering equals 1. If so, then stop this iteration and define the current set of individuals as a subgroup. If not, continue to the next step.

Step 9: Check if the number of individuals in obtained subgroups is less than a pre-specified cutoff by users. If so, then stop this iteration and define the current set of individuals as a subgroup (defined as a group of outliers). If not, continue to the next step.

Step 10: Calculate pairwise F_{ST} for all pairs of subgroups. If F_{ST} is more than a user-specified threshold, then continue to the next iteration in step 1. If not, the pairs with F_{ST} less than the threshold are combined and defined as a single cluster.

Note that IPCAPS methodology combines three stopping criteria: 1) checking whether the EigenFit is lower than a prespecified threshold (*Step 4*), 2) determining whether the fixation index (F_{ST}) value between two clusters is lower than a threshold (*Step 10*), 3) checking whether a number of individuals in each cluster is lower than a customizable cutoff. Regarding the latter, if the minimum cluster size is low (i.e., 3-5), then too many sparse subgroups may be obtained. Hence, a balance needs to be sought between many potentially small, highly homogeneous, clusters or a few less homogeneous clusters that have sufficient power to be followed up for characterization in downstream analyses. When analyzing a dataset with a small number of individuals, for example, <100 individuals, it may be more practical to allow for minimally 5 to 10 individuals per final IPCAPS group. Our findings from an application on 1000 Genomes data (see Section 3) motivates 0.18 as maximum for the EigenFit threshold and the simulation scenario I (supplementary section S4) suggests 0.03 as minimum. The choice of F_{ST} threshold depends on the number of markers and samples available for subtyping. However, we motivate in supplementary section S3 the default of 0.0008.

3. Datasets

To assess the performance of IPCAPS we generated synthetic data with FILEST (*16*) according to 3 main scenarios. Simulation scenario I aimed to investigate a type I error, simulation scenario II aimed to assess the accuracy of IPCAPS, and simulation scenario III targeted quantifying scalability and speed. Cluster agreement between two clustering results was assessed via the Adjusted Rand Index (ARI) using the R Package mclust (*17*). The maximal attainable ARI value is 1, representing an identical match between 2 groups, while a negative value represents a mismatch.

3.1. *Simulation scenario I: test for Type I error*

The objective of simulation scenario I is to examine the type I error rate of our method. Ideally, there should not be any error if we apply IPCAPS to a single homogeneous population. In other words, in this case, the IPCAPS algorithm should only reveal 1 group; the initial population. We compared our method to other iterative pruning-based clustering methods such as ipPCA (*3*, *4*), iNJclust (*7*), and SHIPS (*5*). Moreover, we simulated one population with 500 individuals and 10,000 SNPs without any outliers and did so 100 times (i.e., 100 replicates). The parameter settings for FILEST are listed in Table 1 and the supplementary section S4.

3.2. *Simulation scenario II: test for accuracy*

The objective of simulation scenario II is to determine the accuracy of IPCAPS. Comparative iterative pruning-based methods for clustering are the same as for simulation scenario I: ipPCA, iNJclust, and SHIPS. For scenario II, we simulated 100 replicates of 10,000 SNPs and 500 individuals per population. For the settings SII-1, SII-3 and SII-5, two populations were simulated. We added an additional population in the settings SII-2, SII-4 and SII-6. The adopted F_{ST} values represented pairwise genetic distances as before (Hudson's fixation index) and ranged from 0.0008 to 0.005. We selected the lowest F_{ST} as 0.0008 according to the result in the supplementary section S3, and the highest F_{ST} as 0.005 according to the genetic distance among clearly distinct European populations. To assess the impact of outliers, we added three outliers in the settings SII-3 and SII-4, and five outliers in the settings SII-5 and SII-6. An outlier was considered when it was separated into its own group or grouped with other outliers. All setting parameters are summarized in Table 1 and the supplementary section S5.

3.3. *Simulation scenario III: test for scalability and speed*

The objective of simulation scenario III is to check the scalability and speed of IPCAPS. In particular, we wanted to investigate which of the two factors, the number of individuals or the number of SNPs, has the most impact on computation time. We chose to compare IPCAPS to ipPCA only. The parameter settings for this simulation scenario were as follows. We simulated 100 replicates of two populations while fixing F_{ST} at 0.005. This single fixed value of F_{ST} was motivated by the fact that IPCAPS was able to accurately separate two populations with F_{ST}=0.005. For setting SIII-1, we fixed the number of input SNP to 10,000 and varied the number of individuals from 100 to 10,000. For setting SIII-2, we considered 1,000 individuals and varied the number of SNPs from 25,000 to 100,000. To measure the performance of IPCAPS in terms of computation time, we performed all experiments on the same 64-bit Linux cluster with the 2.2 GHz Intel Xeon 8-core processor and 128 GB of memory per node. Since the cluster was working routinely and we could not control other running processes, we reported the median of execution times from 100 replicates instead of the mean. All parameter settings are summarized in Table 1 and the supplementary section S6.

Table 1. Parameter settings for simulation studies of scenarios I, II, and III. Scenario I contains one setting. Scenario II contains six settings, and Scenario III contains two settings.

<table>
<tr><td rowspan="2">Parameters</td><td colspan="9">Settings</td></tr>
<tr><td>SI</td><td>SII-1</td><td>SII-2</td><td>SII-3</td><td>SII-4</td><td>SII-5</td><td>SII-6</td><td>SIII-1</td><td>SIII-2</td></tr>
<tr><td>No. populations</td><td>1</td><td>2</td><td>3</td><td>2</td><td>3</td><td>2</td><td>3</td><td>2</td><td>2</td></tr>
<tr><td>No. outliers</td><td>0</td><td>0</td><td>0</td><td>3</td><td>3</td><td>5</td><td>5</td><td>0</td><td>0</td></tr>
<tr><td>Population Distance (F_{ST})</td><td>-</td><td colspan="6">0.0008, 0.0009, 0.001, 0.002, 0.003, 0.004, 0.005</td><td>0.005</td><td>0.005</td></tr>
<tr><td>No. individuals per population</td><td>500</td><td colspan="6">500</td><td>100, 2.5k, 5k, 7.5k, 10k</td><td>1k</td></tr>
<tr><td>No. SNPs</td><td>10k</td><td colspan="6">10k</td><td>10k</td><td>25k, 50k, 75k, 100k</td></tr>
<tr><td>No. replications</td><td colspan="9">100</td></tr>
</table>

3.4. *Real-life scenario: application of genome-wide data using the 1000 Genomes Project*

The aim of this experiment is to check the performance of IPCAPS in a big real-life dataset (large matrix calculation usually causes a computational error) and to potentially refine the genetic structure of the 1000 Genomes data in view of the obtained ADMIXTURE profiles (version 1.3.0) (*18*). Initially, we obtained the 1000 Genomes dataset (*19*), which consisted of 3,609 individuals from 26 populations and 78,136,341 SNPs in total. All quality control (QC) steps were carried out in PLINK version 1.9 (*20*). The QC steps consisted in selecting only founders or unrelated individuals (--filter-founders), selecting only autosomal chromosomes 1-22 (--not-chr 0,x,y,xy,mt), filtering out SNPs in linkage disequilibrium (LD) blocks (--indep-pairwise 50 5 0.1), removing SNPs that disagree with the Hardy–Weinberg equilibrium (HWE) testing (--hwe 0.001), allowing individuals with call rate at least 95% (--mind 0.05), filtering out missing genotypes >2% (--geno 0.02), and removing SNPs with low minor allele frequency (MAF) (--maf 0.05). After data QC, there were 2,504 individuals and 127,526 SNPs left. We then performed a population clustering analysis using IPCAPS on the filtered data set after QC steps. Finding actual SNP-based discriminators between IPCAPS clusters was beyond the scope of this study. Since this dataset was huge, it required a lot of memory to perform the analysis. Therefore, all analyses were performed on the 64-bit Linux cluster with the 2.3 GHz Intel Xeon 24-core processor and 512 GB of memory per node.

4. Results

4.1. *Type I error (simulation scenario I)*

From the considered clustering methods, only IPCAPS and SHIPS did not split up the single population into subgroups (average ARI=1). Notably, ipPCA and iNJclust enforced two subgroups (average ARI=0) and 174.79 groups (average ARI=0), respectively. (see supplementary section S4)

Apart from testing for Type I error, we also estimated the minimum EigenFit value from the results of ipPCA because ipPCA forced to split the data into 2 clusters. The average EigenFit value was 0.03, therefore we could use this value as the minimum threshold of EigenFit.

4.2. *Accuracy (simulation scenario II)*

Overall, IPCAPS (red curve in Fig. 1) had optimal performance compared to ipPCA (blue), SHIPS (green), and iNJclust (yellow) in terms of accuracy expressed by average ARI estimated over 100 replicates when comparing observed and expected clustering methods. In particular, IPCAPS performed well with 100% accuracy when F_{ST}=0.002 for all simulation scenarios, while the other strategies performed less for the same F_{ST}=0.002. As for the other strategies, the performance of IPCAPS decreased for decreasing F_{ST}<0.002, although the accuracy reduction was least dramatic for IPCAPS compared to ipPCA, SHIPS, and iNJclust.

In the case of two populations without outliers (setting SII-1, Fig. 1A), IPCAPS and ipPCA gave similar results, but ipPCA performed slightly better for F_{ST}=0.0008. The average ARI of both methods increased to 0.8 when F_{ST}=0.001 and reached 1 when F_{ST}=0.002. SHIPS became highly accurate (ARI=1) only when F_{ST}>=0.004, while iNJclust performed poorly (ARI=0) in this setting.

In the case of three populations without outliers (setting SII-2, Fig. 1B), IPCAPS was more accurate than the other considered methods. The average ARI of IPCAPS reached 1 when F_{ST}=0.002, while the performance of ipPCA dropped in this setting, with ARI reaching 1 from F_{ST}=0.003 onwards. SHIPS showed similar performance in setting SII-2 as in the previous setting, SII-1. The average ARI of iNJclust started to increase when F_{ST}=0.003 and increased up to 0.8 but never reached 1.

In the case of two populations with three and five outliers (settings SII-3 and SII-5, Fig. 1C and 1E), IPCAPS maintained its good performance, similar to the simulation setting SII-1 with two populations and no outliers. The performances of ipPCA and SHIPS dropped in comparison to setting SII-1; iNJclust consistently performed poorly for all F_{ST} in this setting (ARI=0).

In the case of three populations with three and five outliers (settings SII-4 and SII-6, Fig. 1D and 1F), IPCAPS still performed similarly to the corresponding settings without outliers. The performances of ipPCA and SHIPS dropped in comparison to setting SII-2. Interestingly, iNJclust showed increased accuracy for F_{ST}>0.003. However, the average values of ARI of ipPCA, SHIPS, and iNJclust stayed lower than 1 in settings SII-4 and SII-6.

Focusing on simulation settings with outliers and visualizing the number of outliers detected versus F_{ST}, IPCAPS clearly detected the largest number of outliers in comparison to ipPCA, SHIPS, and iNJclust (Fig. 1G, 1H, 1I, and 1J). Recall that an outlier was considered when it was separated into its own group or was grouped with other outliers. Particularly in the settings SII-4 and SII-6 (Fig. 1H and 1J), iNJclust had a hard time identifying any outliers at all. Although ipPCA was able to identify outliers, for all scenarios, it could detect approximately 2 out of 3 in the settings SII-3 and SII-4 (Fig. 1G and 1H), and 4 out of 5 in the settings SII-5 and SII-6 (Fig. 1I and 1J). SHIPS could not detect outliers in the settings SII-3 and SII-4 (Fig. 1G and 1H), but it was able to identify approximately 1 out of 5 in the settings SII-5 and SII-6 (Fig. 1I and 1J).

4.3. *Scalability and speed (simulation scenario III)*

The average execution time of ipPCA (Fig. 1K – blue curve) exponentially grew according to the number of individuals, reaching >24,000 seconds for 10,000 individuals (setting SIII-1). In contrast, the average execution time of IPCAPS (Fig. 1K – red curve) was lower than ipPCA; it reached approximately 2,000 seconds for 10,000 individuals (setting SIII-1). For setting SIII-2 (Fig. 1L), the average execution time of IPCAPS and ipPCA was much lower than for setting SIII-1. The average execution time of ipPCA reached 150 seconds for 100K SNPs, while the average execution time of IPCAPS was slightly lower and less than 150 seconds for 100K SNPs.

4.4. *Real-life scenario: the 1000 Genome Project*

IPCAPS subtyping resulted in 24 groups (excluding the outliers) as shown in Fig. 2. There were five selected populations of East Asian, and IPCAPS could detect four groups (groups 1 to 4) since two closely related Chinese populations were in the same groups (CHB and CHS). Interestingly, the selected four admixed American populations were clustered into five groups (groups 5 to 9) because the Peruvian population (PEL) was mainly separated into two clusters (groups 8 and 9). This was due to the complex admixture found in most of the American populations in that one cluster of PEL had an ancestral background from European (cyan) (group 9), while another cluster of PEL did not (group 8). Five South Asian populations were rather clustered into five clusters. Group 11 was mainly mixed and mainly driven by ITU and STU. Group 12 (BEB) was slightly mixed with East Asian ancestry (light green), and this evidence agreed with what was found in Changmai et al. 2022 (*21*). Groups 10, 13, and 14 (PJL and GIH) were differentiated according to the European ancestry (cyan). Seven African populations were clustered into six groups, and the results agreed with what was described in Chaichoompu et al. 2019 (*22*). Groups 15, 16, and 17 were differentiated by the different admixed proportions of two ancestors (pink and brown). ESN and YRI were clustered in the same groups. ABC and ASW were clustered together but separated into two groups 18 and 19, and they were differentiated by the cyan European ancestor. Group 20, LWK, rather had a unique admixture profile. Five European populations were separated into four clusters (groups 21-24). FIN had a unique ancestral profile (red), as suggested in Wangkumhang et al. 2022 that they were the most distinct group amongst Europeans (*23*). GBR and CEU were in the same group (group 22), unlike IBS and TSI, which had similar ancestral patterns and were differentiated by the other small ancestral parts.

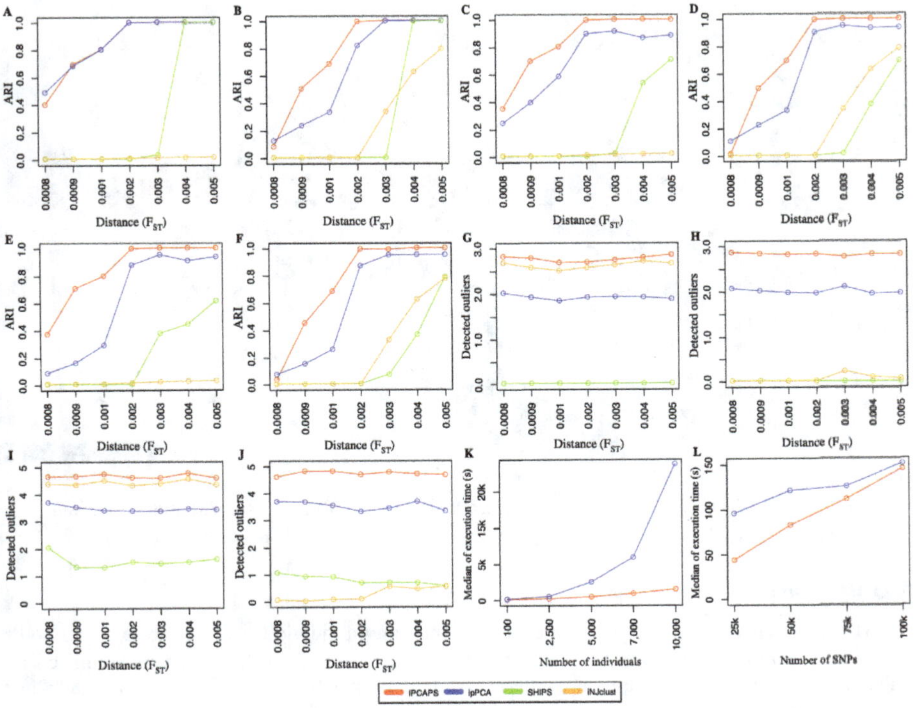

Fig. 1. The simulation results from different scenarios. The clustering accuracy for the simulated datasets without outlier is shown in A (2 populations) and B (3 populations). The clustering accuracy for the simulated datasets with 3 outliers is shown in C (2 populations) and D (3 populations). The clustering accuracy for the simulated datasets with 5 outliers is shown in E (2 populations) and F (3 populations). The number of detected outliers for the simulated datasets with 3 outliers are shown in G (2 populations) and H (3 populations). The number of detected outliers for the simulated datasets with 5 outliers are shown in I (2 populations) and J (3 populations). The median execution time when the number of individuals is scaled is shown in K, and when the number of SNPs is scaled is shown in L. See Table 1 for detailed information for all simulation settings.

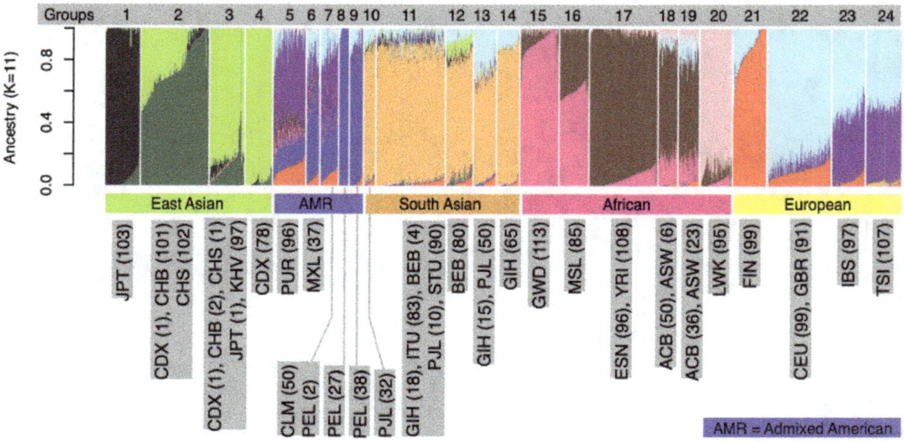

Fig. 2. IPCAPS results of the 1000 Genomes dataset depicted via ADMIXTURE (*18*) profiles (default options). The 24 identified IPCAPS groups are shown in the grey bar (without outliers).

5. Discussions

IPCAPS was generated in the quest for efficient subtyping of individuals at fine scale, using SNPs rather than multilocus haplotypes. It is an iterative clustering algorithm that was templated on ipPCA, yet combines three stopping criteria. As part of the IPCAPS development RubikClust provides a first rough assessment of substructure detection, identifying multi-dimensional outliers. Here, an outlier is an observation that is isolated from other observations in a PC-space. Outliers are collectively removed from further analysis but can be analyzed separately in a sensitivity analysis. The impact of outliers on clustering results with IPCAPS was assessed via several simulation studies, which entailed increasingly complex data structures (simulation scenario II). Among several explored clustering algorithms available from the R environment, MIXMOD served our purposes best, exhibiting excellent performance on complex datasets (see supplementary text S2). Notably, to further increase robustness of final conclusions, rather than choosing one clustering algorithm, multiple ones can be chosen, and a consensus clustering may be derived. The computational burden of IPCAPS depends on the number of individuals due to the dimensionality reduction prior to PCA via the XX^T technique, in which a dimension of the matrix becomes smaller.

EigenFit, which is used as one of the IPCAPS stopping criteria, is motivated by the drawback of EigenDev (*4*). The EigenDev value for a diverse and small subgroup is high and causes the failure in stopping clustering iteration in ipPCA. Hence, we have adjusted the calculation and provided the empirical simulation to check for the minimum threshold of EigenFit (see the section 5.1).

Estimated type I error rates for IPCAPS in our simulation scenario are zero due to the fact that IPCAPS has adopted the F_{ST} threshold of 0.0008 according to sample size and the number of SNPs. Accuracy is defined as the ability to retrieve existing substructure; the adjusted rand index method (ARI) is used to measure accuracy. In all simulation scenarios, IPCAPS generally outperforms ipPCA, SHIPS, and iNJclust. The ipPCA method has a higher average ARI than IPCAPS for F_{ST}=0.008 because ipPCA over separates data as it is observed that Type I error of ipPCA is high (100%). When testing for speed, it is observed that IPCAPS is faster than ipPCA. When dealing with complex population structures in our simulation scenario, IPCAPS delivers satisfactory results. In general, IPCAPS has excellent performance for both fine-level and large-scale settings as supported by experimental results. Initially, the objective of this paper was to develop a tool that deals with fine-level structure. IPCAPS accurately deals with the rough structures by splitting off bigger groups and then zooming in to find additional subtle structures.

Finally, in principle, it is possible to apply IPCAPS methodology to other data types then SNPs, as long as it makes sense to derive PCs, and distance-based stopping criteria (for instance F_{ST}) are adapted to the nature of the data at hand.

6. Conclusions

In this paper, we explained and motivated the components underlying IPCAPS subtyping and for the first time showed extensive simulation studies that underpin its outperformance compared to other iterative subtyping algorithms, namely ipPCA, iNJclust, and SHIPS. The simulated datasets used in all experiments were generated using our own tool FILEST. It allows simulating samples and complex data structures with and without outliers. Furthermore, IPCAPS was applied to big data from the 1000 Genomes project, and it revealed the potential of IPCAPS to detect general population structure, possibly non-linear in nature. Especially for populations in geographically confined regions, IPCAPS was shown to detect meaningful subgroups, which are otherwise hard to detect with classic PCA or ADMIXTURE. We recommend the use of ADMIXTURE or similar software tools to assist in interpreting obtained population subtypes.

7. Supplementary information and availability of software

The supplementary information, the datasets, the experimental scripts, and the results from this paper are publicly available on Zenodo (DOI: 10.5281/zenodo.7141144). IPCAPS is implemented as an R package that is publicly available on the CRAN repository (https://CRAN.R-project.org/package=IPCAPS), and the GitHub repository (https://github.com/kridsadakorn/ipcaps).

Acknowledgments

The authors thank Raphaël Philippart and Alain Empain for critical help with computing clusters at Consortium des Équipements de Calcul Intensif (CÉCI).

References

1. C. Medina-Gomez *et al.*, *Eur. J. Epidemiol.* **30**, 317–330 (2015).
2. C. Finan *et al.*, *Sci. Transl. Med.* **9**, eaag1166 (2017).
3. A. Intarapanich *et al.*, *BMC Bioinformatics.* **10**, 382 (2009).

4. T. Limpiti *et al.*, *BMC Bioinformatics.* **12, 255** (2011).
5. M. Bouaziz, C. Paccard, M. Guedj, C. Ambroise, *PLOS ONE.* **7**, e45685 (2012).
6. R. Tibshirani, G. Walther, T. Hastie, *J. R. Stat. Soc. Ser. B Stat. Methodol.* **63**, 411–423 (2001).
7. T. Limpiti, C. Amornbunchornvej, A. Intarapanich, A. Assawamakin, S. Tongsima, *IEEE/ACM Trans. Comput. Biol. Bioinform.* **11**, 903–914 (2014).
8. K. Chaichoompu *et al.*, *Source Code Biol. Med.* **14** (2019), doi:10.1186/s13029-019-0072-6.
9. R Core Team, R: A Language and Environment for Statistical Computing (2020), (available at https://www.R-project.org).
10. S. C. Heath *et al.*, *Eur. J. Hum. Genet. EJHG.* **16,** 1413–1429 (2008).
11. D. Clayton, *snpStats: SnpMatrix and XSnpMatrix classes and methods* (2015).
12. Y. Qiu, J. Mei, authors of the A. library S. file A. for details, *rARPACK: Solvers for Large Scale Eigenvalue and SVD Problems* (2016; https://CRAN.R-project.org/package=rARPACK).
13. K. Chaichoompu *et al.*, KRIS: Keen and Reliable Interface Subroutines for Bioinformatic Analysis (2021), (available at https://CRAN.R-project.org/package=KRIS).
14. R. Lebret *et al.*, *J. Stat. Softw.* **67** (2015), doi:10.18637/jss.v067.i06.
15. G. Schwarz, *Ann. Stat.* **6**, 461–464 (1978).
16. K. Chaichoompu, F. Abegaz, K. V. Steen, FILEST: Fine-Level Structure Simulator (2018), (available at https://CRAN.R-project.org/package=FILEST).
17. C. Fraley, A. E. Raftery, T. B. Murphy, L. Scrucca, *mclust Version 4 for R: Normal Mixture Modeling for Model-Based Clustering, Classification, and Density Estimation* (Department of Statistics, University of Washington, 2012).
18. D. H. Alexander, J. Novembre, K. Lange, *Genome Res.* **19**, 1655–1664 (2009).
19. A. Auton *et al.*, *Nature.* **526**, 68–74 (2015).
20. S. Purcell, C. Chang, PLINK 1.9. *BGI Cogn. Genomics*, (available at www.cog-genomics.org/plink2).
21. P. Changmai *et al.*, *PLOS Genet.* **18**, e1010036 (2022).
22. K. Chaichoompu *et al.*, *Hum. Genet.* (2019), doi:10.1007/s00439-019-02069-7.
23. P. Wangkumhang, M. Greenfield, G. Hellenthal, *Genome Res.*, in press, doi:10.1101/gr.275994.121.

Precision Medicine: Using Artificial Intelligence to Improve Diagnostics and Healthcare

Michelle Whirl-Carrillo
Department of Biomedical Data Science, Stanford School of Medicine
Stanford, CA, United States
Email: mwcarrilllo@stanford.edu

Steven E. Brenner
University of California, Berkeley
Berkeley, CA, United States
Email: brenner@combio.berkeley.edu

Jonathan H. Chen
Department of Medicine and Center for Biomedical Informatics Research, Stanford School of Medicine
Stanford, CA, United States
Email: jonc101@stanford.edu

Dana C. Crawford
Department of Population and Quantitative Health Sciences, Case Western Reserve University
Cleveland, OH, United States
Email: dcc64@case.edu

Łukasz Kidziński
Bioclinica and Stanford University
Stanford, CA, United States
Email: lukasz.kidzinski@stanford.edu

David Ouyang
Smidt Heart Institute, Cedars-Sinai Medical Center
Los Angeles, CA, United States
Email: david.ouyang@cshs.org

Roxana Daneshjou
Departments of Dermatology and Biomedical Data Science, Stanford School of Medicine
Stanford, CA, United States
Email: roxanad@stanford.edu

Precision medicine requires a deep understanding of complex biomedical and healthcare data, which is being generated at exponential rates and increasingly made available through public biobanks, electronic medical record systems and biomedical databases and knowledgebases. The complexity and sheer amount of data prohibit manual manipulation. Instead, the field depends on artificial intelligence approaches to parse, annotate, evaluate and interpret the data to enable applications to patient healthcare At the 2023 Pacific Symposium on Biocomputing (PSB) session entitled "Precision Medicine: Using Artificial Intelligence (AI) to improve diagnostics and healthcare", we spotlight research that develops and applies computational methodologies to solve biomedical problems.

Keywords: Artificial intelligence; Machine learning; Genomics; Multi-omics

1. Introduction

The goal of precision medicine is to tailor medical care to the individual patient, from disease prevention to diagnosis to treatment. It holds the key to improve healthcare for all, diminishing health disparities. The generation of extensive, comprehensive and diverse medical datasets provide the opportunity to develop tools and methods that will advance the medical field through patient-tailored treatment enabling healthcare equity across diverse populations. Below, we summarize research focusing on methodology development and applications to move personalized medicine forward. Based on the accepted submissions for the Precision Medicine: Using Artificial Intelligence (AI) to improve diagnostics and healthcare session at the Pacific Symposium on Biocomputing (PSB) 2023, computational and AI approaches are being used to advance cancer research, aid in pregnancy-related healthcare, reduce bias in biomedical data, enhance medical imaging and improve immunotherapy strategies.

2. AI-driven tools for improving diagnostics and healthcare

As copious amounts of data are generated at rapidly increasing rates, precision medicine research faces the challenge of integrating across the landscape of "multi's", including multi-omics, multi-models, multi-model systems and multi-sample types. (Acosta) The following submissions highlight greatly needed methods for analysis of integrated data across diverse datasets, and one submission addresses population bias in data.

Hashim et al. developed a self-supervised learning approach for cancer type classification based on multi-omics cancer data, particularly for unannotated or unlabeled data. They applied their pre-training paradigm to The Cancer Genome Atlas pan-cancer dataset. Benefits to their approach is that it can handle missing omics data types and is flexible enough to handle different types of datasets for pre-training and downstream training. (Hashim et al.)

Bhattacharyya et al. integrate multi-omics and model systems to study cellular mechanisms of cancer to discover therapeutic associations. Their hierarchical Bayesian evidence synthesis framework, BaySyn, uses Gaussian process models and is suitable for rich datasets. The authors applied their framework to multi-omic cancer cell line and patient datasets for pan-gynecological cancers, implicating multiple functional genes across cancers. (Bhattacharyya et al.)

Trinh et al. address the problem of using multi-omics data from a study to investigate questions beyond the scope of that study. To do this, they develop trans-omic knowledge transfer modeling and apply it to the case of using information from an ulcerative colitis cohort in the Integrative Human Microbiome Project (IHMP) to understand biomarkers for anti-TNF therapy resistance in a different ulcerative colitis cohort. They discuss the advantages and disadvantages of three different approaches to knowledge transfer modeling: using a supervised classifier, relative separation, and signature transfer. Through the application of these methods, they provide insights into implementing trans-omic, cross-cohort biomarker discovery. (Trinh et al.)

An important aspect of precision medicine is efficiently identifying disease and disease risk in a patient, and subsequently predicting treatments and therapies that will be effective for that person. The following submissions focus on improving methods for detecting and predicting disease and treatment efficacy.

Extending conventional causal inference methods, Aoki and colleagues propose a framework to use neural networks to estimate multi-treatment effect size. By training a neural network with inputs that include treatments, covariates, as well as outcomes, the deep learning approach summarizes the impact of each treatment with the expectation that the latent space distills meaningful information regarding true treatment effect. Using three synthetic datasets with known true treatment effect, the authors show their approach best approximates treatment effect compared multiple standard benchmark causal inference methods. (Aoki et al.)

Machine learning algorithms optimize certain accuracy metrics by finding best low-dimensional representation of the data. While this approach leads to high predictive power, it can lead to biased conclusions when, for example, training data does not represent the target population. This is problem is of particular importance in biomedical data when patient's health is at stake. De Paolis Kaluza et al. propose a method to identify and quantify bias in a setting where labeled data is known to be drawn from a biased population and unlabeled data is drawn from target population. Under a mild assumption that data comes from a mixture of Gaussian distribution, they developed a multi-sample expectation-maximization algorithm to identify and quantify the bias. (De Paolis Kaluza et al., 2023)

In genetic testing for disease diagnosis or risk, genes with functional significance for the given phenotype are tested to identify what variants a patient possesses. Variant classification following guidelines from the American College of Medical Genetics and Genomics (ACMG) and the Association for Molecular Pathology (AMP) (Richards) is used to determine if variants found are potentially pathogenic, benign or a "variant of unknown significance" (VUS). VUS are inconclusive for diagnoses but are commonly assigned due to limited clinical evidence regarding many variants. High throughput assays can be leveraged to molecularly characterize variants lacking sufficient clinical evidence to improve variant classification. The work of Chen and Jain et al. aims to use clinical objectives and *in silico* variant pathogenicity prediction to prioritize genes for high throughput assays. The authors found they could improve on current knowledge-driven and data-driven strategies for variant classification by using a combined score from three metrics quantifying the importance of genes in satisfying specific clinical objectives. (Chen and Jain et al.)

As researchers find ways to vectorize different data modalities we observe more and more creative applications of machine learning for detecting health conditions. In particular, Aryal et al. developed a set of algorithms for quantifying acoustic-linguistic signals and used them to predict status of Alzheimer's disease. Given the dataset of over 1000 patients, they found that in their setting human-engineered linguistic features were more predictive of the disease than acoustic and learned features. (Aryal et al.)

Zhang et al. focused on improving immunotherapy strategies by developing a pipeline for predicting binding affinity for T cell receptor (TCR) and epitope sequences. Computational binding prediction could help streamline the T cell design process. The authors created PiTE -- Pipeline leveraging Transformer-like Encoders -- that uses large numbers of TCR amino acid sequences to pre-train the model and an advanced sequence encoder. (Zhang et al.)

In the past several years, a spotlight has been shown on racial and ethnic disparities in pregnancy-related conditions. (Carty et al.) In fact, pregnancy-related complications and deaths in general in the U.S. continue to rise. (Heavey) The following two submissions discuss computational applications to gestational diabetes and pre-eclampsia.

Mathur et al. demonstrate reasonable and useful applications of Bayesian network modeling approaches that can incorporate both data-driven learning and domain knowledge in the form of network constraints (independence and monotonicity). The methods are well-summarized and demonstrated in a concrete application for gestational diabetes that illustrate the value of multiple different learning and knowledge modeling techniques beyond purely data-driven models. (Mathur et al.)

For many diseases, transcriptional profiling has been used to identify differentially expressed genes (DEGs). The ignorome is the set of genes that have been experimentally identified as associated with disease but for which no established mechanistic relationship exists. In "Knowledge-Driven Mechanistic Enrichment of the Preecomplasia Ignorome", Callahan et al. use a biomedical knowledge graph to gain insights into the molecular mechanisms behind pre-eclampsia and to connect experimental findings with previously described disease mechanisms in the literature. Their model provides an approach that could be generalizable to other complex disease processes. (Callahan et al.)

Additional submissions in this session focus on improving data representation of genomic variation and deep learning segmentation modeling in medical imaging.

In practice, the use of genomics terms and vocabulary can be community or context dependent. Annotation and representation of genetic variants and their states (e.g., genotypes, alleles, haplotypes) vary widely across domains including somatic cancer, Mendelian disease and pharmacogenomics. There are multiple formats for genetic data exchange, some predominantly used in each domain, but each has its limitations especially for application to a different domain. (Pawliczek et al., Holmes et al., den Dunnen et al., Gaedigk et al.) To promote standardized and interoperable representation of genetic variants for precision medicine, the Global Alliance for Genomics and Health (GA4GH) Variation Representation Specification (VRS) developed a Genotype model designed to unambiguously represent the allelic composition of a genetic locus. Here, the Goar et al. describe their Genotype model along with their Haplotype model in the context of several relevant precision medicine settings, including pharmacogenomics. (Goar et al.)

Despite extensive progress in segmentation models in medical imaging, deep learning segmentation models are prone to catastrophic mis-annotation in out-of-domain or foreign examples. Given known clinical priors (such as there is only one prostate or most biological structures are convex), Wooten et al. propose a set of shape features that can identify poor quality segmentation in medical imaging. Features related to area, perimeter, volume, compactness, and convexity are shown to be able to distinguish between acceptable and unacceptable segmentation of the kidney. Using a set of acceptable and unacceptable segmentations of the kidney on CT imaging from radiotherapy treatment plans, the authors show simple heuristics and clustering algorithms can partition between acceptable and unacceptable segmentations, which can be used to quality check deep learning models. (Wooten et al.)

3. Conclusion

Paralleling continued progress in general artificial intelligence, we find there is steady and rapid progress in the application of machine learning to healthcare. Precision medicine is a combination of precision therapeutics - targeting the right treatments to address specific mechanisms of action or response - as well as precision diagnostics - identifying the right patients to the right therapeutics. In this year's session of Precision Medicine: Using Artificial Intelligence to improve diagnostics and healthcare at PSB 2023, we find wide ranging innovations in many modalities and medical datasets. From imaging to genetic data to modeling of clinical treatments, the application of algorithms in the space of healthcare allows a deeper understanding of complex questions.

References

Acosta, J.N., Falcone, G.J., Rajpurkar, P., Topol, E.J. (2022) Multimodal biomedical AI. *Nat Med.*, 28(9):1773-1784. DOI: 10.1038/s41591-022-01981-2

Aoki, R., Chen, Y., Ester, M. (2023) Multi-treatment Effect Estimation from Biomedical Data. *Pacific Symposium on Biocomputing 2023.*

Aryal, S.K., Prioleau, H., Burge, L. (2023) Acoustic-Linguistic Features for Modeling Neurological Task Score in Alzheimer's. *Pacific Symposium on Biocomputing 2023.*

Bhattacharyya, R., Henderson, N., Baladandayuthapani V. (2023) BaySyn: Bayesian Evidence Synthesis for Multi-system Multiomic Integration. *Pacific Symposium on Biocomputing 2023.*

Callahan, T.J., Stefanski, A.L., Kim J.-D., Baumgartner Jr., W.A., Wyrwa, J.M., Hunter, L.E. (2023) Knowledge-Driven Mechanistic Enrichment of the Preeclampsia Ignorome. *Pacific Symposium on Biocomputing 2023.*

Carty, D.C., Mpofu, J.J., Kress, A.C., Robinson, D., Miller, S.A. (2022) Addressing Racial Disparities in Pregnancy-Related Deaths: An Analysis of Maternal Mortality-Related Federal Legislation, 2017-2021. *J Womens Health*, 31(9):122-1231. DOI: 10.1089/jwh.2022.0336

Chen, Y., Jain, S., Zeiberg, D., Iakoucheva, L., Mooney, S.D., Radivojac, P., Pejaver ,V. (2023) Multi-objective prioritization of genes for high-throughput functional assays towards improved clinical variant classification. *Pacific Symposium on Biocomputing 2023.*

De Paolis Kaluza, M.C., Jain, S., Radivojac. P. (2023) An Approach to Identifying and Quantifying Bias in Biomedical Data. *Pacific Symposium on Biocomputing 2023.*

den Dunnen, J.T., Dalgleish, R., Maglott, D.R., et al. HGVS Recommendations for the Description of Sequence Variants: 2016 Update. *Hum Mutat.*, 37(6):564-569. DOI: 10.1002/humu.22981

Gaedigk A., Sangkuhl, K., Whirl-Carrillo, M., et al. The Evolution of PharmVar. *Clin Pharmacol Ther.,* 105(1):29-32. DOI: 10.1002/cpt.1275

Goar, W., Babb, L., Chamala, S., Cline, M., Freimuth, R.R., Hart, R.K., Kuzma, K., Lee, J., Nelson, T., Prlic, A., Riehle, K., Smith, A., Stahl, K., Yates, A.D, Rehm, H., Wagner, A.H. (2023) Development and application of a computable genotype model in the GA4GH Variation Representation Specification. *Pacific Symposium on Biocomputing 2023.*

Hashim, S., Nandakumar, K., Yaqub, M. (2023) Self-omics: A Self-supervised Learning Framework for Multi-omics Cancer Data. *Pacific Symposium on Biocomputing 2023.*

Heavey, E. (2022) Rising US pregnancy-related deaths. *Nursing*, 52(8):36-39. DOI: 10.1097/01.NURSE.0000839800.71201.d8

Holmes, J.B., Moyer, E., Phan, L., et al. SPDI: data model for variants and applications at NCBI. Bioinformatics, 36(6):1902-1907. DOI: 10.1093/bioinformatics/btz856

Mathur, S., Karanam, A., Radivojac, P., Haas, D.M., Kersting, K., Natarajan, S. (2023) Exploiting Domain Knowledge as Causal Independencies in Modeling Gestational Diabetes. *Pacific Symposium on Biocomputing 2023.*

Pawliczek, P., Patel, R.Y., Ashmore, L.R. et al. (2018) ClinGen Allele Registry links information about genetic variants. *Hum Mutat.*, 39(11):1690-1701. DOI: 10.1002/humu.23637

Richards, S., Aziz, N., Bale, S., et al. (2015) Standards and guidelines for the interpretation of sequence variants: a joint consensus recommendation of the American College of Medical Genetics and Genomics and the Association for Molecular Pathology. *Genet Med.,* 17(5):405-424. DOI: 10.1038/gim.2015.30

Trinh, A., Ran, R., Brubaker, D.K. (2023) Trans-Omic Knowledge Transfer Modeling Infers Gut Microbiome Biomarkers of Anti-TNF Resistance in Ulcerative Colitis. *Pacific Symposium on Biocomputing 2023.*

Wooten, Z., Yu, C., Court, L., Peterson, C. (2023) Predictive modeling using shape statistics for interpretable and robust quality assurance of automated contours in radiation treatment planning. *Pacific Symposium on Biocomputing 2023.*

Zhang, P., Bang, S., Lee, H. (2023) PiTE: TCR-epitope binding affinity prediction pipeline using Transformer-based Sequence Encoder. *Pacific Symposium on Biocomputing 2023.*

Self-omics: A Self-supervised Learning Framework for Multi-omics Cancer Data

Sayed Hashim†, Karthik Nandakumar and Mohammad Yaqub
Mohamed Bin Zayed University of Artificial Intelligence
Abu Dhabi, UAE
†*E-mail: sayed.hashim@mbzuai.ac.ae*

We have gained access to vast amounts of multi-omics data thanks to Next Generation Sequencing. However, it is challenging to analyse this data due to its high dimensionality and much of it not being annotated. Lack of annotated data is a significant problem in machine learning, and Self-Supervised Learning (SSL) methods are typically used to deal with limited labelled data. However, there is a lack of studies that use SSL methods to exploit inter-omics relationships on unlabelled multi-omics data. In this work, we develop a novel and efficient pre-training paradigm that consists of various SSL components, including but not limited to contrastive alignment, data recovery from corrupted samples, and using one type of omics data to recover other omic types. Our pre-training paradigm improves performance on downstream tasks with limited labelled data. We show that our approach outperforms the state-of-the-art method in cancer type classification on the TCGA pan-cancer dataset in semi-supervised setting. Moreover, we show that the encoders that are pre-trained using our approach can be used as powerful feature extractors even without fine-tuning. Our ablation study shows that the method is not overly dependent on any pretext task component. The network architectures in our approach are designed to handle missing omic types and multiple datasets for pre-training and downstream training. Our pre-training paradigm can be extended to perform zero-shot classification of rare cancers.

Keywords: Self-supervised Learning; Contrastive Learning; Multi-omics; Cancer Type Classification

1. Introduction

According to WHO, cancer accounted for around 10 million deaths in 2020 or about one in six deaths.[1] Many cancers can be cured with early diagnosis, and effective treatment.[2] Various factors are responsible for late diagnoses, such as symptoms being detected late, lack of access to oncologists, as well as the time & cost involved. It could also be because of vague and unclear symptoms and indistinguishable signs on scans and mammograms.[3] Nevertheless, performing cancer diagnosis in its early stages or even before it starts developing could remarkably improve survival and provide opportunities for more effective treatment. Studies in the areas of biology that end with omics, such as genomics, proteomics, transcriptomics or metabolomics, are called omics sciences. With the advent of Next Generation Sequencing, we have gained access to multiple types of omics data. Each type of omics data reveals different characteristics within the tumour. However, due to the high dimensionality and the numerous different types of omics data, it is nearly impossible for clinicians to analyse multi-omics data. Due to this reason, they tend to focus on analysing the values of specific biomarkers. However, to get a complete picture of a tumour, which is heterogeneous and complex, multi-omics data analysis is vital.

Modern machine learning algorithms, especially deep neural networks, have shown to be able to work well with high-dimensional data. Deep learning has made massive progress in tasks like object recognition, object detection and semantic segmentation in the visual domain. It has also made strides in speech and natural language processing on tasks such as machine translation, speech recognition and question answering. The algorithms developed for the tasks mentioned above require processing high-dimensional inputs. In this work, we developed Self-Supervised Learning (SSL) methods for multi-omics data to provide supervision to the model from unlabelled data. We explored various SSL pretext tasks on top of the usual reconstruction task with autoencoders. Some of the SSL techniques we implemented include contrastive learning, recovering data from its corrupted versions and aligning representations from multi-omics data.

The low-dimensional representations that our model produces from high-dimensional multi-omics data can be considered "computational biomarkers". The model that learns from large datasets gets good at producing such biomarkers and can be used to produce good representations for smaller datasets. Furthermore, as the model learns from tumours diagnosed early, it produces better representations for such tumours. Therefore, even if the dataset at hand does not have samples of tumours that are sequenced early, the fact that it was pre-trained on a large dataset that contains many samples of such tumours makes the model better at early diagnosis.

2. Literature Review

Self-supervised learning (SSL) has been extensively applied in representation learning of data in various domains such as natural language processing[4–6] audio and image.[7–9] These methods mainly use spatial, semantic and temporal structural relationships in the data. This is done through developing novel pretext tasks, data augmentation methods and model architectures. Due to the absence of the relationships mentioned above in tabular data, such methods could be less effective. For instance, augmentation methods used on images, such as scaling and rotation, cannot be directly used on tabular data. SSL techniques have not been explored enough on tabular data due to these reasons.[10]

An autoencoder is a deep network that consists of an encoder and decoder.[11] While the encoder is trained to map the input to a latent representation, the decoder is trained to reconstruct the input from this latent representation. A popular work in images is denoising autoencoders (DAE).[12] It is built on the hypothesis that partially destroyed inputs should result in a similar latent representation as the original inputs. In this work, the authors investigated an autoencoder's robustness to partial demolition of inputs. The input is corrupted and fed to the autoencoder, whose job is to recover the original "clean" input. A group of researchers developed VIME,[10] a novel SSL framework for tabular data. They developed a couple of pretext tasks called feature vector estimation and mask vector estimation. The former aims to reconstruct an input sample from its masked version, while the latter involves predicting the mask vector applied to the sample. In other words, the pretext task is to estimate which features are masked and predict the values of the corrupted features. A work called SubTab focuses on converting the representation learning problem from single-view to multi-view.[13] Here, the features are divided into subsets to produce the various views. The authors claim that this is analogous to cropping images and bagging features in ensemble learning. They demonstrate that the encoder learns more useful representations from a subset of the data than a corrupted version of it. They pre-trained the network on this pretext task and tested its performance on some downstream tasks.

Self-supervised representation learning of multi-omics data is an under-studied area of research. Many methods used for representation learning mainly focus on the integration of multi-omics data. Many integration strategies have been proposed. We will review the integration methods here due to the lack of self-supervised methods. A group developed a group lasso regularised deep learning method for cancer prognosis by integrating multi-omics data using early fusion.[14] They perform various data preprocessing techniques, and the model consists of a few fully connected layers. Another work integrates multi-omics data using standard and disjointed deep autoencoders.[15] Various omics data such as DNA methylation, microRNA expression, mRNA expression and reverse phase protein array data are concatenated before being fed into the autoencoder. A work called OmiEmbed[16] does intermediate multi-omics data integration. It is a multi-task framework that is built on a variational autoencoder. The pretext task here is the reconstruction of three types of omics data: gene expression, microRNA expression and DNA methylation. They show the effectiveness of their method by testing on various downstream tasks. They also developed a multi-task strategy that concurrently trains multiple downstream modules such as survival analysis, cancer type classification and phenotype prediction. Training it this way has shown to perform better than training the downstream modules separately. Late integration of multi-omics data was done in a work that predicts breast cancer prognosis.[17] They perform feature selection and use a deep neural network for the task. Gene expression, copy number alterations and clinical information are fed into three separate networks. Their predictions are combined at the end with a score-fusing technique called weighted linear aggregation.

There exists a lack of studies on self-supervised representation learning of multi-omics data. Studies focusing on adding more pretext tasks on top of the reconstruction task are rare. The usual focus is on integrating the data and less on exploiting inter-omics relationships through constraints and other SSL losses. Moreover, lack of annotated data can be tackled with SSL approaches.

3. Method

3.1. *Dataset*

For our experiments, we used The Cancer Genome Atlas (TCGA) pan-cancer multi-omics dataset.[18] Table 1 gives an overview of the dataset. It is one of the most popular multi-omics datasets. It consists of omics data as well as phenotypic information of patients. We used three types of omics data from the TCGA dataset: DNA methylation, miRNA stem-loop expression, and gene expression. They are 485,577, 1881 and 60,483 dimensional respectively. The dataset contains samples of 33 different tumour types and of normal tissues.

Table 1. An overview of TCGA pan-cancer dataset.

Dataset	TCGA		
Domain		Pan-cancer	
Tumour types		33 + 1(normal) = 34	
Omics data type	Gene exp	DNA methylation	miRNA exp
No of features	60,483	485,577	1881
No of samples	11,538	9736	11,020

3.2. *Data Preprocessing*

We downloaded harmonised data of 3 types of omics data from UCSC Xena data portal.[19] RNA-Seq gene expression dataset comprises 60,483 features, each denoting the expression of a gene. Gene expression level is obtained as the $\log_2$ transformation of fragments per kilobase of transcript per million mapped reads (FPKM) value. miRNA stem-loop expression levels were given as the $\log_2$ transformation of reads per million mapped reads (RPM) value. DNA methylation dataset comprises beta values for each CpG site. Beta values are the ratio of methylated to total array intensity for the corresponding CpG site.[20] Lower beta values mean lower levels of methylation and vice-versa. The beta values missing in the DNA methylation dataset were mean imputed. We removed the means of the three datasets and scaled them to unit variance.

3.3. *Pretext problem formulation*

The architecture we designed for pre-training comprises three autoencoders, one for each type of omics data, and is shown in Fig 1. Our codebase also supports the usage of a common encoder and decoder for all three omic types, but since the inputs of the three omic types are different in size, we used some fully connected layers to downsample them to the same size and the rest of the encoder is shared. The pretext loss minimised during pre-training is a weighted sum of the losses described below. The codebase supports more SSL losses not described here, such as Maximum Mean Discrepancy (MMD) loss and latent reconstruction loss.

3.3.1. *Reconstruction loss*

Let's denote the input data x of ith omic type as x_i and the reconstructed data as x_i'. Let there be N number of omic types. In our case, the value of N is three. As given below, the reconstruction loss can be formulated as the mean squared error loss between input and

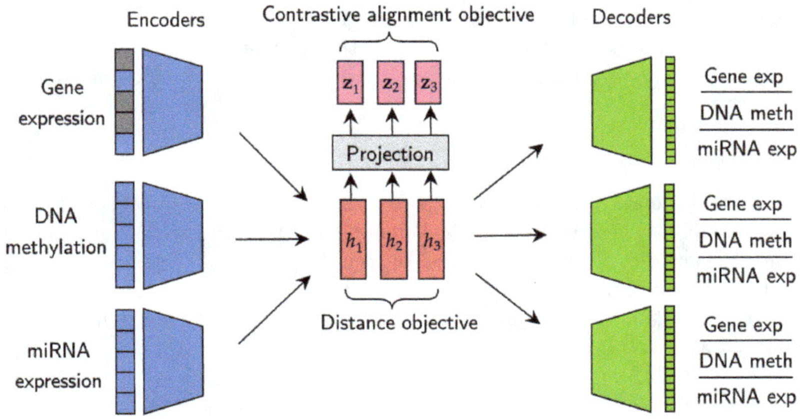

Fig. 1. Pre-training architecture: We partially masked the inputs and fed them to the encoders one by one, producing three latent representations, h_1, h_2 and h_3. These are then passed onto the decoders to reconstruct the entire feature set, including the other two omic types. The latent representations are also fed into a projection layer to compute contrastive alignment objective between each pair of projections, namely (z_1, z_2), (z_1, z_3) and (z_2, z_3). Distance objectives between each pair of latent representations are also minimised. Pre-training also minimises contrastive noise loss, illustrated in Fig 2.

reconstructed omics data.

$$\mathcal{L}_{\text{reconstruction}} = \frac{1}{N} \sum_{i=1}^{N} MSE\left(x_i, x_i'\right) \tag{1}$$

To make the network robust to noise, we performed partial corruption of one omic type and made the network recover the entire feature set, including the other omic types. For this purpose, we divided the almost 60,000-dimensional gene expression data into 23 subsets, each corresponding to the chromosome on which the gene is located. The same is done for around 400,000 dimensional DNA methylation data. The model is then trained to reconstruct the input data when some or all subsets of a specific omic type are masked. The masking methods used are zeroing out and adding Gaussian or swap noise. A random masking method is chosen during each epoch. For instance, 6, 12, 18 random subsets or all 23 subsets of gene expression data can be corrupted. The model can then be asked to reconstruct all the input features, including the corrupted gene expression features and DNA methylation and miRNA expression values. Here, a higher weightage is given in the loss function for recovering the corrupted omic type. Let x_1, x_2 and x_3 be gene expression, DNA methylation and miRNA expression features respectively. If we mask gene expression features, the reconstruction loss can be modified as

$$\mathcal{L}_{\text{reconstruction}} = \frac{1}{N}\left(0.5 * MSE\left(x_1, x_1'\right) + 0.25 * MSE\left(x_2, x_2'\right) + 0.25 * MSE\left(x_3, x_3'\right)\right) \tag{2}$$

Another novel pretext task that we designed is masked subset or chromosome prediction. As described above, gene expression and DNA methylation data were divided into subsets, and random subsets were masked in each epoch. We made the network predict which subsets were masked by feeding the representations from the encoder to a masked chromosome prediction module.

3.3.2. *Contrastive alignment loss*

The latent representations h_1, h_2 and h_3 were passed through a projection network to obtain projections z_1, z_2 and z_3. The alignment loss introduced in CLIP (Contrastive Language-Image Pre-Training)[21] was used to compute alignment between the pairs (z_1, z_2), (z_1, z_3) and (z_2, z_3). The idea is that like text and image provide different types of information about a concept, various omic types contain different information about a patient's tumour. These multiple views are aligned using a contrastive loss.

3.3.3. *Contrastive noise loss*

Let the latent representation from ith omic type x_i be denoted as h_i. By feeding noisy sample $x_i^{'}$ to the same encoder, we can produce $h_i^{'}$. By passing h_i and $h_i^{'}$ through the projection layer, we obtain z_i and $z_i^{'}$ respectively. Contrastive noise loss is computed between each pair $(z_i, z_i^{'})$. This is illustrated in Fig 2. The contrastive noise loss we implemented is the one introduced in the work Barlow Twins.[22] Our codebase also supports the usage of NT-Xent loss[23] and SimSiam loss[24] as both contrastive alignment and noise losses.

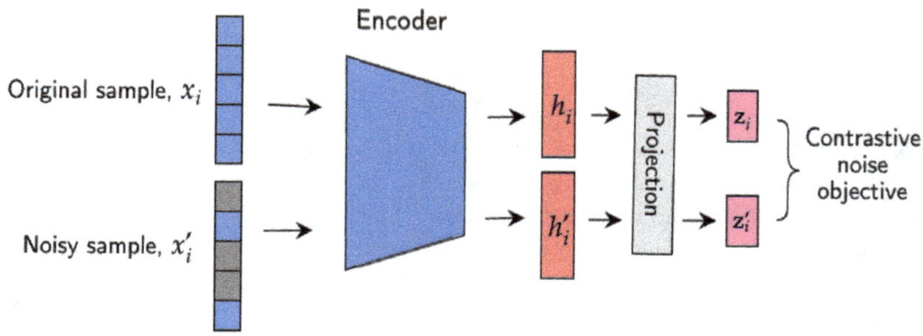

Fig. 2. Illustration of contrastive noise objective: Original and noisy samples are fed to the encoder one after the other to obtain their corresponding representations and projections between which the contrastive noise objective is calculated. This process is repeated for each omic type.

3.3.4. *Distance loss*

Using this loss, the distances between pairs of latent representations (h_1, h_2), (h_2, h_3) and (h_1, h_3) are minimised. This ensures that representations from multiple omic types are consistent with each other. The distance loss can also be computed between the projections. Computing it between latent representations gave better results.

$$\mathcal{L}_{\text{distance}} = MSE(h_1, h_2) + MSE(h_2, h_3) + MSE(h_1, h_3) \tag{3}$$

3.4. *Downstream task: Cancer type classification*

Once the encoders and decoders are trained to minimise the pretext loss, the layers of encoders are frozen and attached to the downstream network to perform cancer type classification, as shown in Fig 3. The dataset consists of 33 cancer types. Each patient's sample is a tissue that could be either normal or cancerous, belonging to one of these classes. The loss function for the downstream classification task is formulated as follows

$$\mathcal{L}_{\text{classification}} = CE(y, y') \tag{4}$$

Here, y is the label, y' the prediction and CE the cross entropy loss.

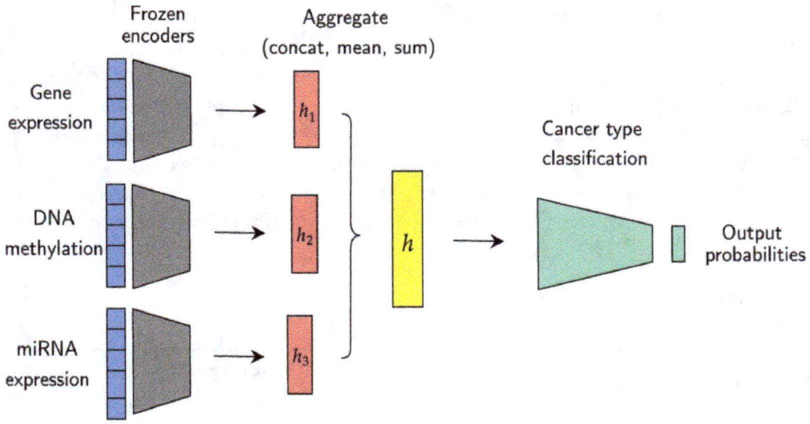

Fig. 3. Downstream module: The encoders are frozen after pre-training and representations from the encoders are aggregated by concatenating them, taking their mean or summing them up. This aggregated representation is then passed through the downstream network to predict the patient's tumour type.

3.4.1. *Handling missing omic types*

Our framework is suitable for handling missing omic types. For pre-training with missing omic types, encoders for only the available omic types can be trained. This is possible since we have separate encoders for each omic type. We can also train the downstream network using new samples that contain missing omic types. For instance, if gene expression is the missing omic type for a new sample from lung tumour, the pre-trained gene expression encoder can be used to generate gene expression representation for this new sample. This representation could be the average gene expression representation of all lung cancer samples. This way, information about the missing omic types can be generated in their absence. Alternatively, we could decide not to use the pre-trained encoder for missing omic types and aggregate representations (mean or sum aggregation) from available omic types. This flexibility allows the usage of datasets which contain different types of omics data for pre-training and downstream training. This is important as datasets usually differ in the type of omics data they contain.

4. Experiments and results

4.1. *Implementation*

Code and links to download the datasets are available at https://github.com/hashimsayed0/self-omics. We used Pytorch Lightning[25] to build the models.

4.2. *Semi-supervised learning*

To evaluate the effect of pre-training, we trained the model in semi-supervised fashion. The model was first pre-trained on the entire training set and was then trained for the downstream task using only part of the training set. The encoders were also kept frozen and not allowed to be optimised for the downstream task. Fig 4 shows the leap in performance provided by our pre-training approach over training the downstream network with random initialisation and OmiEmbed[16] which is the state-of-the-art approach in cancer type classification using multi-omics data. A performance comparison between the methods based on metrics is given in Table 2.

Table 2. Performance metrics of cancer type classification using 1% training data during downstream training.

Method	**Omic type(s)**	**1% training data**				
		Accuracy	**F1**	**AUC**	**Precision**	**Recall**
OmiEmbed	multi-omics (A,B,C)	21.37	7.82	73.58	6.77	14.74
w.o. pretraining	multi-omics (A,B,C)	30.69	19.1	73.03	32.2	22.85
w. pretraining	gene exp. (A)	13.9	4.21	57.99	3.71	9.67
	DNA meth. (B)	32.98	20.47	70.59	21.45	23.66
	miRNA exp. (C)	42.75	27.21	82.51	28.92	32.2
	multi-omics (A,B,C)	**64.45**	**43.33**	**82.95**	**43.99**	**49.83**

4.3. *Ablation study*

We ran experiments to analyse the effects of removing various components of the pretext loss one at a time. This usually helps identify the essential components of the pretext loss and evaluate the method's robustness. Fig 5 shows the effect on downstream performance due to

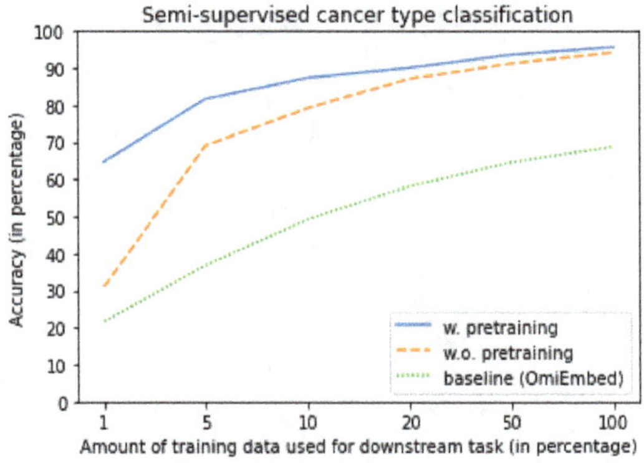

Fig. 4. Semi-supervised cancer type classification performance on multi-omics data: x-axis shows the percentage of training data used during downstream training and the y-axis denotes the accuracy. The encoders were kept frozen during downstream training.

the removal of various components of pre-training loss. The performance is robust to such removals and is not overly dependent on any component.

4.4. *Latent aggregation method*

As we have separate encoders for each omic type, representations from the encoders have to be aggregated to be passed to the downstream network. We experimented with various aggregation methods, including mean, concatenation and sum. Fig 5 shows that concatenation performs slightly better than other methods.

4.5. *t-SNE Visualisation*

To visualise the model's discriminative ability, we fed the latent representations produced by a trained model to t-SNE.[26] Fig 6 shows how the model clusters test samples from the same cancer type together. It is interesting to note how well the model is able to cluster cancer types even using 1% training data for the downstream task.

5. Discussion

By analysing the results of the experiments, it is clear that our approach works well with less training data, thanks to efficient pre-training. Although OmiEmbed performs well with an unfrozen encoder when the whole training set is provided during downstream training, it fails to achieve decent performance when encoder layers are frozen and a limited amount of training data is used. The performance of our approach with frozen encoders is comparable to the performance of OmiEmbed with unfrozen encoder, as reported in their paper.[16] With ablation studies, we show how the model is not entirely dependent on any particular component of the pretext task. The contrastive noise objective helps the encoders become robust to noise

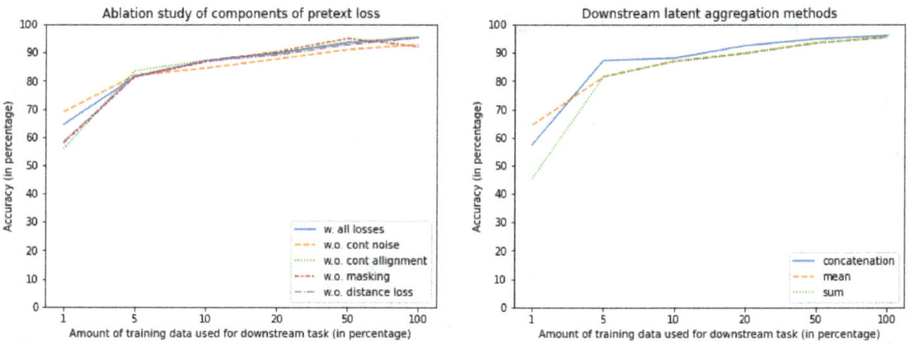

Fig. 5. The plot on the left shows the effect of removing various components of pretext loss, and the one on the right shows the performance variation with different downstream latent aggregation methods. The x-axis shows the percentage of training data used during downstream training, and the y-axis denotes accuracy.

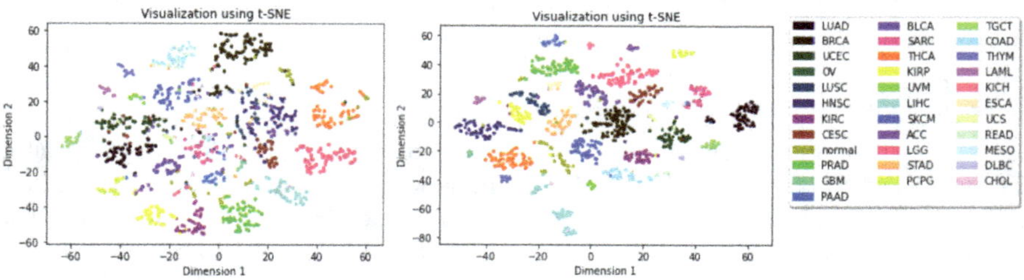

Fig. 6. t-SNE Visualisation: The plot on the left is produced using a model trained on one per cent of training data for downstream training, and the one on the right refers to the model that used the entire training set for downstream training. The legend shows the TCGA codes for the cancer types that the colours represent.

and be able to identify samples from their distorted versions. The contrastive alignment objective makes the encoders learn similar and discriminative information from representations of different omic types of the same patient. Reconstructing the full feature set from the representation of one omic type forces an encoder to learn information about the two other omic types from this omic type. By asking the network to recover masked gene expression data, we make it rely on DNA methylation and miRNA expression data. From our experiments, we found out that masking the latter two omic types did not improve performance. This is also in line with our understanding that gene expression is influenced by DNA methylation and miRNA expression. While there is a significant difference in performance between different experiment settings when less than 10% of training data is used, the performance converges as a higher amount of data is used.

6. Conclusion

We began by discussing various SSL approaches used in tabular domain and methods that integrate multi-omics data. After describing the dataset, we formulated the various components of our pretext task. The main idea behind using these components was to make the encoders learn what is common and specific about different omic types based on patients' profiles. This would help the encoders produce relevant features for the downstream tasks. To evaluate our approach, we designed a semi-supervised framework and ran experiments. We showed that in this framework, our approach outperforms the state-of-the-art method. We performed ablation studies to analyse our approach and its robustness. We then discussed key insights from the results and explained our findings. This work has shown that pre-training with a huge dataset like TCGA with efficient components improves downstream performance in various settings. Our approach also offers the flexibility to use different datasets for pre-training and downstream training and is suitable for handling missing omic types. A limitation of this approach is that the features present in the pre-training dataset need to be available in the downstream dataset to perform pre-training and downstream training on different datasets. Another limitation is that the models trained in this framework contain many parameters and require a good amount of CPU and GPU memory to load the dataset and train the model. This work can be further extended to perform zero-shot classification of rare cancer types. To do this, we need to develop a model that learns about rare cancers from common cancers. This might require representing cancer types like words in latent spaces.[4,5] It could be useful to investigate models like gene2vec[27] for this purpose.

References

1. Who.int, Cancer (2022).
2. H. D. Shukla, J. Mahmood and Z. Vujaskovic, Integrated proteo-genomic approach for early diagnosis and prognosis of cancer, *Cancer Letters* **369**, 28 (2015).
3. S. Huang, J. Yang, S. Fong and Q. Zhao, Artificial intelligence in cancer diagnosis and prognosis: Opportunities and challenges, *Cancer Letters* **471**, 61 (2020).
4. T. Mikolov, K. Chen, G. Corrado and J. Dean, Efficient estimation of word representations in vector space (2013).
5. J. Pennington, R. Socher and C. Manning, GloVe: Global vectors for word representation, in *Proceedings of the 2014 Conference on Empirical Methods in Natural Language Processing (EMNLP)*, (Association for Computational Linguistics, Doha, Qatar, October 2014).
6. J. Devlin, M.-W. Chang, K. Lee and K. Toutanova, Bert: Pre-training of deep bidirectional transformers for language understanding (2018).
7. T. Chen, S. Kornblith, M. Norouzi and G. Hinton, A simple framework for contrastive learning of visual representations, in *Proceedings of the 37th International Conference on Machine Learning*, eds. H. D. III and A. Singh, Proceedings of Machine Learning Research, Vol. 119 (PMLR, 13–18 Jul 2020).
8. J. Grill, F. Strub, F. Altché, C. Tallec, P. H. Richemond, E. Buchatskaya, C. Doersch, B. Á. Pires, Z. D. Guo, M. G. Azar, B. Piot, K. Kavukcuoglu, R. Munos and M. Valko, Bootstrap your own latent: A new approach to self-supervised learning, *CoRR* **abs/2006.07733** (2020).
9. X. Chen, H. Fan, R. B. Girshick and K. He, Improved baselines with momentum contrastive learning, *CoRR* **abs/2003.04297** (2020).
10. J. Yoon, Y. Zhang, J. Jordon and M. van der Schaar, Vime: Extending the success of self-

and semi-supervised learning to tabular domain, in *Advances in Neural Information Processing Systems*, eds. H. Larochelle, M. Ranzato, R. Hadsell, M. Balcan and H. Lin (Curran Associates, Inc., 2020).
11. Y. Bengio, P. Lamblin, D. Popovici and H. Larochelle, Greedy layer-wise training of deep networks *Advances in Neural Information Processing Systems* **19** (MIT Press, 2006).
12. P. Vincent, H. Larochelle, Y. Bengio and P.-A. Manzagol, Extracting and composing robust features with denoising autoencoders *Proceedings of the 25th international conference on Machine learning - ICML '08* (ACM Press, 2008).
13. T. Ucar, E. Hajiramezanali and L. Edwards, Subtab: Subsetting features of tabular data for self-supervised representation learning, *CoRR* **abs/2110.04361** (2021).
14. G. Xie, C. Dong, Y. Kong, J. F. Zhong, M. Li and K. Wang, Group lasso regularized deep learning for cancer prognosis from multi-omics and clinical features, *Genes* **10** (2019).
15. G. Viaud, P. Mayilvahanan and P.-H. Cournède, Representation learning for the clustering of multi-omics data, *IEEE/ACM Transactions on Computational Biology and Bioinformatics* **19**, 135 (2022).
16. X. Zhang, Y. Xing, K. Sun and Y. Guo, Omiembed: A unified multi-task deep learning framework for multi-omics data, *Cancers* **13** (2021).
17. D. Sun, M. Wang and A. Li, A multimodal deep neural network for human breast cancer prognosis prediction by integrating multi-dimensional data, *IEEE/ACM Transactions on Computational Biology and Bioinformatics* **16**, 841 (2019).
18. R. L. Grossman, A. P. Heath, V. Ferretti, H. E. Varmus, D. R. Lowy, W. A. Kibbe and L. M. Staudt, Toward a shared vision for cancer genomic data, *New England Journal of Medicine* **375**, 1109 (2016), PMID: 27653561.
19. M. Goldman, B. Craft, M. Hastie, K. Repečka, F. McDade, A. Kamath, A. Banerjee, Y. Luo, D. Rogers, A. N. Brooks, J. Zhu and D. Haussler, The ucsc xena platform for public and private cancer genomics data visualization and interpretation, *bioRxiv* (2019).
20. N. C. Institute, Bioinformatics pipeline: Methylation liftover pipeline - gdc docs (2021).
21. A. Radford, J. W. Kim, C. Hallacy, A. Ramesh, G. Goh, S. Agarwal, G. Sastry, A. Askell, P. Mishkin, J. Clark, G. Krueger and I. Sutskever, Learning transferable visual models from natural language supervision (2021).
22. J. Zbontar, L. Jing, I. Misra, Y. LeCun and S. Deny, Barlow twins: Self-supervised learning via redundancy reduction, *CoRR* **abs/2103.03230** (2021).
23. K. Sohn, Improved deep metric learning with multi-class n-pair loss objective, in *Advances in Neural Information Processing Systems*, eds. D. Lee, M. Sugiyama, U. Luxburg, I. Guyon and R. Garnett (Curran Associates, Inc., 2016).
24. X. Chen and K. He, Exploring simple siamese representation learning, *CoRR* **abs/2011.10566** (2020).
25. W. Falcon *et al.*, Pytorch lightning, *GitHub. Note: https://github.com/PyTorchLightning/pytorch-lightning* **3** (2019).
26. D. M. Chan, R. Rao, F. Huang and J. F. Canny, t-sne-cuda: Gpu-accelerated t-sne and its applications to modern data (2018).
27. J. Du, P. Jia, Y. Dai, C. Tao, Z. Zhao and D. Zhi, Gene2vec: Distributed representation of genes based on co-expression, *BMC Genomics* **20** (02 2019).

BaySyn: Bayesian Evidence Synthesis for Multi-system Multiomic Integration

Rupam Bhattacharyya[†1], Nicholas Henderson[1] and Veerabhadran Baladandayuthapani[1]
[1]*Department of Biostatistics, University of Michigan, Ann Arbor*
Michigan 48109, USA
[†]*Corresponding Author, EMail: rupamb@umich.edu*

The discovery of cancer drivers and drug targets are often limited to the biological systems - from cancer model systems to patients. While multiomic patient databases have sparse drug response data, cancer model systems databases, despite covering a broad range of pharmacogenomic platforms, provide lower lineage-specific sample sizes, resulting in reduced statistical power to detect both functional driver genes and their associations with drug sensitivity profiles. Hence, integrating evidence across model systems, taking into account the pros and cons of each system, in addition to multiomic integration, can more efficiently deconvolve cellular mechanisms of cancer as well as learn therapeutic associations. To this end, we propose *BaySyn* - a hierarchical Bayesian evidence synthesis framework for multi-system multiomic integration. BaySyn detects functionally relevant driver genes based on their associations with upstream regulators using additive Gaussian process models and uses this evidence to calibrate Bayesian variable selection models in the (drug) outcome layer. We apply BaySyn to multiomic cancer cell line and patient datasets from the Cancer Cell Line Encyclopedia and The Cancer Genome Atlas, respectively, across pan-gynecological cancers. Our mechanistic models implicate several relevant functional genes across cancers such as PTPN6 and ERBB2 in the KEGG adherens junction gene set. Furthermore, our outcome model is able to make higher number of discoveries in drug response models than its uncalibrated counterparts under the same thresholds of Type I error control, including detection of known lineage-specific biomarker associations such as BCL11A in breast and FGFRL1 in ovarian cancers. All our results and implementation codes are freely available via an interactive R Shiny dashboard at tinyurl.com/BaySynApp. The supplementary materials are available online at tinyurl.com/BaySynSup.

Keywords: Additive Gaussian processes, cancer driver genes, gene-drug associations, hierarchical Bayesian variable selection, KEGG gene sets, spike-and-slab priors.

1. Introduction

With the advent of sophisticated techniques and platforms, large-scale datasets covering multiple layers of cellular omics are becoming increasingly available.[1,2] Consistent advancements have been made in the last few years towards adding more dimensions to these high-throughput datasets, namely (1) additional to patient-level disease databases, model systems such as cell lines, patient-derived xenografts and organoids are being studied extensively in context of cancer and other diseases;[3,4] (2) assessing clinical information and therapeutic response with omics data to make pharmacogenomic discoveries is becoming increasingly common.[5,6] Multiple challenges arise during investigations of such datasets, including but not limited to computational inefficiency, complex nature of associations among the omic variables considered, and the biological interpretability and clinical implications of the results.[7] Specifically in context of cancer, the necessity to not only detect biomarker associations with drug/treatment regimens but also to assess the functional relevance and mechanism of such associations is paramount, potentially guiding future therapeutic advances. Thus, novel algorithms that integrate multi-omics patient and model systems profiles can potentially reveal novel biomarkers, drug targets and predictive models in cancer.

Multi-dimensional data integration in cancer To address the wide range of complexity and variability in both detection and management of cancer, a number of multi-omics approaches have been able to uncover intricate molecular mechanisms and discover prognostic candidates.[8] Data integration approaches have proven particularly useful - both vertical (multiple experiments on a common cohort of samples)[9,10] and horizontal (meta-analysis of different cohorts)[11,12] integration methods have been developed.[13] To simultaneously identify pharmacogenomic associations and corresponding functional mechanisms, singular usage of either of these dimensions is insufficient due to the richness of the currently available omics databases. Multi-omics patient databases of cancer such as The Cancer Genome Atlas (TCGA),[14] while rich in transcriptomic, proteomic and other levels of omics profiles, do not typically provide comprehensive and systematic drug response on the same cohort of patients, restricting utilization of these profiles directly in pharmacogenomic contexts. Model systems databases such as the Cancer Cell Line Encyclopedia (CCLE)[15] and Genomics of Drug Sensitivity in Cancer (GDSC)[16] provide both molecular profiles and drug sensitivity information on the same set of models, but the cancer- or lineage-specific sample sizes of such databases are lower than their patient counterparts and association models built solely on them may suffer from the lack of sufficient statistical power to detect all the true signals. In this work, we propose a solution to this, based on a multi-stage hierarchical Bayesian framework that synthesizes information from both patient and model system databases across multiomic levels to improve the identification of novel cancer driver genes and association with drug responses.

A Bayesian evidence synthesis procedure Our integrative framework is called BaySyn: a multi-stage hierarchical Bayesian evidence synthesis pipeline for analysis of multi-system multiomic data. The first stage identifies cancer driver genes by detecting transcriptomic associations with upstream changes, which are then utilized to inform biomarker association models in the second stage to improve selection. Specifically, the first stage uses additive Gaussian process regression models to detect potential nonlinear associations of gene expression data with corresponding copy number and methylation profiles for both cell line cancer lineages and patient cancer types. To tackle the issue of lower sample size in cell line data, we propose multi-lineage versions of these mechanistic models that can deconvolve lineage and upstream main effects as well as any potential interactions, in addition to single-lineage versions of the same. Evidence synthesized across a common pool of genes from the two sources is then used in a calibrated Bayesian variable selection procedure in the second stage to identify genes having high association with an outcome variable of interest, such as drug response data. Specifically, the evidence quantifications from the mechanistic models are used in these outcome models to upweight the prior probability of selection of different biomarkers in a spike-and-slab prior setting. A conceptual schematic of the procedure is presented in Figure 1, providing a high-level summary of the multi-model system evidence synthesis through the mechanistic models and calibrated biomarker selection via the outcome models. We apply our framework to multiomic CCLE and TCGA datasets from pan-gynecological cancers (breast, ovary, and uterus lineages). Our mechanistic models provide cancer-specific and cross-lineage evidence that implicate several relevant functional genes such as PTPN6 and ERBB2 in the KEGG adherens junction gene set. Furthermore, our outcome model is able to make higher number of discoveries in drug response models than its uncalibrated counterparts under the same thresholds of type I error control, including detection of known lineage-specific biomarker associations such as BCL11A in breast and FGFRL1 in ovarian cancers.

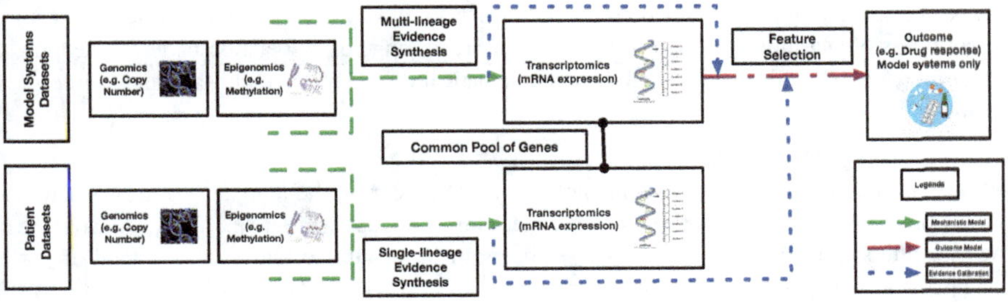

Fig. 1: Conceptual schema of the *BaySyn* framework.

The rest of the paper is organized as follows. Section 2 summarizes the multi-stage data integration framework. Section 3 describes the CCLE and TCGA data processing and analysis procedures, along with summarization of interesting results. We finish with a brief discussion of our proposed procedure and findings in Section 4. All the processed datasets, R codes for the pipeline, and the complete set of real data results are available for access via an interactive R Shiny dashboard at tinyurl.com/BaySynApp. The supplementary materials are available online at tinyurl.com/BaySynSup.

2. Methods

Multi-stage integration pipeline Following Figure 1, for a given set of samples (patients/model systems), we build gene-specific mechanistic models to infer functional relevance of the genes in the samples of interest based on the association of the gene's expression pattern with its upstream covariates such as copy number changes or DNA methylation. Particularly, in case of model systems, certain cancer lineages may contain a low number of samples and the mechanistic models may suffer from a lack of sufficient statistical power to identify true associations with upstream factors. Therefore, we build two versions of the mechanistic models depending on the sample size scenarios - a multi-lineage model that can borrow strength across samples from different lineages (used in this work for modeling the cell line samples; Section 2.1.1), and a single-lineage version that can be applied to a set of samples from a single cancer lineage/type (used in this work in context of the patient samples; Section 2.1.2). Based on statistical summaries of significance of the upstream factors for each gene from these models, we then build the outcome-specific Bayesian hierarchical variable selection models (outcome models, in short; Section 2.2) that can incorporate such prior information and borrow strength to improve selection of genes. The pseudocode for the complete framework is available at Supplementary Notes Section S1.1. The specifics of each type of model are described in full detail in the rest of this section.

2.1. *Mechanistic Models*

For the mechanistic models, we investigate a gene of interest specifically in relation with its upstream factors to detect whether it is a functional driver, and repeat the procedure across the complete pool of genes included in the analyses. This approach offers a highly parallelizable framework, and the efficiency only depends on the computational resources used by each individual model. Further, the class of genomic associations with upstream factors that we are interested in may be highly nonlinear, as has been indicated in past cancer literature.[17,18] Therefore, we intend to equip our models with sufficiently flexible specifications that can identify a broad range of association patterns. Keeping these useful features in mind, we describe the mathematical details of the multi- and single-lineage mechanistic models below.

2.1.1. *Multi-lineage Mechanistic Models*

Notations We begin with setting up some notations. Let M denote the number of lineages across which we intend to borrow strength in a single mechanistic model, and let $\{n_1, \ldots, n_M\}$ denote the lineage-specific sample sizes, with $n = \sum_{c=1}^{M} n_c$ being the total sample size. Across a total of $j \in \{1, \ldots, q\}$ genes, let G_{ij} denote the (continuous) normalized expression data for the jth gene in the ith sample. Let L_i denote the lineage (tissue/cancer type) of the ith sample, and let $\mathbf{U}_{ij} = (U_{ij1}, \ldots, U_{ijp_j})^T$ denote the $p_j \times 1$ vector of upstream information from sample i matched to gene j. Our mechanistic models are gene-specific, allowing different sample sizes for each gene. However, for simplicity of notations, we describe the models assuming a fixed n.

Model structure For the jth gene, we build an additive multi-lineage mechanistic model containing separable components for the main effects of lineage and each upstream covariate, along with any possible interactions of lineage with the upstream factors. Assuming the G_{ij}s to be mean-centered, the general mathematical form of such a model is presented in the following equation.

$$G_{ij} = \underbrace{f_{1j}(L_i)}_{\text{Lineage main effect}} + \underbrace{\sum_{v=1}^{p_j} f_{2jv}(U_{ijv})}_{\text{Upstream main effects}} + \underbrace{\sum_{v=1}^{p_j} f_{3jv}(L_i, U_{ijv})}_{\text{Interaction effects}} + \underbrace{\varepsilon_{ij}}_{\text{Error}}, \forall i \in \{1, \ldots n\}. \tag{1}$$

The simplest choice is to specify each component $f_{\cdot}$ as a linear model. Such models have been explored in context of cancer omics.[19] Although they are computationally simple, they may not be fully able to capture the general range of cellular association patterns. An obvious nonlinear extension is to use splines to construct piece-wise linear mean profiles. Such approaches have also been explored in this context.[20] However, there are multifold challenges – including specifying the number of knots (hence the degree of adaptable nonlinearity) and increasing computational intensity with increasing number of covariates. To build a general class of additive association models while maintaining a reasonable extent of computational efficiency, we use Gaussian process (GP) models.

To build an additive GP model with interaction effects, we adapt an existing approach proposed in context of longitudinal data.[21] In a repeated measures setting, this approach provides a way to incorporate sample-level baseline effects and treatment effects in a nonlinear fashion. We extend this idea to our scenario to include lineage-level baseline effects (treating the experiments on cell lines from the same lineage akin to a repeated experiment setting) and changes in the effects of upstream covariates across different lineages. While samples belonging to cancers sharing some larger group-specific commonalities (e.g. all gynecological cancers) may share patterns of mechanistic impacts of upstream platforms on gene expressions, there may still be cancer-specific differences in the exact effects. Briefly, we use a GP equipped with a zero-sum (zs) kernel for the main effect of the categorical lineage variable, one with an exponentiated quadratic (eq) kernel for the main effects of the continuous upstream variables, and a product of the zs and eq kernels for their interactions, following existing approaches.[21,22] The specifics of the GP model along with the prior choices are described in detail in Supplementary Notes Section S1.2.

Model fitting and hypothesis testing The interest now is in building mechanistic models and testing for different main and interaction effects of interest. We use a dynamic Hamiltonian Monte Carlo (HMC) sampler to obtain draws from the posterior distributions of the parameters. Since we are interested in evaluating the roles of lineage, upstream factors, and any possible interactions in explaining the variability in gene expressions, we are interested in testing the following hypotheses.

(1) **Lineage main effect:** $H_{0Lj} : f_{1j} = \text{constant}$.
(2) **Upstream main effects:** $H_{0Uj} : f_{2jv} = \text{constant}, \forall v \in \{1, \ldots, p_j\}$.
(3) **All upstream effects:** $H_{0UIj} : f_{2jv}, f_{3jv} = \text{constant}, \forall v \in \{1, \ldots, p_j\}$.

To perform these tests, we use model comparison procedures using HMC-based draws of the joint log-posterior function of the parameters in a model. For a model M containing all or some of the components in Equation (1), let $H_{0\bullet}$ be the test of interest and $M_{\bullet}$ be the null model, which is a submodel of M not containing the components set to constant under $H_{0\bullet}$. For example, if we are interested in testing the lineage main effect in a main effects-only model M, $M_{\bullet}$ would be an upstream-only model. We define *pseudo-Bayes factors* ($\text{pBF}_{\bullet j}$s) as scalar summaries of component significance, defined to be the mean difference of the log-posteriors evaluated across the MCMC draws between the two models being compared. The pBFs for the three hypotheses above and for the jth gene are denoted respectively by pBF_{Lj}, pBF_{Uj}, and pBF_{UIj}. Note that these quantities are approximations for the traditional log-Bayes factors (lBFs) for comparing Bayesian models under equal model priors. To compute an lBF, one has to compute the expected posteriors for each model, followed by their log-ratio. Here, we are computing an empirical average of the difference of log-posteriors of the model parameters. The exact expressions of these quantities for a given HMC sample of the parameters are derived in Supplementary Notes Section S1.3. We use standard cut-offs for significance used for lBFs at a $\log_{10}(\bullet)$-scale: < 0.5 (no evidence), $0.5 - 1$ (substantial), $1 - 2$ (strong), and > 2 (decisive).[23] From now on, by pBF we always mean a quantity already in this scale.

Sequential evidence detection To identify driver genes, we quantify evidence of any upstream effect on gene expression untangled from any possible lineage effect. To this end, mimicking classical approaches in regression settings, we follow a sequential scheme as described in Supplementary Figure S1.

(1) Test for any lineage main effect using pBF_{Lj}. If $\text{pBF}_{Lj} \leq 1$, go to Step 2. Else go to Step 3.
(2) Test H_{0Uj} using pBF_{Uj}. Set mechanistic evidence $\mathcal{E}_{j1} = \text{pBF}_{Uj}$.
(3) Test H_{0UIj} using pBF_{UIj}. Set mechanistic evidence $\mathcal{E}_{j1} = \text{pBF}_{UIj}$.

2.1.2. *Single-lineage Mechanistic Models*

These models do not include any lineage main or interaction effects. Thus, from Equation (1), the full models reduce to the following for the jth gene, using same notations as before.

$$G_{ij} = \underbrace{\sum_{\upsilon=1}^{p_j} f_{j\upsilon}(U_{ij\upsilon})}_{\text{Upstream main effects}} + \underbrace{\varepsilon_{ij}}_{\text{Error}}, \forall i \in \{1, \ldots n\}. \tag{2}$$

We use the same eq kernel parametrization for the GP priors on each $f_{\bullet}$ as we used for the $f_{2\bullet}$ components in the multi-lineage models. We now test $H_{0j} : f_{j\upsilon} = \text{constant}, \forall \upsilon \in \{1, \ldots, p_j\}$ for each gene. We compare the full model in Equation (2) with a noise-only null model. The derivation of the corresponding pBF_j is described in Supplementary Notes Section S1.4. We assign the evidence $\mathcal{E}_{j2} = \text{pBF}_j$, as described in Supplementary Figure S1.

2.2. *Outcome Model*

For a given pool of genes, it is possible to compute multiple lines of evidence ($\boldsymbol{\mathcal{E}}_j = (\mathcal{E}_{j1}, \ldots, \mathcal{E}_{jE})^T$ for gene j). For example, for a given gene j, we may compute one pBF from a multi-lineage model built on cell line samples, and another pBF from a single-lineage model built on patient samples ($E = 2$). With interest in some disease- or therapy-related phenotype/outcome Y and the selection of biomarkers associated with it, the goal is to inform the outcome model about any level of evidence captured in these $\mathcal{E}_{je}$s in a covariate-specific way to possibly improve selection.

(1) Sufficiently strong evidence in favor of a covariate $\Longrightarrow$ higher prior probability of inclusion.

(2) Otherwise, a uniform prior is placed on selection/non-selection for that particular covariate.

We utilize a hierarchical Bayesian setting with calibrated spike-and-slab priors, described below. Let Y_i be the mean-centered continuous outcome for the ith sample. Simple extensions to categorical/censored outcomes are possible, but in this work we only focus on continuous outcomes. The mathematical form of the calibrated Bayesian variable selection (cBVS) model is then the following.

$$Y_i = \sum_{j=1}^{q} \underbrace{\beta_j}_{\text{Gene expression coefficients}} G_{ij} + \underbrace{\eta_i}_{\text{Error}}, i \in \{1, \ldots, n\}. \tag{3}$$

Model and prior specifications The errors η_i are iid $\text{N}(0, \tau^2), \forall i \in \{1, ..., n\}$. A standard conjugate prior is used for $\tau^2 \sim \text{Inverse-Gamma}(\frac{\nu}{2}, \frac{\nu\lambda}{2})$. Let $\boldsymbol{\beta} = (\beta_1, \ldots, \beta_q)^T$ denote the q-dimensional vector of regression coefficients. We place a calibrated hierarchical spike-and-slab prior on $\boldsymbol{\beta}$.

$$\begin{aligned} \boldsymbol{\beta}|\boldsymbol{\delta}, \tau &\sim \mathbf{N}_q(\mathbf{0}, \mathbf{D}_{\delta,\tau}), \\ \delta_j|\theta_j &\sim \text{Bernoulli}(\theta_j), \quad \forall j \in \{1, ..., q\}, \\ \theta_j &\sim \text{Beta}\Big(\mathcal{F}(\boldsymbol{\mathcal{E}}_j), \frac{1}{\mathcal{F}(\boldsymbol{\mathcal{E}}_j)}\Big), \quad \forall j \in \{1, ..., q\}. \end{aligned} \tag{4}$$

Here $\mathbf{D}_{\delta,\tau} = \tau^2 \mathbf{A}_\delta$, where $\mathbf{A}_\delta$ is the $q \times q$ diagonal matrix $\mathbf{A}_\delta = \text{diag}\{\delta_1 \upsilon_1 + (1-\delta_1)\upsilon_0, \ldots, \delta_q \upsilon_1 + (1-\delta_q)\upsilon_0\}$ and $\upsilon_1 \geq \upsilon_0 > 0$ are respectively the slab and spike variances. The binary latent variables δ_j are variable inclusion indicators with $\delta_j = 1$ meaning that the jth variable is included in the model. $\mathcal{F}$ is a calibration function mapping the evidence vector $\boldsymbol{\mathcal{E}}_j = (\mathcal{E}_{j1}, \ldots, \mathcal{E}_{jE})^T$ to the prior covariate inclusion probability θ_j. The advantages of the hierarchical formulation (Equation (4)) coupled with the evidence calibration function $\mathcal{F}$ are multifold. First, by adapting $\mathcal{F}$, our framework allows the user to incorporate other significance quantities (such as p-values) into the final outcome model. Any external upstream information, including categorical and continuous covariates, can be used in the mechanistic layer to compute such summary statistics. Finally, by tuning $\mathcal{F}$ appropriately, our framework allows the user to control the impact of the prior information on selection, as we show below. We discuss all these in more detail in Section 4.

Choice of evidence calibration function We use a calibration function $\mathcal{F}$ on $\mathbb{R}^E \rightarrow [0,1]$ to aggregate multi-dimensional prior evidence into a scalar prior probability. To this end, we use a four-parameter logistic map reflecting the maximal evidence across all sources on a continuous and non-decreasing spectrum of evidence strength. The exact mathematical form and the motivation behind this choice are described in Supplementary Notes Section S1.5. Using this function, the calibrated prior means of θ_j (representative values of maximal evidence at the pBF/ $\ln(10)$ scale in parentheses) are as follows: 0.502 (0.25), 0.543 (0.75), 0.726 (1.5), 0.962 (3). As illustrated in Supplementary Figure S2, the corresponding prior distributions of θ_j shift from an uniform prior to one concentrated close to one with increase in prior evidence strength.

Variable selection Inference is centered around the posterior $p(\boldsymbol{\beta}, \boldsymbol{\delta}, \boldsymbol{\theta}, \tau | \boldsymbol{Y}, \boldsymbol{G}, \boldsymbol{\mathcal{E}}, \nu, \lambda, \upsilon_0, \upsilon_1)$, where $\boldsymbol{\beta}, \boldsymbol{\delta}$, and $\boldsymbol{\theta}$ are the $q \times 1$ vectors of all β_js, δ_js, and θ_js respectively, $\boldsymbol{Y}_{n\times 1}$ is the outcome vector, $\boldsymbol{G}_{n\times q}$ is the design matrix, and $\boldsymbol{\mathcal{E}}_{q\times E}$ is the matrix of the $\mathcal{E}_{je}$s. We approximate this using a Gibbs sampler implemented via the *rjags R package*.[24] We obtain posterior estimates of the parameters (i.e., $\hat{\beta}_j$s, $\hat{\theta}_j$s, and $\hat{\tau}$) as their corresponding empirical posterior means. Model selection is performed using the collection of $1 - \hat{\theta}_j$ as p-value type quantities and applying a false discovery rate (FDR) control procedure,[25] described in Supplementary Notes Section S1.6.

3. Multi-system and Multi-platform Integrative Analyses of Pan-Gynecological Cancers

We perform an integrative analysis of cancer cell lines data from CCLE and patient samples from TCGA.[14,15] Using multi-lineage mechanistic models for cell line samples and single-lineage mechanistic models for patient samples, we quantify gene-specific associations of expression with corresponding copy number and methylation data. We then use the pBFs from these two sources to inform and build cBVS models of drug response on gene expression based on the cell line samples. Specifically, our multi-lineage mechanistic models on the cell line samples borrow strength by combining data across three gynecological lineages - breast, ovary, and uterus. The single-lineage mechanistic models on the patient samples are built separately for each of the three corresponding TCGA cancer types by tissue - breast invasive carcinoma (BRCA), ovarian serous cystadenocarcinoma (OV), and uterine carcinosarcoma (UCS). The outcome models on the cell line samples are built in a lineage-specific way for a collection of drugs of interest in gynecological cancers. Our investigations are aimed broadly at answering two sets of questions.

(1) We assess within-system and between-system patterns of functional evidence garnered by the mechanistic models (i.e., a gene may have strong mechanistic evidence of association with the upstream factors for the cell lines only, the patients only, both, or none).
(2) We identify panels of genes whose expressions are associated with responses to specific drugs in the cell line samples, potentially offering novel introspection into treatment selection and the cellular mechanisms/targets of such drugs.

3.1. *Data Processing and Analysis Pipeline*

Multi-omics cell line and patient data Gene expression, copy number, and DNA methylation data on cancer cell lines from CCLE, drug response data from GDSC, along with annotation information to match genes to upstream information, are downloaded from the depmap portal.[26] Gene expression, copy number, and DNA methylation data on TCGA patient samples, along with annotation information matching genes to upstream covariates, are downloaded from the Xena browser.[27] Sample size and other filtering requirements result in a pool of 5,792 genes and 65 drugs to be included in all further analyses, as described in Supplementary Notes Section S1.7. Summary information on each dataset are available in Supplementary Table S1 and Supplementary Figures S3-S8.

BaySyn analysis of gynecological cancers For each gene, a multi-lineage mechanistic model with $M = 3$ (breast, ovary, uterus) is constructed (termed the CL model hereafter) and hypothesis tests are performed as described in Supplementary Figure S1. Further, for each gene, three single-lineage mechanistic models (one for each cancer type – BRCA, OV, UCS) are built on the patient samples and upstream effects are quantified following Supplementary Figure S1. As a post-model fitting investigation, we perform gene set enrichment analyses (GSEA)[28] using these four sets of evidence (CL, BRCA, UCS, OV) for the Kyoto Encyclopedia of Genes and Genomes (KEGG)[29] and gene ontology (GO) gene sets.[30,31] For our analyses, we use the gene set enrichment (GAGE) procedure implemented in the *gage R package* due to the reason that our pBFs are on a different scale than typical expression levels or fold-change summaries.[32] The gene set-specific hypothesis that we test is whether the set in question exhibits significantly higher level of activity as summarized by the evidence statistics compared to the genes outside the gene set, due to the unidirectional nature of the pBFs. For each lineage, drug-specific response association models are built using the cBVS procedure, and variable selection is performed using a 10% FDR control threshold. Illustrative examples of annotated and integrated datasets for each stage of modeling are presented in Supplementary Notes Section S1.8 and Supplementary Figures S9-S11.

3.2. *Results*

Utility of borrowing strength to detect mechanistic evidence Figure 2a summarizes the number of genes inferred to be at the decisive level of evidence (in favor of associations with corresponding upstream covariates) across the three single-lineage models for each TCGA patient cancer type and the multi-lineage model for the cell lines data. The connected dots at the bottom indicate the intersection of the mechanistic models for which the number of genes summarized by the bar height are decisive. The top three combinations of models in terms of detecting decisive evidence all belong to some combination of the TCGA data sets (BRCA only, BRCA and OV, BRCA and UCS - in decreasing order). However, except for the BRCA dataset which utilizes > 750 samples for all genes to build the mechanistic models, the cell lines mechanistic models borrowing strength across three lineages detect more unique signals (4th in the ranking) than the other TCGA datasets. This further validates the utility of building joint nonlinear association models with main and interaction components that can identify shared patterns of association across smaller datasets which would potentially be missed in dataset-specific models. The list of genes uniquely identified by the cell lines mechanistic model is available in Supplementary Table S2.

KEGG gene set enrichment analyses illustrate utility of mechanistic evidences To assess the utility of the mechanistic evidence quantities and to validate their use in future detection of novel

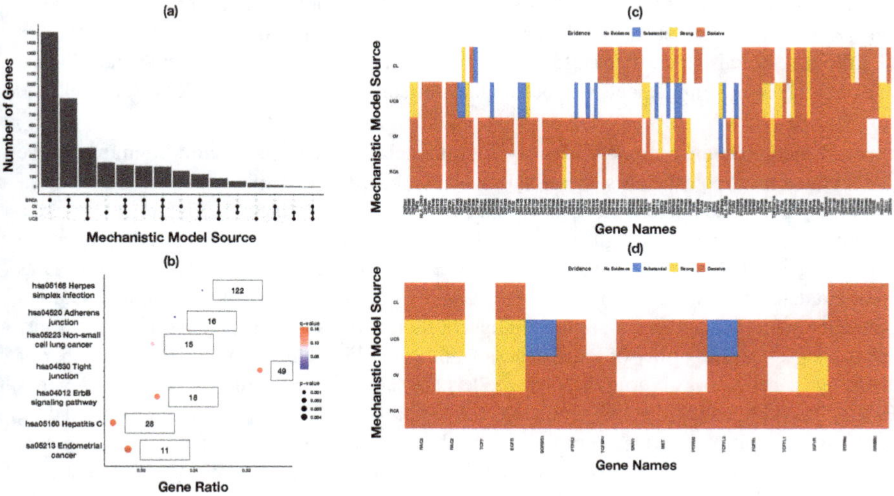

Fig. 2: Mechanistic evidence summary and gene set enrichment results. Panel (a) presents an upset plot of the number of genes at the decisive level of evidence based on the mechanistic models for different intersections of the patient and cell line datasets. Panel (b) presents a dotplot summarizing significance levels for KEGG gene sets. The gene sets are ordered from top to bottom in decreasing order of q-values ($\leq$ 0.2 included). The labels beside the dots indicate set sizes in our analyses. Panels (c) and (d) present heatmaps summarizing levels of mechanistic evidence for the genes in KEGG herpes simplex infection and adherens junction gene sets respectively. Genes in the rows are ordered based on clusters resulting from the evidence statistics.

functional drivers, we perform GSEA using the four evidence sources and the KEGG and GO gene sets. Due to space limitations we only discuss the KEGG results here. The GO results are presented in Supplementary Figures S17-S32. Several KEGG gene sets have been implicated to have significant roles generally in cancer[33,34] and specifically in gynecological cancers.[35–38] The results from our KEGG GSEA are summarized in Figure 2b, exhibiting the seven gene sets with FDR-controlled q-value < 0.2. The gene set-specific mechanistic evidences are summarized in Figure 2c-d for the top two KEGG gene sets; the rest are presented in Supplementary Figures S12-S16. The top gene set identified in the KEGG analyses is the herpes simplex infection pathway (p-value = 3.88×10^{-16}) (Figure 2b). This gene set contains a large cluster of genes exhibiting decisive evidence across majority of the mechanistic models, as can be seen in Figure 2c. Following these genes are two major clusters - one containing genes at the decisive level for the BRCA, OV, and CL mechanistic models, and one containing genes at the decisive level for all three TCGA cancers. The consistent nature of functional evidence across this gene set is in agreement with findings from past investigations - multiple studies have indicated the prognostic value of members of this pathway in gynecological cancers - including breast,[39] ovarian,[40] and endometrial[41] cancer. The second-highest gene set in the KEGG analyses is the adherens junction gene set (p-value = 5.52×10^{-5}) (Figure 2b). The genes PTPN6 and ERBB2 exhibit decisive levels of mechanistic evidence in all four models (Figure 2d).

Different upstream mechanisms of the ERBB2 gene have been implicated in different gynecological cancers, such as copy number changes in ovarian tumors[42] and somatic mutations in breast cancer.[43] The EGFR gene has also shown promise as a potential therapeutic target in multiple gynecological cancers,[44,45] which is in alignment with our findings of some signal in all the TCGA and cell line models (Figure 2d).

Calibrated drug response models identify high-association lineage-specific biomarkers We build calibrated hierarchical Bayesian variable selection-based drug response models for each lineage × drug combination across all 65 drugs and all three cell line lineages. Figure 3a presents a wordcloud where each gene is weighted by the total number of times it is selected in a drug response model at the 10% FDR-controlled cutoff. The genes BAHCC1, ALOX12P2, and SYCP2 emerge as the top candidates, with selection in 14, 12, and 12 models respectively. While this summary allows us to identify general candidates for future pharmacogenomic investigations, it does not indicate any potential lineage-specific utility of these genes. To this end, Figure 3b summarizes the number of times the top genes across all drug response models are selected in each lineage. For breast, genes BAHCC1, BCL11A, and SYCP2 are at the top, with respectively eight, eight, and six detected drug associations. The role of BCL11A in triple-negative breast cancer (TNBC) stemness is well known, and it is considered to be one of the first utilizable targets for treatment of TNBCs.[46] A similar confirmation can be obtained for SYCP2, which has recently been identified as a prognostic biomarker in breast cancer.[47] However, to the best of our knowledge, BAHCC1 has not so far been identified to have breast cancer-specific functional roles, which renders it as a novel detection that deserves deeper investigations. Top genes in the two other lineages also include both novel and known functional drivers - such as ALOX12P2 (nine selections, novel) and FGFRL1 (eight selections, known)[48] for ovary and FBXO17 (seven selections, novel) for uterus.

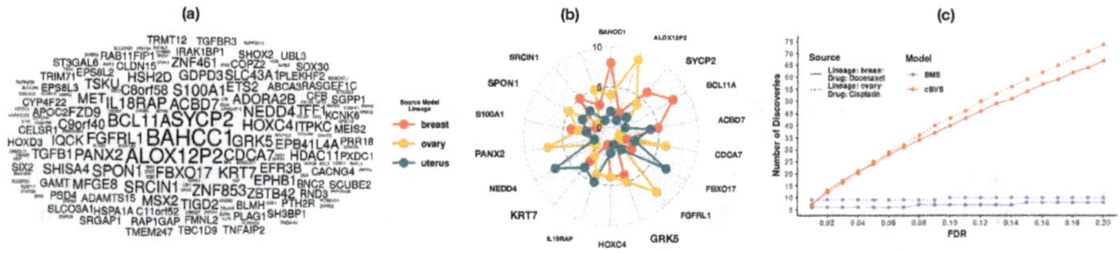

Fig. 3: Drug response model summaries. Panel (a) presents a wordcloud of top genes across all the drug response models (three lineages × 65 drugs). The sizes of the words are proportional to the total number of times across all models that a gene is selected based on a 10% FDR-controlled threshold. Panel (b) presents a radar chart of the top 18 genes (selected in at least nine drug response models) according to the three lineages. Panel (c) presents a discovery plot across increasing FDR control thresholds for the drug docetaxel in lineage breast and the drug cisplatin in lineage ovary. BMS refers to an uncalibrated Bayesian variable selection model based on the Bayesian model averaging procedure (see Supplementary Notes Section S1.9).

Calibration improves statistical power to detect gene-drug associations To assess the discoveries for specific lineage × drug combinations, we focus on two drugs with known use in specific cancer lineages - docetaxel for breast and cisplatin for ovary. The number of discoveries across different FDR thresholds for these are presented in Figure 3c-d and the corresponding discoveries are summarized in Supplementary Tables S3-S4. Similar plots and tables for all other models are available in our R Shiny dashboard at tinyurl.com/BaySynApp. Evidently, compared to an uncalibrated Bayesian variable selection procedure implemented via the BMS R package (see Supplementary Notes Section S1.9), cBVS models make more discoveries at the same level of error control, allowing a continuum of assessment for top candidates emerging across increasing control thresholds. This indicates the utility of synthesizing mechanistic evidence and calibrating the outcome models with such evidences. Several examples of cell lines-based discoveries guided by evidences discovered in patient data emerge. For example, the model for docetaxel response in breast cell lines identify an association with the gene GRK5 at 10% FDR control. Cell lines overexpressing GRK5 have previously been observed to demonstrate an increase in resistance to docetaxel in male gynecological cancers,[49] and our finding suggests that it deserves further investigations in female gynecological cancers as well. Another top discovery at the same FDR threshold is the gene CD83, expression of which is known to be enhanced by docetaxel in metastatic breast cancers.[50] For the response model of cisplatin in the ovarian lineage, multiple solute-carrier family (SLC) genes are selected at the 10% FDR threshold. These genes are known potential biomarkers of ovarian cancer and are under investigation for prognostic utility.[51] Another interesting discovery is that of the CDCA7 gene from the cell division cycle pathway, silencing of which has recently been shown to downregulate cisplatin resistance in lung cancer subtypes, making it a potential therapeutic target.[52] Our finding seems to indicate similar scope in ovarian cancer, demanding further investigation. Notably, all four of these discussed findings had no cell lines-based mechanistic evidence, but had decisive evidence from at least one TCGA source – which further underscores the importance of synthesizing evidence across model systems.

4. Summary and Discussion

We propose BaySyn, a hierarchical multi-stage Bayesian evidence synthesis procedure for multi-system multiomic integration. BaySyn detects functionally relevant driver genes based on their associations with upstream regulators and uses this information to guide variable selection in outcome association models. We apply our framework to multiomic cancer cell line and patient datasets for pan-gynecological cancers. pBFs from the mechanistic layer of BaySyn exhibit high enrichment in previously known KEGG gene sets and detect driver genes known to have functional roles in the cancers studied. Calibrated outcome models for drug responses identify several confirmatory and novel lineage-drug-gene combinations providing further evidence on the profitability of our approach towards future precision oncology endeavors.

Several features of our framework makes it readily adaptable to more general settings and richer datasets. The calibrated spike-and-slab prior can be generalized to include any number (more upstream platforms such as miRNA or mutation) and form (other evidence metrics such as p-values) of prior information by tuning the calibration function accordingly. The outcome model can easily be extended to include other biomarkers such as proteomics. While we use cell lines data to illustrate the integrative approach across model systems, it is straightforward to apply our pipeline to datasets from cancer model systems with higher fidelity to human tumors[53] - such as organoids[54] or patient-derived xenografts[55] - as such databases become increasingly comprehensive and available. Further, both the stages of our framework are highly parallelizable and individual runs are quite efficient - a single gene-specific multi-lineage mechanistic model with interactions takes approximately 20 minutes on average to complete, while a single lineage-drug specific outcome model takes approximately 12 minutes on average (both based on runs on a single core of a 2015 Macbook Air with 8 GB memory and Intel i5 processor). Thus, extending our analyses to include larger gene-drug panels with similar sample sizes is straightforward with existing parallel computing resources.

Limitations and Future Work Certain improvements are of interest given the biological context of our work. First, although we assess mechanistic relevance at a gene-by-gene basis, at a molecular level, genes interact in functional pathways to result in downstream modifications. This motivates joint models for driver genes in a multivariable setting accounting for underlying gene-gene interactions. Second, the relatively low lineage-specific sample sizes in cell lines data make fully Bayesian exploration of the posteriors feasible in the outcome models. Higher data dimensions would result in increased computation times; where-in approximate Bayesian computation schemes such as the E-M based variable selection[56] or variational Bayes[57] would need to be employed. Third, while our framework allows integration of covariate-specific prior information in a variable selection framework, more granular information (both sample- and covariate-specific) may be available, allowing improved learning of the molecular functions driving the changes in an outcome of interest. For example, sample-specific data on tumor heterogeneity may be available, and such data may need to be incorporated in the outcome models driving changes in the covariate effects. Finally, as outlined in Supplementary Notes Section S1.5, in the presence of multiple lines of evidence, how best to aggregate them depends heavily on the context - while multiple possible approaches exist, a case-specific decision must be made to ensure best utilization of the evidences. A data-driven procedure of choosing evidence weights would eliminate this requirement. We leave these tasks for future exploration.

Acknowledgments RB and VB were partially supported by NIH grant R01CA244845-01A1 and VB by P30 CA-046592.

References

1. I. Subramanian et al. *Bioinformatics and biology insights*, 14:1177932219899051, 2020.
2. A. Conesa and S. Beck. *Scientific data*, 6(1):1–4, 2019.
3. B. A. Ruggeri et al. *Biochemical pharmacology*, 87(1):150–161, 2014.
4. J. Kim et al. *Nature Reviews Molecular Cell Biology*, 21(10):571–584, 2020.
5. M. V. Relling and W. E. Evans. *Nature*, 526(7573):343–350, 2015.
6. D. M. Roden et al. *Annals of internal medicine*, 145(10):749–757, 2006.
7. S. Tarazona et al. *Nature Computational Science*, 1(6):395–402, 2021.
8. S. Chakraborty et al. *BioMed research international*, 2018, 2018.
9. A. Kaplan and E. F. Lock. *Cancer informatics*, 16:1176935117718517, 2017.
10. C. Cheng et al. *Integrating Omics Data*, pp. 380, 2015.
11. P. W. Angel et al. *PLoS computational biology*, 16(9):e1008219, 2020.
12. Z. Tu et al. *Integrating Omics Data*, 88:88–109, 2015.
13. G. Tseng et al. *Integrating omics data*. Cambridge University Press, 2015.
14. J. N. Weinstein et al. *Nature genetics*, 45(10):1113–1120, 2013.
15. J. Barretina et al. *Nature*, 483(7391):603–607, 2012.
16. W. Yang et al. *Nucleic acids research*, 41(D1):D955–D961, 2012.
17. H. K. Solvang et al. *BMC bioinformatics*, 12(1):1–12, 2011.
18. K. Litovkin et al. *Journal of cancer research and clinical oncology*, 140(11):1849–1861, 2014.
19. W. Wang et al. *Bioinformatics*, 29(2):149–159, 2013.
20. E. J. McGuffey. *Statistical methods for integrating genomics data*. Texas A&M University, 2015.
21. J. Timonen et al. *Bioinformatics*, 37(13):1860–1867, 2021.
22. C. G. Kaufman and S. R. Sain. *Bayesian Analysis*, 5(1):123–149, 2010.
23. R. E. Kass and A. E. Raftery. *Journal of the american statistical association*, 90(430):773–795, 1995.
24. M. Plummer et al. *Vienna, Austria*, 2016.
25. V. Baladandayuthapani et al. *Journal of the american statistical association*, 105(492):1358–1375, 2010.
26. A. Tsherniak et al. *Cell*, 170(3):564–576, 2017.
27. M. J. Goldman et al. *Nature biotechnology*, 38(6):675–678, 2020.
28. A. Subramanian et al. *Proceedings of the National Academy of Sciences*, 102(43):15545–15550, 2005.
29. M. Kanehisa and S. Goto. *Nucleic Acids Research*, 28(1):27–30, Jan 2000.
30. M. Ashburner et al. *Nature genetics*, 25(1):25–29, 2000.
31. *Nucleic acids research*, 49(D1):D325–D334, 2021.
32. W. Luo et al. *BMC bioinformatics*, 10(1):1–17, 2009.
33. L. Chen et al. *Artificial Intelligence in Medicine*, 76:27–36, 2017.
34. F. Yuan et al. *Mathematical Biosciences* 304:1–8, 2018.
35. A. D. Campos-Parra et al. *Gynecologic oncology*, 143(2):406–413, 2016.
36. X. Yang et al. *OncoTargets and therapy*, 11:1457, 2018.
37. T. Zhang et al. *PLoS One*, 13(5):e0196351, 2018.
38. J. Chen et al. *Medicine*, 99(18), 2020.
39. S. M. Ghouse et al. *Frontiers in oncology*, 10:384, 2020.
40. M. Nakamori et al. *Clinical cancer research*, 9(7):2727–2733, 2003.
41. X.-Y. Zhou et al. *Journal of Clinical Laboratory Analysis*, 36(4):e24315, 2022.
42. I. Dimova et al. *International Journal of Gynecologic Cancer*, 16(1), 2006.
43. J. Y. Hou et al. *Gynecologic Oncology Reports*, 32, 2020.
44. H. D. Reyes et al. *Molecular diagnosis & therapy*, 18(2):137–151, 2014.
45. K. K. Kim et al. *Scientific reports*, 5(1):1–11, 2015.
46. A. Errico. *Nature Reviews Clinical Oncology*, 12(3):127–127, 2015.
47. C. Wu and Y. Tuo. *Future Oncology*, 15(8):817–826, 2019.
48. H. Tai et al. *Journal of immunology research*, 2018, 2018.
49. J. B. Black et al. *Cancer Research*, 78(13_Supplement):LB–312, 2018.
50. M. Buoncervello et al. *Neoplasia*, 14(9):855–IN19, 2012.
51. H. Chen et al. *Annals of Translational Medicine*, 9(15), 2021.
52. W. Zeng et al. 2021.
53. A. Goodspeed et al. *Molecular Cancer Research*, 14(1):3–13, 2016.
54. J. Drost and H. Clevers. *Nature Reviews Cancer*, 18(7):407–418, 2018.
55. F. Invrea et al. *Current opinion in biotechnology*, 63:151–156, 2020.
56. V. Ročková and E. I. George. *Journal of the American Statistical Association*, 109(506):828–846, 2014.
57. C. W. Fox and S. J. Roberts. *Artificial intelligence review*, 38(2):85–95, 2012.

TRANS-OMIC KNOWLEDGE TRANSFER MODELING INFERS GUT MICROBIOME BIOMARKERS OF ANTI-TNF RESISTANCE IN ULCERATIVE COLITIS

Alan Trinh[1,4] Ran Ran[2,4], Douglas K Brubaker[2,3*]
[1]Indiana University School of Medicine, Indianapolis IN, USA. [2]Weldon School of Biomedical Engineering, Purdue University, West Lafayette, IN, USA. [3]Regenstrief Center for Healthcare Engineering, Purdue University, West Lafayette, IN, USA. [4]These Authors Contributed Equally.
*Email: dkbrubak@purdue.edu

A critical challenge in analyzing multi-omics data from clinical cohorts is the re-use of these valuable datasets to answer biological questions beyond the scope of the original study. Transfer Learning and Knowledge Transfer approaches are machine learning methods that leverage knowledge gained in one domain to solve a problem in another. Here, we address the challenge of developing Knowledge Transfer approaches to map trans-omic information from a multi-omic clinical cohort to another cohort in which a novel phenotype is measured. Our test case is that of predicting gut microbiome and gut metabolite biomarkers of resistance to anti-TNF therapy in Ulcerative Colitis patients. Three approaches are proposed for Trans-omic Knowledge Transfer, and the resulting performance and downstream inferred biomarkers are compared to identify efficacious methods. We find that multiple approaches reveal similar metabolite and microbial biomarkers of anti-TNF resistance and that these commonly implicated biomarkers can be validated in literature analysis. Overall, we demonstrate a promising approach to maximize the value of the investment in large clinical multi-omics studies by re-using these data to answer biological and clinical questions not posed in the original study.

Keywords: Trans-omic. Multi-omic. Transfer Learning. Knowledge Transfer. Microbiome. Colitis.

1. Introduction

The generation of matched multi-omics datasets from large clinical cohorts has resulted in identification of novel biomarkers of disease progression and therapeutic response in cancers [1-3], inflammatory [4, 5], and other complex human diseases [6, 7]. The Integrative Human Microbiome Project (iHMP) is a recent effort to understand the complex host and microbiome drivers of inflammatory bowel disease (IBD) [8], type 2 diabetes (T2D) [7], and preterm birth (PTB) [9] through the integration of human multi-omics. The development of computational tools to integrate molecular data across scales [10] and relate signatures to human phenotypes [11] has been a critical parallel and synergistic effort to experimental advances that have expanded the scope of molecular profiling. Because sequencing remains one of the highest costs to scaling clinical multi-omics, patients are recruited with defined criteria to ensure sufficient statistical power to answer the primary study questions. Therefore, though the molecular data in these cohorts are rich in detail and scope, the clinical and phenotypic variables are often sparse and limited in scope.

Transfer Learning, the use of information gained solving one problem to inform the solution of a different one, is a machine learning area suited to maximize the value of the financial, research, and patient efforts required to generate clinical datasets. The profiling of different molecular data types in multi-omic cohorts encode *trans-omic* information that enables correlation of signals across scales. If one of these scales is present in single-omic cohort matched to new phenotypic variables, the trans-omic relationships in the multi-omics study could reveal molecular associations with the phenotypic variables in the single-omic cohort. We term this *Trans-omic Knowledge Transfer* and suggest that this approach represents a largely untapped reservoir of opportunity to reuse data from clinical cohorts to answer questions beyond those posed in the original study.

Here, we examine potential strategies for Trans-omic Knowledge Transfer to associate multi-omic signatures from one cohort of patients to a drug-resistance phenotype in another (Figure 1). Our objective is to identify gut microbial taxa and metabolites in the IBD Multi-omics Database (IBDMDB)[8] predictive of anti-tumor necrosis factor alpha (anti-TNF) therapeutic response in Ulcerative Colitis (UC) patients, a phenotype not in the original IBDMBD data.

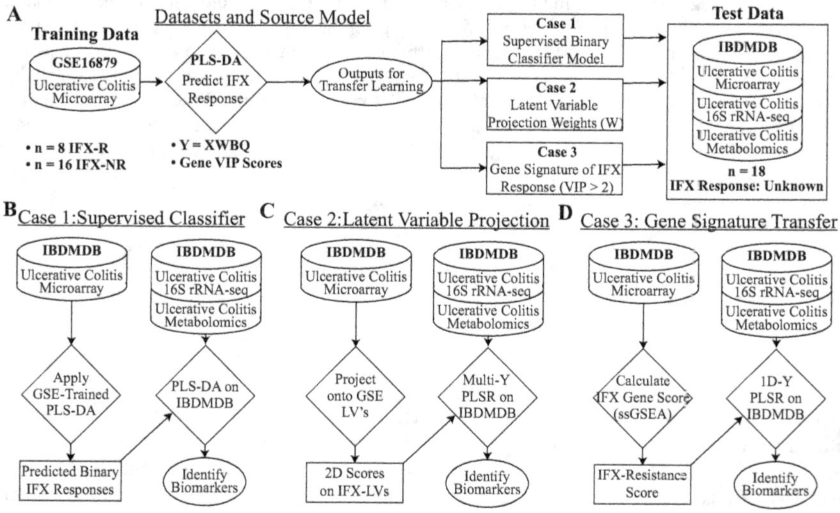

Figure 1. Study Overview. (A) Trans-omic Knowledge Transfer to predict biomarkers of response to an anti-TNF drug (Infliximab: IFX) training on UC patient gene expression data (GSE16879, "GSE-Data") and predicting on a test set (IBDMDB). **(B)** Case 1: Supervised Classifier Transfer. The PLS-DA model constructed on the training data is applied to IBDMDB gene expression data to predict IFX response. New PLS-DA models are constructed to associate microbial taxa and metabolites to the predicted IFX response. **(C)** Case 2: Relative Separation Transfer. The weights matrix *W* is extracted from the GSE-trained PLS-DA model and the IBDMDB gene expression data are projected onto the GSE latent variables (LV). PLS-R models are trained to associate microbial taxa and metabolites to the positions of the IBDMDB samples on the IFX response, GSE-trained LVs. **(D)** Case 3: Signature Transfer. Genes predictive of IFX response in the GSE-trained model are extracted via Variable Importance of Projection (VIP) analysis to define an IFX-response Gene Set. Single Sample Gene Set Enrichment Analysis (ssGSEA) constructs a resistance score for this signature in IBDMDB data. PLS-R models are built to associate taxa and metabolites to the resistance score.

UC is a chronic inflammatory condition of the digestive tract that impacts the large intestine and results in progressively worsening inflammation and intestinal damage [12]. Patients typically progress through a sequence of therapies including antibiotics and general immunosuppressive drugs, to more targeted biologic agents, the most common of which are anti-TNF agents [13]. However, 10-40% [14] of patients will exhibit primary resistance, and up to 50% [15] of initial responders will eventually acquire resistance, depending on the disease type and experiment design.

Therefore, anti-TNF resistance represents a major clinical problem in UC and the identification of microbial and metabolite biomarkers of response could aid in the development of probiotic and prebiotic approaches to enhance response and overcome resistance.

Since information about anti-TNF response is not available in the meta-data for the IBDMDB, we developed three transfer learning approaches to leverage UC patient gene expression data matched to anti-TNF response in another cohort to infer an anti-TNF response gradient and biomarkers in IBDMDB. To compare these approaches, we held the initial model constant, a Partial Least Squares Discriminant Analysis (PLS-DA), and compared three strategies for knowledge transfer we term (1) Supervised Model, (2) Relative Separation, and (3) Signature Transfer. We show how each of these methods enables discovery of cross-cohort biomarkers, assess consistency of different approaches, and offer recommendations on how to generalize these approaches to other classes of machine learning models for trans-omic, cross-cohort biomarker discovery.

2. Methods

2.1 *Datasets – Download and Processing*

Multi-omics data was obtained from the integrated Human Microbiome Project (iHMP) IBD Multi-omics Database [16, 17]. Large intestine samples from Ulcerative colitis and non-IBD control patients were selected if each unique patient had all three of the following data types: gut metabolomics data, 16S rRNA seq data, and colorectal transcriptomics. The cohort consisted of 18 UC patients with all three sets of data. 16S rRNA-seq and gut metabolomic data were log2 normalized, and the transcriptomic data was z-scored normalized. Gene expression data for UC patients matched to Infliximab response information were obtained from Gene Expression Omnibus (GEO) from dataset GSE16879 (N = 24) [18, 19]. Data were log2 RMA normalized [20] and the top 33% of most variable genes were selected for analysis. The IBDMDB gene expression dataset was filtered for just these top 33% of most variable genes from GSE16879 to ensure comparability.

2.2 *Partial Least Squares and Variable Importance of Projection Analysis*

Partial Least Squares Discriminant Analysis (PLS-DA) and Regression (PLS-R) models were trained in MATLAB_R2022a using the 'plsregress' function. For training the initial model with GSE16879 gene expression data, models with 1 to 8 latent variables (LV) were assessed using 6-fold cross-validation. Percent variance explained in Y (infliximab response) and minimized mean squared error (MSE) were examined to select the optimal number of LVs for Knowledge Transfer to the test set. Test set models using metabolomics or microbial taxa information were trained examining 1 to 8 LVs using 6-fold cross-validation and the optimal number of LVs were selected based on percent variance explained and minimized MSE. For gene expression, metabolomics, and 16S rRNA-seq data, predictive features were identified in the PLS models using variable importance of projection (VIP) analysis. A VIP score assesses the weighted variance captured by a feature in a PLS model relative to the total variance captured in the model. A feature with VIP score greater than 1 is considered significantly predictive and higher VIP scores indicate more predictive features.

While other methods for predictive modeling do exist (e.g. random forest, neural networks) that we could examine here, the strength of PLS-DA and PLS-R is the ease of interpretation of the loading coefficients on the latent variables, enabling us to use the inferred biological signatures as validation lists. This is necessary since the nature of Trans-omic Knowledge Transfer involves prediction on a test set for which we cannot know the ground-truth biological signatures.

2.3 ***Case 1: Supervised Classifier Transfer***

Following PLS-DA model training on the GSE16879 gene expression data predicting Infliximab response, the model regression coefficients matrix β, was extracted. We applied β to the z-score normalized IBDMDB gene expression data, filtered for overlapping genes with the top 33% most variable genes, to predict an Infliximab response for the IBDMDB samples. Predicted values greater than 0 were marked as "sensitive" or "1" and less than 0 were marked as "resistant" or "-1". We then used these labels to construct PLS-DA models for the IBDMDB metabolomics and 16S rRNA-seq data predicting the Infliximab response variable. Models were trained and predictive metabolites and microbial taxa were extracted via the procedures described in 2.2.

2.4 ***Case 2: Relative Separation Transfer***

Following PLS-DA model training on the GSE16879 gene expression data predicting Infliximab response, the model weights matrix W was extracted. We multiplied W by the z-score normalized IBDMDB gene expression data, filtered for overlapping genes with the top 33% most variable genes, to predict an Infliximab response for the IBDMDB samples, to infer the scores of IBDMDB samples on GSE16879-trained latent variables. Using this continuous Y matrix, we constructed PLS-R models for the IBDMDB gut metabolomics and 16S rRNA-seq data to predict separation of IBDMDB samples on Infliximab response-associated latent variables. Following model training as described in 2.2 for IBDMDB metabolomics and 16S rRNA-seq data, predictive metabolites and microbial taxa were extracted via VIP analysis.

2.5 ***Case 3: Signature Transfer***

Following PLS-DA model training on the GSE16879 gene expression data predicting Infliximab response, significantly predictive genes were extracted via VIP analysis at a threshold of VIP > 2. These genes were used to define a gene set for analysis via single sample Gene Set Enrichment Analysis (ssGSEA). We analyzed the IBDMDB gene expression data in R (v4.1.1) using the package ssGSEA2.0 to infer patient-specific Infliximab resistance pathway scores. After running ssGSEA2.0, sample-specific Infliximab-resistance scores for the IBDMDB patients were extracted for downstream analysis. We trained PLS-R models with the IBDMDB metabolomics and 16S rRNA-seq data to predict the Infliximab resistance scores. Models were trained and significantly predictive metabolites and microbial taxa were extracted via VIP analysis as described in 2.2.

2.6 ***Data Code Availability***

All data required to reproduce the findings in the manuscript is publicly available through GEO [18] or the IBDMBD [8] portals. All code required to reproduce the findings in this manuscript is available at: https://github.com/WeldonSchool-BrubakerLab/psb2023.git

3. Results

3.1 ***Training the source PLS-DA model on Infliximab Response-Matched Transcriptomics***

We trained a PLS-DA model predicting Infliximab response from large intestine pinch biopsy gene expression data in GSE16879 as the foundational model we held constant in comparing Trans-omic Knowledge Transfer modeling approaches. Processed gene expression data were filtered for the top 33% most variable genes (5,779 genes) as our X-block and a PLS-DA model was trained using a binary Y variable for Infliximab response (Sensitive 1, Resistant -1) (Figure 2A). UC samples primarily separated by Infliximab response on LV1 and a two latent variable model minimized prediction error across 6-fold cross-validation. Using Variable Importance of Projection (VIP) analysis, we identified genes in the model predictive of Infliximab response (2,266 genes VIP > 1) and extracted a 70 gene Infliximab resistance signature (VIP > 1) to define an Infliximab resistance gene set for trans-omic models (Figure 2B-2C). Of those genes, 55 were up-regulated in Infliximab resistant patients relative to sensitive patients.

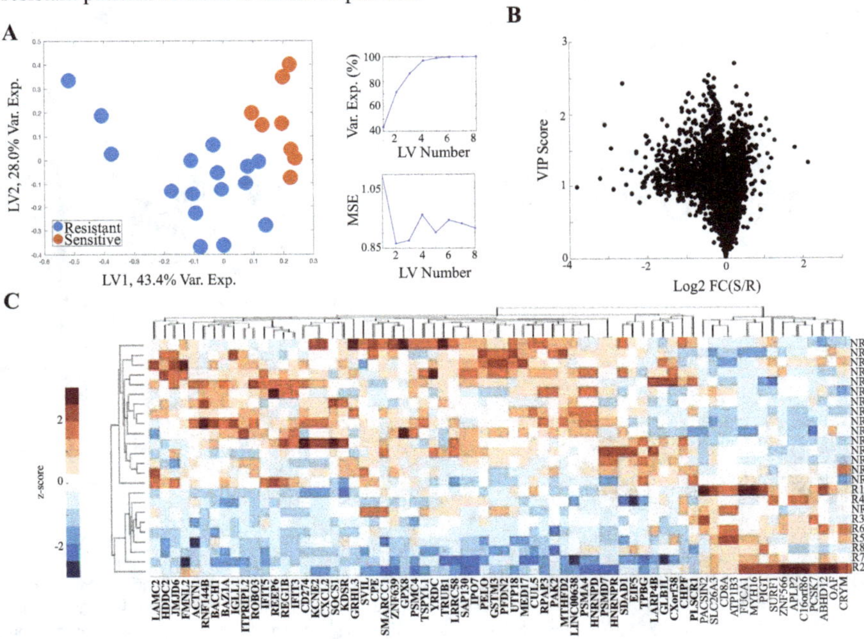

Figure 2. Training the underlying PLS-DA model. (A) Scores of GSE16879 ulcerative colitis samples in PLS-DA latent variables (LV) predicting Infliximab sensitivity or resistance. Two LV were selected explaining 71.4% variance and minimizing MSE. **(B)** Volcano plot of genes by VIP score and log2 fold change between R and NR patients. **(C)** Heatmap of Infliximab response-associated genes at VIP > 2 used to construct the gene set for Case 3: Signature Transfer Modeling. R-Responder, NR- Non-responder or resistant. Bolded genes are up-regulated in Infliximab resistant patients.

3.2 *Inferring Gut Microbial Taxa Predictive of Infliximab Response*

Having trained the initial PLS-DA model predicting Infliximab response from gene expression data in UC patients from GSE16879, we examined three approaches for Trans-omic Knowledge Transfer to identify gut microbial taxa predictive of Infliximab response using gene expression and 16S rRNA-seq data from IBDMDB (Figure 3). For our first case, Supervised Classifier Transfer, we applied the PLS-DA model trained on GSE16879 gene expression data to the IBDMDB gene expression data to predict a binary Infliximab response variable for these patients. Having made this prediction, we trained a new PLS-DA model (2 LV – 73.2% variance explained) predicting

IBDMDB Infliximab response labels from IBDMDB 16S rRNA-seq data (Figure 3A). The microbial taxa information was able to stratify the predicted labels primarily along LV1.

For the second case, Relative Separation Transfer, we applied the weights matrix W from the GSE16879-trained PLS-DA model to the gene expression data from IBDMDB to calculate the scores of IBDMDB samples on GSE16879 latent variables. We then trained a PLS-R model (2 LV – 59.9% variance explained) predicting IBDMDB scores on GSE16879 LV1 and LV2 using IBDMDB 16S rRNA-seq data (Figure 3B). Positive scores on GSE16879 LV1 and LV2 were associated with Infliximab resistance (Figure 2). We observed that these scores were not well stratified by the PLS-R model, but some separation could be observed on 16S rRNA-seq LV1.

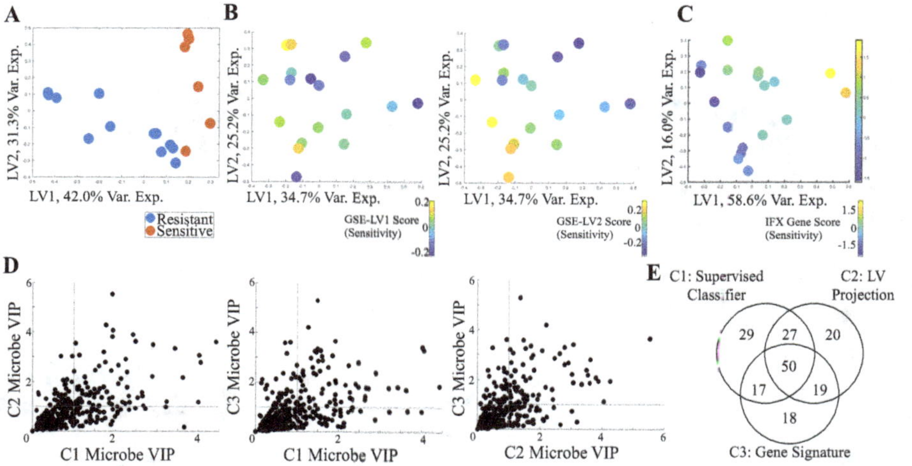

Figure 3. Gut Microbial Predictors of Infliximab Response. (A) Case 1 Supervised Classifier Transfer. Scores plot for a PLS-DA model predicting IBDMDB inferred Infliximab response classes from 16S rRNA-seq data. Infliximab response classes were predicted by applying the GSE16879 trained PLS-DA model to the IBDMDB gene expression data. **(B)** Case 2 Relative Separation Transfer. Scores plot for a PLS-R model trained to predict separation of IBDMDB samples on GSE16879 PLS-DA latent variables from 16S rRNA-seq data. Plots are colored by IBDMDB sample scores on GSE16879 latent variables 1 and 2 inferred using IBDMDB gene expression data. **(C)** Case 3 Signature Transfer: PLS-R model predicting IBDMDB Infliximab resistance gene score from 16S rRNA-seq data. **(D)** Comparison of microbial taxa VIP scores from Case 1 (C1), Case 2 (C2), and Case 3 (C3) PLS Knowledge Transfer models. **(E)** Venn diagram of the number of Infliximab response-associated taxa (VIP > 1) across models.

For the third case, Signature Transfer, we used the 70 genes with VIP scores greater than 2 from the GSE16879 PLS-DA model to define an Infliximab resistance gene set for single sample Gene Set Enrichment Analysis (ssGSEA) of the IBDMDB gene expression data. In brief, ssGSEA calculates an enrichment score for a pathway or gene set, for each sample in a dataset based on the cumulative expression of genes within that sample gene set. Here, we used ssGSEA to calculate an Infliximab resistance score for each sample in the IBDMDB gene expression data and then trained a PLS-R model predicting that score using the IBDMDB 16S rRNA-seq data (Figure 3C). We observed very strong separation of IBDMDB samples by Infliximab resistance scores along the microbial taxa latent variables. Compared to the Supervised Classifier Transfer and Relative Separation Transfer approaches, the model trained using Signature Transfer generated latent variables capturing the greater proportion of variance between samples.

We performed VIP analysis of the microbial taxa in each Knowledge Transfer model to extract Infliximab response-predictive microbial taxa from each approach. When we compared the extracted features across models by VIP score, we observed that there was relatively little consistency between the biomarkers identified by each approach (Figure 3D). This suggests that while all approaches shared the same base-model, a PLS-DA model trained on GSE16879 gene expression data, the specific procedures of trans-omic knowledge transfer strongly influence the downstream-inferred biomarkers. Despite these differences, we were able to identify a core set of 50 microbial taxa associated with Infliximab response across all approaches (Figure 3E). Of these, 18 have been reported to be associated with anti-TNF-α response in clinical studies (Table 1).

Table 1. Bacteria abundance in response to anti-TNF treatment in IBD patients

SILVA Genus	Effect
Subdoligranulum	responder baseline↑[21] responder post-therapy↑ [22]
Blautia	responder baseline↑[23] responder after therapy↓[21, 22]
Butyricicoccus	responder after therapy↑[24]
Fusicatenibacter	responder after therapy↑[22]
Roseburia	responder baseline↑[24] responder after therapy↑[25]
Clostridium sensu stricto 1	responder baseline↑[24]
Faecalibacterium	responder baseline↑[26] responder baseline↑ (F. prausnitzii) [21] responder after therapy↑[22, 25] non-responder after therapy↓[22]
Eubacterium hallii group	responder after therapy↑[22] CD responder after therapy↑[24]
Ruminococcacea NK4A214_group	responder baseline↑[24]
Lachnospiraceae NK4A136 group	responder baseline↑[24]
Eubacterium coprostanoligenes group	responder baseline↑[24]
Dialister	non-responder baseline↑ responder after therapy↓[21]
Ruminococcacea NK4A214 group	responder baseline↑[24]
Coprococcus	responder after therapy↓[21]
Ruminococcus gnavus group	responder after therapy↑[24] responder baseline↑[23]
Dorea	responder baseline↑[23] responder after therapy↑[22]
Bacteroides	relapser baseline↓[27]
Eubacterium rectale	responder baseline↑[28]

Faecalibacterium is one of the most abundant bacterial genera in the human intestine, and *Faecalibacterium prausnitzii* is the only known species in this genus [29]. Its abundance is reduced in both CD and UC [30-34]. Recent literature shows that a higher pre- and post-treatment level of Faecalibacterium correlates to a better anti-TNF-α response [21, 22, 25-27], which may result from the anti-inflammatory effect of a high amount of butyrate produced by *Faecalibacterium prausnitzii* [33]. Furthermore, the pre- and post-treatment level of *Blautia*, *Roseburia*, *Dorea,* and *Ruminococcus gnavus group* is also found to differentiate between anti-TNF-α responders and non-responders [21-25, 28, 35], inferring that they may be useful biomarkers for IBD prognostics.

3.3 *Inferring Gut Metabolites Predictive of Infliximab Response*

Similarly, to the microbial taxa Knowledge Transfer models, we used the PLS-DA model trained on UC patients from GSE16879 to examine Trans-omic Knowledge Transfer approaches to identify gut metabolites predictive of Infliximab response using gene expression and stool metabolomics data from IBDMDB (Figure 4). For Supervised Classifier Transfer, we used the same Infliximab response labels inferred for analysis of the 16S rRNA-seq data to train a new PLS-DA model using the IBDMDB stool metabolomics data to predict the inferred IBDMDB Infliximab response labels (Figure 4A). A two LV model (83.4% variance explained) strongly separated IBDMDB samples by predicted Infliximab response and appeared to capture more total variance explained in these samples than the 16S rRNA-seq PLS model.

For Relative Separation Transfer, we used the same projections of IBDMDB samples onto GSE16879 gene expression latent variables used in for the 16S rRNA-seq models in Figure 3. We trained a PLS-R model (2 LV – 69.9% variance explained) using gut metabolomics to predict IBDMDB scores on GSE16879 latent variables and observed that the metabolomics data produced clearer separation of projection scores and captured more sample-to-sample variance than the 16S rRNA-seq data (Figure 4B). For Signature Transfer, we trained a new PLS-R model predicting the IBDMDB Infliximab resistance gene score from the IBDMDB metabolomics data (2 LV - 86.0% variance explained) and observed strong separation of IBDMDB samples by resistance score on the inferred metabolomics latent variables (Figure 4C). Like the microbial taxa data, the clearest separation between samples and the largest variance explained was attributable to the Signature Transfer methodology. The models using the metabolomics data produced clearer separation between IBDMDB samples than the microbial taxa data in all matched cases, potentially due to the greater percent variance captured in the Y-block by the metabolomics data.

We performed VIP analysis of the metabolites in each Knowledge Transfer model to extract Infliximab response-predictive metabolites from each approach. Just like with the 16S rRNA-seq models, when we compared the metabolites across models by VIP score, we observed that there was relatively little consistency between the biomarkers identified by each approach (Figure 4D). This strengthens our observation that while all approaches shared the same base GSE16879 trained model, the trans-omic knowledge transfer approach strongly influence the downstream-inferred biomarkers. Despite these differences, we identified core set of 44 microbial taxa associated with Infliximab response across all approaches (Figure 4E).

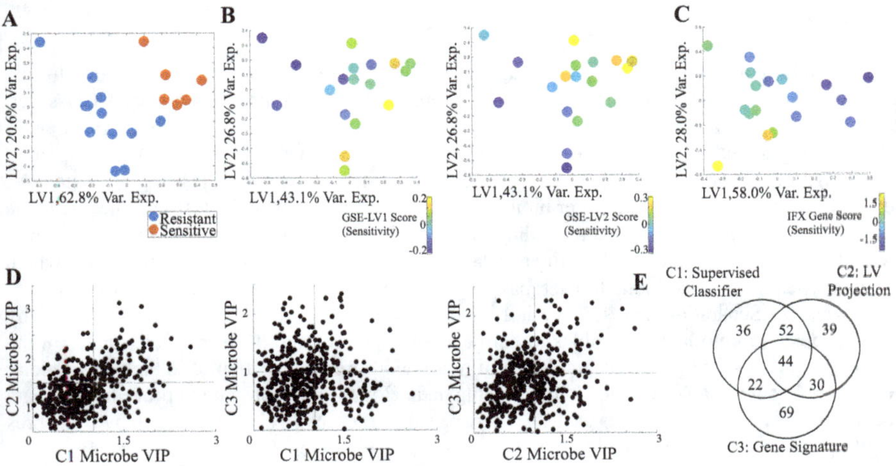

Figure 4. Gut Metabolite Predictors of Infliximab Response. (A) Case 1 Supervised Classifier Transfer. Scores plot for a PLS-DA model predicting IBDMDB inferred Infliximab response classes from gut metabolomics. Infliximab response classes were predicted by applying the GSE16879 trained PLS-DA model to the IBDMDB gene expression data. **(B)** Case 2 Relative Separation Transfer. Scores plot for a PLS-R model trained to predict separation of IBDMDB samples on GSE16879 PLS-DA latent variables from gut metabolomics. Plots are colored by IBDMDB sample scores on GSE16879 latent variables 1 and 2 inferred using IBDMDB gene expression data. **(C)** Case 3 Signature Transfer: PLS-R model predicting IBDMDB Infliximab resistance gene score from gut metabolomics data. **(D)** Comparison of microbial taxa VIP scores from Case 1 (C1), Case 2 (C2), and Case 3 (C3) PLS Knowledge Transfer models. **(E)** Venn diagram of number of Infliximab response-associated taxa (VIP > 1) across models.

Sphingomyelin (d18:1/16:0), a sphingolipid abundant on the apical side of the gastrointestinal epithelial cell membrane and in the myelin sheath of nerve cells [36], significantly increased in the UC mice [37, 38] and ileum of CD human [39]. It was reported that the sphingomyelin level was elevated in anti-TNF-α non-responding IBD patients' serum [40]. This accumulation potentially results from the downregulation of alkaline sphingomyelinase—one of the sphingomyelin digesting enzymes that exhibit anti-inflammatory properties in colitis mice—in IBD [41-43], inferring that the increase of sphingomyelin may correlate to the aggravation of the inflammation, which manifests as the diminished effect of anti-TNF-α. Our model also identified glycine as a core metabolite. It is an amino acid that has been reported to increase in the feces of adult and pediatric IBD patients [44, 45]. The metabolome profile of pediatric Crohn's Disease patients shows a decrease in pediatric CD patients after anti-TNF-α treatment [46]. Given glycine inhibits the TNF-α activity [47], such a decrease could result from the remission. In the same study, sebacic acid, a breakdown product of fatty acids that is normal in urine, was reported to be more abundant in the non-responder. Furthermore, metabolites like leucine, phosphatidylcholine, and arginine are closely related to TNF-α and associated pathways in IBD [48-51]. Their potential as metabolomic predictors of anti-TNF-α response warrants future studies.

4. Discussion

We show that Trans-omic Knowledge Transfer provides a framework for inferring multi-omic biomarkers of phenotypes across cohorts. The approaches we examined, Supervised Classifier, Relative Separation, and Signature Transfer, have methodological and interpretability differences with advantages and disadvantages. Supervised Classifier Transfer is direct application of a supervised model on a test set. New phenotypic labels are inferred in the test set using one data type, and secondary models are built to infer biomarkers in other data types in the test set. The challenge with this approach generally is that the validity of the inferred phenotypic labels cannot be directly assessed and for a binary phenotype, drug resistant or sensitive, the classification threshold at which the phenotypes are defined in the test set may influence the resulting downstream biomarkers.

Relative Separation Transfer partially addresses issues of classification threshold and by using a projection onto latent variables to define a continuum of anti-TNF resistance states in the test set. This allows for continuous modeling of relative differences in samples in the test set along one or more latent variables defined in the training data. However, the projection procedure appears to be the noisiest of the approaches we tested here based on the lack of clear separation by LV scores and interpreting positions on latent variables, rather than a binary phenotype, is challenging.

Signature Transfer is perhaps the most interpretable Knowledge Transfer approach we examined here. Once the gene signature is extracted from the training set, no other features of the model from the training data are retained, all inference of biomarkers is performed in the test set modeling the signature as a dependent variable. The final model thus only aims to characterize the trans-omic relationships in the test set and relative signature score associated with a phenotype. Separation between samples was clearer in this model compared to the Relative Separation approach and the internal consistency of the model mitigates some concerns of predicted class validity in the Supervised Classifier Transfer approach. Though the association of gene signature activity with anti-TNF resistance is still uncertain in this approach, we recommend Signature Transfer as the most rigorous and interpretable Trans-omic Knowledge Transfer approach among those tested here.

Despite the methodological differences in the three approaches, we find that a common set of microbial and metabolite biomarkers of anti-TNF response can be identified. Validation against literature suggests that consensus biomarkers inferred across approaches have potential clinical benefit. A fourth approach to Trans-omic Knowledge Transfer may be to construct multiple models using the same single-omic training and multi-omic test sets and extract the commonly identified trans-omic features for future biological studies. This *Ensemble* approach to Knowledge Transfer may be further augmented by testing multiple classes of prediction models, such as support vector machines, random forests, or neural networks, and extracting the resulting consensus biomarkers.

Our study has some limitations which may be addressed in future studies to extend the approach. While we present important feasibility and proof of concept data here, a disseminatable software toolbox would increase the impact and applicability of our approaches to other problems. Part of this should include additional benchmarking using pairs of multi-omics datasets, varying gene inclusion threshold percent, and withholding select data types to enable more quantitative validation metrics. While not examined here, in principle our frameworks could be expanded to other -omic data types, including proteomics, scRNA-seq, and metagenomics data, provided data types are encoded in latent variables reflective of data-specific distributional properties.

In conclusion, we demonstrate that Trans-omic Knowledge Transfer modeling is a potentially powerful approach for integrating multi-omics and single-omics data across clinical cohorts to discover biomarkers of conditions and phenotypes measured in one or the other cohort. To our knowledge, there are no comparable approaches widely implemented for us to compare our approaches and results to, making this an important first feasibility study of the utility of Trans-omic Knowledge Transfer. The paucity of other methods in this space is likely due to the challenge of validating approaches with quantitative metrics, a limitation we acknowledge and propose a solution to for future methodological studies.

In future work, extensions of this approach could account for cohort-specific covariates in biomarker discover to enhance the robustness of the inferred associations. The ability to re-use clinical multi-omics data to answer novel biological questions adds an important tool to preclinical studies of drug resistance and disease biology. Such methods increase the value of the initial investment to generate the cohort by allowing basic and translational scientists to test new hypotheses through computational models of existing data and to potentially advance new therapies.

5. References

1. Chaudhary, K., et al., *Deep Learning-Based Multi-Omics Integration Robustly Predicts Survival in Liver Cancer.* Clin Cancer Res, 2018. **24**(6): p. 1248-1259.
2. Xiao, Y., et al., *Multi-Omics Profiling Reveals Distinct Microenvironment Characterization and Suggests Immune Escape Mechanisms of Triple-Negative Breast Cancer.* Clin Cancer Res, 2019. **25**(16): p. 5002-5014.
3. Lindskrog, S.V., et al., *An integrated multi-omics analysis identifies prognostic molecular subtypes of non-muscle-invasive bladder cancer.* Nat Commun, 2021. **12**(1): p. 2301.
4. Sacco, K., et al., *Immunopathological signatures in multisystem inflammatory syndrome in children and pediatric COVID-19.* Nat Med, 2022. **28**(5): p. 1050-1062.
5. El Saie, A., et al., *Metabolome and microbiome multi-omics integration from a murine lung inflammation model of bronchopulmonary dysplasia.* Pediatr Res, 2022.
6. Bai, B., et al., *Deep Multilayer Brain Proteomics Identifies Molecular Networks in Alzheimer's Disease Progression.* Neuron, 2020. **105**(6): p. 975-991 e7.
7. Zhou, W., et al., *Longitudinal multi-omics of host-microbe dynamics in prediabetes.* Nature, 2019. **569**(7758): p. 663-671.
8. Schirmer, M., et al., *Dynamics of metatranscription in the inflammatory bowel disease gut microbiome.* Nat Microbiol, 2018. **3**(3): p. 337-346.
9. Fettweis, J.M., et al., *The vaginal microbiome and preterm birth.* Nat Med, 2019. **25**(6): p. 1012-1021.
10. Picard, M., et al., *Integration strategies of multi-omics data for machine learning analysis.* Comput Struct Biotechnol J, 2021. **19**: p. 3735-3746.
11. Chakraborty, S., et al., *Onco-Multi-OMICS Approach: A New Frontier in Cancer Research.* Biomed Res Int, 2018. **2018**: p. 9836256.
12. Head, K.A. and J.S. Jurenka, *Inflammatory bowel disease Part 1: ulcerative colitis--pathophysiology and conventional and alternative treatment options.* Altern Med Rev, 2003. **8**(3): p. 247-83.
13. Rutgeerts, P., S. Vermeire, and G. Van Assche, *Biological therapies for inflammatory bowel diseases.* Gastroenterology, 2009. **136**(4): p. 1182-97.
14. Ben-Horin, S., U. Kopylov, and Y. Chowers, *Optimizing anti-TNF treatments in inflammatory bowel disease.* Autoimmun Rev, 2014. **13**(1): p. 24-30.
15. Papamichael, K. and A.S. Cheifetz, *Therapeutic drug monitoring in inflammatory bowel disease: for every patient and every drug?* Curr Opin Gastroenterol, 2019. **35**(4): p. 302-310.
16. Integrative, H.M.P.R.N.C., *The Integrative Human Microbiome Project: dynamic analysis of microbiome-host omics profiles during periods of human health and disease.* Cell Host Microbe, 2014. **16**(3): p. 276-89.
17. Integrative, H.M.P.R.N.C., *The Integrative Human Microbiome Project.* Nature, 2019. **569**(7758): p. 641-648.
18. Arijs, I., et al., *Mucosal gene expression of antimicrobial peptides in inflammatory bowel disease before and after first infliximab treatment.* PLoS One, 2009. **4**(11): p. e7984.
19. Arijs, I., et al., *Effect of vedolizumab (anti-alpha4beta7-integrin) therapy on histological healing and mucosal gene expression in patients with UC.* Gut, 2018. **67**(1): p. 43-52.
20. Irizarry, R.A., et al., *Exploration, normalization, and summaries of high density oligonucleotide array probe level data.* Biostatistics, 2003. **4**(2): p. 249-64.
21. Ventin-Holmberg, R., et al., *Bacterial and Fungal Profiles as Markers of Infliximab Drug Response in Inflammatory Bowel Disease.* Journal of Crohn's & colitis, 2021. **15**(6): p. 1019-1031.
22. Sanchis-Artero, L., et al., *Evaluation of changes in intestinal microbiota in Crohn's disease patients after anti-TNF alpha treatment.* Scientific Reports, 2021. **11**(1).

23. Park, Y.E., et al., *Microbial changes in stool, saliva, serum, and urine before and after anti-TNF-α therapy in patients with inflammatory bowel diseases.* Scientific Reports, 2022. **12**(1).
24. Dovrolis, N., et al., *The interplay between mucosal microbiota composition and host gene-expression is linked with infliximab response in inflammatory bowel diseases.* Microorganisms, 2020. **8**(3).
25. Wang, Y., et al., *Characteristics of faecal microbiota in paediatric Crohn's disease and their dynamic changes during infliximab therapy.* Journal of Crohn's and Colitis, 2018. **12**(3): p. 337-346.
26. Magnusson, M.K., et al., *Anti-TNF therapy response in patients with ulcerative colitis is associated with colonic antimicrobial peptide expression and microbiota composition.* Journal of Crohn's and Colitis, 2016. **10**(8): p. 943-952.
27. Rajca, S., et al., *Alterations in the intestinal microbiome (Dysbiosis) as a predictor of relapse after infliximab withdrawal in Crohn's disease.* Inflammatory Bowel Diseases, 2014. **20**(6): p. 978-986.
28. Yilmaz, B., et al., *Microbial network disturbances in relapsing refractory Crohn's disease.* Nat. Med, 2019. **25**(2): p.323-336.
29. Lopez-Siles, M., et al., *Faecalibacterium prausnitzii: from microbiology to diagnostics and prognostics.* The ISME Journal 2017 11:4, 2017. **11**(4): p. 841-852.
30. Martinez-Medina, M., et al., *Abnormal microbiota composition in the ileocolonic mucosa of Crohn's disease patients as revealed by polymerase chain reaction-denaturing gradient gel electrophoresis.* Inflam Bowel Dis, 2006. **12**(12): p. 1136-1145.
31. Joossens, M., et al., *Dysbiosis of the faecal microbiota in patients with Crohn's disease and their unaffected relatives.* Gut, 2011. **60**(5): p. 631-637.
32. Machiels, K., et al., *A decrease of the butyrate-producing species roseburia hominis and faecalibacterium prausnitzii defines dysbiosis in patients with ulcerative colitis.* Gut, 2014. **63**(8): p. 1275-1283.
33. Sokol, H., et al., *Faecalibacterium prausnitzii is an anti-inflammatory commensal bacterium identified by gut microbiota analysis of Crohn disease patients.* Proceedings of the National Academy of Sciences of the United States of America, 2008. **105**(43): p. 16731-16736.
34. Swidsinski, A., et al., *Active Crohn's disease and ulcerative colitis can be specifically diagnosed and monitored based on the biostructure of the fecal flora.* Inflammatory Bowel Diseases, 2008. **14**(2): p. 147-161.
35. Sakurai, T., et al., *Mucosal microbiota and gene expression are associated with long-term remission after discontinuation of adalimumab in ulcerative colitis.* Scientific Reports, 2020. **10**(1).
36. Duan, R.D. and Å. Nilsson, *Metabolism of sphingolipids in the gut and its relation to inflammation and cancer development.* Progress in Lipid Research, 2009. **48**(1): p. 62-72.
37. Qi, Y., et al., *PPARα-dependent exacerbation of experimental colitis by the hypolipidemic drug fenofibrate.* American Journal of Physiology - Gastrointestinal and Liver Physiology, 2014. **307**(5): p. 564-573.
38. Fischbeck, A., et al., *Sphingomyelin induces cathepsin D-mediated apoptosis in intestinal epithelial cells and increases inflammation in DSS colitis.* Gut, 2011. **60**(1): p. 55-65.
39. Braun, A., et al., *Alterations of phospholipid concentration and species composition of the intestinal mucus barrier in ulcerative colitis: A clue to pathogenesis.* Inflammatory Bowel Diseases, 2009. **15**(11): p. 1705-1720.
40. Ding, N.S., et al., *Metabonomics and the Gut Microbiome Associated With Primary Response to Anti-TNF Therapy in Crohn's Disease.* Journal of Crohn's & colitis, 2020. **14**(8): p. 1090-1102.
41. Sjöqvist, U., et al., *Chronic Colitis Is Associated With a Reduction of Mucosal Alkaline Sphingomyelinase Activity.* Inflammatory Bowel Diseases, 2002. **8**(4): p. 258-263.
42. Duan, R.D., et al., *Distribution of alkaline sphingomyelinase activity in human beings and animals. Tissue and species differences.* Digestive diseases and sciences, 1996. **41**(9): p. 1801-1806.
43. Andersson, D., et al., *Expression of alkaline sphingomyelinase in yeast cells and anti-inflammatory effects of the expressed enzyme in a rat colitis model.* Digestive Diseases and Sciences, 2009. **54**(7): p. 1440-1448.
44. Bjerrum, J.T., et al., *Metabonomics of human fecal extracts characterize ulcerative colitis, Crohn's disease and healthy individuals.* Metabolomics, 2015. **11**(1): p. 122-133.
45. Kolho, K.L., et al., *Faecal and Serum Metabolomics in Paediatric Inflammatory Bowel Disease.* Journal of Crohn's and Colitis, 2017. **11**(3): p. 321-334.
46. Wang, Y., et al., *Microbial and metabolic features associated with outcome of infliximab therapy in pediatric Crohn's disease.* Gut Microbes, 2021. **13**(1): p. 1-18.
47. Hasegawa, S., et al., *Cysteine, histidine and glycine exhibit anti-inflammatory effects in human coronary arterial endothelial cells.* Clinical and experimental immunology, 2012. **167**(2): p. 269-274.
48. Laplante, M. and D.M. Sabatini, *mTOR signaling in growth control and disease.* Cell, 2012. **149**(2): p. 274-293.
49. Treede, I., et al., *TNF-alpha-induced up-regulation of pro-inflammatory cytokines is reduced by phosphatidylcholine in intestinal epithelial cells.* BMC gastroenterology, 2009. **9**.
50. Treede, I., et al., *Anti-inflammatory effects of phosphatidylcholine.* The Journal of biological chemistry, 2007. **282**(37): p. 27155-27164.
51. Krzystek-Korpacka, M., et al., *Transcriptional and Metabolomic Analysis of L-Arginine/Nitric Oxide Pathway in Inflammatory Bowel Disease and Its Association with Local Inflammatory and Angiogenic Response: Preliminary Findings.* International journal of molecular sciences, 2020. **21**(5).

Multi-treatment Effect Estimation from Biomedical Data

Raquel Aoki†, Yizhou Chen and Martin Ester
School of Computing Science, Simon Fraser University,
Vancouver, British Columbia, Canada
†*E-mail: raoki@sfu.ca*

Several biomedical applications contain multiple treatments from which we want to estimate the causal effect on a given outcome. Most existing Causal Inference methods, however, focus on single treatments. In this work, we propose a neural network that adopts a multi-task learning approach to estimate the effect of multiple treatments. We validated M3E2 in three synthetic benchmark datasets that mimic biomedical datasets. Our analysis showed that our method makes more accurate estimations than existing baselines.

Keywords: Causal Inference, Multiple-treatments, biomedical data

1. Introduction

Consider the following setting: an exploratory study on hearing loss as an Adverse Drug Reaction (ADR) in children under cancer treatment with the drug Cisplatin.[1] While Cisplatin is one of the most effective chemotherapeutic agents for children, reports have also demonstrated that 75-100% of infant patients have hearing loss. Note that patients often receive a drug cocktail, and while a single drug might not lead to ADR, ADR is observed when we have a combination of these drugs. Previous studies[1] pointed out that hearing loss is the result of a combination of factors, such as the patient's age, genetic predisposition, dosage, and exposure to several drugs (more drugs, more heavy metals accumulation in the body, higher the chances of hearing loss). The study's data are the patient's clinical information (low-dimensional), genetic information (high-dimensional), the drugs given to the patient, and the observed ADR.

In Causal Inference notation, the covariates X are the patients' clinical information and genetic information; the outcome of interest Y is the ADR, and each drug is a binary treatment ($\mathcal{T} = [T_0, T_1, ..., T_K]$, where $T_k = 1$ records that the k-th drug was given). Understanding and learning the causal effect of each treatment on the outcome can be used to support doctors in recommending more precise treatments, minimizing ADRs in this example, or maximizing the drug response in other cases. Note that existing treatment effect estimators designed for individual binary treatments could be adopted: For each drug $k \in \{0, ..., K\}$, we fit an estimator using all the other drugs as covariates. However, such an approach assumes the estimator would perform covariate adjustment correctly - and here is where we argue that an estimator that considers the multiple treatments together could be a better alternative for biomedical data.

Recent advances in Machine Learning(ML) are now widely being used to improve Causal Inference methodologies. One example is how ML can improve the covariate adjustment of applications with high-dimensional datasets. Such improvements fit perfectly with the precision medicine vision of developing diagnosis, prognosis, and treatment techniques that consider the individual, often high-dimensional data. Most machine learning methods solve only a single task, i.e. they predict a single target variable. Multi-task learning (MTL) methods,[2] on the other hand, optimize a model to simultaneously solve multiple tasks (or, in our context, treatments). The main argument in favor of MTL is that single-task learning may fail to capture the synergy of multiple treatments, e.g., an additive effect or a genetic predisposition to a certain combination of treatments, but not to individual treatment. Currently, there are only a few methods capable of estimating the causal effect of multiple treatments. Hi-CI[3] considers and models multiple treatments but assumes that only one is assigned to a unit at any given time. The Deconfounder Algorithm (DA),[4] a probabilistic graphical model, works with multiple treatments but has received some recent criticism regarding its assumptions.[5]

Contributions: The main contributions of this paper are as follows:

- We propose the Multi-gate Mixture-of-experts for Multi-treatment Effect Estimation (M3E2), a method to estimate the multi-treatment effect.
- We validate M3E2 in three synthetic datasets that mimic biomedical applications. We also compare our method with three existing baselines.
- We create the repository `github.com/raquelaoki/M3E2` with an implementation of our methods, baselines, and datasets. We also share all the configuration files for reproducibility of our results, with hyperparameters and seeds adopted.

2. Related Work

This work combines the estimation of treatment effects and multi-task learning (MTL).

Estimating Treatment Effects: BART,[6] Causal Forests,[7] CEVAE,[8] and Dragonnet,[9] have explored the estimation of a single treatment effect, using Bayesian Random Forests, Random Forests, VAEs, and neural networks (NN) respectively. The inverse propensity weighting-based methods,[10] meta-learners[11] also focused on binary single-treatments. The Deconfounder Algorithm,[4] Hi-CI,[3] approaches based on the propensity score,[12,13] and others[14–16] aim to estimate multi-treatment effect. However, many of these methods assume that only one treatment is applied to any given unit or consider all the combinatorial interventions, which is infeasible for larger numbers of treatments. Note that several works assume robustness to missing confounders.[4,8,14,17] Their robustness is often built on the assumption that extra information is known, such as a known number of hidden confounders or replacing unobserved confounders with proxies. There are, however, several concerns regarding some of these methods.[5,18] Our proposed method focuses on multiple treatment effect estimation through an outcome model in a multi-task learning neural network architecture and ignorability. By considering all treatments simultaneously, our proposed architecture can learn a better representation of input data and perform a better covariate adjustment than existing baselines.

Multi-task learning (MTL): MTL neural network (NN) architectures aim to optimize a single model for two or more tasks simultaneously. Hard-parameter sharing NN[19] is one of the MTL pillars. Such architecture is composed of a set of layers shared among all tasks and a set of task-specific layers on the top. From the MTL perspective, the Dragonnet[9] has a hard-parameter sharing architecture. Building upon the hard-parameter sharing architectures, the Multi-gate Mixture-of-Experts (MMoE)[20] architecture, where each expert can be seen as a hard-parameter sharing NN, and all the experts are combined through a gate function, which is also trainable. The core idea of such an approach is to improve the model's generalization; plus, it allows experts to specialize in one of the tasks. To put into perspective, an MMoE is to hard-parameter sharing NN what a Random Forest Model is to a Decision Tree. Our proposed method M3E2 uses a MMoE[20] as a component. Our work expands the MMoE architecture to satisfy causal inference assumptions and estimate the multi-treatment effect.

3. MMoE for Multi-treatment Effect Estimation

This section describes our proposed method, M3E2. Its multi-task learning architecture simultaneously predicts the outcome and the propensity scores for each treatment.

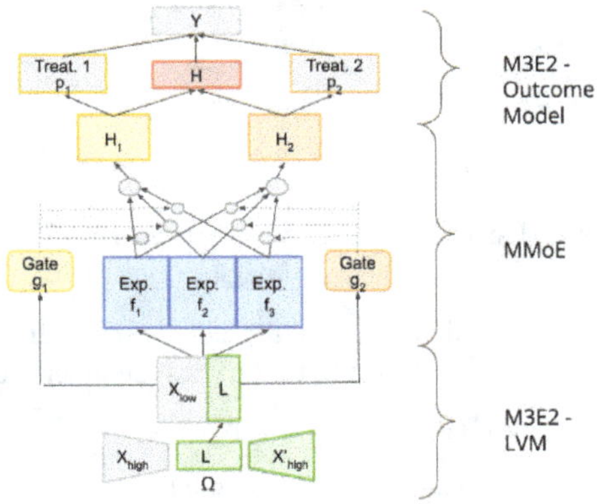

Fig. 1. M3E2 training architecture, for $K = 2$ (two treatments), and 3 experts. It receives as input the covariates $X = [X_{low}, X_{high}]$, and predicts the treatment assignment $\mathcal{T} = \{T_1, ..., T_K\}$ and the outcome Y. The LVM model Ω learns a latent representation L of the high-dimensional covariates X_{high}. The gates g_k, experts $f_e, \forall e \in \{1, 2, 3\}$, and task-specific layers H_1 and H_2 learn a representation H of the input data, and H is used to predict the propensity scores p_1 and p_2 and the outcome Y.

When working with observational studies, one must always describe how the confounders are addressed. Some works assume no unobserved confounders,[6,9,21,22] others try to reduce the bias through latent variables;[4,8,17] while others question if the latent variables are solving the problem at all.[5,18] While exploring alternatives to the ignorability assumption is an interesting research direction, the main focus of this work is the estimation of effect of multiple treatments. Hence, in our work, we assume no unobserved confounders.

Figure 1 illustrates the proposed neural network architecture, with a MMoE,[20] and a Latent Variable Model (LVM) as subcomponents. This architecture predicts $K + 1$ tasks: the outcome Y and K propensity scores p_k. The propensity scores estimate the probability of a treatment being assigned given the covariates ($P(T_k = 1|X)$), and it is important to guarantee the identifiability of the causal effects (Theorem 1). The LVM contributes to the model by efficiently combining low and high-dimensional covariates (section 3.2). The MMoE is an MTL architecture adopted to handle multiple tasks. It contains a combination of experts, gates, and task-specific layers (section 3.3).

One of the strengths of M3E2 is its capacity to estimate the combined effect of a large number of treatments: the M3E2 network only grows linearly with the number of treatments, handling all potential combinations, something that other multi-treatment methods typically struggle to accomplish. Furthermore, the proposed architecture of M3E2 extends the MMoE architecture by incorporating causal inference assumptions through suitable regularizers and adding the outcome model to estimate the treatment effects.

Notation: We define low-dimensional covariates as X_{low} and high-dimensional covariates as X_{high}. An example of the first is clinical variables and, from the latter, genomics information. The split of covariates into low-dimensional and high-dimensional will be explained in Section 3.2. We define the covariates concatenation as $X = [X_{low}, X_{high}]$. The continuous outcome is Y, and K represents the number of treatments. $\mathcal{T} = \{T_0 = t_0, T_1 = t_1, ..., T_K = t_K\}$, where $\mathcal{T}$ could e.g. be the *drug cocktail* taken by a patient.

3.1. *Assumptions*

Assumption 1. Stable Unit Treatment Value Assumption (SUTVA):[23] the response of a particular unit depends only on the treatment(s) assigned, not the treatments of other units.

Assumption 2. Common Confounders and conditional independence:[24] Treatments share confounders. Given the shared confounders, the treatments are independent.

$$T_i \perp T_j | X, \forall i, j \in \{0, ..., K\}, i \neq j$$

Assumption 3. Ignorability - the potential outcome is independent of the treatments given the covariates.

Theorem 1. *Sufficiency of Propensity Score:*[9,25] *If the average treatment effect is identifiable from observational data by adjusting for X, i.e., $ATE = \mathbb{E}_X[\mathbb{E}_Y[Y|X, T = 1] - \mathbb{E}_Y[Y|X, T = 0]]$, then adjusting for the propensity score also suffices:*
$ATE = \mathbb{E}_X[\mathbb{E}_Y[Y|h(X), T = 1] - \mathbb{E}_Y[Y|h(X), T = 0]]$

First, we consider applications with a continuous outcome, binary or continuous treatments, and a set of covariates. Assumption 1 (SUTVA) is standard in Causal Inference. According to SUTVA, the samples are independent and do not interfere with each other. Assumptions 2 and 3 are related to the identifiability of the treatment effect. Assumption 2 assumes no links (dependencies) between the treatments given the covariates, and Assumption 3 assures all back-door paths can be blocked by conditioning on the observed covariates X - guaranteeing the identifiability of the treatment effect.[26] Assumption 2 is also related to multi-task learning (MTL). The ideal use of MTL is when tasks (in our case, treatments) are somehow related. In that case, it is reasonable to assume they also share confounders. The Theorem 1 is presented here as originally proposed, so for the proofs and demonstrations, please check the original publications.[25,27] According to Theorem 1, it suffices to adjust only the information in X that is relevant for predicting the treatment T_k, which is the output of $H_k(X_{L1})$. For multiple treatments, the generalization goes as follows:[27]

$$ATE = E[E[Y|H(X_{L1}), T_1 = t_1, ..., T_K = t_K] - E[Y|H(X_{L1}), T_1 = 1 - t_1, ..., T_K = t_K]]$$

Under these assumptions and theorem, the identifiability comes from the Propensity Score's Sufficiency and the following causal structure: $\mathcal{T} \to Y$, $X \to \mathcal{T}$, $X \to Y$.

3.2. *Latent Variable Model (LVM)*

M3E2 can handle different data types by dividing the input covariates X into two groups, X_{low} and X_{high}. While the Latent Variable Model (LVM) handles the covariates in X_{high}, the X_{low} covariates are fed directly to the experts. The split of the covariates X into X_{low} and X_{high} is defined by the user. Ideally, X_{high} contains high-dimensional covariates, such as gene expression, single-cell data, or image data; and X_{low} contains low-dimensional data, such as clinical variables. Note that, in applications with only one data type, both $X_{low} = \emptyset$ and $X_{high} = X$, and $X_{low} = X$ and $X_{high} = \emptyset$ are acceptable splits.

In applications where $X_{high} \neq \emptyset$, M3E2 uses a LVM to reduce the dimensionality of the covariates in X_{high}. Note that, while there are similarities with other works that adopt proxies to handle unobserved confounders, our LVM component is responsible only for reducing the dimensionality of X_{high}. As described in Section 3.1, our work assumes strong ignorability, a setting with no unobserved confounders. Under strong ignorability, however, we can still have confounding within the observed data. The LVM component, along with the experts, is responsible for extracting a meaningful representation of the input data. These features are used in the covariate adjustment $E[Y|X, T_0, ..., T_k]$, which should close the back-doors and make the treatment effect identifiable. To learn a meaningful representation of X in applications with a mix of high-dimensional and low-dimensional covariates, it was important to find an approach that is capable of combining these different types of covariates. Without the LVM component, the experts could give a disproportional weight to X_{high} covariates, as they would be the majority in X, and even ignore relevant information in X_{low}.

In our experiments, M3E2 adopts an autoencoder with two linear encoder layers and two linear decoder layers. Note, however, that one is free to choose a different architecture or factor model to extract a latent representation of X_{high}. Consider an application with n samples, c_2 columns in X_{high}, c_L as the latent variables size, and the input data X_{high} as a matrix $n \times c_2$. The function $\omega_{enc}(X_{high})$ returns $L_{(n \times c_L)}$, a representation of X_{high} in a lower dimension. Finally, $\omega_{dec}(X_{high})$ returns the reconstructed data X'_{high}, back on $n \times c_2$ space.

3.3. *MMoE Architecture*

In Machine Learning, it is common for a set of shared layers to predict multiple tasks. These architectures are called hard-parameter sharing neural networks. A multi-gate mixture-of-expert (MMoE)[20] architecture contains several experts, where each expert can be seen as a hard-parameter sharing neural network. It was shown that MMoE architectures generalize better,[20] especially in biological applications.[28]

The user defines the number of experts E and the f_e architecture. In the context of multiple treatment effect estimation, the tasks are the propensity score and the outcome Y prediction. The experts' input data is $X_{L1} = [\Omega_{enc}(X_{high}), X_{low}] = [L, X_{low}]$. The ideal number of experts depends on the tasks. Homogeneous tasks might not benefit from many experts and might overfit if the number of experts is too large. Conversely, heterogeneous tasks tend to benefit from a larger number of experts. Note that the definition of homogeneous and heterogeneous tasks is subjective. Here, we define applications whose tasks adopt the same loss as homogeneous tasks. An example would be an application with only classification tasks. On the other hand, heterogeneous task applications contain classification, regression, multi-label, and other potential tasks in the MTL model. The gates control the contribution of each expert to each task. There is a gate g_k per treatment defined as: $g_k(X_{L1}) = softmax(W_K \times X_{L1}), \forall k \in 1, ..., K$, where $W_k \in R^{E \times d}$ is a trainable matrix of weights, E is the number of experts defined by the user, and d is the number of columns in X_{L1}. Finally, note that the gates can be seen as an attention[29] mechanism, learning which experts are more relevant for each task.

3.4. *Task-specific Layers*

The task-specific layers are responsible for predicting the propensity score p_k and the outcome of interest $\hat{Y}$. Each treatment task-specific layer receives as input a weighted average of the experts, where the weights come from the gates associated with that given task. This relationship is formally defined as:

$H_k = h_k(\sum_{e=1}^{E} g_k(X_{L1}) f_e(X_{L1})), \forall k \in \{1, ..., K\}$

In the training phase (Figure 1), the treatment assignment is predicted with the propensity score p_k, estimated as $p_k = P(T_k = t|H_k)$ (for discrete treatments) or $p_k = P(T_k \leq t|H)$ (for continuous treatments using the conditional density $f_{T|X}(t, x)$[30,31]). To estimate the treatment assignment of T_k we only use $H_k, \forall k \in \{1, ..., K\}$. For binary treatments, a softmax activation function will outputs, for each sample, the probability of $P(T_k = 1|H_k)$ and $P(T_k = 0|H_k)$. These predictions are used to calculate the loss of the neural network, as described in Section 3.5. The propensity score losses are used to drive H_k to be sufficient (Theorem 1 - Section 3.1). Note that h_k can be a combination of one or more layers.

Finally, a layer with trainable weights Φ is used to predict the outcome. Consider the input data of this layer as $X_{TH} = [T_1, ..., T_K, H]$, where $T_1, ..., T_K$ are the observed treatment assignments, $H = \frac{\sum_{k=1}^{K} H_k}{K}$, and c_{TH} is the number of columns. The trainable weights layer $\Phi = [\tau_1, \ldots, \tau_k, \ldots, \tau_{c_{TH}}]$ estimates the final outcome as $Y = \Phi \times X_{TH}$. In our context of treatment effect estimation, τ_k is the treatment effect of the treatment k. The Φ works as an outcome model and each weight associated with a $T_i, \forall i \in \{0, ..., K\}$ represents an ATE_i.

Our approach targets additive effect, which is fairly common in biomedical applications.[32] Consider, for example, the ADR study on patients under cancer therapy described in Section 1. Many of these drugs contain heavy metals, and their accumulation can result in adverse drug reactions. Non-linear effects[a] are an interesting extension left for future work.

[a]Note that the linearity only applies to the last layer Φ, not to the autoencoder or the experts.

3.5. *Loss function*

M3E2's loss function is composed of:

(1) Root mean square error loss $\ell_y(Y, \hat{Y}) = RMSE(Y, \hat{Y})$ for continuous outcomes and binary cross-entropy $\ell_y(Y, \hat{Y}) = BCE(Y, \hat{Y})$ for binary outcomes.
(2) Similar to the outcome loss functions, we adopt $\ell_{p_k}(T, T') = RMSE(T_k, \hat{T}_k)$ or/and $\ell_{p_k}(T, T') = BCE(T_k, \hat{T}_k)$ as the propensity score losses, $\forall k \in \{0, ..., K\}$.
(3) $\ell_A(X_{high}, X'_{high}) = RMSE(X_{high}, X'_{high})$ is the autoencoder loss function.
(4) $\frac{1}{2n}\sum_w w^2$ as the L_2 regularization.

As a reminder, while our architecture minimizes the propensity score and the outcome losses, our main target is to obtain estimates of the treatment effects. The treatment effects are a co-product of this model, i.e., the weights associated with the treatments in the trainable layer Φ (See Section 3.4). The model also learns weights in Φ associated with the H; however, these are not considered treatment effects. The total loss is $\mathcal{L} = \alpha\ell_y + \beta\sum_k^K \ell_{p_k} + \gamma\ell_A + \frac{\lambda}{2n}\sum_w w^2$, where α, β and γ are weights. There are two possible ways to define these weights: to adopt them as a hyper-parameter or to adopt an MTL task balancing approach. Modifying both ℓ_{g_k} and ℓ_y to other loss functions is also straightforward.

4. Experiments

In causal inference, the lack of ground truth for real-world applications poses a challenge to its evaluation. Therefore, we adopt three synthetic datasets that have known treatment effects. These synthetic datasets mimic existing biomedical datasets:

- Genome-Wide Association Study (GWAS):[4,33,34] Semi-synthetic sparse dataset with 1000 covariates, 3-10 binary treatments, and continuous outcome. In this dataset, the covariates and treatments are single-nucleotide polymorphisms (SNPs), and the outcome represents a clinical trait. The simulation starts by removing highly correlated SNPs with linkage disequilibrium from the 1000 Genome Project (TGP).[35] Then, a PCA extracts $c = 5$ components from TGP, creating the genetic representation matrix $\Gamma_{v,c}$. The patients' representation matrix is generated as $\Pi_{n,c} \sim 0.9 \times Uniform(0, 0.5)$, where n is the number of desire samples. The covariates are simulated as $X_{n,v} \sim Binomial(1, \Pi_{n,c} \times \Gamma^T_{v,c})$. The set $\mathcal{K}$ contains the index of K columns randomly picked to be treatments. The effect of each covariate is defined as $\tau_i \sim Normal(0, 0.5) \forall i \in \mathcal{K}$(causal effect), else, $\tau_i = 0$ (non-causal effect). Three groups were extracted using k-means(X) to add confounding. Each group $l \in \{1, 2, 3\}$ has an intercept value λ_l and noise distribution $\epsilon \sim Normal(0, \sigma_l)$, $\sigma_l \sim InvGamma(3, 1)$. The outcome is calculated as $Y = \sum_v \tau_v X_{n,v} + \lambda_{l_n} + \epsilon$.
- Copula:[32] This recently proposed dataset also mimics a Genome-Wide Association Study. The Copula, unlike the GWAS dataset, features a fully synthetic dataset. We adopted the setting with four treatments and non-linear outcomes. The covariates are generated as $X_{n,v} \sim Normal(0, \sigma)$, where n is the sample size and v the number of covariates. The treatments are simulated as $T_{n,l} = PCA_1(X_{n,v}) + \epsilon_t, \forall l \in \{1, 2, 3, 4\}$, $\epsilon_t \sim Normal(0, \sigma_t)$, and $Y = 3 \times T_1 - T_2 + T_3 I_{T_3 > 0} + 0.7 \times T_3 I_{T_3 \leq 0} - 0.06 \times T_4 - 4 \times T_1^2 + 2.8 \times \sum_v X_{n,v} + \epsilon_y$, $\epsilon_y \sim Normal(0, \sigma_y)$. The causal effects are $\tau = [1, 0.25, -0.2, 0.1]$.

- IHDP:[6,8,9] the Infant Health and Development Program (IHDP) is a traditional benchmark for single binary treatments. It is supposed to mimic a study on infant development. In that study, the treatment was assigned ($T = 1$) if the child had special care/home visits from a trained provider. The outcome Y is cognitive test scores, and the goal is to measure the causal effect of the home visits. This benchmark contains ten replications of such a study, with 24 covariates and a continuous outcome. We adopt this dataset to compare our proposed method with some of the single-treatment baselines that have been previously evaluated on the IHDP benchmark datasets. [b]

Due to the synthetic nature of the datasets adopted [c], we can calculate the mean absolute error (MAE) between the estimated treatment effect and the true treatment effect. Defining τ_k as the true treatment effect of T_k, and $\hat{\tau}_k$ as its estimated value by one of the methods. As we have multiple treatment effects, we report their average error $\frac{\sum_{k=0}^{K}|\tau_k - \hat{\tau}_k|}{K}$, where K is the total number of treatments. We repeat each combination of (*data* $\times$ *model* $\times$ *setting*) $B = 20$ times, and in our plots, we show the MAE calculated over all these runs:

$$MAE = \sum_{b=0}^{B} \left(\frac{\sum_{k=0}^{K} |\tau_k - \hat{\tau}_k|}{K} \right) \frac{1}{B} \tag{1}$$

A good estimator has estimates close to the true treatment effect values; therefore, *low MAE values are desirable.* We adopt an experimental setting similar to the multi-task learning settings,[20] where the proposed multi-task learning method is compared with other multi-task learning methods and single-task learning models. Among our baselines, the DA[4] is the only method that can estimate the effect of multiple treatments with one model. The CEVAE[8] and Dragonnet[9] are single-treatment methods. We used the author's implementation of the baselines when available. For single-treatment baselines, the multiple treatment effects were estimated as follows: to estimate τ_1, the baseline methods receive as input T_1 as the treatment assignment, and the columns $T_0, T_2, ..., T_K$ are added to X_{low}. We follow this setup for all K treatments. We also performed experiments with BART. However, since CEVAE and Dragonnet achieved better performance results in the recent publications,[8,9] and BART performed poorly on the GWAS and Copula datasets, we decided not to discuss BART in the experimental section.

4.1. *Overall Performance*

Figure 2 shows, for each dataset, the average MAE across all settings. Our proposed method, M3E2, clearly outperforms all baselines on the multi-treatment datasets GWAS and COPULA. On IHDP, a single-treatment dataset, M3E2 was outperformed by Dragonnet, yet, it was better than the other two baselines. Note that our results for Dragonnet on IHDP match the results previously reported,[9] and the estimators' larger variance on the IHDP dataset can be explained by the scale of the true treatment effect. Our main take from Figure 2 is that our method outperforms all the baselines on its ideal use-case: applications with multiple treatment effects.

---

[b]Implementation available at `github.com/AMLab-Amsterdam/`
[c]Implementation available at `github.com/raquelaoki/CompBioAndSimulated_Datasets`

In single-treatment applications, while achieving reasonable results, simpler architectures that target single-treatment estimation like the Dragonnet tend to achieve better performance.

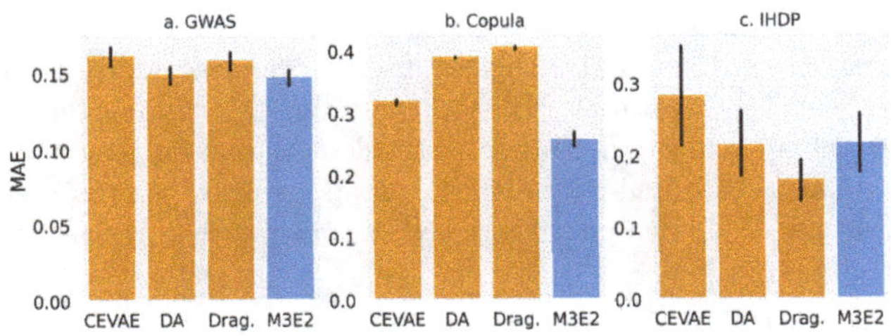

Fig. 2. MAE barplots of the M3E2 and baseline methods. Small MAE values are desirable. The black line indicates a 95% confidence interval.

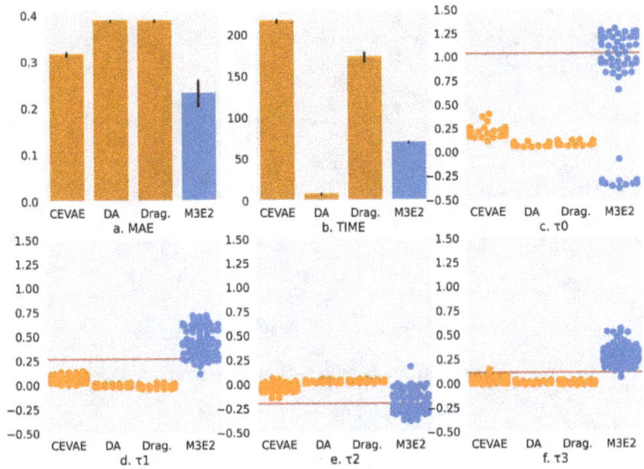

Fig. 3. Copula results for one simulated dataset ($n = 10000, k = 4, v = 10$) with 24 independent repetitions of each model. The baselines' results are shown in orange, our results are in blue, and the red line shows the true effect (c-f).

Figure 3 shows a deeper analysis of the Copula dataset. Figure 3.a shows that M3E2 has the lowest MAE values compared to the other baselines. Figure 3.b shows the total run time of each method in seconds. As a reminder, both DA and M3E2 fit one model for all treatments; Dragonnet and CEVAE, on the other hand, fit one model for each treatment. DA, a probabilistic model, has the fastest running time; M3E2 has the lowest running time among the NN methods. A comparison between the true τ (line in red) and the estimated treatment effects (dots) is shown in Figures 3.c-f. Note that for τ_0 and τ_2, M3E2 is the only method whose estimates are centered around the true value. For τ_1 and τ_3, M3E2 overestimates the treatment effects, yet, it still produces reasonably good estimates. Overall, M3E2 has a good performance. However, we noticed two limitations: First, M3E2 has a larger variance than the other methods; second, for some runs, it estimated values very far from the true treatment effect τ_0. Considering our baselines, while they have a smaller variance, we noticed that DA and Dragonnet often estimated the treatment effect as 0, indicating that these methods might fail to estimate the treatment effect in this dataset correctly, despite achieving reasonable predictive performance. CEVAE was the second-best method; still, its results were never centered around the true values (red lines) and often underestimated the magnitude of the treatment effect.

4.2. *Impact of Dataset Parameters*

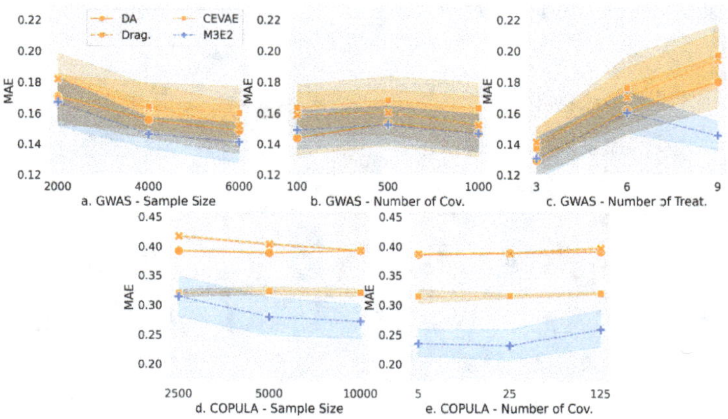

Fig. 4. Impact of the dataset parameters in estimating multiple treatment effects.

We also explored the impact of the dataset parameters in estimating the multiple treatment effects. We focused on three parameters: the sample size, number of treatments, and covariates. Figure 4 shows, in detail, the average MAE and the 95% confidence interval (colored area) for the several settings. Figure 4.*a* and 4.*d* show the impact of the sample size on the GWAS and Copula dataset, respectively. Our proposed method, M3E2, is the method that benefits the most from increasing the sample size. We noticed that all methods are robust to the increase in the number of covariates (Figures 4.b and 4.e), with M3E2 having a small increase on MAE on the Copula dataset with 125 covariates. The most surprising result of all is shown in Figure 4.c. The MAE increases in all baselines with the increase in the number of treatments. Nevertheless, M3E2 achieves better results with nine treatments than with six treatments. Such a result shows that, while the methods are similar regarding the dataset impact on MAE and are quite robust to variations in the number of covariates, M3E2 significantly outperforms all other methods when a larger number of treatment effects are considered.

5. Discussion and Conclusion

In this paper, we have investigated the problem of estimating the effect of multiple treatments in observational data, a setting often found in biomedical applications. To address current limitations, we proposed the M3E2, a multiple treatment effect estimator that uses a MTL neural network architecture. One of the main advantages of M3E2 is its flexibility, as several of its subcomponents can be replaced by alternative implementations, e.g., by different experts, latent variable models, or propensity score predictors. We experimentally compared M3E2 against three baselines on three synthetic benchmark datasets that mimic biomedical applications. The online repository `github.com/raquelaoki/M3E2` contains the code to replicate all the experiments, and we put extra effort into making the M3E2 implementation agnostic to the application; therefore, its deployment in other applications should be straightforward. M3E2 demonstrated promising experimental results and strong evidence that MTL contributed to more accurate estimates of the treatment effects. Nevertheless, there remain several directions for future research. As discussed in Section 3.1, our method assumes ignorability, which is quite limiting in real-life applications. M3E2 also inherits the limitations of other MTL models, in particular, the susceptibility to imbalanced tasks and overfitting. All strengths and limitations considered, we believe that M3E2 has a very good use case with manageable limitations. In future research, we want to apply our proposed method to a real-world dataset that records adverse drug reactions in therapies for treating cancer in infants, moving a step forward toward the precision medicine goal of providing the *right drug at the right dose to the right patient*.[36]

References

1. B. I. Drögemöller, G. E. Wright, C. Lo, T. Le, B. Brooks, A. P. Bhavsar, S. R. Rassekh, C. J. Ross and B. C. Carleton, Pharmacogenomics of cisplatin-induced ototoxicity: Successes, shortcomings, and future avenues of research, *Clinical Pharmacology & Therapeutics* **106**, 350 (2019).
2. S. Ruder, An overview of multi-task learning in deep neural networks, *arXiv preprint arXiv:1706.05098* (2017).
3. A. Sharma, G. Gupta, R. Prasad, A. Chatterjee, L. Vig and G. Shroff, Hi-ci: Deep causal inference in high dimensions, in *Proceedings of the 2020 KDD Workshop on Causal Discovery*, 2020.
4. Y. Wang and D. M. Blei, The blessings of multiple causes, *Journal of the American Statistical Association* , 1 (2019).
5. A. D'Amour, On multi-cause causal inference with unobserved confounding: Counterexamples, impossibility, and alternatives, *arXiv preprint arXiv:1902.10286* (2019).
6. J. L. Hill, Bayesian nonparametric modeling for causal inference, *Journal of Computational and Graphical Statistics* **20**, 217 (2011).
7. S. Wager and S. Athey, Estimation and inference of heterogeneous treatment effects using random forests, *Journal of the American Statistical Association* **113**, 1228 (2018).
8. C. Louizos, U. Shalit, J. M. Mooij, D. Sontag, R. Zemel and M. Welling, Causal effect inference with deep latent-variable models, in *NeurIPS*, 2017.
9. C. Shi, D. Blei and V. Veitch, Adapting neural networks for the estimation of treatment effects, in *NeurIPS*, 2019.
10. M. A. Hernán and J. M. Robins, Estimating causal effects from epidemiological data, *Journal of Epidemiology & Community Health* **60**, 578 (2006).
11. A. Curth and M. van der Schaar, Nonparametric estimation of heterogeneous treatment effects: From theory to learning algorithms, in *AISTATS*, 2021.

12. M. Lechner, Identification and estimation of causal effects of multiple treatments under the conditional independence assumption, 43 (2001).
13. M. J. Lopez and R. Gutman, Estimation of causal effects with multiple treatments: a review and new ideas, *Statistical Science* , 432 (2017).
14. W. Miao, W. Hu, E. L. Ogburn and X. Zhou, Identifying effects of multiple treatments in the presence of unmeasured confounding, *Journal of the American Statistical Association* , 1 (2021).
15. A. Tanimoto, T. Sakai, T. Takenouchi and H. Kashima, Regret minimization for causal inference on large treatment space, in *AISTATS*, 2021.
16. Z. Qian, A. Curth and M. van der Schaar, Estimating multi-cause treatment effects via single-cause perturbation, in *NeurIPS*, 2021.
17. A. Mastouri, Y. Zhu, L. Gultchin, A. Korba, R. Silva, M. J. Kusner, A. Gretton and K. Muandet, Proximal causal learning with kernels: Two-stage estimation and moment restriction, *NeurIPS* (2021).
18. S. Rissanen and P. Marttinen, A critical look at the consistency of causal estimation with deep latent variable models, *NeurIPS* **34** (2021).
19. R. Caruana, Multitask learning: A knowledge-based source of inductive bias, *ICML* (1993).
20. J. Ma, Z. Zhao, X. Yi, J. Chen, L. Hong and E. H. Chi, Modeling task relationships in multi-task learning with multi-gate mixture-of-experts, in *ACM SIGKDD*, 2018.
21. U. Shalit, F. D. Johansson and D. Sontag, Estimating individual treatment effect: generalization bounds and algorithms, in *ICML*, 2017.
22. A. N. Glynn and K. M. Quinn, An introduction to the augmented inverse propensity weighted estimator, *Political analysis* **18**, 36 (2010).
23. D. B. Rubin, Randomization analysis of experimental data: The fisher randomization test comment, *Journal of the American Statistical Association* **75**, 591 (1980).
24. R. Ranganath and A. Perotte, Multiple causal inference with latent confounding, *arXiv preprint arXiv:1805.08273* (2018).
25. P. R. Rosenbaum and D. B. Rubin, The central role of the propensity score in observational studies for causal effects, *Biometrika* **70**, 41 (1983).
26. J. Pearl, Causal diagrams for empirical research, *Biometrika* **82**, 669 (1995).
27. G. W. Imbens, The role of the propensity score in estimating dose-response functions, *Biometrika* **87**, 706 (2000).
28. R. Aoki, F. Tung and G. L. Oliveira, Heterogeneous multi-task learning with expert diversity, *IEEE/ACM Transactions on Computational Biology and Bioinformatics* (2022).
29. A. Vaswani, N. Shazeer, N. Parmar, J. Uszkoreit, L. Jones, A. N. Gomez, Ł. Kaiser and I. Polosukhin, Attention is all you need, *NeurIPS* **30** (2017).
30. K. Hirano and G. W. Imbens, The propensity score with continuous treatments, *Applied Bayesian modeling and causal inference from incomplete-data perspectives* **226164**, 73 (2004).
31. L. Nie, M. Ye, qiang liu and D. Nicolae, Varying coefficient neural network with functional targeted regularization for estimating continuous treatment effects, in *ICLR*, 2021.
32. J. Zheng, A. D'Amour and A. Franks, Copula-based sensitivity analysis for multi-treatment causal inference with unobserved confounding, *arXiv preprint arXiv:2102.09412* (2021).
33. M. Song, W. Hao and J. D. Storey, Testing for genetic associations in arbitrarily structured populations, *Nature genetics* **47**, 550 (2015).
34. R. Aoki and M. Ester, Parkca: Causal inference with partially known causes, *Pac Symp Biocomputing* (2021).
35. G. P. Consortium, A. Auton, L. Brooks, R. Durbin, E. Garrison and H. Kang, A global reference for human genetic variation, *Nature* **526**, 68 (2015).
36. F. S. Collins and H. Varmus, A new initiative on precision medicine, *New England journal of medicine* **372**, 793 (2015).

An Approach to Identifying and Quantifying Bias in Biomedical Data

M. Clara De Paolis Kaluza, Shantanu Jain, Predrag Radivojac
Northeastern University, Boston, MA 02115, U.S.A.

Data biases are a known impediment to the development of trustworthy machine learning models and their application to many biomedical problems. When biased data is suspected, the assumption that the labeled data is representative of the population must be relaxed and methods that exploit a typically representative unlabeled data must be developed. To mitigate the adverse effects of unrepresentative data, we consider a binary semi-supervised setting and focus on identifying whether the labeled data is biased and to what extent. We assume that the class-conditional distributions were generated by a family of component distributions represented at different proportions in labeled and unlabeled data. We also assume that the training data can be transformed to and subsequently modeled by a nested mixture of multivariate Gaussian distributions. We then develop a multi-sample expectation-maximization algorithm that learns all individual and shared parameters of the model from the combined data. Using these parameters, we develop a statistical test for the presence of the general form of bias in labeled data and estimate the level of this bias by computing the distance between corresponding class-conditional distributions in labeled and unlabeled data. We first study the new methods on synthetic data to understand their behavior and then apply them to real-world biomedical data to provide evidence that the bias estimation procedure is both possible and effective.

Keywords: Bias detection, bias estimation, semi-supervised learning

1. Introduction

The development and application of machine learning methods have become commonplace in biomedical sciences and have the potential to transform clinical care.[1,2] Many of those predictive modeling approaches take place in a binary semi-supervised setting; that is, where the prediction outcome is dichotomized and the available data for training and evaluation contains samples of labeled and unlabeled examples. One such scenario is the prediction of the effect of genomic variants as pathogenic or benign, where labeled data contains pathogenic (positive) and benign (negative) variants from databases such as ClinVar[3] and the unlabeled data is often a large reference set of observed variants such as gnomAD.[4]

A traditional approach in semi-supervised learning is to assume that the labeled data is representative of unlabeled data, thus requiring little sophistication during model development, model selection, and performance evaluation. However, a distinguishing feature of real biomedical data is that the labeled examples may not be representative of the unlabeled data; that is, the labeled data may be biased.[5] Data biases can have adverse effects on the ability of models to be optimized for the unlabeled data at hand and can also lead to poor estimation

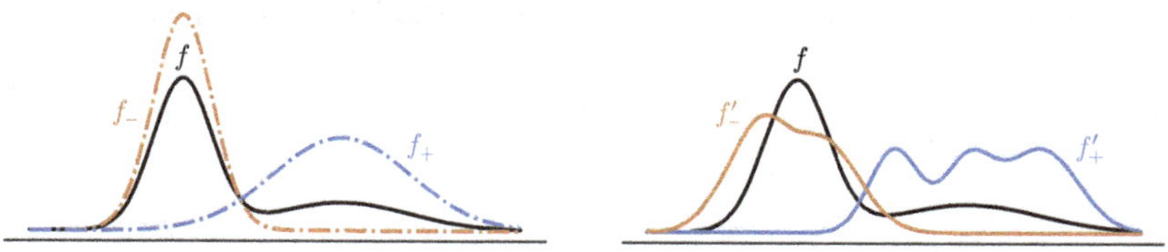

Fig. 1: An illustration of bias in labeled data. Left: unbiased (unobserved, dash-dotted lines) distributions of positive (f_+) and negative (f_-) classes that comprise the (observed, solid line) unbiased mixture distribution $f = \alpha f_+ + (1-\alpha)f_-$, drawn here with $\alpha = 0.3$. Right: the same unbiased observed mixture f together with biased observed distributions of positive (f'_+) and negative (f'_-) classes. The objective of this work is to use datasets from (f, f'_+, f'_-) to estimate the existence and extent of the differences between f_+ and f'_+ and between f_- and f'_-.

of a classifier's performance on a reference distribution.[6] More generally, biased data presents an obstacle to the development of trustworthy methods that are necessary for the societal acceptance of machine learning-based predictive technologies.[7,8]

Learning under sample selection bias is a well-known problem.[9] Early approaches relaxed the assumption of fully representative data by assuming the same class-conditional distributions in labeled and unlabeled data, thus reducing the problem of posterior estimation to estimation of class priors in unlabeled data.[10,11] Other approaches consider situations where at least one class-conditional distribution from which the labeled data is generated is representative of its unlabeled counterpart.[12–15] While such methods have advanced the treatment of sample selection bias, we are not aware of methods that can identify whether and to what extent labeled data differs from unlabeled data for a general form of bias.

The objective of this work is to develop a statistical test for identifying biased labeled data while simultaneously quantifying the level of bias. We assume that the real-world data can be transformed and subsequently modeled using nested mixtures of multivariate Gaussian distributions; that is, with both positive and negative samples being Gaussian mixtures themselves. We then model these class-conditional distributions in both labeled and unlabeled data by the shared underlying component distributions, but permit the proportions at which the data is sampled from those component distributions to differ between labeled and unlabeled data. We finally develop an expectation-maximization (EM) algorithm that learns both individual and shared parameters from the combined data which allows us to identify and quantify bias. Our experiments on synthetic and real-world data demonstrate the ability of this procedure to detect bias and provide useful information to data scientists in their workflows.

2. Problem Formulation

We consider the binary classification problem where input features $x \in \mathbb{R}^D$ are used to predict class label $y \in \mathcal{Y} = \{-,+\}$, where $+$ and $-$ represent the positive and negative class, respectively. Let $p(x,y)$ be the unknown joint distribution that governs how x appears in nature or in a target population of interest and its relationship with y. We refer to $p(x,y)$ as the unbiased distribution, where we expect a classifier to perform optimally. Let $f_+(x) = p(x|y=+)$ and $f_-(x) = p(x|y=-)$ denote the positive and negative class-conditional distributions, respectively. Let $f(x) = p(x)$ denote the marginal distribution over x and $\alpha = p(y = +)$ be the probability that a random point from $p(x, y)$ is positive, the class prior for the positive class. It can be shown that f is a mixture distribution with components f_+ and f_- and mixing proportions α and $1 - \alpha$, respectively; i.e.,

$$f(x) = \alpha f_+(x) + (1 - \alpha) f_-(x). \tag{1}$$

Let L^+ and L^- represent sets of positive and negative labeled examples, respectively and U represent a set of unlabeled examples, available for training. Though we observe examples drawn randomly from $f(x)$ in U, unlike the standard classification setting, we might not observe labeled examples drawn randomly from $f_+(x)$ and $f_-(x)$. Instead L^+ and L^- are drawn from potentially biased class-conditional distributions $f'_+(x)$ and $f'_-(x)$, respectively (Fig. 1). We use the term bias here in a purely statistical sense; the labeled positives and negatives in the observed data are systemically different from those in the unlabeled data such that they cannot be interpreted to be drawn i.i.d. from the same distribution. In this work, we are interested in detecting and quantifying the extent to which the examples in L^+ and L^- differ from the positives and negatives in U, without the knowledge of the class labels in U.

2.1. *Assumptions*

If $f'_+(x)$ and $f'_-(x)$ are arbitrarily different from $f_+(x)$ and $f_-(x)$, respectively, detecting and quantifying the bias is an intractable problem. Fortunately, for most practical settings the biased and unbiased distributions are related. In this work, we employ a (G)aussian (c)omponent-based "(m)ixing (b)ias" assumption (MB-GC),[16] relating the biased and unbiased distributions. Formally, we assume both $f_+(x)$ and $f'_+(x)$ can be expressed as mixtures with the same K^+ shared Gaussian component distributions, but with differing mixing proportions. $f_-(x)$ and $f'_-(x)$ are assumed to be related in the same manner with K^- shared Gaussian components. Mathematically,

$$f_*(x) = \sum_{k \in \mathcal{K}^*} w_k^* \phi_k^*(x) \quad \text{and} \quad f'_*(x) = \sum_{k \in \mathcal{K}^*} v_k^* \phi_k^*(x), \tag{MB-GC}$$

where $*$ is a placeholder for $+$ or $-$; $\mathcal{K}^* = \{1, 2, \ldots, K^*\}$; $\boldsymbol{w}^* = [w_k^*]_{k \in \mathcal{K}^*}$ and $\boldsymbol{v}^* = [v_k^*]_{k \in \mathcal{K}^*}$ are probability vectors; i.e., $w_k^*, v_k^* \geq 0$, $\sum_{j \in \mathcal{K}^*} w_j^* = 1$ and $\sum_{j \in \mathcal{K}^*} v_j^* = 1$; and $\phi_k^*(x) = \phi(x; \mu_k^*, \Sigma_k^*)$ is the D-dimensional Gaussian density function with mean μ_k^* and covariance Σ_k^*. We use the shorthand $\boldsymbol{\mu}^* = \{\mu_k^*\}_{k \in \mathcal{K}^*}$ and $\boldsymbol{\Sigma}^* = \{\Sigma_k^*\}_{k \in \mathcal{K}^*}$ to group the parameters.

It is important to mention that a parametric approximation of the distributions becomes a universal nonparametric approximator as $K^+, K^- \to \infty$.[17] However, picking a large number of components may lead to a complex model prone to overfitting and identifiability issues. We therefore restrict ourselves to a relatively small number of components, up to eight, in each class-conditional representation, as in the parametric paradigm.

Since Gaussian mixture models are effective up to a moderate number dimensions, for high-dimensional data, we employ the MB-GC assumption after dimensionality reduction. Conceptually, we interpret the input feature $x \in \mathbb{R}^D$ as a low-dimensional representation of D_r-dimensional raw features ($D_r > D$) in such cases. It is conceivable that neither the raw features nor the dimensionality-reduced features appear exactly as Gaussian mixtures, especially with a small number of components. In spite of this limitation, we argue that the modern representation learning approaches[18,19] can be used to learn embeddings that do satisfy that property, potentially making our assumptions and methods even more effective.

2.2. *Quantifying Bias*

Although various distance measures can be used,[20] we quantify the bias between f_+ and f'_+ as the area under the ROC curve (AUC) of an optimal binary classifer, or a score function $s : \mathbb{R}^D \to \mathbb{R}$, between them. Based on the probabilistic interpretation of AUC,[21] it is the probability that a randomly drawn example from f_+ achieves a higher score than a randomly drawn example from f'_+, as per an optimal score function. Mathematically, for $\mathcal{S}$ being the family of all real-valued score functions defined on $\mathbb{R}^D$,

$$\text{AUC}(f_+, f'_+) = \max_{s\in\mathcal{S}} \text{AUC}_s(f_+, f'_+),$$

where, correcting for ties, $\text{AUC}_s(f_+, f'_+) = p(s(X_{f_+}) > s(X_{f'_+})) + \frac{1}{2}p(s(X_{f_+}) = s(X_{f'_+}))$; X_{f_+} and $X_{f'_+}$ are random variables distributed according to f_+ and f'_+, respectively. Note that AUC is symmetric; i.e., $\text{AUC}(f_+, f'_+) = \text{AUC}(f'_+, f_+)$. It ranges from 0.5 to 1, with a higher value indicating a larger difference between the two distributions and consequently a larger bias. Typically, values between 0.5 and 0.6 are considered to be small enough that the distributions can be interpreted to be practically indistinguishable. A value of 1 corresponds to a perfect classifier; that is, a situation when the supports between f'_+ and f_+ are distinct. Thus, in this work, a value of 0.5 indicates no bias and a value of 1 indicates maximum bias (Fig. 2).

If samples from f_+ and f'_+ were available, $\text{AUC}(f_+, f'_+)$ could be estimated by first training a classifier to separate the samples, and then computing AUC in the standard manner as the area under the ROC curve. Though a sample from f_+ is not readily available, such a sample is procured using the approach presented in Methods. The bias between f_- and f'_- can be quantified as $\text{AUC}(f_-, f'_-)$ and estimated similarly.

3. Methods

In order to detect and quantify the bias, we derive an expectation-maximization (EM) algorithm from multi-sample Gaussian mixtures. Under the MB-GC assumptions each of L^+, L^- and U contain examples drawn i.i.d. from a Gaussian mixture. Formally,

$$\forall x \in L^*,\ x \sim \sum_{k\in\mathcal{K}^*} v_k^* \phi_k^*(x) \qquad \forall x \in U,\ x \sim \sum_{k\in\mathcal{K}^+} \alpha w_k^+ \phi_k^+(x) + \sum_{k\in\mathcal{K}^-} (1-\alpha) w_k^- \phi_k^-(x),$$

where the second equation for the distribution of U is obtained by combining MB-GC assumptions with Eq. 1 and $*$ is a placeholder for $+$ or $-$. Note that the resultant distribution is a mixture of $K^+ + K^-$ components. The combined data log-likelihood is given by

$$\begin{aligned}\mathcal{L}(\boldsymbol{\theta}; L^+, L^-, U) = &\sum_{x\in L^+} \log\left(\sum_{k\in\mathcal{K}^+} v_k^+ \phi_k^+(x)\right) + \sum_{x\in L^-} \log\left(\sum_{k\in\mathcal{K}^-} v_k^- \phi_k^-(x)\right) \\ &+ \sum_{x\in U} \log\left(\sum_{k\in\mathcal{K}^+} \alpha w_k^+ \phi_k^+(x) + \sum_{k\in\mathcal{K}^-} (1-\alpha) w_k^- \phi_k^-(x)\right),\end{aligned}$$

where $\boldsymbol{\theta} = \{\alpha, \boldsymbol{w}^+, \boldsymbol{w}^-, \boldsymbol{v}^+, \boldsymbol{v}^-, \boldsymbol{\mu}^+, \boldsymbol{\mu}^-, \boldsymbol{\Sigma}^+, \boldsymbol{\Sigma}^-\}$ represent all unknown parameters. To obtain the maximum likelihood estimates of the parameters, we derive the following update equations, under the EM framework.

$$\hat{\alpha} = \frac{1}{|U|}\sum_{x\in U}\sum_{k\in\mathcal{K}^+}\omega_k^+(x;\check{\boldsymbol{\theta}}), \qquad \hat{w}_k^* = \frac{1}{\check{\alpha}^*|U|}\sum_{x\in U}\omega_k^*(x;\check{\boldsymbol{\theta}}), \qquad \hat{v}_k^* = \frac{1}{|L^*|}\sum_{x\in L^*}\nu_k^*(x;\check{\boldsymbol{\theta}})$$
$$\hat{\mu}_k^* = \frac{\sum_{x\in U}\omega_k^*(x;\check{\boldsymbol{\theta}})x + \sum_{x\in L^*}\nu_k^*(x;\check{\boldsymbol{\theta}})x}{\sum_{x\in U}\omega_k^*(x;\check{\boldsymbol{\theta}}) + \sum_{x\in L^*}\nu_k^*(x;\check{\boldsymbol{\theta}})} \tag{EM-update}$$
$$\hat{\Sigma}_k^* = \frac{\sum_{x\in U}\omega_k^*(x;\check{\boldsymbol{\theta}})(x-\check{\mu}_k^*)(x-\check{\mu}_k^*)^T + \sum_{x\in L^*}\nu_k^*(x;\check{\boldsymbol{\theta}})(x-\check{\mu}_k^*)(x-\check{\mu}_k^*)^T}{\sum_{x\in U}\omega_k^*(x;\check{\boldsymbol{\theta}}) + \sum_{x\in L^*}\nu_k^*(x;\check{\boldsymbol{\theta}})},$$

where $\check{}$ and $\hat{}$ are used to represent the current and updated parameters, respectively, during an EM iteration; $\alpha^+ = \alpha$ and $\alpha^- = 1-\alpha$; $\omega_k^*(x;\boldsymbol{\theta})$ is the probability that a given $x \in U$ comes from ϕ_k^*; similarly, $\nu_k^*(x;\boldsymbol{\theta})$ is the probability that a given $x \in L^*$ comes from ϕ_k^*; i.e.,

$$\omega_k^*(x;\boldsymbol{\theta}) = \frac{\alpha^* w_k^* \phi(x;\mu_k^*,\Sigma_k^*)}{\sum_{k\in\mathcal{K}^+}\alpha w_k^+\phi(x;\mu_k^+,\Sigma_k^+) + \sum_{k\in\mathcal{K}^-}(1-\alpha)w_k^-\phi(x;\mu_k^-,\Sigma_k^-)}$$
$$\nu_k^*(x;\boldsymbol{\theta}) = \frac{v_k^*\phi(x;\mu_k^*,\Sigma_k^*)}{\sum_{k\in\mathcal{K}^*}v_k^*\phi(x;\mu_k^*,\Sigma_k^*)}.$$

Starting with an initial value, as discussed in Section 3.3, the parameters in $\boldsymbol{\theta}$ are iteratively updated using Eq. EM-update until convergence, when the relative change in the log-likelihood, $(\mathcal{L}(\hat{\boldsymbol{\theta}};L^+,L^-,U) - \mathcal{L}(\check{\boldsymbol{\theta}};L^+,L^-,U))/\mathcal{L}(\check{\boldsymbol{\theta}};L^+,L^-,U)$, is less than a small predefined threshold (δ) or until the number of iterations reaches a predefined maximum (I).

3.1. *Estimating Bias*

Once $\boldsymbol{\theta}$ is estimated, we use the estimated value of $\boldsymbol{w}^+$ to infer the distribution of the unbiased positives, f_+, as per Eq. MB-GC. In order to estimate the bias in the labeled positive sample, we first subsample from U, to procure a set, $\hat{L}^+$, representing estimated f_+. To this end, we use the responsibility, $r^+(x;\theta) = \sum_{k\in\mathcal{K}^+}\omega_k^+(x;\theta)$, giving the probability that a given $x \in U$ is a positive. Precisely, $\forall x \in U$, if

$$\text{Bernoulli}(r^+(x;\theta)) = \begin{cases} 1 & \text{add } x \text{ to } \hat{L}^+, \\ 0 & \text{discard } x, \end{cases}$$

where $r^+(x;\theta)$ is used as the success probability of the Bernoulli distribution. Once $\hat{L}^+$ is procured, we estimate the bias, $\text{AUC}(f_+, f'_+)$, by training a classifier between L^+ and $\hat{L}^+$ treated as positives and negatives, respectively, and compute the AUC using the classifier's score function. The bias in L^- can be similarly estimated using the responsibility $r^-(x;\theta) = \sum_{k\in\mathcal{K}^-}\omega_k^-(x;\theta)$ to subsample $\hat{L}^-$ from U and then computing the AUC for a classifier trained to separate $\hat{L}^-$ and L^-. For a dataset $S = (L^+, L^-, U)$, we denote the estimated bias as $\text{Bias}_{\text{est}}(S)$.

3.2. *Detecting Bias*

We focus the subsequent presentation on bias detection in L^+ only; the detection of bias in L^- can be approached similarly. Due to model misspecification and errors in the parameter and bias estimation, a bias higher than 0.5 is likely to be estimated, when, in fact, the data is unbiased. To mitigate this issue, we introduce a bias threshold, $\tau \in [0.5, 1]$, and interpret a dataset to contain bias only if its estimated bias is above τ. A higher value of τ would decrease the probability that an unbiased dataset is detected to have bias (type-1 error), $e(\tau)$. However, it will also decrease the probability that a biased dataset is detected to have bias (power), $q(\tau)$. To achieve a low type-1 error and a high power, we determine an appropriate value of τ by controlling for type-1 error on synthetic datasets; see Synthetic Data.

Let $\mathcal{S}_{\text{syn}}^{\text{ub}}$ and $\mathcal{S}_{\text{syn}}^{\text{b}}$ be two families of unbiased and biased synthetic datasets, respectively, where each dataset is of the form (L^+, L^-, U) and bias is defined as per the current context. Let $e_{\text{syn}}(\tau) = |\{\text{Bias}_{\text{est}}(S) \geq \tau,\ S \in \mathcal{S}_{\text{syn}}^{\text{ub}}\}|/|\mathcal{S}_{\text{syn}}^{\text{ub}}|$ and $q_{\text{syn}}(\tau) = |\{\text{Bias}_{\text{est}}(S) \geq \tau,\ S \in \mathcal{S}_{\text{syn}}^{\text{b}}\}|/|\mathcal{S}_{\text{syn}}^{\text{b}}|$ be the fraction of unbiased and biased synthetic datasets with estimated bias above τ, respectively. We define $\tau_\eta = \min_\tau e_{\text{syn}}(\tau) \leq \eta$ as a suitable threshold for which type-1 error computed w.r.t $\mathcal{S}_{\text{syn}}^{\text{ub}}$ is η (typically, $\eta \in [0, 0.1]$); i.e., $e_{\text{syn}}(\tau_\eta) = \eta$. The power computed w.r.t. $\mathcal{S}_{\text{syn}}^{\text{b}}$ at τ_η is $q_{\text{syn}}(\tau_\eta)$. Using this framework, for any real-world dataset $S = (L^+, L^-, U)$, we enable computing a p-value for bias detection as p-value$(S) = e_{\text{syn}}(\text{Bias}_{\text{est}}(S))$, the proportion of unbiased synthetic datasets estimated to have a bias above $\text{Bias}_{\text{est}}(S)$.

Note that estimates of type-1 error, power and p-value computed w.r.t. synthetic datasets are representative of their true values to the extent that they capture the diversity of the real-world datasets. In addition to explicitly diversifying the synthetic datasets to a feasible extent, we address this issue by also estimating type-1 error and power w.r.t. selected unbiased and biased real-world datasets, still using the synthetic data threshold; see Data and Results.

3.3. *Implementation Details*

Initialization Parameter estimates of our algorithm are likely sensitive to the initial parameters; it is known to be the case for the standard EM algorithm (GMM) for a single Gaussian mixture sample.[22,23] Because we have access to labeled data, we leverage it for parameter initialization. However, in order to introduce more diversity to initialization across multiple restarts, we do not use parameters estimates on only labeled data as our initial parameters; e.g., by using parameters from GMM on each L^*. Instead, we initialize parameters in the following steps. (1) Run GMM with K^* components on L^* to obtain initial estimates of $\boldsymbol{v}^*$, for $* \in \{+, -\}$ and save the location parameter estimates $\boldsymbol{u}^* = \{u_k^*\}_{k \in \mathcal{K}^*}$. (2) Run k-means++[24] on unlabeled data U with $K^+ + K^-$ centers. Sort the centers based on the minimum distance to any location in $\boldsymbol{u}^+$. Pick the top K^+ centers to initialize $\boldsymbol{\mu}^+$ and the remaining centers as $\boldsymbol{\mu}^-$. (3) Compute the distance from unlabeled points $x \in U$ to each of the $K^+ + K^-$ centers and assign them to the closest one. This gives an assignment for all points to a cluster which has already been assigned as positive or negative. (4) Use the assignments to compute $\alpha = \frac{\sum_{k \in \mathcal{K}^+} |A_k^+|}{|U|}$, $w_k^* = \frac{|A_k^*|}{\sum_{k \in \mathcal{K}^*} |A_k^*|}$ and $\Sigma_k^* = \frac{1}{|A_k^*|} \sum_{x \in A_k^*} (x_i - \mu_k^*)(x_i - \mu_k^*)^T$, where A_k^+ (A_k^-) indicate points assigned to the k-th positive (negative) cluster.

Model Selection Parameter estimation with EM algorithms when the number of components is unknown is not trivial and many methods exist for model selection.[25,26] We employ the one-fold cross-validation-based information criterion (CVIC)[25] for model selection by running our EM optimization for various values of K^+, K^- and selecting the model that achieves the highest log-likelihood on a validation set.

Hyper-parameters We assume $K \equiv K^+ = K^-$ for convenience in experimentation. We use the maximum number of iterations $I = 2000$ and the convergence threshold $\delta = 10^{-8}$ for termination. We run the estimation on each dataset 20 times with different random seeds.

4. Data

4.1. *Synthetic Data*

To find appropriate bias thresholds and evaluate our method, we generate synthetic Gaussian mixture datasets, following MB-GC assumptions, from known parameters. This allows us to control bias directly and evaluate performance for different levels of bias in the dataset.

Here f_+ and f_- are both K-component Gaussian mixtures. Their parameters are determined by a given AUC(f_+, f_-) range (e.g., $[0.65, 0.7]$) and mutual irreducibility parameters, support ($\sigma = 0.01$) and pairwise responsibility threshold ($\rho = 0.9$), governing the overlap between each pair of components. Let ϕ_i and ϕ_j be two of the $2K$ components and let Z_i and Z_j be samples of 1000 examples each, drawn from ϕ_i and ϕ_j, respectively. If more than σ fraction of points in Z_i have $\phi_i(\cdot) \geq \rho(\phi_i(\cdot) + \phi_j(\cdot))$ and, similarly, more than σ fraction of points in Z_j have $\phi_j(\cdot) \geq \rho(\phi_i(\cdot) + \phi_j(\cdot))$, then ϕ_i and ϕ_j are considered to be approximately mutually irreducible.[27] Starting with random values for the location and shape parameters for each component as well as the mixing proportions $\boldsymbol{w}^+$ and $\boldsymbol{w}^-$ of the two mixtures (drawn from a flat Dirichlet distribution), the parameters are perturbed until AUC(f_+, f_-), evaluated with $f_+(\cdot)/f_-(\cdot)$ as the score function (known to be optimal), lies in the desired range and all pairs of the $2K$ components are approximately mutually irreducible w.r.t. σ and ρ.

We generate 1000 unbiased datasets for each combination of dimensions $D \in \{1, 2, 8, 16\}$ and number of components $K \in \{2, 4, 8\}$. The class prior α is sampled uniformly from the range $[0.01, 0.99]$ for each dataset. Seven AUC(f_+, f_-) ranges, $[0.65, 0.7], [0.7, 0.75], \ldots, [0.95, 1]$ are approximately equally represented in the 1000 datasets for each setting. For the unbiased datasets, f'_+ and f'_- are set equal to f_+ and f_-, respectively.

To evaluate performance of bias estimation against known values of bias, we generate 1750 datasets for each dimension and number of components for varying levels of bias AUC(f_+, f'_+) between 0.5 and 1 (Fig. 2b). First α, f_+ and f_- are generated as for the unbiased data, where the seven AUC(f_+, f_-) ranges are equally represented across the 1750 datasets. A desired range of bias is achieved by drawing random mixing proportions, $\boldsymbol{v}^+$, from a flat Dirichlet distribution until AUC(f_+, f'_+) computed with the optimal score function $f_+(\cdot)/f'_+(\cdot)$ is in the target bias range. The five bias ranges $[0.5, 0.6], [0.6, 0.7], \ldots, [0.9, 1]$ are equally represented across the datasets. For simplicity, f'_- is set equal to f_-.

Each dataset has 100,000 unlabeled points from $f = \alpha f_+ + (1-\alpha) f_-$ and 5,000 labeled points from each f'_+ and f'_- with the chosen parameters. Figure 2a shows examples of 1D distributions for different values of AUC(f_+, f_-) within the range we use to sample synthetic data. These examples illustrate the complexity of synthetic datasets; even for higher AUC(f_+, f_-), the positive and negative distributions are not easily distinguished.

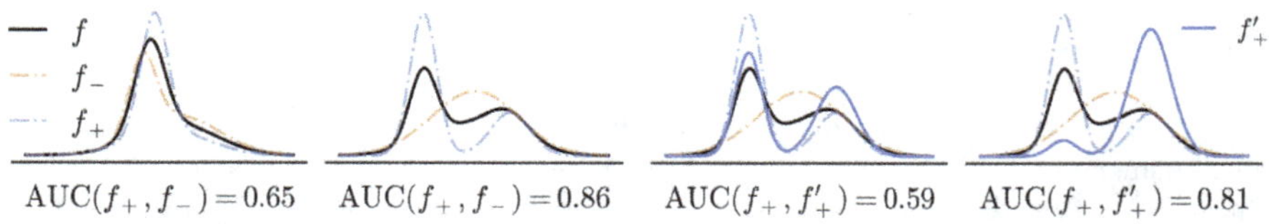

(a) Positive f_+ and negative f_- classes (b) Bias in positive samples

Fig. 2: Synthetic data in one dimension. Examples of (a) low and high AUC(f_+, f_-) and (b) low and high bias AUC(f_+, f'_+). Unlabeled mixtures f shown here with $\alpha = 0.5$ in all cases.

4.2. *Biomedical Data*

We selected 8 biomedical datasets from the the UCI Machine Learning Repository[28] to apply our methods. The following datasets were used, with a note that for each we give the number of examples, the fraction of examples from the positive class (α) and the number of features D in parentheses: Activity recognition with healthy older people using a wearable sensor[29] (52481, 0.29, 8), Epileptic Seizure Recognition[30] (11500, 0.18, 178), Smartphone-Based Recognition of Human Activities and Postural Transitions[31] (10929, 0.16, 561), Mushroom[28] (8124, 0.21, 126), HIV-1 protease cleavage[32] (6590, 0.20, 160), Splice-junction Gene Sequences[33] (3190, 0.24, 287), Parkinsons Telemonitoring[34] (5875, 0.48, 20), and Physicochemical Properties of Protein Tertiary Structure[28] (45730, 0.13, 9).

Datasets were constructed by assigning one class as positive and the remaining as negative for multi-class data or setting a threshold for regression data. For each problem, 100 unbiased datasets were generated by selecting a subset of labeled points uniformly. We generate 250 biased datasets for each biological dataset through Markov sampling. First a point x_i is selected uniformly at random from the positive class. The same point is resampled with some probability p_{stay} and a new point x_j is selected with probability $1 - p_{\text{stay}}$. The transition probability $\Pr(x_j|x_i)$ is proportional to the inverse of the squared Euclidean distance between points $||x_i - x_j||^2$. Since the true bias cannot be measured directly, we use the probability of resampling p_{stay} as a proxy for bias. Higher values of p_{stay} correspond to higher bias in labeled data since the feature space will be less uniformly sampled (Fig. 3). In each case, 20% of points are held out as a validation set used for model selection. We reduce the dimensionality with PCA for datasets with more than 8 features.

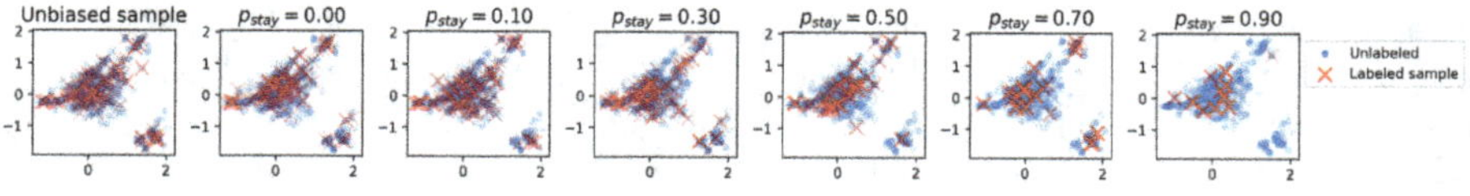

Fig. 3: Unbiased (far left) and biased samples from the dataset HIV[32] with varying probability of resampling a point p_{stay}. Features are illustrated projected onto the first two principal components.

5. Experiments

Empirical Null Distribution and Bias Threshold We use synthetic Gaussian mixture datasets to determine the bias threshold for a range of dimensions $D \in \{1, 2, 8, 16\}$ and number of components $K \in \{2, 4, 8\}$. We consider bias in positive class, but the method for estimating bias in the negative class or both would follow the same process. We run the EM optimization on each unbiased dataset to estimate all unknown parameters, $\boldsymbol{\theta}$. We use the estimated parameters $\widehat{\boldsymbol{\theta}}$ to compute the estimated bias for the positive class, $\text{AUC}(\widehat{f_+}, \widehat{f'_+})$, where $\widehat{\cdot}$ indicates the parameters estimated by the optimization procedure and the distributions parameterized by them. The true bias $\text{AUC}(f_+, f'_+)$ for these datasets is exactly 0.5 since the distributions are identical (no bias), but because there is error in the estimation $\widehat{\boldsymbol{\theta}}$, $\text{AUC}(\widehat{f_+}, \widehat{f'_+}) \geq 0.5$. For each setting of dimension D and number of components K used to generate the datasets, we determine $\tau_\eta(D, K)$ for $\eta \in \{0.05, 0.10\}$ of datasets with $\text{AUC}(\widehat{f_+}, \widehat{f'_+}) \geq \tau_\eta(D, K)$.

Model Selection To apply the appropriate bias threshold $\tau_\eta(D, K)$ to any data it is important to know the number of components that best represent the data and use the threshold found for that setting (dimension is known). However, the true or best value of K is not generally known for any dataset. We evaluate the effect of unknown K for finding the threshold τ_η by running the optimization on unbiased datasets for $K \in \{2, 4, 8\}$ on all datasets, regardless of which value was used to generate the data. For each dataset, we compute the estimated parameters log-likelihood on a validation set and choose the model that maximizes the value. The validation set is generated with the same parameters as the original dataset.

Bias Quantification and Detection To evaluate our method in detecting and estimating bias, we run our EM optimization algorithm on synthetic and biological datasets with varying amount of bias and report the estimated bias. For synthetic data where the true bias is known, we evaluate power for each level of type-1 error, $\eta \in \{0.05, 0.10\}$. Ground truth biased datasets $\mathcal{B}$ are those where the true bias $\text{AUC}(f_+, f'_+) > 0.5$, for K number of components. Predicted biased datasets $\widehat{\mathcal{B}}$ are those where $\text{AUC}(\widehat{f_+}, \widehat{f'_+}) \geq \tau_\eta(D, \widehat{K})$ for $\widehat{K}$ selected through model selection. Power is estimated as $q(\tau) = |\widehat{\mathcal{B}}|/|\mathcal{B}|$.

6. Results and Discussion

Figure 4 illustrates the thresholds found for each dimension and number of components. When the number of components, K, is smaller, parameter estimation more reliably estimates the bias lower. As the number of dimensions and number of components increases, so does the complexity of the optimization problem and the estimated value of bias. These results suggest the utility of finding dimension- and component-specific thresholds, and the empirical null distribution for ascertaining bias.

Results on quantification of bias on synthetic (Fig. 5) and biomedical (Fig. 6) data show increasing estimated bias as true bias increases. Note that for biomedical datasets the true bias is unknown and p_{stay} is not a direct measurement of bias; different data sets have different levels of compactness in their feature space. Since the sampling probability is proportional to the inverse distance between points, the bias is also dependent on the density of points. Bias will

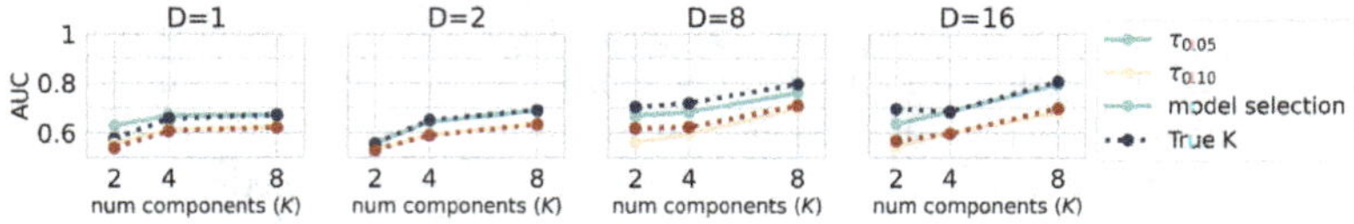

Fig. 4: Bias ($\text{AUC}(f_+, f'_+)$) thresholds found from parameter estimation on unbiased data sets.

differ across datasets for the same value of p_{stay} and estimated bias cannot be directly compared between datasets. However, for each datasets bias should increase as the sampling less uniform, *i.e.* p_{stay} increases. In synthetic data, we see excellent power (Fig. 7) for the type-1 error of 0.05 across all levels of bias, dimensionality D and the number of components (K) per class-conditional distribution. We also see for high-bias datasets ($\text{AUC}(f_+, f'_+) \geq 0.9$) on datasets with two components, that some datasets have a low estimated bias. Our investigation showed that to generate datasets with high bias and few components, the mixing proportions w_k^+ or v_k^+ must be very skewed, making the optimization difficult, sometimes unrealistically so. For one dimension, the average minimum value of the smallest w_k^+ for datasets with $\text{AUC}(f_+, f'_+) \geq 0.9$ is 0.01, 0.07 for $0.8 \leq \text{AUC}(f_+, f'_+) < 0.9$, and 0.19-0.23 for $\text{AUC}(f_+, f'_+) < 0.8$.

Figure 7 shows the power for bias detection on synthetic datasets for type-1 error $\eta \in \{0.05, 0.10\}$. For each setting we see generally higher power in bias detection as the true bias increases. For higher type-1 error, the detection achieves a higher power. Again there is a drop in performance for $K = 2$ in high-bias datasets due to the challenging nature of these datasets.

For real datasets we also show that our estimation of α and negative bias is not generally affected by increasingly biased samples of the positive class (Fig. 6, middle and bottom rows, respectively). Our EM algorithm is still able to detect that the set of unbiased labels from the negative class are truly unbiased (a low value of $\text{AUC}(\widehat{f_-}, \widehat{f'_-})$). The estimation for bias for negative class in UCI results is consistently better than the estimation of bias for unbiased positive samples because α is always less than or equal to 0.5. Higher estimated bias in negatives seems to be correlated with overestimation of the class prior α, particularly exemplified in the parkinsons dataset.

7. Conclusion

Despite a broad awareness that biased data may adversely impact the deployment of machine learning tools in biomedicine, there is a surprising dearth of methods built to ascertain the existence and the level of bias in available data. We set out to address this deficiency by developing and extensively evaluating a bias estimation method based on reasonable assumptions. We used synthetic and real-world biomedical data to show that technologies for bias detection and ultimately correction can be realistically implemented in future data processing pipelines.

Code

The source code for this project is available at `https://github.com/claradepaolis/bi-est`

Acknowledgements

The authors acknowledge the support by the NIH grants U01HG012022 and R01HD101246.

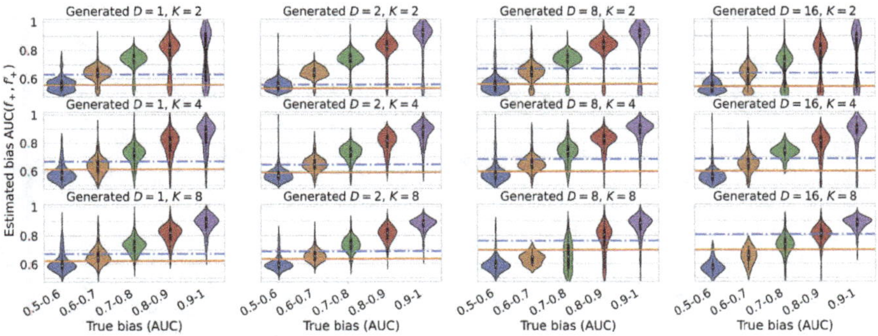

Fig. 5: Estimated bias on Gaussian mixtures with varying true bias AUC(f_+, f'_+). Bias thresholds $\tau_{0.05}, \tau_{0.10}$ shown as dash-dotted and solid lines, respectively.

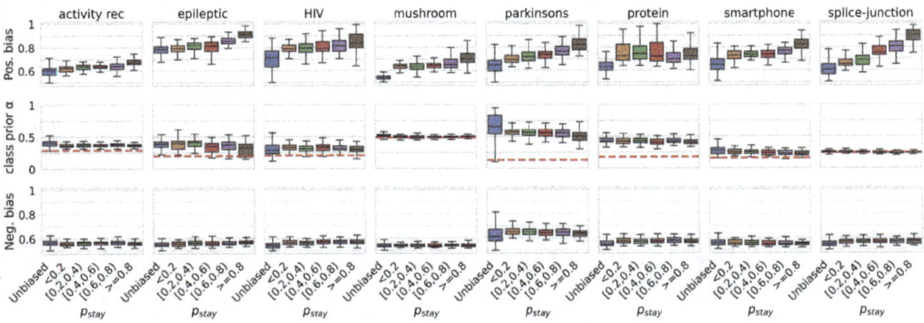

Fig. 6: Bias and parameter estimation for biomedical datasets. Each column shows results for samples from each dataset. Top: Bias estimation for positive class for unbiased (leftmost) and biased sampled datasets for increasing levels of p_{stay}, corresponding to larger bias. Middle: Estimation of the class prior α with true value shown as dashed line. Bottom: Bias estimation for negative class, which is unbiased in each case.

References

1. K. B. Johnson *et al.*, *Clin Transl Sci* **14**, 86 (2021).
2. P. Rajpurkar *et al.*, *Nat Med* **28**, 31 (2022).
3. M. J. Landrum *et al.*, *Nucleic Acids Res* **44**, D862 (2016).
4. K. J. Karczewski *et al.*, *Nature* **581**, 434 (2020).
5. T. Stoeger *et al.*, *PLoS Biol* **16**, p. e2006643 (2018).
6. B. Yu and K. Kumbier, *Proc Natl Acad Sci U S A* **117**, 3920 (2020).
7. L. Szabo, Artificial intelligence is rushing into patient care–and could raise risks, *Scientific American* **12** (2019).
8. R. Schwartz *et al.*, *Draft NIST Special Publication 1270* (2021).
9. J. Heckman, *Econometrica* **47**, 153 (1979).

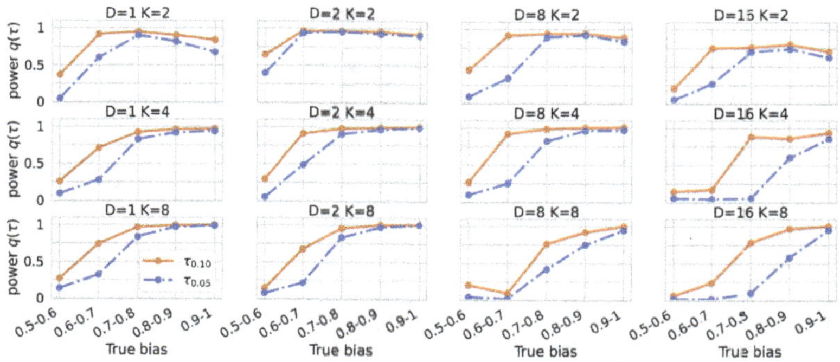

Fig. 7: Power $q(\tau)$ of bias prediction for type-1 error $\eta \in \{0.05, 0.10\}$ on unbiased datasets.

10. S. Vucetic and Z. Obradovic, Classification on data with biased class distribution, in *ECML*, 2001.
11. M. Saerens *et al.*, *Neural Comput* **14**, 21 (2002).
12. B. Zadrozny, Learning and evaluating classifiers under sample selection bias, in *ICML*, 2004.
13. J. Huang *et al.*, Correcting sample selection bias by unlabeled data, in *NeurIPS*, 2006.
14. C. Cortes *et al.*, Sample selection bias correction theory, in *ALT*, 2008.
15. Y. G. Hsieh *et al.*, Classification from positive, unlabeled and biased negative data, in *ICML*, 2019.
16. S. Jain *et al.*, Class prior estimation with biased positives and unlabeled examples, in *AAAI*, 2020.
17. W. Feller, *An introduction to probability and its applications* (Wiley, 1966).
18. M. Śmieja *et al.*, *IEEE Trans Neural Netw Learn Syst* **32**, 3930 (2020).
19. Y. Uğur *et al.*, *Entropy* **22**, p. 213 (2020).
20. M. M. Deza and E. Deza, *Encyclopedia of distances* (Springer, 2013).
21. J. Hanley and B. J. McNeil, *Radiology* **143**, 29 (1982).
22. G. J. McLachlan and T. Krishnan, *The EM algorithm and extensions* (Wiley, 2007).
23. J.-P. Baudry and G. Celeux, *Stat Comput* **25**, 713 (2015).
24. S. Vassilvitskii and D. Arthur, k-means++: The advantages of careful seeding, in *SODA*, 2006.
25. G. J. McLachlan and S. Rathnayake, *WIREs Data Mining Knowl Discov* **4**, 341 (2014).
26. T. Huang *et al.*, *Stat Sin* **27**, 147 (2017).
27. S. Jain *et al.*, Estimating the class prior and posterior from noisy positives and unlabeled data, in *NeurIPS*, 2016.
28. D. Dua and C. Graff, UCI machine learning repository (2017).
29. R. L. S. Torres *et al.*, Sensor enabled wearable RFID technology for mitigating the risk of falls near beds, in *RFID*, 2013.
30. R. G. Andrzejak *et al.*, *Phys Rev E* **64**, p. 061907 (2001).
31. J.-L. o. Reyes-Ortiz, *Neurocomputing* **171**, 754 (2016).
32. T. Rögnvaldsson *et al.*, *Bioinformatics* **31**, 1204 (2015).
33. M. Noordewier *et al.*, Training knowledge-based neural networks to recognize genes in DNA sequences, in *NeurIPS*, 1990.
34. A. Tsanas *et al.*, *IEEE Trans Biomed Eng* **57**, 884 (2010).

Multi-objective prioritization of genes for high-throughput functional assays towards improved clinical variant classification

Yile Chen[1†], Shantanu Jain[2†], Daniel Zeiberg[2], Lilia M. Iakoucheva[3], Sean D. Mooney[1], Predrag Radivojac[2*], Vikas Pejaver[4*]

[1] *University of Washington, Seattle, WA,* [2] *Northeastern University, Boston, MA,* [3] *University of California San Diego, La Jolla, CA,* [4] *Icahn School of Medicine at Mount Sinai, New York, NY*

The accurate interpretation of genetic variants is essential for clinical actionability. However, a majority of variants remain of uncertain significance. Multiplexed assays of variant effects (MAVEs), can help provide functional evidence for variants of uncertain significance (VUS) at the scale of entire genes. Although the systematic prioritization of genes for such assays has been of great interest from the clinical perspective, existing strategies have rarely emphasized this motivation. Here, we propose three objectives for quantifying the importance of genes each satisfying a specific clinical goal: (1) Movability scores to prioritize genes with the most VUS moving to non-VUS categories, (2) Correction scores to prioritize genes with the most pathogenic and/or benign variants that could be reclassified, and (3) Uncertainty scores to prioritize genes with VUS for which variant pathogenicity predictors used in clinical classification exhibit the greatest uncertainty. We demonstrate that existing approaches are sub-optimal when considering these explicit clinical objectives. We also propose a combined weighted score that optimizes the three objectives simultaneously and finds optimal weights to improve over existing approaches. Our strategy generally results in better performance than existing knowledge-driven and data-driven strategies and yields gene sets that are clinically relevant. Our work has implications for systematic efforts that aim to iterate between predictor development, experimentation and translation to the clinic.

Keywords: Multiplexed Assays of Variant Effect; MAVE; clinical variant classification; variant pathogenicity prediction, gene prioritization.

1. Introduction

The American College of Medical Genetics and Genomics (ACMG) and the Association for Molecular Pathology (AMP) have developed guidelines to standardize the practice of clinical variant classification and interpretation.[1] These guidelines group the disparate sources of information about a genetic variant into different lines of evidence, weigh them in terms of evidential strength, and provide rules to combine these differently weighted lines of evidence to assign a variant to one of five classes: pathogenic, likely pathogenic, benign, likely benign or a variant of uncertain significance (VUS). Despite the tremendous progress that the ACMG/AMP guidelines have brought about, a substantial number of variants, particu-

† These authors contributed equally

∗ To whom correspondence should be addressed (vikas.pejaver@mssm.edu) larly missense, remain VUS due to the limited availability of evidence.[2] Furthermore, variants assigned to the remaining four classes are often reclassified due to initial misclassification.[3]

Among the evidential lines, functional evidence derived from *in vitro* assays holds the potential to address aforementioned challenges, as they are weighted highly in the ACMG/AMP guidelines. In particular, multiplexed assays of variant effects (MAVEs) can query the functional impact of all possible amino acid substitutions at every position in a protein within a single assay, allowing for the construction of a variant effect map for all missense variants for a gene.[4,5] However, only a limited number of genes have been assayed with the explicit intent of addressing the goal of clinical variant interpretation.

Historically, the selection of genes for MAVEs and functional characterization has been driven by study-specific motivations, including the study of sequence-structure-function relationships,[6] the characterization of biologically or medically important genes[7] and the development of new technology.[8] This is typically done on the basis of prior knowledge and expertise and is likely to recapitulate preferences for well-studied genes.[9] With the accumulation of large numbers of clinically interpreted variants in knowledgebases such as ClinVar,[10] it is now feasible to devise data-driven strategies to more directly address clinical objectives when prioritizing genes for MAVEs. To date, only one study has sought to systematically prioritize genes explicitly for clinical decision-making.[2] This study proposed a difficulty-adjusted impact score (DAIS) that accounted for the number of VUS in each gene, after adjusting for gene length, and up-weighted those that appeared in multiple patients and for which classifications were most likely to be impacted upon adding new functional evidence.

To the best of our knowledge, none of these strategies have incorporated computational predictors of variant pathogenicity. Variant pathogenicity predictors assign scores to each variant indicative of their pathogenicity based on different features such as sequence context, evolutionary history, protein structure and function, among others.[11] Recent work has suggested that at appropriate score thresholds, some predictors can provide strong evidence for both pathogenicity and benignity as per the ACMG/AMP guidelines.[12] This motivates an alternative strategy that uses computational variant pathogenicity predictors to guide the selection of genes for MAVEs such that when functional and predictive evidence are combined, they will be of sufficient strength to impact the overall clinical classifications of a large set of variants across different genes.

Here, we define three objectives for gene prioritization for MAVEs that improve clinical variant classification and operationalize these objectives through the use of variant pathogenicity predictors. We formalize the process of prioritizing genes for MAVEs solely from the perspective of clinical variant classification and define three objectives (two direct and one indirect) that are desirable in this context. The first two were devised to (1) move the most VUS towards more definitive classifications of pathogenicity or benignity, and (2) reassess and possibly correct existing classifications of the highest numbers of pathogenic and/or benign variants. The third objective emphasizes the use of MAVEs as a means to improve pathogenicity predictors themselves, which in turn, when combined with MAVE data can reclassify VUS. We then quantify to what extent the genes that have already been assayed in the literature or are registered to be assayed by MAVEs fulfill these objectives, along with other potential strategies that one could adopt. Finally, we present and evaluate alternative strategies to prioritize genes such that these objectives are optimized individually and when combined.

2. Methods

2.1. *Data collection*

ClinVar variants. We extracted all missense variants in ClinVar (October 2021) and separated them by the category of clinical significance: Pathogenic (P), Likely Pathogenic (LP), Benign (B), Likely Benign (LB), variants of uncertain significance (VUS), and variants with conflicting interpretations of pathogenicity for each gene. The ClinVar data set contained 11,281 genes with 402,721 missense variants (Supp. Table 1).

gnomAD variants. VUS in ClinVar are likely to accumulate in a biased manner due to differences in the frequency with which different genes are tested. At the gene-level, variants in population-scale sequencing resources such as gnomAD accumulate in a less biased manner as all genes are likely to be uniformly sampled. To this end, we extracted missense variants from gnomAD (v2.1.1 GRCh38 dataset) as an additional set of variants that are not annotated as P, LP, B or LB.[13] Only variants with genotype quality (GQ) $\geq$ 20 and depth (DP) $\geq$ 10 were retained. We identified 17,988 genes that had 4,542,252 missense variants.

Genes with MAVEs. We extracted genes from three resources: MaveDB,[14] VariantEffect (`https://github.com/VariantEffect/MaveReferences`), and MaveRegistry,[15] to create a representative set of genes with functional data. The first two record and maintain information on which genes have been subject to MAVEs either by submission to the resource or by reviewing the literature. MaveRegistry hosts information on which genes are currently being assayed or are expected to be assayed in the near future. After accounting for overlaps between these resources, we were left with a set of 94 assayed genes.

2.2. *Data pre-processing*

We treated P, LP, and P/LP as a single pathogenic category; B, LB, and B/LB as a single benign category; VUS and conflicting interpretations of pathogenicity as the VUS category. Motivated by the clinical objectives that we define in Section 2.4, we only retained genes that had at least one VUS and at least one pathogenic or benign variant in the ClinVar data set, reducing our data set to 3,981 genes. Considering the increased difficulty in mapping variant effects for longer proteins, we removed genes that were longer than genes previously assayed by MAVEs. We also removed genes that were shorter than those previously assayed because these genes may have had too few known variants to justify prioritization for MAVEs. Only genes that appeared in both ClinVar and gnomAD were considered and variants that were recorded in both databases were removed from gnomAD data so as to avoid double-counting when scoring. The set of genes remaining after these pre-processing steps (3,829 genes with 321,619 VUS/P/B variants and 1,161,072 gnomAD variants) served as our starting gene set.

2.3. *Obtaining calibrated REVEL scores*

REVEL is a meta-predictor that combines scores from multiple pathogenicity predictors and has been shown to perform well for clinical variant interpretation.[11] For each variant in all data sets, we extracted REVEL scores by mapping the chromosomal position and amino acid alteration to REVEL's prediction tables.[11] However, REVEL scores themselves are not calibrated for clinical use and our formulations for clinical objectives require that prediction scores best approximate the posterior probability of pathogenicity/benignity (Section 2.4). Therefore, we obtained a mapping of all possible REVEL scores to local posterior probability of pathogenicity and benignity from Pejaver *et al.*[12] We then recorded these local posterior probabilities for all variants in this study and used them in all analyses.

2.4. *Gene prioritization objectives: a clinical perspective*

From a clinical perspective, the overall goal of gene prioritization is to make definitive and accurate classifications for more variants appearing in patient populations, when combining new functional evidence and existing evidence. This includes: (1) assisting the movement of VUS to pathogenic and benign classes, (2) correcting for errors in current pathogenic and benign classifications and (3) improving predictors to assist clinical decision making. To operationalize these objectives we rely on pathogenicity predictions from REVEL for variants in ClinVar and gnomAD over a subset of ClinVar genes. While ClinVar variants are the most relevant to the clinical goal, we include gnomAD variants to account for biases in ClinVar VUS annotations that arise out of the preferential testing of some genes over others. We refer to this combined set of ClinVar VUS and gnomAD variants as the *unlabeled set* of variants.

Let $\mathcal{G}$ be a subset of ClinVar genes filtered based on constraints related to assay feasibility and other attributes of interest (Sections 2.1, 2.2). For a gene $g \in \mathcal{G}$, let $\mathcal{P}(g)$, $\mathcal{B}(g)$ be the set of variants in g annotated as P/LP and B/LB in ClinVar, respectively. Let $\mathcal{U}(g)$ be the *unlabeled* set of variants, i.e., the combined set of ClinVar VUS and gnomAD variants for gene g. For a variant v, let $\rho(v)$ be a variant's probability of pathogenicity, estimated by explicitly calibrating a predictor's pathogenicity scores on a set of pathogenic and benign variants, i.e., $\rho(v) = p(v \text{ is pathogenic} \mid \text{REVEL}(v))$ (Section 2.3). We then define three prioritization objectives, each serving different purposes in relation to our overall goal.

(a) **Movability.** We define movability as the 'movement' of a variant from a VUS annotation to a non-VUS (P, LP, B, LB) annotation when additional functional evidence is collected. This is similar to a previous definition[2] but allows for the incorporation of prediction outputs more explicitly towards the reduction of VUS annotations. To have maximal impact on the reclassification of VUS, we aim to prioritize genes that contain the highest expected number of movable variants, i.e., the expected number of pathogenic/benign variants among a gene's unlabeled variants. Since annotating new pathogenic variants and new benign ones have different benefits, we propose two movability scores for each gene: the *movability-to-P score* and the *movability-to-B score*, and calculate them as follows:

$$\text{Move}_{\mathcal{P}}(g) = \sum_{v \in \mathcal{U}(g)} \rho(v) \quad \text{and} \quad \text{Move}_{\mathcal{B}}(g) = \sum_{v \in \mathcal{U}(g)} 1 - \rho(v)$$

Optimizing this objective can also benefit the objective of improving predictors (see below), as it is expected to increase the number of P/LP and B/LB variants available for training.

(b) **Correction.** We define the 'correction' of a variant's clinical annotation as the update of an existing P/LP classification to B/LB/VUS or of an existing B/LB classification to P/LP/VUS, when additional functional evidence is collected. To have maximal impact on pathogenic or benign variants that may be currently misclassified, we want to prioritize those genes that contain the highest expected number of variants whose clinical classification ought to be corrected, i.e., the expected number of pathogenic (benign) variants among a gene's variants annotated as benign (pathogenic). Again, since there are differences in importance between correcting misclassifications of pathogenic variants and benign ones, we propose two correction scores for each gene: the *correction-of-P score* and the *correction-of-B score*, and calculate them as follows:

$$\text{Correct}_{P}(g) = \sum_{v \in \mathcal{P}(g)} 1 - \rho(v) \quad \text{and} \quad \text{Correct}_{B}(g) = \sum_{v \in \mathcal{B}(g)} \rho(v)$$

(c) **Predictor improvement.** Though not obvious, increasing the number of VUS with more certain predictions towards benignity or pathogenicity has a significant role to play in moving more VUS to a non-VUS (P, LP, B, LB) annotation. If the improvement in the prediction of a VUS is large enough, it may directly provide an additional line of evidence that may be enough to push it to a non-VUS annotation. Furthermore, an improved prediction on variants from the same gene, might make the gene more likely to be assayed by an experimentalist motivated by the movability objective defined above. The new functional evidence thus obtained would help its movement to a non-VUS annotation.

In order to increase the number of VUS with more certain predictions, the predictors themselves ought to be improved. To that end, we intend to generate more functional evidence for unlabeled variants (VUS and gnomAD variants) with uncertain predictions and we prioritize genes with high average uncertainty over their unlabeled variant set. The new functional evidence accrued on these variants would help improve the predictors, either by incorporating it as a feature while training a pathogenicity predictor or via transfer learning from function to disease domain. Note that the improvement in the predictor thus obtained is not restricted to the assayed variants, but also to other variants due to the predictor's generalization capabilities. Inspired by the entropy-based uncertainty sampling approach in the active learning literature,[16] we prioritize genes for predictor improvement based on the average entropy of prediction on a gene's unlabeled variants. Intuitively, the criterion prioritizes genes having a higher fraction of unlabeled variants with calibrated pathogenicity score close to 0.5. Formally, we define the average entropy of a gene, adjusted for the number of unlabeled variants, as

$$\text{Entropy}_{\text{adj}}(g) = \sum_{v \in \mathcal{U}(g)} \frac{-\rho(v)\log_2 \rho(v) - (1-\rho(v))\log_2(1-\rho(v))}{|\mathcal{U}(g)|} \left(1 + \lambda \frac{\log_2 |\mathcal{U}(g)|}{\log_2 |\max_{h \in \mathcal{G}} \mathcal{U}(h)|}\right)$$

In this expression, the term $\left(1 + \lambda \frac{\log_2 |\mathcal{U}(g)|}{\log_2 |\max_{h \in \mathcal{G}} \mathcal{U}(h)|}\right)$, with $\lambda \in [0, 1]$, serves as an adjustment factor that prevents genes with very small number of unlabeled variants from being prioritized. The log scale gives genes with many unlabeled variants only a small advantage. The hyperparameter λ can be further used to moderate the advantage given to genes with a large number of unlabeled variants. In this work, we choose $\lambda = 1$.

2.5. *Gene prioritization strategies and their comparison*

There are several possible strategies to prioritize genes for high-throughput functional assays. We describe a diverse set of prioritization strategies below.

(1) **Knowledge- or expert-driven.** The set of 94 assayed genes described in Section 2.1 serve as an appropriate proxy for expert-driven gene prioritization. After applying the pre-processing steps described in Section 2.2, we were left with a set of 68 genes. This set is referred to as the *assayed* set. In addition, we simulated knowledge-driven selection in a simple manner by prioritizing genes in terms of the collective knowledge that we have about them. Here, we used publication counts as reported by PubMed (`https://ftp.ncbi.nlm.nih.gov/gene/DATA/gene2pubmed.gz`) in July 2022. We refer to this gene set as the *highest publications* set.

(2) **Data-driven.** In this strategy, knowledgebases such as ClinVar are explicitly queried and genes are prioritized based on the numbers of variants of interest observed in them. For instance, genes with a high number of VUS are of particular interest because of the challenges in classifying such variants. We constructed a gene set ranked by the highest number of unlabeled variants (VUS and gnomAD). We refer to this gene set as the *highest unlabeled variants* set. Similarly, one may be interested in genes with the most number of VUS along with P/LP variants. We also constructed a gene set ranked by the highest total of VUS and P/LP. We refer to this gene set as the *highest non-benign variants* set.

    Previous work introduced two sophisticated strategies to prioritize genes for MAVEs in addition to the number of ClinVar VUS in a gene.[2] The movability- and reappearance-weighted impact score (MARWIS) incorporated patient data from Invitae to define variants' movability and reappearance and give extra weight for reappearing and movable VUS. The other score, difficulty-adjusted impact score (DAIS) was a specialized version of MARWIS that was adjusted for protein length. DAIS was deemed to be better-performing in practice and a set of 100 genes with the highest DAIS was made available to the community. After applying the pre-processing steps in Section 2.2 to this set, 94 genes remained. We refer to this gene set as the *DAIS* set.

(3) **Single score optimization.** We constructed five gene sets by directly optimizing the five scores, derived to increase movability, correction and predictor improvement (Section 2.6). For each score, we picked the top-K genes to create a gene set of length K. We refer to the resulting five gene sets as the *highest movability-to-P*, the *highest movability-to-B*, *highest correction-of-P*, *highest correction-of-B* and the *highest uncertainty* sets. As these gene sets represent the best selection for their corresponding score, no other gene set can be better w.r.t. that score.

(4) **Multiple score optimization.** In order to obtain a single gene set that improves on all three objectives simultaneously, we implemented an approach to optimize a weighted combination of the five scores. The weights are learnt to incentivize improvement over the *assayed* gene set on all five scores (Section 2.6). The resultant gene set is referred to as the *combined score* set. This gene set makes tradeoffs between the five scores depending on how well the *assayed* gene set performs on each score.

(5) **Random selection.** To create a baseline gene set of length K, we sampled K genes

randomly from the starting gene set and refer to this gene set as the *random* set.

We evaluated these different strategies by computing their score distributions in terms of $Move_P(g)$, $Move_B(g)$, $Correct_P(g)$, $Correct_B(g)$, and $Entropy_{adj}(g)$. Then, we tested whether the single score optimization strategy was significantly better than all other strategies using one-sided Wilcoxon rank-sum tests. We also tested whether the multiple score optimization strategy was better than those that were used to generate the *assayed* and *DAIS* gene sets. To ensure a fair comparison, we only compared gene sets of the same length. Since the *assayed* and *DAIS* are extant gene sets of fixed length, they determined the length constraints on the remaining gene sets. For comparisons with the *assayed* set, K was set to 68, and for those with the *DAIS* set, K was set to 94.

2.6. *Multiple score optimization*

Let $\mathcal{G}$ be a starting set of genes available to be assayed. Let $\mathcal{A} \subseteq \mathcal{G}$ (e.g., *assayed* set) be an existing gene set of length K, determined to be suitable for assaying based on some criteria. We present an approach to create a novel gene set optimized to improve over $\mathcal{A}$, w.r.t. the five scores, derived to increase movability, correction and predictor improvement (Section 2.4). Let $\boldsymbol{w} = [w_i]_{i=1}^5$ be a weight vector with five non-negative entries such that $\sum_{i=1}^5 w_i = 1$. Let S_1, S_2, S_3, S_4 and S_5 be short-hands for $\text{Move}_P, \text{Move}_B, \text{Correct}_P, \text{Correct}_B$, and $\text{Entropy}_{\text{adj}}$, respectively. We define the combined weighted score as

$$\text{Combined}_{\boldsymbol{w}}(g) = \textstyle\sum_{i=1}^5 w_i \overline{S}_i(g)$$

where $\overline{S}(g)$ denotes a score $S(g)$ after z-score normalization on the entire gene set $\mathcal{G}$. The normalization ensures that the scores are on the same scale, which in turn allows us to define an optimization criteria that treats each score equally. It also allows the weights to be on the same scale, which makes it easier to find a good solution. In order to learn the optimal $\boldsymbol{w}$, we first create a sample, W, containing 10^5 candidate weights from Dirichlet$(1,1,1,1,1)$, a uniform distribution over the space of five dimensional probability vectors. For each candidate $\boldsymbol{w} \in W$, we sort the genes in $\mathcal{G}$ in the decreasing order of $\text{Combined}_{\boldsymbol{w}}(g)$. The top K genes are picked in a candidate gene set $\mathcal{O}_{\boldsymbol{w}}^K$. For a set of numbers X, let Median(X) and Prctile$_{90}(X)$ denote the median and the 90th percentile of those numbers. For $G \subseteq \mathcal{G}$, let $\overline{S}_i(G)$ denote the set containing the ith normalized score evaluated on genes in G. If the median or the 90th percentile of any normalized score on $\mathcal{O}_{\boldsymbol{w}}^K$ is less than that on $\mathcal{A}$, then discard $\boldsymbol{w}$, i.e., for any i, if $\text{Median}(\overline{S}_i(\mathcal{O}_{\boldsymbol{w}}^K)) < \text{Median}(\overline{S}_i(\mathcal{A}))$ or $\text{Prctile}_{90}(\overline{S}_i(\mathcal{O}_{\boldsymbol{w}}^K)) < \text{Prctile}_{90}(\overline{S}_i(\mathcal{A}))$, then discard $\boldsymbol{w}$. This ensures that each remaining weight leads to a gene set with higher median and 90th percentile on each of the five score distributions compared to the $\mathcal{A}$. Let W_{good} be the set of remaining candidate weights. If $W_{\text{good}} \neq \emptyset$, a $\boldsymbol{w} \in W_{\text{good}}$ is guaranteed to give a better gene set than $\mathcal{A}$ on each of the five scores. In order to select an optimum weight from W_{good}, we define the following optimization criteria to find weights that lead to largest cumulative increase in the the normalized score medians compared to $\mathcal{A}$:

$$C(\boldsymbol{w}) = \textstyle\sum_{i=1}^5 \left[\text{Median}(\overline{S}_i(\mathcal{O}_{\boldsymbol{w}}^K)) - \text{Median}(\overline{S}_i(\mathcal{A}))\right].$$

The optimum weights are given by $\boldsymbol{w}_{\text{opt}} = \text{argmax}_{\boldsymbol{w} \in W_{\text{good}}} C(\boldsymbol{w})$. The corresponding gene set, $\mathcal{O}_{\boldsymbol{w}_{\text{opt}}}^K$ is the optimal gene set, referred to as the *combined score* set. Note that if a gene set of a different size, $K_1 \neq K$, is needed, the top K_1 genes sorted based on $\text{Combined}_{\boldsymbol{w}_{\text{opt}}}(g)$ are selected. The resultant set is referred to as $\mathcal{O}^{K_1}_{\boldsymbol{w}_{\text{opt}}}$.

2.7. *Functional and phenotypic enrichment analyses*

To evaluate the biological and clinical relevance of the multiple score optimization strategy, we ranked all genes by their *combined score* and conducted a functional enrichment analysis on the top 100 genes using the *g:GOSt* function in the gProfiler web-server.[17] We used our starting gene set of 3,829 genes as the background set. Any Gene Ontology (GO) and Human Phenotype (HP) Ontology terms that were significantly enriched in the top 100 genes, after correcting for multiple hypothesis testing (P-value < 0.05) were recorded.

3. Results

3.1. *Multiple score optimization outperforms knowledge-driven and simple data-driven strategies*

We compared multiple gene sets (see Section 2.5), constructed through diverse prioritization strategies on the five scores, covering the three clinical objectives: movability, correction and

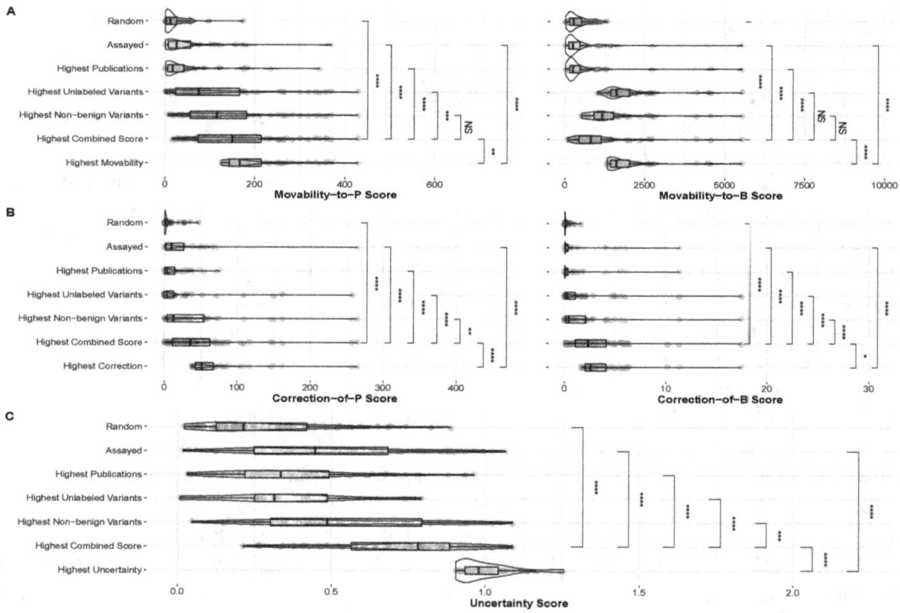

Fig. 1. **Score distributions 68-gene sets constructed based on seven prioritization strategies. A.** Score distribution of movability to pathogenic (left) and benign (right), **B.** Score distribution of correction of pathogenic (left) and benign (right) variants, **C.** Uncertainty score distribution.

predictor improvement (Figure 1). All the sets in this comparison had 68 genes, to be consistent with the *assayed* set. Unsurprisingly, for any given score, the *highest single score* gene set, being the best set for the score, outperformed all other gene sets. As expected, the *combined score* set performed better than the *assayed* gene set because it was explicitly constructed to improve over the *assayed* set. Overall, the *combined score* set performed better than all other gene sets except the respective highest single score sets. There were two exceptions to this. In the case of *movability-to-B* score, the *combined score* set did not perform better than the *highest unlabeled variants* and *highest non-benign variants* gene sets, suggesting that the number of unlabeled variants may be a strong determinant of *movability-to-B* due to the high prior probability of benignity in general. In particular, the scope of improvement in *movability-to-B* score over the *highest unlabeled variants* set is limited as can be observed in comparison to *highest movability-to-B* set, the best possible set for that score. Furthermore, among all comparisons of the *combined score* where it performs better, it does so with statistical significance, except in one case: comparison with *highest non-benign variants* set on *movability-to-P* score.

The *assayed* set performed slightly better than *random* on most scores. Moreover, its score distributions were far away from that of the corresponding *highest single score* set. This suggests that there is a huge scope of improvement on the set of genes currently being assayed, with respect to clinical objectives. On all score criteria, the performance of the *highest publication* set is quite similar to that of the *assayed* set. This is consistent with the previous observation that genes with fewer publications are less likely to be functionally tested.[9]

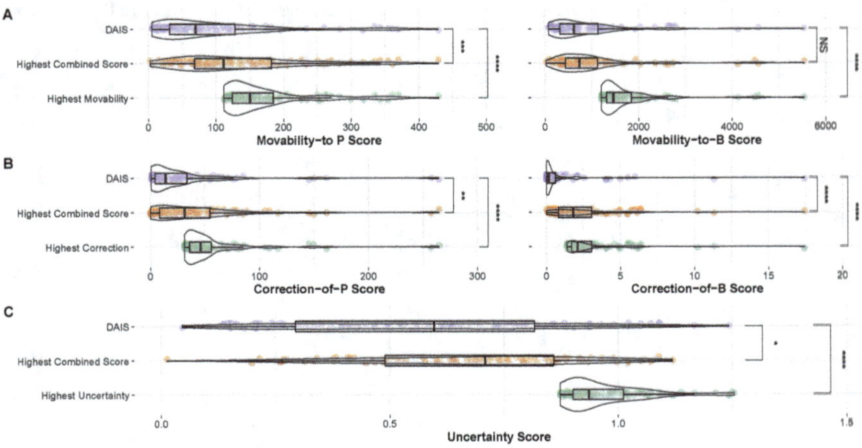

Fig. 2. **Score distributions for top 94 genes prioritized by our proposed strategies and by existing data-driven strategies. A.** Score distribution of movability to pathogenic (left) and benign (right), **B.** Score distribution of correction of pathogenic (left) and benign (right) variants, **C.** Uncertainty score distribution. DAIS, 94 genes out of the top 100 genes ranked by the difficulty-adjusted impact score.[2]

3.2. *Multiple score optimization outperforms existing clinically motivated prioritization strategies*

We next compared our single and multiple score optimization strategies to a previously proposed strategy that explicitly aimed to improve clinical variant classification, DAIS[2] (Figure 2). Since the DAIS set comprised of 94 genes, we considered the top 94 genes with the highest single and combined scores. The single and multiple score optimization strategies yielded statistically significant improvements over DAIS in all situations, with one exception. When considering the *movability-to-B* score, the *combined score* set showed improvement over DAIS, although not significantly, similar to our observations in Section 3.1.

3.3. *Multiple score optimization yields clinically relevant genes*

We characterized the properties of the highest-scoring genes in the *combined score* set and investigated to what extent our strategy aligned with biomedical interests. Among the top 20 genes, six genes were in our *assayed* gene set, and 12 genes were also prioritized by DAIS, albeit with differences in ranking (Table 1). All identified genes generally have a large number of variants recorded in ClinVar and gnomAD, with the exception of *SCN10A*, which has no

Table 1. Missense variant counts and scores for the top 20 genes from the *combined score* gene set. Similar counts and scores are available for all genes in this study here: `https://igvfgenecard.shinyapps.io/GeneCardApp/` Genes in bold were also present in the *assayed* set. The Movability and Correction scores are rounded to the closest integer. The Combined score is given as the weighted sum of the five scores after z-score normalization. The weights for *movability-to-P*, *movability-to-B*, *correction-of-P*, *correction-of-B*, and *uncertainty* were 0.143, 0.160, 0.380, 0.310, and 0.006, respectively.

		DAIS	ClinVar					Movability		Correction		Entropy	
Rank	Gene	rank	P/LP	B/LB	VUS	gnomAD	Total	to P	to B	of P	of B	adjusted	Combined
1	*TSC2*	32	80	185	2178	273	2716	318	2035	29	17	0.8	13.3
2	***BRCA1***	10	120	206	2817	160	3303	181	2727	71	11	0.5	10.5
3	***LDLR***	40	635	62	564	176	1437	155	547	265	4	0.9	10.1
4	*FBN1*	39	873	17	1338	536	2764	335	1451	257	2	0.9	9.9
5	***BRCA2***	9	57	236	5453	325	6071	173	5533	37	6	0.3	7.5
6	*IDS*	1055	120	57	49	125	351	32	134	39	10	0.7	7.0
7	*MYH7*	2	271	17	1284	297	1869	355	1129	150	2	1.1	6.7
8	*SCN1A*	66	452	39	670	361	1522	283	683	146	3	1.0	6.6
9	*NF1*	11	232	19	2750	224	3225	261	2632	162	0	0.5	6.4
10	***MSH2***	4	73	26	1757	123	1979	369	1409	28	6	1.0	5.9
11	*COL4A5*	1839	414	87	66	372	939	72	347	80	6	0.7	5.6
12	*SCN8A*	468	122	44	346	250	762	125	438	43	6	0.9	5.3
13	***SCN5A***	63	83	33	1058	386	1560	361	998	23	5	1.0	5.3
14	*MLH1*	8	122	33	1103	80	1338	175	957	62	4	0.8	5.0
15	*SCN10A*	391	0	55	381	831	1267	226	930	0	6	0.8	4.8
16	*FLNA*	211	32	85	560	493	1170	150	858	16	6	0.8	4.7
17	*CACNA1S*	323	12	44	393	777	1226	251	858	3	6	0.9	4.7
18	*FBN2*	155	33	58	708	1005	1804	300	1331	13	5	0.9	4.6
19	***TP53***	1	143	76	717	27	963	176	525	54	4	1.0	4.5
20	*ABCA4*	130	235	17	582	845	1679	252	1110	109	0	0.8	4.3

variants classified as pathogenic or likely pathogenic. In addition, our *combined score* also prioritized important genes that may have been overlooked previously. For example, IDS, which has more than 200 IDS variants were found in Hunter syndrome patients[18] was ranked

6th. *COL4A5*, with over 400 variants thata cause Alport syndrome, was (ranked 11th). Many sodium voltage-gated channels (*SCN*)-related genes were also ranked within the top 20, and mutations in these genes can lead to channel defects and cause channelopathies.[19] Since the objective of improving predictors may not necessarily yield genes that are clinically relevant, we systematically explored the functional and phenotypic characteristics associated with the *combined score* set. We conducted an enrichment analysis on the top 100 genes ranked by their combined score and reported significantly enriched GO terms and the 40 most significant HP terms (Supp. Figure 1A). This top-100 gene set was enriched in many biological processes such as neuronal action, membrane depolarization, and molecular functions such as multiple channel activities and transmembrane transporter activity. From the phenotypic perspective, enriched high-level HP terms included abnormalities of different organ systems such as skin, gastrointestinal tract, nervous system, among others (Supp. Figure 1B). More specific HP terms included cardiovascular related disease, limitation of mobility, and stroke, among others.

4. Discussion

Genetic and genomic testing are now routinely used in healthcare systems to provide diagnoses and infer lifetime risk for disease symptoms, particularly in the identification of hereditary susceptibility to cancer, metabolic conditions, intellectual and physical developmental disorders, among others. The classification of genetic variants detected in a patient's gene panel or genome is a key step in this context. In this regard, our study presented three objectives that explicitly captured the goal of improving clinical classification of variants and derived five scores to operationalize them. We derived an optimal gene set for each score and also derived a *combined score* gene set by optimizing a weighted combination of the five scores to explicitly improve over the existing *assayed* set.

As expected, all single score optimization strategies, led to the best performance on the corresponding score. More importantly, evaluating the existing approaches relative to the single score optimization, demonstrated a considerable performance gap, suggesting a significant scope of improvement on each objective. Even though our *combined score* gene set was obtained by optimizing directly over the three objectives relative to the *assayed* set, its observed improvement over the *assayed* and DAIS gene sets on all scores is not entirely obvious due to the inherent trade-offs between the objectives (movability vs. predictor improvement). This is a further testament to the scope of simultaneous improvement on all objectives along with an approach that demonstrably does so.

DAIS, a more sophisticated strategy, presented higher scores in general but did not outperform our approach. Unlike DAIS, our approach does not use any proprietary patient data, but despite this, one-third of our genes overlapped with the DAIS set. Our approach can be potentially complementary to DAIS, since we accounted for conflicting variants, incorporated non-VUS and less biased gnomAD variants and focused on correction and predictor improvement as objectives. Another strength of our strategy is its interpretability. The *movability* scores and *correction* scores are interpreted as the expected number of pathogenic or benign variants, and the *uncertainty* score as predictive uncertainty. In addition, our approach for multiple score optimization could be easily extended to incorporate other scores such as DAIS, if appropriate data were available, or could directly optimize the combined score to improve over both the assayed and DAIS sets.

Though our movability objective quantifies the expected number unlabeled variants in a gene that are pathogenic (or benign), it is possible that after running a given assay the number of variants moved to the P/LP (B/LB) categories as per the ACMG/AMP guidelines might differ. This might happen either because the assay might not capture the functional mechanism that leads to the disease, or the strength of the new evidence combined with existing evidence might not be enough to move the variant. Without functional assay outcomes, this is difficult to discern and is a limitation of our study. In future, when additional information on an assay's relevance to specific diseases is available, refined criteria that take that information into account might better quantify the movement. Similarly, if all existing evidence for a variant is accessible, the criteria may be refined to take it into account, as done so by Kuang et al.[2] Our study is currently limited in this regard, as ClinVar does not detail which specific lines of evidence were used to classify a variant. Similar considerations apply to the correction scores as well.

In conclusion, we defined three objectives in terms of improving clinical classification by using variant pathogenicity predictors. Our final *combined* scores provided a list of prioritized genes for MAVEs but this list will keep updating with iterated future work between prediction and experimentation. All data sets, analysis scripts, and supplementary results for this study can be accessed here: `https://github.com/strongbeamsprout/Gene-Prioritization`.

5. Acknowledgments

This work was supported by National Institutes of Health grant U01 HG012022.

References

1. S. Richards et al. *Genet. Med.*, 17(5):405–424, 2015.
2. D. Kuang et al. . *Bioinformatics*, 36(22-23):5448–5455, 2020.
3. S. M. Harrison and H. L. Rehm. *Genome Med.*, 11(1):72, 2019.
4. D. M. Fowler and S. Fields. *Nat. Methods*, 11(8):801–807, 2014.
5. J. Weile and F. P. Roth. *Hum. Genet.*, 137(9):665–678, 2018.
6. P. A. Romero et al. *Proc. Natl. Acad. Sci. U.S.A*, 112(23):7159–7164, 2015.
7. X. Jia et al. *Am. J. Hum. Genet.*, 108(1):163–175, 2021.
8. K. A. Matreyek et al. *Nat. Genet.*, 50(6):874–882, 2018.
9. T. Stoeger et al. *PLoS Biol.*, 16(9):e2006643, 2018.
10. M. J. Landrum et al. *Nucleic Acids Res.*, 46(D1):D1062–D1067, 2018.
11. N. M. Ioannidis et al. *Am. J. Hum. Genet.*, 99(4):877–885, 2016.
12. V. Pejaver et al. *bioRxiv*, 10.1101/2022.03.17.484479, 2022.
13. K. J. Karczewski et al. *Nature*, 581(7809):434–443, 2020.
14. D. Esposito et al. *Genome Biol.*, 20(1):223, 2019.
15. D. Kuang et al. *Bioinformatics*, 37(19):3382–3383, 2021.
16. B. Settles. *Synthesis lectures on artificial intelligence and machine learning*, 6(1):1–114, 2012.
17. U. Raudvere et al. . *Nucleic Acids Res.*, 47(W1):W191–W198, 2019.
18. V. Ricci et al. *Am. J. Med. Genet. A*, 120A(1):84–87, 2003.
19. M. de Lera Ruiz and R. L. Kraus. *J. Med. Chem.*, 58(18):7093–7118, 2015.

Acoustic-Linguistic Features for Modeling Neurological Task Score in Alzheimer's

Saurav K. Aryal† Howard Prioleau and Legand Burge
EECS, Howard University,
Washington, DC 20059, USA
†*E-mail: saurav.aryal@howard.edu*
https://howard.edu/

The average life expectancy is increasing globally due to advancements in medical technology, preventive health care, and a growing emphasis on gerontological health. Therefore, developing technologies that detect and track aging-associated disease in cognitive function among older adult populations is imperative. In particular, research related to automatic detection and evaluation of Alzheimer's disease (AD) is critical given the disease's prevalence and the cost of current methods. As AD impacts the acoustics of speech and vocabulary, natural language processing and machine learning provide promising techniques for reliably detecting AD. We compare and contrast the performance of ten linear regression models for predicting Mini-Mental Status Exam scores on the ADReSS challenge dataset. We extracted 13000+ handcrafted and learned features that capture linguistic and acoustic phenomena. Using a subset of 54 top features selected by two methods: (1) recursive elimination and (2) correlation scores, we outperform a state-of-the-art baseline for the same task. Upon scoring and evaluating the statistical significance of each of the selected subset of features for each model, we find that, for the given task, handcrafted linguistic features are more significant than acoustic and learned features.

1. Introduction

People are living longer due to advancements in medical technology, preventive health care, and a growing emphasis on gerontological health. The Administration for Community Living estimates that by 2020, 77 million people in the United States will be 60 years of age or older. Hence, developing technologies that detect and track aging-associated disease in cognitive function among older adult populations is imperative.

For decades scientists have examined the association between psychological well-being and cognition. In prior research, gerontologists have identified a significant relationship between mental acuity, loneliness and depression, and social engagement among older adults. Specifically, late-life dementia has been associated with extended periods of loneliness in older adults.[1] Another cognition study,[2] conducted a longitudinal study of adults aged 60 years or older living in North Manhattan, New York, and who were randomly selected from a dementia registry. Their study assessed the association between depressed mood and the onset of dementia. Physicians collected neuropsychological data to assess the degree of decreased cognitive function and determine the risk of dementia. Study results indicated that of the 1,070 participants, 218 (20%) met the criteria for dementia at baseline assessment. Among the 852 participants that did not have dementia, depressive symptoms were common among those with cognitive impairment. Two years after the baseline data collection, follow-up data were collected on 478 participants who did not have dementia from the baseline collection. A comparison of baseline and follow-up results concluded that of the 478 participants (93%), the depressed mood was associated with dementia and exhibited symptoms of Alzheimer's disease.[2]

Before the turn of the last century, the only way to ascertain if a person has AD was via posthumous autopsy. Currently, as per the National Institute of Health (NIH), medical professionals ask the patient and their caregivers about overall health, medications, diet, medical history, and changes in behavior and personality. They may also administer a psychiatric evaluation to determine confounding causes and conduct tests on memory, problem-solving, attention, counting, language, blood, urine, and other standard medical tests. Finally, performing computed tomography (CT), magnetic resonance imaging (MRI), or positron emission tomography (PET) supports an AD diagnosis or rules out other plausible causes.[3] While there are other methods, such as accumulation of amyloid plaques and associated genes, these methods may not be entirely accurate[4].[5] Nonetheless, all methods listed are cost-prohibitive or require at least one dedicated medical professional. Consequently, researchers have been studying and modeling non-invasive methods using speech and linguistic features that do not necessitate human intervention to detect and evaluate AD patients. In addition, caregivers experience feelings of depression and being overwhelmed when caring for an older adult lacking social support mechanisms and are predominantly female and overwhelmingly low-income.[1]

Thus, with an aging world population negatively impacted by the symptoms associated with cognitive decline and an overwhelmed caregiving profession, research into technologies to help alleviate these issues is necessary. As AD affects the acoustics of speech[6] and vocabulary,[7] natural language processing and machine learning provide promising techniques for reliably detecting AD. While significant work has been done on detecting AD, this paper will evaluate and score mental status with ten different linear regression models using a combination of handcrafted or learned acoustic-linguistic features. The statistical significance and relevance of each selected feature are also studied.

The rest of the paper covers a review of related works in Section 2. The models, dataset, feature extraction, feature selection, and training-testing protocol are detailed in Section 3. The performance of our models and features are compared to a state-of-the-art baseline linear model in section 4. The final section outlines the conclusion and future work.

2. Related Works

There has been significant research into the symptoms and manifestations of Alzheimer's Disease (AD) in medical literature and AD detection in interdisciplinary research. The review of relevant literature will be divided into two subsections: the first will cover the well-known acoustic-lingual expression of AD in patients, and the second will cover models and techniques currently used for evaluating and detecting AD. Furthermore, the first subsection helps establish the relevance of acoustic and linguistic features for AD progression, whereas the second subsection supports the reasoning behind our methodology.

2.1. *Acoustic and Linguistic Features in AD*

The relation between loss of memory and AD-associated neurodegeneration is well established. Recent research has studied acoustic and verbal aberrations present in patients with AD. In particular, dysarthria/slurring, stuttering, monotony, higher delay, and associated acoustic features with AD.[7] Additionally, linguistic features such as paucity of words or aggramatism are also present with AD.[6,8] In severe cases, sentences uttered may comprise only nouns; articles, auxiliary verbs, and inflectional affixes are absent or replaced in lesser forms. Unsurprisingly, multiple approaches have utilized acoustic and linguistic features for the automatic detection of AD. We will discuss a few of these approaches in the following subsection.

2.2. *Contemporary Models and Techniques for AD Evaluation*

Speech has been used to distinguish between healthy and AD patients.[9] Some researchers have focused on developing dedicated machine learning model architectures[10–12] while others have focused on language models to classify AD.[13] Some research has been focused on extracting acoustic and textual features that capture information indicative of AD, such as the length of segments and the amount of silence.[13] Other researchers have used linguistic and audio features extracted from English speech.[14,15] Prosodic features have been extracted from English speech[16–18] and so have paralinguistic acoustic features.[19] Other approaches have attempted to focus on collecting speech from people performing multiple normative tasks to improve generalizability.[20] However, most of these approaches utilize unbalanced, non-standardized, and proprietary datasets, which hampers their reproducibility and generalizability. We suggest the reader peruse this survey[21] to get a better understanding of these approaches.

In 2020, The ADReSS Challenge[22] defined shared tasks and standardized datasets with predefined metrics. Different approaches for automated recognition of AD based on spontaneous speech and transcripts can be compared with two tasks: AD Classification (AD vs. not-AD) and the neuropsychological score regression. The challenge provided a baseline using standard machine learning models such as Random Forest and k-Nearest Neighbors on classification metrics (accuracy, precision, recall, F-1) and regression Root Mean Square Error (RMSE) scores. More details pertaining to the dataset are discussed in the Methodology section.

Since the release of the dataset, significant work has been done on the classification task,[23–25] the regression task,[26] or both.[27–30] Of the two tasks, a high degree of accuracy 83% to 92.84% has been obtained on the classification task. However, the regression task, being the more challenging of the two, still has room for improvement and is the focus of this paper. Of the approaches reviewed, the lowest RMSE score of 4.56 was acheived on both training and testing sets and utilizes a linear Ridge Regressor model on a set of the 30 best correlating features.[27] We refer to this work as the baseline and state-of-art for the comparison of our model and feature set through the remainder of the paper.

3. Methodology

The models, dataset, feature extraction, feature selection, and training-testing protocol are detailed in the following subsections. All of the tasks performed were performed on a standard personal laptop machine or a Google Collaboratory notebook.[31] No specific accelerators are required, however, feature extraction, feature selection, and training-testing could be sped up through the utilization of more computing cores.

3.1. *The ADReSS Dataset and Metrics*

To enable comparison with the baseline, the ADReSS Challenge dataset[22] is utilized. This dataset comprises of audio recordings, transcripts from patients performing the Cookie Theft task from the Boston Diagnostic Aphasia exam.[32] Also provided with the dataset are metadata relating to the subject's age, gender and Mini Mental Status Examination (MMSE) score for both non-AD and AD patients. The regression task for this paper is associated with predicting these MMSE score based on the given audio recording and transcripts. Although the MMSE was originally designed to screen for dementia, it is an instrument currently used extensively to assess cognitive status in clinical settings.[33] According to the Alzheimer's Association (2020), an MMSE score of 20–24 corresponds to mild dementia, 13–20 corresponds to moderate dementia, and a score < 12 is severe dementia.

Furthermore, the dataset comes divided into a Train Set (108 patients - 54 non-AD and 54 AD) and a Test Set (48 patients - 24 non-AD and 24 AD). As per the original challenge's guidelines and our baseline, the RMSE is used to determine and compare the performance of our approach. Since the dataset comes with many-to-one mapping of audio file to transcript files, in contrast to previous work, we opted to consider each unique audio-transcript file pair as a distinct observation. While this approach does limit us to shorter audio files with few utterances per file, the number of observations increases to 1447 for training and 569 for testing.

3.2. *Modeling and Train-Validation-Test Protocol*

Although the we were able to increase the sample size by considering audio-transcript file pairs, the number is still smaller than is demanded by most deep learning methods. While work such as[34] has been done on small sample learning, these methods are still a black box. Interpretability is required to evaluate the association between features and the output of the model. While conventional, non-linear machine learning models such as Random Forest and k-Nearest Neighbors were originally the benchmark provided with the dataset,[22] they have been outperformed by the baseline's linear models[27] likely owing to the small sample size. Thus, we also opt for linear modeling. Similar to,[27] we use regression models with in-built regularization or specific optimizations namely Ridge.[35] Additionally, we also employ Lasso,[36] ElasticNet,[37] LassoLars,[38] Bayesian Ridge,[39] Bayesian Automatic Relevance Determination,[40] Orthogonal Matching Pursuit,[41] Huber,[42] TheilSen,[43] and Stochastic Gradient Descent optimization.[44] The models were trained and evaluated using a combination of the BSD-licensed scikit-learn,[45] numpy,[46] seaborn,[47] scipy,[48] and pandas[49] package, and the PSF-licensed matplotlib.[50] The ISF-licensed regressors[51] was used to evaluate the statiscal signficance of each selected feature . Beyond the default, the hyperparameters for each model can be found through the Appendix.

The training and testing protocol utilizes the provided disjoint sets provided with the dataset. Similar to the baseline, each model is trained using Leave One Subject Out (LOSO) Cross Validation on the training set and the RMSE is evaluated on both the training and test set. Of the models, Ridge, Lasso, ElasticNet, LassoLars, and Orthogonal Matching Pursuit's

L1 or L2 regularization parameters were evaluated during this cross-validation. Additionally, a random 80-20 train-validation split of only the training set is used for feature selection.

3.3. *Feature Extraction, Pre-processing, and Feature Selection*

3.3.1. *Feature Extraction*

To learn from both the audio recording and text transcripts, feature extraction is necessary. The dataset provides audio broken up into normalized audio chunks of the subject's sentences/utterances. Text from each participant's transcripts was combined into one large string separated by a new line for linguistic feature extraction. To aid in our feature extraction a combination of software, and python libraries was used. Each of these third-party software, libraries, and their associated licenses are detailed in the Appendix.

We further classify each feature into Audio Features and Linguistic Features. Each of these features may also either be handcrafted or learned. In total, each audio-transcript pair produced just over 13,000 features. To the best of our knowledge, a significant subset of these features are novel applications for the current task of MMSE score prediction.

* **Audio Features** (11,659 Features):

The learned audio features derived from audio recordings include Articulation,[52,53] Phonation,[52,54] and Prosody[52,55] Features. Articulation features are made up of Bark band energies. Phonation features are composed up of pitch perturbation quotient, logarithmic energy, and derivatives of fundamental frequencies account for 28 features. Prosody features, based on energy and duration, include 103 features. The handcrafted audio features include spectral, Mel Frequency Cepstral Coefficients (MFCCs), and Chroma Vector/Deviation features. While all together these features total to 138, we utilized 80 different combinations of frame sizes and overlaps when the average feature are calculated. This was done to find the optimal frame size and overlap which would provide the most significant association with the given task during feature selection.

* **Linguistic Features** (1,693 Features) Linguistic features include, but are not limited to, Word/Sentence Count, Vocab Set, reading scales, and emotion analysis. These features were all extracted from the textual transcript files and totaled up to 1,693 features.

3.3.2. *Pre-processing*

Since audio data was retrieved from a normalized chunks no further pre-processing was required beyond feature extraction. Each participant's transcript was parsed and combined into one large string separated by a new line characters which was used for linguistic feature extraction. Lacking previous background and for convenient modeling, the features were divided by the maximum value. The scaled features were normalized as required by the modeling library before training. No other pre-processing was performed.

3.3.3. *Feature Selection*

While extracting over 13,000 features provides us with a significant amount of data. Linear models, even with strong regularization, tend to get over-parameterized at this scale and

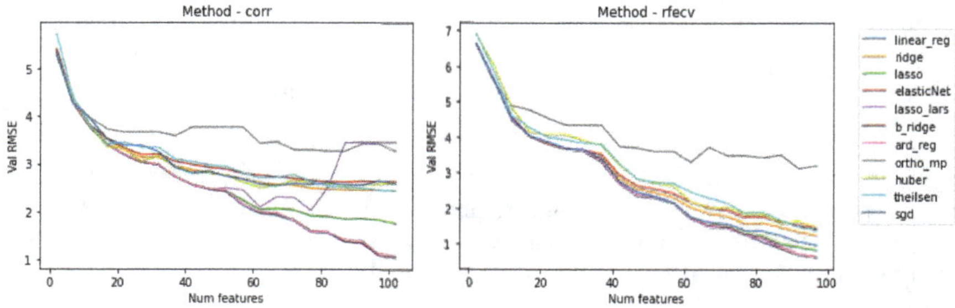

Fig. 1. Validation RMSE vs Num Features using Correlation and Recursive Elimination

require specific adaptation. Thus, we opt to select a subset of 100 due to limitations in available computing power and time. We utilized two methods from[45] for selecting the best features for this problem: (1) Recursive Feature Elimination using a standard Linear Regression estimator and (2) Correlation Scores. For the first method, the best set of features which decreased the RMSE on a standard linear regression model trained on 80% of the training set and minimized RMSE on the 20% validation set was used. We could not get to 100 features since the method only lets us select a minimum number of features required and outputted a set of features > 100. For the second method, we simply selected a the top 100 most correlated features with the output. In order, to further simply the model we trained and validated the models on features from the top 2 features until the all top 100 features selected by the algorithms. Plots of validation RMSE for each of the methods can be seen in Figure 1. As expected, the error does incrementally decrease with the addition of each feature. However, we are better suited taking a cut off around at a few feature after the steep decrease in RMSE. We chose to set this limit at 54 features which is half the number of subjects in the training set. Lacking precedence, we used P-values < 0.05 and coefficient > 0.01 were considered significant. Given page limitations, model summaries, source code, and additional plots are provided via the Appendix. In the following section, we will cover the results of our modeling experiments and perform comparisons with the baseline.

4. Results

All of the models using features selected by both RFECV and Correlation outperformed the baseline model on the training set. Of these models, the standard linear regression model performed the best with an RMSE improvement of 2.37 compared to the baseline of 4.56. The RMSE plot for each model can be seen in Figure 2.

However, for the test set, not all models outperformed the baseline. Interestingly, none of the models which used features selected by recursive elimination outperformed the baseline whereas five models using correlation features outperformed the baseline despite the two methods having an overlap of 17 features selected out of the total 54. Of these models that outperformed the baseline, the stochastic gradient descent optimized model performed the

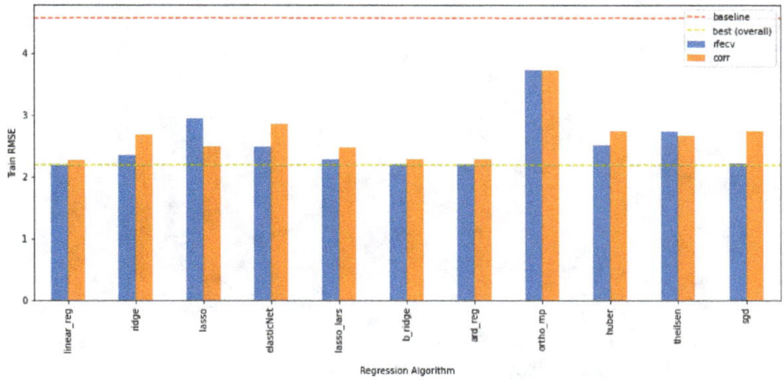

Fig. 2. Train RMSE for each model and each feature selection method

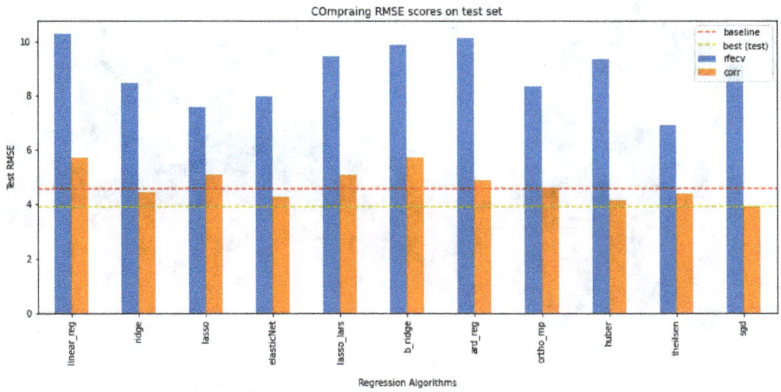

Fig. 3. Test RMSE for each model and each feature selection method

best with an RMSE improvement of 0.66 compared to the baseline RMSE of 4.56. The plot of RMSE can be seen in Figure 3.

Upon a closer look into the the box in Figure 4 and histogram plots in Figure 5 of the residuals of each of the models that outperformed the baseline, we notice that stochastic gradient descent optimization has the most reliable performance. However, the range of prediction is currently too large and unreliable in all of these models for real world application.

Moreover, of the 54 features selected by the methods, it was noticed that all were handcrafted linguistic features related to word usage, readability, and character frequencies. This observation is inline with the observations of both the baseline and speech pathological research[6,8] that linguistic features are better predictors for this task in comparison to acoustic features and is supported. Details results of feature selection can be found via the Appendix

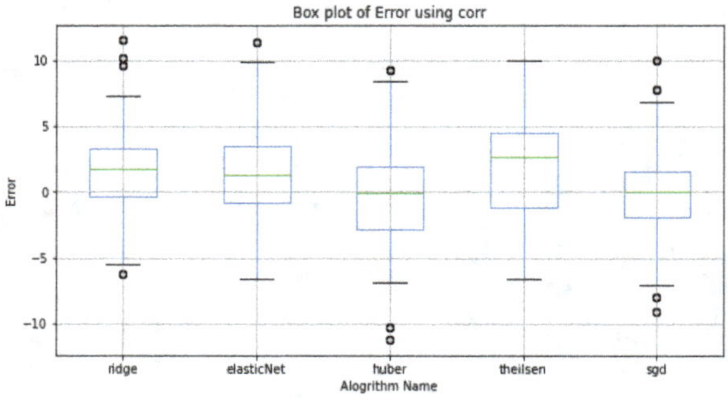

Fig. 4. Boxplot of Residuals on the Test set

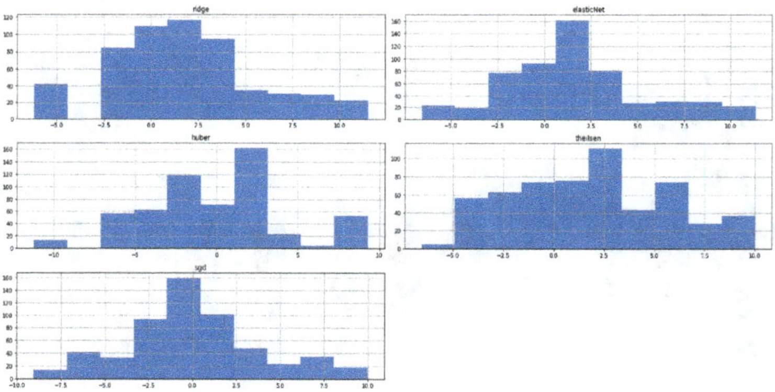

Fig. 5. Histogram of Residuals on the Test set

5. Limitations and Future Work

The major limitation of this work stems from data source. Since the dataset consists of audio recordings of the participants performing a specific task, it is unlikely these findings may be generalizable to recordings that are not obtained from the same task or for non-native English speakers. Furthermore, the standardization based on this task might also explain the proclivity of models to find significance of linguistic features over acoustic features for the prediction of MMSE scores. It is possible that other modes of data capture may be better suited to a general approach for evaluating AD patients.[20]

Although the current dataset is remarkable, the sample size limits researchers from fully realizing and utilizing the most recent advancement in machine learning. While approaches such as early stopping and dropouts could be utilizes, one must question the external validity of such approaches within such a small sample size. Perhaps research into small sample size algorithms[34] could be applied; however the issues related to interpretability still persists.

Contemporary research has shown the continued need to advance further the study of aging-associated disease effects on cognitive impairment in older adults.[56] Researchers studied older adults who were already enrolled in research projects investigating the onset of Alzheimer's Disease (AD) on cognition under the assumption that the Functional Activities Questionnaire (FAQ) using the Instrumental Activities of Daily Living (IADL) scale to detect and track diminishing capability in managing and remembering daily household tasks and personal responsibilities. Difficulties in managing IADL identified in the FAQ proved helpful in detecting and tracking changes in cognition in healthy older adults at risk for Alzheimer's Disease.[57] Furthermore, social determinants of health such as transportation, education, diet, and other daily factors negatively impact a person's health outlook. Black and Brown persons in the United States are adversely affected by schooling, diet, and disease symptoms associated with hypertension and diabetes that might cause cognitive decline.[58] To further improve the reliability of the models social determinants, facial features, depression, and other correlates can be considered in conjunction with an in-home monitoring and audio-video capture device.

While we do believe that this paper sufficiently advance the state-of-the-art for this task, explores the largest feature space to date, and guides us towards automating the diagnosis of AD and modeling of cognitive status in the elderly, we must note that with automation we should not intend to replace trained medical professionals. We firmly believe that any technology stemming from research should be used as a tool to guide, assist, and ease medical professionals and caregivers to provide the best care possible.

6. Conclusion

While we were able to outperform the baseline with 5 different models, the performance of these models are still not fully suited for real world application. More research needs to be done to find models that work on low resource problems such as neurological evaluation of AD patients using audio and textual features.

7. Acknowledgement

This project was supported (in part) by the National Institute on Minority Health and Health Disparities of the National Institutes of Health under Award Number 2U54MD007597, and the Office of Data Science Strategy of the National Institutes of Health under OTA OT2 OD32581-01, and a 2021 Amazon Research Award. The content is solely the responsibility of the authors and does not necessarily represent the official views of the funding organizations.

8. Appendix

All supplemental materials can be found in the link below: https://bit.ly/3Skbaij

References

1. R. S. Wilson, K. R. Krueger, S. E. Arnold, J. A. Schneider, J. F. Kelly, L. L. Barnes, Y. Tang and D. A. Bennett, Loneliness and Risk of Alzheimer Disease, *Archives of General Psychiatry* **64**, 234 (February 2007).

2. D. P. Devanand, M. Sano, M.-X. Tang, S. Taylor, B. J. Gurland, D. Wilder, Y. Stern and R. Mayeux, Depressed mood and the incidence of alzheimer's disease in the elderly living in the community, *Archives of general psychiatry* **53**, 175 (1996).
3. How Is Alzheimer's Disease Diagnosed? | National Institute on Aging.
4. K. R. Thomas, K. J. Bangen, A. J. Weigand, E. C. Edmonds, C. G. Wong, S. Cooper, L. Delano-Wood, M. W. Bondi and f. t. A. D. N. Initiative, Objective subtle cognitive difficulties predict future amyloid accumulation and neurodegeneration, *Neurology* **94**, e397 (January 2020), Publisher: Wolters Kluwer Health, Inc. on behalf of the American Academy of Neurology Section: Article.
5. M. Giri, M. Zhang and Y. Lü, Genes associated with Alzheimer's disease: an overview and current status, *Clinical Interventions in Aging* **11**, 665 (May 2016).
6. F. Rudzicz, G. Hirst, P. van Lieshout, G. Penn, F. Shein, A. Namasivayam and T. Wolff, Torgo database of dysarthric articulation (2012).
7. I. Ferrer, A. Aymami, A. Rovira and J. M. Grau Veciana, Growth of abnormal neurites in atypical Alzheimer's disease, *Acta Neuropathologica* **59**, 167 (September 1983).
8. J. O. d. Lira, T. S. C. Minett, P. H. F. Bertolucci and K. Z. Ortiz, Analysis of word number and content in discourse of patients with mild to moderate alzheimer's disease, *Dementia & neuropsychologia* **8**, 260 (2014).
9. M. L. B. Pulido, J. B. A. Hernández, M. Á. F. Ballester, C. M. T. González, J. Mekyska and Z. Smékal, Alzheimer's disease and automatic speech analysis: A review, *Expert Systems with Applications* **150**, p. 113213 (July 2020).
10. J. Chen, J. Zhu and J. Ye, An attention-based hybrid network for automatic detection of alzheimer's disease from narrative speech., in *INTERSPEECH*, (Not Available, 2019).
11. Y.-W. Chien, S.-Y. Hong, W.-T. Cheah, L.-C. Fu and Y.-L. Chang, An Assessment System for Alzheimer's Disease Based on Speech Using a Novel Feature Sequence Design and Recurrent Neural Network, in *2018 IEEE International Conference on Systems, Man, and Cybernetics (SMC)*, (Not Available, 2018). ISSN: 2577-1655.
12. L. Liu, S. Zhao, H. Chen and A. Wang, A new machine learning method for identifying Alzheimer's disease, *Simulation Modelling Practice and Theory* **99**, p. 102023 (February 2020).
13. Z. Guo, Z. Ling and Y. Li, Detecting Alzheimer's Disease from Continuous Speech Using Language Models, *Journal of Alzheimer's Disease* **70**, 1163 (January 2019), Publisher: IOS Press.
14. K. C. Fraser, J. A. Meltzer and F. Rudzicz, Linguistic Features Identify Alzheimer's Disease in Narrative Speech, *Journal of Alzheimer's Disease* **49**, 407 (January 2016), Publisher: IOS Press.
15. G. Gosztolya, V. Vincze, L. Tóth, M. Pákáski, J. Kálmán and I. Hoffmann, Identifying Mild Cognitive Impairment and mild Alzheimer's disease based on spontaneous speech using ASR and linguistic features, *Computer Speech & Language* **53**, 181 (January 2019).
16. R. Nagumo, Y. Zhang, Y. Ogawa, M. Hosokawa, K. Abe, T. Ukeda, S. Sumi, S. Kurita, S. Nakakubo, S. Lee, T. Doi and H. Shimada, Automatic Detection of Cognitive Impairments through Acoustic Analysis of Speech, *Current Alzheimer Research* **17**, 60 (January 2020).
17. Y. Qiao, X.-Y. Xie, G.-Z. Lin, Y. Zou, S.-D. Chen, R.-J. Ren and G. Wang, Computer-Assisted Speech Analysis in Mild Cognitive Impairment and Alzheimer's Disease: A Pilot Study from Shanghai, China, *Journal of Alzheimer's Disease* **75**, 211 (January 2020), Publisher: IOS Press.
18. R. Ossewaarde, R. Jonkers, F. Jalvingh and R. Bastiaanse, Classification of Spontaneous Speech of Individuals with Dementia Based on Automatic Prosody Analysis Using Support Vector Machines (SVM), in *The Thirty-Second International Flairs Conference*, (Not Available, 2019).
19. F. Haider, S. de la Fuente and S. Luz, An Assessment of Paralinguistic Acoustic Features for Detection of Alzheimer's Dementia in Spontaneous Speech, *IEEE Journal of Selected Topics in Signal Processing* **14**, 272 (February 2020), Conference Name: IEEE Journal of Selected Topics in Signal Processing.
20. A. Balagopalan, J. Novikova, F. Rudzicz and M. Ghassemi, *The Effect of Heterogeneous Data for*

Alzheimer's Disease Detection from Speech, Tech. Rep. arXiv:1811.12254, arXiv (November 2018), arXiv:1811.12254 [cs, eess, stat] type: article.
21. S. de la Fuente Garcia, C. W. Ritchie and S. Luz, Artificial intelligence, speech, and language processing approaches to monitoring alzheimer's disease: a systematic review, *Journal of Alzheimer's Disease* **78**, 1547 (2020).
22. S. Luz, F. Haider, S. de la Fuente, D. Fromm and B. MacWhinney, Alzheimer's dementia recognition through spontaneous speech: The adress challenge, *arXiv preprint arXiv:2004.06833* (2020).
23. E. Edwards, C. Dognin, B. Bollepalli, M. K. Singh and V. Analytics, Multiscale system for alzheimer's dementia recognition through spontaneous speech., in *INTERSPEECH*, (Not Available, 2020).
24. J. Yuan, Y. Bian, X. Cai, J. Huang, Z. Ye and K. Church, Disfluencies and fine-tuning pre-trained language models for detection of alzheimer's disease., in *INTERSPEECH*, (Not Available, 2020).
25. A. Pompili, T. Rolland and A. Abad, The INESC-ID Multi-Modal System for the ADReSS 2020 Challenge (May 2020).
26. S. Farzana and N. Parde, Exploring mmse score prediction using verbal and non-verbal cues., in *INTERSPEECH*, (Not Available, 2020).
27. A. Balagopalan, B. Eyre, F. Rudzicz and J. Novikova, To bert or not to bert: comparing speech and language-based approaches for alzheimer's disease detection, *arXiv preprint arXiv:2008.01551* (2020).
28. M. S. S. Syed, Z. S. Syed, M. Lech and E. Pirogova, Automated screening for alzheimer's dementia through spontaneous speech., in *INTERSPEECH*, (Not Available, 2020).
29. T. Searle, Z. Ibrahim and R. Dobson, Comparing natural language processing techniques for alzheimer's dementia prediction in spontaneous speech, *arXiv preprint arXiv:2006.07358* (2020).
30. G. Soğancıoğlu, O. Verkholyak, H. Kaya, D. Fedotov, T. Cadée, A. A. Salah and A. Karpov, Is everything fine, grandma? acoustic and linguistic modeling for robust elderly speech emotion recognition, *arXiv preprint arXiv:2009.03432* (2020).
31. E. Bisong, Google Colaboratory, in *Building Machine Learning and Deep Learning Models on Google Cloud Platform: A Comprehensive Guide for Beginners*, ed. E. Bisong (Apress, Berkeley, CA, 2019) pp. 59–64.
32. B. MacWhinney, The childes project: Tools for analyzing talk: Volume i: Transcription format and programs, volume ii: The database (2000).
33. R. Y. Wood, K. K. Giuliano, C. U. Bignell and W. W. Pritham, Assessing cognitive ability in research: use of mmse with minority populations and elderly adults with low education levels., *Journal of Gerontological Nursing* **32**, 45 (2006).
34. R. Keshari, S. Ghosh, S. Chhabra, M. Vatsa and R. Singh, Unravelling small sample size problems in the deep learning world, in *2020 IEEE Sixth International Conference on Multimedia Big Data (BigMM)*, (Not Available, 2020).
35. D. W. Marquardt and R. D. Snee, Ridge regression in practice, *The American Statistician* **29**, 3 (1975).
36. J. Ranstam and J. Cook, Lasso regression, *Journal of British Surgery* **105**, 1348 (2018).
37. H. Zou and T. Hastie, Regularization and variable selection via the elastic net, *Journal of the royal statistical society: series B (statistical methodology)* **67**, 301 (2005).
38. R. J. Tibshirani and J. Taylor, The solution path of the generalized lasso, *The annals of statistics* **39**, 1335 (2011).
39. C. M. Bishop and N. M. Nasrabadi, *Pattern recognition and machine learning* (Springer, 2006).
40. D. Wipf and S. Nagarajan, A new view of automatic relevance determination, *Advances in neural information processing systems* **20** (2007).
41. T. Blumensath and M. E. Davies, On the difference between orthogonal matching pursuit and

orthogonal least squares (2007).
42. A. Owen, A robust hybrid of lasso and ridge regression (technical report) (2006).
43. X. Wang, X. Dang, H. Peng and H. Zhang, The theil-sen estimators in multiple linear regression models, *Manuscript available at: http://home. olemiss. edu/˜ xdang/papers/MTSE. pdf* (2009).
44. L. Bottou, Stochastic gradient descent tricks, in *Neural networks: Tricks of the trade*, (Springer, 2012) pp. 421–436.
45. F. Pedregosa, G. Varoquaux, A. Gramfort, V. Michel, B. Thirion, O. Grisel, M. Blondel, P. Prettenhofer, R. Weiss, V. Dubourg, J. Vanderplas, A. Passos, D. Cournapeau, M. Brucher, M. Perrot and E. Duchesnay, Scikit-learn: Machine learning in Python, *Journal of Machine Learning Research* **12**, 2825 (2011).
46. C. R. Harris, K. J. Millman, S. J. van der Walt, R. Gommers, P. Virtanen, D. Cournapeau, E. Wieser, J. Taylor, S. Berg, N. J. Smith, R. Kern, M. Picus, S. Hoyer, M. H. van Kerkwijk, M. Brett, A. Haldane, J. F. del Río, M. Wiebe, P. Peterson, P. Gérard-Marchant, K. Sheppard, T. Reddy, W. Weckesser, H. Abbasi, C. Gohlke and T. E. Oliphant, Array programming with NumPy, *Nature* **585**, 357 (September 2020).
47. M. L. Waskom, seaborn: statistical data visualization, *Journal of Open Source Software* **6**, p. 3021 (2021).
48. P. Virtanen, R. Gommers, T. E. Oliphant, M. Haberland, T. Reddy, D. Cournapeau, E. Burovski, P. Peterson, W. Weckesser, J. Bright, S. J. van der Walt, M. Brett, J. Wilson, K. J. Millman, N. Mayorov, A. R. J. Nelson, E. Jones, R. Kern, E. Larson, C. J. Carey, İ. Polat, Y. Feng, E. W. Moore, J. VanderPlas, D. Laxalde, J. Perktold, R. Cimrman, I. Henriksen, E. A. Quintero, C. R. Harris, A. M. Archibald, A. H. Ribeiro, F. Pedregosa, P. van Mulbregt and SciPy 1.0 Contributors, SciPy 1.0: Fundamental Algorithms for Scientific Computing in Python, *Nature Methods* **17**, 261 (2020).
49. T. pandas development team, pandas-dev/pandas: Pandas (February 2020).
50. J. D. Hunter, Matplotlib: A 2d graphics environment, *Computing in Science & Engineering* **9**, 90 (2007).
51. N. Haas, regressors: Easy utilities for fitting various regressors, extracting stats, and making relevant plots.
52. J. C. Vásquez-Correa, J. Orozco-Arroyave, T. Bocklet and E. Nöth, Towards an automatic evaluation of the dysarthria level of patients with parkinson's disease, *Journal of communication disorders* **76**, 21 (2018).
53. J. R. Orozco-Arroyave, J. C. Vásquez-Correa, J. F. Vargas-Bonilla, R. Arora, N. Dehak, P. S. Nidadavolu, H. Christensen, F. Rudzicz, M. Yancheva, H. Chinaei *et al.*, Neurospeech: An open-source software for parkinson's speech analysis, *Digital Signal Processing* **77**, 207 (2018).
54. T. Arias-Vergara, J. C. Vásquez-Correa and J. R. Orozco-Arroyave, Parkinson's disease and aging: analysis of their effect in phonation and articulation of speech, *Cognitive Computation* **9**, 731 (2017).
55. N. Dehak, P. Dumouchel and P. Kenny, Modeling prosodic features with joint factor analysis for speaker verification, *IEEE Transactions on Audio, Speech, and Language Processing* **15**, 2095 (2007).
56. Z. Li, Z. Zhang, Y. Ren, Y. Wang, J. Fang, H. Yue, S. Ma and F. Guan, Aging and age-related diseases: from mechanisms to therapeutic strategies, *Biogerontology* **22**, 165 (April 2021).
57. G. A. Marshall, A. S. Zoller, N. Lorius, R. E. Amariglio, J. J. Locascio, K. A. Johnson, R. A. Sperling, D. M. Rentz and for the Alzheimer's Disease Neuroimaging Initiative, Functional Activities Questionnaire Items that Best Discriminate and Predict Progression from Clinically Normal to Mild Cognitive Impairment, *Current Alzheimer Research* **12**, 493 (June 2015).
58. G. Landsberg, Therapeutic options for cognitive decline in senior pets, *Journal of the American Animal Hospital Association* **42**, 407 (2006).

PiTE: TCR-epitope Binding Affinity Prediction Pipeline using Transformer-based Sequence Encoder

Pengfei Zhang [1,2], Seojin Bang [2§] and Heewook Lee [1,2 †]

[1] *School of Computing and Augmented Intelligence*
Arizona State University, Tempe, AZ, United States
[†] *E-mail: heewook.lee@asu.edu*

[2] *Biodesign Institute*
Arizona State University, Tempe, AZ, United States

Accurate prediction of TCR binding affinity to a target antigen is important for development of immunotherapy strategies. Recent computational methods were built on various deep neural networks and used the evolutionary-based distance matrix BLOSUM to embed amino acids of TCR and epitope sequences to numeric values. A pre-trained language model of amino acids is an alternative embedding method where each amino acid in a peptide is embedded as a continuous numeric vector. Little attention has yet been given to summarize the amino-acid-wise embedding vectors to sequence-wise representations. In this paper, we propose PiTE, a two-step pipeline for the TCR-epitope binding affinity prediction. First, we use an amino acids embedding model pre-trained on a large number of unlabeled TCR sequences and obtain a real-valued representation from a string representation of amino acid sequences. Second, we train a binding affinity prediction model that consists of two sequence encoders and a stack of linear layers predicting the affinity score of a given TCR and epitope pair. In particular, we explore various types of neural network architectures for the sequence encoders in the two-step binding affinity prediction pipeline. We show that our Transformer-like sequence encoder achieves a state-of-the-art performance and significantly outperforms the others, perhaps due to the model's ability to capture contextual information between amino acids in each sequence. Our work highlights that an advanced sequence encoder on top of pre-trained representation significantly improves performance of the TCR-epitope binding affinity prediction*.

Keywords: TCR; epitope; binding affinity prediction; sequence encoder.

1. Introduction

T cells play fundamental roles in the adaptive immune system. T cell receptor (TCR) is a cell surface protein complex that binds to peptides presented by antigen presenting cells (APCs) via major histocompatibility complex (MHC, pMHC is the peptide-MHC multimers that are presented to T cells).[1] A successful binding and recognition of a foreign antigen triggers an immune response to defend our body from the invaders. The binding is essentially determined

§Now at Google.
*Code and models are publicly available at `https://github.com/Lee-CBG/PiTE`

by two short amino acid chains.[2] One is an epitope, a part of antigen peptides bound within pMHC presented by APCs and a TCR is the counterpart. Of a TCR, the complementarity-determining region 3 (CDR3) of TCR β chain is known to be the most important part that interacts with its cognate epitope pairs.[2–4]

Accurate prediction of TCR binding affinity to a target epitope is a critical step to unraveling the underlying binding mechanisms. Especially, the ability to predict computationally is extremely valuable as it can automate screening of cognate TCRs for an epitope of interest. Computational screening of a confident candidate set of TCRs for a target epitope can dramatically reduce the time and the cost of wet lab assays, thereby further enabling rapid development of personalized immunotherapy.[5,6]

Many machine learning models to predict the binding affinity of TCR and epitope sequences have been developed.[7–14] While earlier models such as TCRex[8] and TCRGP[7] utilized random forest and gaussian process respectively, more recent models leveraged a large capacity of deep neural networks. For example, NetTCR[9] and NetTCR2.0[10] were built on multiple convolutional neural network (CNN) layers with different sizes of filters to encode each sequence followed by dense layers to predict the binding affinity scores between the encoded sequences. To accommodate the amino acid sequential data, ERGO[11] utilized a long-short term memory (LSTM)[15] layer followed by a multi-layer perceptron. Similarly, TITAN[12] and ATM-TCR[13] leveraged the attention mechanism.[16]

The first step to process the input for these machine learning models is translating string representation of peptides (both TCR and epitope sequences) into a real-valued numeric vector. Overwhelmingly many models[7–10,12] map each amino acid in a TCR (or epitope) sequence to a predefined vector of numeric values using evolutionary-based distance matrices BLOSUM.[17] However, the models using BLOSUM-based embedding suffer from limited performance, especially when predicting binding affinity for out-of-sample epitopes[13] not present in the training data the models were trained on.

In order to improve generalized prediction performance, several amino acids embedding models have been proposed.[11,14,18,19] These models were trained on a large number of unpaired TCR sequences by considering the input sequence itself as the supervision signal. Among these, especially the embedding models[14,19] whose architectures were inspired by language representation models such as Bert[20] and ELMo[21] have shown to learn more effective contextualized embeddings for TCR and epitope sequences and improved prediction performance. Typically, such models yield a larger size of embedding vectors than those of BLOSUM-based method. Average pooling has been commonly used to reduce the size of the embedding model outputs and enable training a binding affinity prediction model with less computational burden. However, it wipes off position-specific information and degrades prediction performance because it averages vectors over all amino acids.

We propose `PiTE`, a **Pi**peline leveraging **T**ransformer-like **E**ncoders to predict the binding affinity between a pair of TCR and epitope sequences. Our pipeline consists of two parts: (1) amino acids embedding for each TCR and epitope, and (2) binding affinity prediction between the two sequences. First, we use a pre-trained embedding model to map string representations of amino acids sequences (e.g., `GLCTLVAML`) to a sequence of real-valued vectors. It leverages a large number of unlabeled TCR sequences to train an embedding model, and learn contextual representations of TCRs and epitopes using a bidirectional LSTM architecture. Second, we train a binding affinity prediction model that takes a pair of TCR and epitope embeddings as an input and returns a binding affinity score between those two sequences. `PiTE` encodes TCR and epitope amino acids embeddings using two sequence encoders, respectively, and determines the binding affinity between those two sequences using multiple linear layers. In particular, we explore various different types of neural network architectures to encode each sequence on top of existing embedding models. We highlight the importance of an advanced sequence encoder to boost the performance of the TCR-epitope binding affinity prediction.

2. Data

2.1. *Positive Sample Collection*

To train our models, we sampled TCR-epitope pairs with known binding affinity from three publicly available databases–IEDB,[22] VDJdb,[23] and McPAS.[24] Pairs with MHC class I type epitopes and TCRβ CDR3 sequences were used in our analysis. In this paper, TCR sequence refers to CDR3 unless otherwise stated. Sequences containing wildcard amino acids, such as `*` and `X` were excluded. After removing duplicates from three databases, a total of 150,008 unique TCR-epitope pairs known to bind were obtained.

2.2. *Negative Sample Generation*

While there is real negative binding data,[10] the dataset only covers a limited number of epitopes (19 epitopes), we strictly generated the same number of negative samples so that our data have an 1:1 ratio of positive and negative samples. In detail, we collected TCR sequences from TCR repertoires of healthy controls in ImmunoSEQ[25] portal. We then replaced TCRs of the positive TCR-epitope pairs with TCRs randomly selected from the healthy controls, resulting in 150,008 negative TCR-epitope pairs. Combining our collected positive pairs and generated negative pairs, we had 300,016 unique TCR-epitope pairs in total.

2.3. *Training and Testing Set Split*

The binding characteristic of TCRs and epitopes is many-to-many, which means a TCR can bind to multiple epitopes and an epitope can bind to multiple TCRs. Considering that our dataset has 290,683 unique TCRs and 982 unique epitopes, it is highly likely that an epitope can be found in both training and testing sets if we randomly split the sets. It is less likely that a TCR present in both training and testing sets, but this can still happen. Therefore, the random split of training and testing sets cannot properly measure generalization performance of our model on novel TCRs and epitopes. In order to measure generalization performance on novel TCRs and epitopes, we followed two dataset splitting approaches used in ATM-TCR:[13] the TCR split and the epitope split. In the TCR split, no testing TCRs ever appeared in the training set, allowing us to evaluate the performance of binding affinity prediction models on out-of-sample TCRs. Similarly, in the epitope split, no testing epitopes ever appeared in the training set, allowing us to evaluate the performance on out-of-sample epitopes.

3. Methods

PiTE consists of two parts: amino acid embedding and TCR-epitope binding affinity prediction (see Fig. 1). In the TCR (or epitope) amino acids embedding part, we use a pre-trained embedding model to map a TCR (or epitope) sequence of string representation of amino acids to a sequence of real-valued vectors. In the binding affinity prediction part, we train a variety of different binding affinity prediction models, which composed of two sequence encoders (one for TCR and the other for epitope) and a block of linear classification layers. In particular, we are interested in how different types of encoders would perform in summarization of amino-acid-wise embedding vectors into a sequence-wise representation.

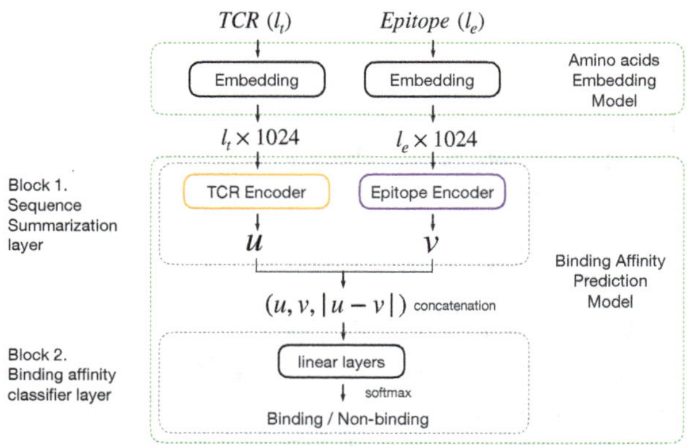

Fig. 1. PiTE pipeline: A TCR sequence with length of l_t is first fed to the amino acids embedding model. Each amino acid is embedded as a 1×1024 vector, hence a TCR sequence is embedded as a $l_t \times 1024$ matrix. Similarly, an epitope sequence with length l_e is embedded as a $l_e \times 1024$. These embeddings are then passed into each sequence encoder to obtain the summarized representation u and v for the TCR and epitope sequence, respectively. Finally, u, v, and their absolute subtraction $|u - v|$ are concatenated, and fed to two linear layers followed by a softmax activation function to predict the binding affinity between the TCR and epitope sequences. Note sequence encoder layers and binding affinity classifier layer are trained together as one binding affinity prediction model.

3.1. *Amino Acids Embedding*

Amino acid embedding is a process to map each amino acid in a TCR (or epitope) sequence to a real-valued vector. Recently, amino acid embedding models[11,14,18,19] leveraging a large number of (unlabeled) TCR sequences have shown great advantages over the BLOSUM-based models. We use a pre-trained amino acids embedding model[19] trained on unlabeled TCR sequences collected from ImmunoSEQ portal. The embedding model adopted the overall architecture from a widely used language representation model, ELMo,[21] with different layer sizes. Note that this paper does not aim to find an optimal architecture for amino acid embedding. We use this model because it performs the best on our dataset, but it can be replaced by any other state-of-the-art embedding models such as TCR-Bert[14] and DeepTCR.[18]

The embedding model serves as a feature extractor that maps each amino acid in a string representation of TCR (or epitope) sequence to a numeric vector of size of 1×1024. Therefore, a TCR sequence of length l_t is represented by a sequence of embedding vectors (i.e., a matrix of size $l_t \times 1024$). Similarly, an epitope sequence of length l_e is represented by a sequence of embedding vectors (i.e., a matrix of size $l_e \times 1024$). These embeddings will serve as the input of the binding affinity prediction model. Since the binding affinity prediction model requires the input to have the same shape and size, we align TCRs and epitopes using the IMGT approach with a predefined length l. If the length of the TCR sequence (l_t) is longer than l, we remove an embedding vector of the amino acid from the end until it equals l. Otherwise, we append zeros to the end of embedding vectors to ensure the embedding length is l. We predefine l as 22 for both the TCR and epitope sequences. This preprocessing step is applied before feeding the TCR (or epitope) embeddings into our sequence encoder except for the baseline average pooling encoder.

3.2. *TCR-epitope Binding Affinity Prediction*

3.2.1. *Sequence Encoders*

Average pooling (baseline): Average pooling is a pooling technique that projects a high dimensional matrix to a low dimensional one by averaging values with regards to some feature dimension. It has been commonly used for obtaining sequence representations from the output of amino acids embedding models. It helps to reduce the dimension of the amino acid embedding of which the size is generally larger than the BLOSUM embedding. We used an average pooling with regards to the length dimension as the baseline for sequence encoders. In detail, we performed the average pooling on each embedding of TCRs with the size $l_t \times 1024$, and obtained a summarized TCR sequence representation with the size 1×1024. Similarly, we obtained a summarized epitope sequence representation with the size 1×1024. It helps to handle various lengths of TCR (or epitope) sequences by reducing the dimension of their amino acids embedding size.

Transformers: Transformer[16] is a deep learning model using an encoder-decoder structure that leverages multi-head self-attention mechanism to learn contextual representation of texts. Although it was originally designed for machine translation, it and its variants have been achieving revolutionary performances in many other natural language processing tasks such as question answering, text generation, and textual entailment.[20,26]

We use a multi-head self-attention module for sequence encoders, which is similar to Transformer encoder. The attention module allows the model to attend different amino acid residues of a TCR (or epitope) sequence based on their contextual relationship. In detail, the module takes three types of vectors as input: a query vector Q, a key vector K, and a value vector V. Each vector is defined by a linear projection of a TCR (or epitope) embedding, and each element in the projection matrix is considered as a model parameter. Then the scaled dot-product of Q and K determines the strength of contextual relationship between different amino acid residues. The self-attention layer is then calculated by the following equation:

$$Attention(Q, K, V) = Softmax\left(\frac{QK^T}{\sqrt{d_k}}\right)V.$$

The multi-head self-attention layer is defined as a concatenation of multiple self-attention layers. Taking an embedded TCR sequence ($l_t \times 1024$) as an example, we first feed it into a multi-head attention layer with two heads followed by a dropout layer[27] with a rate of 0.1 and a layer-wise normalization.[28] The output of which is then served as the input for a feed-forward layer followed by another dropout layer with a rate of 0.1 and a layer-wise normalization. Finally, a SiLU[29] activation function followed by a global max pooling layer is used to produce a 1×1024 summarized representation for the TCR sequence. Similarly, we generate a 1×1024 sized representation for the epitope sequence.

BiLSTMs: LSTM[15] is a type of recurrent neural networks designed for dealing with long-term dependencies in sequential data and have been commonly used to process protein or genomic sequences.[11,30] Evidence has shown that BiLSTMs with max-pooling achieved overall better performance than other recurrent units such as vanilla LSTMs and GRUs[31] for sentence encoding in natural language process.[32] We therefore select a BiLSTM structure as one of our sequence encoders. A BiLSTM layer consists of two LSTM layers in opposite directions: the forward layer and the backward layer. The forward LSTM layer is used to predict the current state given previous ones by feeding the input sequence in order, and the backward LSTM layer is used for producing the current state given the future ones by feeding the input sequence reversely. In this way, a BiLSTM layer can learn features from both directions.

In detail, taking an epitope sequence with length l_e as an example, we first use a biLSTM layer with 32 units to encode the epitope sequence, followed by a time-distributed linear layer with 256 neurons. The output vector size is $l_e \times 256$. We then feed this vector to a SiLU activation function[29] and global max pooling layer as it has been shown the global max-pooling achieves better encoding results in general.[32] The final outputed representation vector is 1×256 for the epitope sequence. Similarly, the representation size for a TCR sequence is also 1×256.

CNNs: CNNs are a type of neural networks using convolution operations to extract high-level features in image processing.[33] CNNs have achieved excellent performances in many computer vision tasks involving videos or images.[34,35] A recent work suggested that CNNs could also perform well even when dealing with sequential data such as protein sequences.[36] Specifically, they trained a ByteNet-based[37] CNN model on protein data and showed that their CNN model achieved comparable performance with Transformers. We thereby design an CNN-based architecture for the sequence encoders using ByteNet.

A ByteNet block consists of 3 one-dimensional CNN layers, each of which is followed by a batch normalization[38] layer and GeLU[39] activation function. The number of filters for these three CNN layers are 256, 512, and 1024, respectively. The first and third CNN layers with both kernel sizes and stride steps being 1 are utilized to process the sequential TCR and epitope sequences. The middle CNN layer is a dilated CNN[40] with a kernel size of 5 and stride step of 1, and it is used to expand the receptive field of input sequence covered without pooling to learn global context information. The input and output of each block are added together, and serve as the input for the next block. Four blocks are used in total. The dilation rate for the dilated CNN layer in each block increases by a factor of 2, ranging from 2 to 16.

Taking a TCR amino acids embedding ($l_t \times 1024$) as an example, we first feed it into an 1D CNN layer with 256 filters followed by a GeLU activation function and another 1D CNN layer with 512 filters. Batch normalization and a GeLU activation function are then applied. The output of which is then feed into a 1D CNN layer with 1024 filters followed by 4 continuous ByteNet blocks. We use the final output of these ByteNets as the summarized representation for TCR or epitope sequences. The size of summarized representation is 1×1024.

3.2.2. *Linear Prediction Layers*

On top of the sequence encoders, we stack two dense layers for determining the TCR-epitope binding affinity score between two sequence representations. The classifier takes a pair of summarized TCR and epitope representation vectors as the input and predicts the probability (0–1) that they are binding to each other. Taking a summarized TCR sequence representation (denoted as u) obtained from the baseline sequence encoder (size of 1×1024) as an example, a summarized epitope sequence representation is also 1×1024 size (denoted as v). We first concatenate u, v, and their absolute subtraction $|u - v|$ together, resulting in a 1×3072 input vector under baseline circumstance. The reason we include $|u - v|$ into the concatenation is that we aim to force the model to not only learn features from TCR and epitope sequences but also pay attention to the difference between them. We then feed this input vector into a linear layer with 1024 neurons, followed by a batch normalization,[38] a 0.3 rate dropout[27] and a SiLU[29] activation function. The output of which is then passed into another linear layer with a single neuron followed by a softmax function to produce a binding affinity score ranging from 0 to 1.

4. Experiments

We compared four different sequence summarizing encoders, including average pooling as baseline, our Transformer-based, BiLSTM-based, and CNN-based sequence encoders. We trained the sequence encoders together with a two-layer neural network that concatenates output representations of the encoders and predicts the binding affinity of TCR and epitope pairs.

4.1. *Implementation Details*

We trained TCR-epitope binding prediction models using adam[41] optimizer and binary cross-entropy loss with a learning rate of 0.001 and a batch size of 32. An early stopping method was used to avoid over-fitting. It stops training if the validation loss has not decreased for the last 30 epochs or the epoch become larger than 200. For each type of the sequence encoder, we listed the size of summarized representations (u for a TCR sequence and v for an epitope sequence showed in Fig. 1), as well as the total number of trainable parameters in the TCR-epitope binding affinity prediction models in Table 1. Note that the summarized representation size of our BiLSTM-based method is 1×256, which is one fourth of other methods. We intentionally designed in this way to build a lite sequence encoder for comparison purposes. We trained each model for 10 runs and reported mean and standard deviation of AUC, precision, and recall scores. We tuned the number of heads in the multi-head attention layers and the size of binary classification layers, and selected values achieving the highest AUC in epitope split (Supplementary table 1). Each run took less than 1 day to finish on a NVIDIA RTX 2080 GPU with 11 GB memory. All our code was developed upon Tensorflow.[42]

Table 1. Summarized representation size of different sequence encoder and trainable parameters of TCR-epitope binding affinity prediction models. We show number of total trainable parameters in the prediction model and trainable parameters in encoder layers in parentheses.

Sequence Encoder Structure	Representation Size	Trainable Parameters (in encoders)
Average Pooling (Baseline)	1×1024	3,149,825 (0)
Transformer	1×1024	20,082,753 (16,932,928)
BiLSTMs	1×256	1,364,993 (574,464)
CNNs	1×1024	11,430,657 (8,280,832)

4.2. *Results and Discussion*

Our Transformer-based sequence encoder significantly outperforms the rest three methods. To visually compare performances of different sequence encoders, we showcased the ROC curves for both TCR and epitope split in Fig. 2. It was constructed by plotting the true positive rate against the false positive rate. A model is considered to have good performance if its ROC curve is close to the top-left corner. As seen in Fig. 2, we found that our transformer-based model outperformed the other three methods under both TCR and epitope split settings, indicating that it can summarize the TCR and epitope amino acids embedding better. It may be because the multi-head attention mechanism assists to learn contextual information between amino acids. We also compared the AUC, precision, and recall scores of the methods in Fig. 2. The mean values across 10 runs are shown on top of each bar in Fig. 2. The height of error bars represents the standard deviation over 10 runs. A two-sample paired t-test was carried out for statistical significance testing. A p-value less than 0.05 means a significant performance difference, otherwise, we considered it an statistically equivalent. We showed that our Transformer-based model significantly outperformed both the baseline and BiLSTM-based method in TCR and epitope split. In detail, our Transformer-based method achieved a 97.48% AUC score in TCR split, outperforming baseline and BiLSTM-based methods by 3 and 2 points, respectively. Similarly, even bigger performance gains were observed in the epitope split. The Transformer-based method reached a 89.83% AUC score which surpassed the baseline and BiLSTM-methods by around 5 and 4 points, respectively. Our comparison results suggested that Transformer-based sequence encoder can best summarize TCR (or epitope) representations.

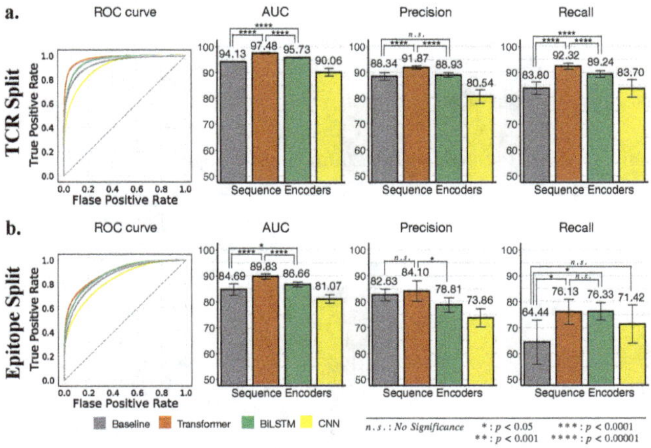

Fig. 2. Performance of the TCR-epitope binding affinity prediction models using variety of different sequence encoders in **a.** TCR split and **b.** Epitope split.

The choice of model architecture can be more important than the number of model parameters. Our BiLSTM-based method significantly outperformed the baseline method in both TCR split and epitope splits as well. As seen in Fig. 2, it achieved a 95.73% AUC score in the TCR split, which is 1 point higher than the baseline of which the number of trainable parameters are three times larger (Table. 1). We also observed that the current size of BiLSTM-based method performed similar with a larger size BiLSTM model (representation size 1×1024). The large BiLSTM model achieved an AUC of 95.52% in the TCR split, and of 87.13% in the epitope split, showing that increasing the number of parameters in BiLSTM is not a significant factor for improving the prediction performance. Moreover, we also observed that CNN may not be an optimal structure for summarizing TCR or epitope sequences. It performed significantly worse than baseline in both TCR split and epitope split. The AUC score dropped around 4 points to 90.06% and 81.07% compared to baseline in both TCR and epitope split, respectively. While the CNN-based model contains three more times parameters than the baseline method, it failed to summarize better embeddings for sequences. It may be because the the CNN-based model focused on leaning local contextual information but not on global contextual information. All those results showed that carefully selecting the neural network structure can make great improvement for TCR-epitope binding affinity prediction than simply increasing model capacities.

The Transformer-based method performs best on most individual out-of-sample epitopes. To take a closer look at our models' performance on individual unseen epitopes, we further compared AUC scores of each epitopes having the top 20 frequency in the epitope split (Table. 2). For each epitope, we highlighted the highest AUC score across four models in bold. We found that our Transformer-based method achieved the highest AUC scores in 17 out of 20 epitopes. Apart from the first two epitopes, the Transformer-based and BiLSTM-based model surpassed the baseline for the other 18 epitopes. The CNN-based model, on the other hand, generally performed worse than baseline. Overall, the comparison results of individual epitopes was consistent with our observation in Fig 2.

Table 2. AUC scores for Top 20 frequent epitopes in testing set

Epitopes	Number of TCRs	Baseline	Transformers	BiLSTM	CNNs
MIELSLIDFYLCFLAFLLFLVLIML	23146	**74.37**	60.05	68.81	64.94
GILGFVFTL	10802	**85.93**	80.75	83	78.82
LLWNGPMAV	4716	79.75	**89.51**	87.41	75.75
LSPRWYFYYL	3502	71.19	**93.69**	80.62	78.67
VQELYSPIFLIV	2126	77.99	**92.86**	89.56	80.67
GMEVTPSGTWLTY	1990	74.88	**93.17**	86.19	76.99
ELAGIGILTV	1970	86.86	**90**	88.84	82.29
YEDFLEYHDVRVVL	1752	81.06	**96.58**	92.76	75
FLPRVFSAV	1734	78.78	**89.16**	84.49	75.38
MPASWVMRI	1558	75.61	**89.74**	81.26	75.23
FPPTSFGPL	1362	79.01	**93.18**	86.79	80.92
YEQYIKWPWYI	1074	67.88	**95.63**	87.25	77.1
VLHSYFTSDYYQLY	970	79.18	**86.5**	86.09	79.39
KTAYSHLSTSK	952	59.14	**80.68**	78.79	70.59
CRVLCCYVL	870	71.04	80.35	**80.92**	75.64
ILGLPTQTV	472	78.39	**95.34**	93.65	75.43
FIAGLIAIV	406	77.1	**93.35**	82.52	66.26
SMWSFNPETNIL	398	80.66	**92.72**	89.45	81.41
ILHCANFNV	398	80.16	**95.98**	90.46	85.18
FTISVTTEIL	396	76.27	**94.45**	88.39	80.31

5. Conclusions

This paper proposed PiTE, a pipeline that achieved a state-of-the-art performance for the TCR-epitope binding affinity prediction problem. In particular, we explored various types of neural network architectures for the sequence encoders that can be used on top of the existing embedding models. We showed that the Transformer-based method achieved the best performance. Our experimental evidence showed that the performance can be further boosted with more advanced structure of sequence encoders.

References

1. C. Szeto, C. A. Lobos, A. T. Nguyen and S. Gras, TCR recognition of peptide–MHC-I: Rule makers and breakers, *International Journal of Molecular Sciences* **22**, p. 68 (2020).
2. M. Krogsgaard and M. M. Davis, How T cells 'see' antigen, *Nature Immunology* **6**, 239 (2005).
3. M. M. Davis and P. J. Bjorkman, T-cell antigen receptor genes and T-cell recognition, *Nature* **334**, 395 (1988).

4. J. L. Xu and M. M. Davis, Diversity in the CDR3 region of VH is sufficient for most antibody specificities, *Immunity* **13**, 37 (2000).
5. C. Graham, R. Hewitson, A. Pagliuca and R. Benjamin, Cancer immunotherapy with CAR-T cells–behold the future, *Clinical Medicine* **18**, p. 324 (2018).
6. L. Zhao and Y. J. Cao, Engineered T cell therapy for cancer in the clinic, *Frontiers in Immunology* **10**, p. 2250 (2019).
7. E. Jokinen, J. Huuhtanen, S. Mustjoki, M. Heinonen and H. Lähdesmäki, Predicting recognition between T cell receptors and epitopes with TCRGP, *PLoS Computational Biology* **17**, p. e1008814 (2021).
8. S. Gielis, P. Moris, W. Bittremieux, N. De Neuter, B. Ogunjimi, K. Laukens and P. Meysman, Detection of enriched T cell epitope specificity in full T cell receptor sequence repertoires, *Frontiers in Immunology* **10**, p. 2820 (2019).
9. V. I. Jurtz, L. E. Jessen, A. K. Bentzen, M. C. Jespersen, S. Mahajan, R. Vita, K. K. Jensen, P. Marcatili, S. R. Hadrup, B. Peters *et al.*, NetTCR: sequence-based prediction of TCR binding to peptide-MHC complexes using convolutional neural networks, *BioRxiv* , p. 433706 (2018).
10. A. Montemurro, V. Schuster, H. R. Povlsen, A. K. Bentzen, V. Jurtz, W. D. Chronister, A. Crinklaw, S. R. Hadrup, O. Winther, B. Peters *et al.*, NetTCR-2.0 enables accurate prediction of TCR-peptide binding by using paired TCRα and β sequence data, *Communications Biology* **4**, 1 (2021).
11. I. Springer, H. Besser, N. Tickotsky-Moskovitz, S. Dvorkin and Y. Louzoun, Prediction of specific TCR-peptide binding from large dictionaries of TCR-peptide pairs, *Frontiers in Immunology* , p. 1803 (2020).
12. A. Weber, J. Born and M. Rodriguez Martínez, TITAN: T-cell receptor specificity prediction with bimodal attention networks, *Bioinformatics* **37**, i237 (2021).
13. M. Cai, S. Bang, P. Zhang and H. Lee, Atm-tcr: Tcr-epitope binding affinity prediction using a multi-head self-attention model, *Frontiers in Immunology* **13** (2022).
14. K. Wu, K. E. Yost, B. Daniel, J. A. Belk, Y. Xia, T. Egawa, A. Satpathy, H. Y. Chang and J. Zou, TCR-BERT: learning the grammar of T-cell receptors for flexible antigen-binding analyses, *bioRxiv* (2021).
15. S. Hochreiter and J. Schmidhuber, Long short-term memory, *Neural Computation* **9**, 1735 (1997).
16. A. Vaswani, N. Shazeer, N. Parmar, J. Uszkoreit, L. Jones, A. N. Gomez, Ł. Kaiser and I. Polosukhin, Attention is all you need, *Advances in Neural Information Processing Systems* **30** (2017).
17. S. Henikoff and J. G. Henikoff, Amino acid substitution matrices from protein blocks, *Proceedings of the National Academy of Sciences* **89**, 10915 (1992).
18. J.-W. Sidhom, H. B. Larman, D. M. Pardoll and A. S. Baras, DeepTCR is a deep learning framework for revealing sequence concepts within T-cell repertoires, *Nature Communications* **12**, 1 (2021).
19. P. Zhang, S. Bang, M. Cai and H. Lee, Cracking TCR-epitope interactions using language model representations, *Under review* .
20. J. Devlin, M.-W. Chang, K. Lee and K. Toutanova, BERT: Pre-training of deep bidirectional transformers for language understanding, in *Proceedings of the 2019 Conference of the North American Chapter of the Association for Computational Linguistics: Human Language Technologies*, (Association for Computational Linguistics, Minneapolis, Minnesota, June 2019).
21. M. E. Peters, M. Neumann, M. Iyyer, M. Gardner, C. Clark, K. Lee and L. Zettlemoyer, Deep contextualized word representations (2018), NAACL.
22. R. Vita, S. Mahajan, J. A. Overton, S. K. Dhanda, S. Martini, J. R. Cantrell, D. K. Wheeler, A. Sette and B. Peters, The immune epitope database (IEDB): 2018 update, *Nucleic Acids Research* **47**, D339 (2019).
23. M. Shugay, D. V. Bagaev, I. V. Zvyagin, R. M. Vroomans, J. C. Crawford, G. Dolton, E. A.

Komech, A. L. Sycheva, A. E. Koneva, E. S. Egorov *et al.*, VDJdb: a curated database of T-cell receptor sequences with known antigen specificity, *Nucleic Acids Research* **46**, D419 (2018).
24. N. Tickotsky, T. Sagiv, J. Prilusky, E. Shifrut and N. Friedman, McPAS-TCR: a manually curated catalogue of pathology-associated T cell receptor sequences, *Bioinformatics* **33**, 2924 (2017).
25. S. Nolan, M. Vignali, M. Klinger, J. N. Dines, I. M. Kaplan, E. Svejnoha, T. Craft, K. Boland, M. Pesesky, R. M. Gittelman *et al.*, A large-scale database of T-cell receptor beta (TCRβ) sequences and binding associations from natural and synthetic exposure to SARS-CoV-2, *Research Square* (2020).
26. T. Brown, B. Mann, N. Ryder, M. Subbiah, J. D. Kaplan, P. Dhariwal, A. Neelakantan, P. Shyam, G. Sastry, A. Askell *et al.*, Language models are few-shot learners, *Advances in Neural Information Processing Systems* **33**, 1877 (2020).
27. N. Srivastava, G. Hinton, A. Krizhevsky, I. Sutskever and R. Salakhutdinov, Dropout: a simple way to prevent neural networks from overfitting, *The Journal of Machine Learning Research* **15**, 1929 (2014).
28. J. L. Ba, J. R. Kiros and G. E. Hinton, Layer normalization, *arXiv:1607.06450* (2016).
29. S. Elfwing, E. Uchibe and K. Doya, Sigmoid-weighted linear units for neural network function approximation in reinforcement learning, *Neural Networks* **107**, 3 (2018).
30. M. Heinzinger, A. Elnaggar, Y. Wang, C. Dallago, D. Nechaev, F. Matthes and B. Rost, Modeling aspects of the language of life through transfer-learning protein sequences, *BMC Bioinformatics* **20**, 1 (2019).
31. K. Cho, B. Van Merriënboer, D. Bahdanau and Y. Bengio, On the properties of neural machine translation: Encoder-decoder approaches, *arXiv:1409.1259* (2014).
32. A. Conneau, D. Kiela, H. Schwenk, L. Barrault and A. Bordes, Supervised learning of universal sentence representations from natural language inference data, in *Proceedings of the 2017 Conference on Empirical Methods in Natural Language Processing*, September 2017.
33. Y. LeCun, B. Boser, J. S. Denker, D. Henderson, R. E. Howard, W. Hubbard and L. D. Jackel, Backpropagation applied to handwritten zip code recognition, *Neural Computation* **1**, 541 (1989).
34. J. Deng, W. Dong, R. Socher, L.-J. Li, K. Li and L. Fei-Fei, ImageNet: A large-scale hierarchical image database, in *2009 IEEE conference on computer vision and pattern recognition*, 2009.
35. A. Krizhevsky, I. Sutskever and G. E. Hinton, ImageNet classification with deep convolutional neural networks, *Advances in Neural Information Processing Systems* **25** (2012).
36. K. K. Yang, A. X. Lu and N. K. Fusi, Convolutions are competitive with transformers for protein sequence pretraining, *bioRxiv* (2022).
37. N. Kalchbrenner, L. Espeholt, K. Simonyan, A. v. d. Oord, A. Graves and K. Kavukcuoglu, Neural machine translation in linear time, *arXiv:1610.10099* (2016).
38. S. Ioffe and C. Szegedy, Batch normalization: Accelerating deep network training by reducing internal covariate shift, in *International Conference on Machine Learning*, 2015.
39. D. Hendrycks and K. Gimpel, Gaussian error linear units (GELUs), *arXiv:1606.08415* (2016).
40. F. Yu and V. Koltun, Multi-scale context aggregation by dilated convolutions, in *International Conference on Learning Representations (ICLR)*, May 2016.
41. D. P. Kingma and J. Ba, Adam: A method for stochastic optimization, in *ICLR (Poster)*, 2015.
42. M. Abadi, A. Agarwal, P. Barham, E. Brevdo, Z. Chen, C. Citro, G. S. Corrado, A. Davis, J. Dean, M. Devin, S. Ghemawat, I. Goodfellow, A. Harp, G. Irving, M. Isard, Y. Jia, R. Jozefowicz, L. Kaiser, M. Kudlur, J. Levenberg, D. Mané, R. Monga, S. Moore, D. Murray, C. Olah, M. Schuster, J. Shlens, B. Steiner, I. Sutskever, K. Talwar, P. Tucker, V. Vanhoucke, V. Vasudevan, F. Viégas, O. Vinyals, P. Warden, M. Wattenberg, M. Wicke, Y. Yu and X. Zheng, TensorFlow: Large-scale machine learning on heterogeneous systems (2015).

Exploiting Domain Knowledge as Causal Independencies in Modeling Gestational Diabetes

Saurabh Mathur[1], Athresh Karanam[1], Predrag Radivojac[2],David M. Haas[3], Kristian Kersting[4] and Sriraam Natarajan[1]

[1]*Department of Computer Science, University of Texas at Dallas, Richardson, TX 70580, USA*

[2]*Northeastern University, Boston, MA 02115, USA*

[3]*Indiana University School of Medicine Indianapolis, IN 46202, USA*

[4]*Department of Computer Science, TU Darmstadt, and Hessen Center for AI (hessen.AI), Darmstadt, Germany*

We consider the problem of modeling gestational diabetes in a clinical study and develop a domain expert-guided probabilistic model that is both interpretable and explainable. Specifically, we construct a probabilistic model based on causal independence (Noisy-Or) from a carefully chosen set of features. We validate the efficacy of the model on the clinical study and demonstrate the importance of the features and the causal independence model.

Keywords: Probabilistic Models, Bayesian networks

1. Introduction

We consider the problem of predicting the onset of gestational diabetes mellitus (GDM) from a combination of risk factors and a polygenic risk score. To this effect, we consider data from the **Nulliparous Pregnancy Outcomes Study: Monitoring Mothers-to-Be** (nuMoM2b[1]) study and develop a probabilistic model for modeling GDM. While the success of deep learning methods[2] in medical tasks[3] has significantly increased the interest in machine learning based methods, these models suffer from the twin problems of being data-hungry and uninterpretable. While quite powerful in their classification abilities, these models are not easy to be employed in decision-making systems that require human interaction.

Consequently, we propose a probabilistic learning method that can effectively and efficiently incorporate domain knowledge. Inspired by previous work in probabilistic learning with expert knowledge,[4,5] we develop a framework for modeling GDM from a few risk factors including Age, BMI, metabolism, family history, blood pressure, etc, and combine the results with a polygenic risk score.

Specifically, our work considers two types of knowledge - causal independencies and qualitative influences. Causal independencies[6–9] specify sets of risk factors (called random variables in probabilistic learning terminology) that are independent of each other when affecting the target. The idea here is that each of these variables has an independent effect on the target – for instance, BMI and age affect GDM independently – and their effects can be combined by a probabilistic combination function. One such example is Noisy-Or. The advantage of such independencies lies in the fact that they lead to a drastic reduction in the number of parameters needed to learn the model.

While powerful, specifying only causal independencies could be insufficient. As an example, consider age and BMI as risk factors for GDM. While both these risk factors could be independent, when they both are higher, the risk of GDM could be increased. This information is not captured by simple causal independencies. To model such knowledge, earlier methods employ the use of qualitative constraints.[4,10,11] A qualitative constraint could be a monotonic statement of the form *as X increases Y increases.* For instance, in our task, it is easy to specify that as age increases the risk of GDM increases.

Inspired by our prior work,[5] we combine these two types of domain knowledge to learn a probabilistic model for predicting GDM from the nuMoM2b data and employ the use of polygenic risk score to provide a prior over the incidence of GDM. Specifically, we take the view of a temporal model due to Heckerman and Breese[6] and combine the influence due to the different risk factors using Noisy-Or. For each of these risk factors, we also employ monotonicity constraints whenever applicable. Our empirical evaluations demonstrate that the proposed method with the knowledge from domain experts outperforms probabilistic learning only from data and is comparable with the best machine learning methods that are not interpretable or interactive.

To summarize, we make the following key contributions: (1) We view the problem of modeling GDM using a probabilistic lens and in the presence of domain expert knowledge in the form of qualitative constraints and causal independencies. (2) We take the temporal view and derive the gradients for learning the probabilistic model. (3) We evaluate the algorithm on a real GDM study and establish its effectiveness.

2. Data description

The **Nulliparous Pregnancy Outcomes Study: Monitoring Mothers-to-Be** (nuMoM2b[1]) study was established to study individuals without previous pregnancy lasting 20 weeks or more (nulliparous) and to elucidate factors associated with adverse pregnancy outcomes. The study enrolled a racially/ethnically/geographically diverse population of 10,038 nulliparous women with singleton gestations. The enrolled participants were followed for the duration of their pregnancy and visits were scheduled four times during the pregnancy: 6 weeks 0 days through 13 weeks 6 days estimated gestational age (EGA), 16 weeks 0 days through 21 weeks 6 days EGA, 22 weeks 0 days through 29 weeks 6 days EGA, and at the time of delivery. Our subset has 7 variables - *BMI, PRS, METs, Age, Hist, PCOS, HiBP.*

For our work, we excluded 193 cases where women were diagnosed with pregestational diabetes. Additionally, 3,368 cases with missing features in the dataset were excluded. In our experiments, we use two cohorts. Figure 1 illustrates the mechanism for choosing these cohorts.

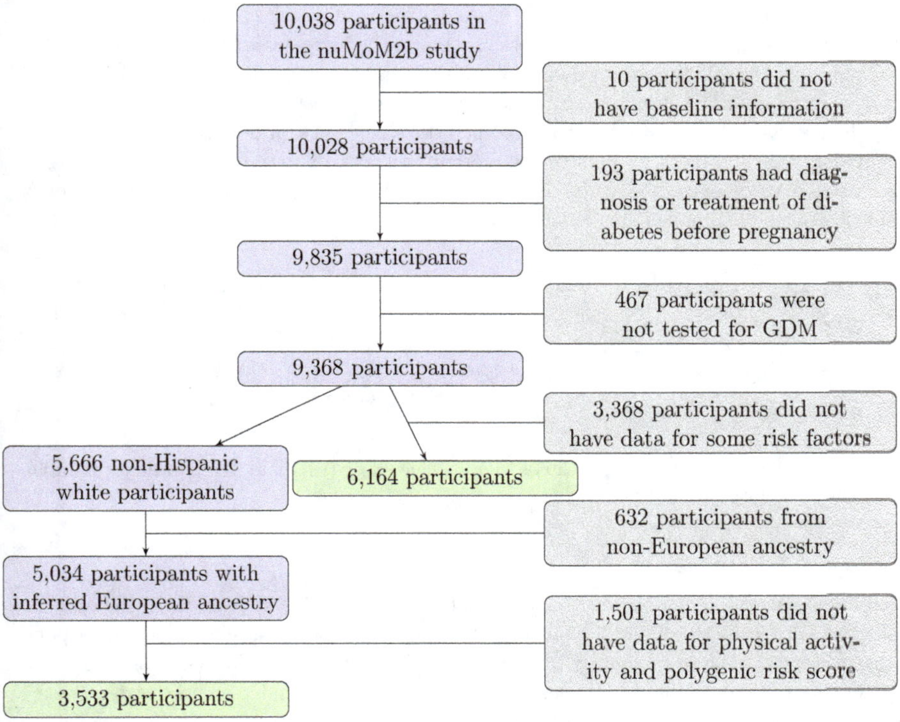

Fig. 1. Flowchart illustrating the process of selecting the cohorts for our experiments. The two sub-cohorts used in our experiments are indicated in green.

A sub-cohort of 3,533 non-Hispanic white participants with European ancestry was used for experiments involving *PRS* and a cohort of 6,164 participants was used for experiments not involving *PRS*. Of the 7 variables, *Hist, PCOS, HiBP* are binary, *Age* is discrete while *BMI, PRS and METs* are continuous. *Age* was categorized into 4 values based on quantiles to limit the number of possible values. The continuous variables *BMI, PRS, and METs* were discretized into 5 categories based on quantiles.

3. Background: Knowledge-guided learning

We now present the necessary background on the two types of expert knowledge that we consider in this work – qualitative influences and causal independencies.

3.1. *Qualitative influence*

A qualitative influence (QI) statement[10] indicates the effect of change in one or more factor(s) on a target.[5] We focus on one particular type of QI: *monotonicty. Monotonicity* represents a direct relationship between two variables: "As BMI increases, neck circumference increases" indicates that the probability of greater neck circumference increases with an increase in BMI. Note that while the QI statements do not directly specify the quantitative relationships (i.e., the precise probabilities), they specify how the conditional distribution ($P(circumference \mid BMI)$) changes as the value of BMI changes. Such statements are quite natural to be specified in many domains, and more so, in medicine. Formally, a *monotonic influence* (MI) of variable X on variable Y, denoted $X \overset{M+}{\prec} Y$ (or its inverse $X \overset{M-}{\prec} Y$), indicates that higher values of X stochastically result in higher (or lower) values of Y.

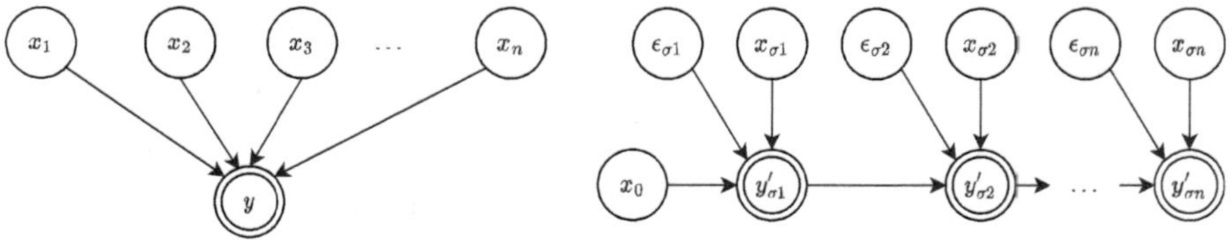

Fig. 2. A belief network for multiple causes and a single effect (left) and Temporal interpretation of Independence of causal influence (right).

3.2. *Causal Independence*

Causal independence, in simple terms, states that (1) the effect is independent of the order in which causes are introduced, and (2) the impact of a single cause on the effect does not depend on what other causes have previously been applied. This definition facilitates a (probabilistic) belief network representation that is consistent with a set of causal independence statements.[6,7] The Noisy-Or model, illustrated in Figure 3, belongs to a class of causal interactions which are characterized by the independence of causal inputs. The belief network in Figure 2 represents a general multiple-cause interaction wherein n causes influence a single effect (target variable) y. While this representation provides an intuitive way to capture the causal interaction between the risk factors x_i and the target variable, it requires 2^n parameter assessments for binary variables - one parameter for each instantiation of the causes. This leads to an exponentially large number of examples required to learn a robust conditional distribution.

Akin to conditional independence assumptions in Bayesian networks, causal independence assumptions allow efficient parameter learning by causing an exponential reduction in the total number of model parameters as compared to the case of general multiple-cause interaction. Concretely, the presence of independence of causal influences allows us to represent the belief network in Figure 2 on the left as the temporal network on the right, for any ordering of causes $\sigma = \{\sigma 1, \ldots, \sigma n\}$. Here, the unobserved effect variable at a timestep $y'_{\sigma i}$ is defined as a deterministic function of the cause $x_{\sigma i}$, the previous state of the effect $y'_{\sigma i-1}$ and $\epsilon_{\sigma i}$, a dummy variable representing the uncertainty. Finally, x_0 represents all causes not considered in the model and $y'_{\sigma n}$ is the observed effect variable. This relation can be expressed as

$$y'_{\sigma 1} = h_\sigma(x_0, x_{\sigma 1}, \epsilon_{\sigma 1}) \tag{1}$$

$$y'_{\sigma i} = h_\sigma(y'_{\sigma i-1}, x_{\sigma i}, \epsilon_{\sigma i}), \ \forall i \in \{2, \ldots, n\} \tag{2}$$

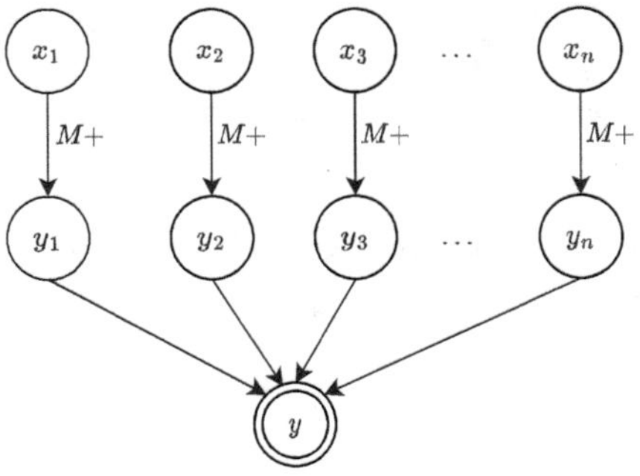

Fig. 3. The Noisy-Or model

For the case where h_σ is the Noisy-Or function, the temporal belief network is equivalent to the Noisy-Or model shown in Figure 3. The number of parameters in the Noisy-Or model is linear in the number of causes, n, while it is exponential in the original model.

Causal independence statements, in conjunction with qualitative influence statements, allow the injection of rich domain knowledge into an interpretable model while ensuring feasible parameter learning from data. We build upon prior work[5] in employing this knowledge in the context of GDM modeling.

4. Causal independencies with qualitative constraints for modeling GDM

Given: A set of causally independent risk factors $\mathbf{X}$ for the target GDM Y and a set of qualitative influences C
To Do: Learn an interpretable model $\mathfrak{m}$ that models the conditional probability of a target variable given the risk factors.

As mentioned earlier, $\mathbf{X}$ is the set of risk factors $\langle BMI, PRS, METs, Age, Hist, PCOS, HiBP\rangle$ while Y denotes GDM. So the goal of our work is to learn $P(GDM \mid \mathbf{X})$ given the constraints C. In the rest of this section, we use $\mathbf{X}$ and Y instead of specific risk factors and GDM to demonstrate the generality of the approach.

In the Noisy-Or model, the target variable is activated if any of the causes is active, unless the active causes are inhibited. Formally, the probability of a cause being active is called the *link probability* and we parameterize it using the sigmoid function σ, i.e., $P(Y_i = 1 \mid X_i = x_i) = \sigma(w_i x_i + b_i)$, $\forall i \in \{1, \ldots, n\}$. The key assumption of the Noisy-Or model is that the inhibitory effect for each cause is independent. Consequently, we parameterize these *inhibition probabilities* as $P(Y = 0 \mid Y_i = 1) = \sigma(q_i)$, $\forall i \in \{1, \ldots, n\}$. Finally, the target variable may still be activated even if none of the causes are active. This is called *leakage* and represents all other possible causes that are not included as risk factors. We parameterize the leak probability as $P(Y = 1 \mid Y_1 = 0, \ldots, Y_n = 0) = \sigma(q_l)$. Thus, the target distribution under Noisy-Or is

$$P(Y = 1 \mid \mathbf{X} = x) = 1 - (1 - q_l) \prod_{i=1}^{n} (P(Y_i = 1 \mid X_i = x_i) q_i + P(Y_i = 0 \mid X_i = x_i)) \tag{3}$$

Following previous work,[4,5] we define positive (or negative) monotonic influence $X_i \overset{M+}{\prec} Y$ (or $X_i \overset{M-}{\prec} Y$) as $P(Y_i = 0 \mid X_i = a) \leq P(Y_i = 0 \mid X_i = b) \;\; \forall a, b \in domain(X_i), a > b$ (or a < b). The Noisy-Or model with monotonic influences is shown in Figure 3.

4.1. *Parameter Learning under monotonicity constraints*

The log-likelihood under the Noisy-Or model can be written as:

$$\begin{aligned}\mathcal{L}(\mathbf{w}, \mathbf{b}, \mathbf{q}, q_l; \mathcal{D}) &= \sum_{j=1}^{N} \log P(Y = y^{(j)} \mid \mathbf{X} = x^{(j)}) \\ &= \sum_{j=1}^{N} y^{(j)} \log(1 - P(Y = 0 \mid \mathbf{X} = x^{(j)})) + (1 - y^{(j)}) \log P(Y = 0 \mid \mathbf{X} = x^{(j)})\end{aligned} \tag{4}$$

We encode the monotonic influences as the margin constraints $\delta_i^{a,b} \leq 0$ where:

$$\delta_i^{a,b} = \begin{cases} P(Y_i = 0 \mid X_i = a) - P(Y_i = 0 \mid X_i = b) + \epsilon & X_i \overset{M+}{\prec} Y \in C \\ -P(Y_i = 0 \mid X_i = a) + P(Y_i = 0 \mid X_i = b) + \epsilon & X_i \overset{M-}{\prec} Y \in C \\ 0 & otherwise \end{cases}$$

Intuitively, if the monotonicity constraint is satisfied, $\delta \leq 0$ while if the constraint is violated, $\delta > 0$. ϵ is a small margin. Now using these constraints, we define the penalty function, $\zeta_i^{a,b} = I_{\delta_i^{a,b} > 0} {\delta_i^{a,b}}^2$. Intuitively, the penalty is applied if the constraint is violated and is equal to the square of the magnitude of the violation. Essentially, the model will not penalize the cases where the constraints are satisfied (for instance, if the constraint on BMI is satisfied when the parameters are learned, the penalty for that parameter = 0).

Including the penalty function, the final objective that is to be maximized is

$$J(\mathbf{w}, \mathbf{b}, \mathbf{q}, q_l; D) = \mathcal{L}(\mathbf{w}, \mathbf{b}, \mathbf{q}, q_l; D) - \lambda \sum_{i=1}^{n} \sum_{a>b} \zeta_i^{a,b}$$

where, λ is the penalty weight. The first term is the classic log-likelihood that is computed using the different conditional distributions and the second term is simply the sum of the non-zero penalties weighted by a constant λ. Recall that $\mathbf{w}$ and $\mathbf{b}$ are the link probability parameters, and $\mathbf{q}$ and q_l are inhibition probability and the leak probability parameters respectively. Intuitively, the penalty function serves as a regularizer that forces the model to satisfy the constraints as much as possible given the data.

The advantage of this formalism is that since it is a weighted combination,**the data could be noisy or the constraints could be incorrect**. The model can simply trade-off between the data and constraints accordingly. Exploring the case when both data and domain expert are noisy is outside the scope of this work. Thus, the model is robust to both data noise and expert advice noise. λ could be chosen by cross-validation, but, in our experiments and in prior work,[5] the model is robust to the choice of λ as long as it is not close to 0 or 1.

4.2. *Derivation of the gradients of the log-likelihood term*

First, we define the following intermediate gradient terms:

$$U_j = \frac{\partial \log P(Y = y^{(j)} \mid \mathbf{X} = x^{(j)})}{\partial P(Y = 0 \mid \mathbf{X} = x^{(j)})} = \frac{-y^{(j)}}{P(Y = 1 \mid \mathbf{X} = x^{(j)})} + \frac{1 - y^{(j)}}{P(Y = 0 \mid \mathbf{X} = x^{(j)})}$$

$$Q_{lj} = \frac{\partial P(Y = 0 \mid X = x^{(j)})}{\partial q_l} = -\frac{P(Y = 0 \mid X = x^{(j)})\sigma'(q_l)}{1 - q_l}$$

$$Q_{ij} = \frac{\partial P(Y = 0 \mid X = x^{(j)})}{\partial q_i} = \frac{P(Y = 0 \mid \mathbf{X} = x^{(j)}))P(Y_i = 1 \mid X_i = x_i^{(j)})\sigma'(q_i)}{P(Y_i = 1 \mid X_i = x_i^{(j)})q_i + P(Y_i = 0 \mid X_i = x_i^{(j)})}$$

$$V_{ij} = \frac{\partial P(Y = 0 \mid \mathbf{X} = x^{(j)})}{\partial P(Y_i = 1 \mid X_i = x_i^{(j)})} = \frac{P(Y = 0 \mid \mathbf{X} = x^{(j)})(q_j - 1)}{P(Y_i = 1 \mid X_i = x_i^{(j)})q_i + P(Y_i = 0 \mid X_i = x_i^{(j)})}$$

$$W_{ij} = \frac{\partial P(Y_i = 1 \mid X_i = x_i^{(j)})}{\partial w_i} = \sigma'(w_i x_i + b_i)x_i$$

$$B_{ij} = \frac{\partial P(Y_i = 1 \mid X_i = x_i^{(j)})}{\partial b_i} = \sigma'(w_i x_i + b_i)$$

Here, U_j is the gradient of the log-likelihood of the jth data example with respect to the probability that the target Y is 0 (i.e., the case where $GDM = false$). Q_lj and Q_ij, V_ij are the gradients of the probability that the target is 0 ($GDM = false$) for the jth data example with respect to the leak parameter q_l, the inhibition parameter q_i, and the link probability $P(Y_i = 1 \mid X_i = x_i^{(j)})$ respectively. W_ij and B_ij are the gradients of the link probability $P(Y_i = 1 \mid X_i = x_i^{(j)})$ with respect to its parameters w_i and b_i respectively. Finally σ' is the gradient of the sigmoid function $\sigma'(x) = \sigma(x)(1 - \sigma(x))$.

The gradients of the log-likelihood function with respect to the link parameters w_i and b_i can be computed in terms of U_j, V_{ij}, W_{ij} and B_{ij} as

$$\begin{aligned}
\frac{\partial \mathcal{L}(\mathbf{w}, \mathbf{b}, \mathbf{q}, q_l; \mathcal{D})}{\partial w_i} &= \sum_{j=1}^{N} \frac{\partial \log P(Y = y^{(j)} \mid \mathbf{X} = x^{(j)})}{\partial w_i} \\
&= \sum_{j=1}^{N} \frac{\partial \log P(Y = y^{(j)} \mid \mathbf{X} = x^{(j)})}{\partial P(Y = 0 \mid \mathbf{X} = x^{(j)})} \frac{\partial P(Y = 0 \mid \mathbf{X} = x^{(j)})}{\partial P(Y = 1 \mid X_i = x_i^{(j)})} \frac{\partial P(Y_i = 1 \mid X_i = x_i^{(j)})}{\partial w_i} \\
&= \sum_{j=1}^{N} U_j V_{ij} W_{ij}
\end{aligned} \tag{5}$$

$$
\begin{aligned}
\frac{\partial \mathcal{L}(\mathbf{w}, \mathbf{b}, \mathbf{q}, q_l; \mathcal{D})}{\partial b_i} &= \sum_{j=1}^{N} \frac{\partial \log P(Y = y^{(j)} \mid \mathbf{X} = x^{(j)})}{\partial b_i} \\
&= \sum_{j=1}^{N} \frac{\log P(Y = y^{(j)} \mid \mathbf{X} = x^{(j)})}{\partial P(Y = 0 \mid X = x^{(j)})} \frac{\partial P(Y = 0 \mid X_i = x^{(j)})}{\partial P(Y_i = 1 \mid X_i = x_i^{(j)})} \frac{\partial P(Y_i = 1 \mid X_i = x_i^{(j)})}{\partial b_i} \\
&= \sum_{j=1}^{N} U_j V_{ij} B_{ij}
\end{aligned}
\tag{6}
$$

The gradients of the log-likelihood function with respect to the inhibition and leak parameters q_i and q_l can be computed in terms of U_j, Q_{ij} and Q_{lj} as

$$
\begin{aligned}
\frac{\partial \mathcal{L}(\mathbf{w}, \mathbf{b}, \mathbf{q}, q_l; \mathcal{D})}{\partial q_i} &= \sum_{j=1}^{N} \frac{\partial \log P(Y = y^{(j)} \mid \mathbf{X} = x^{(j)})}{\partial q_i} \\
&= \sum_{j=1}^{N} \frac{\partial \log P(Y = y^{(j)} \mid \mathbf{X} = x^{(j)})}{\partial P(Y = 0 \mid \mathbf{X} = x^{(j)})} \frac{\partial P(Y = 0 \mid \mathbf{X} = x^{(j)})}{\partial q_i} \\
&= \sum_{j=1}^{N} U_j Q_{ij}
\end{aligned}
\tag{7}
$$

$$
\begin{aligned}
\frac{\partial \mathcal{L}(\mathbf{w}, \mathbf{b}, \mathbf{q}, q_l; \mathcal{D})}{\partial q_l} &= \sum_{j=1}^{N} \frac{\partial \log P(Y = y^{(j)} \mid \mathbf{X} = x^{(j)})}{\partial q_l} \\
&= \sum_{j=1}^{N} \frac{\partial \log P(Y = y^{(j)} \mid \mathbf{X} = x^{(j)})}{\partial P(Y = 0 \mid \mathbf{X} = x^{(j)})} \frac{\partial P(Y = 0 \mid \mathbf{X} = x^{(j)})}{\partial q_l} \\
&= \sum_{j=1}^{N} U_j Q_{lj}
\end{aligned}
\tag{8}
$$

4.3. *Derivation of the gradients of the penalty term*

The gradients of the penalty function are given by

$$
\begin{aligned}
\frac{\partial \zeta_i^{a,b}}{\partial w_i} &= \frac{\partial \zeta_i^{a,b}}{\delta_i^{a,b}} \frac{\delta_i^{a,b}}{\partial w_i} \\
&= I_{\delta_i^{a,b}>0}\ 2\delta_i^{a,b} \frac{\delta_i^{a,b}}{\partial w_i} \\
&= I_{\delta_i^{a,b}>0} \begin{cases} \frac{P(Y_i=0|X_i=a)}{\partial w_i} - \frac{P(Y_i=0|X_i=b)}{\partial w_i} + \epsilon & X_{i\prec}^{M+} Y \in C \\ -\frac{P(Y_i=0|X_i=a)}{\partial w_i} + \frac{P(Y_i=0|X_i=b)}{\partial w_i} + \epsilon & X_{i\prec}^{M-} Y \in C \\ 0 & otherwise \end{cases} \\
&= I_{\delta_i^{a,b}>0} \begin{cases} \sigma'(w_i a + b_i)a - \sigma'(w_i b + b_i)b + \epsilon & X_{i\prec}^{M+} Y \in C \\ -\sigma'(w_i a + b_i)a + \sigma'(w_i b + b_i)b + \epsilon & X_{i\prec}^{M-} Y \in C \\ 0 & otherwise \end{cases}
\end{aligned}
\tag{9}
$$

$$
\begin{aligned}
\frac{\partial \zeta_i^{a,b}}{\partial b_i} &= \frac{\partial \zeta_i^{a,b}}{\delta_i^{a,b}} \frac{\delta_i^{a,b}}{\partial w_i} \\
&= I_{\delta_i^{a,b}>0}\ 2\delta_i^{a,b} \frac{\delta_i^{a,b}}{\partial b_i} \\
&= I_{\delta_i^{a,b}>0} \begin{cases} \frac{P(Y_i=0|X_i=a)}{\partial b_i} - \frac{P(Y_i=0|X_i=b)}{\partial b_i} + \epsilon & X_{i\prec}^{M+} Y \in C \\ -\frac{P(Y_i=0|X_i=a)}{\partial b_i} + \frac{P(Y_i=0|X_i=b)}{\partial b_i} + \epsilon & X_{i\prec}^{M-} Y \in C \\ 0 & otherwise \end{cases} \\
&= I_{\delta_i^{a,b}>0} \begin{cases} \sigma'(w_i a + b_i) - \sigma'(w_i b + b_i) + \epsilon & X_{i\prec}^{M+} Y \in C \\ -\sigma'(w_i a + b_i) + \sigma'(w_i b + b_i) + \epsilon & X_{i\prec}^{M-} Y \in C \\ 0 & otherwise \end{cases}
\end{aligned}
\tag{10}
$$

Using these gradients, we solve the maximization problem using the L-BFGS-B algorithm, increasing the value of λ until the solution satisfies all the constraints[a]. The high-level flowchart of our model construction is presented in Figure 4. Given the entire GDM data set, after preprocessing and obtaining the causal independencies, we construct the smaller data set where we learn the model such that the qualitiative constraints are satisfied. The final model is then evaluated on the test set and the results are presented in the next section.

5. Experimental evaluation

Our experiments explicitly aim at answering the following questions,

Q1: Does inclusion of QIs improve model performance over a base model that does not have background knowledge in the form of QIs?

[a]The code is available at `https://github.com/saurabhmathur96/noisy_or`

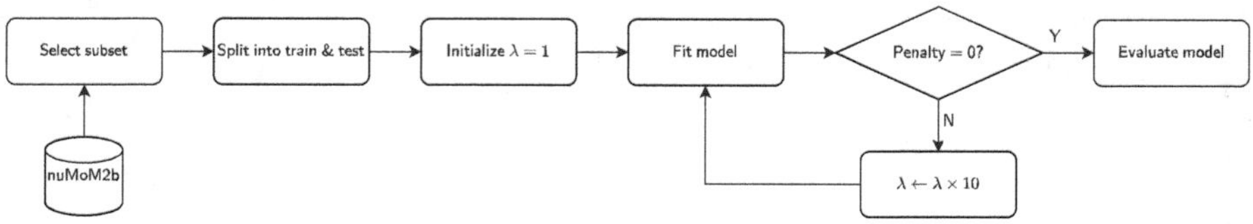

Fig. 4. Flowchart for the Noisy-Or model construction process

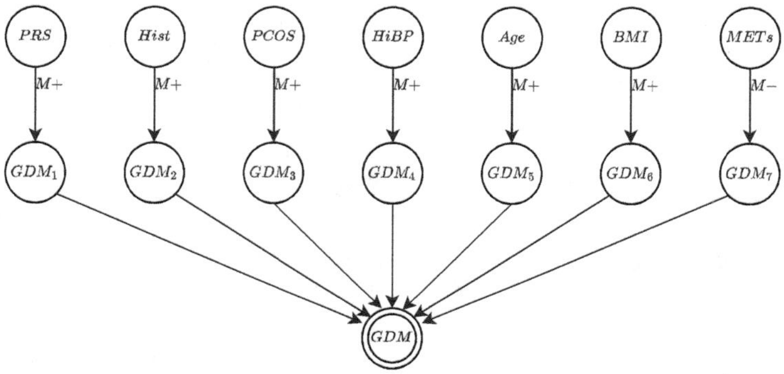

Fig. 5. Noisy-OR model used for the GDM dataset. Both QIs and causal independence knowledge are incorporated in this model. This representation shows that *PRS, Hist, PCOS, HiBP, Age and BMI* have a positive monotonic influence on GDM whereas *METs* have a negative monotonic influence. Additionally, all the risk factors are causally independent in this model.

Q2: Can our proposed model incorporate causal independencies to efficiently estimate model parameters without significantly losing performance?

We evaluate our proposed approach on two sub-cohorts in the nuMoM2b study - one sub-cohort with *PRS* as a risk factor and one without it - as described in section 2. The domain knowledge in the form of causal independencies and QIs were provided by our domain expert Dr. Haas. Figure 5 presents our proposed noisy-OR model that incorporates this domain knowledge for the task of GDM prediction given the 7 risk factors.

To answer the first question, we train noisy-OR models for the two cohorts with and without the inclusion of QIs. Figure 6 presents the AUC-ROC[12] for our model trained on each of the sub-cohorts. In the case of the sub-cohort using the *PRS* (bottom in Figure 6), it can be clearly noted that incorporating QIs improves AUC-ROC from 0.6409 ± 0.0408 to 0.7371 ± 0.0149. In the sub-cohort not using the *PRS*, incorporating QIs improves the AUC-ROC from 0.6640 ± 0.0079 to 0.6863 ± 0.0091. It is evident from these charts that the inclusion of QIs as domain knowledge improves model performance. This analysis helps us answer Q1. Our proposed approach can effectively incorporate QIs to improve model performance.

To answer the second question, we compare our proposed approach to a strong discriminative baseline: gradient boosted trees (GBT). Figure 6 presents a comparison of our model with the baseline for the two sub-cohorts (left and center). GBT achieves AUC-ROC scores of 0.7261 ± 0.0174 and 0.6831 ± 0.0130 for the sub-cohort with and without PRS, respectively. This is comparable to the performance of our proposed approach when QIs are incorporated. However, unlike the noisy-OR model, GBT does not make any causal independence assumptions and hence has no causal meaning and is much more difficult to interpret. This analysis helps us answer Q2. Our proposed model can incorporate causal independencies to allow feasible parameter learning without losing model performance as compared to models that do not make causal independence assumptions.

To summarize, our experiments on two sub-cohorts of the GDM dataset suggest that our proposed approach can leverage domain knowledge in the form of QIs and causal independencies to effectively and efficiently learn an interpretable model without losing model performance as compared to a strong discriminative baseline that is uninterpretable.

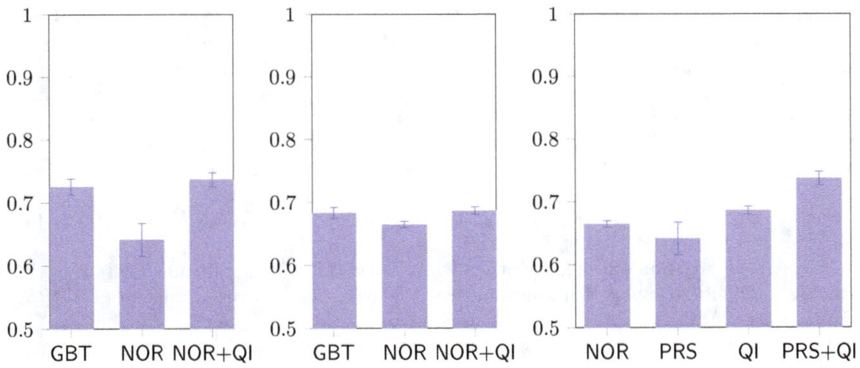

Fig. 6. The AUC-ROC scores for the Noisy OR model (NOR) as compared to the Gradient Boosted Trees model (GBT) with PRS (left) and without PRS (center). The AUC-ROC scores for the Noisy OR model (NOR) in the presence of PRS and Qualitative Influences (right). The bars show the mean score over 10 boostrap samples and the error bars show the standard deviation.

6. Conclusion

We adapted the use of qualitative constraints and causal independencies to build an interpretable and explainable probabilistic model for modeling GDM given a **small number of risk factors**. We presented the learning method that learned the parameters of the model. Our empirical evaluations on nuMoM2b dataset clearly demonstrated that the use of the two types of constraints yielded better results than learning only from data and most importantly, exhibit similar performance as the state-of-the-art machine learning algorithm. Extending the model to include more risk factors is an immediate research direction. Learning a fully generative model such as Bayesian network would provide valuable insights in the interactions between risk factors. Finally, evaluating the learned models on larger and diverse data such as EHRs remains an interesting future direction.

Acknowledgements

The authors acknowledge the support by the NIH grant R01HD101246. KK acknowledges the support of the Hessian Ministry of Higher Education, Research, Science and the Arts (HMWK) in Germany, project "The Third Wave of AI". DH acknowledges the support from the Eunice Kennedy Shriver National Institute of Child Health and Human Development (NICHD): U10 HD063037, Indiana University. The authors are thankful and acknowledge the support of Rashika Ramola, Rafael Guerrero and Hoyin Chu for sharing the data and the PRS scores used in evaluation.

References

1. D. M. Haas, C. B. Parker *et al.*, A description of the methods of the nulliparous pregnancy outcomes study: monitoring mothers-to-be (numom2b), *American journal of obstetrics and gynecology* **212** (2015).
2. I. Goodfellow, Y. Bengio and A. Courville, *Deep Learning* (MIT Press, 2016). `http://www.deeplearningbook.org`.
3. S. K. Zhou, H. Greenspan, C. Davatzikos, J. S. Duncan, B. van Ginneken, A. Madabhushi, J. L. Prince, D. Rueckert and R. M. Summers, A review of deep learning in medical imaging: Image traits, technology trends, case studies with progress highlights, and future promises (2020).
4. E. E. Altendorf, A. C. Restificar and T. G. Dietterich, Learning from sparse data by exploiting monotonicity constraints, in *UAI*, (AUAI Press, 2005).
5. S. Yang and S. Natarajan, Knowledge intensive learning: Combining qualitative constraints with causal independence for parameter learning in probabilistic models, in *ECML-PKDD*, (Springer, 2013).
6. D. Heckerman and J. S. Breese, A new look at causal independence, *CoRR* **abs/1302.6814** (2013).
7. S. Srinivas, A generalization of the noisy-or model, in *UAI*, (Morgan Kaufmann, 1993).
8. J. Vomlel, Exploiting functional dependence in bayesian network inference, *CoRR* **abs/1301.0609** (2013).
9. J. Pearl, *Probabilistic reasoning in intelligent systems - networks of plausible inference* (Morgan Kaufmann, 1989).
10. M. P. Wellman, Fundamental concepts of qualitative probabilistic networks, *Artif. Intell.* **44**, 257 (1990).
11. A. J. Feelders and L. C. van der Gaag, Learning bayesian network parameters with prior knowledge about context-specific qualitative influences, in *UAI*, (AUAI Press, 2005).
12. J. A. Hanley and B. J. McNeil, The meaning and use of the area under a receiver operating characteristic (roc) curve., *Radiology* **143**, 29 (1982).

Knowledge-Driven Mechanistic Enrichment of the Preeclampsia Ignorome

Tiffany J. Callahan[1,2†], Adrianne L. Stefanski[2], Jin-Dong Kim[3],
William A. Baumgartner Jr.[2], Jordan M. Wyrwa[4], Lawrence E. Hunter[2]

[1]*Department of Biomedical Informatics, Columbia University, New York, NY USA*
[2]*Computational Bioscience Program, University of Colorado Anschutz Medical Campus, Aurora, CO USA*
[3]*Database Center for Life Science, Research Organization of Information and Systems, Kashiwa, Japan*
[4]*Department of Physical Medicine and Rehabilitation, School of Medicine, University of Colorado Anschutz Medical Campus, Aurora, CO USA*
†*Email: tc3206@cumc.columbia.edu*

Preeclampsia is a leading cause of maternal and fetal morbidity and mortality. Currently, the only definitive treatment of preeclampsia is delivery of the placenta, which is central to the pathogenesis of the disease. Transcriptional profiling of human placenta from pregnancies complicated by preeclampsia has been extensively performed to identify differentially expressed genes (DEGs). The decisions to investigate DEGs experimentally are biased by many factors, causing many DEGs to remain uninvestigated. A set of DEGs which are associated with a disease experimentally, but which have no known association to the disease in the literature are known as the ignorome. Preeclampsia has an extensive body of scientific literature, a large pool of DEG data, and only one definitive treatment. Tools facilitating knowledge-based analyses, which are capable of combining disparate data from many sources in order to suggest underlying mechanisms of action, may be a valuable resource to support discovery and improve our understanding of this disease. In this work we demonstrate how a biomedical knowledge graph (KG) can be used to identify novel preeclampsia molecular mechanisms. Existing open source biomedical resources and publicly available high-throughput transcriptional profiling data were used to identify and annotate the function of currently uninvestigated preeclampsia-associated DEGs. Experimentally investigated genes associated with preeclampsia were identified from PubMed abstracts using text-mining methodologies. The relative complement of the text-mined- and meta-analysis-derived lists were identified as the uninvestigated preeclampsia-associated DEGs (n=445), i.e., the preeclampsia ignorome. Using the KG to investigate relevant DEGs revealed 53 novel clinically relevant and biologically actionable mechanistic associations.

Keywords: Preeclampsia; Knowledge Graphs; Knowledge-based Enrichment; Ignorome.

1. Introduction

Preeclampsia has been known since Hippocrates described it in 400 BC and remains a leading cause of maternal and fetal morbidity and mortality.[1,2] Preeclampsia is a hypertensive, multisystemic disorder with an unknown etiology and variable maternal and fetal manifestations.[3] Maternally, preeclampsia presents as both hypertension and proteinuria, but can quickly progress to affect the kidneys, brain, and liver and in severe cases, results in thrombocytopenia, stroke, visual disturbance, renal failure, placental abruption, seizure, and death.[4] Fetal consequences of preeclampsia are a function of gestational age and the severity of the mother's condition, which may include intrauterine growth restriction (IUGR), prematurity, and perinatal death.[5]

Mechanistically, preeclampsia is thought to be partially caused by alterations in circulating angiogenic factors like vascular endothelial growth factor (VEGF), which is known to tightly regulate angiogenesis,[6] and triggers the development of organs. Preeclampsia is caused when free levels of transforming growth factor β (TGFβ), placental growth factor (PIGF), and VEGF are decreased, due to increased levels of antiangiogenic factors like soluble FMS-like tyrosine kinase 1 (Sflt-1) and Endoglin (sEng).[7] Despite extensive research and an in-depth understanding of the pathophysiology of preeclampsia, clinicians remain unable to prevent this disease.[8] One advantage of preeclampsia research is that upon termination of a pregnancy and/or delivery, the placenta is a non-vital organ and biopsies can be performed.[9] Even with this advantage and the sizable collection of transcriptomic data deposited in the public domain that has resulted from it, individual studies and many recent meta-analyses have not made much progress in furthering our understanding of effective prevention or treatment of preeclampsia.

In similarly complex diseases like asthma, strategies to identify relevant genes have yielded novel mechanistic insight into previously ignored genes.[10] The ignorome is defined as the portion of a gene signature shown to be significantly associated with a specific disease, but without a published mechanistic link — and often without any published disease association. Recently, researchers discovered that the top 5% of statistically significant differentially expressed genes (DEGs) were responsible for 70% of the published literature for a given disease.[11] Further examination of ignorome genes revealed no differences between the published and ignored genes in terms of their connectivity in co-expression networks; the biggest factor as to whether or not a gene was well-represented in the literature was its date of discovery.[11]

Preeclampsia has an extensive body of scientific literature, a large pool of DEG data, and only one definitive treatment. Given the rate at which science advances, tools facilitating knowledge-based analyses may be a valuable resource to support discovery and improve our understanding of this disease. Knowledge-based clinical research, and its ability to integrate disparate data from many sources in order to suggest underlying mechanisms of action, provides a potentially powerful new avenue to obtain mechanistic insight into experimental findings, such as in the enrichment of DEG lists. Very few DEGs are examined after an initial experiment because experimental follow-up is difficult and expensive, and nonsignificant DEGs are often investigated because prioritization approaches are generally based on experimental signal (e.g., effect size) rather than on existing knowledge. The goal of this paper was to demonstrate how a large-scale heterogeneous biomedical knowledge graph (KG) could be used to identify novel preeclampsia mechanisms from previously analyzed transcriptomic experiments.

2. Methods

The preeclampsia ignorome was identified in two steps: (i) identification of preeclampsia DEGs from multi-platform microarray meta-analysis and (ii) identification of genes associated with preeclampsia in the literature. The preeclampsia ignorome was generated from the set difference of the gene lists generated by these steps. Supplemental Material, code, and data are publicly available (http://tiffanycallahan.com/ignorenet/). Please see the analysis workflow readme (https://github.com/callahantiff/ignorenet/blob/master/analyses/preeclampsia/README.md) for information on the algorithms and data sources (KGs and gene lists) used for this analysis.

2.1. *Identification of the Preeclampsia Molecular Signature*

In collaboration with a PhD-level molecular biologist (ALS) who specializes in reproductive science, a meta-analysis was performed to identify relevant transcriptomic data on the Gene Expression Omnibus (GEO). Using the keyword "preeclampsia", publicly available human experiments deposited in GEO were examined. The initial set of identified studies were further reviewed for the following criteria to ensure: (i) processed samples were from a human placenta biopsy (i.e., chorionic villi, decidua basalis, and placenta); (ii) samples were processed using Agilent, Affymetrix, Applied Biosystems, Illumina, or NimbleGen; and (iii) studies provided normalized data and/or DEG lists. Each study's normalized data were processed using standard R pipelines using the ignorenet library (https://github.com/callahantiff/ignorenet). The final gene list was assembled by selecting significant DEGs ($p<0.05$) in at least 50% of the studies.

2.2. *Identification of Genes Associated with Preeclampsia in the Literature*

To identify known preeclampsia genes two strategies were employed: (i) **Literature-Driven.** This strategy aimed to identify relevant genes via keyword search against PubTator,[12] DisGeNET,[13] and Malacards (implemented 08-11/2017).[14] For this step, all queried results were manually verified for accuracy (i.e., verified that hits obtained were actually to preeclampsia and the associated keywords and were not errors or mismatches to closely associated synonyms or acronyms) and all valid associations were used to create a final unique list of genes; and (ii) **Gene-Driven.** This strategy aimed to identify relevant articles by querying 18 keywords in addition to the the preeclampsia molecular signature DEGs against PubAnnotation.[15] Similar to the Literature-Driven Approach, all results were manually verified for accuracy and all associations were used to create a final unique list of genes. See the Supplemental Material for keyword lists.

2.3. *Evaluation*

2.3.1. *Knowledge Graph Node Embeddings*

A v1.0 PheKnowLator KG[16] built using Linked Open Data and Open Biological and Biomedical Ontology Foundry ontologies was used for this analysis. The core set of ontologies included phenotypes (Human Phenotype Ontology [HP][17]), diseases (Human Disease Ontology [DOID][18]), and biological processes, molecular functions, and cellular components (Gene Ontology [GO][19]). Genes, pathways, and chemicals were added to the core set of ontologies to form the foundation of the KG which was extended by adding relations between phenotypes, diseases, and GO biological processes, molecular functions, and cellular components. Node embeddings were derived using C++ implementation of DeepWalk (hyperparameter settings suggested by developers: 512 dimensions, 100 walks, a walk length of 20, and a sliding window length of 10).[20]

2.3.2. *Visualizations*

Node embeddings were visualized using the t-distributed stochastic neighbor embedding (t-SNE) algorithm.[21] Experiments were performed to identify the best hyperparameter setting (perplexity=50). Node embeddings and ignorome genes were overlaid and visually inspected.

2.3.3. *Enrichment*

Using the node embeddings, the 100 nearest disease, drug, gene, GO concepts, pathway, and phenotype (i.e., domains) annotations for each ignorome gene as measured by pairwise cosine similarity (i.e., L2-normalized dot product of embedding vectors: $k(x, y) = \frac{xy^{T}}{||x||y||}$)[22] of the node embeddings were obtained. Annotations were reviewed by a PhD molecular biologist specializing in reproductive science (ALS; 08-09/2021). To determine if they occurred by chance, we:

1. Examined the overlap between the top-100 closest associations to each ignorome gene in the expert-verified list and the associations generated when enriching the preeclampsia ignorome using ToppGene;[23]
2. Computed how often the reviewed associations occurred by chance in 1,000 ignorome-sized random samples drawn from all non-ignorome genes represented in the KG. For each sample, the top-100 closest annotations to each gene, by domain were obtained and the number of annotations that overlapped with the expert-verified list was recorded. P-values were obtained for each domain by dividing the number of overlapping annotations out of the 1,000 samples, where a p-value of 0.05 indicates a 50 in 1,000 chance of observing a sample annotation that overlaps with the expert-verified annotations.

3. Results

3.1. *The Preeclampsia Ignorome*

As shown in Figure 1, there were 68 studies returned from the domain-expert review of GEO (Supplemental Table 1). Of these, 12 studies were determined to be eligible for inclusion in the current project (Supplemental Table 2). Processing these studies led to a sample of 548 DEGs, which appeared in 50% of the studies. The Gene-Driven strategy returned 1,962 articles which resulted in a total of 417 known preeclampsia genes. The Literature-Driven strategy returned 1,102 articles and 658 genes. These lists were combined and yielded a total of 946 unique genes associated with preeclampsia in the literature. Of the 548 genes identified as the preeclampsia molecular signature, 103 were found in the list of genes associated with preeclampsia in the literature, leaving 445 DEGs with no known literature evidence (i.e., "PE Ignorome" or non-overlapping blue circle of Figure 1). The remaining 843 genes associated with preeclampsia in the literature not found in the list of experimentally-derived genes are those that were found in less than 50% of studies, were not transcriptionally regulated, or played a role in the placenta.

The preeclampsia ignorome genes were examined for associations to other diseases in the literature. Figure 2, illustrates the number of articles from Malacards, DisGeNET, PubAnnotation, and PubTator that annotated each preeclampsia gene and the number of annotations to diseases other than preeclampsia that were found for each ignorome gene. Supplemental Table 3 contains the list of gene symbols binned by article count. As shown in Figure 2 (a), most genes were cited by fewer than 20 articles and less than 20 of the ignorome genes were cited more than 100 times. Among the genes cited 100 or more times were BRAF (n=2,749), TARDBP (n=694), and IDHI (n=564). Figure 2 (b) illustrates the most frequently annotated diseases, which included neoplasms (n=1,778), mental disorders (n=280), and congenital diseases (n=272).

The PheKnowLator KG contained 128,286 nodes and 3,203,264 edges. The following 10 edge types, (ordered by frequency): drug-disease (n=1,216,900), drug-pathway (n=711,043), gene-gene (n=594,100), gene-go concept (n=265,002), gene-phenotype (n=120,288), gene-pathway (n=107,029), pathway-disease (n=106,727), disease-phenotype (n=43,817), gene-disease (n=20,452), and pathway-go concept (n=17,906), were used for the current analysis. The t-SNE plot is shown in Supplemental Figure 1 with nodes colored by node type and the preeclampsia genes marked using gold stars. As expected, most entities appeared closer to entities of a similar type than entities of other types except for GO concepts and phenotypes.

3.2. *Preeclampsia Ignorome Gene Enrichment*

Performing enrichment analysis on the preeclampsia ignorome genes using ToppGene returned 4,098 annotations ($p<0.001$ or Q-value Bonferroni <0.05). The annotations included four diseases,

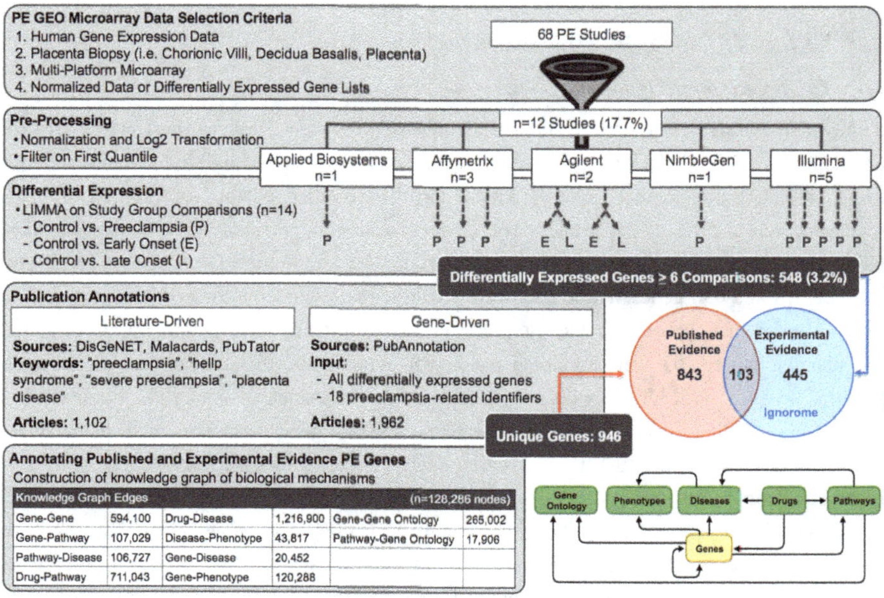

Fig. 1. Overview of Results for Finding the Preeclampsia Ignorome. The figure provides an overview of the procedures utilized in order to obtain the preeclampsia ignorome. Acronyms - PE: Preeclampsia.

3,667 drugs, 248 genes, 116 GO biological processes, 44 GO cellular components, 19 GO molecular functions, and no pathways or phenotypes. PheKnowLator node embeddings were used to annotate the preeclampsia ignorome genes by obtaining the 100 closest entities in vector space, which resulted in a total of 19 diseases (average similarity of 0.37 and frequency of 1.0 across the preeclampsia genes), 521 drugs (average similarity of 0.37 and frequency of 1.08 across the preeclampsia genes), 1,060 GO concepts (average similarity of 0.38 and frequency of 1.49 across the preeclampsia genes), 563 pathways (average similarity of 0.44 and frequency of 2.29 across the preeclampsia genes), and 64 phenotypes (average similarity of 0.30 and frequency of 1.0 across the preeclampsia genes). None of the identified diseases, GO concepts, pathways, or phenotypes overlapped with the ToppGene annotations, but seven of the identified drugs and 188 of the identified genes did.

The reproductive science expert reviewed the KG-derived annotations and provided explanations using her domain expertise and rigorous literature review, which resulted in the validation of 53 annotations and included five phenotypes (Supplemental Table 4), 10 pathways (Supplemental Table 5), 10 drugs (Supplemental Table 6), 10 genes (Supplemental Table 7), 10 GO concepts (Supplemental Table 8), and eight diseases (Supplemental Table 9). The expert spent

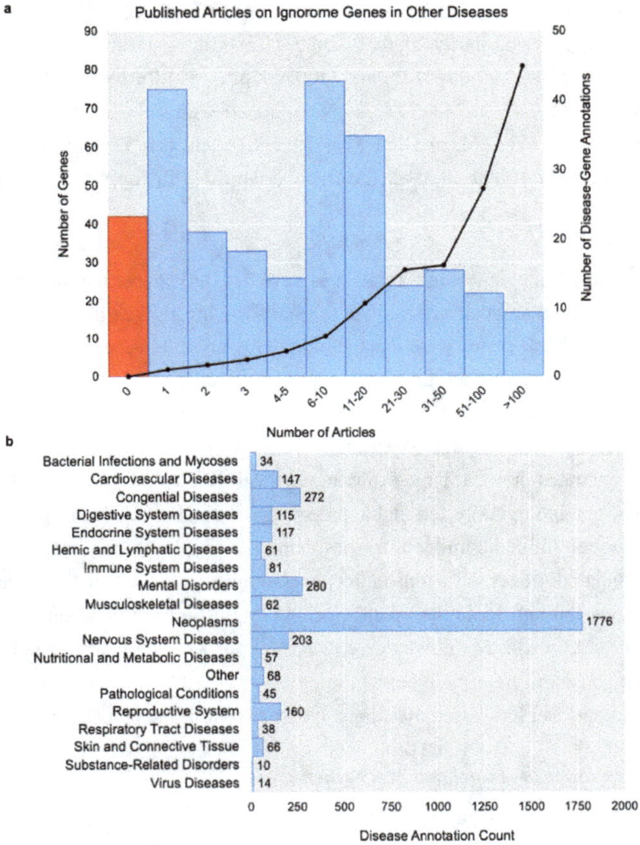

Fig. 2. Preeclampsia Ignorome Gene Annotations in Other Diseases. (a) illustrates the literature coverage of the 445 preeclampsia ignorome genes to other diseases. The x-axis represents the number of disease-annotated articles for each gene. The left y-axis shows the number of genes as bars, where the red bar contains the number of genes with no literature annotations to any disease. The right y-axis shows the number of diseases annotated to each preeclampsia gene and the number of annotations to diseases other than preeclampsia that were found for each ignorome gene in the literature. (b) Plots the counts of literature annotations to high-level disease categories.

~six hours on this task, noting that the drug and disease associations were the most challenging and time consuming to review. For all tables, evidence is provided in the form of mechanistic explanations and includes support from peer reviewed articles. None of the expert-reviewed annotations occurred by chance (*ps<0.005*): (i) **Diseases.** 485 concepts with an average similarity of 0.40 (0.26-0.77); (ii) **Drugs.** 8,371 concepts with an average similarity of 0.41 (0.25-0.69); (iii) **Genes.** 23,728 concepts with an average similarity of 0.47 (0.24-0.93); (iv) **GO Concepts.** 15,447 concepts with an average similarity of 0.39 (0.25-0.77), four overlapped with ToppGene (i.e., GO:0000398, GO:0005747, GO:0070125, and GO:0005833); (v) **Pathways.** 1,671 concepts with an average similarity of 0.45 (0.24-0.77), four overlapped with ToppGene (i.e., R-HSA-194840, R-HSA-611105, R-HSA-5419276, and R-HSA-6799198]); and (vi) **Phenotypes.** 3,080 concepts with an average similarity of 0.36 (0.25-0.63), one overlapped with ToppGene (i.e., HP:0008316).

4. Discussion

Recent examination of the ignorome genes has revealed an interesting phenomena; the only difference between the genes that are frequently published for a given disease and those that are not is the date in which the genes were discovered.[11] This presents new exciting opportunities for discovery, especially with respect to improving our understanding of complex diseases like preeclampsia. Given the rate at which science advances and the volume of data that is generated as a result, tools facilitating knowledge-based analyses are valuable resources to support discovery. This paper demonstrates how a large-scale biomedical KG could be used to identify novel clinically relevant and biologically actionable preeclampsia mechanisms from previously analyzed experiments. Although limited, similar work has demonstrated the value of using KGs to generate new disease-associated genes,[25,26] drug-target interactions,[27] and evaluate the consistency of genome annotations through biological pathways.[28] A big difference between these methods and ours is the depth and breadth of knowledge covered by our KG and that we are able to generate explanations that consist of multiple types of biological entities. To the best of our knowledge, our work is the first to perform KG-based mechanistic enrichment of the preeclampsia ignorome.

4.1. *Novel Preeclampsia-Associated Mechanisms*

Precise characterization of phenotypes will require the ability to identify and understand complicated biological relationships. Our novel preeclampsia ignorome associations required fairly complicated explanations. A few relevant results from each domain are described below.

Phenotypes. These associations present new opportunities to enrich our understanding of the phenotypic variance within preeclampsia. There were many interesting associations, but one of the most relevant was PPM1K to *Elevated Plasma Branched Chain Amino Acids*. Examining this mechanism closer revealed that the disruption of PPM1K results in an increase of branched chain amino acids, which can result in oxidative stress, insulin resistance, and eventually obesity, by activation of the mammalian target of rapamycin complex 1 (mTORC1) signaling.[29] mTORC1 signaling is vital for communicating placental growth factor signaling and when reduced in IUGR pregnancies, has been found to impair mitochondrial respiration and lead to placental insufficiency.[30] While mitochondrial dysfunction is known to be central to preeclampsia pathophysiology,[31] the role of PPM1K in preeclampsia has yet to be thoroughly examined.

Pathways. Associations within this domain highlight potential new avenues of investigation for specific gene targets within pathways that are known to play a role in preeclampsia. Three associations are highlighted: (i) MFAP5 and FBLN5 to the *Elastic Fibre Formation pathway* – this pathway is altered in umbilical cord vessels from pregnancies complicated by preeclampsia,[32] but the exact molecular mechanism causing the alteration is unknown; (ii) ADAMTSL3 and SPON1 to *Diseases Associated with O-glycosylation of Proteins* – it is known that altered o-glycosylation is associated with aberrant immune cell dynamics at the maternal-fetal interface[33] and in severe preeclampsia, altered glycosylation of maternal plasma proteins is associated with increased monocyte adhesion;[34] and (iii) TCP1, RGS11, and TBCD to *Protein Folding*; the impact of aberrant protein folding on preeclampsia is well documented[35] but the roles of TCP1, RGS11, and TBCD in this pathway are not fully understood.

Drugs. The association of MME to *anti-asthmatic agents* may provide an avenue for drug repurposing. Membrane matrix remodeling is critical to placental development[36] and women who experience asthma during pregnancy have an increased risk of developing preeclampsia.[37] While beta-adrenergic agonists such as ritodrine and terbutaline have been used for the management of asthma and preterm labor, it is unclear as to whether or not anti-asthmatic medications could reduce the risk of preeclampsia.[38]

Genes. Associations within this domain may provide a deeper understanding of the molecular landscape of preeclampsia by helping researchers identify relevant, yet understudied genes, for example, the associations from PLOD1, FBLN5, and PTGDS to PLOD2. These associations are supported by evidence that PLOD2 is a protein that is upregulated in trophoblast stem cells cultured under hypoxic conditions.[39]

GO Concepts. These associations may highlight opportunities to bridge findings across domains, for example, the associations between ACTR3, NEBL, ACTR3B, MYO1B, COBLL1, ZNF185, and ITPRID2 to the GO Molecular Function *Actin Filament Binding*. Preeclampsia is associated with altered actin polymerization via endothelial protein C receptor.[40] Traditionally, actin has been studied via cell biology or histology but a deeper examination of these associations within the biological context of preeclampsia has the potential to connect the findings derived from these disconnected studies.

Diseases. By enriching microarray data derived from placental samples with KG-based mechanisms it is possible to identify diseases that occur later in life, but which are likely to be associated with fetal exposure to maternal preeclampsia. For example, the association between STS and *Attention Deficit Hyperactivity Disorder* (ADHD); STS dysfunction causes ADHD[41] and offspring of preeclamptic mothers[41] are more likely to be diagnosed with ADHD.[42]

4.2. *Preeclampsia Ignorome Enrichment*

Examining differences in the enrichment of GO annotations relevant to preeclampsia revealed some interesting insights. For example, *Placenta Development* included 25 genes associated with preeclampsia in the literature, 10 genes with both literature and experimental evidence, but none were ignorome genes. This finding confirms our expectations – a lot of genes known to impact placental development exist and many have been investigated experimentally. In contrast, the *Cell Surface Receptor Signaling Pathway* included genes from all three of the aforementioned groups, supporting our observation that the things enriched for this biological process are over-studied. Only ~10% of the ignorome genes (n=42) had no other disease annotations when examining the coverage of ignorome genes in the literature. This leaves a significant body of literature spanning a wide-range of diseases, which would take a substantial amount of time and domain expertise, a task which is often out-of-scope for most researchers.

4.3. *Limitations and Future Work*

Our work has important limitations: (i) all analyses were performed using data available in 2017. More data has likely become available since then, but re-analysis of these data was not feasible; (ii) microarray data were only obtained from GEO. It is important to explore other repositories and other types of molecular data; (iii) the pipeline depends on tools like PubTator to review the literature and domain experts to formulate explanations for annotation. Incorporation of more advanced models and pipelines would improve scalability and reduce bias; (iv) our results require additional validation (i.e., wet lab and sensitivity analysis/ablation studies) before the full utility of our approach can be determined; and (v) the PheKnowLator Ecosystem is new and while preliminary studies have suggested it produces robust KGs additional experiments are warranted. Future work aims to address these limitations and will explore advanced algorithms to process novel associations like natural language generators.

5. Conclusion

Large-scale biomedical KGs new opportunities to improve our understanding of complex diseases, like preeclampsia. With assistance from a domain expert, we propose potential mechanistic explanations for 53 new associations between preeclampsia ignorome genes. These mechanistic explanations represent biologically-actionable discoveries that await further investigation in the hopes of finding a means to prevent preeclampsia.

Acknowledgements

This work was supported by the National Library of Medicine (T15LM009451).

References

1. Ghulmiyyah L, Sibai B. Maternal mortality from preeclampsia/eclampsia. Semin Perinatol. 2012;36:56–9.
2. The Medical Works of Hippocrates: A New Translation from the Original Greek Made Especially for English Readers. JAMA. 1951;147(15):1506–1506.
3. Bell MJ. A historical overview of preeclampsia-eclampsia. J Obstet Gynecol Neonatal Nurs. 2010;39:510–8.
4. Hod T, Cerdeira AS, Karumanchi SA. Molecular Mechanisms of Preeclampsia. Cold Spring Harb Perspect Med. 2015;5.
5. de Souza Rugolo LMS, Bentlin MR, Trindade CEP. Preeclampsia: Effect on the Fetus and Newborn. Neoreviews. 2011;12:e198–206.
6. Adair TH, Montani JP. Overview of Angiogenesis. Morgan & Claypool Life Sciences; 2010.
7. Levine RJ, Lam C, Qian C, et al. Soluble endoglin and other circulating antiangiogenic factors in preeclampsia. N Engl J Med. 2006;355:992–1005.
8. Roberts JM, Bell MJ. If we know so much about preeclampsia, why haven't we cured the disease? J Reprod Immunol. 2013;99:1–9.
9. Maltepe E, Fisher SJ. Placenta: the forgotten organ. Annu Rev Cell Dev Biol. 2015;31:523–52.
10. Riba M, Garcia Manteiga JM, Bošnjak B, et al. Revealing the acute asthma ignorome: characterization and validation of uninvestigated gene networks. Sci Rep. 2016;6:24647.
11. Pandey AK, Lu L, Wang X, et al. Functionally enigmatic genes: a case study of the brain ignorome. PLoS One. 2014;9:e88889.
12. Wei CH, Kao HY, Lu Z. PubTator: a web-based text mining tool for assisting biocuration. Nucleic Acids Res. 2013;41:W518–22.
13. Piñero J, Bravo À, Queralt-Rosinach N, Gutiérrez-Sacristán A, et al. DisGeNET: a comprehensive platform integrating information on human disease-associated genes and variants. Nucleic Acids Res. 2017;45:D833–9.
14. Rappaport N, Nativ N, Stelzer G, et al. MalaCards: an integrated compendium for diseases and their annotation. Database. 2013;2013:bat018.
15. Kim JD, Cohen KB, Kim JJ. PubAnnotation-query: a search tool for corpora with multi-layers of annotation. BMC Proc. 2015;9(5):A3.
16. Callahan TJ, Tripodi IJ, Hunter LE, et al. The Phenotype Knowledge Translator (PheKnowLator) Ecosystem. https://zenodo.org/communities/pheknowlator-ecosystem
17. Köhler S, Gargano M, Matentzoglu N, et al. The Human Phenotype Ontology in 2021. Nucleic Acids Res. 2021;49:D1207–17.
18. Schriml LM, Arze C, Nadendla S, et al. Disease Ontology: a backbone for disease semantic integration. Nucleic Acids Res. 2012;40:D940–6.
19. The Gene Ontology Consortium. The Gene Ontology Resource: 20 years and still GOing strong. Nucleic Acids Res. 2019;47:D330–8.
20. Tsitsulin A. deepwalk-c. GitHub. https://github.com/xgfs/deepwalk-c
21. van der Maaten L, Hinton GE. Visualizing High-Dimensional Data Using t-SNE. J Mach Learn Res. 9:2579–605.
22. Manning CD, Raghavan P, Schütze H. Introduction to Information Retrieval. Cambridge University Press; 2008.
23. Chen J, Bardes EE, Aronow BJ, Jegga AG. ToppGene Suite for gene list enrichment analysis and candidate gene prioritization. Nucleic Acids Res. 2009;37:W305–11.

24. Wagner LK. Diagnosis and management of preeclampsia. Am Fam Physician. 2004;70:2317–24.
25. Nunes S, Sousa RT, Pesquita C. Predicting Gene-Disease Associations with Knowledge Graph Embeddings over Multiple Ontologies. arXiv. 2021.
26. Hu J, Lepore R, Dobson RJB, et al. DGLinker: flexible knowledge-graph prediction of disease–gene associations. Nucleic Acids Res. 2021;49:W153–61.
27. Alshahrani M, Almansour A, Alkhaldi A, et al. Combining biomedical knowledge graphs and text to improve predictions for drug-target interactions and drug-indications. PeerJ. 2022;10:e13061.
28. Mercier J, Josso A, Médigue C, Vallenet D. GROOLS: reactive graph reasoning for genome annotation through biological processes. BMC Bioinformatics. 2018;19:132.
29. Lynch CJ, Adams SH. Branched-chain amino acids in metabolic signalling and insulin resistance. Nat Rev Endocrinol. 2014;10:723–36.
30. Rosario FJ, Gupta MB, Myatt L, et al. Mechanistic Target of Rapamycin Complex 1 promotes the expression of genes encoding Electron Transport Chain proteins and stimulates oxidative phosphorylation in primary human trophoblast cells by regulating mitochondrial biogenesis. Sci Rep. 2019;9:246.
31. Smith AN, Wang X, Thomas DG, et al. The role of mitochondrial dysfunction in preeclampsia: Causative factor or collateral damage? Am J Hypertens. 2021;34:442–52.
32. Junek T, Baum O, Läuter H, et al. Pre-eclampsia associated alterations of the elastic fibre system in umbilical cord vessels. Anat Embryol. 2000;201:291–303.
33. Borowski S, Tirado-Gonzalez I, Freitag N, et al Altered glycosylation contributes to placental dysfunction upon early disruption of the NK cell-DC dynamics. Front Immunol. 2020;11:1316.
34. Flood-Nichols SK, Kazanjian AA, Tinnemore D, et al. Aberrant glycosylation of plasma proteins in severe preeclampsia promotes monocyte adhesion. Reprod Sci. 2014;21:204–14.
35. Gerasimova EM, Fedotov SA, Kachkin DV, et al. Protein misfolding during pregnancy: New approaches to preeclampsia diagnostics. Int J Mol Sci. 2019;20:6183.
36. O'Connor BB, Pope BD, Peters MM, et al. The role of extracellular matrix in normal and pathological pregnancy: Future applications of microphysiological systems in reproductive medicine. Exp Biol Med. 2020;245:1163–74.
37. Rudra CB, Williams MA, Frederick IO, Luthy DA. Maternal asthma and risk of preeclampsia: a case-control study. J Reprod Med. 2006;51:94–100.
38. Mayer C, Apodaca-Ramos I. Tocolysis. In: StatPearls. Treasure Island (FL): 2021.
39. Chakraborty D, Cui W, Rosario GX, et al. HIF-KDM3A-MMP12 regulatory circuit ensures trophoblast plasticity and placental adaptations to hypoxia. Proc Natl Acad Sci USA. 2016;113:E7212–21.
40. Wang H, Wang P, Liang X, et al. Down-regulation of endothelial protein C receptor promotes preeclampsia by affecting actin polymerization. J Cell Mol Med. 2020;24:3370–83.
41. Stergiakouli E, Langley K, Williams H, et al. Steroid sulfatase is a potential modifier of cognition in attention deficit hyperactivity disorder. Genes Brain Behav. 2011;10:334–44.
42. Dachew BA, Scott JG, Mamun A, Alati R. Pre-eclampsia and the risk of attention-deficit/hyperactivity disorder in offspring: Findings from the ALSPAC birth cohort study. Psychiatry Res. 2019;272:392–7.

Development and application of a computable genotype model in the GA4GH Variation Representation Specification

Wesley Goar[1], Lawrence Babb[2], Srikar Chamala[3], Melissa Cline[4], Robert R. Freimuth[5], Reece K. Hart[6], Kori Kuzma[1], Jennifer Lee[7], Tristan Nelson[8], Andreas Prlić[9], Kevin Riehle[10], Anastasia Smith[1], Kathryn Stahl[1], Andrew D. Yates[11], Heidi L. Rehm[2,12], Alex H. Wagner[1,13]

[1]Institute for Genomic Medicine, Nationwide Children's Hospital, Columbus, OH; [2]Broad Institute of MIT and Harvard, Cambridge, MA; [3]Department of Pathology and Laboratory Medicine, Children's Hospital Los Angeles, Los Angeles,CA; [4]UC Santa Cruz Genomics Institute, Santa Cruz, CA; [5]Department of Artificial Intelligence & Informatics, Center for Individualized Medicine, Mayo Clinic; [6]MyOme, Inc, San Carlos, CA; [7]Sequencing.com, Los Angeles, CA; [8]Geisinger, Danville, PA; [9]Invitae, San Francisco, CA; [10]Baylor College of Medicine, Houston, TX; [11]European Molecular Biology Laboratory, European Bioinformatics Institute, Wellcome Genome Campus, Cambridge, UK; [12]Massachusetts General Hospital, Boston, MA; [13]Department of Pediatrics & Biomedical Informatics, The Ohio State University College of Medicine, Columbus, OH

As the diversity of genomic variation data increases with our growing understanding of the role of variation in health and disease, it is critical to develop standards for precise inter-system exchange of these data for research and clinical applications. The Global Alliance for Genomics and Health (GA4GH) Variation Representation Specification (VRS) meets this need through a technical terminology and information model for disambiguating and concisely representing variation concepts. Here we discuss the recent Genotype model in VRS, which may be used to represent the allelic composition of a genetic locus. We demonstrate the use of the Genotype model and the constituent Haplotype model for the precise and interoperable representation of pharmacogenomic diplotypes, HGVS variants, and VCF records using VRS and discuss how this can be leveraged to enable interoperable exchange and search operations between assayed variation and genomic knowledgebases.

Keywords: Genomics, GA4GH, VRS, Genotype, Haplotype, Allele, HGVS, VCF

1. Introduction

Representation of genomic variation as recorded in genomic data systems is highly varied and complex, involving the computable formalization of imprecise concepts with imprecise definitions for data exchange between systems. Several well-known formats and tools have been developed for exchanging some common forms of variation, including the Variant Call Format (VCF)[1], the Human Genome Variation Society (HGVS) variant nomenclature[2], the NCBI Sequence-Position-Deletion-Insertion (SPDI) data model[3] and the ClinGen Allele Registry web service[4], among others[5–8]. Despite this, these common fit-for-purpose variation models use unaligned terminologies, conventions, and assumptions that make it challenging to losslessly convert information between formats. More pressingly, these formats are difficult to extend to domain-specific requirements for variation representation across different communities, promoting further division of terms, information models, and exchange formats for genomic variation[9,10].

The precise conceptual representation of variation is important for the application of computational methods in assessing human genomic variation in a clinical context. When studying rare diseases and cancers, clinical evaluation of patients increasingly includes interrogation of patient genomes for variants of potential clinical significance. Often, these assays will be highly targeted to query only those specific regions of interest, providing only partial information for clinical reporting. In some cases, observation of a variant allele is reported only as "heterozygous" (the presence of at least two different alleles at a genomic locus), "homozygous" (multiple copies of an allele at a locus with no other alleles), or "hemizygous" (an allele describing a locus for which there is only one total allele). These reports often omit further information regarding the total number of alleles at the locus or (for heterozygous variants) the composition of other alleles.

These abbreviated representations of human genotypes are imprecise, implying a diploid genotype when the patient may have aneuploidy caused by large-scale structural variation[11] and/or meiotic nondisjunction[12], typically resulting in abnormal phenotypes and disease. Heterozygous genotypes described in this way further connote the presence of a reference-agreement allele, though this too is not necessarily the case. To complicate the matter further, the manner in which variants are reported relies on an understood meaning of terms such as *allele*, *genotype*, and *haplotype*, which have similar but distinct meanings across different genomic communities and laboratories.

Clinical evaluation of genomic biomarkers also extends to drug response evidence, which can vary widely between individuals. In order to better understand how genetic information contributes to this variability, the pharmacogenomics (PGx) community collected evidence to gauge how genetic variants within a patient contribute to the overall responsiveness of a patient to different drugs[13]. Evidence from PGx knowledgebases can provide important information regarding drug toxicity and response within a patient, allowing for a more personalized treatment[14].

One class of biomarkers describing PGx knowledge are "Star (*) Alleles", which were first used to identify or denote alleles within the CYP gene family[15]. The results of PGx assays are often reported as diplotypes (pairs of haplotypes) due to the human genome being diploid[10]. The association of diplotypes and phenotypes enables the identification of pharmacogenetic interactions. For the assessment of PGx diplotypes, the most widely used nomenclature system for PGx alleles is the domain-specific "star" (*) system[16]. Due to the complex nature of PGx alleles and clinical assays, there continues to be ambiguity that can make it difficult to utilize PGx data in practice[17–24]. Some of these challenges were highlighted by the Centers for Disease Control and Prevention's (CDC) Genetic Testing Reference Material (GeT-RM) Coordination Program test for clinical PGx genetic testing[25,26]. The results of this study demonstrate many inconsistencies due to a lack of a unified and standardized nomenclature system and different PGx designs. To help overcome the challenges regarding PGx data, the Clinical Pharmacogenetics Implementation Consortium was created to help educate and facilitate the use of PGx data in clinical settings[19,27–29]. Despite this, challenges remain in aligning PGx Star Alleles and other clinical biomarker domains[30]. Notably, there is a "*" representation that is called a spanning deletion in VCF, describing overlapping deletion Alleles at sites of other variants in a VCF file[31].

To address the challenge of aligning the disparate genotype variation representations found in clinical reports, existing genomic variant exchange formats, and the PGx community, the Global Alliance for Genomics and Health (GA4GH)[32] Genomic Knowledge Standards (GKS) Work Stream developed the Variation Representation Specification (VRS; vrs.ga4gh.org)[33] to enable the reliable and precise exchange of variation between computer systems. The GA4GH VRS standard leverages a clearly defined terminology and information model, a value object design philosophy, and fully-specified JSON Schema, which allows it to meet these diverse use cases through modular variation representation. The VRS design philosophy makes it well-suited to describing complex variation concepts using a standard, computationally defined set of objects, enabling precise semantics and improving FAIR genomic data exchange. In this manuscript we describe a new model for representing genotypes using VRS, and demonstrate applications of this model to structure related concepts in other systems, including VCF, HGVS, and PGx Star Alleles.

2. Results

2.1. *A landscape analysis of genotype concepts across communities*

We first surveyed the requirements of genotype variation data as represented by large-scale genomic data standards (i.e. VCF), clinical reports (HGVS), and knowledgebases containing PGx (Star Allele) and/or variant-disease evidence (HGVS). We analyzed the conceptual alignment of terms from each specification to existing concepts in VRS to inform a conceptual framework for genotype representation (**Figure 1**).

The simplest conceptual unit of variation is the "small variant", a contiguous sequence change (typically fewer than 50 residues in length) often referred to simply as a "variant" or "allele". This is the fundamental unit of the Variant Call Format (VCF), used for representing variants called from high-throughput sequencing data. Each record within a VCF contains an identified variant with its corresponding position and the reference (also called "wild type") allele it was called against, along with other relevant information including the genotype. The VCF specification defines an allele as, "representing single genetic haplotypes (A, T, ATC)"[34], which aligns with the NCBI definition of a Contextual Allele[3]. The HGVS nomenclature uses the aligned term "variant" to describe a small variant but differentiates this from the term "Allele" (as described below). The PGx nomenclature describes this as a "sequence variation"[35], and also differentiates this from a broader definition for "allele" (also discussed below). In VRS, this fundamental concept is termed an Allele[33], and is defined as *the state of a molecule at a contiguous segment of a biological sequence*.

A broader concept, in which several small variants occurring on the same molecule (*in-cis*) are described together similarly goes by several different definitions among the genomics community. In the VCF specification, this concept is a *haplotype*, defined as "a set of variants which are known to be on the same chromosome in the germline genome". This aligns to the ClinGen concept of a "haplotype" and a "star allele" in the PGx community. HGVS also terms this an "allele", defined as "a series of variants on one chromosome"[36]. An HGVS Allele may represent a series of changes *in-cis*, and variants are considered different Alleles when on different chromosomes (i.e. *in-trans*). In addition, the HGVS nomenlcature may represent a set of variants with uncertain phase. The *in-cis* variation concept in VRS is termed Haplotype[33], defined as *a set of non-overlapping Allele members that co-occur on the same molecule*.

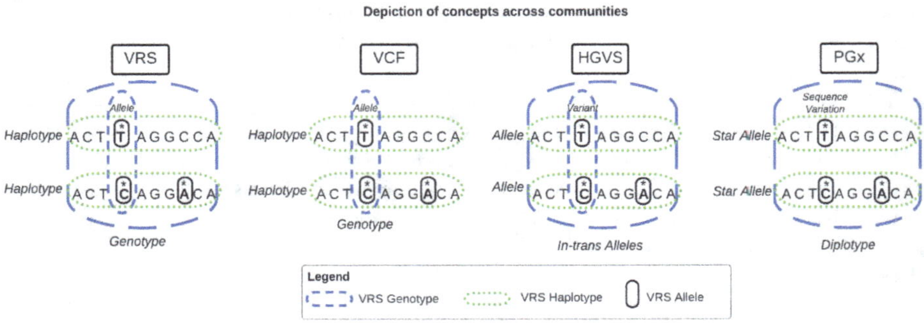

Fig 1. *Genomics Concepts across Communities*
Communities use different terms for similar concepts. These concepts are represented with respect to VRS nomenclature while using terminology from each community. Among these standards, the VRS Genotype (blue dashes) aligns most closely to in-trans HGVS Alleles, VCF genotypes, and PGx diplotypes. Similarly, HGVS Alleles, VCF Haplotypes, and PGx Star Alleles are all aligned to the VRS Haplotype (green dots). Finally, a VRS Allele is conceptually aligned with a VCF allele, an HGVS variant, and a PGx "sequence variation" (black circles). HGVS and VRS genotypes are illustrated with both broad and narrow representations (blue dashes), as they may represent either.

To model a Genotype in VRS, we built upon these concepts and analyzed the use of "genotype" or similar terms as described in other community standards. The VCF genotype is defined as: "an assignment of alleles for each chromosome of a single named sample at a particular locus." The reference allele in a VCF is encoded using a 0, while alternate alleles use 1, 2, etc. For example, in a diploid variant call, a heterozygous reference and alternate allele genotype would be encoded as 0/1 or a heterozygous alternate 1 and alternate 2 allele genotype would be encoded as 1/2. A homozygous alternate allele genotype is annotated as 1/1. Haploid variant calls only contain a single allele, while a triploid variant call would contain three alleles (e.g 0/0/1). An unphased genotype is represented using the "/" whereas a genotype with known phasing uses a "|" (e.g. 1 | 0).

The HGVS nomenclature doesn't use the term genotype, but (as described above) *in-trans* alleles are conceptually aligned with the common meaning of the term[36]. The use of "heterozygous" and "homozygous" as free text are used in some clinical reports[37] accompanying an HGVS variant, in lieu of a formal HGVS trans-allele structure. This observation illuminated a key modeling requirement to capture the concept of heterozygous alleles within a genotype while lacking complete information about the constituent members.

We evaluated how PGx Star Alleles were represented within genotypes, and found that PGx evidence may be associated with a specific genotype representation described as a diplotype (a diploid genotype). Similarly, PGx evidence at the Star Allele level can be described naturally by a VRS Haplotype. This conceptual design benefits from a diploid constraint, and was well-suited to our starting model for Genotype (see **Methods**). We kept these diplotypes as an example case for testing in developing a VRS Genotype model.

2.2. *The VRS Genotype information model and supporting classes*

To develop the Genotype information model in VRS, we evaluated the definitions and constraints of the Allele and Haplotype models identified in our landscape analysis. The VRS Haplotype class had previously been defined as "a set of non-overlapping Allele members that co-occur on the same molecule", but Haplotypes were allowed to contain a minimum of one Allele, designed to capture a semantic distinction between an Allele and a single-Allele Haplotype. However, after evaluating related concepts in the community, it was decided that the Haplotype information model should be updated to require at least two Allele members. This was informed by the lack of a distinction between a single-Allele Haplotype and an isolated Allele in other systems.

As a result of our modeling, we defined Genotype as "a quantified set of Molecular Variation associated with a genomic locus", where *Molecular Variation* collectively refers to VRS Alleles, Haplotypes, and future classes of variation that exist on a contiguous molecule. This is in contrast to VRS *Systemic Variation* (including concepts such as Genotype and Copy Number Variation) which describe variation across several molecules within a system. We aligned this genotype definition with an information model that is flexible enough to capture the cross-domain concerns identified in our landscape analysis. As noted, some specifications (e.g. VCF and HGVS) distinguish between genotypes with and without known *in-trans* phasing. The GA4GH Variation Representation team is working on a generalized phasing model that captures the semantics of phasing, and has opted to define this independent of the Genotype model.

Each Molecular Variant constituting a Genotype is contained within an associated *Genotype Member* object to quantify the Molecular Variant present at a genomic locus (**Figure 2**). This provides a convenient mechanism for compactly representing identical Molecular Variation at a locus as well as expressing uncertainty in the count of that variation through the application of Definite Range or Indefinite Range objects[33]. The count attributes of the Genotype Member and Genotype classes also enable compact representation of Molecular Variation in polyploid genomes and reflect similar conceptual structures designed for this purpose[38].

In addition, a count field exists at the Genotype level for expressing the total copies of the genomic locus as described by the Genotype Members. The Genotype count value could be greater (but never less) than the summation of counts across Genotype Members. In such cases, the difference conveys additional unspecified Molecular Variation that is expected to exist but is not explicitly represented. This feature allows for precisely representing ambiguity in genotype concepts when not all Molecular Variation are reported.

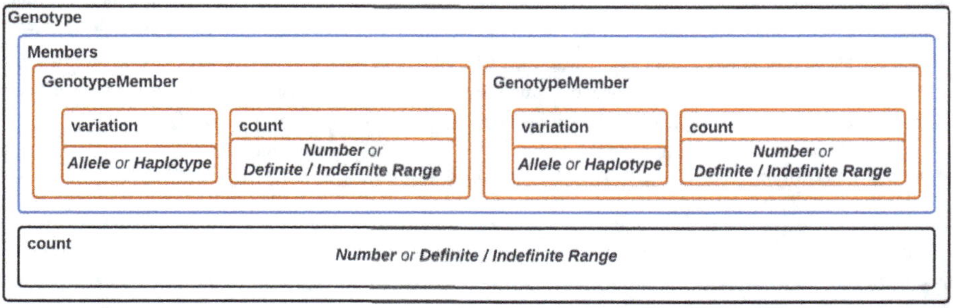

Fig 2. *Genotype Class in VRS*
The Genotype class in VRS must contain at least one member consisting of an Allele or Haplotype and its count of occurrences within the system. This can be represented by an integer Number or as a Definite/Indefinite Range. The Genotype also has a count, representing the expected total of the genotype's molecule in the system, expressed as an integer or as a definite/indefinite range. This allows the user to describe what is known regarding the genotype without making an inference. For example, a user could add a single Genotype Member with a count = 1 and have the Genotype count = 2 to represent that there are additional molecular variations expected to exist but they are not explicitly described by the user or data.

2.3. *Applications of the Genotype information model*

We evaluated how this structure provides the flexibility to represent concepts from a simple two allele genotype or a diplotype composed of a single Allele in-trans with a haplotype. The two-Allele genotype example is exemplified by a common VCF record pattern, where two or more VCF Alleles are expressed *in-trans* independent of *in-cis* phasing with neighboring Alleles (e.g. 0/1). In this case, each VCF Allele is expressed as a VRS Allele, put into a Genotype Member object with count=1, and both of those Genotype Members added to a Genotype with count=2 (**Figure 3A**). We also developed a utility for annotating VCF records with VRS Alleles (see **Methods**) to assist Genotype reconstruction from single-sample and multi-sample VCFs.

A more complex scenario was tested on the *CYP2C19 *1/*17* diplotype (**Figure 3B**) as represented by changes from a reference sequence. Initialization of this process requires selection of a sequence context for describing the constituent variants. In this example we selected the GRCh38 genomic reference[39]. It is important that a genomic DNA sequence is used in this step, as Star Alleles include variation in regulatory and intronic regions and representation of intronic variation with respect to a cDNA sequence (e.g. RefSeq NM_ sequences) is dependent upon an inferred alignment of these variants to a genomic reference. VRS Alleles were constructed on the selected reference sequence, and *in-cis* Alleles were subsequently grouped into VRS Haplotypes. The count of each Molecular Variation (in this example, one Haplotype representing a *CYP2C19 *1* Star Allele and one Haplotype representing a *CYP2C19 *17* Star Allele) is specified using the Genotype Member class. These Genotype Members are assembled into a Genotype and the overall count (2) of alleles at the locus is recorded, explicitly indicating a diploid state at this locus.

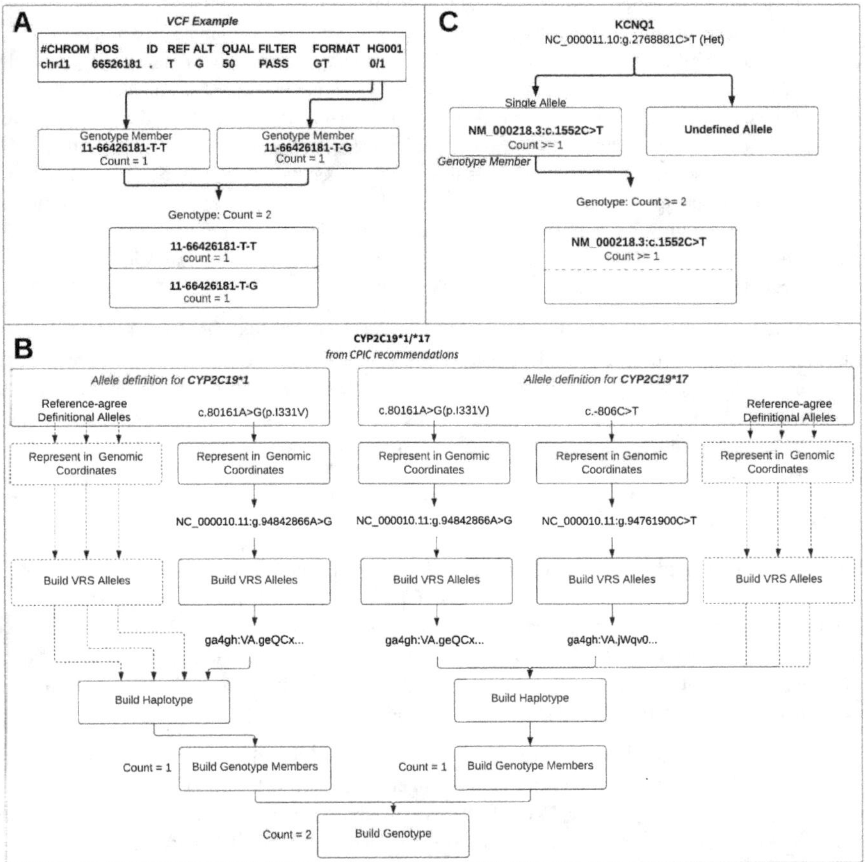

Fig 3. *Visualization of Genotypes in VRS*
Variants are represented in their genomic coordinates and then normalized and translated into their VRS-allele ID's using VRS-Python. **A**. Representation of a 0/1 Genotype from a VCF. **B**. CYP2C19*1 is composed of a single variant and can be placed into a Genotype Member with a count of 1. CYP2C19*17 contains two variants *in-cis* which needs to be represented by a Haplotpye and then placed into a Genotype Member with count = 1. These two genotype members are then used to construct the genotype shown above with a total copy count of 2. A Star Allele representation incorporating reference-agree VRS Alleles is depicted with dashed lines. **C.** Representation of a heterozygous variant from an eMerge report.

Nuances to the use and meaning of the VRS Genotype model for representing Star Alleles were captured in discussion with members of the PGx informatics community. While the VRS Genotype model faithfully represents the variants for these Star Alleles as displayed in PharmVar, the meaning of these PGx Star Alleles and how they should be assessed is more complex than simply observing the described collection of non-reference allele variants. The Star Allele model also assumes that there is an associated set of definitive locations that have been assayed (and are expected to be reference-agree) to properly assign Star Allele Haplotypes from patient sequencing data. To address this, we leveraged the Allele design of VRS to demonstrate a data structure to efficiently communicate this nuance between systems using both variant and reference-agree Alleles (**Figure 3B** and **Methods**). This has the added benefit of preserving the context under which Star Alleles are described, aiding reinterpretation and data reuse as additional Star Alleles are discovered and the number of definitive sites increase.

Finally, we tested this model on Genotypes with missing members to illustrate how this model captures those annotations. Starting with an eMERGE-seq panel report[37], we create a Genotype from a heterozygous variant report with only one allele described. We used the VRS Indefinite Range concept[33] to express the heterozygous variant as observed at least once at a genomic locus with at least two alleles (**Figure 3C**). An alternative could also be to infer a diploid state for this report, in which case we would represent this as a variant observed once at a locus of two alleles.

2.4. *Implementation support*

The definition and information model for Genotypes has been implemented in documentation at vrs.ga4gh.org, structured in JSON Schema at github.com/ga4gh/vrs and implemented in Python at github.com/ga4gh/vrs-python/tree/pgx. We have also created example PGx jupyter notebooks to demonstrate how to create and use Genotypes and other VRS components within VRS-Python to build and search Star Alleles at github.com/ga4gh/vrs-python/blob/pgx/notebooks/PGx.ipynb, alongside methods for VCF and HGVS translation to VRS at github.com/ga4gh/vrs-python/blob/pgx/notebooks/Extras.ipynb.

In addition to the static examples available above, this and other VRS-Python notebooks can be run from a local copy of the vrs-python repository or using zero-install cloud-based notebooks hosted at mybinder.org/v2/gh/ga4gh/vrs-python/pgx. The cloud-based notebooks are a simple mechanism for newcomers to interactively test the functionality and scope of VRS-Python and associated VRS models by leveraging our publicly accessible REST APIs to support services. A user may follow the examples provided within the notebooks to gain an understanding of VRS and can even edit or add cells to further explore VRS using their own data or examples.

3. Discussion

Defining a model for genotype representation required careful conceptual alignment and semantic precision for interoperability of this model with similar concepts across different communities. We found that while the VRS, VCF, HGVS, and PGx communities have some differences between the terms allele, haplotype, and genotype, there are shared conceptual relationships describing the *in-cis* and *in-trans* representation of sequence variants at a genomic locus. We found that these shared conceptual models enabled a unified computational structure for interchangeable and lossless description of these concepts between systems, advancing our ability to automate scalable evidence search operations between assayed data and genomic knowledgebases.

The VRS Genotype model explicitly captures the count of individual alleles and all expected alleles at a locus as independent values, allowing for the flexible description of genomic loci and enabling precise forms of ambiguity using VRS Definite Range and Indefinite Range quantifiers. We demonstrated how this allows for reconstruction of ambiguity as derived from clinical reports and representation of Genotypes of ambiguous ploidy. We also illustrated how this model enables lossless capture of the VCF record-level genotype model, and like VCF, this provides a straightforward mechanism for representation of alleles at polyploid loci. In addition, we showed how the Genotype model enables the representation of diplotypes as expressed in PGx resources. We also illustrated how this model can be extended using the modular design of VRS to associate Genotypes with additional necessary elements for precisely-defined representations of PGx Star Alleles. Together, these findings provide a template for the flexible use of VRS Genotypes across various genomics communities with domain-specific requirements.

Our future efforts will focus on extending our VCF-annotation tool to include the ability to annotate VRS genotypes in VCF files. We will also be applying the VRS genotype model to the ClinVar database. In addition, the GA4GH Variation Representation team will be implementing a phasing model to explicitly capture *in-trans* and *in-cis* semantics for Variation collections, that will allow for richer expression of Genotypes with validated *in-trans* relationships.

Prior to this work, data exchange between PGx and other genomic communities has been somewhat challenging. VRS allows us to precisely describe the genotypes within PGx data, VCF files, and lab reports using a shared syntax, opening an avenue for advanced queries, search operations, and machine learning by improving interoperability between disparate clinical assays and knowledgebases.

4. Methods

4.1. *Community modeling and use case discussions*

The Genotype model was initially discussed and revisited on several occasions during the development of VRS, and an initial model was under consideration for the VRS 1.2 release. This initial model was a structure containing a set of Haplotypes and was designed to represent the set as an *in-trans* model. This model was unwieldy due to the lack of support for Molecular Variation counts or total Molecular Variant count at a locus.

In July 2022, the GA4GH sponsored a VRS hackathon at the Intelligent Systems for Molecular Biology 2022 Annual Conference in Madison, Wisconsin. During the hackathon, modeling of the Genotype class was selected as a preferred topic, and participants in this activity worked together to evaluate the Genotype model and its relation to similar concepts in different communities, including immunogenomic and pharmacogenomic use cases. The group discussed the concepts of alleles, genotypes, and haplotypes and how they are related to one another to determine the best way to precisely model a genotype within VRS. Multiple examples from clinical reports, genomic assay results, and genomic knowledgebases were chosen to test and revise the ideas proposed. Once the group finalized the VRS Genotype model, they used the model to describe PGx alleles using VRS to test the model for interoperability between assayed PGx data and pharmacogenomic knowledge bases.

4.2. *Community Review*

Community involvement and review is a critical component of developing standards that are meant for the global community. We presented the new VRS genotype model during the July 18th and July 25th GA4GH Variation Representation meetings, and with the VCF community maintainers on the GA4GH July 27th VRS/VCF alignment call to receive feedback from interested community members and domain experts. We also sent an open call for review to the GA4GH community for comments and questions during our open review period. The community comments for the review of this model were documented online at github.com/ga4gh/vrs/pull/394.

4.3. *VRS-VCF annotation tool*

The VRS-VCF annotation tool allows users to annotate the reference and alternate alleles of a VCF record with VRS. The VRS allele identifier is stored in the INFO field of the VCF and an optional pickle file containing the entire VRS object can be created for all the annotated records. The VRS allele identifier can then be used for precise and speedy lookup of information from databases utilizing VRS, which drastically simplifies the variant annotation process. The tool is open-source and readily available online at github.com/ga4gh/vrs-python/blob/main/src/ga4gh/vrs/extras/vcf_annotation.py.

4.4. *Software availability*

All code supporting the development, documentation, implementation, and validation of the VRS Genotype model is available online at GitHub as indicated throughout the text, under the permissive Apache 2.0 open source license.

5. Acknowledgments

The authors thank Li Gong, Teri E. Klein, Ryan Whaley, and Michelle Whirl-Carillo (Stanford University) for important discussions and critical feedback that substantially advanced this work. WAG & AHW were supported by the National Human Genome Research Institute (NHGRI) award R35HG011949. LB & HR were supported by the NHGRI award U24HG006834. MSC was supported by the National Cancer Institute (NCI) award U01CA242954-01. RRF & KR were supported by the NHGRI award U41HG006834. RRF was supported by the NHGRI award R35HG011899. KR was supported by the NHGRI awards U41HG009649, U41HG009650. ADY was supported by the Wellcome Trust [WT222155/Z/20/Z] and the European Molecular Biology Laboratory. RKH was supported by ClinGen, Invitae, Inc, and MyOme, Inc.

Bibliography

1. Danecek, P. *et al.* The variant call format and VCFtools. *Bioinformatics* **27**, 2156–2158 (2011).
2. den Dunnen, J. T. *et al.* HGVS Recommendations for the Description of Sequence Variants: 2016 Update. *Hum. Mutat.* **37**, 564–569 (2016).
3. Holmes, J. B., Moyer, E., Phan, L., Maglott, D. & Kattman, B. SPDI: data model for variants and applications at NCBI. *Bioinformatics* **36**, 1902–1907 (2020).
4. Pawliczek, P. *et al.* ClinGen Allele Registry links information about genetic variants. *Hum. Mutat.* **39**, 1690–1701 (2018).
5. Sherry, S. T. *et al.* dbSNP: the NCBI database of genetic variation. *Nucleic Acids Res.* **29**, 308–311 (2001).
6. Fokkema, I. F. A. C. *et al.* LOVD v.2.0: the next generation in gene variant databases. *Hum. Mutat.* **32**, 557–563 (2011).
7. International Standing Committee on Human Cytogenomic Nomenclature. *ISCN 2020: An International System for Human Cytogenomic Nomenclature (2020)*. (Karger, 2020).
8. Quinlan, A. R. & Hall, I. M. BEDTools: a flexible suite of utilities for comparing genomic features. *Bioinformatics* **26**, 841–842 (2010).
9. Wagner, A. H. *et al.* A harmonized meta-knowledgebase of clinical interpretations of somatic genomic variants in cancer. *Nat. Genet.* **52**, 448–457 (2020).
10. Kalman, L. V. *et al.* Pharmacogenetic allele nomenclature: International workgroup recommendations for test result reporting. *Clin. Pharmacol. Ther.* **99**, 172–185 (2016).
11. Escaramís, G., Docampo, E. & Rabionet, R. A decade of structural variants: description, history and methods to detect structural variation. *Brief. Funct. Genomics* **14**, 305–314 (2015).
12. Angell, R. First-meiotic-division nondisjunction in human oocytes. *Am. J. Hum. Genet.* **61**, 23–32 (1997).
13. Jones, D. S. How personalized medicine became genetic, and racial: Werner Kalow and the formations of pharmacogenetics. *J. Hist. Med. Allied Sci.* **68**, 1–48 (2013).
14. Sim, S. C., Altman, R. B. & Ingelman-Sundberg, M. Databases in the area of pharmacogenetics. *Hum. Mutat.* **32**, 526–531 (2011).
15. Nebert, D. W. Suggestions for the nomenclature of human alleles: relevance to ecogenetics, pharmacogenetics and molecular epidemiology. *Pharmacogenetics* **10**, 279–290 (2000).
16. Robarge, J. D., Li, L., Desta, Z., Nguyen, A. & Flockhart, D. A. The Star-Allele Nomenclature: Retooling for Translational Genomics. *Clinical Pharmacology & Therapeutics* vol. 82 244–248 Preprint at https://doi.org/10.1038/sj.clpt.6100284 (2007).
17. Swen, J. J. *et al.* Translating pharmacogenomics: challenges on the road to the clinic. *PLoS Med.* **4**, e209 (2007).
18. Scott, S., Abul-Husn, N., Obeng, A. O., Sanderson, S. & Gottesman, O. Implementation and utilization of genetic testing in personalized medicine. *Pharmacogenomics and Personalized Medicine* 227 Preprint at https://doi.org/10.2147/pgpm.s48887 (2014).
19. Relling, M. V. & Klein, T. E. CPIC: Clinical Pharmacogenetics Implementation Consortium of the Pharmacogenomics Research Network. *Clin. Pharmacol. Ther.* **89**, 464–467 (2011).
20. Lee, K. C., Ma, J. D. & Kuo, G. M. Pharmacogenomics: Bridging the gap between science and practice. *Journal of the American Pharmacists Association* vol. 50 e1–e17 Preprint at

https://doi.org/10.1331/japha.2010.09124 (2010).

21. Ma, J. D., Lee, K. C. & Kuo, G. M. Clinical application of pharmacogenomics. *J. Pharm. Pract.* **25**, 417–427 (2012).
22. Stanek, E. J. *et al.* Adoption of pharmacogenomic testing by US physicians: results of a nationwide survey. *Clin. Pharmacol. Ther.* **91**, 450–458 (2012).
23. Malentacchi, F. *et al.* Is laboratory medicine ready for the era of personalized medicine? A survey addressed to laboratory directors of hospitals/academic schools of medicine in Europe. *Clinical Chemistry and Laboratory Medicine (CCLM)* vol. 53 Preprint at https://doi.org/10.1515/cclm-2015-0171 (2015).
24. Hess, G. P., Fonseca, E., Scott, R. & Fagerness, J. Pharmacogenomic and pharmacogenetic-guided therapy as a tool in precision medicine: current state and factors impacting acceptance by stakeholders. *Genet. Res.* **97**, e13 (2015).
25. Pratt, Zehnbauer, Wilson & Baak. Characterization of 107 genomic DNA reference materials for CYP2D6, CYP2C19, CYP2C9, VKORC1, and UGT1A1: a GeT-RM and Association for .... *The Journal of molecular*.
26. Pratt, V. M. *et al.* Characterization of 137 Genomic DNA Reference Materials for 28 Pharmacogenetic Genes. *The Journal of Molecular Diagnostics* vol. 18 109–123 Preprint at https://doi.org/10.1016/j.jmoldx.2015.08.005 (2016).
27. Gaedigk, A., Whirl-Carrillo, M., Pratt, V. M., Miller, N. A. & Klein, T. E. PharmVar and the Landscape of Pharmacogenetic Resources. *Clin. Pharmacol. Ther.* **107**, 43–46 (2020).
28. Whirl-Carrillo, M. *et al.* Pharmacogenomics knowledge for personalized medicine. *Clin. Pharmacol. Ther.* **92**, 414–417 (2012).
29. Relling, M. V. *et al.* New Pharmacogenomics Research Network: An Open Community Catalyzing Research and Translation in Precision Medicine. *Clin. Pharmacol. Ther.* **102**, 897–902 (2017).
30. Caudle, K. E. *et al.* Standardization can accelerate the adoption of pharmacogenomics current status and the path forward. *Pharmacogenomics* **19**, 847–860 (2018).
31. GATK Documentation Team. Spanning or overlapping deletions (* allele). *Genome Analysis Toolkit* https://gatk.broadinstitute.org/hc/en-us/articles/360035531912-Spanning-or-overlapping-deletions-allele-.
32. Rehm, H. L. *et al.* GA4GH: International policies and standards for data sharing across genomic research and healthcare. *Cell Genom* **1**, 100029 (2021).
33. Wagner, A. H. *et al.* The GA4GH Variation Representation Specification: A computational framework for variation representation and federated identification. *Cell Genomics* **1**, (2021).
34. Global Alliance for Genomics and Health. *The Variant Call Format Specification - VCFv4.3 and BCFv2.2*. https://samtools.github.io/hts-specs/VCFv4.3.pdf (2022).
35. PharmVar. https://www.pharmvar.org/criteria.
36. Sequence Variant Nomenclature. https://varnomen.hgvs.org/recommendations/DNA/variant/alleles/.
37. Murugan, M. *et al.* Genomic considerations for FHIR®; eMERGE implementation lessons. *J. Biomed. Inform.* **118**, 103795 (2021).
38. Clevenger, J. P., Korani, W., Ozias-Akins, P. & Jackson, S. Haplotype-Based Genotyping in Polyploids. *Front. Plant Sci.* **9**, 564 (2018).
39. Schneider, V. A. *et al.* Evaluation of GRCh38 and de novo haploid genome assemblies demonstrates the enduring quality of the reference assembly. *Genome Res.* **27**, 849–864 (2017).

Predictive modeling using shape statistics for interpretable and robust quality assurance of automated contours in radiation treatment planning

Zachary T. Wooten
Department of Statistics, Rice University, 6100 Main St.
Houston, TX 77005, USA
Email: ztw5@rice.edu

Cenji Yu and Laurence E. Court
Department of Radiation Physics, The University of Texas MD Anderson Cancer Center,
1400 Pressler St. Houston, TX 77030, USA
Email: cyu4@mdanderson.org, lecourt@mdanderson.org

Christine B. Peterson
Department of Biostatistics, The University of Texas MD Anderson Cancer Center,
1400 Pressler St. Houston, TX 77030, USA
Email: cbpeterson@mdanderson.org

Deep learning methods for image segmentation and contouring are gaining prominence as an automated approach for delineating anatomical structures in medical images during radiation treatment planning. These contours are used to guide radiotherapy treatment planning, so it is important that contouring errors are flagged before they are used for planning. This creates a need for effective quality assurance methods to enable the clinical use of automated contours in radiotherapy. We propose a novel method for contour quality assurance that requires only shape features, making it independent of the platform used to obtain the images. Our method uses a random forest classifier to identify low-quality contours. On a dataset of 312 kidney contours, our method achieved a cross-validated area under the curve of 0.937 in identifying unacceptable contours. We applied our method to an unlabeled validation dataset of 36 kidney contours. We flagged 6 contours which were then reviewed by a cervix contour specialist, who found that 4 of the 6 contours contained errors. We used Shapley values to characterize the specific shape features that contributed to each contour being flagged, providing a starting point for characterizing the source of the contouring error. These promising results suggest our method is feasible for quality assurance of automated radiotherapy contours.

Keywords: Shape statistics; Contour quality assurance; Medical imaging; Random forest.

1. Introduction

Segmenting anatomical structures in medical images is a critical step in radiation treatment planning, as treatment plans are optimized to achieve a high radiation dose to tumor while sparing nearby organs at risk. Recently, increasing effort has been put into automating the contouring process, as this would save clinicians time, reduce human error, and enhance access to radiation therapy in low-resource environments [1]. Deep learning methods like convolutional neural networks (CNN) have revolutionized the automation of contouring. While the results from these methods are promising, they provide no measures to indicate uncertainty or low confidence in challenging cases. Deep learning methods can make mistakes in image segmentation and contouring, particularly when faced with real data that do not resemble instances in their training data. It is of critical importance to avoid contouring errors in radiotherapy planning, as contouring mistakes could lead to overdosage of organs at risk. Currently, automatically generated contours must be manually reviewed for errors. Creating an automated contour review process to find and flag problematic contours would be a more objective and efficient approach.

Some approaches have been proposed to tackle this challenge. McIntosh et al. (2013) used a groupwise conditional random forest to detect contour errors based on imaging features [2], while Hui et al. (2018) showed that volumetric features of a set of contours can be used to fit univariate parametric distributions and find outliers on each feature [3]. Rhee et al. (2019) showed promising results using a second CNN-based model for flagging unacceptable contours [4]. However, relying on a similar approach for contouring and quality assurance may create redundancy, as similar methods may fail in similar ways.

We propose an orthogonal method for flagging unacceptable contours that only uses shape features of the contour without relying on deep learning methods or image features. This approach was chosen to allow our method to be applicable across various imaging systems, as image intensity and radiomic features depend heavily on the platform used for image acquisition. Our method accurately flags erroneous contours based on aspects of the resulting shapes, avoiding dependence on the imaging modality. Specifically, we trained a random forest classifier on shape features of kidney contours and compared its performance to alternative machine learning methods in correctly flagging unacceptable contours. We demonstrate its application to an external data set, where we identify potential contouring errors and characterize the shape features that informed these predictions.

2. Background

2.1 Shape features

Shape features are quantitative summaries that aim to characterize the geometric aspects of an object. Existing works on shape analysis, including Dryden [5] and Wirth [6], provide numerous examples of shape features that can be used to describe various geometric properties. Here, we rely on the features listed in Table 1.

Since several of these shape features require computing the convex hull of an object, we provide some additional discussion of the convex hull and its properties. The convex hull of an object is the smallest convex shape that contains the object, as illustrated in Figure 1a. The area is the shaded portion, while the convex area is the portion within the convex hull, shown as a dotted outline. Furthermore, the perimeter of the shape is calculated from the outline of the shaded object, whereas the convex perimeter is calculated from the outline of the convex hull.

Additional features of interest include sphericity, which describes how closely the shape resembles a sphere (or circle in two dimensions) and is a ratio of the minimum radius to the maximum radius. Naturally, for a circle, the minimum and maximum radii are the same. Hence the farther this ratio deviates from 1, the less circular the shape. Figure 1b illustrates how the minimum and maximum radii used in computing this shape statistic would be calculated.

Table 1. Shape features and their descriptions

Shape Feature	Description	Formula
Area	Number of pixels/voxels in a shape	
Perimeter	Length of number of pixels/voxels in the boundary of the object	
Minimum Radius	Shortest radius value from the center of shape to boundary	
Mean Radius	Average radius value from the center of shape to boundary	
Max Radius	Largest radius value from the center of shape to boundary	
Centroid Size	Square root of the sum of squared Euclidean distances from each landmark to the centroid [5]	$\sqrt{\sum_{i=1}^{k} \|\|(X)_i - \bar{X}\|\|^2}$
Compactness	The ratio of the area of an object to the area of a circle with the same perimeter	$\frac{4\pi * \text{Area}}{(\text{Perimeter})^2}$
Sphericity	The degree to which an object approaches the shape of a sphere	$\frac{\text{Min Radius}}{\text{Max Radius}}$
Convexity	The relative amount that an object differs from a convex object	$\frac{\text{Convex Perimeter}}{\text{Perimeter}}$
Solidity	The ratio of the area of an object to the area of a convex hull of the object	$\frac{\text{Area}}{\text{Convex Area}}$
Roundness	The ratio of the area of an object to the area of a circle with the same convex perimeter	$\frac{4\pi * \text{Area}}{(\text{Convex Perimeter})^2}$

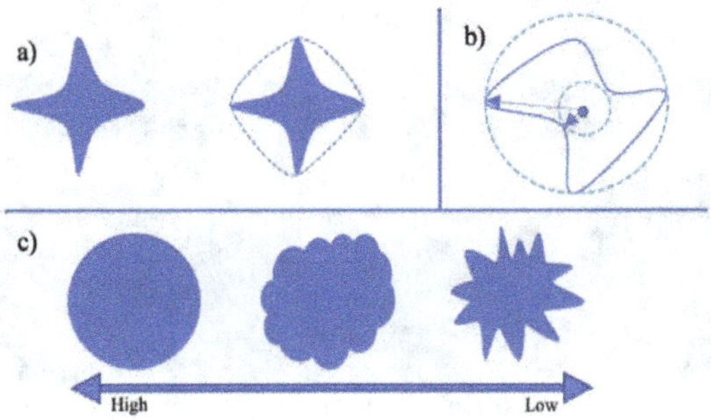

Fig 1. a) Shape with convex hull; b) Sphericity is the ratio of a shape's minimum and maximum radii; c) Shapes decreasing in value from left to right for compactness, convexity, solidity, and roundness.

Finally, we include the shape features compactness, convexity, solidity, and roundness. These four shape features take values from 0 to 1, where a higher value indicates the shape is smoother and less spiky than lower values. In Figure 1c, we see the circle on the left would have the highest value on these four shape statistics, and the irregular shape on the right would have the lowest value.

3. Methods

3.1 Training dataset

Our training data was obtained from CT scans for cervix radiotherapy treatment planning. Here we focus on contouring of the kidney; since most patients have two kidneys, this yields two structures per patient plan. The contours were generated by the Radiation Plan Assistant (RPA) [7], using a deep learning model based on a CNN algorithm. In total, we obtained 260 clinically acceptable contours using the RPA. A dosimetrist then manually created erroneous contours of several of the same kidney structures, yielding 52 unacceptable contours. Figure 2 provides an illustrative example showing acceptable and unacceptable contours of a patient's kidney. Typically, an organ at risk will be reflected in multiple image slices, where each slice captures a view of the patient's anatomy for a given orientation and depth.

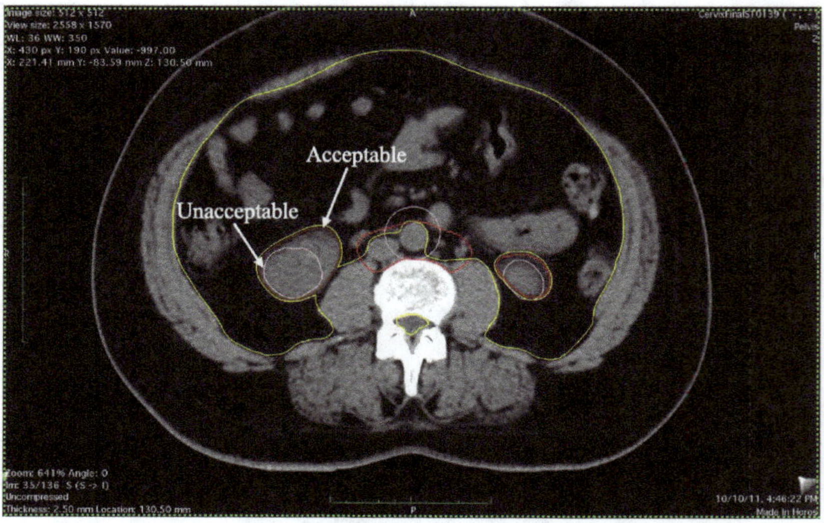

Fig. 2. An axial view of a cervix radiation treatment plan with organ structures contoured

To extract the contour for downstream analysis, we created a mask for the organ on a 512 by 512 voxel grid. The entries in the corresponding binary matrix representation were set to 1 if the voxel coordinate was contained within the contour boundary, and otherwise set to 0. We repeated this for every axial slice in the plan until we had a complete three-dimensional array of the organ structure. The dimension of each voxel was 1.27mm x 1.27 mm x 2.5 mm.

3.2 Extracting shape features

We now describe how the shape features described analytically in Table 1 were computed in practice. We extracted shape features from the contours using R by inputting the binary matrix representation of the contour mask into various functions. The functions assume there is a single, closed contour. The perimeter and compactness of a contour were calculated by counting the number of voxels on its edge. We relied on the *EBImage* package to calculate the minimum, mean, and maximum radii, by finding the midpoint of the contour and the radii to each edge voxel [8]. With the radii values we calculated sphericity. We calculated the convex hull of a contour using the *chull* function in the *grDevices* package that returns coordinates of the convex hull [9]. We calculated the area and convex area of a contour using the *concaveman* package [10]. Finally, we relied on the *shapes* package to calculate the centroid size [11]. We captured these shape features for every slice in the patient's radiotherapy treatment plan, resulting in a vector of values for each feature across slices.

3.3 Histogram and volumetric features

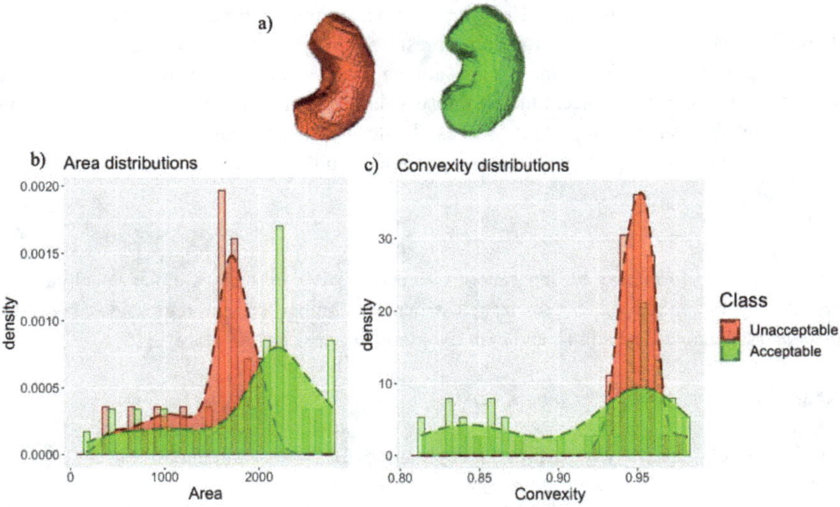

Fig. 3. a) 3D rendering of the unacceptable (red) and acceptable (green) contours of the right kidney; b) distributions of the areas; c) distributions of convexity.

A challenge in treating these shape features as predictors in a model is that the organ structures vary in size across patients, resulting in vectors of different lengths. For example, some structures could be defined in 50 slices, while others could be defined in 100 slices. In addition, values from neighboring slices tend to be highly correlated. To construct a consistent set of summary features, we relied on histogram features which summarize the distribution of shape values for each organ.

Specifically, we take all the values from a specific shape feature, and we calculate the minimum, 1st quartile, median, mean, 3rd quartile, maximum, and standard deviation. Figure 3 illustrates an unacceptable and an acceptable 3D structure, along with the shape feature distributions for area and convexity. Here, we can see a distinct difference in the shape feature distributions. We augmented our feature set by including volume, surface area, and the volume to surface area ratio. This resulted in a total of 80 features per structure.

3.4 Machine learning classifier

3.4.1 The random forest algorithm

Random forests are a popular machine learning algorithm that use an ensemble of decision trees [12]. Each tree casts a vote for the most popular class per input vector. The trees in the random forest are created by partitioning the feature space into rectangular regions on a randomly chosen set of features called nodes. Based on an optimization criterion, the tree splits at a particular value in the feature space. The decision trees created are "weak learners," meaning a single tree alone would have poor accuracy in classification. However, together the trees break up the feature space uniquely and make powerful predictions. Random forests are robust to challenging settings, and can accommodate non-linear effects, interactions among features, and correlated predictors. In addition to strong predictive performance, random forests can provide insight on the relative importance of predictors through variable importance scores. To develop our random forest model, we used the *randomForest* package in R with 500 trees and 16 node splits per tree.

3.4.2 Comparators

To assess the performance of the random forest relative to that of other machine learning approaches, we applied other popular classifiers including logistic regression, lasso logistic regression [13], naïve Bayes [14], and extreme gradient boosting (XGBoost) [15].

3.4.3 Model training and performance metrics

To train the classifiers, we performed repeated 5-fold cross validation on all 312 kidney observations. For each fold we used roughly 80% of the data as a training set and 20% of the data as a test set. Performance metrics including the area under the curve (AUC) for the receiver operating characteristic (ROC) and precision-recall (PR) curves were computed on each test set and averaged over folds and replicates. We also computed the sensitivity and specificity using a default threshold value of 0.5 and an optimized threshold obtained using Youden's Index.

3.4.4 Shapley values

In a machine learning framework, the Shapley value can be used to explain model predictions by calculating each feature's contribution in a particular instance [16]. The contribution for a given feature is calculated by removing that feature from the model and seeing how the prediction value changes. If removing a feature drastically changes the prediction, then that feature would have a large Shapley value. Importantly, unlike variable importance scores, which provide a single ranking of features for the entire data set, Shapley values are case-specific. Using the *shapr* package in R, we applied this framework to identify key features driving the model predictions [17]. The resulting Shapley values were plotted as a bar chart to provide a starting point for identifying why specific contours were flagged.

4. Results

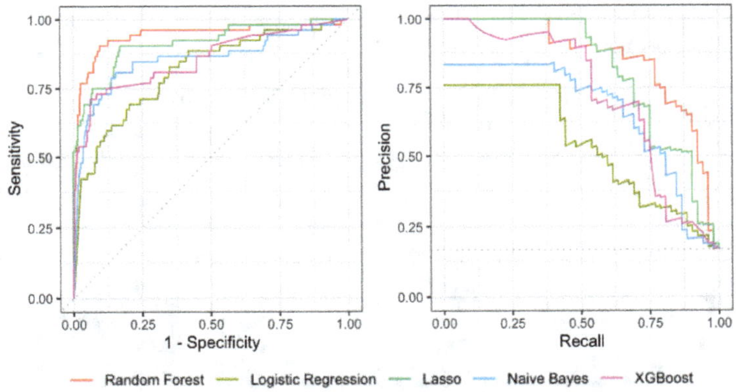

Fig. 4. ROC and PR Curves of various classifiers

In Table 2, we provide a summary of predictive performance in terms of the AUC for the ROC and PR curves, sensitivity and specificity using a threshold of 0.50, and sensitivity and specificity using an optimized threshold from Youden's index (indicated by subscripts). The metrics in Table 2 reflect

Table 2. Performance metrics from 10 iterations of five-fold cross validation

Classifier	Random Forest	Logistic Regression	Lasso	Naïve Bayes	XGBoost
AUC_{roc}	0.937 (± 0.008)	0.809 (± 0.013)	0.912 (± 0.009)	0.849 (± 0.008)	0.831 (± 0.020)
AUC_{pr}	0.828 (± 0.022)	0.506 (± 0.033)	0.829 (± 0.011)	0.647 (± 0.018)	0.655 (± 0.067)
$Specificity_{0.50}$	0.977 (± 0.005)	0.861 (± 0.014)	0.271 (± 0.019)	0.920 (± 0.004)	0.970 (± 0.011)
$Sensitivity_{0.50}$	0.608 (± 0.016)	0.640 (± 0.060)	0.983 (± 0.014)	0.692 (± 0.013)	0.571 (± 0.044)
$Specificity_{yi}$	0.883 (± 0.042)	0.817 (± 0.072)	0.902 (± 0.057)	0.878 (± 0.030)	0.879 (± 0.101)
$Sensitivity_{yi}$	0.889 (± 0.053)	0.733 (± 0.076)	0.808 (± 0.043)	0.816 (± 0.062)	0.719 (± 0.103)

averages over 10 replicates of five-fold CV. The AUC for the ROC curve summarizes predictive performance in terms of sensitivity and specificity across a range of threshold values. The PR curve is like the ROC curve but focuses on the trade-off between precision (also known as positive predictive value) and recall (also known as sensitivity). The PR curve is particularly useful in characterizing classification accuracy for imbalanced data sets. The proposed random forest prediction model outperformed the other classifiers with a cross-validated AUC_{roc} value of 0.937 and one of the highest AUC_{pr} value of 0.828 (similar to the value achieved by lasso logistic regression). Figure 4 shows illustrative ROC and PR curves from one replicate of the five-fold CV. In Table 2, we also provide sensitivity and specificity for specific cut-off values, where an instance is considered as flagged if its predicted value is above the threshold. We considered 0.50 as a standard cut-off and an optimized cut-off obtained using Youden's Index. In the radiation therapy quality assurance setting, a more sensitive classifier is preferred to ensure that concerning cases will get additional review. The random forest with Youden's index performed very well in this regard, achieving a sensitivity of 0.889. To illustrate, figure 5 shows the probabilities of each contour from the random forest trained on the entire dataset. Contours with probabilities above the threshold values are flagged as unacceptable. Shape features and code to reproduce analysis provided at: https://github.com/wootz101/QA_Contours

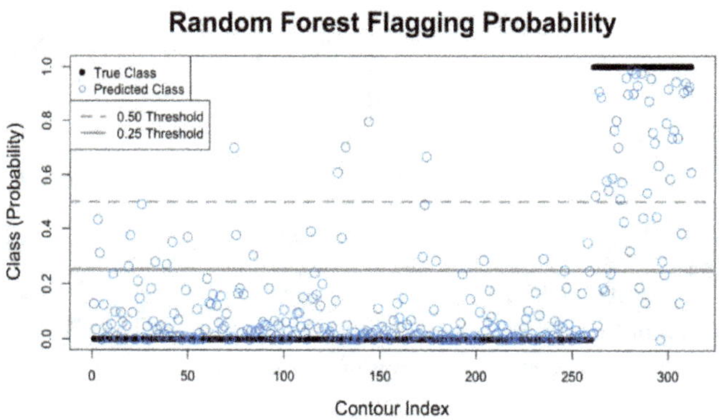

Fig 5. Random forest probabilities in blue with example thresholds in grey; the true class is marked in black, where acceptable contours have a value of 0 and unacceptable contours have a value of 1. The index range of 1-260 correspond to acceptable contours and 261-312 correspond to unacceptable contours.

5. Application to unlabeled data

Table 3. Error Rates

Model	Ground Truth	Not Flagged	Flagged	Class Error
80 Variable	Acceptable	255	5	1.9%
	Unacceptable	16	36	30.8%
Top 10 Variable	Acceptable	250	10	3.8%
	Unacceptable	15	37	28.8%

Based on these results, the random forest prediction method performed well at discerning acceptable vs. unacceptable contours in a cross-validation setting. We then sought to assess the utility of this approach when applied to a new external data set. To do so, we first trained a final random forest model using the entire dataset of 312 kidney contours, using the same parameters as before. Training on the full dataset, the random forest performs well with a total accuracy of 93.27% and an AUC value of 0.937, with a false positive rate of 1.9% and a false negative rate of 30.8%. Table 3 gives further information on the random forest's error rates based on a 50% threshold.

5.1 Variable importance

The random forest is a useful classifier in this regard as it also provides a measure of feature importance. Table 4 shows the top ten variables of importance by their inclusion mean decrease in accuracy percent.

Table 4. Importance measure

1st	2nd	3rd	4th	5th
Sphericity (Max) 2.7%	Min Radius (Min) 1.6%	Centroid (SD) 1.2%	Min Radius (SD) 1.2%	Area (SD) 1.1%
6th	7th	8th	9th	10th
Perimeter (SD) 1.1%	Mean Radius (SD) 0.9%	Max Radius (Median) 0.7%	Area (Min) 0.6%	Solidity (Mean) 0.6%

The *shapr* package in R is limited to 13 variables as the computation time increases exponentially with the number of variables. Therefore, we constructed a new random forest that only uses these top 10 shape histogram features to accommodate the software and hardware constraints. We used 500 trees and 8 node splits per tree as parameters. We lowered the node splits from 16 to 8 because we went from 80 to 10 input features. Trimming down the original model is an important step in order to use Shapely values to interpret why a contour gets flagged. Table 3 shows the performance of the random forest when we scale down from 80 features to the top 10. These results indicate the top 10 variable random forest model performs similarly to the full 80 variable model. In fact, the top 10 model is slightly more sensitive in flagging unacceptable contours.

5.2 Unlabeled dataset

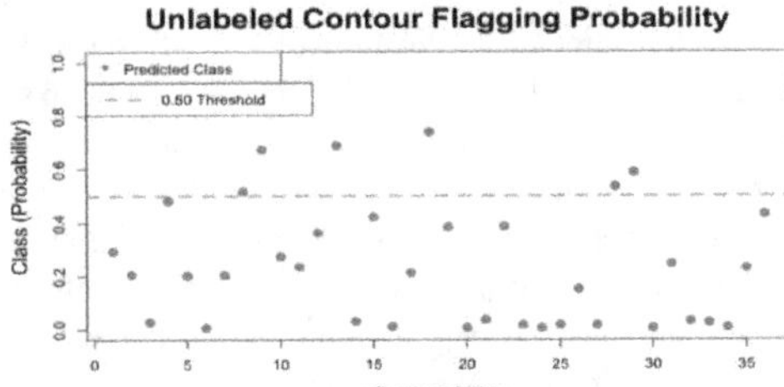

Fig 6. Probability of unacceptable contours from unlabeled dataset

We obtained an external data set of 18 radiation treatment plans for cervical cancer radiotherapy. The voxel dimensions of these plans were 1.172 mm x 1.172 mm x 2.5 mm. From these plans, we extracted 36 kidney contours. These independent test contours were previously unseen and so were considered unlabeled data. We extracted the shape features as previously described and applied our trained random forest to obtain model predictions. Figure 6 shows the estimated probabilities of each contour being unacceptable for use in radiotherapy planning. A total of 6 contours were flagged with a probability > 0.5.

5.3 Shapley values of flagged contours

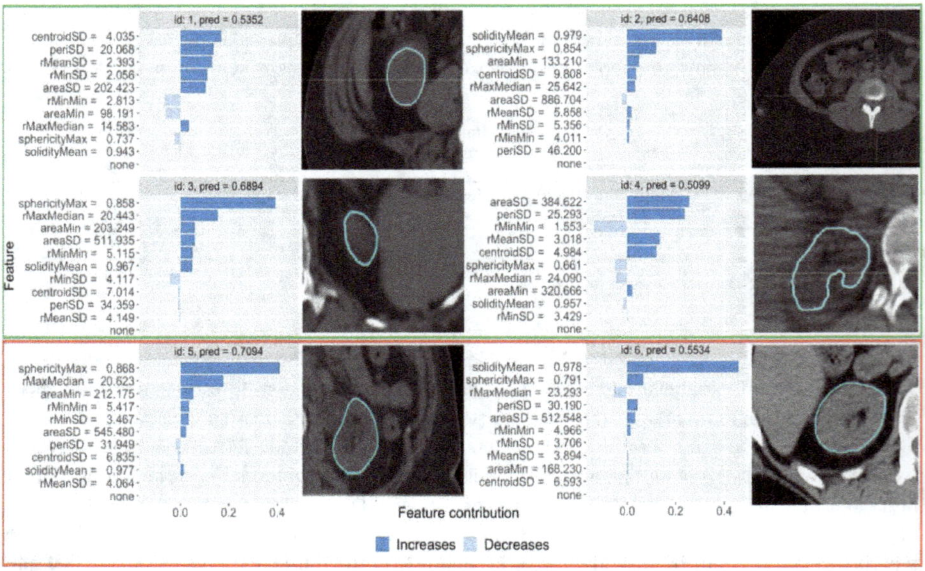

Fig 7. Shapley values show the impact each feature has on the overall prediction for the corresponding contour, with dark blue increasing and light blue decreasing the prediction of an error. The id: 1-4 are correctly flagged and outlined in green, and id: 5-6 are incorrectly flagged and outlined in red.

As would happen in the potential clinical application of our approach, an expert reviewer then inspected the flagged contours to simulate the clinical workflow. Of the 6 contours flagged, 4 were found to contain errors including over-contouring and under-contouring of the kidney region. Figure 7 shows the Shapley values of each variable for the flagged contours along with example images of the unacceptable kidney contours that were correctly flagged and the acceptable kidney contours that were incorrectly flagged. The errors in these contours are visually noticeable, with under-contouring being the most common error. Using the Shapley values, we can interpret how the deep learning contour erred. For instance, examining the Shapley value plot and corresponding contour for id: 1, we see the random forest model flagged the contour because the contour's centroid size, perimeter, mean radius, and minimum radius had low standard deviations. The generated contour was indeed under-contoured which explains its out of distribution metrics. For id: 2, the contour had minor errors as it didn't contour the beginning of the kidney which resulted in a large mean solidity value. Hence, we see there is no contour in the medical image for id: 2 where there should be one. We see in id: 3 the Shapley value plots indicate that the maximum sphericity value was too high. The kidney was over-contoured on this patient which led to a highly spherical shape that the random forest noticed and flagged. For id: 4 we see that the area standard deviation and perimeter standard deviation values for the contour were too low, causing it to be flagged. Low standard deviation of area and perimeter would indicate that the area and perimeter values varied less from slice to slice than they did for acceptable contours. This real data application highlights the feasibility of our approach for radiotherapy quality assurance.

Our method also has limitations and sometimes generates false positives. We see in id: 5 the contour was flagged due to its high maximum sphericity value, however, there were no contouring errors found. This false positive is particularly interesting because it has the highest prediction value for being flagged. False positives are to be expected due to the inherent variation in human anatomy; our expert reviewer noted that in this instance the kidney structure was completely connected to a neighboring structure. The connectedness of the structure might lead to some variation in contouring. While this contour is safe for clinical use, it is challenging for both humans and machines to distinguish the ground truth border for this patient. For id: 6 the solidity mean value was too high which caused the contour to be flagged even though there were no errors.

6. Discussion

We have shown that training a random forest on shape features of contours is a viable method of contour quality assurance. Our method is novel and would be robust to differences in imaging platform or imaging processing steps in that it only requires shape features, and no imaging or radiomic features. Classification of contours using shape features could be useful in other contexts beyond radiation treatment planning; in particular, segmentation of the brain is a key task in the analysis of MRI data, while automatic detection of objects in images is a critical step in the development of automated driving systems. In both cases, critical structures identified using deep learning or other automated tools could potentially be distinguishable using shape features.

One of the limitations in this study is that the unacceptable contours used in the training data were created by hand. Since only acceptable contours are used in clinical radiotherapy treatment planning, real-world cases of unacceptable contours are difficult to obtain. Our method provides basic annotations to characterize which features drove the model predictions. More detailed information, including the spatial locations with potential errors, would enhance the interpretation of results. We plan to explore methods to enable location-specific annotation within contours in future work. Furthermore, we plan to explore how this method performs across other imaging platforms.

7. Acknowledgements

ZTW was partially supported by NIH/NCI training grant T32 CA096520 and NSF GRFP Grant No. 1842494. CBP was partially supported by NIH/NCI CCSG P30 CA016672 (Biostatistics Resource Group) and by a grant from Varian Medical Systems.

8. Bibliography

[1] McCarroll RE, Beadle BM, Balter PA, et al. (2018) Retrospective validation and clinical implementation of automated contouring of organs at risk in the head and neck: a step toward automated radiation treatment planning for low-and middle-income countries. *J Glob Oncol.* 4:1-11.
[2] McIntosh C, Svistoun I, Purdie TG. (2013) Groupwise conditional random forests for automatic shape classification and contour quality assessment in radiotherapy planning. *IEEE Trans Med Imaging.* **32**(6):1043-1057.
[3] Hui CB, Nourzadeh H, Watkins WT, et al. (2018) Quality assurance tool for organ at risk delineation in radiation therapy using a parametric statistical approach. *Med Phys.* **45**(5):2089-2096.
[4] Rhee DJ, Cardenas CE, Elhalawani H, et al. (2019) Automatic detection of contouring errors using convolutional neural networks. *Med Phys.* **46**(11):5086-5097.
[5] Dryden IL, Mardia KV. (2016) *Statistical Shape Analysis with Applications in R.* Wiley, 2nd edition.
[6] Wirth MA. (2004) Shape Analysis & Measurement. University of Guelph. Accessed online at http://www.cyto.purdue.edu/cdroms/micro2/content/education/wirth10.pdf.
[7] Kisling K, McCarroll R, Zhang L, et al. (2018) Radiation planning assistant - a streamlined, fully automated radiotherapy treatment planning system. *J Visualized Exp.* 134:e57411.
[8] Pau G, Fuchs F, Sklyar O, Boutros M, and Huber W (2010): EBImage - an R package for image processing with applications to cellular phenotypes. *Bioinformatics*, **26**(7), pp. 979-981, 10.1093/bioinformatics/btq046
[9] R Core Team (2020). R: A language and environment for statistical computing. *R Foundation for Statistical Computing*, Vienna, Austria.
[10] Gombin J, Vaidyanathan R and Agafonkin V (2020). concaveman: A Very Fast 2D Concave Hull Algorithm. R package version 1.1.0.
[11] Dryden IL (2019). shapes: Statistical Shape Analysis. R package version 1.2.5.
[12] Breiman L. (2001) Random Forests. *Machine Learning*, **45**(1): 5-32.
[13] Friedman J, Hastie T, Tibshirani R (2010). "Regularization Paths for Generalized Linear Models via Coordinate Descent." *Journal of Statistical Software*, **33**(1), 1–22.
[14] Majka M (2019). _naivebayes: High Performance Implementation of the Naive Bayes Algorithm in R_. R package version 0.9.7
[15] Chen T, Guestrin C. XGBoost: A scalable tree boosting system. In Proceedings of the 22nd ACM SIGKDD International Conference on Knowledge Discovery and Data Mining, 2016 Aug 13 (pp. 785-794).
[16] Cohen S, Ruppin E, Dror G. (2005) Feature selection based on the Shapley value. *In Other Words*, 665-670.
[17] Sellereite N, Jullum M and Redelmeier A (2021). shapr: Prediction Explanation with Dependence-Aware Shapley Values. R package version 0.2.0.

SALUD: Scalable Applications of cLinical risk Utility and preDiction

Pankhuri Singhal
Perelman School of Medicine, University of Pennsylvania
Philadelphia, PA 19104, USA
Email: singhalp@pennmedicine.upenn.edu

Yogasudha Veturi
The Pennsylvania State University
University Park, PA 16801, USA
Email: yzv101@psu.edu

Renae Judy
Department of Surgery, Perelman School of Medicine, University of Pennsylvania
Philadelphia, PA 19104, USA
Email: renae.judy@pennmedicine.upenn.edu

Yoson Park
Internal Medicine Research Unit, Pfizer Inc
Boston, MA 02139, USA
Email: yoson.park@gmail.com

Marijana Vujkovic
Department of Genetics, Perelman School of Medicine, University of Pennsylvania
Philadelphia, PA 19104, USA
Email: vujkovic@pennmedicine.upenn.edu

Olivia Veatch
Department of Psychiatry & Behavioral Sciences, and Molecular & Integrative Physiology at the University of Kansas Medical Center
Kansas, MO 66103, USA
Email: oveatch@kumc.edu

Rachel Kember
Department of Psychiatry, Perelman School of Medicine, University of Pennsylvania
Philadelphia, PA 19104, USA
Email: rkember@pennmedicine.upenn.edu

Shefali Setia Verma
Department of Pathology and Laboratory Medicine, Perelman School of Medicine, University of Pennsylvania 19104, USA
Philadelphia, PA
Email: shefali.setiaverma@pennmedicine.upenn.edu

This PSB 2023 session discusses challenges in clinical implication and application of risk prediction models, which includes but is not limited to: implementation of risk models, responsible use of polygenic risk scores (PGS), and other risk prediction strategies. We focus on the development and use of new, scalable methods for harmonizing and refining risk prediction models by incorporating genetic and non-genetic risk factors, applying new phenotyping strategies, and integrating clinical factors and biomarkers. Lastly, we will discuss innovation in expanding the utility of these prediction models to underrepresented populations. This session focuses on the overarching theme of enabling early diagnosis, and treatment and preventive measures related to complex diseases and comorbidities.

Keywords: Risk Prediction, risk factors, clinical implementation polygenic risk scores, complex human diseases

1. Introduction:

Genetic variants each harboring small phenotypic effects are shown to collectively contribute to complex trait and disease risk. Genome-wide association studies (GWAS), a mainstay of genetics research, are widely used to identify such common genetic variants (single nucleotide polymorphisms or SNPs) that convey increased or decreased risk for complex traits in populations. Due to the polygenic nature of complex traits, reliably predicting disease susceptibility or risk often requires studies of large sample sizes. To address this, large biobanks such as the Million Veteran Program (MVP) and UK Biobank, and consortia such as the Global Lipids Genetics Consortium (Graham et al., 2021), Global Biobank Meta-Analysis Initiative (Zhou et al., 2021), and Genetic Investigation of Anthropometric Traits (Yengo et al., 2018), among several others, have been successful at identifying and validating genetic components of complex traits based on sample sizes ranging from hundreds of thousands to over a million. Nevertheless, identifying people at risk of disease prior to the presentation of symptoms remains one of the main challenges and goals of precision medicine. Countless hours and resources are spent in understanding the pathophysiology of complex diseases and identifying clinical, genetic, and exposure risk factors that influence the risk of prevalent diseases that substantially impact public health such as breast cancer, coronary artery disease (CAD), obesity, and type 2 diabetes.

Consequently, estimating the disease risk of patients based on their common genetic variants by aggregating the weighted sum of the trait-affected alleles from GWAS into polygenic scores [PGS, also known as genetic risk scores (GRS) or polygenic risk scores (PRS)] has gained popularity (Wand et al., 2021). PGS provides an opportunity to estimate an individual's genetic risk (or predisposition) for complex diseases or traits. This is set as a non-modifiable lifetime risk and could be utilized prior to symptom onset to improve patients' health by predicting relatively modifiable factors such as lifestyle, nutrition, clinical, and other cumulative non-genetic risks that may act over multiple years (Torkamani et al., 2018). PGS capture a larger proportion of genetic liability than individual SNPs alone and have already been used to identify patients with disease risk equivalent to monogenic mutations, predict mortality, identify cases with earlier disease onset, and provide evidence for cross-trait associations. Recently, focus and interest have shifted from the theoretical application of PGS post hoc in large populations to the implementation of these methods for individual patients in clinical practices. Risk models such as BOADECIA for breast cancer (Lee et al., 2019) and cardioriskSCORE for CAD include PGS along with other clinical risk factors such as family history. Models for cancer risk have been integrated into wider gene screening panels such as PGLNext and ColoNext that test a subset of genes to provide cancer-type specific testing as a consumer product.

We are in a golden digital age for medicine in which individuals have access to their health records and genetic data at their fingertips. There is a strong public interest in better understanding personal genetics made clear in the various companies that have been founded in the last decade to bridge the gap between consumer and clinician. Companies like 23&Me provide genetic insight into trait and disease risks, while others focus on aspects of genetics including ancestry, embryo screening, fertility, cancer risk, allergy predispositions, diet optimization and weight loss, immune health, and cardiovascular event prediction. PGS have become a particular focus area of the health technology sector as a means of data-driven disease prevention. Numerous companies are geared towards providing genetics-based health risk predictions based on the application of PGS. These have been designed not only for the average individual but also for companies looking to build wellness incentive programs within their own businesses. Some PGS-focused companies provide risk score prediction as a clinical tool or platform for health systems and healthcare providers to implement in their clinics and hospitals. The wide scope of commercial applications underscores the keen interest in exploring genetic risk prediction. The direct-to-consumer model, however, comes with a great responsibility to critically examine the methodology with respect to health equity and diversity.

Despite recent advancements, a number of aspects of PGS require evaluation. PGS generated from currently available GWAS typically explain only a small proportion, 2-10%, of trait variation (Stringer et al., 2011). Moreover, a disproportionate majority (>78%) of participants in genetic studies are of European descent, limiting applications of PGS for many traits to individuals from this ancestry only (Sirugo et al., 2019). Also, many questions remain regarding best practices for the harmonization of multiple risk factors into clinically relevant models, particularly when including genetic factors in non-European populations or in longitudinal cumulative risk predictions.

Consented EHR-linked biobanks provide a vast and continuously growing repository of longitudinal data on diverse clinical populations that can fuel clinical, genetic, and epidemiologic research. Risk prediction models are not limited to a single phenotype or to a cross-sectional analysis of patient health. With the availability of multidimensional genomic and EHR data, longitudinal and time-series analyses can be conducted to investigate patient disease trajectories (Jensen et al., 2014). Complex genetic diseases often do not present phenotypically in the same way, in the same timeframe, in all patients (Woodward et al., 2022). Understanding which types of individuals develop certain conditions– and when– is essential for prognostics and disease prevention. Moreover, linking phenotypic patterns with genetic underpinnings can improve the predictive power of risk models. Such integrated risk prediction could be built upon a variety of machine learning methodologies and clinical and genomic data types. This is especially useful for understanding both the etiological basis for disease comorbidity and the architecture of disease co-occurrence (Monchka et al., 2022). Various network and statistical approaches have been applied to determine shared genetic components of comorbid conditions and the interactions between disease-associated gene products (Barabási et al., 2011). Leveraging longitudinal data in these analyses can provide a predictive aspect for disease onset. In addition, other kinds of omics data (e.g., transcriptomics, proteomics, metabolomics) can explain variance attributable to genetics as well as some lifestyle/environmental factors (Kim et al., 2015). Furthermore, the fact that EHR data are collected in real-world clinical settings makes them particularly valuable for research aimed at reflecting population diversity.

2. Overview of the contributions

The SALUD session keynote talk by Dr. Cooke-Bailey entitled "Pause, Reflect, Redirect: Clinical Scalability of Genetic Risk Scores Remains Limited due to Lack of Diversity" will focus on the utility of risk scores across disease, model, and scope of genetic data, as well as and what remains lacking across the breadth of these approaches in clinical scalability and broad applicability. While future GRS and PRS may serve as surrogate measures for disease risk, the current landscape leaves much room for improvement in clinical implementation across different ancestral groups. Key to realizing the true power of clinical and genetic risk models is intentional focus on improving representation of data from populations that have historically been underrepresented in research. This session will be focused on the utility of risk scores across several common and complex disorders as described briefly below.

One of the goals of precision medicine is to be able to stratify patients based on their genetic risk for a disease using GRS to inform future screening and intervention strategies. However, the variants used to calculate these scores are often based on European (EUR) ancestry individuals, limiting their clinical utility. Study titled "*Diversity is key for cross-ancestry transferability of glaucoma genetic risk scores in Hispanic Veterans in the Million Veteran Program*" by *Waksmunski et al.* addresses the challenges of applying GRS in complex conditions like primary open-angle glaucoma (POAG). POAG disproportionately affects individuals of African and Hispanic (HIS) ancestries. This study evaluates the risk stratification performance of POAG GRS based on cross-ancestry variants in EUR and HIS individuals.

Abdominal aortic aneurysms (AAA) are common enlargements of the abdominal aorta which can grow larger until rupture, often leading to death. Recent large-scale genome-wide association studies have identified genetic loci associated with AAA risk. Study titled "*Predictive models for abdominal aortic aneurysms using polygenic scores and PheWAS- derived risk factors*" by *Hellwege et al.* combines known risk factors, PRS, and precedent clinical diagnoses from electronic health records (EHR) to develop predictive models for AAA. The resulting models improve identification of people at risk of a AAA diagnosis compared with existing guidelines.

Study titled "*Quantifying factors that affect polygenic risk score performance across diverse ancestries and age groups for body mass index*" by *Hui and Xiao et al.* addresses the challenge of limited transferability of PRS across groups that differ in ancestry or sample characteristics. To evaluate these factors in the PRS generation process, the authors quantified the effects of ancestry, genome-wide association study summary statistics sample size, and LD reference panel on PRS performance. This was done using a cross-ancestry and age-specific approach. PRS for body mass index (BMI) was generated for this analysis. Furthermore, comorbidities and clinical associations in electronic health records with PRS for BMI were explored.

Late-onset Alzheimer's disease (LOAD) is a polygenic disorder with a long prodromal phase, making early diagnosis challenging. PRS leverage combined effects of many loci to predict LOAD risk, but often lack sensitivity to preclinical disease changes, limiting clinical utility. Study titled

"*Resilience polygenic risk score may be sensitive to preclinical disease changes*" by *Eissman et al.* generates a resilience phenotype to model better-than-expected cognition given LOAD biomarker levels in order to bolster preclinical polygenic risk prediction. The resulting LOAD PRS and resilience PRS models together are evaluated for prediction of preclinical disease status among dementia-free and biomarker-positive individuals.

3. Conclusion

Developing accurate risk prediction models for disease is one of the main goals of precision medicine. The addition of genetic data to these models could enhance their performance. However, there are many questions about appropriate implementation, interpretation, and derivation of genetic risk prediction models. The studies presented in this session explore these issues by combining genetic scores with known risk factors to test the improvement in performance, enhance transferability of genetic scores in diverse ancestries, and evaluate the ability of models including genetic scores to predict preclinical disease status. This research is essential as we move towards incorporating genetic risk prediction models in clinical practice.

4. Acknowledgements

PS is supported by F31AG069441-01.

References

1. Barabási, A. L., Gulbahce, N., & Loscalzo, J. (2011). Network medicine: A network-based approach to human disease. In *Nature Reviews Genetics* (Vol. 12, Issue 1, pp. 56–68). https://doi.org/10.1038/nrg2918
2. Graham, Sarah E., et al. "The power of genetic diversity in genome-wide association studies of lipids." *Nature* 600.7890 (2021): 675-679.
3. Jensen, A. B., Moseley, P. L., Oprea, T. I., Ellesøe, S. G., Eriksson, R., Schmock, H., Jensen, P. B., Jensen, L. J., & Brunak, S. (2014). Temporal disease trajectories condensed from population-wide registry data covering 6.2 million patients. *Nature Communications*, *5*. https://doi.org/10.1038/ncomms5022
4. Kim, D., Joung, J. G., Sohn, K. A., Shin, H., Park, Y. R., Ritchie, M. D., & Kim, J. H. (2015). Knowledge boosting: A graph-based integration approach with multi-omics data and genomic knowledge for cancer clinical outcome prediction. *Journal of the American Medical Informatics Association*, *22*(1), 109–120. https://doi.org/10.1136/amiajnl-2013-002481
5. Lee, Andrew, et al. "BOADICEA: a comprehensive breast cancer risk prediction model incorporating genetic and nongenetic risk factors." *Genetics in Medicine* 21.8 (2019): 1708-1718.
6. Monchka, B. A., Leung, C. K., Nickel, N. C., & Lix, L. M. (2022). The effect of disease co-occurrence measurement on multimorbidity networks: a population-based study. *BMC Medical Research Methodology*, *22*(1). https://doi.org/10.1186/s12874-022-01607-8

7. Sirugo, G., Williams, S. M., & Tishkoff, S. A. (2019). The Missing Diversity in Human Genetic Studies. *Cell*, *177*(1), 26–31. https://doi.org/10.1016/j.cell.2019.02.048
8. Stringer, S., Wray, N. R., Kahn, R. S., & Derks, E. M. (2011). Underestimated effect sizes in GWAS: fundamental limitations of single SNP analysis for dichotomous phenotypes. *PloS One*, *6*(11), e27964. https://doi.org/10.1371/journal.pone.0027964
9. Torkamani, Ali, Nathan E. Wineinger, and Eric J. Topol. "The personal and clinical utility of polygenic risk scores." *Nature Reviews Genetics* 19.9 (2018): 581-590.
10. W and, H., Lambert, S. A., Tamburro, C., Iacocca, M. A., O'Sullivan, J. W., Sillari, C., Kullo, I. J., Rowley, R., Dron, J. S., Brockman, D., Venner, E., McCarthy, M. I., Antoniou, A. C., Easton, D. F., Hegele, R. A., Khera, A. v., Chatterjee, N., Kooperberg, C., Edwards, K., … Wojcik, G. L. (2021). Improving reporting standards for polygenic scores in risk prediction studies. In *Nature* (Vol. 591, Issue 7849, pp. 211–219). Nature Research. https://doi.org/10.1038/s41586-021-03243-6
11. Woodward, A. A., Urbanowicz, R. J., Naj, A. C., & Moore, J. H. (2022). Genetic heterogeneity: Challenges, impacts, and methods through an associative lens. In *Genetic Epidemiology*. John Wiley and Sons Inc. https://doi.org/10.1002/gepi.22497
12. Yengo, Loic, et al. "Meta-analysis of genome-wide association studies for height and body mass index in~ 700000 individuals of European ancestry." *Human molecular genetics* 27.20 (2018): 3641-3649.
13. Zhou, Wei, and Global Biobank Meta-analysis Initiative. "Global Biobank Meta-analysis Initiative: Powering genetic discovery across human diseases." *medRxiv* (2021).

Diversity is key for cross-ancestry transferability of glaucoma genetic risk scores in Hispanic Veterans in the Million Veteran Program

Andrea R. Waksmunski

Cleveland Institute for Computational Biology, Department of Population and Quantitative Health Sciences, Case Western Reserve University, Wolstein Research Building, 2103 Cornell Road, Cleveland, OH 44106, USA, axw360@case.edu

Tyler G. Kinzy

Cleveland Institute for Computational Biology, Department of Population and Quantitative Health Sciences, Case Western Reserve University, Wolstein Research Building, 2103 Cornell Road, Cleveland, OH 44106, USA, tgk18@case.edu
Research Service, VA Northeast Ohio Healthcare System, 10701 East Blvd, Cleveland, OH 44106, USA

Lauren A. Cruz

Cleveland Institute for Computational Biology, Department of Population and Quantitative Health Sciences, Case Western Reserve University, Wolstein Research Building, 2103 Cornell Road, Cleveland, OH 44106, USA, lac140@case.edu

Cari L. Nealon

Eye Clinic, VA Northeast Ohio Healthcare System, 10701 East Blvd, Cleveland, OH 44106, USA, Cari.Nealon@va.gov

Christopher W. Halladay

Center of Innovation in Long Term Services and Supports, Providence VA Medical Center, 830 Chalkstone Ave, Providence, RI 02908, USA, Christopher.Halladay@va.gov

Scott A. Anthony

Eye Clinic, VA Northeast Ohio Healthcare System, 10701 East Blvd, Cleveland, OH 44106, USA, Scott.Anthony@va.gov

Paul B. Greenberg

Ophthalmology Section, Providence VA Medical Center, 830 Chalkstone Ave, Providence, RI 02908, USA
Division of Ophthalmology, Alpert Medical School, Brown University, 222 Richmond St, Providence, RI 02903 USA, paul_greenberg@brown.edu

Jack M. Sullivan

Ophthalmology Section, Research Service, VA Western NY Healthcare System, 3495 Bailey Ave, Buffalo, NY 14215, USA, JackMSullivanMDPhD@yahoo.com

Wen-Chih Wu

Cardiology Section, Medical Service, Providence VA Medical Center, 830 Chalkstone Ave, Providence, RI 02908, USA, wen-chih_wu@brown.edu

---

Sudha K. Iyengar

Cleveland Institute for Computational Biology, Department of Population and Quantitative Health Sciences, Case Western Reserve University, Wolstein Research Building, 2103 Cornell Road, Cleveland, OH 44106, USA, ski@case.edu

Research Service, VA Northeast Ohio Healthcare System, 10701 East Blvd, Cleveland OH 44106, USA

Dana C. Crawford

Cleveland Institute for Computational Biology, Department of Population and Quantitative Health Sciences, Case Western Reserve University, Wolstein Research Building, 2103 Cornell Road, Cleveland, OH 44106, USA, dcc64@case.edu

Research Service, VA Northeast Ohio Healthcare System, 10701 East Blvd, Cleveland, OH 44106, USA

Neal S. Peachey

Research Service, VA Northeast Ohio Healthcare System, 10701 East Blvd, Cleveland, OH 44106, USA, Neal.Peachey@va.gov

Cole Eye Institute, Cleveland Clinic Foundation, 2022 East 105th Street Cleveland, OH 44195, USA

Department of Ophthalmology, Cleveland Clinic Lerner College of Medicine of Case Western Reserve University, 9501 Euclid Ave, Cleveland, OH 44195, USA

Jessica N. Cooke Bailey

Cleveland Institute for Computational Biology, Department of Population and Quantitative Health Sciences, Case Western Reserve University, Wolstein Research Building, 2103 Cornell Road, Cleveland, OH 44106, USA, jnc43@case.edu

Research Service, VA Northeast Ohio Healthcare System, 10701 East Blvd, Cleveland, OH 44106, USA

Consortium Author: VA Million Veteran Program

A major goal of precision medicine is to stratify patients based on their genetic risk for a disease to inform future screening and intervention strategies. For conditions like primary open-angle glaucoma (POAG), the genetic risk architecture is complicated with multiple variants contributing small effects on risk. Following the tepid success of genome-wide association studies for high-effect disease risk variant discovery, genetic risk scores (GRS), which collate effects from multiple genetic variants into a single measure, have shown promise for disease risk stratification. We assessed the application of GRS for POAG risk stratification in Hispanic-descent (HIS) and European-descent (EUR) Veterans in the Million Veteran Program. Unweighted and cross-ancestry meta-weighted GRS were calculated based on 127 genomic variants identified in the most recent report of cross-ancestry POAG meta-analyses. We found that both GRS types were associated with POAG case-control status and performed similarly in HIS and EUR Veterans. This trend was also seen in our subset analysis of HIS Veterans with less than 50% EUR global genetic ancestry. Our findings highlight the importance of evaluating GRS based on known POAG risk variants in different ancestry groups and emphasize the need for more multi-ancestry POAG genetic studies.

Keywords: Genetic risk score, primary open-angle glaucoma, ancestral diversity

1. Introduction

Primary open-angle glaucoma (POAG) is the leading cause of irreversible blindness globally (1,2). To mitigate severe POAG outcomes, early intervention is essential (3). POAG is a complex disease with a substantial genetic component (4,5). Comprehensively evaluating individual genetic profiles via genetic risk scores (GRS) may enable POAG risk stratification (6). Specifically, in the era of precision medicine, it is possible that individuals with high genetic risk for developing POAG and experiencing more aggressive disease course could be eligible for earlier and more frequent comprehensive eye examinations and be prioritized for early intervention.

While showing promising clinical utility for diseases with complex disease etiology, GRS are not without limitations (7–9). Historically, studies that inform which variants are included in GRS have been predominantly performed on data from individuals of European descent (EUR), regardless of whether disease burden is highest in EUR or other ancestries (10). GRS also lack cross-ancestry generalizability (9). Although POAG burden is higher in Hispanic (HIS) and African-descent (AFR) individuals (11), most POAG genetic studies have been reported in EUR individuals. Additionally, HIS individuals have a high degree of genetic admixture shaped by Native American, EUR, and AFR ancestries (12), which presents a possible limitation for the clinical use of GRS. We previously found that performance of a POAG GRS was significantly diminished in AFR Veterans compared to EUR Veterans in the Million Veteran Program (MVP) (13). To overcome limitations of contemporary GRS, representation of ancestral diversity in genetic studies must increase. The most recent genome-wide POAG analysis was a cross-ancestry meta-analysis of over 34,000 cases and nearly 350,000 controls that identified 127 POAG-associated loci (14). While this dataset predominantly included EUR individuals, it also included individuals of Asian and African descent (14), representing an important step towards increasing ancestral diversity in POAG genetic studies.

Large-scale, multi-ancestry biobanks linked to electronic health records (EHR) offer another way to increase diversity in genetic studies. We accessed the MVP, which is an ongoing US-based observational research program and mega-biobank funded by the Department of Veterans Affairs (VA) Office of Research and Development (15). To date, over 800,000 Veterans with linked genetic, EHR, health survey, and other clinical data have been enrolled in the MVP (15,16). Representation of diverse ancestral populations (16) is prominent in the MVP; about 29% of participants are from ancestries that have been historically underrepresented in genetic studies, including HIS (16).

In this study, we sought to assess the cross-ancestry transferability of a POAG GRS in HIS and EUR Veterans in the MVP. Among POAG cases and controls in the MVP, we calculated GRS based on 127 variants identified in the 2021 cross-ancestry POAG meta-analysis (14). Finally, we evaluated the GRS performance for POAG case classification in HIS and EUR Veterans.

2. Methods

2.1. *Study demographics*

We classified POAG cases and controls with a previously published algorithm developed in the VA (17) and applied to the MVP as previously described (13). Ancestry groups were defined using the Harmonized Ancestry and Race/Ethnicity (HARE) algorithm (18), which classifies an individual's

HARE group based on the correspondence of their self-identified race/ethnicity and genetically inferred ancestry.

2.2. *GRS calculations and association tests*

We calculated 127-variant GRS for HIS and EUR Veterans in the MVP. GRS were either unweighted or weighted by published cross-ancestry effect estimates (14) as shown in Equations 1 and 2, respectively. Risk alleles were defined by having odds ratios greater than 1 in the cross-ancestry analysis (14).

$$GRS_{unweighted(i)} = \sum_{j=1}^{k} M_{ij} \tag{1}$$

where M = risk allele dosage, i = individual, k = 127 variants

$$GRS_{weighted(i)} = \sum_{j=1}^{k} \beta_j M_{ij} \tag{2}$$

where M = risk allele dosage, i = individual, k = 127 variants, β=log(odds ratio)

We tested for association between the GRS and POAG via logistic regression-based analyses using unadjusted models as well as models adjusting for age, sex, and 10 sample-specific principal components (PCs).

2.3. *GRS performance for POAG risk stratification in the MVP*

We compared POAG case classification across GRS deciles and evaluated GRS model performance with area under the curve (AUC) estimates from receiver operating characteristic (ROC) curves, as previously described (13). To elucidate the contributions of each model variable, we estimated the proportion of POAG variance explained by: (i) age, (ii) age and sex, (iii) age, sex, and 10 PCs, and (iv) age, sex, 10 PCs, and each GRS (unweighted and weighted). Coefficients of determination (R^2) were calculated on the observed scale (Nagelkerke's) and the liability scale using a fixed disease prevalence of 2.4% (19) as well as increases in R^2 with the addition of each variable to the model.

2.4. *Subset analyses based on global genetic ancestry*

HIS Veterans are more genetically admixed than EUR Veterans (18); thus, we evaluated GRS performance in a subset of HIS Veterans with less than 50% EUR global genetic ancestry (GGA) as determined via the ADMIXTURE software program (20). We compared these subset results to the full MVP HIS POAG case-control dataset.

3. Results

3.1. *POAG cases and controls in the MVP*

Applying the above-described phenotype and ancestry group definitions to the MVP, our dataset included 3,347 HIS Veterans (382 cases; 2,965 controls) and 62,193 EUR Veterans (3,382 cases; 58,811 controls) (Table 1). Nearly all the study participants were male (Table 1). Among EUR Veterans, 96.48% of POAG cases and 97.76% of controls were male ($p < 0.05$; Table 1); whereas, among HIS Veterans, 97.12% of POAG cases and 98.01% of controls were male ($p > 0.05$; Table 1). Although the average ages of EUR POAG cases and controls were not significantly different, HIS POAG cases were about 2 years younger, on average, than HIS controls ($p < 0.05$; Table 1).

Table 1. POAG case-control demographics in the MVP. The *p*-values shown were from Welch's t-test for age and chi-square test for sex. SD: Standard deviation.

	HIS				EUR			
	Cases	Controls	Total	*p*-value	Cases	Controls	Total	*p*-value
N (% total)	382 (11.41)	2,965 (88.59)	3,347 (100)		3,382 (5.44)	58,811 (94.56)	62,193 (100)	
Age (SD)	70.24 (9.70)	72.16 (7.23)	71.94 (7.57)	0.0002	73.32 (9.55)	73.11 (7.3)	73.12 (7.44)	0.2021
N Males (% total)	371 (97.12)	2,906 (98.01)	3,277 (97.91)	0.3402	3,263 (96.48)	57,496 (97.76)	60,759 (97.69)	1.8×10^{-6}

3.2. *GRS calculations and association tests*

We detected association between the 127-variant GRS and POAG case-control status in HIS and EUR Veterans in the MVP. Unweighted and weighted GRS were significantly associated with POAG status in both EUR and HIS Veterans ($p < 0.05$) (Table 2). Although effect estimates were comparable between both datasets for each GRS type, the association signals were more pronounced in the analyses of EUR Veterans compared to HIS Veterans (Table 2).

Table 2. Association test results for unadjusted and adjusted models for unweighted and weighted GRS in HIS and EUR Veterans in the MVP. Effect estimates are calculated as log(odds ratio) for a 1 standard deviation increase in the GRS.

Population	Model	GRS Type	Effect Estimate	Standard Error	z value	*p*-value
HIS	Unadjusted	Unweighted	0.55	0.057	9.56	1.18×10^{-21}
		Weighted	0.61	0.058	10.54	5.37×10^{-26}
	Adjusted	Unweighted	0.54	0.059	9.20	3.54×10^{-20}
		Weighted	0.61	0.060	10.16	3.13×10^{-24}
EUR	Unadjusted	Unweighted	0.56	0.018	30.63	5.65×10^{-206}
		Weighted	0.61	0.018	34.43	7.62×10^{-260}
	Adjusted	Unweighted	0.56	0.018	30.64	3.36×10^{-206}
		Weighted	0.61	0.018	34.40	2.28×10^{-259}

3.3. *GRS performance for POAG risk stratification in the MVP*

POAG case proportions generally increased across GRS deciles for both EUR and HIS Veterans (Figure 1). In the top deciles, a higher proportion of EUR POAG cases were consistently categorized compared to HIS POAG cases (Figure 1).

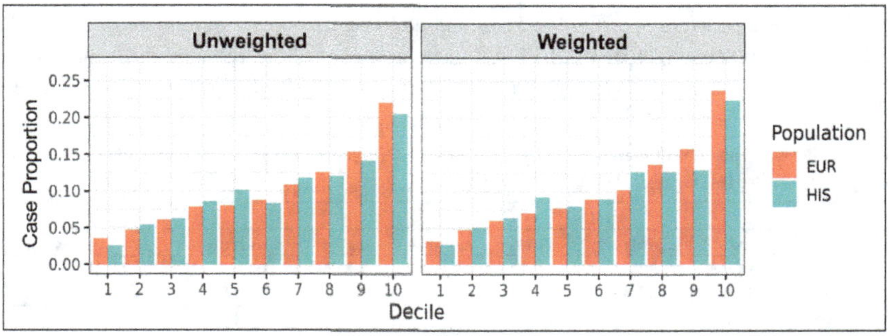

Fig. 1. Case proportions for EUR and HIS Veterans in the MVP for the unweighted and weighted GRS.

For both weighted and unweighted approaches, when we specifically compared the top GRS decile to the bottom 90%, we observed ~3-fold higher odds of POAG case classification for both GRS types in the top decile for both EUR and HIS Veterans (Table 3; Figure 2).

Table 3. Odds ratios (OR) comparing the top GRS decile to bottom 90% in HIS and EUR Veterans.

Population	GRS Type	OR (95% CI)	*p*-value
HIS	Unweighted	2.70 (2.03-3.56)	3.20×10^{-12}
	Weighted	3.11 (2.35-4.07)	4.63×10^{-16}
EUR	Unweighted	2.74 (2.51-2.98)	2.26×10^{-116}
	Weighted	3.03 (2.78-3.29)	9.05×10^{-147}

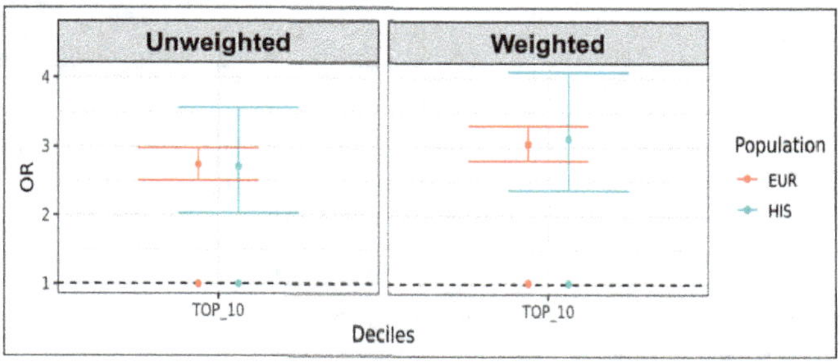

Fig. 2. Comparison of the top GRS decile versus the bottom 90% of the GRS distribution for unweighted and weighted GRS in EUR and HIS Veterans in the MVP.

We found no statistically significant difference in GRS performance based on ROC curve comparisons between HIS and EUR Veterans (AUC range: 0.65-0.69) (Figure 3). This trend was observed for both unadjusted (Figure 3A) and adjusted models (Figure 3B).

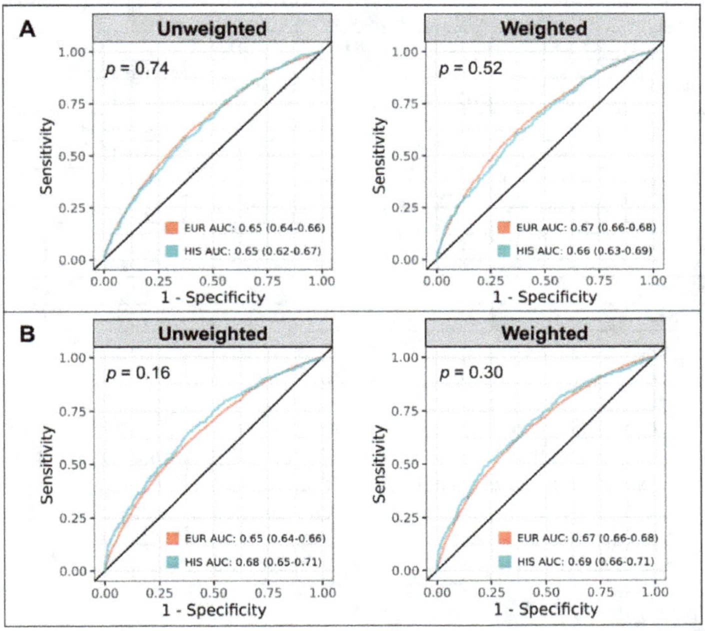

Fig. 3. ROC curve comparisons for (A) unadjusted and (B) adjusted models for unweighted and weighted GRS in HIS and EUR Veterans in the MVP. The *p*-values shown were calculated from DeLong's comparison of ROC curves.

3.4. *Proportion of variance explained by model variables*

We found that coefficients of determination (R^2) on the observed (Nagelkerke's) and liability scales were less than 0.1 for all the model variable combinations that we evaluated in our adjusted analyses (Table 4). Covariates alone (age, sex, and 10 PCs) explained a higher proportion of POAG variance in HIS Veterans (Nagelkerke's $R^2 = 0.034$; liability $R^2 = 0.030$) than in EUR Veterans (Nagelkerke's $R^2 = 0.002$; liability $R^2 = 0.0023$) (Table 4). Adding the GRS (unweighted and weighted) to the model resulted in similar increases in R^2 in HIS and EUR Veterans (Table 4).

Table 4. Coefficients of determination (R^2) on the observed scale (Nagelkerke's) and the liability scale for model variables in our adjusted GRS models for HIS and EUR Veterans in the MVP.

	HIS		EUR	
Model Variables	**Nagelkerke's R^2 (Observed Scale)**	**Liability R^2**	**Nagelkerke's R^2 (Observed Scale)**	**Liability R^2**
Age	0.013	0.012	0.0001	0.0001
Age+Sex	0.014	0.012	0.0011	0.0013
Age+Sex+10PCs	0.034	0.030	0.0020	0.0023
Age+Sex+10PCs+Unweighted GRS	0.085	0.076	0.047	0.054
Age+Sex+10PCs+Weighted GRS	0.096	0.086	0.058	0.067
R^2 Increase				
Unweighted GRS	0.051	0.046	0.045	0.052
Weighted GRS	0.062	0.056	0.056	0.065

3.5. *Subset analyses based on global genetic ancestry*

Among the 382 HIS POAG cases and 2,965 HIS controls in the MVP, a subset (220 POAG cases and 1,486 controls) had less than 50% EUR GGA (Figure 4). On average, cases in the GGA-based HIS subset were about 70 years old, while controls were about 72 years old ($p = 0.0018$). ROC curves for the GGA-based subset were comparable to those for the full HIS POAG case-control dataset (Table 5).

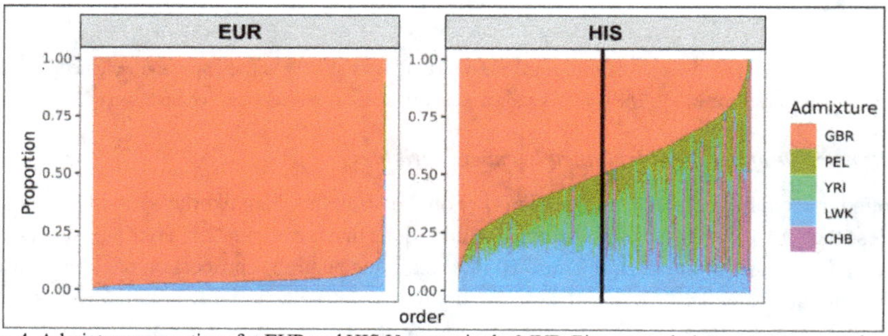

Fig. 4. Admixture proportions for EUR and HIS Veterans in the MVP. Five-way admixture was computed with ADMIXTURE using five 1000 Genomes reference groups (GBR: British in England and Scotland; PEL: Peruvian in Lima, Peru; YRI: Yoruba in Ibadan, Nigeria; LWK: Luhya in Webuye, Kenya; CHB: Han Chinese in Beijing, China). The vertical black line denotes 50% GBR; HIS Veterans to the right of the line were included in the subset analyses.

Table 5. Comparison of ROC curves for full HIS case-control dataset and GGA-based HIS subset.

GRS Type	**Area Under the Curve (95% CI)**		**DeLong's Comparison of ROC curves**
	HIS	**HIS Subset**	***p*-value**
Unweighted	0.65 (0.62-0.67)	0.63 (0.59-0.67)	0.61
Weighted	0.66 (0.63-0.69)	0.65 (0.61-0.69)	0.84

4. Discussion

In this study, we confirmed that GRS based on 127 POAG risk variants identified through cross-ancestry meta-analysis performed similarly in HIS and EUR Veterans in the MVP. We also observed this trend in our subset analyses based on GGA. However, it is important to note that across the highest GRS deciles, a higher proportion of EUR POAG cases were categorized compared to HIS POAG cases in the MVP. This emphasizes the need for more inclusive POAG genetics studies to improve the development of equitable risk prediction models based on genetic data.

The genetic etiology of POAG is complex with heritability estimates from twin studies and GWAS ranging from 0.26 to 0.93 (21–27). To date, over 125 genomic variants have been implicated in the genetic architecture of POAG, but these individual variants only moderately influence disease risk and only account for about 10% of the additive genetic variance of POAG (5,14). Rather than investigating single genetic variant associations, we performed logistic regression-based association analyses on unweighted and weighted GRS in HIS and EUR Veterans and found that both GRS types strongly associated with POAG case-control status in these groups (Table 2). However, when we examined the proportion of POAG variance explained by model variables, we observed varied effects of the addition of covariates alone compared to the combination of covariates and GRS in HIS and EUR Veterans (Table 4). This trend was also observed in our prior study, where covariates were more informative for POAG variance in AFR Veterans while GRS were more informative for EUR Veterans in the MVP (13). We hypothesize that this could be partially explained by the significant difference in the average ages of the AFR (13) and HIS POAG cases and controls (Table 1). Additionally, while the variants included in the 127-variant GRS were identified from a cross-ancestry meta-analysis (14), the variants may still be more informative for EUR individuals than individuals of other ancestries due to the high proportion of EUR individuals included in that study.

Based on our ROC curve comparisons and case classification evaluations, the performance of the 127-variant GRS was not significantly different between HIS and EUR Veterans (Figures 1 and 3). This is in stark contrast to our prior work, which found that GRS performance was significantly reduced when applied to AFR Veterans compared to EUR Veterans (13). Similar trends have been observed in the application of polygenic risk scores (PRS) for coronary heart disease in EUR, HIS, and AFR individuals (28,29) as well as for breast cancer in HIS individuals with varying proportions of EUR and Native American ancestry (30). It was hypothesized that the similar PRS performance in HIS and EUR individuals was attributable to the masking of the breadth of diversity in the HIS group (31), which is more genetically admixed (32). To interrogate this in our study, we evaluated GRS performance in a subset of HIS Veterans with less than 50% EUR GGA and did not detect a significant difference between the full and subset analyses (Table 5). Because AFR and HIS Veterans have a higher admixture proportion than EUR Veterans in the MVP (18), future work should consider the contributions of local genetic ancestry in POAG GRS performance.

While this study describes the application of GRS to a large multi-ancestry POAG case-control dataset, it has limitations. Nearly all the MVP-enrolled Veterans in this study were male due to demographic trends in the US military (15). While previous studies have estimated higher POAG prevalence in males than females (19), future work should evaluate GRS performance in a sex-balanced dataset to ensure that their application is equitable. Also, although this study examined

GRS in both EUR and HIS Veterans, there are substantially more EUR Veterans than HIS Veterans in our analyses. We also limited our GRS to 127 risk variants identified in the largest-to-date multi-ancestry POAG GWAS (14), and we were unable to assess GRS weighted by ancestry-specific effect estimates because the previously published meta-analysis did not include HIS individuals (14). Future studies examining a larger portion of the genetic architecture of POAG in multi-ancestry datasets should be prioritized to facilitate the construction of more informative GRS.

In summary, based on our knowledge of the current GRS limitations (e.g., dearth of diversity in GWAS and lack of transferability of GRS across different ancestries) and what we learned from this study, it is clear that POAG genomics studies need to increase the inclusion of diverse ancestral groups, especially those who have been historically underrepresented in research. This will hopefully improve understanding of the complex genetic architecture of POAG and ensure that GRS can be equitably introduced to the clinic for POAG risk stratification, especially for HIS and AFR individuals for whom POAG burden is higher.

5. Acknowledgments

This research is based on data from the MVP, Office of Research and Development, Veterans Health Administration, and was supported by award I01 BX004557. A full consortium acknowledgment for the MVP can be found in our prior publication (13). This publication does not represent the views of the Department of Veteran Affairs or the United States Government. We are grateful to the VINCI and GENISIS support teams and the MVP Core Statistical Analysis team for their contributions to this study. We also appreciate the Veterans who enrolled in the MVP. This work was also funded by the Cleveland Institute for Computational Biology, NIH Core Grants (P30 EY025585, P30 EY011373), and unrestricted grants from Research to Prevent Blindness to Case Western Reserve University (CWRU), Cleveland Clinic Lerner College of Medicine of CWRU, and the University of Buffalo. A.R.W. was supported by the CWRU Visual Sciences Training Program (T32 EY 7157-19) and CWRU Clinical and Translational Scientist Training Program (TL1 TR 002549-04). L.A.C. was supported by the National Heart, Lung, and Blood Institute (T32 HL 0075-67). This publication was made possible by the Clinical and Translational Science Collaborative of Cleveland (UL1TR0002548) from the National Center for Advancing Translational Sciences (NCATS) component of the National Institutes of Health and NIH roadmap for Medical Research. This work made use of the High Performance Computing Resource in the Core Facility for Advanced Research Computing at Case Western Reserve University.

References

1. Quigley, H.A. and Broman, A.T. (2006) The number of people with glaucoma worldwide in 2010 and 2020. *British Journal of Ophthalmology*, **90**, 262–267.
2. Tham, Y.C., Li, X., Wong, T.Y., Quigley, H.A., Aung, T. and Cheng, C.Y. (2014) Global prevalence of glaucoma and projections of glaucoma burden through 2040: a systematic review and meta-analysis. *Ophthalmology*, **121**, 2081–2090.
3. Caprioli, J. (2013) Glaucoma: a disease of early cellular senescence. *Invest Ophthalmol Vis Sci*, **54**, ORSF60–ORSF67.
4. Wiggs, J.L. and Pasquale, L.R. (2017) Genetics of glaucoma. *Hum Mol Genet*, **26**, R21–R27.

5. Choquet, H., Wiggs, J.L. and Khawaja, A.P. (2020) Clinical implications of recent advances in primary open-angle glaucoma genetics. *Eye*, **34**, 29–39.
6. Torkamani, A., Wineinger, N.E. and Topol, E.J. (2018) The personal and clinical utility of polygenic risk scores. *Nat Rev Genet*, **19**, 581–590.
7. Adeyemo, A., Balaconis, M.K., Darnes, D.R., Fatumo, S., Granados Moreno, P., Hodonsky, C.J., Inouye, M., Kanai, M., Kato, K., Knoppers, B.M., *et al.* (2021) Responsible use of polygenic risk scores in the clinic: potential benefits, risks and gaps. *Nat Med*, **27**, 1876–1884.
8. Lewis, A.C.F., Green, R.C. and Vassy, J.L. (2021) Polygenic risk scores in the clinic: Translating risk into action. *Human Genetics and Genomics Advances*, **2**, 100047.
9. Martin, A.R., Kanai, M., Kamatani, Y., Okada, Y., Neale, B.M. and Daly, M.J. (2019) Clinical use of current polygenic risk scores may exacerbate health disparities. *Nat Genet*, **51**, 584–591.
10. Sirugo, G., Williams, S.M. and Tishkoff, S.A. (2019) The Missing Diversity in Human Genetic Studies. *Cell*, **177**, 26–31.
11. National Eye Institute (NEI) (2019) Glaucoma Data and Statistics. Glaucoma Data and Statistics https://www.nei.nih.gov/learn-about-eye-health/resources-for-health-educators/eye-health-data-and-statistics/glaucoma-data-and-statistics.
12. Bryc, K., Velez, C., Karafet, T., Moreno-Estrada, A., Reynolds, A., Auton, A., Hammer, M., Bustamante, C.D. and Ostrer, H. (2010) Genome-wide patterns of population structure and admixture among Hispanic/Latino populations. *Proc Natl Acad Sci U S A*, **107**, 8954–8961.
13. Waksmunski, A.R., Kinzy, T.G., Cruz, L.A., Nealon, C.L., Halladay, C.W., Simpson, P., Canania, R.L., Anthony, S.A., Roncone, D.P., Rogers, L.S., *et al.* (2022) Glaucoma genetic risk scores in the Million Veteran Program. *Ophthalmology*, online ahead of print.
14. Gharahkhani, P., Jorgenson, E., Hysi, P., Khawaja, A.P., Pendergrass, S., Han, X., Ong, J.S., Hewitt, A.W., Segre, A. v, Rouhana, J.M., *et al.* (2021) Genome-wide meta-analysis identifies 127 open-angle glaucoma loci with consistent effect across ancestries. *Nat Commun*, **12**, 1258.
15. Gaziano, J.M., Concato, J., Brophy, M., Fiore, L., Pyarajan, S., Breeling, J., Whitbourne, S., Deen, J., Shannon, C., Humphries, D., *et al.* (2016) Million Veteran Program: A mega-biobank to study genetic influences on health and disease. *J Clin Epidemiol*, **70**, 214–223.
16. Hunter-Zinck, H., Shi, Y., Li, M., Gorman, B.R., Ji, S.-G., Sun, N., Webster, T., Liem, A., Hsieh, P., Devineni, P., *et al.* (2020) Genotyping Array Design and Data Quality Control in the Million Veteran Program. *Am J Hum Genet*, **106**, 535–548.
17. Nealon, C.L., Halladay, C.W., Kinzy, T.G., Simpson, P., Canania, R.L., Anthony, S.A., Roncone, D.P., Sawicki Rogers, L.R., Leber, J.N., Dougherty, J.M., *et al.* (2021) Development and Evaluation of a Rules-based Algorithm for Primary Open-Angle Glaucoma in the VA Million Veteran Program. *Ophthalmic Epidemiol*, 1–9.
18. Fang, H., Hui, Q., Lynch, J., Honerlaw, J., Assimes, T.L., Huang, J., Vujkovic, M., Damrauer, S.M., Pyarajan, S., Gaziano, J.M., *et al.* (2019) Harmonizing Genetic Ancestry and Self-identified Race/Ethnicity in Genome-wide Association Studies. *Am J Hum Genet*, **105**, 763–772.
19. Zhang, N., Wang, J., Li, Y. and Jiang, B. (2021) Prevalence of primary open angle glaucoma in the last 20 years: a meta-analysis and systematic review. *Sci Rep*, **11**, 13762.

20. Alexander, D.H., Novembre, J. and Lange, K. (2009) Fast model-based estimation of ancestry in unrelated individuals. *Genome Res*, **19**, 1655–1664.
21. Asefa, N.G., Neustaeter, A., Jansonius, N.M. and Snieder, H. (2019) Heritability of glaucoma and glaucoma-related endophenotypes: Systematic review and meta-analysis. *Surv Ophthalmol*, **64**, 835–851.
22. Sanfilippo, P.G., Hewitt, A.W., Hammond, C.J. and Mackey, D.A. (2010) The heritability of ocular traits. *Surv Ophthalmol*, **55**, 561–583.
23. Springelkamp, H., Hohn, R., Mishra, A., Hysi, P.G., Khor, C.C., Loomis, S.J., Bailey, J.N., Gibson, J., Thorleifsson, G., Janssen, S.F., *et al.* (2014) Meta-analysis of genome-wide association studies identifies novel loci that influence cupping and the glaucomatous process. *Nat Commun*, **5**, 4883.
24. Springelkamp, H., Iglesias, A.I., Mishra, A., Hohn, R., Wojciechowski, R., Khawaja, A.P., Nag, A., Wang, Y.X., Wang, J.J., Cuellar-Partida, G., *et al.* (2017) New insights into the genetics of primary open-angle glaucoma based on meta-analyses of intraocular pressure and optic disc characteristics. *Hum Mol Genet*, **26**, 438–453.
25. Choquet, H., Thai, K.K., Yin, J., Hoffmann, T.J., Kvale, M.N., Banda, Y., Schaefer, C., Risch, N., Nair, K.S., Melles, R., *et al.* (2017) A large multi-ethnic genome-wide association study identifies novel genetic loci for intraocular pressure. *Nat Commun*, **8**, 2108.
26. Ge, T., Chen, C.Y., Neale, B.M., Sabuncu, M.R. and Smoller, J.W. (2017) Phenome-wide heritability analysis of the UK Biobank. *PLoS Genet*, **13**, e1006711.
27. Polubriaginof, F.C.G., Vanguri, R., Quinnies, K., Belbin, G.M., Yahi, A., Salmasian, H., Lorberbaum, T., Nwankwo, V., Li, L., Shervey, M.M., *et al.* (2018) Disease Heritability Inferred from Familial Relationships Reported in Medical Records. *Cell*, **173**, 1692-1704 e11.
28. Fahed, A.C., Aragam, K.G., Hindy, G., Chen, Y.D.I., Chaudhary, K., Dobbyn, A., Krumholz, H.M., Sheu, W.H.H., Rich, S.S., Rotter, J.I., *et al.* (2021) Transethnic Transferability of a Genome-Wide Polygenic Score for Coronary Artery Disease. *Circ Genom Precis Med*, **14**, E003092.
29. Dikilitas, O., Schaid, D.J., Kosel, M.L., Carroll, R.J., Chute, C.G., Denny, J.A., Fedotov, A., Feng, Q.P., Hakonarson, H., Jarvik, G.P., *et al.* (2020) Predictive Utility of Polygenic Risk Scores for Coronary Heart Disease in Three Major Racial and Ethnic Groups. *Am J Hum Genet*, **106**, 707–716.
30. Shieh, Y., Fejerman, L., Lott, P.C., Marker, K., Sawyer, S.D., Hu, D., Huntsman, S., Torres, J., Echeverry, M., Bohórquez, M.E., *et al.* (2020) A Polygenic Risk Score for Breast Cancer in US Latinas and Latin American Women. *JNCI: Journal of the National Cancer Institute*, **112**, 590–598.
31. Clarke, S.L., Huang, R.D.L., Hilliard, A.T., Tcheandjieu, C., Lynch, J., Damrauer, S.M., Chang, K.-M., Tsao, P.S. and Assimes, T.L. (2022) Race and Ethnicity Stratification for Polygenic Risk Score Analyses May Mask Disparities in Hispanics. *Circulation*, **146**, 265–267.
32. Bryc, K., Durand, E.Y., Macpherson, J.M., Reich, D. and Mountain, J.L. (2015) The Genetic Ancestry of African Americans, Latinos, and European Americans across the United States. *Am J Hum Genet*, **96**, 37.

Predictive models for abdominal aortic aneurysms using polygenic scores and PheWAS-derived risk factors[a]

Jacklyn N. Hellwege[†]
Division of Genetic Medicine, Department of Medicine, Vanderbilt Genetics Institute
Vanderbilt University Medical Center
2525 West End Ave. Ste 700, Nashville, TN, 37203, USA
Email: jacklyn.hellwege@vumc.org

Chad Dorn
Department of Biomedical Informatics, Vanderbilt University Medical Center
2525 West End Ave. Ste 1500, Nashville, TN, 37203, USA
Email: chad.a.dorn@vumc.org

Marguerite R. Irvin
Department of Epidemiology, University of Alabama at Birmingham,
Birmingham, AL 35233, USA
Email: irvinr@uab.edu

Nita A. Limdi
Department of Neurology, University of Alabama at Birmingham,
Birmingham, AL 35233, USA
Email: nlimdi@uabmc.edu

James Cimino
Informatics Institute, University of Alabama at Birmingham,
Birmingham, AL 35233, USA
Email: jamescimino@uabmc.edu

T. Mark Beasley
Department of Biostatistics, University of Alabama at Birmingham,

[a]Some of the datasets used for analyses were obtained from Vanderbilt University Medical Center's BioVU which is supported by institutional funding, 1S10RR025141-01, and by the CTSA grant UL1TR000445 from NCATS/NIH. The eMERGE Network is funded by the following grants: U01HG8657 (Kaiser Washington/University of Washington); U01HG8685 (Brigham and Women's Hospital); U01HG8672 (Vanderbilt University Medical Center); U01HG8666 (Cincinnati Children's Hospital Medical Center); U01HG6379 (Mayo Clinic); U01HG8679 (Geisinger Clinic); U01HG8680 (Columbia University Health Sciences); U01HG8684 (Children's Hospital of Philadelphia); U01HG8673 (Northwestern University); U01HG8701 (Vanderbilt University Medical Center serving as the Coordinating Center); U01HG8676 (Partners Healthcare/Broad Institute); and U01HG8664 (Baylor College of Medicine).
[†]Work partially supported by K12 HD04348.

Birmingham, AL, 35233, USA.
Email: mbeasley@uab.edu

Philip S. Tsao
VA Palo Alto Health Care System
Stanford Cardiovascular Institute, Department of Medicine, Stanford University School of Medicine, Stanford, CA, 94305, USA
Email: ptsao@stanford.edu

Scott M. Damrauer
Corporal Michael J. Crescenz VA Medical Center
Department of Genetics, Department of Surgery, University of Pennsylvania Perelman School of Medicine Philadelphia, PA, 19104, USA
Email: Scott.Damrauer@pennmedicine.upenn.edu

Dan M. Roden
Division of Clinical Pharmacology, Department of Medicine; Department of Pharmacology; Department of Biomedical Informatics; Vanderbilt Genetics Institute; Vanderbilt University Medical Center
2215 Garland Ave., Nashville, TN, 37203, USA
Email: dan.roden@vumc.org

Digna R. Velez Edwards
Division of Quantitative Science, Department of Obstetrics and Gynecology, Department of Biomedical Informatics, Vanderbilt Genetics Institute, Vanderbilt University Medical Center
2525 West End Ave. Ste 600, Nashville, TN, 37203, USA
Email: digna.r.velez.edwards@vumc.org

Wei-Qi Wei
Department of Biomedical Informatics, Vanderbilt University Medical Center
2525 West End Ave. Ste. 1500, Nashville, TN, 37203, USA
Email: wei-qi.wei@vumc.org

Todd L. Edwards
Division of Epidemiology, Vanderbilt Genetics Institute, Vanderbilt University Medical Center
2525 West End Ave. Ste 600, Nashville, TN, 37203, USA
Email: todd.l.edwards@vumc.org

Abdominal aortic aneurysms (AAA) are common enlargements of the abdominal aorta which can grow larger until rupture, often leading to death. Detection of AAA is often by ultrasonography and screening recommendations are mostly directed at men over 65 with a smoking history. Recent large-scale genome-wide association studies have identified genetic loci associated with AAA risk. We combined known risk factors, polygenic risk scores (PRS) and precedent clinical diagnoses from electronic health records (EHR) to develop predictive models for AAA, and compared performance against screening recommendations. The PRS included genome-wide summary statistics from the Million Veteran Program and FinnGen (10,467 cases, 378,713 controls of European ancestry), with optimization in Vanderbilt's BioVU and validated in the eMERGE Network, separately across both White and Black participants. Candidate diagnoses were identified through a temporally-oriented

Phenome-wide association study in independent EHR data from Vanderbilt, and features were selected via elastic net. We calculated C-statistics in eMERGE for models including PRS, phecodes, and covariates using regression weights from BioVU. The AUC for the full model in the test set was 0.883 (95% CI 0.873-0.892), 0.844 (0.836-0.851) for covariates only, 0.613 (95% CI 0.604-0.622) when using primary USPSTF screening criteria, and 0.632 (95% CI 0.623-0.642) using primary and secondary criteria. Brier scores were between 0.003 and 0.023 for our models indicating good calibration, and net reclassification improvement over combined primary and secondary USPSTF criteria was 0.36-0.60. We provide PRS for AAA which are strongly associated with AAA risk and add to predictive model performance. These models substantially improve identification of people at risk of a AAA diagnosis compared with existing guidelines, with evidence of potential applicability in minority populations.

Keywords: Abdominal Aortic Aneurysm, Polygenic Scores, Prediction, Precision Medicine

1. Introduction

Abdominal aortic aneurysms (AAA) is a common and life-threatening condition in which enlargement of the abdominal aorta can lead to a deadly rupture. Rupture is associated with a mortality rate as high as 81%, including mortality of over 50% even among individuals that rupture in a hospital setting[1]. Current estimates suggest that approximately 4% of the US population over 65 has an AAA, and 41,000 deaths a year are attributed to AAA complications[2,3]. Based on AHA 2019 Heart Disease and Stroke statistics, the prevalence of AAA ranges from 1.3% in males 45-54 years old to 12.5% in males 75-84 years old[4]. For females, the prevalence ranges from 0% in the youngest to 5.2% in the oldest age groups[4].

Common risk factors for AAA risk are race, age, sex, smoking behavior, atherosclerosis, hypertension, and hyperlipidemia[5-7]. A family history of AAA is associated with an adjusted OR of 2.17[8]. Factors associated with aorta diameter from Mendelian randomization studies include pulse pressure, triglycerides, and height[9]. An estimate of SNP-based heritability for AAA is not available, however, heritability of AAA is estimated to be as high as 70%[10]. Multiple genome-wide association studies have been conducted and have detected 24 distinct loci[11-15]. These observations provide a basis for including genetic information in prediction of future AAA events.

There are no currently available pharmacological therapies for prevention or treatment of AAA. When discovered, AAA cases are monitored using periodic ultrasounds, where the goal is to observe AAA expansion until the risk of rupture is deemed to be larger than the risks posed by surgical repair[16], which for many patients is when the diameter reaches 5.5 cm[17]. AAA cases are most often either discovered incidentally by abdominal imaging for some other indication, or by screening programs that target specific high-risk groups.

Current US Preventative Services Task Force (USPSTF) guidelines focus on screening men between 65 and 75 years of age with a history of smoking[18]. In a recent large retrospective study of almost 291,850 AAA hospitalizations, 23% were women, and over 60% were not between 65 and 75 years of age[19]. USPSTF recommendations are not derived from statistical models and may underserve understudied groups or individuals who are at unusually high risk for their demographic category due to an accumulation of known and unknown risk factors.

Strong racial disparities have been observed in prevalence, risk, and response to surgical treatments in AAA patients[20,21]. These important and poorly understood aspects of AAA epidemiology are often neglected in screening guidelines. Because effective AAA management depends on detection, this opportunity for improving the screening strategy has the potential to save lives, many of whom are in underserved groups. In this paper, we leverage prior GWAS of AAA and electronic health records (EHR) linked to genetic information to develop predictive models that outperform the USPSTF guidelines in identifying high-risk individuals and evaluating the performance of polygenic predictors in multiple ancestral groups.

2. Methods

2.1. *Synthetic Derivative*

The Synthetic Derivative (SD) is a deidentified mirror of EHR at Vanderbilt University Medical Center (VUMC) with records for >3 million patients dating to January 1990 and updated regularly.

2.2. *BioVU*

The BioVU DNA Repository is a subset of the SD at VUMC with linkage to individuals' DNA samples. A detailed description of the database and how it is maintained has been published elsewhere[22,23]. BioVU participant DNA samples were genotyped on a custom Illumina Multi-Ethnic Genotyping Array (MEGA-ex; Illumina Inc., San Diego, CA, USA). Quality control included excluding samples or variants with missingness rates above 2%. Samples were also excluded if consent had been revoked, sample was duplicated, or failed sex concordance checks. Imputation was performed on the Michigan Imputation Server (MIS) v1.2.4[24] using Minimac4 and the Haplotype Reference Consortium (HRC) panel v1.1[25]. AAA cases were identified using phecodes[26,27]: 2 or more instances of an International Classification of Diseases (ICD) version 9 or 10 diagnostic code for AAA, while controls were those without any ICD codes for AAA or phecodes in range 440-449.9 (Diseases of Arteries, Arterioles, and Capillaries). Individuals with one AAA ICD code were excluded. Smoking status was defined using ICD codes.

2.3. *eMERGE*

The eMERGE Network is a consortium of several EHR-linked biorepositories formed with the goal of developing approaches for the use of the EHR in genomic research[28,29]. Consortium membership has evolved over eMERGE's 11-year history, with many sites contributing data: Group Health/University of Washington, Marshfield Clinic, Mayo Clinic, Northwestern University, Vanderbilt University, Children's Hospital of Philadelphia (CHOP), Boston Children's Hospital (BCH), Cincinnati Children's Hospital Medical Center (CCHMC), Geisinger Health System, Mount Sinai School of Medicine, Harvard University and Columbia University. The eMERGE study was approved by the Institutional Review Board at each site and all methods were performed in accordance with the relevant guidelines and regulations. Participants at all sites provided written informed consent. AAA cases and controls were defined as in BioVU.

2.4. *Genome-wide Summary Statistics*

We combined genome-wide summary statistics for AAA from the Million Veteran Program[11] and FinnGen[30] for a total of 10,467 cases and 378,713 controls of European ancestry) using fixed-effects inverse-variance weighted meta-analysis implemented in METAL[31].

2.5. *Polygenic Score Development*

PRSs were constructed using PRS-CS[32] software and PLINK2[33], followed by p-value thresholding (range: $p=1$ - 5×10^{-8}) as in Ref[34]. Optimal p-value thresholds were 1.0 in Whites and $p<5\times10^{-3}$ in Blacks, as determined by maximal variance explained in BioVU (0.76% and 0.59%, respectively).

2.6. *Identification of phecode risk factors*

We extracted all diagnostic codes from individuals in the SD who were not part of the BioVU MEGA genotyped set who classified as either a case or control for AAA status. Codes for AAA cases were censored following the earliest AAA diagnosis code – i.e. all diagnoses post-AAA were removed, in order to capture only those diagnoses which preceded AAA diagnosis and represent potential risk factors for subsequent diagnosis of AAA. We performed a phenome-wide association study[35] (PheWAS) on this temporally-censored dataset with AAA as the outcome with each phecode status used as predictor, adjusted for age and sex, stratified by self-reported race/ethnicity. Bonferroni correction was used to set significance thresholds to identify significant phecodes.

2.7. *Selection of independent components with elastic nets*

We used elastic net models with 10-fold cross validation in BioVU to estimate feature weights, implemented in the glmnet R package[36,37] for selection of candidate risk features derived from the temporal PheWAS in the SD. Among the variables considered were 196 candidate phecodes (significant in at least one temporal PheWAS), age, sex, BMI, smoking status, race, and ethnicity. Individuals missing status (with only one AAA ICD code or an exclusion code) were classified with controls (using probit linkages) in a case-cohort design to allow simultaneous modeling of phecodes.

2.8. *Predictive models*

Prediction of AAA diagnoses in eMERGE data used logistic regression implemented in R, and evaluated area under the receiver operator curve (pROC package), net reclassification index (nricens package), and Brier scores. Phecodes selected from the elastic net were included alongside age, sex, BMI, smoking status, polygenic scores, and principal components of ancestry.

3. Results

3.1. *Polygenic risk score development, performance, and association with AAA*

We performed meta-analysis of MVP and FinnGen summary statistics for AAA using a fixed-effects inverse-variance weighted method in METAL. Polygenic scores were constructed using PRS-CS to generate weights, followed by p-value thresholding. The optimal p-value threshold was 1.0 in non-Hispanic Whites (NHW), while the optimal threshold in non-Hispanic Blacks (NHB) was $p<5\times10^{-3}$ as determined by maximal variance explained in BioVU (0.76% and 0.59%, respectively; Table 1); at these thresholds, the PRSs contained 1,118,966 and 12,314 SNPs, respectively.

Table 1. Variance explained across PRS p-value thresholds in BioVU Non-Hispanic Whites and Blacks

RACE	1	0.5	5.0E-02	5.0E-03	5.0E-04	5.0E-05	5.0E-06	5.0E-07	5.0E-08
NHW	**0.0076**	0.0070	0.0072	0.0062	0.0056	0.0042	0.0039	0.0031	0.0014
NHB	0.0018	0.0021	0.0018	**0.0059**	0.0032	0.0021	0.0023	0.0012	0.00001

We observed increasing odds of AAA in eMERGE by PRS of both scores when modeled adjusting for age, sex, body mass index (BMI), and 10 principal components (Figure 1). In NHW, the scores were both significant (p-value =< 2e-16) and each explained 0.014% of the variance, while in NHB only the p<5e-3 score (PRS-B) was significant (p-value = 0.0028). When modeled as deciles, associations trended toward higher odds ratios at higher deciles for both PRS in NHW, but more consistently in NHB with the p=5e-3 PRS (Figure 1). The 95th and higher percentile vs. the rest odds ratios were 2.45 (95% Confidence Interval [CI]: 2.09-2.88; p-value $<2x10^{-16}$) and 2.11 (95% CI 0.84-5.31; p-value = 0.11) for NHW and NHB subsets, respectively, for the p=1 score (Table 2). For the $p=5x10^{-3}$ PRS, the odds ratios were 2.2 (95% CI: 1.87-2.59; p-value $<2x10^{-16}$) and 3.34 (95% CI 1.49-7.47; p-value = 0.003) for NHW and NHB subsets, respectively.

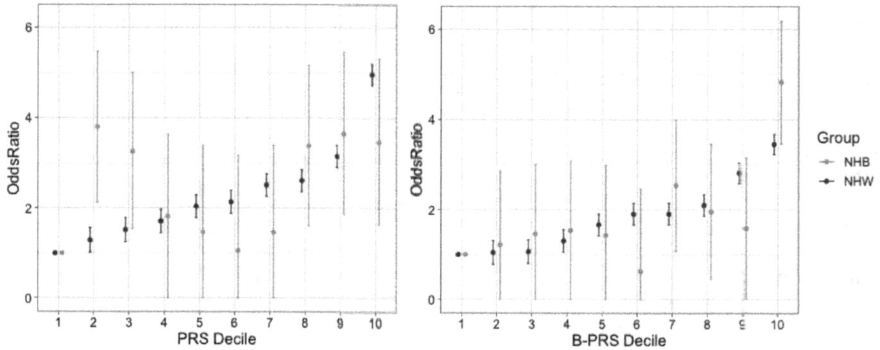

Figure 1. Odds ratios for AAA with p=1 PRS (A) and p=5e-3 PRS (B) deciles in eMERGE

Table 2. Association between AAA PRS and AAA outcome in eMERGE

RACE	CASES / CONTROLS	P=1 PRS OR (95% CI)	P=1 PRS P-VALUE	P=5E-3 PRS-B OR (95% CI)	P=5E-3 PRS-B P-VALUE
NHW	2,165 / 42,843	2.45 (2.09-2.88)	**$<2.0x10^{-16}$**	2.20 (1.87-2.59)	**$<2.0x10^{-16}$**
NHB	42 / 4,492	2.11 (0.84-5.31)	0.11	3.34 (1.49-7.47)	**0.003**

Each PRS modeled as top 5% of distribution compared to remainder. Covariates included age, sex, BMI and 10 principal components of ancestry.

3.2. *Identification of phecode diagnosis risk factors*

In order to identify risk-associated diagnoses which precede AAA diagnosis/events, we performed a temporally-censored PheWAS. Within the Vanderbilt Synthetic Derivative dataset, we censored any diagnosis codes occurring after an ICD code for AAA, and performed a PheWAS using AAA as the outcome and each phecode as the predictor. Atherosclerosis phecodes were broadly significant, while Kawasaki disease was significant only in NHB individuals. In total, 192 phecodes were significant in analyses of NHW, 10 in NHB, 3 in Hispanic and none in non-Hispanic Asian (NHA) (Table 3). In total, 196 phecodes were significantly associated in at least one analysis. All significant phecodes were included as components in the elastic net.

Table 3. Feature-identifying PheWAS in Vanderbilt Synthetic Derivative

RACE	CASES	CONTROLS	PHECODES ANALYZED	SIGNIFICANT PHECODES
NHW	4,416	1,202,332	1866	192
NHB	292	166,170	1860	10
NHA	23	23,490	1802	0
Hispanic	31	47,003	1843	3

Of 202 variables (196 Phecodes) included in the elastic net, 87 were retained in the model- four *a priori* variables (smoking status, median BMI, age, and gender), and 83 Phecode diagnoses. 67 of 87 features were negatively associated, that is, diagnosis of a preceding Phecode was associated with a reduced risk of AAA diagnosis. Chromosomal abnormalities and genetic disorders diagnoses (phecode 758) had the largest weighting in the elastic net model, despite being generally uncommon in the population studied (0.04%). Evaluation of the 83 phecodes indicated several hierarchical codes which were collapsed to select independent features, resulting in a final set of 68 phecodes.

3.3. *Predictive models*

We validated our AAA risk prediction models developed in BioVU using external data to evaluate its discrimination and calibration. We benchmarked our models to the performance of the USPTF screening criteria. A sparse model containing age, sex, BMI, smoking status and principal components of ancestry performed substantially better than USPTF screening criteria, with AUCs over 0.8 in all three groups compared to AUCs ranging from 0.55-0.63 for USPTF primary and secondary criteria (Table 4, Figure 2). The AUCs when including PRS and covariates were 0.846

Table 4. AUC (CI) for predictive models fit in BioVU and applied to eMERGE

MODEL	ALL	NHW	NHB
USPTF-B	0.613 (0.604-0.622)	0.614 (0.605-0.623)	0.545 (0.504-0.586)
USPTF-C	0.632 (0.623-0.642)	0.632 (0.622-0.642)	0.594 (0.539-0.650)
COV	0.844 (0.836-0.851)	0.838 (0.830-0.845)	0.819 (0.765-0.873)
PHE	0.859 (0.849-0.870)	0.853 (0.842-0.864)	0.807 (0.732-0.883)
PHE+COV	0.883 (0.874-0.893)	0.877 (0.868-0.887)	0.758 (0.659-0.857)
PRS	0.494 (0.484-0.505)	0.598 (0.586-0.610)	0.531 (0.448-0.613)
PRS+COV	0.836 (0.829-0.844)	0.846 (0.838-0.854)	0.820 (0.766-0.874)
FULL	**0.883 (0.874-0.893)**	**0.877 (0.868-0.887)**	**0.758 (0.659-0.857)**
PRS-B	0.533 (0.522-0.544)	0.601 (0.589-0.613)	0.580 (0.498-0.662)
PRS-B+COV	0.846 (0.839-0.854)	0.846 (0.838-0.853)	0.830 (0.776-0.874)
FULL-B	**0.883 (0.873-0.892)**	**0.880 (0.870-0.890)**	**0.758 (0.659-0.857)**

PRS: Best performing PRS overall; PRS-B/FULL-B: models including p<5e-3 optimal PRS in NHB

(0.839-0.854), 0.846 (0.838-0.853) and 0.830 (0.776-0.884) for the entire dataset, in NHW, and in NHB respectively. Adding phecode predictors to the models improved AUCs further: 0.883 (0.873-0.892), 0.880 (0.870-0.890) in the entire data and NHW set, respectively, but not in NHB (AUC = 0.758 (0.659-0.857).

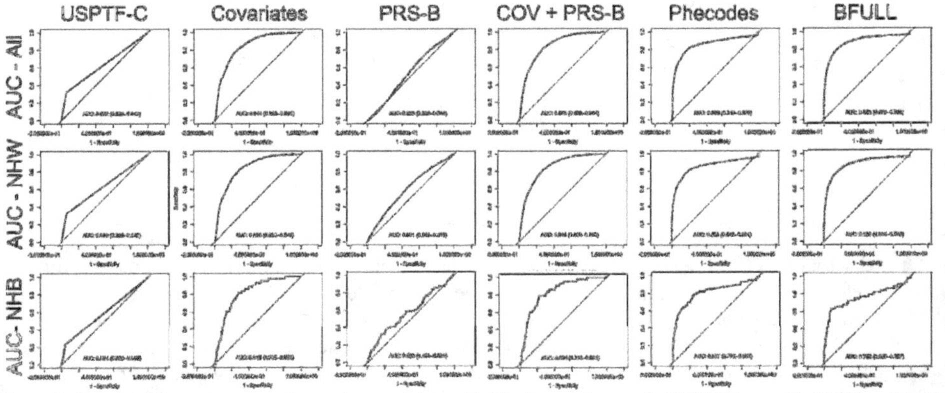

Figure 2. Receiver-operator curve plots using models applied in (top to bottom:) eMERGE overall, NHW and NHB for (left to right:) USPTF primary+secondary guidelines, covariates only, PRS-B only, covariates + PRS-B, phecodes only, and full models (covariates, PRS-B, and phecodes).

We evaluated model reclassification and calibration using net reclassification indices (NRI) and Brier scores, respectively. Generally, although model calibration was very good for the full models (0.003-0.023; Table 5), inclusion of both PRS and phecode predictors to models using covariates had a moderate impact on reclassification indices (0.23) in combined datasets, with larger impacts in NHB (Table 6). The NRIs from these data compared to USPTF guidelines is striking, with covariates alone having an NRI of 0.20-0.37, and full models 0.46-0.83.

Table 5. Brier scores for various models in eMERGE

MODEL	ALL	NHW	NHB
FULL	0.021	0.023	0.0032
FULL-B	0.021	0.023	0.0030

4. Discussion

We have integrated a variety of data types to construct models for predicting AAA diagnoses across multiple EHR systems. Our polygenic scores for AAA, despite being developed using only European-ancestry genetic data, associated with AAA in NHB as well as NHW, and are being made available through the polygenic score catalog (pgscatalog.org). Addition of the PRS in the entire eMERGE dataset had a small negative effect on the model (ΔAUC = -0.008), however the model improved in the NHW and NHB strata separately, as did all PRS-B models.

Our study suggests an enhanced disease screening program of asymptomatic individuals who would otherwise be considered lower risk by USPTF guidelines would substantially improve AAA detection in the US population. Even covariates alone perform substantially better than the USPTF guidelines, similar to what has been shown in a recent UK Biobank study with a simple predictive

Table 6. NRI for predictive models in eMERGE compared with USPSTF screening criteria

MODELS	EMERGE	EMERGE NHW	EMERGE NHB
USPTF C : B	0	0	0
COV : USPTF B	0.37	0.31	0.20
COV : USPTF C	0.37	0.31	0.20
PRS+COV : COV	0.025	0.031	0.008
PRS-B+COV : COV	0.018	0.024	0.048
FULL : COV	0.23	0.25	0.61
BFULL : COV	0.23	0.24	0.63
FULL : USPTF B	0.60	0.50	0.82
FULL : USPTF C	0.60	0.50	0.82
BFULL : USPTF B	0.60	0.46	0.83
BFULL : USPTF C	0.60	0.46	0.83

PRS: Best performing PRS overall; PRS-B/FULL-B: models including p<5e-3 PRS (optimal in NHB).

model that lacked variables for genetics, sex, or race[38]. This demonstrates the principle that opportunities exist to substantially improve the public health impact of AAA. Clinical decision support tools for identifying patients for AAA screening based on USPTF guidelines have existed for over a decade[39-42], however, recent reports indicate that even those fitting USPTF criteria remain unlikely to receive screening (only 13% of eligible patients within ≥ two years)[43]. Importantly, these studies focused on male patients, while in both BioVU and eMERGE, females made up 23-25% of the AAA cases, higher than the 17% observed in the UK Biobank risk prediction study[38].

A critical aspect of implementing predictive models that rely on multiple structured data elements and complex calculations is scalability. Compared with the USPSTF guidelines, which are straightforward to incorporate into clinical practice, implementing the models we present here would require that calculations be integrated into EHR systems. Ideally risk determinations would be presented to the clinical practitioner in real time during an encounter with a patient. Given the significant discrimination improvement over USPSTF criteria, and examples of implementation for other traits[44], we believe that real-time risk evaluation is feasible. Enhanced screening seems unlikely to lead to unnecessary invasive clinical procedures, as previous meta-analyses indicate that repair of small unruptured aneurysms had no advantage over routine ultrasound surveillance[45].

Recent studies have explored integration of imaging-derived parameters in prediction of AAA growth, rupture and mortality[46-49]. While our analyses rely on diagnostic codes and demographic information, our overarching goal is to identify potentially high-risk individuals for AAA screening via imaging. The goals of these approaches are distinct: identification of who is likely to develop AAA and who among AAA patients requires intervention. Restriction to extant structured data in the EHR improves the likelihood and feasibility of implementation of models in the clinical setting.

Our study is most limited by sample counts for most diverse racial/ethnic groups being too small to include as separate strata. This is concerning due to racial/ethnic differences in screening prevalence but also in clinical presentation, treatment, and mortality following surgical repair[19-21,50,51]. We were able to include NHB individuals in all phases of this analysis, and confirmed that performance of USPTF criteria is lower in this group[19,43,51], but that clinically meaningful prediction (AUC>0.8) were attainable using either basic covariates or medical diagnoses.

Our results in eMERGE NHB participants incorporating phecodes suggested that despite use of cross-validation, our models from BioVU were likely overfit due to sparseness of NHB participants relative to the number of terms estimated. Larger numbers of NHB participants would facilitate improved models, however, we observed good discriminative performance compared with USPTF.

Predictive models including a PRS optimized in NHB individuals resulted in models that performed nearly equally as well in NHW but provided modest improvements in NHB. This is unusual for genetic studies based solely on European-ancestry participants[52] but suggests that risk variants may persist across diverse populations, making prediction of events easier. Although the PRS alone was little better than chance at predicting AAA diagnosis, including covariates was sufficient to yield clinical utility[53]. Future work evaluating scalability and incorporating sex-stratified estimates into models will enhance quality of prediction and clinical implementation.

In summary, we provide predictive models and polygenic scores for AAA which strongly associated with and predict AAA risk in multiple populations. These models substantially improve identification of people at risk of a AAA diagnosis compared with existing guidelines.

References

1. Dua A, et al. Epidemiology of aortic aneurysm repair in the United States from 2000 to 2010. *J Vasc Surg.* 2014;59(6):1512-1517.
2. Summers KL, et al. Evaluating the prevalence of abdominal aortic aneurysms in the United States through a national screening database. *J Vasc Surg.* 2021;73(1):61-68.
3. Stuntz M. Modeling the Burden of Abdominal Aortic Aneurysm in the USA in 2013. *Cardiology.* 2016;135(2):127-131.
4. Benjamin EJ, et al. Heart Disease and Stroke Statistics-2019 Update: A Report From the American Heart Association. *Circulation.* 2019;139(10):e56-e528.
5. Lo RC, et al. Abdominal aortic aneurysms in women. *J Vasc Surg.* 2016;63(3):839-844.
6. Jahangir E, et al. Smoking, sex, risk factors and abdominal aortic aneurysms: a prospective study of 18 782 persons aged above 65 years in the Southern Community Cohort Study. *Journal of epidemiology and community health.* 2015;69(5):481-488.
7. Pleumeekers HJ, et al. Aneurysms of the abdominal aorta in older adults. The Rotterdam Study. *Am J Epidemiol.* 1995;142(12):1291-1299.
8. Ye Z, et al. Family history of atherosclerotic vascular disease is associated with the presence of abdominal aortic aneurysm. *Vasc Med.* 2016;21(1):41-46.
9. Portilla-Fernandez E, et al. Genetic and clinical determinants of abdominal aortic diameter: genome-wide association studies, exome array data and Mendelian randomization study. *Hum Mol Genet.* 2022.
10. Wahlgren CM, et al. Genetic and environmental contributions to abdominal aortic aneurysm development in a twin population. *J Vasc Surg.* 2010;51(1):3-7; discussion 7.
11. Klarin D, et al. Genetic Architecture of Abdominal Aortic Aneurysm in the Million Veteran Program. *Circulation.* 2020;142(17):1633-1646.
12. Jones GT, et al. Meta-Analysis of Genome-Wide Association Studies for Abdominal Aortic Aneurysm Identifies Four New Disease-Specific Risk Loci. *Circ Res.* 2017;120(2):341-353.
13. Bradley DT, et al. A variant in LDLR is associated with abdominal aortic aneurysm. *Circ Cardiovasc Genet.* 2013;6(5):498-504.
14. Bown MJ, et al. Abdominal aortic aneurysm is associated with a variant in low-density lipoprotein receptor-related protein 1. *Am J Hum Genet.* 2011;89(5):619-627.

15. Gretarsdottir S, et al. Genome-wide association study identifies a sequence variant within the DAB2IP gene conferring susceptibility to abdominal aortic aneurysm. *Nat Genet.* 2010;42(8):692-697.
16. Chaikof EL, et al. The Society for Vascular Surgery practice guidelines on the care of patients with an abdominal aortic aneurysm. *J Vasc Surg.* 2018;67(1):2-77.e72.
17. Kent KC. Clinical practice. Abdominal aortic aneurysms. *N Engl J Med.* 2014;371(22):2101-2108.
18. Guirguis-Blake JM, et al. Primary Care Screening for Abdominal Aortic Aneurysm: Updated Evidence Report and Systematic Review for the US Preventive Services Task Force. *Jama.* 2019;322(22):2219-2238.
19. Li SR, et al. Epidemiology of age-, sex-, and race-specific hospitalizations for abdominal aortic aneurysms highlights gaps in current screening recommendations. *J Vasc Surg.* 2022.
20. Deery SE, et al. Racial disparities in outcomes after intact abdominal aortic aneurysm repair. *J Vasc Surg.* 2018;67(4):1059-1067.
21. Williams TK, et al. Disparities in outcomes for Hispanic patients undergoing endovascular and open abdominal aortic aneurysm repair. *Ann Vasc Surg.* 2013;27(1):29-37.
22. Pulley J, et al. Principles of human subjects protections applied in an opt-out, de-identified biobank. *Clinical and translational science.* 2010;3(1):42-48.
23. Roden DM, et al. Development of a large-scale de-identified DNA biobank to enable personalized medicine. *Clinical pharmacology and therapeutics.* 2008;84(3):362-369.
24. Das S, et al. Next-generation genotype imputation service and methods. *Nat Genet.* 2016;48(10):1284-1287.
25. McCarthy S, et al. A reference panel of 64,976 haplotypes for genotype imputation. *Nat Genet.* 2016;48(10):1279-1283.
26. Wu P, et al. Mapping ICD-10 and ICD-10-CM Codes to Phecodes: Workflow Development and Initial Evaluation. *JMIR Med Inform.* 2019;7(4):e14325.
27. Wei WQ, et al. Evaluating phecodes, clinical classification software, and ICD-9-CM codes for phenome-wide association studies in the electronic health record. *PLoS One.* 2017;12(7):e0175508.
28. Gottesman O, et al. The Electronic Medical Records and Genomics (eMERGE) Network: past, present, and future. *Genetics in medicine : official journal of the American College of Medical Genetics.* 2013;15(10):761-771.
29. McCarty CA, et al. The eMERGE Network: a consortium of biorepositories linked to electronic medical records data for conducting genomic studies. *BMC medical genomics.* 2011;4:13.
30. Kurki MI, et al. FinnGen: Unique genetic insights from combining isolated population and national health register data. *medRxiv.* 2022:2022.2003.2003.22271360.
31. Willer CJ, et al. METAL: fast and efficient meta-analysis of genomewide association scans. *Bioinformatics.* 2010;26(17):2190-2191.
32. Ge T, et al. Polygenic prediction via Bayesian regression and continuous shrinkage priors. *Nature communications.* 2019;10(1):1776.
33. Chang CC, et al. Second-generation PLINK: rising to the challenge of larger and richer datasets. *GigaScience.* 2015;4:7.
34. Manca R, et al. The neural signatures of psychoses in Alzheimer's disease: a neuroimaging genetics approach. *European archives of psychiatry and clinical neuroscience.* 2022.

35. Carroll RJ, et al. R PheWAS: data analysis and plotting tools for phenome-wide association studies in the R environment. *Bioinformatics.* 2014;30(16):2375-2376.
36. Simon N, et al. Regularization Paths for Cox's Proportional Hazards Model via Coordinate Descent. *J Stat Softw.* 2011;39(5):1-13.
37. Friedman J, et al. Regularization Paths for Generalized Linear Models via Coordinate Descent. *J Stat Softw.* 2010;33(1):1-22.
38. Welsh P, et al. Derivation and Validation of a 10-Year Risk Score for Symptomatic Abdominal Aortic Aneurysm: Cohort Study of Nearly 500 000 Individuals. *Circulation.* 2021;144(8):604-614.
39. Chaudhry R, et al. Use of a Web-based clinical decision support system to improve abdominal aortic aneurysm screening in a primary care practice. *J Eval Clin Pract.* 2012;18(3):666-670.
40. Hye RJ, et al. Leveraging the electronic medical record to implement an abdominal aortic aneurysm screening program. *J Vasc Surg.* 2014;59(6):1535-1542.
41. Eaton J, et al. Effect of visit length and a clinical decision support tool on abdominal aortic aneurysm screening rates in a primary care practice. *J Eval Clin Pract.* 2012;18(3):593-598.
42. Lee ES, et al. Implementation of an aortic screening program in clinical practice: implications for the Screen For Abdominal Aortic Aneurysms Very Efficiently (SAAAVE) Act. *J Vasc Surg.* 2009;49(5):1107-1111.
43. Anjorin AC, et al. Underutilization of Guideline-based Abdominal Aortic Aneurysm Screening in an Academic Health System. *Ann Vasc Surg.* 2022;83:184-194.
44. Pasley J. Predicting blood clots before they happen in pediatric patients. *VUMC Reporter.* May 28, 2021, 2021. https://news.vumc.org/2021/05/26/predicting-blood-clots-before-they-happen-in-pediatric-patients/.
45. Ulug P, et al. Surgery for small asymptomatic abdominal aortic aneurysms. *Cochrane Database Syst Rev.* 2020;7(7):Cd001835.
46. Dong H, et al. MR Elastography of Abdominal Aortic Aneurysms: Relationship to Aneurysm Events. *Radiology.* 2022;304(3):721-729.
47. Lorandon F, et al. Scannographic Study of Risk Factors of Abdominal Aortic Aneurysm Rupture. *Ann Vasc Surg.* 2021;73:27-36.
48. Jalalzadeh H, et al. Estimation of Abdominal Aortic Aneurysm Rupture Risk with Biomechanical Imaging Markers. *J Vasc Interv Radiol.* 2019;30(7):987-994.e984.
49. Hirata K, et al. Machine Learning to Predict the Rapid Growth of Small Abdominal Aortic Aneurysm. *J Comput Assist Tomogr.* 2020;44(1):37-42.
50. Ribieras AJ, et al. Racial disparities in presentation and outcomes for endovascular abdominal aortic aneurysm repair. *J Vasc Surg.* 2022.
51. Barshes NR, et al. Racial and ethnic disparities in abdominal aortic aneurysm evaluation and treatment rates in Texas. *J Vasc Surg.* 2022;76(1):141-148.e141.
52. Martin AR, et al. Clinical use of current polygenic risk scores may exacerbate health disparities. *Nature genetics.* 2019;51(4):584-591.
53. Lambert SA, et al. Towards clinical utility of polygenic risk scores. *Hum Mol Genet.* 2019;28(R2):R133-r142.

Quantifying factors that affect polygenic risk score performance across diverse ancestries and age groups for body mass index

Daniel Hui[1]*, Brenda Xiao[1]*, Ozan Dikilitas[2], Robert R. Freimuth[3], Marguerite R. Irvin[4], Gail P. Jarvik[5], Leah Kottyan[6], Iftikhar Kullo[7], Nita A. Limdi[8], Cong Liu[9], Yuan Luo[10], Bahram Namjou[11], Megan J. Puckelwartz[12], Daniel Schaid[13], Hemant Tiwari[14], Wei-Qi Wei[15], Shefali Verma[16], Dokyoon Kim[17], Marylyn D. Ritchie[18]**

[1]*Graduate Program in Genomics and Computational Biology, University of Pennsylvania, Philadelphia, PA, USA*

[2]*Department of Internal Medicine, Department of Cardiovascular Medicine, Clinician-Investigator Training Program, Mayo Clinic, Rochester MN*

[3]*Department of Artificial Intelligence and Informatics, Mayo Clinic, Rochester, MN, USA*

[4]*Department of Epidemiology, University of Alabama at Birmingham, Birmingham, AL, United States*

[5]*Departments of Medicine and Genome Sciences, University of Washington, Seattle WA, USA*

[6]*Center for Autoimmune Genomics and Etiology, Department of Pediatrics, University of Cincinnati, Cincinnati, OH, USA*

[7]*Division of Cardiovascular Diseases, Mayo Clinic, Rochester, MN 55905, USA*

[8]*Department of Neurology & Epidemiology, University of Alabama at Birmingham, Birmingham, AL, USA*

[9]*Department of Biomedical Informatics, Columbia University, New York, NY, USA*

[10]*Department of Preventive Medicine (Health and Biomedical Informatics), Northwestern University, Chicago, IL USA*

[11]*Department of Pediatrics, University of Cincinnati, Cincinnati, OH, USA*

[12]*Department of Pharmacology, Northwestern University, Chicago, IL USA*

[13]*Division of Biomedical Statistics and Informatics, Department of Health Sciences Research, Mayo Clinic, Rochester, MN 55905, USA*

[14]*Department of Biostatistics, University of Alabama at Birmingham, Birmingham, AL, United States*

[15]*Department of Biomedical Informatics, Vanderbilt University Medical Center, Nashville, TN, USA*

[16]*Department of Pathology and Laboratory Medicine, Perelman School of Medicine, University of Pennsylvania, Philadelphia, PA, USA*

[17]*Department of Biostatistics, Epidemiology and Informatics, Institute for Biomedical Informatics, Perelman School of Medicine, University of Pennsylvania, Philadelphia, PA, USA*

[18]*Department of Genetics, Institute for Biomedical Informatics, Perelman School of Medicine, University of Pennsylvania, Philadelphia, PA, USA*

Email: marylyn@pennmedicine.upenn.edu

*Equal contributions to the manuscript

**Corresponding author

Polygenic risk scores (PRS) have led to enthusiasm for precision medicine. However, it is well documented that PRS do not generalize across groups differing in ancestry or sample characteristics e.g., age. Quantifying performance of PRS across different groups of study participants, using genome-wide association study (GWAS) summary statistics from multiple ancestry groups and sample sizes, and using different linkage disequilibrium (LD) reference panels may clarify which factors are limiting PRS transferability. To evaluate these factors in the PRS generation process, we generated body mass index (BMI) PRS (PRS_{BMI}) in the Electronic Medical Records and Genomics (eMERGE) network (N=75,661). Analyses were conducted in two ancestry groups (European and African) and three age ranges (adult, teenagers, and children). For PRS_{BMI} calculations, we evaluated five LD reference panels and three sets of GWAS summary statistics of varying sample size and ancestry. PRS_{BMI} performance increased for both African and European ancestry individuals using cross-ancestry GWAS summary statistics compared to European-only summary statistics (6.3% and 3.7% relative R^2 increase, respectively, $p_{African}$=0.038, $p_{European}$=6.26x10^{-4}). The effects of LD reference panels were more pronounced in African ancestry study datasets. PRS_{BMI} performance degraded in children; R^2 was less than half of teenagers or adults. The effect of GWAS summary statistics sample size was small when modeled with the other factors. Additionally, the potential of using a PRS generated for one trait to predict risk for comorbid diseases is not well understood especially in the context of cross-ancestry analyses – we explored clinical comorbidities from the electronic health record associated with PRS_{BMI} and identified significant associations with type 2 diabetes and coronary atherosclerosis. In summary, this study quantifies the effects that ancestry, GWAS summary statistic sample size, and LD reference panel have on PRS performance, especially in cross-ancestry and age-specific analyses.

Keywords: polygenic risk scores (PRS), risk prediction, transferability, diversity

Introduction

Polygenic risk scores (PRS) provide individualized genetic estimates of a phenotype by aggregating genetic effects across hundreds or thousands of loci, typically from genome-wide association studies (GWAS). PRS are potentially a powerful source of increased prediction performance, even when combined with family history (1,2). However, in recent years it has become increasingly apparent that performance of PRS is substantially reduced when the ancestry of the individuals in whom prediction is being done differs from the ancestry of the individuals from the GWAS used to generate SNP weights used for PRS construction. For instance, when using GWAS from European ancestry individuals, the prediction accuracy of polygenic scores in individuals of African or Hispanic/Latino ancestry have a relative performance of 25% and 65% compared to performance in European ancestry individuals (3). Additionally, evidence exists suggesting that for some traits, such as adiposity traits, this disparity may be further exacerbated by environmental, demographic, or social risk factors (including age, physical activity, smoking status, and alcohol use (4–7)). For example, differences in the genetic architecture of body mass index (BMI) have been shown to differ between age groups (8–11). Thus, the performance of PRS for BMI is also affected by the age of the individuals used in the GWAS and the study data where the PRS is evaluated (12). Broad-sense heritability estimates for BMI in adults ranges from 40%-90% when estimated in adults of different cohorts even of homogeneous ancestry (13); even if heritability estimates are similar across populations, genetic architecture and enrichment for variants in different functional categories may still differ (14,15).

Several outstanding questions surrounding PRS, especially within the context of adiposity traits and BMI, warrant further investigation. For instance, when cross-ancestry summary statistics (i.e., those including individuals of multiple ancestry groups in the GWAS) are available, can they be used to improve prediction performance in individuals from one or more different ancestry groups? We need a more thorough evaluation of the potential prediction performance gain (or loss) in African ancestry individuals when cross-ancestry GWAS summary statistics are used to estimate the SNP weights. In addition, we need to improve our understanding of the impact of the composition of the linkage disequilibrium (LD) reference panel in combination with cross-ancestry GWAS summary statistics on PRS prediction performance. For prediction of BMI specifically, how does prediction performance differ for individuals in different age groups, especially those who are not adults (i.e., less than age 18)?

Additionally, how much these different variables impact the PRS performance when considered together is important to explore. Developing a deeper understanding of which features (ancestry of individuals in the GWAS, ancestry of the individuals generating the LD references panel, ancestry of the study data, age of the study data) have the greatest impact of PRS performance will help the field develop future studies and strategies around clinical risk prediction with PRS. The degree to which increased GWAS sample size increases prediction performance regardless of these other factors is also important to determine. Finally, there is potential for using a PRS generated for one trait to predict risk for comorbid traits. Understanding how much the different elements of PRS generation affects associations with clinical comorbidities of obesity is of great importance for precision medicine.

We comprehensively investigated the influence of these factors on the performance of PRS using the Electronic Medical Records and Genomics (eMERGE) Network dataset. eMERGE is an NIH funded consortium that combines participants from multiple electronic health record (EHR) linked biobanks (16). In the present study, we included 75,661 individuals of diverse ancestry and age (14% African ancestry, 55% female, and 12% children age < 13). These individuals were from the eMERGE III imputed array dataset (N=83,717) (dbGaP Study: phs001584.v2.p2), estimated European or African ancestry, and had BMI measurements available. For these analyses, we used published BMI GWAS summary statistics from the GIANT (Genetic Investigation of ANthropometric Traits) consortium, an international consortium that primarily studies anthropometric traits, which included participants (max N=339,224, mean N per variant=226,960) from European, African, and Asian ancestry groups (17). We also used summary statistics from a European ancestry BMI GWAS (18) in UK Biobank (UKBB) individuals (N=339,721), which was conducted using both the full sample size of the European ancestry UKBB, as well as after down-sampling to the same number of individuals in the GIANT GWAS. This comparison allowed us to better evaluate whether it was the ancestry composition or the sample size of the dataset where the GWAS summary statistics were derived that affected the results of the PRS performance. We calculated PRS for BMI (PRS_{BMI}) across 90 different combinations of analyses (described more in Methods) – six different groupings based on ancestry and age, five different LD reference panels (of varying ancestry and from three different cohorts), and the three mentioned sets of GWAS summary statistics. We then statistically compared the different sets of analyses to see what factors most influence PRS_{BMI} performance across various groupings of individuals based on ancestry and age. Lastly, we also tested the association of the best performing PRS_{BMI} with common comorbidities across ancestry groups to identify the clinical relevance of the PRS_{BMI} in phenotypes derived from an Electronic Health Record (EHR). Investigation of these variables elucidates our understanding of the factors that affect PRS performance and transferability across ancestries and populations, especially within the context of BMI, as well as the potential of using PRS_{BMI} to predict risk for comorbid disease.

Methods

Overall study design

The electronic Medical Records and Genomics (eMERGE) network dataset is an NIH funded consortium that combines participants from multiple electronic health record (EHR) linked biobanks. In this study, we included 75,661 individuals with available genetic and phenotypic data. The individuals in the eMERGE dataset include multiple ancestry groups – genetically inferred ancestry was assigned by the eMERGE consortium (16) – and a large age distribution (14% African ancestry, 19% less than age 18, Figure 1). Briefly, we calculated PRS_{BMI} for all individuals within each combination where the following elements of the model varied: 1) LD panels that differed in ancestry, 2) GWAS summary statistics with variable ancestry composition, and 3) GWAS summary statistics for two different sample sizes. The details for each of these are provided more below. The data was also split by ancestry and age group, and we statistically compared PRS_{BMI} performance between all the different groups – in total, 90 sets of PRS_{BMI} were calculated separately and then compared. We first estimated the effect and significance of each variable (i.e., ancestry of GWAS summary statistics and test data, LD panel ancestry, size of GWAS summary statistics, and age of test individuals) on PRS performance. Next, we estimated how much each variable affects PRS_{BMI} performance when all are modeled together, and finally we analyzed the potential clinical associations by testing the PRS_{BMI} for association with common comorbid conditions from the EHR. For the primary results related to LD panel or ancestry of summary statistics and test data, we restricted analyses to adults as the other age groups were limited in sample size. In the following sections, we describe all these elements in more detail.

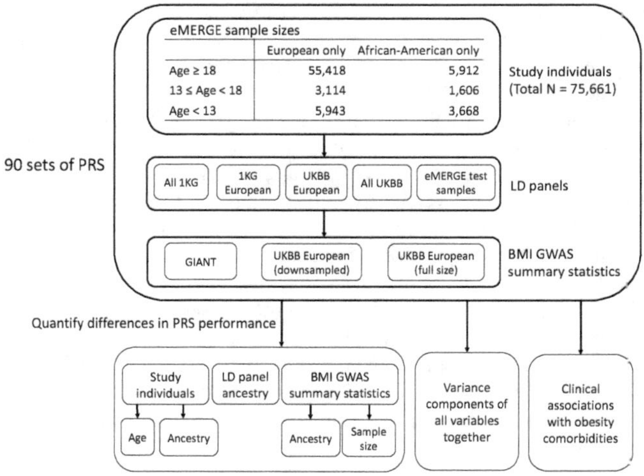

Figure 1. Flowchart of project. Max size of LD panel was 5,000 individuals. UK Biobank (UKBB) European GWAS summary statistics were down-sampled to the mean sample size per variant of GIANT (N=226,960), full size of UKBB European was N=377,921. 1000 Genomes is abbreviated as 1KG.

Summary statistics to generate PRS_{BMI}

We obtained published GWAS summary statistics from the GIANT consortium (17) to use as one set of BMI GWAS summary statistics. Up to 322,154 adults of European ancestry, as well as an additional 17,072 adults of non-European ancestry (adults of African, East Asian, and South Asian ancestry), were included in the GIANT GWAS analysis.

For the second set of summary statistics, we performed a GWAS in the individuals of European ancestry from the UK Biobank (UKBB). Individuals were first filtered by low quality samples (sex mismatch between genetically inferred and self-reported, variant missingness > 5%), relatedness (no 2nd degree relatives or higher), and within the White British ancestry subset (with these individuals being defined by UKBB and selected based on self-reports and genetically determined ancestry) (18); a total of 377,921 individuals initially remained. Variants were filtered on imputation quality score (using the INFO metric (19)) > 0.30, and minor allele frequency > 1% within this subset of individuals. In addition, we generated a second set of GWAS summary statistics from the UKBB, where we randomly down-sampled individuals to the sample size in the GIANT GWAS dataset (N=226,960). In each UKBB GWAS, data processing and modeling were performed similarly as in the GIANT GWAS – summary statistics were calculated using linear regression, with age, age^2, sex, and the first 5 genetic principal components (PCs) included as covariates. BMI, defined as weight in kilograms divided by squared height in meters, was first inverse-rank normal transformed.

After calculation of BMI GWAS summary statistics in each of the two datasets of UKBB individuals of European ancestry, we harmonized variants across all datasets used (UKBB, eMERGE, GIANT, and 1000 Genomes Phase 3). For the remainder of downstream analyses, we kept only those variants that were present in all datasets, and additionally excluded any strand-ambiguous SNPs (alleles A/T or C/G), and retained only biallelic variants; in total, 2,014,457 variants were retained for analyses.

LD reference panels

Five different LD reference panels were used for each set of PRS_{BMI} calculations: 1) all of 1000 Genomes ($1KG_{All}$) (N=2,504), 2) 1000 Genomes European ancestry ($1KG_{EUR}$) (N=503), 3) 5,000 randomly selected European ancestry individuals from the UK Biobank ($UKBB_{EUR}$), 4) 5,000 randomly selected individuals from all of UK Biobank ($UKBB_{All}$), and 5) up to 5,000 randomly selected individuals from the dataset for which PRS_{BMI} were being calculated for in the eMERGE dataset (referred to as test data henceforward). These panels were chosen to test for differences in ancestry distribution and sample size on PRS performance.

Statistical methods

PRS software

For each comparison set, PRS_{BMI} were calculated using pruning and thresholding method via PRSice v2.1.9 (20). We chose to use PRSice due to the flexibility it provides in choosing external LD panels and allowed us to easily include multi-ancestry LD panels in our analyses. Default parameters were used in all analyses (clumping performed in 250 kb windows using an R^2 of 0.1, p-value step size of 0.00005 between p-values of .0001 up to .10 and step size of .0001 between p-values of .10 up to .50).

Statistical comparisons

Incremental R^2 for PRS_{BMI} was calculated by subtracting the R^2 using a model with only the covariates from the R^2 of the model using the covariates and the PRS_{BMI} (the default option in PRSice). Statistical differences between model performances from different iterations were determined using the Wilcoxon rank-sum test to compare the distributions of the squared residuals generated from the model for all individuals in the iteration; for comparisons between the same set of individuals, the paired Wilcoxon rank-sum test was used. When testing which of the five LD panels performed the best, we used a Bonferroni-corrected threshold of 0.05/10 = 0.005 (ten comparisons between five LD panels). When comparing the best performing PRS_{BMI} across ancestries and summary statistics using their best LD panel, we used a Bonferroni threshold of 0.05/25 = 0.002 (25 comparisons between the five LD panels used).

Proportion of variance explained by each individual variable

We modeled all evaluated features together in the following linear regression model:

$$R^2 \sim LD\ panel + N_{Sumstat} + Age_{Test} + Ancestry_{Sumstat} + Ancestry_{Test} + Ancestry_{Sumstat} * Ancestry_{Test}$$

Where the *Sumstat* subscript is defined as a set of GWAS summary statistics, and the *Test* subscript is defined as a set of test individuals that PRS prediction is being assessed in. We quantified the variance in R^2 that could be explained by each of these different variables using type II sum of squares from ANOVA. The sum of squares of variables involving ancestry were summed together; an interaction term between summary statistics ancestry and test data ancestry was included to identify whether the ancestry of summary statistics and test data matched.

Association of PRS_{BMI} with comorbidities

We selected the ten most frequent Phecodes (21) from the EHR data in the eMERGE dataset (which includes obesity as a positive control) to test their association with the PRS_{BMI}. For each Phecode, individuals were classified as a case for the condition if there was at least one occurrence of the respective Phecode in their EHR record; individuals were classified as a control for that condition if there was no occurrence of the Phecode. This classification is a rule-of-one instance of a Phecode to define case status. For each eMERGE ancestry subgroup, we selected the best performing PRS_{BMI} i.e., the PRS_{BMI} with the highest R^2, and tested the association of the PRS_{BMI} with these ten clinical conditions using a logistic regression model. PRS_{BMI} was first mean-centered and standard deviation was set to 1. Sex, age, age^2, and the first five genetic PCs were included as covariates.

Data visualization

The 'ggplot2' R package was used for plotting, with the 'geom_signif' package used to include significance bars. The association results were plotted using PheWAS-View (22).

Results

Effect of LD panel

For adults of African ancestry, when using the down-sampled UKBB GWAS summary statistics, using either cross-ancestry or African ancestry test data LD panels significantly improved PRS_{BMI} performance compared to European ancestry LD panels (Figure 2). When using the UKBB summary statistics, the top PRS_{BMI} R^2 was 0.0140 using the test data as LD panel, while the second-best performing LD panel (UKBB European) had an R^2 of 0.0109 ($p = 4.94 \times 10^{-20}$). When using the GIANT summary statistics, the top PRS_{BMI} R^2 was 0.0149 using $1KG_{All}$ as the reference panel. The PRS_{BMI} calculated using the best European ancestry panel ($1KG_{EUR}$) resulted in a R^2 of 0.0141, but this difference between these two reference panels was not Bonferroni significant (p = 0.037). However, the $1KG_{all}$ LD panel performed significantly better than the two UKBB LD panels ($UKBB_{All}$: $R^2 = 0.0134$, $p = 3.65 \times 10^{-5}$; UKBB European: $R^2 = 0.0128$, p =

$3.65x10^{-9}$). The test data LD panel performed the second-best with an R^2 of 0.0142, and significantly outperformed the UKBB European LD panel ($p = 4.78x10^{-5}$). For adults of European ancestry, we observed more significant differences in performance when using the GIANT summary statistics compared to the down-sampled UKBB summary statistics. The $1KG_{All}$ LD panel performed the best with a R^2 of 0.0612. It also significantly outperformed all other LD panels ($1KG_{EUR}$: $R^2 = 0.0560$, $p = 5.54x10^{-104}$; Test data: $R^2 = 0.0564$, $p = 6.50x10^{-67}$; $UKBB_{All}$: $R^2 = 0.0561$, $8.09x10^{-107}$; $UKBB_{EUR}$: $R^2 = 0.0561$, $p = 3.02x10^{-77}$). We note that this increase was larger when using the GIANT summary statistics but was still present when using the UKBB summary statistics. When using the UKBB summary statistics, the choice of LD panel had a much smaller impact on prediction performance. While the $1KG_{All}$ LD panel performed the best, the difference in performance was much less significant between the next best performing LD panel ($R^2_{1KG_{All}} = 0.0590$, $R^2_{UKBB_{All}} = 0.0583$, $p = 3.48x10^{-4}$). The difference between the best and worst performing scores – LD panel using 1KG all versus 1KG European – was also much less significant ($p= 1.15x10^{-12}$). These results suggest that the choice of LD panel particularly matters when calculating PRS_{BMI} using cross-ancestry GWAS, or for African ancestry individuals when the GWAS summary statistics are derived from European ancestry individuals.

However, we did observe a slight decrease in the impact of the choice of LD panel when using the full UKBB summary statistics for adults; again, the largest differences were observed in adults of African ancestry, but differences in performance across LD panels were not as significant. The test LD panel performed second best with the $1KG_{EUR}$ LD panel performing best ($R^2_{Test} = 0.0197$, $R^2_{1KG_{EUR}} = 0.0200$, $p = 0.18$). The $1KG_{All}$ LD panel was the worst performing LD panel with an R^2 of 0.0185, and this difference between the $1KG_{EUR}$ LD panel was significant after multiple hypothesis correction ($p = 5.08x10^{-7}$).

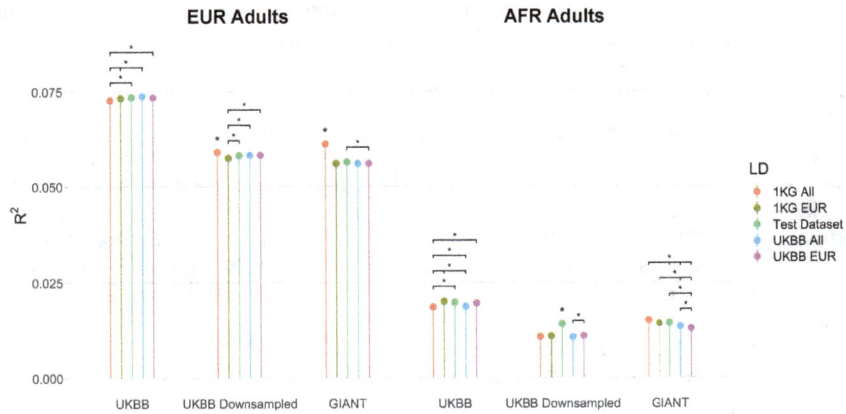

Figure 2. PRS R^2 values across all runs in adults. Asterisks without bars indicate significantly different R^2 values between the other 4 LD panels used. Bars are present for significant differences between specific R^2 values.

Effect of summary statistics and ancestry of test data

As expected, the R^2 values of the PRS_{BMI} were significantly higher when calculated for European ancestry adults than adults of African ancestry, even when using the cross-ancestry GIANT summary statistics (Figure 2). When using the GIANT summary statistics, the best performing PRS_{BMI} in adults of European ancestry had an R^2 of 0.0612, which was significantly higher than the R^2 from the best performing PRS_{BMI} in African ancestry adults ($R^2 = 0.0149$, $p < 4.9x10^{-324}$).

In African ancestry adults, the R^2 when using the GIANT summary statistics was higher than the R^2 when using the down-sampled UKBB summary statistics with their respective best LD panel (GIANT ($1KG_{All}$ LD panel): $R^2 = 0.0149$, UKBB (test data LD panel): $R^2 = 0.0140$; $p = 0.038$). This difference was not statistically significant after multiple hypothesis correction. However, the GIANT summary statistics with the $1KG_{All}$ LD panel did significantly outperform the UKBB summary statistics with all other LD panels. When keeping the LD panel constant, the PRS_{BMI} calculated using the GIANT summary statistics resulted in higher R^2 than using the UKBB summary statistics for all LD panels except for the test data LD panel, and this difference was statistically significant for the $1KG_{All}$ ($p = 1.55x10^{-33}$), $1KG_{EUR}$ ($p = 6.78x10^{-18}$), and $UKBB_{All}$ ($p = 1.28x10^{-15}$) LD panels. Somewhat surprisingly, we observed higher R^2 values for European ancestry adults when using the cross-ancestry GIANT summary statistics versus the down-sampled European UKBB summary statistics ($R^2_{GIANT} = 0.0612$ versus $R^2_{UKBB} = 0.0590$), with this difference being statistically significant ($p = 6.26x10^{-4}$); the best performing LD panel for both set of summary statistics was $1KG_{All}$.

We also compared prediction performance in all individuals using the full (N=377,921) European UKBB GWAS versus the European UKBB GWAS down-sampled to GIANT's sample size (N=226,960) (Figure 2, Supplemental Table 1). For consistency, UKBB European individuals were used for the European test ancestry comparisons, and for the African ancestry comparisons the test sets (i.e., African ancestry LD panels) were used as LD panels. Uniformly across test ancestry and age groups, we observed higher and statistically significant increases in R^2.

Prediction performance across different age groups

Across different ancestries and summary statistics, we broadly observed similar R^2 values for adults and teenagers, with substantially reduced performance in children (Supplemental Figure 1). R^2 values in children were consistently less than half of that in adults and teenagers, with differences in R^2 values for adults and teenagers being minimal (except in the case of African ancestry individuals using the GIANT summary statistics, with teenagers having more than double the R^2 of adults). Somewhat surprisingly, teenagers consistently had higher R^2 than adults across all analyses, although these differences were much less significant than those compared with children.

Proportion of variance explained by each assessed factor

While we observed significant differences due to ancestry, age, and number of individuals used to calculate summary statistics, we aimed to quantify the effect of these different variables on PRS_{BMI} performance when considered together (Table 1). We observed that 89.5% of the variance in PRS_{BMI} R^2 could be explained using these variables, indicating that the majority of the effects of LD panel, ancestry, age, and sample size could be explained through linear relationships with PRS_{BMI} R^2. In the context of these comparisons, the ancestry of the summary statistics or test data accounts for 55.1% of the variance explained in PRS_{BMI} R^2. Choice of LD panel and age of test individuals accounted for similar amounts of variance explained in PRS_{BMI} R^2 (16.5% and 15.9%, respectively), while the number of individuals used to calculate the GWAS summary statistics only accounted for 1.9% of variance explained in PRS_{BMI} R^2. Per previous sections, while number of individuals used for summary statistics resulted in significant differences in PRS_{BMI} performance, its overall impact when modeled jointly with all the other factors in the context of these analyses seemed to be small.

Variable	Proportion of explained variance
Ancestry of summary statistics or test data	0.5510
Choice of LD reference panel	0.1650
Age of test individuals	0.1590
N individuals used to calculate summary statistics	0.0195
Residuals (unexplained variance)	0.1050

Table 1. Proportion of variance in R^2 that can be explained by different variables using type II sum of squares from ANOVA.

PRS_{BMI} *association with comorbid traits*

To determine whether the PRS_{BMI} was associated with clinical comorbidities, we performed a Phenome-Wide Association Study for ten clinical conditions (Supplemental Table 2, described more in Methods). Here, the PRS_{BMI} was tested for association with diagnosis codes (Phecodes) to evaluate whether the polygenic background for BMI associates with these clinical diagnoses. The PRS_{BMI} was significantly associated with several of the most frequent Phecodes in eMERGE, particularly in European adults (Figure 3a). As expected, obesity had the strongest association with PRS_{BMI} in all ancestry groups ($p_{EUR} < 4.9x10^{-324}$; $p_{AFR} = 5.17x10^{-8}$); this was a positive control. In European ancestry individuals, the best performing PRS_{BMI} was also significantly positively associated with type 2 diabetes ($p_{EUR} = 1.04x10^{-102}$), essential hypertension ($p_{EUR} = 7.12x10^{-56}$), coronary atherosclerosis ($p_{EUR} = 3.61x10^{-26}$), hyperlipidemia ($p_{EUR} = 4.38x10^{-16}$), depression ($p_{EUR} = 1.95x10^{-13}$), hypercholesteremia ($p_{EUR} = 3.64x10^{-15}$), asthma ($p_{EUR} = 3.13x10^{-13}$), and diverticulosis ($p_{EUR} = 0.0017$). These associations were less statistically significant in African ancestry individuals, which had much lower sample size, and many associations were no longer significant after Bonferroni correction. Only type 2 diabetes ($p_{AFR} = 1.2x10^{-5}$) and coronary atherosclerosis ($p_{AFR} = 0.001$) were significantly associated with the PRS_{BMI} in African ancestry adults. We also looked at the prevalence of each condition per PRS quintile for the most significantly associated conditions (Figure 3b). The case prevalence generally increased in higher PRS_{BMI} quintile groups for conditions significantly associated with the PRS_{BMI}, a trend matching the results we obtained from the association analysis. Phenotypes with downward trends were not significantly associated with PRS_{BMI}, and low sample sizes in earlier quintile groups may have contributed to this seemingly decreasing prevalence. We performed similar analyses in teens and children but identified no statistically significant associations (results not shown). The much smaller sample sizes of the Phecodes in these age groups may have also contributed to the lack of statistically significant results – most of these diagnoses are adult-onset conditions.

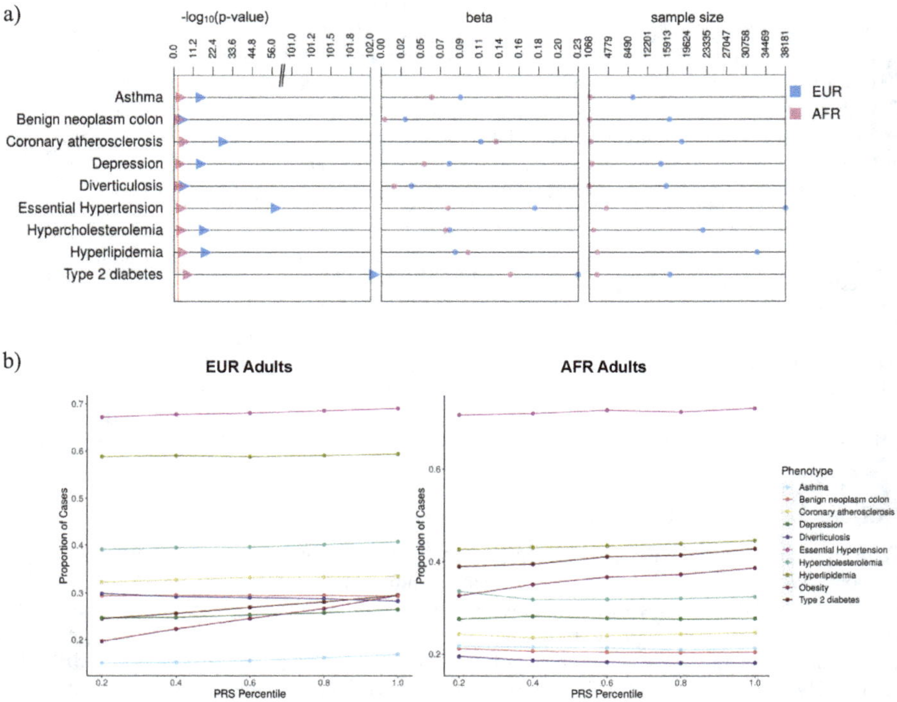

Figure 3. a) Best PRS_{BMI} associations with top 9 most prevalent conditions overall in eMERGE adults. Note the association with obesity is not included in the plot because the p-value in European ancestry individuals was $p_{EUR} < 4.9 \times 10^{-324}$ which was off the scale of the plot. b) Prevalence plots of significantly associated conditions in eMERGE adults by best performing PRS quintile

Discussion

Somewhat unintuitively, African ancestry LD panels performed best for African ancestry individuals, regardless of whether European ancestry or cross-ancestry GWAS summary statistics were used. We observed minimal impact of the choice of LD panel when both test data and summary statistics were of European ancestry. These results suggest that as long as either the test data or GWAS summary statistics are of similar ancestry, or the test data and LD panel are of similar ancestry, the difference in PRS performance may be minimal as compared to if all the GWAS summary statistics, test data, and LD panel are all of the same ancestry. We also observed significantly decreased PRS performance in children compared to adults and teens, with the GWAS used in this study being conducted on adult populations.

While the findings in this study highlight many important strategies for performing PRS in different ancestry and age groups, there are limitations that should be addressed in future studies.

First, inclusion of analyses that evaluate how different proportions of non-European ancestry individuals affect the prediction performance of PRS would be useful. The GIANT summary statistics we used in this study are only about 6% non-European ancestry. It may be useful to see how the PRS prediction performance changes in both non-European and European ancestry datasets as a function of the proportion of non-European ancestry samples included in the GWAS. Such analyses may be possible by combining African ancestry individuals from these different datasets. These analyses will be possible once larger datasets that include non-European ancestry cohorts are publicly available or could be tested by analyzing other traits with larger African ancestry GWAS. Future analyses could also include sex-stratified GWAS and comparison sets to evaluate the influence of sex on PRS_{BMI} performance. Finally, repeating these types of analyses with different PRS methods would be useful as novel PRS methods are being developed on a regular basis, many of which incorporate ancestry in different ways.

Overall, this study demonstrates the importance of expanding non-European ancestry data resources for PRS, specifically in the generation of GWAS summary statistics and LD reference panels. Failure to do so reduces the impact of PRS in diverse populations and increases the potential for continued health disparities, especially in precision medicine where genetics is being integrated into clinical care.

Description of supplemental data

Supplemental data include one figure and two tables (https://upenn.box.com/s/7cec571ltjkcyv409vwi7w9t0stkvo12).

Declaration of author competing interests

Authors have no competing interests to declare.

Data and code availability

Code supporting the current study are available from the corresponding author on request.

Acknowledgements

eMERGE Network (Phase III): This phase of the eMERGE Network was initiated and funded by the NHGRI through the following grants: U01HG8657 (Group Health Cooperative/University of Washington); U01HG8685 (Brigham and Women's Hospital); U01HG8672 (Vanderbilt University Medical Center); U01HG8666 (Cincinnati Children's Hospital Medical Center); U01HG6379 (Mayo Clinic); U01HG8679 (Geisinger Clinic); U01HG8680 (Columbia University Health Sciences); U01HG8684 (Children's Hospital of Philadelphia); U01HG8673 (Northwestern University); U01HG8701 (Vanderbilt University Medical Center serving as the Coordinating Center); U01HG8676 (Partners Healthcare/Broad Institute); and U01HG8664 (Baylor College of Medicine). UK Biobank: All data for this cohort pertained to project 32133 – "Integration of multi-organ imaging phenotypes, clinical phenotypes, and genomic data". MDR would also like to acknowledge NIH AI077505.

References

1. Truong B, Zhou X, Shin J, Li J, van der Werf JHJ, Le TD, et al. Efficient polygenic risk scores for biobank scale data by exploiting phenotypes from inferred relatives. Nat Commun. 2020 Jun 17;11(1):3074.
2. Margaux L.A. Hujoel, Po-Ru Loh, Benjamin M. Neale, Alkes L. Price. Incorporating family history of disease improves polygenic risk scores in diverse populations. Available from: https://www.biorxiv.org/content/10.1101/2021.04.15.439975v1

3. Martin AR, Kanai M, Kamatani Y, Okada Y, Neale BM, Daly MJ. Clinical use of current polygenic risk scores may exacerbate health disparities. Nat Genet. 2019 Apr;51(4):584–91.
4. Rask-Andersen M, Karlsson T, Ek WE, Johansson Å. Gene-environment interaction study for BMI reveals interactions between genetic factors and physical activity, alcohol consumption and socioeconomic status. PLoS Genet. 2017 Sep;13(9):e1006977.
5. Robinson MR, English G, Moser G, Lloyd-Jones LR, Triplett MA, Zhu Z, et al. Genotype-covariate interaction effects and the heritability of adult body mass index. Nat Genet. 2017 Aug;49(8):1174–81.
6. Sulc J, Mounier N, Günther F, Winkler T, Wood AR, Frayling TM, et al. Quantification of the overall contribution of gene-environment interaction for obesity-related traits. Nat Commun. 2020 Mar 13;11(1):1385.
7. Justice AE, Winkler TW, Feitosa MF, Graff M, Fisher VA, Young K, et al. Genome-wide meta-analysis of 241,258 adults accounting for smoking behaviour identifies novel loci for obesity traits. Nat Commun. 2017 Apr 26;8:14977.
8. Helgeland Ø, Vaudel M, Juliusson PB, Lingaas Holmen O, Juodakis J, Bacelis J, et al. Genome-wide association study reveals dynamic role of genetic variation in infant and early childhood growth. Nat Commun. 2019 Oct 1;10(1):4448.
9. Vogelezang S, Bradfield JP, Ahluwalia TS, Curtin JA, Lakka TA, Grarup N, et al. Novel loci for childhood body mass index and shared heritability with adult cardiometabolic traits. PLoS Genet. 2020 Oct;16(10):e1008718.
10. Couto Alves A, De Silva NMG, Karhunen V, Sovio U, Das S, Taal HR, et al. GWAS on longitudinal growth traits reveals different genetic factors influencing infant, child, and adult BMI. Sci Adv. 2019 Sep;5(9):eaaw3095.
11. Choh AC, Lee M, Kent JW, Diego VP, Johnson W, Curran JE, et al. Gene-by-age effects on BMI from birth to adulthood: the Fels Longitudinal Study. Obes Silver Spring Md. 2014 Mar;22(3):875–81.
12. Mostafavi H, Harpak A, Agarwal I, Conley D, Pritchard JK, Przeworski M. Variable prediction accuracy of polygenic scores within an ancestry group. eLife. 2020 Jan 30;9:e48376.
13. Elks CE, den Hoed M, Zhao JH, Sharp SJ, Wareham NJ, Loos RJF, et al. Variability in the heritability of body mass index: a systematic review and meta-regression. Front Endocrinol. 2012;3:29.
14. Galinsky KJ, Reshef YA, Finucane HK, Loh PR, Zaitlen N, Patterson NJ, et al. Estimating cross-population genetic correlations of causal effect sizes. Genet Epidemiol. 2019 Mar;43(2):180–8.
15. Shi H, Gazal S, Kanai M, Koch EM, Schoech AP, Siewert KM, et al. Population-specific causal disease effect sizes in functionally important regions impacted by selection. Nat Commun. 2021 Feb 17;12(1):1098.
16. Stanaway IB, Hall TO, Rosenthal EA, Palmer M, Naranbhai V, Knevel R, et al. The eMERGE genotype set of 83,717 subjects imputed to ~40 million variants genome wide and association with the herpes zoster medical record phenotype. Genet Epidemiol. 2019 Feb;43(1):63–81.
17. Locke AE, Kahali B, Berndt SI, Justice AE, Pers TH, Day FR, et al. Genetic studies of body mass index yield new insights for obesity biology. Nature. 2015 Feb 12;518(7538):197–206.
18. Bycroft C, Freeman C, Petkova D, Band G, Elliott LT, Sharp K, et al. The UK Biobank resource with deep phenotyping and genomic data. Nature. 2018 Oct;562(7726):203–9.
19. Howie BN, Donnelly P, Marchini J. A flexible and accurate genotype imputation method for the next generation of genome-wide association studies. PLoS Genet. 2009 Jun;5(6):e1000529.
20. Euesden J, Lewis CM, O'Reilly PF. PRSice: Polygenic Risk Score software. Bioinforma Oxf Engl. 2015 May 1;31(9):1466–8.
21. Wu P, Gifford A, Meng X, Li X, Campbell H, Varley T, et al. Mapping ICD-10 and ICD-10-CM Codes to Phecodes: Workflow Development and Initial Evaluation. JMIR Med Inform. 2019 Nov 29;7(4):e14325.
22. Pendergrass SA, Dudek SM, Crawford DC, Ritchie MD. Visually integrating and exploring high throughput Phenome-Wide Association Study (PheWAS) results using PheWAS-View. BioData Min. 2012 Jun 8;5(1):5.

Polygenic resilience score may be sensitive to preclinical Alzheimer's disease changes

Jaclyn M. Eissman[1,2], Greyson Wells[1], Omair A. Khan[3], Dandan Liu[3], Vladislav A. Petyuk[4], Katherine A. Gifford[1], Logan Dumitrescu[1,2], Angela L. Jefferson[1], and Timothy J. Hohman[1,2†]

[1]*Vanderbilt Memory and Alzheimer's Center, Vanderbilt University Medical Center, Nashville, TN 37212, USA*

[2]*Vanderbilt Genetics Institute, Vanderbilt University Medical Center, Nashville, TN 37212, USA*

[3]*Department of Biostatistics, Vanderbilt University Medical Center, Nashville, TN 37212, USA*

[4]*Biological Sciences Division and Environmental Molecular Sciences Laboratory, Pacific Northwest National Laboratory, Richland, WA 99354, USA*

[†]*Email: timothy.j.hohman@vumc.org*

Late-onset Alzheimer's disease (LOAD) is a polygenic disorder with a long prodromal phase, making early diagnosis challenging. Twin studies estimate LOAD as 60-80% heritable, and while common genetic variants can account for 30% of this heritability, nearly 70% remains "missing". Polygenic risk scores (PRS) leverage combined effects of many loci to predict LOAD risk, but often lack sensitivity to preclinical disease changes, limiting clinical utility. Our group has built and published on a resilience phenotype to model better-than-expected cognition give amyloid pathology burden and hypothesized it may assist in preclinical polygenic risk prediction. Thus, we built a LOAD PRS and a resilience PRS and evaluated both in predicting cognition in a dementia-free cohort (N=254). The LOAD PRS had a significant main effect on baseline memory (β=-0.18, P=1.68E-03). Both the LOAD PRS (β=-0.03, P=1.19E-03) and the resilience PRS (β=0.02, P=0.03) had significant main effects on annual memory decline. The resilience PRS interacted with CSF Aβ on baseline memory (β=-6.04E-04, P=0.02), whereby it predicted baseline memory among Aβ+ individuals (β=0.44, P=0.01) but not among Aβ- individuals (β=0.06, P=0.46). Excluding *APOE* from PRS resulted in mainly LOAD PRS associations attenuating, but notably the resilience PRS interaction with CSF Aβ and selective prediction among Aβ+ individuals was consistent. Although the resilience PRS is currently somewhat limited in scope from the phenotype's cross-sectional nature, our results suggest that the resilience PRS may be a promising tool in assisting in preclinical disease risk prediction among dementia-free and Aβ+ individuals, though replication and fine-tuning are needed.

Keywords: Alzheimer's disease, polygenic risk, resilience, preclinical, cognition

1. Introduction

Late-onset Alzheimer's disease (LOAD) is a highly polygenic disorder, characterized by a neuropathological cascade resulting in neurodegeneration and cognitive impairment.[1] Notably, LOAD is characterized by a long prodromal phase in which pathology begins to accumulate prior to the onset of clinical disease. The prodromal stage thus represents decades of pathological changes before cognitive deficits are detected (e.g., dementia), making early clinical dementia diagnosis quite challenging,[1] yet imperative. Additionally, LOAD is a highly heritable trait, with twin studies estimating LOAD heritability to be 60-80%,[2,3] though the source for much of the genetic variation driving LOAD heritability has yet to be elucidated.[2,3] Genome-wide association studies (GWAS) have been integral in beginning to uncover narrow-sense heritability, defined as the additive genetic component of heritability. As of 2022, LOAD GWAS have identified and replicated 33 risk and protective loci.[2,4] However, the effect sizes of known LOAD GWAS loci are small to moderate,[5] accounting for ~8% of total LOAD heritability, with ~6% out of this ~8% coming from the *APOE* ε2 and ε4 risk and protective alleles.[5] Furthermore, studies have estimated the portion of LOAD narrow-sense heritability driven by common variants in the population, including and in addition to *APOE*. For example, Ridge and colleagues calculated that ~30% of LOAD phenotypic variance can be explained by a summation of effects of common GWAS variants,[5] suggesting a substantial heritable component remains unexplained or missing.

In recent years, LOAD polygenic risk scores (PRS) have leveraged the effects of multiple genetic loci to predict LOAD risk, but these PRS have not had expected clinical utility. One reason is that LOAD PRS are often built from case/control GWAS, which may represent later-stage disease processes, resulting in a loss of sensitivity when applied to preclinical disease.[6] Thus, LOAD PRS may be most beneficial in identifying symptomatic MCI or LOAD cases.[6] At the same time, some studies have found that LOAD PRS can be built in a sensitive manner to predict MCI or LOAD risk in younger, dementia-free individuals.[7,8] Yet, it also remains unclear if LOAD PRS hold more predictive power than simply predicting genetic risk from *APOE* genotype alone. Many studies have found that LOAD PRS hold predictive power for LOAD risk above and beyond *APOE* genotype,[9,10] while other studies have found that *APOE* genotype is still the best predictor.[6,11]

While neuropathology is a hallmark of LOAD and other related disorders, it is notable that a subset of individuals can maintain normal cognition in the face of neuropathology. In fact, ~30% of elderly adults who meet NIA-AA Reagan neuropathological criteria for AD at autopsy remain cognitively unimpaired throughout life.[12,13] These elderly individuals are characterized as "resilient" in frameworks of cognitive reserve and resilience.[14,15] Our group has defined a continuous measure of resilience, representing better-than-expected cognition given amyloid pathology burden, and leveraged this measure for genomic analysis.[16] The purpose of our original resilience GWAS was to identify common genetic variants that relate to cognition in the face of amyloid. By design, the residual metric of resilience is not correlated with amyloid, but is strongly predictive of future memory performance among people who are Aβ+.[16,17] Notably, we found resilience to be 20-25% heritable,[17] and found it has a genetic architecture distinct from that of clinical AD.[17]

However, to our knowledge, very few studies have examined polygenic resilience scores for complex traits, but these few have laid a framework for polygenic resilience scores as a tool to study complex, heritable traits. In 2021, Hess and colleagues created a method of calculating a "polygenic resilience score" for schizophrenia. In brief, this method takes marginal SNP effects from a trait, builds a weighted summary score from these SNP associations, and then selects the controls and the cases with the highest scores.[18] Hou and colleagues applied this method to look at LOAD in the context of resilience and observed that a higher polygenic resilience score was associated with lower LOAD risk penetrance among high-risk LOAD individuals.[19] A caveat of Hou and colleague's study is that their findings attenuated when only examining their score among high-risk *APOE* ε4 carriers, and Hou et al. reiterates that PRS contributions above and beyond *APOE* is mixed in the literature.[19]

Additionally, a limitation of this polygenic resilience score method is that it uses trait-based GWAS and binning to determine "resilient" individuals, limiting the scope of the analysis.

We felt we could extend the polygenic resilience score framework by 1) leveraging our continuous, quantitative resilience phenotype 2) clarifying if a resilience PRS could predict risk above and beyond *APOE* 3) examine the relationship of a resilience PRS with amyloid pathology, which has been scarcely analyzed in LOAD PRS studies. Thus, we generated a LOAD[4] PRS and a cognitive resilience[17] PRS. In a dementia-free cohort, we assessed the association of each PRS with baseline memory and with annual memory decline and tested to see if amyloid modified the association of each PRS with memory performance. We hypothesized that while the LOAD PRS would be useful in predicting annual memory decline due to neuropathological build up, the resilience PRS would be more predictive of baseline memory in the presence of amyloid pathology, by differentiating the heterogeneity in memory performance among Aβ+ individuals.

2. Methods

2.1. *Participants*

Participants were recruited as part of a case-control, longitudinal, observational design study, the Vanderbilt Memory and Aging Project (VMAP) which takes place at the Vanderbilt University Medical Center in Nashville, Tennessee.[20] VMAP began in 2012 and recruited individuals who were 60+ years of age, English speakers, had auditory/visual capacity for testing, and had a study partner. Each participant was given a Clinical Dementia Rating (CDR) interview and NIA-AA criteria was leveraged to classify individuals into cognitively unimpaired or mild cognitive impairment (MCI).[20] All protocols for the VMAP cohort were IRB-approved and informed consent for each participant was obtained prior to enrollment. Please see **Table 1** for an overview of the VMAP cohort.

Table 1. VMAP Cohort Demographics.

Cohort Characteristics	
Number of participants	334
Number of participants with genetic data	76.05% (254)
Total number of visits	3.83 +/- 0.76
Longitudinal follow-up (years)	2.27 +/- 1.97
Demographics and Health Characteristics	
Age at baseline (years)	72.74 +/- 6.89
Sex (% female)	27.54% (92)
Education (years)	16.13 +/- 2.56
APOE ε4 (% positive)	26.35% (88)
Amyloid status (% positive)	49.70% (166)
Diagnosis at baseline (% MCI)	29.34% (98)

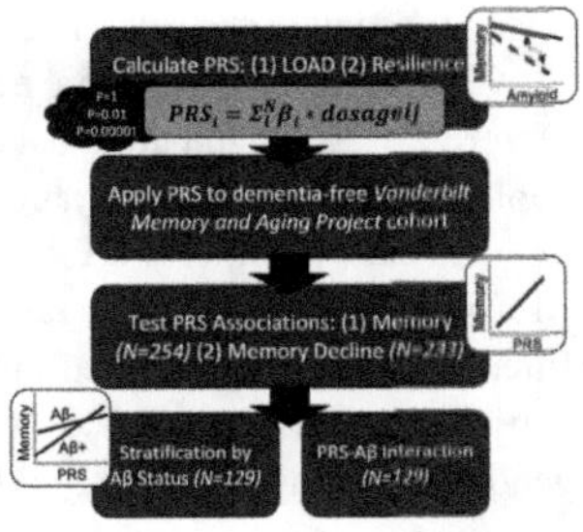

Figure 1. Flow-chart summary of analytical workflow.

2.2. *Cerebrospinal fluid amyloid*

A subset of participants (N=155) consented to and successfully completed lumbar puncture. Cerebral spinal fluid (CSF) was collected, spun down, and supernatant was analyzed through enzyme-linked immunosorbent assays (ELISA). One assay conducted was the INNOTEST® β-

AMYLOID$_{(1-42)}$, which includes autoantibodies for neo-epitopes of amino acids 1 and 42 of the Aβ1-42 amino acid peptides, ensuring specificity for Aβ1-42 peptides. Binarized amyloid status was determined for each participant based on CSF Aβ1-42 measurements. A published cut-point of CSF Aβ1-42 530ng/L was implemented, thus defining Aβ+ individuals with CSF Aβ1-42 values under 530ng/L.[21] A more detailed protocol is described in a prior paper by our group.[20]

2.3. *Neuropsychological composites*

Participants completed a series of neuropsychological tests that covered domains including memory, and a memory composite score was defined in a prior paper by our group.[22] Memory composites were calculated from item-level data, to reduce multiple testing burden. The composite score leveraged test item-level data from the California Verbal Learning Test, Second Edition, and the Biber Figure Learning Test. Composite scores were calculated with a bifactor latent variable model, and final memory composite scores were on a z-score scale.[22]

2.4. *Genetic data quality control and imputation*

Individuals consenting to genotyping (N=333) were genotyped from whole blood on the Illumina MEGA^{EX} genotyping array. Raw genetic data were processed as follows. First, variant-level filtering removed variants with >5% missingness, <1% minor allele frequency (MAF), and non-autosomal variants. Next, sample-level filtering removed individuals with >1% missingness, those who were related, those with mismatched self-reported and genetically determined sex, and heterozygosity outliers. Then genetic data were filtered to keep self-reported non-Hispanic white individuals, and genetic ancestry outliers (e.g., principal component analysis – PCA) were removed. Variants were also filtered for Hardy-Weinberg equilibrium (HWE) exact test $P<1x10^{-6}$. Finally, genetic data were lifted over to hg38 and compared and aligned to the Trans-Omics for Precision Medicine (TOPMed) reference panel,[23–25] dropping variants that failed lift-over or mismatched with the reference panel.

Cleaned genetic data were next phased (Eagle phasing) and imputed on the TOPMed imputation server.[23–25] Raw, imputed data were filtered to remove variants with an imputed $R^2<0.8$ or duplicated/multi-allelic variants. Additionally, original genotypes were merged back in with the imputed data. Another HWE exact test was performed filtering for $P<1x10^{-6}$, and variants with MAF <1% were removed. Once again, genetic ancestry outliers determined by a PCA were subsequently filtered. The final, cleaned, imputed VMAP genetic data included 255 non-Hispanic white participants and 8,689,730 variants. Additionally, *APOE* genotypes were determined by the TaqMan genotyping assay for rs7412 and rs429358 performed on DNA extracted from whole blood.[20]

2.5. *Statistical analyses*

See **Figure 1** for an overview of our analytical plan.

2.5.1. *Polygenic risk score generation*

Two PRS were calculated leveraging Kunkle et al. LOAD case/control genome-wide meta-analysis[4] and our group's recent genome-wide meta-analysis on resilience[17]. No participants in VMAP were included in either of the original GWAS. First, when applicable, GWAS were lifted to hg38. Next, GWAS variants were compared to the VMAP genetic data. Any ambiguous, palindromic variants were filtered out. Then overlapping variants between the GWAS and the VMAP genetic data were retained and then were compared for variants on opposite strands between the GWAS and the genetic data, and strand differences were resolved. Then, linkage disequilibrium (LD) clumping was performed with PLINK[26] in the VMAP genetic data (r^2=0.5, window=250kb), to choose the variant with the most significant phenotypic association within each genetically-linked genomic region. Each PRS was built with three different P-value thresholds: P=1, P=0.01, and P=0.00001, wherein variants were included in the PRS only if their phenotypic association was less than the given threshold. The LD-clumped genetic data were then leveraged to calculate each PRS with PLINK's profile function[27] which calculates scores as follows: Weights were retrieved from the variant associations with LOAD or with resilience from the respective GWAS. For each variant the given weight was multiplied by 0, 1, or 2, based on how many risk alleles an individual had. The summation of this process results in a summary score for an individual. Since *APOE* polymorphism is a robust risk factor for LOAD, PRS were calculated with and without the *APOE* region, defined by a 1Mb region up- and downstream of the *APOE* gene.

2.5.2. *Baseline and longitudinal linear models*

We performed a series of linear models and linear mixed effects models in R (v. 4.2) for each PRS. Fixed effects in our models included baseline age, self-reported sex, and the given PRS. Linear mixed effects models included a PRS-by-interval term, where interval was determined by the difference between a participant's age at each cognitive visit and their baseline age. Additionally, linear mixed effects models allowed slope and intercept to vary for each participant. In addition, we performed identical sets of models with the addition of a PRS-by-amyloid term in linear models and a PRS-by-amyloid-by-interval term for linear mixed effects models, with amyloid measured by the CSF Aβ1-42 assay outlined above. The outcome of our models were baseline memory or annual memory decline for linear models and linear mixed effect models, respectively. Each set of models above was performed again stratifying by amyloid status. Sensitivity analyses were performed for all models leveraging PRS generated without the *APOE* region.

3. Results

We performed a series of linear models and linear mixed effects models investigating each PRS association with baseline memory or annual memory decline, respectively. All main effect associations are presented in **Figure 2** and/or **Table 2**. The LOAD PRS had a significant main effect on baseline memory (**Figure 2A; Table 2**), but when *APOE* was excluded from the PRS, this result attenuated to nonsignificant

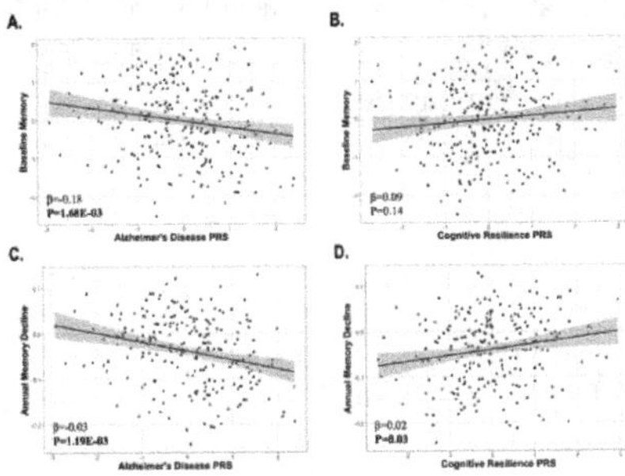

Figure 2. Main effect PRS associations (P=0.01 threshold; with *APOE*) with baseline memory (A, B) and annual memory decline (C, D).

(**Table 2**). Both the LOAD PRS (**Figure 2C; Table 2**) and the resilience PRS (**Figure 2D; Table 2**) had significant main effects on annual memory decline irrespective of *APOE* inclusion in PRS.

Next, we performed a second series of models with a PRS-by-CSF-Aβ interaction term to determine if amyloid modified the association of each PRS with memory performance. Additionally, we performed amyloid status-stratified models to determine if Aβ- individuals or Aβ+ individuals (or neither) were driving any observed significant interactions. All CSF-Aβ interaction and amyloid-status stratified results are presented in **Figure 3** and/or **Table 2**.

The LOAD PRS did not interact with CSF Aβ on either baseline memory (**Figure 3A; Table 2**) or annual memory decline (**Figure 3C; Table 2**), and this was consistent when *APOE* was excluded from PRS (**Table 2**). However, the LOAD PRS significantly predicted annual memory decline more strongly among Aβ+ individuals (**Figure 3C; Table 2**), albeit this result is difficult to interpret with the PRS-by-CSF-Aβ interaction term being nonsignificant. The resilience PRS significantly interacted with CSF Aβ on baseline memory (**Figure 3B; Table 2**), whereby it significantly predicted baseline memory among Aβ+ individuals (**Figure 3B; Table 2**) but not among Aβ- individuals (**Figure 3B; Table 2**). These results remained consistent when *APOE* was excluded.

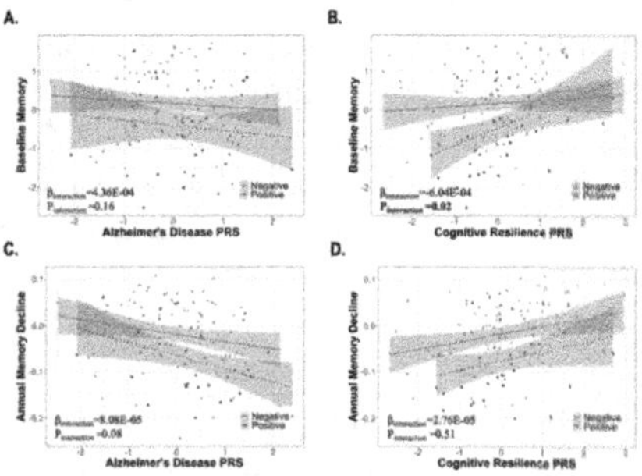

Figure 3. PRS associations (P=0.01 threshold; with *APOE*) with baseline memory (A, B) and annual memory decline (C, D) stratified by Aβ status.

In addition to the PRS with a P=0.01 threshold which are presented in the figures, we tested two other P-value thresholds: P=1 and P=0.00001 (**Table 2**). All results were consistent across all three thresholds unless denoted in the following paragraph. The LOAD PRS without *APOE* fell just under significance in the main effect association on annual memory decline at the P=1 and P=0.00001 thresholds. The resilience PRS did not have a main effect on annual memory decline at P=1 or P=0.00001 (with or without *APOE*). Additionally, the resilience PRS-by-CSF-Aβ interaction trended significant at P=1, but still significantly predicted baseline memory among Aβ+ individuals. Lastly, both the LOAD PRS and the resilience PRS varied by threshold – and by *APOE* inclusion for the LOAD PRS – in predicting annual memory decline among Aβ- individuals and/or among Aβ+ individuals.

Table 2. PRS Associations with Baseline Memory and Annual Memory Decline.

				Baseline Memory					
PRS		***Main Effect***		***Aβ*PRS***		***Aβ-***		***Aβ+***	
PRS	Threshold	β	P	β	P	β	P	β	P
LOAD	P=1	-0.13	***0.03***	2.73E-04	0.41	-0.11	0.21	-0.10	0.59
LOAD	P=0.01	-0.18	***1.68E-03***	4.36E-04	0.16	-0.08	0.37	-0.13	0.47
LOAD	P=0.00001	-0.25	***4.00E-05***	5.70E-04	0.13	0.02	0.87	-0.11	0.57
Resilience	P=1	0.09	0.12	-4.97E-04	0.08	0.10	0.21	0.57	***1.33E-03****
Resilience	P=0.01	0.09	0.14	-6.04E-04	***0.02****	0.06	0.46	0.44	***0.01****
Resilience	P=0.00001	0.01	0.88	-7.83E-04	***0.02****	-0.09	0.30	0.52	***0.02****

Annual Memory Decline									
PRS		***Main Effect***		***Aβ*PRS***		***Aβ-***		***Aβ+***	
PRS	Threshold	β	P	β	P	β	P	β	P
LOAD	P=1	-0.02	***0.02***	2.59E-05	0.63	-0.03	***0.04****	-0.05	***0.01****
LOAD	P=0.01	-0.03	***1.19E-03****	8.08E-05	0.08	-0.03	*0.09#*	-0.05	***0.01****
LOAD	P=0.00001	-0.03	***8.66E-04***	7.16E-05	0.21	-0.01	*0.54#*	-0.02	0.23
Resilience	P=1	4.74E-03	0.60	3.66E-05	0.42	9.88E-04	0.94	0.04	***4.69E-02****
Resilience	P=0.01	0.02	***0.03****	2.76E-05	0.51	0.03	***0.02****	0.02	0.36
Resilience	P=0.00001	0.01	0.39	-6.30E-05	0.25	-2.41E-03	0.87	0.08	***6.60E-04****

*Note: P-values with * remain significant without APOE; # significant without APOE only*

4. Discussion

We built a LOAD PRS and a cognitive resilience PRS and evaluated each PRS in predicting memory outcomes among dementia-free elderly individuals. Both sets of PRS provided useful information and performed best in the spheres most closely related to the original phenotype in the GWAS. The LOAD PRS was predictive of annual memory decline in the whole sample and more strongly among Aβ+. In contrast, the resilience PRS was a particularly strong predictor of baseline memory in the presence of amyloid pathology, reflecting that the original phenotype was built to represent better-than-expected memory performance among those with high levels of AD biomarkers. Together, our findings suggest that the complementary information of a resilience PRS could improve preclinical prediction. It also highlights the need to expand sample sizes allowing for incorporation of longitudinal cognitive data into genetic studies of resilience to improve polygenic risk score applications in the future.

4.1. *LOAD PRS is a strong predictor of annual cognitive decline in later stages of disease*

Our main effect findings (**Figure 2; Table 2**) highlight that the LOAD PRS had a significant main effect on both baseline memory and annual memory decline. While the LOAD PRS did not interact with CSF Aβ on baseline memory or annual memory decline (**Figure 3; Table 2**), it more strongly predicted annual memory decline among Aβ+ individuals. LOAD PRS associations with cognitive decline have been replicated in other studies. For example, Kauppi and colleagues found that an AD PRS significantly predicted cognitive decline in a cohort of cognitive unimpaired individuals.[28] Ge and colleagues determined that a LOAD PRS predicted cognitive decline among Aβ+ cognitively unimpaired and MCI individuals.[29] Likewise, both Tan et al. and Desikan et al. observed that a polygenic hazard score was associated with cognitive decline.[30–32] More specifically, Tan et al. found that those that had a high polygenic hazard score, indicative of high polygenic risk for LOAD, and who were Aβ+, showed steeper cognitive decline.[30–32] Taken together, it may be that the LOAD PRS reflects a number of heterogeneous routes to cognitive impairment that includes AD neuropathology, but also includes some non-AD processes. All the studies mentioned as well as ours, found consistent associations with cognitive decline and stronger associations among Aβ+ individuals than among Aβ- individuals, though the difference in our non-demented cohort was negligible at best. It is notable that we did not observe a LOAD PRS-Aβ interaction. Perhaps the LOAD PRS models later stages of disease where Aβ accumulation has already occurred in many individuals and is but one contributor, while other pathways downstream and parallel to amyloidosis are primarily contributing to cognitive decline. This idea was posited by Carrasquillo and colleagues[6] (and others) and appears to be supported by our findings.

4.2. *Resilience PRS is a strong predictor of cognition in earlier stages of disease*

Only the resilience PRS significantly interacted with Aβ on memory performance, whereby it predicted baseline memory among Aβ+ individuals but not among Aβ- individuals. (**Figure 3; Table 2**). Notably, previous studies are mixed regarding if LOAD polygenic risk associates with Aβ burden. Multiple studies have found associations between LOAD PRS and amyloid positivity, including Mormino and colleagues who also observed an association between their LOAD PRS and cognitive decline.[7,27,33] Other studies have found no association between a LOAD PRS and amyloid positivity, or an association that attenuated when *APOE* was excluded.[11,29,34,35] It is noteworthy that Ge and colleagues found no association between the LOAD PRS and baseline Aβ, but did find an association of the LOAD PRS with cognitive decline among Aβ+.[29] Ebenau and colleagues comment on the mixed literature surrounding LOAD PRS association with Aβ positivity, pointing to heterogeneity in Aβ progression across diagnostic status as a potential reason for disagreement.[33]

Our original resilience phenotype was designed to predict better-than expected cognition in the presence of amyloid pathology.[16] This matches what we are seeing with the resilience PRS, and the cross-sectional result we see with the PRS matches the cross-sectional nature of the phenotype.[16] A recent study showed that a LOAD PRS enriched for amyloid-positivity-associated loci was associated with cognitive decline, whereas simply a LOAD PRS was not associated.[36] This highlights that loci driving amyloidosis, which begins earlier in disease progression, may not be the same loci driving clinical dementia (downstream).[36] To address this limitation, the resilience PRS may be a complementary tool in this case, as based on our novel results, it can selectively predict baseline memory among Aβ+ individuals (**Figure 3; Table 2**). Since much of the elderly population is living with neuropathology,[12] determining those most at risk for future cognitive decline is imperative. Whereas the LOAD PRS may be working through amyloid pathology, performing similarly irrespective of amyloid pathology, the resilience PRS, in contrast, may be interacting with amyloid pathology, predicting genetic risk above and beyond amyloid pathology. It is noteworthy that all individuals in the VMAP cohort were dementia-free. Thus, our resilience PRS may be a tool that can best predict genetic risk for cognitive deficits among biomarker-positive individuals while they are still in the preclinical stage of disease. Our promising initial results indicate that we may have developed a novel PRS that 1) does not lose predictive power among those with Aβ pathology 2) performs its best among this high-risk Aβ+ group, separating them out from those in the elderly population who may or may not have Aβ in their brain, and 3) performs robustly irrespective of an individual's future clinical diagnosis. Replicating our findings, incorporating longitudinal data into resilience models, and increasing sample size will be necessary to fine-tune this PRS.

4.3. *PRS including more variants may have predictive power beyond the APOE locus*

Over the last decade of PRS as a tool for LOAD risk prediction, there has been much debate regarding if a LOAD PRS has more predictive power than *APOE* genotype alone. Studies have been mixed, with many demonstrating that LOAD PRS associate with LOAD risk and LOAD-endophenotypes above and beyond *APOE*,[9,27,37] while some studies show that LOAD PRS without *APOE* attenuate to nonsignificant in predicting LOAD risk or endophenotype levels.[11,29,34] However, some of the studies that found PRS to contribute to risk prediction beyond that of *APOE* still underscore that *APOE* is contributing a large amount to polygenic risk.[9,37] One study positing that a LOAD PRS has predictive power beyond *APOE* also stated that 43.8% of the 61.0% total predictive power of the LOAD PRS on conversion from MCI to LOAD was coming from *APOE* alone.[9] Notably, our resilience PRS findings remained consistent when *APOE* was removed from PRS calculations, which makes sense as the resilience phenotype attempts to regress out effects of amyloidosis[17] which are often driven by *APOE*.[34] A resilience PRS like the one we built in this study may be promising in terms of its ability to predict LOAD-related cognitive outcomes above and beyond that of *APOE* but replicating our findings and larger sample sizes for future resilience GWAS are needed to fully elucidate this theory.

In addition, there is no gold standard for a singular P-value threshold to leverage for LOAD PRS calculations. Two recent studies examined LOAD PRS at a variety of different thresholds. Ge and colleagues observed fairly consistent results across thresholds spanning from $P=0.01$ to $P=1x10^{-7}$.[38] Another study observed that distinguishing between cognitively unimpaired and LOAD participants was best with a threshold of $P=0.01$, and in fact predictive power plateaued after $P=0.01$.[27] In this study, we tested three thresholds: $P=1$, $P=0.01$, and $P=0.00001$. Our results were mostly consistent across the three thresholds, but the resilience PRS at $P=0.01$ seemed to best predict annual memory decline. Overall, our results combined with some previous studies suggest that perhaps allowing for inclusion of more loci that fall below the stringent genome-wide threshold captures a wider variety of processes contributing to complex trait risk.[18,19,27]

4.4. *Strengths and weaknesses*

Our study had multiple strengths. We leveraged a deeply-phenotyped cohort, the Vanderbilt Memory and Aging Project. This cohort has many important features including participants free of dementia, baseline biomarker status for participants, and longitudinal measurements of memory composite scores. However, our study did have some limitations. Our resilience PRS was not built with inclusion of measures of tau pathology or other known age-related neuropathologies. Sample size is a limiting factor for these measures of pathology, but as sample sizes increase in these cohorts, we plan to incorporate other pathology measures into our resilience models in addition to amyloid. Additionally, our sample size (in VMAP) was limited to those consenting to genotyping, neuropsychological testing, and lumbar puncture. Our study was limited to non-Hispanic white individuals, attenuating the generalizability of our findings to other populations. Currently, genetic data is becoming available for individuals across multiple ancestry groups, allowing groups including ours to expand diversity in GWAS studies, including cross-ancestry approaches. With more diverse GWAS, future studies will be able to build PRS in multiple ancestry groups, which will aid in our understanding of AD genetic risk in diverse populations. Lastly, some of the PRS associations reported in this study did not survive correction for multiple comparisons with the false discovery rate (FDR<0.05) procedure, likely due to power and sample size constraints of the original GWAS. The sample sizes of individuals with cognition, genotyping, and neuropathology data are ever increasing, which we are leveraging to increase our sample sizes for our resilience GWAS, and this will contribute to increased power in an analysis like this one in the future.

4.5. *Conclusions*

Although our study needs to be replicated, we find our initial novel findings to be promising that a cognitive resilience PRS may serve as a complementary clinical tool with a LOAD PRS in identifying those most at risk for future cognitive decline while individuals are still in the preclinical and prodromal stages of LOAD.

5. Acknowledgements

Study data were obtained from the Vanderbilt Memory and Aging Project (VMAP). Data were collected by Vanderbilt Memory and Alzheimer's Center Investigators at Vanderbilt University Medical Center. This work was supported by NIA grants R01-AG034962, R01-AG056534, R01-AG062826, K24-AG046373, and Alzheimer's Association IIRG-08-88733. This work was additionally supported by: Swedish Research Council #2018-02532, Swedish Research Council #2018-02532, European Research Council, #681712, Swedish State Support for Clinical Research, #ALFGBG-720931, Swedish State Support for Clinical Research, #ALFGBG-720931, U24-AG074855, R01-AG061518, R01-AG061518, P20-AG068082, U01-AG068057, R21-AG059941, K01-AG049164, K12-HD043483, HHSN311201600276P, RF1-AG059869, R01-AG073439, and T32-GM080178.

References

1. Jack CR, Knopman DS, Jagust WJ, et al. Hypothetical model of dynamic biomarkers of the Alzheimer's pathological cascade. *The Lancet Neurology*. 2010;9(1):119.
2. Bellenguez C, Küçükali F, Jansen IE, et al. New insights into the genetic etiology of Alzheimer's disease and related dementias. *Nat Genet*. 2022;54(4):412-436. doi:10.1038/s41588-022-01024-z
3. Gatz M, Reynolds CA, Fratiglioni L. Role of genes and environments for explaining alzheimer disease. *Archives of General Psychiatry*. 2006;63(2):168-174.
4. Kunkle BW, Grenier-Boley B, Sims R, et al. Genetic meta-analysis of diagnosed Alzheimer's disease identifies new risk loci and implicates Aβ, tau, immunity and lipid processing. *Nature genetics*. 2019;51(3):414-430. doi:10.1038/s41588-019-0358-2
5. Ridge PG, Mukherjee S, Crane PK, Kauwe JSK. Alzheimer's disease: analyzing the missing heritability. *PloS one*. 2013;8(11):e79771.
6. Carrasquillo MM, Crook JE, Pedraza O, et al. Late-onset Alzheimer's risk variants in memory decline, incident mild cognitive impairment, and Alzheimer's disease. *Neurobiol Aging*. 2015;36(1):60-67. doi:10.1016/j.neurobiolaging.2014.07.042
7. Li WW, Wang Z, Fan DY, et al. Association of Polygenic Risk Score with Age at Onset and Cerebrospinal Fluid Biomarkers of Alzheimer's Disease in a Chinese Cohort. *Neurosci Bull*. 2020;36(7):696-704. doi:10.1007/s12264-020-00469-8

8. Logue MW, Panizzon MS, Elman JA, et al. Use of an Alzheimer's disease polygenic risk score to identify mild cognitive impairment in adults in their 50s. *Mol Psychiatry*. 2019;24(3):421-430. doi:10.1038/s41380-018-0030-8
9. Chaudhury S, Brookes KJ, Patel T, et al. Alzheimer's disease polygenic risk score as a predictor of conversion from mild-cognitive impairment. *Transl Psychiatry*. 2019;9(1):154. doi:10.1038/s41398-019-0485-7
10. Ware EB, Faul JD, Mitchell CM, Bakulski KM. Considering the APOE locus in Alzheimer's disease polygenic scores in the Health and Retirement Study: a longitudinal panel study. *BMC Med Genomics*. 2020;13(1):164. doi:10.1186/s12920-020-00815-9
11. Darst BF, Koscik RL, Racine AM, et al. Pathway-Specific Polygenic Risk Scores as Predictors of Amyloid-β Deposition and Cognitive Function in a Sample at Increased Risk for Alzheimer's Disease. *J Alzheimers Dis*. 2017;55(2):473-484. doi:10.3233/JAD-160195
12. Sonnen JA, Santa Cruz K, Hemmy LS, et al. Ecology of the aging human brain. *Archives of neurology*. 2011;68(8):1049-1056.
13. Driscoll I, Troncoso J. Asymptomatic Alzheimers Disease: A Prodrome or a State of Resilience? *Current Alzheimer Research*. 2011;8(4):330-335.
14. Stern Y, Arenaza-Urquijo EM, Bartrés-Faz D, et al. Whitepaper: Defining and investigating cognitive reserve, brain reserve, and brain maintenance. *Alzheimer's & Dementia*. 2020;16(9):1305-1311. doi:https://doi.org/10.1016/j.jalz.2018.07.219
15. Arenaza-Urquijo EM, Vemuri P. Improving the resistance and resilience framework for aging and dementia studies. *Alzheimer's research & therapy*. 2020;12(1):41. doi:10.1186/s13195-020-00609-2
16. Hohman TJ, McLaren DG, Mormino EC, Gifford KA, Libon DJ, Jefferson AL. Asymptomatic Alzheimer disease: Defining resilience. *Neurology*. 2016;87(23):2443-2450.
17. Dumitrescu L, Mahoney ER, Mukherjee S, et al. Genetic variants and functional pathways associated with resilience to Alzheimer's disease. *Brain*. 2020;143(8):2561-2575. doi:10.1093/brain/awaa209
18. Hess JL, Tylee DS, Mattheisen M, et al. A polygenic resilience score moderates the genetic risk for schizophrenia. *Mol Psychiatry*. 2021;26(3):800-815. doi:10.1038/s41380-019-0463-8
19. Hou J, Hess JL, Armstrong N, et al. Polygenic resilience scores capture protective genetic effects for Alzheimer's disease. *Transl Psychiatry*. 2022;12(1):296. doi:10.1038/s41398-022-02055-0
20. Jefferson AL, Gifford KA, Acosta LMY, et al. The Vanderbilt Memory & Aging Project: Study Design and Baseline Cohort Overview. *Journal of Alzheimer's Disease*. 2016;(Preprint):1-20.
21. Skillbäck T, Farahmand BY, Rosén C, et al. Cerebrospinal fluid tau and amyloid-β1-42 in patients with dementia. *Brain*. 2015;138(Pt 9):2716-2731. doi:10.1093/brain/awv181
22. Kresge HA, Khan OA, Wagener MA, et al. Subclinical Compromise in Cardiac Strain Relates to Lower Cognitive Performances in Older Adults. *Journal of the American Heart Association*. 2018;7(4). doi:10.1161/jaha.117.007562
23. Das S, Forer L, Schonherr S, et al. Next-generation genotype imputation service and methods. *Nature genetics*. 2016;48(10):1284-1287. doi:10.1038/ng.3656

24. Fuchsberger C, Abecasis GR, Hinds DA. minimac2: faster genotype imputation. *Bioinformatics*. 2014;31(5):782-784. doi:10.1093/bioinformatics/btu704
25. Taliun D, Harris DN, Kessler MD, et al. Sequencing of 53,831 diverse genomes from the NHLBI TOPMed Program. *bioRxiv*. Published online January 1, 2019.
26. Chang CC, Chow CC, Tellier LC, Vattikuti S, Purcell SM, Lee JJ. Second-generation PLINK: rising to the challenge of larger and richer datasets. *GigaScience*. 2015;4(1). doi:10.1186/s13742-015-0047-8
27. Mormino EC, Sperling RA, Holmes AJ, et al. Polygenic risk of Alzheimer disease is associated with early- and late-life processes. *Neurology*. 2016;87(5):481-488. doi:10.1212/wnl.0000000000002922
28. Kauppi K, Rönnlund M, Nordin Adolfsson A, Pudas S, Adolfsson R. Effects of polygenic risk for Alzheimer's disease on rate of cognitive decline in normal aging. *Transl Psychiatry*. 2020;10(1):250. doi:10.1038/s41398-020-00934-y
29. Ge T, Sabuncu MR, Smoller JW, Sperling RA, Mormino EC. Dissociable influences of APOE epsilon4 and polygenic risk of AD dementia on amyloid and cognition. *Neurology*. 2018;90(18):e1605-e1612. doi:10.1212/wnl.0000000000005415
30. Tan CH, Hyman BT, Tan JJX, et al. Polygenic hazard scores in preclinical Alzheimer disease. *Annals of neurology*. 2017;82(3):484-488. doi:10.1002/ana.25029
31. Desikan RS, Fan CC, Wang Y, et al. Genetic assessment of age-associated Alzheimer disease risk: Development and validation of a polygenic hazard score. *PLoS medicine*. 2017;14(3):e1002258. doi:10.1371/journal.pmed.1002258
32. Tan CH, Bonham LW, Fan CC, et al. Polygenic hazard score, amyloid deposition and Alzheimer's neurodegeneration. *Brain*. 2019;142(2):460-470. doi:10.1093/brain/awy327
33. Ebenau JL, van der Lee SJ, Hulsman M, et al. Risk of dementia in APOE ε4 carriers is mitigated by a polygenic risk score. *Alzheimers Dement (Amst)*. 2021;13(1):e12229. doi:10.1002/dad2.12229
34. Leonenko G, Shoai M, Bellou E, et al. Genetic risk for alzheimer disease is distinct from genetic risk for amyloid deposition. *Ann Neurol*. 2019;86(3):427-435. doi:10.1002/ana.25530
35. Tan CH, Fan CC, Mormino EC, et al. Polygenic hazard score: an enrichment marker for Alzheimer's associated amyloid and tau deposition. *Acta Neuropathologica*. 2018;135(1):85-93. doi:10.1007/s00401-017-1789-4
36. Xicota L, Gyorgy B, Grenier-Boley B, et al. Association of APOE-Independent Alzheimer Disease Polygenic Risk Score With Brain Amyloid Deposition in Asymptomatic Older Adults. *Neurology*. Published online May 23, 2022:10.1212/WNL.0000000000200544. doi:10.1212/WNL.0000000000200544
37. Karlsson IK, Escott-Price V, Gatz M, et al. Measuring heritable contributions to Alzheimer's disease: polygenic risk score analysis with twins. *Brain Commun*. 2022;4(1):fcab308. doi:10.1093/braincomms/fcab308
38. Ge T, Sabuncu MR, Smoller JW, Sperling RA, Mormino EC. Dissociable influences of APOE epsilon4 and polygenic risk of AD dementia on amyloid and cognition. *Neurology*. 2018;90(18):e1605-e1612. doi:10.1212/wnl.0000000000005415

TOWARDS ETHICAL BIOMEDICAL INFORMATICS: LEARNING FROM OLELO NOEAU, HAWAIIAN PROVERBS

Peter Y. Washington

Department of Information & Computer Sciences, University of Hawaii at Manoa
Honolulu, HI 96822, USA
Email: pyw@hawii.edu

Noelani Puniwai

Kamakakuokalani, University of Hawaii at Manoa
Honolulu, HI 96822, USA
Email: npuniwai@hawaii.edu

Martina Kamaka

Department of Native Hawaiian Health, University of Hawaii at Manoa
Honolulu, HI 96822, USA
Email: martinak@hawaii.edu

Gamze Gürsoy

Department of Biomedical Informatics, Columbia University
New York, NY 10032, USA
Email: ggursoy@nygenome.org

Nicholas Tatonetti

Department of Biomedical Informatics, Columbia University
New York, NY 10032, USA
Email: nick.tatonetti@columbia.edu

Steven E. Brenner

Department of Plant & Microbial Biology, University of California, Berkeley
Berkeley, CA 94720, USA
Email: brenner@compbio.berkeley.edu

Dennis P. Wall

Department of Pediatrics (Systems Medicine), Biomedical Data Science, and Psychiatry & Behavioral Sciences, Stanford University
Stanford, CA, 94305, USA
Email: dpwall@stanford.edu

Innovations in human-centered biomedical informatics are often developed with the eventual goal of real-world translation. While biomedical research questions are usually answered in terms of how a method performs in a particular context, we argue that it is equally important to consider and formally evaluate the ethical implications of informatics solutions. Several new research paradigms have arisen as a result of the consideration of ethical issues, including but not limited for privacy-preserving computation and fair machine learning. In the spirit of the Pacific Symposium on Biocomputing, we discuss broad and fundamental principles of ethical biomedical informatics in terms of Olelo Noeau, or Hawaiian proverbs and poetical sayings that capture Hawaiian values. While we emphasize issues related to privacy and fairness in particular, there are a multitude of facets to ethical biomedical informatics that can benefit from a critical analysis grounded in ethics.

Keywords: Ethics; Bioethics; Privacy; Fairness; Bias; Biomedical Data Science; Pono

1. Introduction

The field of biomedical informatics is intrinsically tied to ethics, as a large portion of innovations are developed for the explicit purpose of advancing human health. However, every innovation involves a wide array of stakeholders, such as clinicians, patients, family members of the patients, healthy individuals whose data are used to support an informatics solution, and many others. A solution that improves the health of one stakeholder may harm or put at risk another stakeholder in often inadvertent and subtle ways.

Considering the ethics of biomedical informatics solutions may lead to varying conclusions depending on the ethical framework used to conduct the analysis. Utilitarianism, for example, is a framework centered around doing the greatest amount of good for the largest number of people. Deontological ethics, by contrast, centers around doing the morally right action regardless of the number of people affected. One can propose countless examples of decisions that may align with one ethical theory but directly conflict with another. For example, collecting large swaths of training data that contain protected health information may be ideal from a utilitarian standpoint, as the model would be used to help a large number of people, but might be unethical from a deontological view without extensive privacy protections in place.

Here, we consider another ethical perspective: Olelo Noeau, or Native Hawaiian proverbs that capture Native Hawaiian values and the Hawaiian worldview. The Pacific Symposium on Biocomputing (PSB) takes place in Hawaii every year. As such, we center this introduction on a discussion of Native Hawaiian values as they relate to the field of biomedical informatics. While we acknowledge that many Native Hawaiian values have variety and layers to their meaning, for our purposes, we will focus on the more commonly understood meanings of these phrases. We summarize relevant Olelo Noeau for biomedical informatics in Table 1.

Table 1. Correspondence between either Olelo Noeau and analogous ethical considerations in biomedical informatics research.

Olelo Noeau	English interpretation	Relevant Hawaiian concepts, values	Analogue in Biomedical Informatics
Ike aku, ike mai, kokua aku kokua mai; pela iho la ka nohona ohana	Recognize and be recognized, help and be helped; such is family life.	Ohana, Laulima	Inclusiveness, Human-Centered Design Utilitarian ethics, Collaboration
Ike i ke au nui me ke au iki	Know the big current and the little current	Pono	Equity, Fairness
Kanukanu, huna i ka meheu, i ka maawe alanui o Kapuukolu	Covering with earth, hiding the footprints on the narrow trail of Kapuukolu	Kapu	Respect for privacy and sanctity
He waiwai nui ka lokahi	Unity is a precious possession	Lokahi	Balance of traditional performance metrics, privacy, and fairness

2. Ike aku, ike mai, kokua aku kokua mai; pela iho la ka nohona ohana. Family life requires an exchange of mutual help and recognition.

Ohana, the word for family, is one of the key Hawaiian principles that defines Hawaiian culture. The Hawaiian proverb "*Ike aku, ike mai, kokua aku, kokua mai; pela iho la ka nohona ohana*" literally describes the importance of a human-centered design process - "*recognize and be recognized, help and be helped; such is family life*" [1]. Native Hawaiian social structure is centered around extended families. For example, illnesses affect the entire Ohana because what impacts one impacts all. Laulima is also a pillar of Hawaiian culture: goals must be achieved by collaboration and cooperation. Traditionally, survival depended on this.

Following this ideal, one might suggest that biomedical informatics solutions should be developed with to work for all stakeholders, regardless of socioeconomic, demographic, political, or geographic factors. This includes involving all stakeholders in the development and design process, often with the aid of established human-centered design practices.

Digital solutions for various health conditions often and increasingly incorporate informatics solutions. For example, the SuperpowerGlass system developed by some of the authors at Stanford [2] was initially designed using in-person human-centered design sessions with participants. Before even the first quantitative feasibility study was conducted, iterative design sessions with participants were completed, and parent and child stakeholders were extensively interviewed by the study team [3-4]. Qualitative feedback was collected and coded to inform the updated design decisions of future iterations of the wearable therapeutic [5]. Only after these design sessions was the SuperpowerGlass system tested in feasibility studies [6-8] and a formal randomized controlled trial [9]. The process of co-designing with the end users of a medical solution can prevent situations where extensive time and effort is put into developing elaborate solutions that are ultimately disregarded by patients and clinicians as being unusable or unethical.

3. Ike i ke au nui me ke au iki. Know the big current and the little current.

The Hawaiian proverb "*Ike i ke au nui me ke au iki*" translates to "*know the big current and the little current*" in English, meaning that it is valuable to recognize the importance of all knowledge, be it small or large [1]. Ensuring the dialogue of data sources and data analysis is inclusive of all supports this ideal.

Similarly, the concept of Pono refers to the ideal balance of equity and abundance among all living and non-living entities [19]. A Pono concept is larger than the defense of right conduct that structures our conversations around ethics and ensures that our motivation in seeking pono is for the prosperity of all communities.

Fairness in machine learning is particularly important in the contexts of biology, medicine, and health. Machine learning models that make a diagnostic prediction, for example, can be problematic if the level of fidelity of the prediction of disease status is inconsistent across demographic groups. Machine learning classifiers are limited by the input data that are used to train them, and in many instances, the training data are unbalanced and biased. Due to differences in representation levels at the granularity of a hospital, city, or country, it may be impossible to collect balanced data sets without discarding large amounts of data from the majority class. Recent algorithmic techniques enable increased fairness, including data augmentation to upsample the underrepresented groups [10-12], enforcing a flavor of fairness in the loss function or otherwise imposing an algorithmic constraint [13-14], or post-processing methods for redefining the prediction thresholds for a black box model [15-17]. Some argue that beyond issues with data are fundamental biases in the quantitative methodologies themselves, which can put underserved populations at a disadvantage. Maggie Walter and Chris Andersen explore this topic in "Indigenous Statistics: A Quantitative Research Methodology" [18], discussing issues such as the inherent power dynamics between non-

Indigenous and Indigenous populations in statistical and policy discourse and ways that data collection methods are designed to only collect data of certain types.

4. Kanukanu, huna i ka meheu, i ka maawe alanui o Kapuukolu. Covering with earth, hiding the footprints on the narrow trail of Kapuukolu.

This Hawaiian proverb shares a value of privacy and guarding of personal information from those who pry. "In ancient times a person who did not want to be traced by his footsteps carefully eradicated them as he went" [1]. While these ideals can extend to a variety of topics in biomedical informatics, we hone in on respect of the participants whose data are used to develop biomedical innovations. We discuss respect for privacy in particular, which is the greatest concern of participants who share their data.

The concept of Kapu similarly reflects the respect required of personal data and the privilege of working with information that can be identifiable [47]. Kapu references not only the interaction with the dataset, but the ability to safeguard, protect and honor that which comprises the sacredness and dignity of each individual.

Biomedical data are sensitive by definition, often containing protected health information and identifiable information. It is crucial to share these data with the broader community in order to advance scientific progress [20-21]. However, the potential for data breaches must be accounted for. In biomedical informatics, avenues for potential breaches extend beyond traditional hacking and computer security issues. Risks specific to this field include but are not limited to identifying the genome of a single individual from within a larger dataset [22-25], cross-referencing multiple databases using demographic and familial information [26-27], inherently identifying multimedia datasets [28-32], and performing diagnostic assessments with humans in the loop [33-38]. Other considerations are the management of very small data sets, since the careless release of these could compromise not only privacy, but also dignity of subjects. Current solutions to these issues include homomorphic encryption [39-41], running privacy audits through bioinformatics tools [42-43], data sanitization [44], and differential privacy [45], and federated learning [46].

5. He waiwai nui ka lokahi; Unity is a precious possession. (Lokahi as it relates to Balance and Harmony)

Lokahi is the concept of balance; in the Native Hawaiian worldview it incorporates the balance between spirituality (Akua), humankind (Kanaka), and nature (Aina). These three pillars of Lokahi are embodied in the Lokahi triangle (Figure 1). The values of the Lokahi triangle are central to the Hawaiian notion of holistic health, including in contemporary health practices in Hawaii [48].

Lokahi is encompassed in the Hawaiian proverb "*He waiwai nui ka lokahi*", or "*unity is a precious possession*" [1]. Lokahi translates directly to ethical biomedical informatics as the marriage of traditional performance metrics (such as accuracy, mean squared error, F1-score, and AUROC) with metrics that contain an ethical component (such as attack success rate for privacy and demographic parity for fairness). Often, these metrics can be at direct odds with each other. For example, it has been repeatedly documented that improving fairness can often detriment model performance and vice versa [49-55]. Considering our framework perspective, consideration for what is ultimately the best solution for this concept is the one that does the pono (proper) thing and finds a way to balance both.

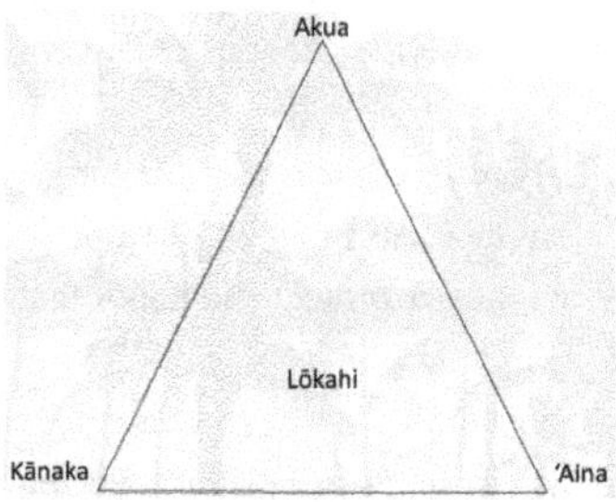

Fig. 1. Lokahi triangle, consisting of spirituality (akua), humankind (Kanaka), and nature (Aina). Together, these elements represent balance.

6. Closing Thoughts

We emphasize that the Hawaiian cultural concepts are not simply words/phrases but ways of living. Biomedical informatics is a discipline that is inherently human-centered, and yet the quantitative logistics of the field can stray far from this central core, resulting in researchers forgetting the ethical implications of their work. We hope that this short piece will inspire PSB attendees to become Alakai, or leaders, in the incorporation of values-driven perspective in all facets of biomedical informatics research. Doing so could help avoid ethical complications and setbacks while ensuring inclusivity, respect for not only our populations but also in our field, and equity. We close with a proverb that we hope all attendees will follow: "*O ka pono ke hana ia a iho mai na lani*" [1], meaning "*continue to do good until the heavens come down to you*", or "*blessings come to those who persist in doing good.*"

7. Acknowledgements

This work was supported in part by funds to DPW from the National Institutes of Health (R01LM013364).

8. Author Contributions

PYW, NP, and MK focused on the conceptual translation of these proverbs to biomedical informatics. All authors collaborated on the early stages of session design and perspective.

References

1. Pukui, Mary Kawena (editor, and translator). ʻŌlelo Noʻeau: Hawaiian Proverbs & Poetical Sayings. Bishop Museum Press, 1983.
2. Kline, Aaron, Catalin Voss, Peter Washington, Nick Haber, Hessey Schwartz, Qandeel Tariq, Terry Winograd, Carl Feinstein, and Dennis P. Wall. "Superpower glass." GetMobile: Mobile Computing and Communications 23, no. 2 (2019): 35-38.
3. Voss, Catalin, Peter Washington, Nick Haber, Aaron Kline, Jena Daniels, Azar Fazel, Titas De et al. "Superpower glass: delivering unobtrusive real-time social cues in wearable systems." In Proceedings of the 2016 ACM International Joint Conference on Pervasive and Ubiquitous Computing: Adjunct, pp. 1218-1226. 2016.
4. Washington, Peter, Catalin Voss, Nick Haber, Serena Tanaka, Jena Daniels, Carl Feinstein, Terry Winograd, and Dennis Wall. "A wearable social interaction aid for children with autism." In Proceedings of the 2016 CHI Conference Extended Abstracts on Human Factors in Computing Systems, pp. 2348-2354. 2016.
5. Washington, Peter, Catalin Voss, Aaron Kline, Nick Haber, Jena Daniels, Azar Fazel, Titas De, Carl Feinstein, Terry Winograd, and Dennis Wall. "SuperpowerGlass: a wearable aid for the at-home therapy of children with autism." Proceedings of the ACM on interactive, mobile, wearable and ubiquitous technologies 1, no. 3 (2017): 1-22.
6. Daniels, Jena, Nick Haber, Catalin Voss, Jessey Schwartz, Serena Tamura, Azar Fazel, Aaron Kline et al. "Feasibility testing of a wearable behavioral aid for social learning in children with autism." Applied clinical informatics 9, no. 01 (2018): 129-140.
7. Daniels, Jena, Jessey N. Schwartz, Catalin Voss, Nick Haber, Azar Fazel, Aaron Kline, Peter Washington, Carl Feinstein, Terry Winograd, and Dennis P. Wall. "Exploratory study examining the at-home feasibility of a wearable tool for social-affective learning in children with autism." NPJ digital medicine 1, no. 1 (2018): 1-10.
8. Daniels, Jena, Jessey Schwartz, Nick Haber, Catalin Voss, Aaron Kline, Azar Fazel, Peter Washington et al. "5.13 Design and efficacy of a wearable device for social affective learning in children with autism." Journal of the American Academy of Child & Adolescent Psychiatry 56, no. 10 (2017): S257.

9. Voss, Catalin, Jessey Schwartz, Jena Daniels, Aaron Kline, Nick Haber, Peter Washington, Qandeel Tariq et al. "Effect of wearable digital intervention for improving socialization in children with autism spectrum disorder: a randomized clinical trial." JAMA pediatrics 173, no. 5 (2019): 446-454.
10. Pastaltzidis, Ioannis, Nikolaos Dimitriou, Katherine Quezada-Tavarez, Stergios Aidinlis, Thomas Marquenie, Agata Gurzawska, and Dimitrios Tzovaras. "Data augmentation for fairness-aware machine learning: Preventing algorithmic bias in law enforcement systems." In 2022 ACM Conference on Fairness, Accountability, and Transparency, pp. 2302-2314. 2022.
11. Sharma, Shubham, Yunfeng Zhang, Jesús M. Ríos Aliaga, Djallel Bouneffouf, Vinod Muthusamy, and Kush R. Varshney. "Data augmentation for discrimination prevention and bias disambiguation." In Proceedings of the AAAI/ACM Conference on AI, Ethics, and Society, pp. 358-364. 2020.
12. Yang, Suorong, Weikang Xiao, Mengcheng Zhang, Suhan Guo, Jian Zhao, and Furao Shen. "Image Data Augmentation for Deep Learning: A Survey." arXiv preprint arXiv:2204.08610 (2022).
13. Bellamy, Rachel KE, Kuntal Dey, Michael Hind, Samuel C. Hoffman, Stephanie Houde, Kalapriya Kannan, Pranay Lohia et al. "AI Fairness 360: An extensible toolkit for detecting and mitigating algorithmic bias." IBM Journal of Research and Development 63, no. 4/5 (2019): 4-1.
14. Berk, Richard, Hoda Heidari, Shahin Jabbari, Matthew Joseph, Michael Kearns, Jamie Morgenstern, Seth Neel, and Aaron Roth. "A convex framework for fair regression." arXiv preprint arXiv:1706.02409 (2017).
15. Kim, Michael P., Amirata Ghorbani, and James Zou. "Multiaccuracy: Black-box post-processing for fairness in classification." In Proceedings of the 2019 AAAI/ACM Conference on AI, Ethics, and Society, pp. 247-254. 2019.
16. Lohia, Pranay K., Karthikeyan Natesan Ramamurthy, Manish Bhide, Diptikalyan Saha, Kush R. Varshney, and Ruchir Puri. "Bias mitigation post-processing for individual and group fairness." In Icassp 2019-2019 ieee international conference on acoustics, speech and signal processing (icassp), pp. 2847-2851. IEEE, 2019.
17. Petersen, Felix, Debarghya Mukherjee, Yuekai Sun, and Mikhail Yurochkin. "Post-processing for individual fairness." Advances in Neural Information Processing Systems 34 (2021): 25944-25955.
18. Walter, Maggie, and Chris Andersen. Indigenous statistics: A quantitative research methodology. Routledge, 2016.
19. Chun, Malcolm Nāea. Pono: The way of living. CRDG, 2006.

20. Arellano, April Moreno, Wenrui Dai, Shuang Wang, Xiaoqian Jiang, and Lucila Ohno-Machado. "Privacy policy and technology in biomedical data science." Annual review of biomedical data science 1 (2018): 115.
21. Knoppers, Bartha Maria, and Michael JS Beauvais. "Three decades of genetic privacy: a metaphoric journey." Human Molecular Genetics 30, no. R2 (2021): R156-R160.
22. Church, G. et al. Public access to genome-wide data: five views on balancing research with privacy and protection. PLoS Genet. 5, e1000665 (2009).
23. Homer, Nils, Szabolcs Szelinger, Margot Redman, David Duggan, Waibhav Tembe, Jill Muehling, John V. Pearson, Dietrich A. Stephan, Stanley F. Nelson, and David W. Craig. "Resolving individuals contributing trace amounts of DNA to highly complex mixtures using high-density SNP genotyping microarrays." PLoS genetics 4, no. 8 (2008): e1000167.
24. Im, Hae Kyung, Eric R. Gamazon, Dan L. Nicolae, and Nancy J. Cox. "On sharing quantitative trait GWAS results in an era of multiple-omics data and the limits of genomic privacy." The American Journal of Human Genetics 90, no. 4 (2012): 591-598.
25. Lunshof, J.E., Chadwick, R., Vorhaus, D.B. & Church, G.M. From genetic privacy to open consent. Nat. Rev. Genet. 9, 406–411 (2008).
26. Gymrek, Melissa, Amy L. McGuire, David Golan, Eran Halperin, and Yaniv Erlich. "Identifying personal genomes by surname inference." Science 339, no. 6117 (2013): 321-324.
27. Sweeney, Latanya. "Simple demographics often identify people uniquely." Health (San Francisco) 671, no. 2000 (2000): 1-34.
28. Kalantarian, Haik, Khaled Jedoui, Peter Washington, Qandeel Tariq, Kaiti Dunlap, Jessey Schwartz, and Dennis P. Wall. "Labeling images with facial emotion and the potential for pediatric healthcare." Artificial intelligence in medicine 98 (2019): 77-86.
29. Kalantarian, Haik, Peter Washington, Jessey Schwartz, Jena Daniels, Nick Haber, and Dennis P. Wall. "Guess what?." Journal of healthcare informatics research 3, no. 1 (2019): 43-66.
30. Kalantarian, Haik, Khaled Jedoui, Peter Washington, and Dennis P. Wall. "A mobile game for automatic emotion-labeling of images." IEEE transactions on games 12, no. 2 (2018): 213-218.
31. Kalantarian, Haik, Peter Washington, Jessey Schwartz, Jena Daniels, Nick Haber, and Dennis Wall. "A gamified mobile system for crowdsourcing video for autism research." In 2018 IEEE international conference on healthcare informatics (ICHI), pp. 350-352. IEEE, 2018.
32. Kalantarian, Haik, Khaled Jedoui, Kaitlyn Dunlap, Jessey Schwartz, Peter Washington, Arman Husic, Qandeel Tariq, Michael Ning, Aaron Kline, and Dennis Paul Wall. "The performance of emotion classifiers for children with parent-reported autism: quantitative feasibility study." JMIR mental health 7, no. 4 (2020): e13174.

33. Leblanc, Emilie, Peter Washington, Maya Varma, Kaitlyn Dunlap, Yordan Penev, Aaron Kline, and Dennis P. Wall. "Feature replacement methods enable reliable home video analysis for machine learning detection of autism." Scientific reports 10, no. 1 (2020): 1-11.
34. Tariq, Qandeel, Jena Daniels, Jessey Nicole Schwartz, Peter Washington, Haik Kalantarian, and Dennis Paul Wall. "Mobile detection of autism through machine learning on home video: A development and prospective validation study." PLoS medicine 15, no. 11 (2018): e1002705.
35. Washington, Peter, Emilie Leblanc, Kaitlyn Dunlap, Yordan Penev, Aaron Kline, Kelley Paskov, Min Woo Sun et al. "Precision telemedicine through crowdsourced machine learning: testing variability of crowd workers for video-based autism feature recognition." Journal of personalized medicine 10, no. 3 (2020): 86.
36. Washington, Peter, Qandeel Tariq, Emilie Leblanc, Brianna Chrisman, Kaitlyn Dunlap, Aaron Kline, Haik Kalantarian et al. "Crowdsourced privacy-preserved feature tagging of short home videos for machine learning ASD detection." Scientific reports 11, no. 1 (2021): 1-11.
37. Washington, Peter, Emilie Leblanc, Kaitlyn Dunlap, Yordan Penev, Maya Varma, Jae-Yoon Jung, Brianna Chrisman et al. "Selection of trustworthy crowd workers for telemedical diagnosis of pediatric autism spectrum disorder." In BIOCOMPUTING 2021: Proceedings of the Pacific Symposium, pp. 14-25. 2020.
38. Washington, Peter, Haik Kalantarian, Qandeel Tariq, Jessey Schwartz, Kaitlyn Dunlap, Brianna Chrisman, Maya Varma et al. "Validity of online screening for autism: crowdsourcing study comparing paid and unpaid diagnostic tasks." Journal of medical Internet research 21, no. 5 (2019): e13668.
39. Gürsoy, Gamze, Eduardo Chielle, Charlotte M. Brannon, Michail Maniatakos, and Mark Gerstein. "Privacy-preserving genotype imputation with fully homomorphic encryption." Cell Systems 13, no. 2 (2022): 173-182.
40. Sarkar, Esha, Eduardo Chielle, Gamze Gürsoy, Oleg Mazonka, Mark Gerstein, and Michail Maniatakos. "Fast and scalable private genotype imputation using machine learning and partially homomorphic encryption." IEEE Access 9 (2021): 93097-93110.
41. Sarkar, Esha, Eduardo Chielle, Gamze Gursoy, Leo Chen, Mark Gerstein, and Michail Maniatakos. "Scalable privacy-preserving cancer type prediction with homomorphic encryption." arXiv preprint arXiv:2204.05496 (2022).
42. Emani, Prashant S., Gamze Gürsoy, Andrew Miranker, and Mark B. Gerstein. "PLIGHT: A tool to assess privacy risk by inferring identifying characteristics from sparse, noisy genotypes." bioRxiv (2021).

43. Gürsoy, Gamze, Tianxiao Li, Susanna Liu, Eric Ni, Charlotte M. Brannon, and Mark B. Gerstein. "Functional genomics data: privacy risk assessment and technological mitigation." Nature Reviews Genetics 23, no. 4 (2022): 245-258.
44. Gürsoy, Gamze, Prashant Emani, Charlotte M. Brannon, Otto A. Jolanki, Arif Harmanci, J. Seth Strattan, J. Michael Cherry, Andrew D. Miranker, and Mark Gerstein. "Data sanitization to reduce private information leakage from functional genomics." Cell 183, no. 4 (2020): 905-917.
45. Dwork, Cynthia. "Differential privacy: A survey of results." In International conference on theory and applications of models of computation, pp. 1-19. Springer, Berlin, Heidelberg, 2008.
46. Khanna, Amol, Vincent Schaffer, Gamze Gürsoy, and Mark Gerstein. "Privacy-preserving Model Training for Disease Prediction Using Federated Learning with Differential Privacy." In 2022 44th Annual International Conference of the IEEE Engineering in Medicine & Biology Society (EMBC), pp. 1358-1361. IEEE, 2022.
47. Chun, Malcolm Naea. No na mamo: Traditional and contemporary Hawaiian beliefs and practices. Honolulu, HI: University of Hawaii Press, 2011.
48. Chang, Healani K. "Hawaiian health practitioners in contemporary society." *Pacific Health Dialog* 8, no. 2 (2001): 260-273.
49. Calmon, Flavio, Dennis Wei, Bhanukiran Vinzamuri, Karthikeyan Natesan Ramamurthy, and Kush R. Varshney. "Optimized pre-processing for discrimination prevention." *Advances in neural information processing systems* 30 (2017).
50. Caton, Simon, and Christian Haas. "Fairness in machine learning: A survey." *arXiv preprint arXiv:2010.04053* (2020).
51. Corbett-Davies, Sam, Emma Pierson, Avi Feller, Sharad Goel, and Aziz Huq. "Algorithmic decision making and the cost of fairness." In *Proceedings of the 23rd acm sigkdd international conference on knowledge discovery and data mining*, pp. 797-806. 2017.
52. Dwork, Cynthia, Moritz Hardt, Toniann Pitassi, Omer Reingold, and Richard Zemel. "Fairness through awareness." In *Proceedings of the 3rd innovations in theoretical computer science conference*, pp. 214-226. 2012.
53. Hardt, Moritz, Eric Price, and Nati Srebro. "Equality of opportunity in supervised learning." *Advances in neural information processing systems* 29 (2016).
54. Mehrabi, Ninareh, Fred Morstatter, Nripsuta Saxena, Kristina Lerman, and Aram Galstyan. "A survey on bias and fairness in machine learning." *ACM Computing Surveys (CSUR)* 54, no. 6 (2021): 1-35.
55. Zliobaite, Indre. "On the relation between accuracy and fairness in binary classification." *arXiv preprint arXiv:1505.05723* (2015).

The Effect of AI-Enhanced Breast Imaging on the Caring Radiologist-Patient Relationship

Arianna Bunnell*
Information & Computer Science, University of Hawaiʻi at Mānoa
Honolulu, HI 96822, USA
Email: abunnell@hawaii.edu

Sharon Rowe
Philosophy, University of Hawaiʻi at Mānoa
Honolulu, HI 96822, USA

AI has shown radiologist-level performance at diagnosis and detection of breast cancer from breast imaging such as ultrasound and mammography. Integration of AI-enhanced breast imaging into a radiologist's workflow through the use of computer-aided diagnosis systems, may affect the relationship they maintain with their patient. This raises ethical questions about the maintenance of the radiologist-patient relationship and the achievement of the ethical ideal of shared decision-making (SDM) in breast imaging. In this paper we propose a caring radiologist-patient relationship characterized by adherence to four care-ethical qualities: attentiveness, competency, responsiveness, and responsibility. We examine the effect of AI-enhanced imaging on the caring radiologist-patient relationship, using breast imaging to illustrate potential ethical pitfalls.

Drawing on the work of care ethicists we establish an ethical framework for radiologist-patient contact. Joan Tronto's four-phase model offers corresponding elements that outline a caring relationship. In conjunction with other care ethicists, we propose an ethical framework applicable to the radiologist-patient relationship. Among the elements that support a caring relationship, attentiveness is achieved after AI-integration through emphasizing radiologist interaction with their patient. Patients perceive radiologist competency by effective communication and medical interpretation of CAD results from the radiologist. Radiologists are able to administer competent care when their personal perception of their competency is unaffected by AI-integration and they effectively identify AI errors. Responsive care is reciprocal care wherein the radiologist responds to the reactions of the patient in performing comprehensive ethical framing of AI recommendations. Lastly, responsibility is established when the radiologist demonstrates goodwill and earns patient trust by acting as a mediator between their patient and the AI system.

Keywords: Care ethics; Breast imaging; Computer aided diagnosis

* To whom correspondence should be addressed.

1. Background

1.1. *Artificial Intelligence in breast imaging*

AI is widely applied to diagnostic and screening breast imaging, across almost all modalities. AI for clinical use can be subdivided into computer-aided detection (CADe), diagnosis (CADx), and exam triage (CADt) systems[1]. The first CADe system for screening mammography, designed to mark mammograms in areas of suspicion before review by a radiologist, was approved by the FDA in 1998[2]. By 2008, CADe was used in 70% of screening and 48% of diagnostic mammography patient visits in hospitals[3]. AI-enabled breast imaging CADe and CADx systems can be classified as *standalone* and *reader aid* systems[4]. Standalone AI-enabled CADs are designed to provide a diagnosis on their own, while reader aid systems are designed to assist a radiologist in establishing a diagnosis.

Recently, there has been a flood of research investigating deep learning-based solutions for breast imaging for cancer risk prediction, diagnosis and prognosis, and in predicting treatment response[1,5-7]. Deep learning has shown performance consistent with radiologists at cancer detection and diagnosis in 2D and 3D mammography[8-10], ultrasound[11,12], and MRI[13] in research settings. Deep learning-based CADe and CADx systems have the potential to both reduce the workload on radiologists by accurately diagnosing simple cases and advance breast imaging as AI can pick up on image characteristics not obvious to human radiologists. However, in reducing the workload on radiologists, a deep learning-based CADe/x system removes the opportunity for the radiologist to exercise fundamental diagnostic skills in their clinical practice.

1.2. *The ethical ideal: shared decision-making*

We identify shared decision-making (SDM) as an ethical ideal for healthcare delivery. SDM has the ultimate aim of cultivating a partnership between patient and radiologist. SDM is promoted by both the Radiological Society of North America's *Radiology Cares* campaign[14] and the American College of Radiology's Imaging 3.0™[15]. SDM literature in breast imaging, specifically mammography, places particular emphasis on the following three components of care delivery[16]:

1. *Information Delivery and Patient Education:* The first step to informed consent and treatment under SDM is patient education through presentation of risks and benefits associated with imaging. A personal breast cancer risk assessment is also recommended to contextualize imaging and treatment options[17,18]. Effective information delivery can involve risk scoring, visual aids, and real-world examples in addition to verbal delivery by the radiologist. In addition, information delivery should involve discussion of CADs.
2. *Interpersonal Radiologist-Patient Communication:* Open, honest communication between radiologist and patient is essential to SDM. Verbal, nonverbal and paraverbal physician communication effect patient trust, comfort, and visit satisfaction[19]. Radiologists can contribute to effective communication through asking questions and attentive, empathetic listening. SDM involves patients and radiologists interacting in a democratic manner, with equal gravity given to radiologist and patient.

3. *Framework of the Decision:* SDM requires that treatment decisions be situated in the patient's values, understanding, and background[16]. The patient must understand that the decision to undergo imaging is their choice to make after communication of risks and benefits. The nature of informed consent regarding AI is an open research area[20-23]. SDM should be adapted to patient cultural background and mindful of possible language barriers between radiologist and patient. Patient trust in their radiologist, patient-perceived radiologist expertise, and patient misunderstanding around the role of AI and CADs can all be barriers to decision framing and interpersonal communication.

We introduce care ethics and its goal to foster caring relationships as an ethical framework that supports SDM.

2. Care Ethics

Care ethics has been developed as an alternative to principle-based theories that have historically dominated biomedical and healthcare ethical thinking. In the past 20 years, care ethics has been increasingly applied to a range of healthcare issues, particularly in nursing ethics[24-26]. Care ethics begins with the assumption that moral responsibility derives from our nature as embodied, interdependent, relational beings. As such, we all experience some level of vulnerability during our lifetimes that puts us in need of care from others. Valorizing relationships and recognizing the work of care is a central tenet. Rather than considering how universal principles enter into ethical decision-making, care ethics takes a contextual point of view, seeing moral dilemmas as arising from concrete situations in the context of particular relationships. This shifts the emphasis of moral questions away from "What principles establish my moral obligations?" to "How can I best meet my caring responsibilities in this context?"

Joan Tronto distinguishes between two senses of care: as an action and as a disposition. To provide a useable framework for navigating the complex terrain of caring processes, she identifies four phases that ideally play out in all caring relationships. These are caring about (becoming aware and attending to a need for care); caring for (assuming responsibility to meet such a need); caregiving (the actual work of care, which requires knowledge and judgment); and care receiving (a complex dynamic involving the shared moral burden between the cared for and caregiver). She also identifies four elements of care—attentiveness, competence, responsibility, and responsiveness—that refer to the disposition of those involved in caring relationships[27].

Tronto observes that almost all medical care is "necessary care." Since it is not care one can provide for oneself, it involves the development of a caring physician-patient relationship: "In such settings [those wherein one cannot care for oneself] there is always a power imbalance between care providers and care receivers"[27]. This inherent power imbalance, wherein a radiologist has substantial societal authority and epistemological advantage over their patient, creates a cautionary situation for the reciprocal nature of an ideal caring relationship. When AI is introduced through a CADe/x/t system, further complications arise in that the epistemological authority of the radiologist may be challenged and opportunities for strengthening of the radiologist-patient relationship are removed. In this context, we take breast radiology as a suitable clinical lens for considering the ethical implications resulting from the use of AI-based CADe/x/t systems in breast imaging, due to care ethics' emphasis on the radiologist-patient relationship.

3. The Caring Radiologist-Patient Relationship

3.1. *Assumptions*

For the purposes of the bioethical analysis in this paper, we identify key assumptions about the roles of both the radiologist and CADe/x/t systems in breast imaging. Firstly, we assume that only healthcare professionals interact directly with the CADe/x/t system. Secondly, we assume that the system being used falls into either the CADx or the CADe classifications (the combination of which is referred to as CAD henceforth). We make this assumption because it is possible that through the use of a CADt system, a radiologist may never see their patient's imaging, which eliminates the opportunity to exercise a crucial part of the competency quality of care, restricting the development of the radiologist-patient relationship. We also assume that all CADs involve the use of AI and that the patient is aware of the use of CAD in their examination. Finally, we assume that the radiologist is involved with image acquisition, image analysis, and communication of results to the patient. This does not entail that the radiologist necessarily acquire the images themselves, nor that the radiologist initially or exclusively communicates results to the patient.

The 21st Century Cures Act requires radiology records be made available to patients as soon as information is in the patient's electronic health record[28]. This is consistent with our assumptions, as long as the radiologist communicates with the patient in a reasonable timeframe. However, immediate release of imaging may expose the patient to CAD results (for example, automated breast density assessment from mammography) before radiologist contact. This may cause the patient to question the competency of the radiologist and damage the radiologist-patient relationship. This is further reason to have the radiologist engaged in caring communication with the patient.

3.2. *Developing the idea of caring relationships*

Virginia Held argues that the central focus of care ethics is "the compelling moral salience of attending to and meeting the needs" of particular others for whom we take responsibility[29]. Complimenting Tronto's position that a care ethic is a relational ethic, Nel Noddings and Vrinda Dalmiya develop care ethics along an "individualistic, dyadic model"[30,31]. This person-to-person model is conducive to discussing radiologist-patient interaction. Thomas Randall identifies attentiveness, mutual concern, responsiveness, and trustworthiness as values integrated in good caring. He finds mutual concerns to be "expressed between related beings when there exists a shared interest to make possible the cooperation required to develop and sustain association for the benefit of all involved"[32]. This focuses attentiveness on the part of both radiologist and patient. It engenders trustworthiness in support of a robust and positive relationship supportive for follow up care. This is particularly important for *responsiveness*, which focuses on how a patient responds and whether their needs are met by the care given. It requires paying close attention, honed listening skills, receptiveness, and understanding[33]. A caring relationship between the radiologist and the patient can thus be characterized by adherence to the four elements identified by Tronto: attentiveness, competence, responsiveness, and responsibility, throughout the stages of caring about, caring for, taking care of, and care receiving. Tronto emphasizes the mediating role of communication in care ethics, highlighting such facets of caring such as empathy, attentive listening, and expressions of sympathy and concern from the caregiver.

The following sections explore how Tronto's four caring elements play out in a breast imaging workflow adhering to the previously stated assumptions.

3.3. *Attentiveness*

When one is attentive, the need for care is recognized so caring can begin. Attentiveness does not only trigger the beginning of care; empathetic and enthusiastic listening is an act of care itself[34]. Radiologists care attentively when they listen to their patients and examine symptoms and imaging carefully and without bias. In adhering to SDM, a radiologist allows a patient to express their need for care in their own terms. To strengthen reciprocity in the radiologist-patient relationship, patients can cultivate attentive care by communicating their needs and concerns openly, asking questions, listening in turn, and adhering to their treatment plan.

Attentiveness is of particular importance in breast imaging, where patients may identify palpable lumps or other symptoms during self-examination and need to communicate concerns to their care provider. Breast cancer and breast imaging can be an emotional experience for patients; the connections of the breast to motherhood and sexuality can make seeking care for breast-related concerns embarrassing or anxiety-inducing[35]. This adds to the vulnerability of the patient and must be recognized in attentive breast imaging care, as patients may not be comfortable expressing their need for care candidly. An attentive radiologist observes possibly minute indications of patient condition and adjusts caregiving, particularly the communication of results, in kind.

CADs can disrupt attentiveness in the radiologist-patient relationship. Essentially, there are two designs for CADs in clinical practice, 1) the radiologist needs to interact directly with the CAD during a patient encounter (when the radiologist is performing diagnostic imaging themselves, such as an ultrasound follow-up to mammography), and 2) the CAD is used out of sight of the patient. In this first situation, the opportunity to interact with the CAD during the patient appointment is encountered, and the interaction between radiologist and patient is interrupted. When the radiologist is interacting with the CAD, they are not serving as a physician, but as a technician. This fragmentation of roles can lead to disinterestedness in serving as a physician when interacting with the CAD[36]. Aside from role-switching when interacting with CAD, if used in real-time, radiologists may possibly need to input data, trigger analysis, or actively identify lesions in certain CADx systems. This reduces the amount of time spent face-to-face with patients and can damage the patient's perception of the radiologist's attentiveness. Over-interaction with results from non-real-time CAD produces similar damage to the attentive quality of care. Patients can receive attentive care by the caring radiologist choosing to keep CAD interaction to a minimum during patient encounters, or relegating CAD to non-real-time use, such as in exams performed by a radiology technician.

3.4. *Competence*

After identifying that caring needs to occur, for care to be competent, the caregiver needs to be able to administer the needed care well. Requiring ethical care to be competent recognizes that care ethics does not simply involve good intentions but also requires knowledge, judgement, and skillful execution. Competent caring in breast imaging involves, but is not limited to, maintaining technical competence by staying up to date with new technologies, adhering to reporting standards such as those set forth by the American College of Radiology's Breast Imaging Reporting & Data System[37], and deferring to other physicians or diagnostic tools when necessary. The relational nature of ethical care requires not only that the radiologist administer care well, but that the patient perceives care as competent. Thus, competent caring also involves maintaining patient trust in the radiologist. Medically correct care administered without the perception of competency damages trust and cannot be ethical care. Administering competent care also involves clear, empathetic communication of imaging results at a level appropriate for the patient.

CADs can impact both perception and realization of a radiologist's competency in caring. When a CAD is introduced into the breast imaging workflow, there is a risk of skill erosion, wherein the radiologist loses some or all of their ability to interpret imaging without the use of the CAD. Skill erosion can also occur when new radiologists are not taught the skills which are now being addressed by the CAD. For example, less emphasis may be placed on developing the skills for precise lesion delineation, because this is a common feature of CADe systems. Medical skill erosion, not specific to radiology, has been well-documented as a response to new clinical technology and is an oft-cited professional consequence of incorporating clinical decision support systems into medical practice[38-40].

The ethical question is then whether or not skill erosion challenges the ability of the radiologist to provide competent care. We propose that it does not. The competency requirement of care entails that radiologists evolve with developments in medicine so they provide the best care available to their patient. If we accept that a CADx system diagnoses breast cancer from mammography with higher sensitivity and specificity than the radiologist, then, if the radiologist neglects to defer to the CADx when inspecting imaging, the quality of care suffers. Misdiagnosis can be extremely traumatic for the patient in the case of a false positive, with negative psychological effects lasting up to three years[35], and deadly in the case of a false negative. Thus, it is essential in maintaining a healthy, caring radiologist-patient relationship that a diagnosis be as accurate as possible, and this implies the use of the CADx system.

Accepting that a particular CAD provides a better diagnosis does not necessitate skill erosion. Radiologists may maintain their imaging inspection skills by either examining imaging for a selection of patients without use of the CAD, or ensuring they inspect imaging independently before referring to the CAD. Two concerns present themselves here: The former option may harm a subset of patients and is unethical unless the patients give their informed consent after an SDM-adherent discussion of risks and benefits. The latter slows down the radiologist at best, and at worst subjects patients to over-testing. In the event that the CAD is removed from the medical practice, it is the radiologist who is responsible for "upskilling" to maintain a high quality of care.

The inclusion of a reading aid-style CAD in a breast imaging workflow presents opportunity for disagreement between the radiologist and the CAD. Without the opportunity for follow-up discussion and explanation as one would have with a human collaborator, this can challenge the radiologist's perception of their own competency[41,42]. However, this need not directly affect the caring radiologist-patient relationship, unless the self-perceived skills of the radiologist affect their patient interactions. On the contrary, referring to the CAD adds to the radiologist-patient relationship in much the same way that consulting with another radiologist would. A critical component of providing competent care is knowing when to defer decision-making to others.

The perception of radiologist competency by patients is essential to maintaining a caring relationship. In order to accept care, the more vulnerable care-receiver must trust the caregiver. The inclusion of CAD in the clinical breast imaging environment can damage a patient's trust in the competency of their radiologist. If a CAD is referred to for all imaging results, or if CAD results are presented with minimal explanation of medical significance from the radiologist, there is a risk of seeing the radiologist as just an intermediary between the patient and the computer system[43]. A particular risk to patient perception of radiologist competency arises when CAD results are made available automatically to the patient, before the radiologist can make contact. In this scenario, the patient receives medical information without input from the radiologist, establishing a pseudo computer-patient relationship, in which the computer is presented as competent. When a patient finds a computer to be more competent than the radiologist there is risk to the radiologist-patient relationship (examples from other fields[44-46]). To maintain the perception of competency, radiologists need to be skilled empathetic listeners and communicators, not only with respect to medical knowledge and CAD results[47], but also in person-to-person interactions. If the radiologist and the CAD system agree, radiologists give ethical care when they communicate CAD results effectively. When the patient receives CAD results independently, then the radiologist may maintain the perception of competency by providing adequate medical framing of CAD decisions. If they do not agree, the radiologist may need to compete with a patient's perception of an established epistemic authority in CAD (Note that we are not explicitly referring to explainable AI technologies here, but the skill of the radiologist in communicating diagnostic results in terms appropriate for the patient).

3.5. *Responsiveness*

The responsive element refers to the complex dynamic between caregiver and care-receiver. It implies a shared ethical responsibility, requiring that attention be paid to both the patient and their responses to the care administered. Responsiveness recognizes the vulnerability of the patient and places a particular emphasis on understanding what is being expressed by the patient throughout all stages of care. Both patient and radiologist have a role in responsive care. Medical care can be administered according to best practices, attentively and competently, but as soon as the response of a patient is not considered and care adjusted accordingly, the care can end in moral failure. For example, a patient who is uncomfortable with the breast compression involved in mammography and communicates this discomfort may not continue to be ethically treated. A care-ethical response would involve discussing alternative imaging modalities, and/or adjusting the procedure (or pre-procedural communication) to make the patient more comfortable.

Responsive care encourages dialogue consistent with the ethical ideal of SDM. Patients must feel comfortable expressing their response to care and radiologists must demonstrate that they adjust caregiving to patient response. Responsive caring also necessitates that patient values are incorporated into caregiving. Attitudes around and adoption of mammography have been shown to vary based on patient cultural background[48-50] and a responsive caregiver will adjust their practice and communication to best suit their patient. Radiologist's opportunities to provide responsive care are expanded with the integration of CAD systems, particularly when patients are exposed to CAD results before radiologist communication can occur. Radiologists display responsive care when they modify their communication of CAD results to both the epistemological position and emotional state resulting from previous discovery of CAD results.

However, responsive care can be harmed by CAD usage in clinical breast imaging practice. The application of patient values relating to diagnosis and treatment decisions requires the ethical implications and explanation for these decisions be communicated to the patient. For example, women with different backgrounds may react differently to being told that there is a 2% chance of malignancy in an identified breast lesion, and a recommendation of follow-up imaging or biopsy. CAD decisions are not *a priori* centered around patient value-systems. This risks placing the entire burden of ethical contextualization on the patient.

A patient's capacity to be engaged in responsive care can be further harmed by CAD integration when there is no avenue for the patient to provide feedback on the quality of care they are receiving directly to the CAD. For this reason, the CAD can never assume a role as a moral agent, from a care ethics perspective. We argue that feedback and dialogue with the radiologist is crucial and some may see it as an appropriate substitute for providing feedback to the CAD, especially in the situation where the CAD is serving as a reader aid to the radiologist. We disagree, on the grounds that dialogue about quality of care and accurate diagnosis should be provided to every entity that is making decisions. Patient and radiologist feedback could be incorporated into CADs through closed-loop designs where feedback is used to improve performance. Furthermore, for care to be responsive, the caregiver needs to react to feedback from the care-receiver. The ethical, caring patient cannot receive care from a CAD without substantial radiologist intervention to bridge the ethical gap between CAD output and patient values.

3.6. *Responsibility*

When considering care ethics as a professional ethical framework, we draw attention to the distinction of care ethics as a *responsibility-based* ethical theory, as opposed to more traditional *obligation-based* ethical theories. A care ethics approach to moral decision making involves asking how decisions fulfill our responsibility to maintain caring relationships[51]. By contrast, obligation-based ethical theory asks how decisions influence what we owe to others, thus distancing ourselves from our interpersonal relationships. Defining care ethics as responsibility-based in healthcare assumes practitioners are responsible for the care of their patients as a result of the physician-patient relationship. Radiologists are not care-ethically obligated to administer treatment to their patient; however, they are responsible for how their treatment (and the patient's outcome) will influence not only the radiologist-patient relationship but also the wide network of professional and personal relationships linking the radiologist and patient. Responsible care involves a reciprocal effort on the part of the patient to be open to receiving care.

Radiologists demonstrate responsible care simply by taking it upon themselves to care for their patients. We believe this responsibility need not erode with the use of CAD but can evolve to include more non-medical aspects of care. Radiologists who specialize in breast imaging have unique opportunities to interact with patients in both performing imaging and communicating results. As the medical needs of a patient are met, the radiologist can focus on more humanistic aspects of their practice. The responsibility of radiologists to attend to the emotional and mental wellbeing of their patient through the skills of communication, listening, and empathy is no less a responsibility than diagnosis and treatment. If we take as given that ethical actions are grounded in healthy, caring relationships, it seems obvious that maintaining the radiologist-patient relationship is essential to ethical breast imaging care. It may therefore be necessary for radiologists to shift their focus from medical skills to their less-technical, more caring skills, precisely because CAD are incapable of forming relationships, and thus cannot function as moral agents from a care ethics perspective[43].

Consideration of CAD errors draws particular attention to the breast radiologist's care-ethical *responsibility* for their patient. CAD may be susceptible to errors due to dataset shift in deployment due to unrepresentative training data and differences in data acquisition methods, among other hard-to-detect reasons[52]. A caring radiologist must be sufficiently *competent* to identify CAD errors and trust their own judgement[53,54]. Furthermore, a responsible radiologist must safeguard their patient from erroneous CAD output to maintain trustworthiness and goodwill towards the patient. Thus, within a care context the radiologist is *responsible* for the effects CAD may have on their patient's diagnosis, and thus must engage in AI/CAD safety and monitoring protocols.

Patients need to trust that their radiologist is administering responsible care. This grounds the radiologist-patient relationship. Trust implies an assumption of goodwill between parties involved. Radiologist-patient trust can be fostered through accurate diagnoses, open communication, and empathetic listening. CAD can harm this trust because the patient cannot trust the CAD, which is serving as an extension of the radiologist in making diagnosis decisions. A distinction can be made between reliability and trustworthiness where consistency in decisions and behavior is a condition of reliability, but does not necessarily imply trustworthiness[55]. Trustworthy AI initiatives that focus on the removal of bias contribute to reliability under this framework.

CAD in itself cannot add to the perception of radiologist trustworthiness, since goodwill and responsibility towards the patient cannot be assumed. The CAD and the radiologist are not the same entity. The radiologist may be trusted while the CAD is not. However, while the CAD is advising the radiologist in image interpretation, it serves as an extension of the radiologist. Trust cannot be established in a radiologist who relies exclusively on CAD to make decisions in their practice. Therefore, the radiologist must be present to compensate for CAD's inability to demonstrate goodwill to patients and safeguard them from CAD unreliability and errors; for example, when identifying and communicating why a CAD recommendation has been dismissed, as with unorthodox breast placement, where CAD is known to be unreliable.

4. Conclusion

CAD can reduce some of the burden on radiologists for diagnostic decision-making in breast imaging but is not wholly consistent with the caring radiologist-patient relationship without considerable adaption of radiologist care patterns. The potential diagnostic accuracy and speed of CAD in breast imaging is impossible for human radiologists to replicate, and the potential for CAD to lessen imaging quality/frequency gaps in low-resource settings is groundbreaking. To deny patients the opportunity to receive timely care and the most correct diagnosis would be blatantly unethical. The perspective of care ethics requires maintenance of responsive relationships in which conflicts can be resolved without damage to the continuing relationship[56]. Radiologist maintenance of the radiologist-patient relationship involves administrating attentive care through disengagement with CAD during patient encounters, demonstrating competency through effective communication of CAD results, providing comprehensive ethical framing of CAD output, and establishing responsibility through caution in applying CAD diagnoses.

References

1.Hickman SE, Baxter GC, Gilbert FJ. Adoption of artificial intelligence in breast imaging: evaluation, ethical constraints and limitations. *British journal of cancer*. 2021;125(1):15-22. doi:10.1038/s41416-021-01333-w

2.Keen JD, Keen JM, Keen JE. Utilization of Computer-Aided Detection for Digital Screening Mammography in the United States, 2008 to 2016. *Journal of the American College of Radiology*. 2018;15(1):44-48. doi:10.1016/j.jacr.2017.08.033

3.Rao VM, Levin DC, Parker L, Cavanaugh B, Frangos AJ, Sunshine JH. How Widely Is Computer-Aided Detection Used in Screening and Diagnostic Mammography? *Journal of the American College of Radiology*. 2010/10/01/ 2010;7(10):802-805. doi:https://doi.org/10.1016/j.jacr.2010.05.019

4.Freeman K, Geppert J, Stinton C, et al. Use of artificial intelligence for image analysis in breast cancer screening programmes: systematic review of test accuracy. *BMJ*. 2021-09-01 2021:n1872. doi:10.1136/bmj.n1872

5.Le EPV, Wang Y, Huang Y, Hickman S, Gilbert FJ. Artificial intelligence in breast imaging. *Clinical radiology*. 2019;74(5):357-366. doi:10.1016/j.crad.2019.02.006

6.Hu Q, Giger ML. Clinical Artificial Intelligence Applications: Breast Imaging. *Radiologic Clinics of North America*. 2021/11/01/ 2021;59(6):1027-1043. doi:https://doi.org/10.1016/j.rcl.2021.07.010

7.Bhowmik A, Eskreis-Winkler S. Deep learning in breast imaging. *BJR open*. 2022;4(1)doi:10.1259/bjro.20210060

8.Shen L. End-to-end training for whole image breast cancer diagnosis using an all convolutional design. *arXiv preprint arXiv:171105775*. 2017;

9.Schaffter T, Buist DS, Lee CI, et al. Evaluation of combined artificial intelligence and radiologist assessment to interpret screening mammograms. *JAMA network open*. 2020;3(3):e200265-e200265.

10.Rodriguez-Ruiz A, Lång K, Gubern-Merida A, et al. Stand-Alone Artificial Intelligence for Breast Cancer Detection in Mammography: Comparison With 101 Radiologists. *JNCI: Journal of the National Cancer Institute*. 2019-09-01 2019;111(9):916-922. doi:10.1093/jnci/djy222

11.Zhuang Z, Li N, Joseph Raj AN, Mahesh VG, Qiu S. An RDAU-NET model for lesion segmentation in breast ultrasound images. *PloS one*. 2019;14(8):e0221535.

12.Shen Y, Shamout FE, Oliver JR, et al. Artificial intelligence system reduces false-positive findings in the interpretation of breast ultrasound exams. *Nature Communications*. 2021-12-01 2021;12(1)doi:10.1038/s41467-021-26023-2

13.Zhou J, Luo LY, Dou Q, et al. Weakly supervised 3D deep learning for breast cancer classification and localization of the lesions in MR images. *Journal of Magnetic Resonance Imaging*. 2019;50(4):1144-1151.

14.Patient-centered care. Radiological Society of North America. Accessed July 26, 2022. https://www.rsna.org/practice-tools/patient-centered-care

15.Imaging 3.0. American College of Radiology. Accessed July 26, 2022. https://www.acr.org/Practice-Management-Quality-Informatics/Imaging-3

16.Dubenske LL, Schrager SB, Hitchcock ME, et al. Key Elements of Mammography Shared Decision-Making: a Scoping Review of the Literature. *Journal of General Internal Medicine*. 2018-10-01 2018;33(10):1805-1814. doi:10.1007/s11606-018-4576-6

17.Mcclintock AH, Golob AL, Laya MB. Breast Cancer Risk Assessment. *Mayo Clinic Proceedings*. 2020-06-01 2020;95(6):1268-1275. doi:10.1016/j.mayocp.2020.04.017
18.Siu AL. Screening for Breast Cancer: U.S. Preventive Services Task Force Recommendation Statement. *Annals of Internal Medicine*. 2016-02-16 2016;164(4):279. doi:10.7326/m15-2886
19.Thompson TL. Interpersonal Communication and Health Care. 1994.
20.Astromskė K, Peičius E, Astromskis P. Ethical and legal challenges of informed consent applying artificial intelligence in medical diagnostic consultations. *AI & SOCIETY*. 2021;36(2):509-520.
21.Group CAoRAIW. Canadian Association of Radiologists white paper on ethical and legal issues related to artificial intelligence in radiology. *Canadian Association of Radiologists' Journal*. 2019;70(2):107-118.
22.Cohen IG. Informed consent and medical artificial intelligence: What to tell the patient? *Geo LJ*. 2019;108:1425.
23.D'Antonoli TA. Ethical considerations for artificial intelligence: An overview of the current radiology landscape. *Diagnostic and Interventional Radiology*. 2020;26(5):504.
24.Edwards SD. Three versions of an ethics of care. *Nursing philosophy*. 2009;10(4):231-240. doi:10.1111/j.1466-769X.2009.00415.x
25.Lachman VD. Applying the ethics of care to your nursing practice. *Medsurg nursing*. 2012;21(2):112-116.
26.Green B. Applying Feminist Ethics of Care to Nursing Practice. *Journal of Nursing & Care*. 2012;1(3)doi:10.4172/2167-1168.1000111
27.Tronto JC. Consent as a Grant of Authority: A Care Ethics Reading of Informed Consent. Cambridge University Press; 2008:182-198.
28.21st Century Cures Act, 114-255 (Rep. Bonamici S 2016). 01/06/2015.
29.Held V. *The ethics of care : personal, political, and global*. Oxford University Press; 2006.
30.Noddings N. *Caring: a relational approach to ethics & moral education*. 2nd ed. University of California Press; 2013.
31.Dalmiya V. Why Should a Knower Care? *Hypatia*. 2002;17(1):34-52. doi:10.1111/j.1527-2001.2002.tb00678.x
32.Randall TE. Justifying partiality in care ethics. *Res Publica*. 2020;26(1):67-87.
33.Maio G. Fundamentals of an ethics of care. *Care in healthcare*. 2018:51-63.
34.Klaver K, Baart A. Attentiveness in care: Towards a theoretical framework. *Nursing Ethics*. 2011-09-01 2011;18(5):686-693. doi:10.1177/0969733011408052
35.Parker LM, Carter SM. Ethical and Societal Considerations in Breast Cancer Screening. 2016:347-374.
36.Lysaght T, Lim HY, Xafis V, Ngiam KY. AI-Assisted Decision-making in Healthcare: The Application of an Ethics Framework for Big Data in Health and Research. *Asian bioethics review*. 2019;11(3):299-314. doi:10.1007/s41649-019-00096-0
37.CJ DO, EA S, EB M, Morris EA, al. e. *ACR BI-RADS ® Atlas, Breast Imaging Reporting and Data System*. American College of Radiology; 2013.
38.Lu J. Will Medical Technology Deskill Doctors? *International education studies*. 2016;9(7):130. doi:10.5539/ies.v9n7p130
39.Rinard RG. Technology, Deskilling, and Nurses: The Impact of the Technologically Changing Environment. *Advances in Nursing Science*. 1996;18(4):60-69.

40.Sinagra E, Rossi F, Raimondo D. Use of Artificial Intelligence in Endoscopic Training: Is Deskilling a Real Fear? *Gastroenterology*. 2021-05-01 2021;160(6):2212. doi:10.1053/j.gastro.2020.12.065
41.Grote T, Berens P. On the ethics of algorithmic decision-making in healthcare. *Journal of medical ethics*. 2020;46(3):205-211. doi:10.1136/medethics-2019-105586
42.Di Nucci E. Should we be afraid of medical AI? *Journal of medical ethics*. 2019;45(8):556-558. doi:10.1136/medethics-2018-105281
43.Cartolovni A, Tomicic A, Lazic Mosler E. Ethical, legal, and social considerations of AI-based medical decision-support tools: A scoping review. *International journal of medical informatics (Shannon, Ireland)*. 2022;161:104738-104738. doi:10.1016/j.ijmedinf.2022.104738
44.Longoni C, Cian L. Artificial intelligence in utilitarian vs. hedonic contexts: The "word-of-machine" effect. *Journal of Marketing*. 2022;86(1):91-108.
45.Larkin C, Drummond Otten C, Árvai J. Paging Dr. JARVIS! Will people accept advice from artificial intelligence for consequential risk management decisions? *Journal of Risk Research*. 2022;25(4):407-422.
46.Yang C, Hu J. When do consumers prefer AI-enabled customer service? The interaction effect of brand personality and service provision type on brand attitudes and purchase intentions. *Journal of Brand Management*. 2022;29(2):167-189.
47.Ferretti A, Schneider M, Blasimme A. Machine Learning in Medicine: Opening the New Data Protection Black Box. *European Data Protection Law Review*. 2018;doi:10.3929/ethz-b-000296449
48.Cadet TJ, Bakk L, Stewart K, Maramaldi P. Older Hispanic Women and Breast Cancer Screening: Do Cultural Factors Matter? *Journal of ethnic & cultural diversity in social work*. 2017;26(4):382-398. doi:10.1080/15313204.2017.1315627
49.Russell KM, Monahan P, Wagle A, Champion V. Differences in health and cultural beliefs by stage of mammography screening adoption in African American women. *Cancer*. 2007-01-15 2007;109(S2):386-395. doi:10.1002/cncr.22359
50.Simon CE. Breast Cancer Screening: Cultural Beliefs and Diverse Populations. *Health & social work*. 2006;31(1):36-43. doi:10.1093/hsw/31.1.36
51.Tronto JC. *Moral boundaries : a political argument for an ethic of care*. Routledge; 1993.
52.Liu X, Glocker B, Mccradden MM, Ghassemi M, Denniston AK, Oakden-Rayner L. The medical algorithmic audit. *The Lancet Digital Health*. 2022-05-01 2022;4(5):e384-e397. doi:10.1016/s2589-7500(22)00003-6
53.Tschandl P, Rinner C, Apalla Z, et al. Human–computer collaboration for skin cancer recognition. *Nature Medicine*. 2020-08-01 2020;26(8):1229-1234. doi:10.1038/s41591-020-0942-0
54.Gaube S, Suresh H, Raue M, et al. Do as AI say: susceptibility in deployment of clinical decision-aids. *npj Digital Medicine*. 2021-12-01 2021;4(1)doi:10.1038/s41746-021-00385-9
55.Kerasidou C, Kerasidou A, Buscher M, Wilkinson S. Before and beyond trust: reliance in medical AI. *Journal of medical ethics*. 2021:medethics-2020-107095. doi:10.1136/medethics-2020-107095
56.Tronto JC. Beyond gender difference to a theory of care. *Signs: journal of women in culture and society*. 1987;12(4):644-663.

Federated Learning for Sparse Bayesian Models with Applications to Electronic Health Records and Genomics

Brian Kidd[1], Kunbo Wang[2], Yanxun Xu[2], Yang Ni[1,†]

[1]Department of Statistics, Texas A&M University, College Station, Texas 77843, USA
[2]Department of Applied Mathematics and Statistics, Johns Hopkins University, Baltimore, MD 21218, USA
[†]Correspondence: yni@stat.tamu.edu

Federated learning is becoming increasingly more popular as the concern of privacy breaches rises across disciplines including the biological and biomedical fields. The main idea is to train models locally on each server using data that are only available to that server and aggregate the model (not data) information at the global level. While federated learning has made significant advancements for machine learning methods such as deep neural networks, to the best of our knowledge, its development in sparse Bayesian models is still lacking. Sparse Bayesian models are highly interpretable with natural uncertain quantification, a desirable property for many scientific problems. However, without a federated learning algorithm, their applicability to sensitive biological/biomedical data from multiple sources is limited. Therefore, to fill this gap in the literature, we propose a new Bayesian federated learning framework that is capable of pooling information from different data sources without breaching privacy. The proposed method is conceptually simple to understand and implement, accommodates sampling heterogeneity (i.e., non-iid observations) across data sources, and allows for principled uncertainty quantification. We illustrate the proposed framework with three concrete sparse Bayesian models, namely, sparse regression, Markov random field, and directed graphical models. The application of these three models is demonstrated through three real data examples including a multi-hospital COVID-19 study, breast cancer protein-protein interaction networks, and gene regulatory networks.

Keywords: Causal discovery; Distributed computation; Graphical models; Privacy; Sparse regression.

1. Introduction

Sparse models such as sparse regression and graphical models have been extensively studied and find numerous applications in biological and biomedical sciences such as biomarker identification for electronic health records data[1] and reverse-engineering gene regulatory networks for genomic data.[2] Sparse Bayesian models not only provide point estimation but also naturally quantify the estimation uncertainty, which facilitates interpretation especially for models that have moderate to large numbers of parameters. Shrinkage and variable selection priors have been developed for this purpose including the horseshoe prior,[3] the Bayesian lasso,[4] the spike-and-slab prior,[5] and the thresholding prior.[6] In this article, we study the sparse Bayesian models under the federated learning setting where data are distributed across multiple local sources (called local servers hereafter) and the goal is to perform global inference that pools information from local servers without breaching the local data privacy. Typical application includes privacy-preserved analyses of electronic health records data across multiple hospitals or medical centers where data may be limited in size in each site (hence independent analysis in each site would lack statistical power) but cannot be shared across sites due to the sensitivity of protected health information.

Federated learning is an emerging area and finds many applications especially in health.[7–9] Essentially, the idea is to train models locally on each server using data that are only available to that server and then send model information (instead of any private data) to a central server for aggregation. The central server subsequently sends the aggregated model information back to local servers. The exchange of information between the central and local servers can be an iterative process depending on the communication cost and the design of the federated learning algorithm.[10] Another interesting line of federated learning research considers heterogeneous scenarios where the data distributions may be different across local servers.[11] In general, methods developed for federated learning could be applied for distributing computational tasks on massive data, but the opposite is not true as distributed computing does not generally preserve privacy of the local data.

This article particularly focuses on Bayesian methods, which typically provide more natural uncertainty quantification than the frequentist counterpart. Bayesian inference, however, often requires running a long Markov chain Monte Carlo (MCMC) algorithm to achieve practical convergence, which can be time-consuming. Therefore, Bayesian distributed computing has been developed to improve the computational efficiency through parallelization. One such line of research is so-called consensus Monte Carlo for which MCMC is run on each local server without communication among the servers and the Monte Carlo samples are only aggregated at the end.[12–18] Intuitively, the idea is to divide the posterior into separate sub-posteriors to be computed on each local server; then the research question becomes how to effectively combine these local chains into a single posterior. However, in many situations (e.g. the local data being heterogeneous or highly non-Gaussian), consensus Monte Carlo may not have good empirical performance,[19] but work is continuing to attempt to overcome these issues.[20] There are also methods that run multiple chains with somewhat frequent communication during the course of MCMC.[19,21,22] These methods are potentially useful for federated learning but require carefully crafted MCMC methods to protect privacy. Another line of research involves using a distributed version of stochastic gradients within Langevin Dynamics (i.e., Langevin Monte Carlo),[23] which subsamples each local dataset for gradient approximation. In fact, multiple methods have applied the distributed stochastic gradients idea to federated learning.[24,25] However, gradient does not exist for discrete parameters such as variable selection indicators in sparse models, which is the main focus of this article. Lastly, Bayesian neural networks have seen recent advancements in the federated learning setting where the aggregation is achieved through fitting parametric or nonparametric models to local network parameters.[26,27] While useful for neural networks, it is not straightforward to extend their methods to other models including sparse models such as sparse regression and graphical models.

Our paper demonstrates how basic MCMC algorithms can be used within the federated learning setting by reformulating the model and adding an explicit layer for pooling the local models. As the order of MCMC updating steps can be interchanged, the communication between local servers and the global server can be reduced by running multiple local steps per global aggregation. Through multiple sparse models and real data examples, we show the simplicity and broad applicability of the proposed method.

2. Method

2.1. Overall Framework

We first introduce the proposed federated learning framework for Bayesian models. Later, we will provide several concrete examples illustrating the application of the proposed framework to three specific sparse Bayesian models – sparse regression, Markov random field, and directed graphical models.

Let $\boldsymbol{D}_1, \boldsymbol{D}_2, \ldots, \boldsymbol{D}_M$ denote M datasets and let $\boldsymbol{D} = \{\boldsymbol{D}_1, \ldots, \boldsymbol{D}_M\}$ be the collection of all datasets. If they are available on the same computing server (i.e., under the non-federated learning setting) and if they are independent and identically distributed (iid), then a single probability model can be used to model $\boldsymbol{D}$, $\boldsymbol{D} \sim P(\boldsymbol{D}|\boldsymbol{\theta}) = \prod_{k=1}^{M} P(\boldsymbol{D}_k|\boldsymbol{\theta})$, which is schematically represented by a directed acyclic graph in Figure 1(a). However, this model has two obvious downsides under the federated learning setting: (i) $\boldsymbol{D}_k$ is only available on the local server $k = 1, \ldots, M$ and cannot be shared with other servers due to privacy concerns, etc; and (ii) $\boldsymbol{D}_1, \ldots, \boldsymbol{D}_M$ may not be iid. A naive approach to address these two concerns is to consider M independent probability models (Figure 1(b)), one for each local server, $\boldsymbol{D}_k \sim P(\boldsymbol{D}_k|\boldsymbol{\theta}_k)$. This approach does not provide a joint inference across datasets, which can result in statistically inefficient inference and poor interpretation of model parameters. To provide joint inference while preserving privacy, federated learning approaches have been developed. For example, one may aggregate the estimates of $\boldsymbol{\theta}_1, \ldots, \boldsymbol{\theta}_M$ using some deterministic function $\boldsymbol{\theta} = f(\boldsymbol{\theta}_1, \ldots, \boldsymbol{\theta}_M)$ such as average for continuous parameters and majority vote for discrete parameters. Such deterministic approach is often ad hoc (e.g., lack of finite-sample theoretical justification) and generally does not propagate estimation uncertainty from local parameters $\boldsymbol{\theta}_1, \ldots, \boldsymbol{\theta}_M$ to the global parameter $\boldsymbol{\theta}$. In this article, we will instead consider a probabilistic aggregation approach, which overcomes all the aforementioned limitations. The proposed approach is conceptually simple and natural for Bayesian models. Consider the following hierarchical model, for $k = 1, \ldots, M$,

$$\boldsymbol{D}_k \sim P(\boldsymbol{D}_k|\boldsymbol{\theta}_k), \quad \boldsymbol{\theta}_k \sim P(\boldsymbol{\theta}_k|\boldsymbol{\theta}), \quad \boldsymbol{\theta} \sim P(\boldsymbol{\theta}).$$

Given appropriate choices of $P(\boldsymbol{\theta}_k|\boldsymbol{\theta})$ and $P(\boldsymbol{\theta})$ (to be discussed later), this conceptually simple hierarchical model provides a principled recipe to probabilistically aggregate local information through the posterior distribution $P(\boldsymbol{\theta}|\boldsymbol{\theta}_1, \ldots, \boldsymbol{\theta}_M) \propto P(\boldsymbol{\theta}) \prod_{k=1}^{M} P(\boldsymbol{\theta}_k|\boldsymbol{\theta})$, which directly provides point and interval estimation of $\boldsymbol{\theta}$ through e.g., the posterior mean and the credible interval. Algorithmically, by exploiting the conditional independence of $\boldsymbol{\theta}_k$ and $\boldsymbol{D}_{-k}$ given $\boldsymbol{\theta}$ (subscript "$-k$" means removing $\boldsymbol{D}_k$ from $\boldsymbol{D}$), the computation is trivially parallelizable at the local level and no data ever need to be passed to the global server, hence preserving privacy;

see Figure 1(c). In Algorithm 1, we outline the federated learning MCMC pseudocode, which highlights the local parallelizability and privacy protection (there is no data sharing, and the shared parameters are not observation-level parameters).

The aggregation via the posterior distribution depends crucially on the choices of the prior distribution of local parameters given the global parameter $P(\boldsymbol{\theta}_k|\boldsymbol{\theta})$ and the prior distribution of the global parameter $P(\boldsymbol{\theta})$. Three properties are deemed desirable: (i) $P(\boldsymbol{\theta}_k|\boldsymbol{\theta})$ should encourage $\boldsymbol{\theta}_k$ to tightly concentrate around $\boldsymbol{\theta}$ so that $\boldsymbol{\theta}$ can be interpreted as a global version of local server-specific parameters $\boldsymbol{\theta}_1, \dots, \boldsymbol{\theta}_M$, (ii) $P(\boldsymbol{\theta}_k|\boldsymbol{\theta})$ should also allow occasional deviation of $\boldsymbol{\theta}_k$ from $\boldsymbol{\theta}$ if $\boldsymbol{D}_k$ strongly supports it, which accommodates non-iid scenarios, and (iii) $P(\boldsymbol{\theta})$ should encourage sparsity in $\boldsymbol{\theta}$ for better model interpretability. To make the discussion concrete, we now consider three specific sparse Bayesian models. For ease of exposition, we start with a sparse regression model.

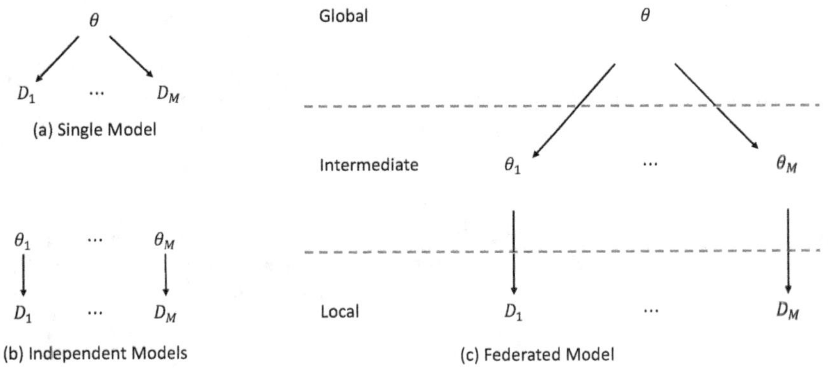

Fig. 1: Illustration of (a) a single model, (b) independent models, and (c) a federated model. The arrows represent the direct dependencies among the variables. The federated model has three levels: global, intermediate, and local. The parameters at the intermediate level are passed from local servers to the global server whereas the data never leave the local servers.

2.2. Example 1: Federated Sparse Regression

2.2.1. Sparse Regression

Let $\boldsymbol{D}_k = (\boldsymbol{X}_{ki}, Y_{ki})_{i=1}^{n_k}$ for $k = 1, \dots, M$ denote the local server-specific dataset with n_k observations where $\boldsymbol{X}_{ki} = (X_{ki1}, \dots, X_{kip})^T$ is p-dimensional covariate vector and Y_{ki} is the response variable for $i = 1, \dots, n_k$. Consider the following server-specific regression model,

$$Y_{ki} = \boldsymbol{X}_{ki}^T \boldsymbol{\theta}_k + \epsilon_{ki}, \tag{1}$$

for $k = 1, \dots, M$ and $i = 1 \dots, n_k$, where $\boldsymbol{\theta}_k = (\theta_{k1}, \dots, \theta_{kp})^T$ is the regression coefficient vector and $\epsilon_{ki} \sim N(0, \sigma_k^2)$ is a normal error term. For simplicity, we do not make joint inference on σ_k^2 as the parameter of interest of a regression model is typically the regression coefficient $\boldsymbol{\theta}_k$; but

Algorithm 1 General Algorithm

Input: $\boldsymbol{D}_k$ and hyperparameters
Output: Monte Carlo samples of $\boldsymbol{\theta}_1, \ldots, \boldsymbol{\theta}_M$ and $\boldsymbol{\theta}$

```
Initialize θ^(0) on the global server
for t in 1,...,T do                                                    ▷ MCMC iterator
    parfor k in 1...,M do                                              ▷ Parallel for-loop
        Send the global parameter θ^(t-1) to local server k
        Sample θ_k^(t)|D_k, θ^(t-1) ~ P(θ_k|D_k, θ^(t-1)) on local server k ▷ Local Update
        Send θ_k^(t) to the global server
    end parfor
    Sample θ^(t) ~ P(θ|θ_1^(t),...,θ_M^(t)) on the global server        ▷ Global Aggregation
end for
```

if desired, our method can be easily extended for joint inference of σ_k^2. In many applications, not all covariates are predictive of the response variable and, correspondingly, $\boldsymbol{\theta}_k$ is assumed to be sparse, i.e., most of the entries $\boldsymbol{\theta}_k$ are zero or very close to zero.

2.2.2. Prior

We now specify the prior distributions $P(\boldsymbol{\theta}_k|\boldsymbol{\theta})$, $P(\boldsymbol{\theta})$, and $P(\sigma_k^2)$. To achieve the fist two desired properties outlined at the end of Section 2.1, we impose an element-wise mean-shifted horseshoe prior for $\boldsymbol{\theta}_k$, which is centered around the global parameter $\boldsymbol{\theta}$,

$$\theta_{kj}|\theta_j \sim N(\theta_j, \lambda_{kj}^2\tau_j^2),$$
$$\lambda_{kj}, \tau_j \sim C^+(0,1),$$

where $C^+(0,1)$ is the standard half-Cauchy distribution. The mean-zero horseshoe prior[28,29] has been extensively studied in the sparse regression model, which is capable of shrinking small coefficients aggressively towards zero while leaving large coefficients untouched. Our use of mean-shifted horseshoe prior aggressively shrinks local parameter θ_{kj} towards the global parameter θ_j but still allows substantial deviation if data dictates so.

To encourage sparsity, we assume a spike-and-slab prior[5] on the global parameter with a beta-Bernoulli hyperprior,

$$\theta_j|\gamma_j \sim \gamma_j N(0, \eta_j) + (1-\gamma_j)N(0, c_0\eta_j),$$
$$\gamma_j \sim \text{Bernoulli}(\rho), \quad \rho \sim \text{beta}(a_\rho, b_\rho),$$

where c_0 is fixed small constant (e.g., 0.01) and γ_j is a binary indicator variable, which equals 1 if θ_j is significantly away from 0 and equals 0 if θ_j is so small that it can be safely treated as zero without affecting the model fit. The prior specification is completed with conjugate inverse-gamma priors for variance parameters $\sigma_k^2 \sim IG(a_\sigma, b_\sigma)$ and $\eta_j \sim IG(a_\eta, b_\eta)$.

In summary, the local horseshoe prior shrinks local parameters towards the global parameter (i.e., the aggregation) and the global spike-and-slab prior induces sparsity.

2.2.3. MCMC

We expand the "Local Update" and the "Global Aggregation" steps of Algorithm 1 for sparse regression model in Algorithms 2 and 3, respectively. Note that for the sampling of horseshoe-related parameters, we utilize the parameter expansion technique.[30] Also note that one can opt to run multiple local update steps per each global aggregation due to the standard Markov chain theory; see the for-loop in Algorithm 2.

Algorithm 2 Local Update for Sparse Regression

```
for ℓ in 1, ..., L do
    Sample ν_kj ~ IG(1, 1 + λ_kj^{-2})                                        ▷ Parameter Expansion[30]
    Sample λ²_kj ~ IG[1, ν_kj^{-1} + (θ_kj − θ_j)²/(2τ²_j)]
    Sample θ_k ~ f(θ_k) ∝ ∏_{i=1}^{n_k} N(Y_ki | X_ki^T θ_k, σ²_k) ∏_{j=1}^{p} N(θ_kj | θ_j, λ²_kj τ²_j)
    Sample σ²_k ~ IG(a_σ + n_k/2, b_σ + Σ_{i=1}^{n_k} (Y_ki − X_ki^T θ_k)²/2)
end for
```

for ℓ in $1,\ldots,L$ do
- Sample $\nu_{kj} \sim IG(1, 1+\lambda_{kj}^{-2})$ ▷ Parameter Expansion[30]
- Sample $\lambda_{kj}^2 \sim IG\big[1, \nu_{kj}^{-1} + (\theta_{kj}-\theta_j)^2/(2\tau_j^2)\big]$
- Sample $\boldsymbol{\theta}_k \sim f(\boldsymbol{\theta}_k) \propto \prod_{i=1}^{n_k} N(Y_{ki}|\boldsymbol{X}_{ki}^T\boldsymbol{\theta}_k, \sigma_k^2) \prod_{j=1}^{p} N(\theta_{kj}|\theta_j, \lambda_{kj}^2\tau_j^2)$
- Sample $\sigma_k^2 \sim IG(a_\sigma + n_k/2, b_\sigma + \sum_{i=1}^{n_k}(Y_{ki} - \boldsymbol{X}_{ki}^T\boldsymbol{\theta}_k)^2/2)$

end for

Algorithm 3 Global Aggregation for Sparse Regression

- Sample $\xi_j \sim IG(1, 1+\tau_j^{-2})$ ▷ Parameter Expansion[30]
- Sample $\tau_j^2 \sim IG\big[(M+1)/2, \xi_j^{-1} + \sum_{k=1}^{M}(\theta_{kj}-\theta_j)^2/\lambda_{kj}^2\big]$
- Sample $\boldsymbol{\theta} \sim f(\boldsymbol{\theta}) \propto \prod_{j=1}^{p}\big[N(\theta_j|0, c_0^{1-\gamma_j}\eta)\prod_{k=1}^{M} N(\theta_{kj}|\theta_j, \lambda_{kj}^2\tau_j^2)\big]$
- Sample $\eta \sim IG\big[a_\eta + p/2, b_\eta + \sum_{j=1}^{p}\theta_j^2/c_0^{1-\gamma_j}\big]$
- Sample $\gamma_j \sim \text{Bernoulli}(q_j)$ with $q_j = \frac{\rho N(\theta_j|0,\eta)}{\rho N(\theta_j|0,\eta)+(1-\rho)N(\theta_j|0,c_0\eta)}$
- Sample $\rho \sim \text{beta}(a_\rho + \sum_{j=1}^{p}\gamma_j, b_\rho + p - \sum_{j=1}^{p}\gamma_j)$

2.3. Example 2: Federated Markov Random Field

The sparse regression model in Section 2.2 can be extended to the sparse Gaussian Markov random field model (also known as the Gaussian graphical model), which can also be worked out in a federated learning setting. Let $\boldsymbol{D}_k = (\boldsymbol{Y}_{ki})_{i=1}^{n_k}$ for $k = 1,\ldots,M$ where $\boldsymbol{Y}_{ki} = (Y_{ki1},\ldots,Y_{kip})^T$ is a random vector whose conditional independence relationships are of interest. We assume a centered multivariate Gaussian distribution,

$$\boldsymbol{Y}_{ki} \sim N(0, \boldsymbol{\Omega}_k^{-1}), \tag{2}$$

with precision (inverse covariance) matrix $\boldsymbol{\Omega}_k = [\omega_{kjh}]_{j=1,h=1}^{p,p}$. If $\omega_{kjh} = 0$, then Y_{kj} and Y_{kh} are conditionally independent given all the other variables. Often, such conditional independence relationships are represented by an undirected graph/network where nodes represent the random variables and two nodes are connected $j - h$ by an undirected edge if and only if $\omega_{kjh} \neq 0$. Interestingly, Gaussian Markov random field is closely related to sparse regression, which leads to the so-called neighborhood selection method.[31] Note that the joint distribution

(2) implies the conditional distribution of Y_{kij} given all the other variables,

$$Y_{kij} = \boldsymbol{Y}_{ki,-j}^T \boldsymbol{\theta}_{kj} + \epsilon_{kij}, \tag{3}$$

with $\boldsymbol{\theta}_{kj} = -\boldsymbol{\Omega}_{k,-j,j}/\omega_{kjj}$ and $\epsilon_{kij} \sim N(0, \omega_{kjj}^{-1})$, which is exactly a regression model with response Y_{kij} and covariates $\boldsymbol{Y}_{ki,-j}$. Therefore, $\omega_{kjh} = 0$ if and only if $\theta_{kjh} = 0$. Consequently, estimating a sparse precision matrix $\boldsymbol{\Omega}_k$ reduces to estimating the set of sparse regression coefficient for p independent regressions. Hence, the proposed federated learning algorithm for sparse regression can be applied in parallel to (3) for $j = 1, \ldots, p$. One caveat is that the neighborhood selection method has no guarantee of the symmetry of $\boldsymbol{\Omega}_k$ but simple post-processing procedures based on union or intersection can be used to obtain a consensus undirected graph.[31]

2.4. Example 3: Federated Directed Graphical Models

Markov random field is useful for investigating symmetric association but cannot be used to identify causal relationships, which are asymmetric (cause and effect are not exchangeable). Directed graphical models[32,33] are popular tools for discovering causality (i.e., generating plausible causal hypotheses in an exploratory fashion). Consider the following structural equation model,[34,35]

$$\boldsymbol{Y}_{ki} = \boldsymbol{Y}_{ki}\boldsymbol{\theta}_k + \boldsymbol{E}_{ki}, \tag{4}$$

where $\boldsymbol{\theta}_k = [\theta_{kjh}]_{j=1,h=1}^{p,p}$ is the causal effect matrix and $\boldsymbol{E}_{ki} = (\epsilon_{ki1}, \ldots, \epsilon_{kip})^T \sim N(0, \boldsymbol{\Sigma}_{ki})$ is the normally-distributed error vector with diagonal covariance $\boldsymbol{\Sigma}_{ki}$. Under the causal Markov assumption,[32,33] we say Y_{kh} is a direct cause of Y_{kj} if $\theta_{kjh} \neq 0$, which can be represented by an arrow $j \leftarrow h$ in a directed graph/network. The error distribution induce a distribution for $\boldsymbol{Y}_{ki}$,

$$\boldsymbol{Y}_{ki} \sim N(0, (\boldsymbol{I} - \boldsymbol{\theta}_k)^{-1}\boldsymbol{\Sigma}_{ki}(\boldsymbol{I} - \boldsymbol{\theta}_k)^{-T}),$$

where $\boldsymbol{I}$ is a $p \times p$ identity matrix. Note that for observational data, the causal relationships may not be identifiable due to Markov equivalence. To ensure identifiability, various methods have been developed. As an example, we take advantage of the non-Gaussianity for causal identifiability.[36] Specifically, we assume each diagonal entry of $\boldsymbol{\Sigma}_{ki}$ to be exponentially distributed, which induces a marginal Laplace distribution for ϵ_{kij} for $j = 1, \ldots, p$. We remark that the popular causal discovery method, Bayesian network, is a special case of the directed graphical model considered here by restricting the graph to be acyclic. Because biological systems tend to have feedback loops, we do not make such restriction. The price to pay is that we lose conjugacy but the proposed federated learning framework is still applicable with a minor tweak: replace the Gibbs sampling of $\boldsymbol{\theta}_k$ in Algorithm 2 by a Metropolis step. Specifically, we propose a new value $\boldsymbol{\theta}_k^\star$ from some proposal density $q(\cdot)$ such as normal, which could depend on the value of $\boldsymbol{\theta}_k$ from the last iteration. Then we accept $\boldsymbol{\theta}_k^\star$ with probability $\min(1, a)$ with

$$a = \frac{q(\boldsymbol{\theta}_k) N(0, (\boldsymbol{I} - \boldsymbol{\theta}_k^\star)^{-1}\boldsymbol{\Sigma}_{ki}(\boldsymbol{I} - \boldsymbol{\theta}_k^\star)^{-T}) \prod_{j \neq h} N(\theta_{kjh}^\star | \theta_{jh}, \lambda_{kjh}^2 \tau_{jh}^2)}{q(\boldsymbol{\theta}_k^\star) N(0, (\boldsymbol{I} - \boldsymbol{\theta}_k)^{-1}\boldsymbol{\Sigma}_{ki}(\boldsymbol{I} - \boldsymbol{\theta}_k)^{-T}) \prod_{j \neq h} N(\theta_{kjh} | \theta_{jh}, \lambda_{kjh}^2 \tau_{jh}^2)}.$$

3. Numerical Studies

We demonstrate the proposed methods with three real data examples. Simulation results are provided in the Supplementary Materials `https://www.dropbox.com/s/5cl1ag92otaos54/kidd_supp.pdf?dl=0`.

3.1. Johns Hopkins COVID-19 Data - Federated Sparse Regression

COVID-19 (a coronavirus) has been a recent pandemic receiving a great amount of attention worldwide. We analyze the COVID-19 clinical data electronically recorded in four Johns Hopkins' hospitals (i.e., $M = 4$). Each hospital provides 100-150 patients, leading to a total sample size of 552. Due to the sensitive protected health information, data cannot be easily shared across hospitals for the purpose of statistical analyses but local computation within each hospital is feasible. Therefore, this data provide an excellent opportunity to illustrate the practical utility of the proposed federated learning method.

An important marker for COVID-19 is the arterial oxygen saturation (S_aO_2, our response variable), which, unfortunately, is difficult to measure. Instead, because of its non-invasiveness, the peripheral oxygen saturation (S_pO_2, our main covariate) is often used as a proxy measurement for S_aO_2. We will apply the federated sparse regression model to the Johns Hopkins data to examine the association between S_pO_2 and S_aO_2 in COVID-19 patients while adjusting for eight variables commonly collected at doctors visits: temperature in Celsius (Temp_C), mean arterial pressure (MAP), gender, age, and race, hemoglobin count (HGB), bilirubin levels, and creatinine levels. Dummy variable coding is used for gender (Male) and race (Race_b (Black), Race_h (Hispanic), Race_a (Asian)).

We run the federated learning algorithm with $T = 1000$ global aggregation and $L = 100$ local updates per each global aggregation. We report the posterior mean of $\boldsymbol{\theta}$ and posterior inclusion probability (PIP) in Table 1. PIP is defined as the posterior mean of γ_j and a large value indicates high significance of X_j. As expected, S_pO_2 is the most significant predictor of S_aO_2 with PIP=0.777, which demonstrates that the proposed federated sparse regression has the potential to identify important variable by pooling information from multiple local servers without breaching privacy.

3.2. Breast Cancer Protein-Protein Interaction Networks - Federated Markov Random Field

Breast cancer is one of the most prevalent types of cancer, affecting over 5% of women in the United States throughout their lives. Since cancer is a genetic disease, modern treatment of breast cancer relies heavily on the fundamental understanding of genetic architecture of breast cancer tissues. Therefore, it is crucial to understand genetic networks at different levels such as gene and protein levels. In this section, to demonstrate federated Markov random field, we consider a Reverse Phase Protein Array data from the The Cancer Proteome Atlas.[37] Protein expression data are extracted from 7 sites with over 50 observations (the biggest site has 149 observations). We focus our analysis on $p = 11$ breast cancer-related proteins.[38] We reported PIP of all pairs of proteins in Figure 2(a) with darker color corresponding to higher PIP. The most significant interaction, STK11 and CDKN1B, is biologically plausible as STK11 is known

Table 1: COVID-19 data

Covariate	$\boldsymbol{\theta}$	PIP
S_pO_2	0.673	0.777
Age	-0.002	0.032
MAP	0.006	0.048
Temp_C	0.152	0.306
HGB	0.029	0.123
Bilirubin	-0.013	0.157
Creatinine	-0.017	0.090
Male	0.013	0.142
Race_b	-0.003	0.216
Race_h	-0.007	0.178
Race_a	-0.037	0.217

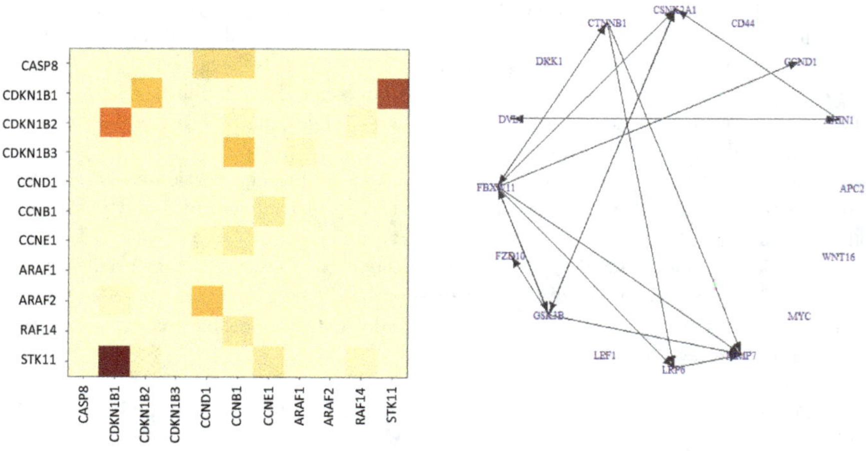

(a) Protein-protein interaction network

(b) Gene regulatory network

Fig. 2: Breast cancer genetic networks.

to phosphorylate CDKN1A[39] and CDKN1A and CDKN1B belong to the same family of CDK inhibitor. The next most significant association is between CDKN1B1 and CDKN1B2, which is also not surprising given they are the variants of the same protein CDKN1B. As we noted before, Figure 2(a) is not symmetric due to the artifact of neighborhood selection.[31] It can be symmetrized if desired by taking the maximum or minimum of PIP for each pair of pairs.

3.3. Breast Cancer Gene Regulatory Networks - Federated Directed Graphical Models

To demonstrate federated directed graphical models, we consider the breast cancer gene expression data obtained from the Genomic Data Commons project of the National Cancer Institute.[40] The consortium hosts data generated from over 45 different sites. We restrict our analysis to the 10 sites with over 50 observations, leading to total sample size 901 with the largest site having 227 observations and two others having over 100 observations each.

We focus our analysis on the WNT/β-catenin signaling pathway known to be critical for breast cancer development.[41] Particularly, $p = 16$ genes emphasized in the recent review paper[41] are considered. We present the estimated gene regulatory network in Figure 2(b) where Bayesian false discovery rate control[42] is used to threshold the PIP to obtain the sparse network.

Some feedback loops are interesting. For example, DVL1 is known to inactivate AXIN1, but our analysis also shows a direct feedback from AXIN1 to DVL1, which requires further experimental validation. In addition, the regulatory relationship from CTNNB1 to MMP7 also matches the existing biological knowledge that MMP7 is a downstream effect of CTNNB1.[43]

4. Discussion

We have brought sparse Bayesian models into the realm of federated learning. The proposed method is conceptually simple and allows for data heterogeneity (i.e., non-iid observations) and proper uncertainty quantification. By switching the MCMC order and updating local models multiple times between global server updates, we manage to the limit the communication cost while maintaining theoretical convergence (as MCMC eventually converges regardless of the update order). Through real data examples, we show the applicability of the proposed method for sparse regression, Markov random field, directed graphical models.

There are several future directions. First, we have only considered linear models for both regression and graphical models. Nonlinearity can be incorporated by spline basis expansion.[44] Second, some variables may not be measured in certain sites. By pooling the covariance information together through federated learning, one can impute these missing variables under the missing at random assumption. Preliminary simulations (not shown) support this idea. Third, we have focused on the federated learning setting where there is a central server. It would be interesting to extend our current approach to the scenarios where there is no central server and only pairwise direct communication among local serves is possible.

References

1. Y. Ni, F. C. Stingo, M. J. Ha, R. Akbani and V. Baladandayuthapani, Bayesian hierarchical varying-sparsity regression models with application to cancer proteogenomics, Journal of the American Statistical Association 114, 48 (2019).
2. J. Choi, R. Chapkin and Y. Ni, Bayesian causal structural learning with zero-inflated Poisson Bayesian networks, Advances in Neural Information Processing Systems 33, 5887 (2020).
3. C. M. Carvalho, N. G. Polson and J. G. Scott, The horseshoe estimator for sparse signals, Biometrika 97, 465 (2010).
4. T. Park and G. Casella, The bayesian lasso, Journal of the American Statistical Association 103, 681 (2008).

5. E. I. George and R. E. McCulloch, Variable selection via Gibbs sampling, Journal of the American Statistical Association 88, 881 (1993).
6. Y. Ni, F. C. Stingo and V. Baladandayuthapani, Bayesian graphical regression, Journal of the American Statistical Association 114, 184 (2019).
7. Y. Wu, X. Jiang, J. Kim and L. Ohno-Machado, Grid binary logistic regression (glore): building shared models without sharing data, Journal of the American Medical Informatics Association 19, 758 (2012).
8. Y. Li, X. Jiang, S. Wang, H. Xiong and L. Ohno-Machado, Vertical grid logistic regression (vertigo), Journal of the American Medical Informatics Association 23, 570 (2016).
9. J. Xu, B. S. Glicksberg, C. Su, P. Walker, J. Bian and F. Wang, Federated learning for healthcare informatics, Journal of Healthcare Informatics Research 5, 1 (2021).
10. T. Li, A. K. Sahu, A. Talwalkar and V. Smith, Federated learning: Challenges, methods, and future directions, IEEE Signal Processing Magazine 37, 50 (2020).
11. Y. Laguel, K. Pillutla, J. Malick and Z. Harchaoui, A superquantile approach to federated learning with heterogeneous devices, in 2021 55th Annual Conference on Information Sciences and Systems (CISS), 2021.
12. X. Wang and D. B. Dunson, Parallelizing MCMC via Weierstrass sampler, arXiv preprint arXiv:1312.4605 (2013).
13. S. Srivastava, V. Cevher, Q. Dinh and D. Dunson, WASP: Scalable Bayes via barycenters of subset posteriors, in Artificial Intelligence and Statistics, 2015.
14. S. L. Scott, A. W. Blocker, F. V. Bonassi, H. A. Chipman, E. I. George and R. E. McCulloch, Bayes and big data: The consensus Monte Carlo algorithm, International Journal of Management Science and Engineering Management 11, 78 (2016).
15. C. Nemeth and C. Sherlock, Merging MCMC subposteriors through Gaussian-process approximations, Bayesian Analysis 13, 507 (2018).
16. Y. Ni, Y. Ji and P. Müller, Consensus Monte Carlo for random subsets using shared anchors, Journal of Computational and Graphical Statistics 29, 703 (2020).
17. Y. Ni, D. Jones and Z. Wang, Consensus variational and Monte Carlo algorithms for Bayesian nonparametric clustering, in 2020 IEEE International Conference on Big Data (Big Data), 2020.
18. Y. Ni, P. Müller, M. Diesendruck, S. Williamson, Y. Zhu and Y. Ji, Scalable Bayesian nonparametric clustering and classification, Journal of Computational and Graphical Statistics 29, 53 (2020).
19. L. J. Rendell, A. M. Johansen, A. Lee and N. Whiteley, Global consensus Monte Carlo, Journal of Computational and Graphical Statistics 30, 249 (2020).
20. D. Mesquita, P. Blomstedt and S. Kaski, Embarrassingly parallel MCMC using deep invertible transformations, in Uncertainty in Artificial Intelligence, 2020.
21. A. Chowdhury and C. Jermaine, Parallel and distributed MCMC via shepherding distributions, in International Conference on Artificial Intelligence and Statistics, 2018.
22. V. Plassier, M. Vono, A. Durmus and E. Moulines, DG-LMC: A turn-key and scalable synchronous distributed MCMC algorithm via Langevin Monte Carlo within Gibbs, in International Conference on Machine Learning, 2021.
23. S. Ahn, B. Shahbaba and M. Welling, Distributed stochastic gradient MCMC, in International Conference on Machine Learning, 2014.
24. K. El Mekkaoui, D. Mesquita, P. Blomstedt and S. Kaski, Federated stochastic gradient Langevin dynamics, in Uncertainty in Artificial Intelligence, 2021.
25. M. Vono, V. Plassier, A. Durmus, A. Dieuleveut and E. Moulines, QLSD: Quantised Langevin stochastic dynamics for Bayesian federated learning, in International Conference on Artificial Intelligence and Statistics, 2022.
26. H.-Y. Chen and W.-L. Chao, FedBE: Making Bayesian model ensemble applicable to federated

learning, arXiv preprint arXiv:2009.01974 (2020).
27. M. Yurochkin, M. Agarwal, S. Ghosh, K. Greenewald, N. Hoang and Y. Khazaeni, Bayesian nonparametric federated learning of neural networks, in International Conference on Machine Learning, 2019.
28. C. M. Carvalho, N. G. Polson and J. G. Scott, Handling sparsity via the horseshoe, in Artificial Intelligence and Statistics, 2009.
29. A. Bhadra, J. Datta, N. G. Polson and B. Willard, Lasso meets horseshoe: A survey, Statistical Science 34, 405 (2019).
30. E. Makalic and D. F. Schmidt, A simple sampler for the horseshoe estimator, IEEE Signal Processing Letters 23, 179 (2015).
31. N. Meinshausen and P. Bühlmann, High-dimensional graphs and variable selection with the lasso, The Annals of Statistics 34, 1436 (2006).
32. P. Spirtes, C. N. Glymour, R. Scheines and D. Heckerman, Causation, Prediction, and Search (MIT press, 2000).
33. J. Pearl, Causality: Models, Reasoning and Inference, 2nd edn. (Cambridge University Press, USA, 2009).
34. P. Spirtes, Directed cyclic graphical representations of feedback models, in Proceedings of the Eleventh Conference on Uncertainty in Artificial Intelligence, UAI'95 (Morgan Kaufmann Publishers Inc., San Francisco, CA, USA, 1995).
35. T. Richardson, A discovery algorithm for directed cyclic graph, in Proceedings of the Twelfth International Conference on Uncertainty in Artificial Intelligence, UAI'961996.
36. G. Lacerda, P. L. Spirtes, J. Ramsey and P. O. Hoyer, Discovering cyclic causal models by independent components analysis, in Proceedings of the Twenty-Fourth Conference on Uncertainty in Artificial Intelligence, 2008.
37. J. Li, Y. Lu, R. Akbani, Z. Ju, P. L. Roebuck, W. Liu, J.-Y. Yang, B. M. Broom, R. G. Verhaak, D. W. Kane et al., TCPA: a resource for cancer functional proteomics data, Nature methods 10, 1046 (2013).
38. M. Kim, J. Park, M. Bouhaddou, K. Kim, A. Rojc, M. Modak, M. Soucheray, M. J. McGregor, P. O'Leary, D. Wolf et al., A protein interaction landscape of breast cancer, Science 374, p. eabf3066 (2021).
39. R. Esteve-Puig, R. Gil, E. Gonzalez-Sanchez, J. J. Bech-Serra, J. Grueso, J. Hernandez-Losa, T. Moline, F. Canals, B. Ferrer, J. Cortes et al., A mouse model uncovers lkb1 as an uvb-induced dna damage sensor mediating cdkn1a (p21waf1/cip1) degradation, PLoS Genetics 10, p. e1004721 (2014).
40. R. L. Grossman, A. P. Heath, V. Ferretti, H. E. Varmus, D. R. Lowy, W. A. Kibbe and L. M. Staudt, Toward a shared vision for cancer genomic data, New England Journal of Medicine 375, 1109 (2016).
41. Y. Feng, M. Spezia, S. Huang, C. Yuan, Z. Zeng, L. Zhang, X. Ji, W. Liu, B. Huang, W. Luo et al., Breast cancer development and progression: Risk factors, cancer stem cells, signaling pathways, genomics, and molecular pathogenesis, Genes & Diseases 5, 77 (2018).
42. P. Müller, G. Parmigiani and K. Rice, FDR and Bayesian multiple comparisons rules, in Proceedings of the 8th Valencia World Meeting on Bayesian Statistics, (Oxford University Press, 2006).
43. M. Kanehisa, M. Furumichi, Y. Sato, M. Ishiguro-Watanabe and M. Tanabe, KEGG: integrating viruses and cellular organisms, Nucleic acids research 49, D545 (2021).
44. Y. Ni, F. C. Stingo and V. Baladandayuthapani, Bayesian nonlinear model selection for gene regulatory networks, Biometrics 71, 585 (2015).

Not in my AI: Moral engagement and disengagement in health care AI development*

Ariadne A. Nichol, Meghan C. Halley, Carole A. Federico*, and Mildred K. Cho†
Stanford Center for Biomedical Ethics, Stanford University
Stanford, CA 94305, USA
Email: micho@stanford.edu

Pamela L. Sankar†
Department of Medical Ethics & Health Policy, University of Pennsylvania
Philadelphia, PA 19104, USA

Machine learning predictive analytics (MLPA) are utilized increasingly in health care, but can pose harms to patients, clinicians, health systems, and the public. The dynamic nature of this technology creates unique challenges to evaluating safety and efficacy and minimizing harms. In response, regulators have proposed an approach that would shift more responsibility to MLPA developers for mitigating potential harms. To be effective, this approach requires MLPA developers to recognize, accept, and act on responsibility for mitigating harms. In interviews of 40 MLPA developers of health care applications in the United States, we found that a subset of ML developers made statements reflecting moral disengagement, representing several different potential rationales that could create distance between personal accountability and harms. However, we also found a different subset of ML developers who expressed recognition of their role in creating potential hazards, the moral weight of their design decisions, and a sense of responsibility for mitigating harms. We also found evidence of moral conflict and uncertainty about responsibility for averting harms as an individual developer working in a company. These findings suggest possible facilitators and barriers to the development of ethical ML that could act through encouragement of moral engagement or discouragement of moral disengagement. Regulatory approaches that depend on the ability of ML developers to recognize, accept, and act on responsibility for mitigating harms might have limited success without education and guidance for ML developers about the extent of their responsibilities and how to implement them.

Keywords: Machine learning, Moral disengagement, Moral awareness, Regulation, Safety, Ethics

* C.A.F. was supported on a training grant from the National Institutes of Health (T32 HG008953).

† This work was supported by grants from The Greenwall Foundation and the National Institutes of Health (R01HG010476)

1. Introduction

Machine learning (ML) is increasingly utilized in health care, but can pose a variety of harms and raise ethical concerns. (Chen et al., 2021) Yet, unique features of ML create challenges to evaluating its safety and efficacy and minimizing harms. (Char, Shah, & Magnus, 2018 ; London, 2022) Proposed regulatory approaches designed to meet these challenges would shift the locus of responsibility for assessing and mitigating potential harms to ML developers. (US Food & Drug Administration, 2018, 2019, 2021) The success of such an approach would depend on the ability of ML developers to recognize, accept, and act on responsibility for mitigating harms. Other research suggests that the environment of computer science and software development could contribute to deflection of responsibility for harms (Gotterbarn, 2001; Vakkuri, Kemell, Jantunen, & Abrahamsson, 2020) in ways that are at odds with the culture of health care. We previously found that developers or machine learning-based predictive analytics for health care (MLPA) recognized a wide range of potential harms to individuals, social groups, and to the health care system. (Nichol, 2022) In addition, some developers were able to identify drivers of these harms and strategies to respond to these drivers through the development process. Those findings suggested that some MLPA developers acknowledge harms of their products and recognize strategies to mitigate those harms. However, recognition of the potential for harms and their mitigators is insufficient to prevent manifestation of harms if developers do not have moral awareness – the appreciation that there is an ethical aspect to the decisions that *they* make. According to the Rest Model, there are four components of ethical decision-making: (1) moral awareness, (2) moral judgment, (3) moral intention, and (4) moral action. (Narvaez & Rest, 1995) That is, developers would, at the very least, have to accept responsibility for identifying and minimizing harms as a prerequisite for taking appropriate action. We present a new analysis of previously-collected data from interviews of health care MLPA developers in the US (Nichol, 2022) which examines developers' perceptions of moral awareness and responsibility.

2. Methods

2.1. *Recruitment*

We recruited individuals from July 2019 to July 2020 who were working for U.S.-based organizations involved in developing MLPA tools for use in health care settings. We selected individual organizations based on our previously published analysis of the landscape of predictive analytics in health care (Nichol et al., 2021) which included a range of organizational types and sizes. The sample consisted of computer software and information technology companies, including those specifically focused on health care, as well as health insurers and hospital systems. In addition, we classified organizations by size based on number of employees (1-50, 51-1,000, over 1,000), as specified in the LinkedIn page for each organization. We identified 96 organizations, of which we selected 15 that were representative of the range of organizations, both in terms of type and size. (Table 1)

From these organizations, we identified potential participants through LinkedIn, reviewing search results by organization for key words such as data scientist, software engineer, or manager. We contacted individuals to participate through LinkedIn's direct messaging feature. To identify additional participants, we also used a snowball sampling approach. (Bernard, 2006) To examine the MLPA development process from different perspectives, we intentionally included participants representing a variety of roles, including data scientists, software engineers, project managers and executive leaders, among others. Individuals were offered a $100 electronic gift card for participation. Our study was approved by the Institutional Review Boards of Stanford University and the University of Pennsylvania.

2.2. *Data collection*

Each participant completed a one-hour semi-structured interview through video conference. Interviews were conducted by one of two members of the research team (AAN or MCH). We iteratively developed the interview guide through pilot interviews with MLPA developers with familiarity with health care ML, and who were not included in the final sample. The interview guide included questions on the participants' background and training, company and MLPA product goals in health care, facilitators and barriers to product development, potential benefits and harms of these products, and views on their regulation and oversight.

2.3. *Data analysis*

Interviews were audio-recorded, transcribed verbatim and de-identified. We analyzed the data using the mixed-method analytic software Dedoose™ 8.3, using standard qualitative data analysis methods (Miles, Huberman, & Saldana, 2019) based on grounded theory. (Strauss & Corbin, 1997) To generate the initial codebook, all team members reviewed a subset of interview transcripts and generated a list of key concepts identified in the data. The team then iteratively refined the codebook through multiple rounds of provisional coding. Once the codebook was finalized, at least two team members independently coded each interview to enhance rigor and reliability, resolving any coding differences through team consensus. To further examine participant perceptions of the potential harms of MLPA in health care, and their attitudes toward regulation and oversight, we then reviewed all data coded to these topics across all participants to identify consistency and variability in narratives both within and across participants.

3. Results

3.1. *Participant characteristics*

40 of 76 MLPA developers contacted responded (52.6%). The majority (n=29, 72.5%) of participants worked at health care-oriented computer software and information technology companies. Almost two thirds (n=25) of participants held roles that involved both working directly

with data in MLPA development and other functions, such as leadership. Sixteen participants occupied high-level management roles. Thirty-five percent held health-related advanced degrees.

3.2. *Developer perspectives on responsibility*

In analyzing our interview data on developer perspectives on potential harms and benefits of their products, we found statements revealing their perspectives on roles and responsibilities to mitigate harms even though we did not ask about them directly. Some respondents indicated a sense of moral sensitivity or awareness that included recognition of moral issues and empathy with others' points of view, (Narvaez & Rest, 1995) and some of those reflected recognition of the developer's role in addressing these issues. Others made statements that minimized harmful impacts of their products or their responsibilities to mitigate them. Examples of these statements are described below.

3.3. *Moral disengagement*

Many developers made statements recognizing the potential harms from use of ML in health care, especially to patients, such as bias, loss of privacy, or inaccurate output of models. However, a subset of these statements also indicated minimization of harms or deflection of responsibility for preventing or mitigating them. We identified eight different subtypes of "moral disengagement" statements that created moral distance between their actions and harms or responsibility. (Table 2) These eight types of moral distancing or disengagement could be grouped into two categories: (1) rationalizations for, or minimization of harms of AI in health care applications (minimizing risk), or (2) minimization of the developer's role in addressing or mitigating harms (minimizing responsibility).

Examples of each of the eight subtypes of moral disengagement statements are shown in Table 2, and the label we gave to each subtype. Some of these statements compared the harms of ML to those in other contexts such as social media, or financial data and asserted that there was no difference between those contexts and health care (Subtype: ***No difference***). Others favorably compared the harms of ML to current practices in health care (***Status quo is worse)***. Some of the harms of ML were recognized but were either believed to be justified by benefits (***Risks justify benefits***), minimized by being characterized as being irrelevant to the interviewee's work product (***Not in my AI***), or by downplaying the role of ML in health care, usually by locating ultimate decision-making authority with a clinician (**ML doesn't make decisions**). Similarly, other statements suggested that the harms of developers' products were not characteristics of the products themselves but arose from how they were used or misused (***Off-label use***). Finally, another type of statement stressed the role of regulation in assuring that harms would be minimized or prevented (***Regulation prevents harms***).

3.4. *Moral awareness and engagement*

In contrast, other participants made statements reflecting not only a recognition of the potential for their work to cause harm, but that their decisions had moral implications for which developers had responsibility. There was almost no overlap between the set of participants who made statements indicating moral disengagement and those who made statements indicating moral engagement, which were defined as statements indicating awareness of a moral issue, statements recognizing the potential for conflicting interests leading to a moral dilemma, statements acknowledging responsibility, and statements indicating that responsibility aligned with personal values. Almost all statements indicating awareness of a moral issue also acknowledged some responsibility of ML developers, or at least recognized the role of developers in potentially causing harm.

> *You know, for some of these indications there are very negative effects to incorrectly identifying a person, either positively or negatively. Say the treatment for a certain indication puts somebody under a lot of duress and if we falsely flag somebody as having that indication then the culpability of that duress, you know, at least partly does lay on our shoulders.* (Participant 8)

Another participant demonstrated their awareness of a moral issue, as well as recognition of the link between design decisions and harms.

> *It's hard to realize that hey, somebody could actually not get treatment or a claim for somebody could be denied because you built a claims adjudicator algorithm, so that compass I think exists with us because you can fine tune your algorithm to be let's say more precise or be more specific, or like for precision recall, and both have different implications.* (Participant 24)

This participant went on to acknowledge not only the link between developers' algorithmic design decisions and effects on patients, but also the power and implied responsibility conferred by the data scientist's specialized knowledge.

> *Now, a data scientist has tremendous powers here because like your stakeholders don't really understand what precision recall is and where that threshold should be, so it's up to you to use your own judgment and say, you know what, actually I think I would rather that people have their claims paid than denied, so I will just tune it for true-positives.* (Participant 24)

A few of these participants also recognized moral differences of ML in the health care context: *...but there's a lot of consequences in telling people to do the wrong thing in healthcare.* (Participant 3) Others made statements reflecting a sense of responsibility for ensuring that their products would be of benefit to patients, and that fulfilling that responsibility was not only aspirational, but a requirement, and one that aligned with personal values.

> *But, you know, my hope is that also the people on the plans, like the members, will also benefit from these products. If I didn't think that they were going to be also benefiting from these products, then I probably wouldn't be working at [respondent's company].* (Participant 26)

Another participant also expressed that the purpose of their product was to benefit patients: *This is why we're here. This is why we're doing this is to help people. And I would like to think that we're helping people.* (Participant 25) But this participant also described a sense of internal conflict about their goals: *...that's a fine line to walk every day, right, because at the end of the day like we're B2B products.* (Participant 25)

It was striking that many of the statements indicated recognition of the potential for conflicting interests leading to a moral dilemma, primarily financial interests: *...a lot of times you're just seeing predictive models being built for... based on cost, right... it's a very easy... easily understood outcomes, and then that leads to all sorts of potentially irrelevant or even slightly harmful socially or clinically sort of predictions being made.* (Participant 5) This participant indicated taking action to mitigate the potential harm: ... *there was a separate analytics team ... who did the predictive modeling work. But we were involved to help them determine some of the more useful inputs and also the outcome of interest, and we did steer them away from cost-based outcomes.*

However, several participants expressed discomfort with harms that could be inflicted by users of their products, and a lack of knowledge or ability to prevent those harms. *What are the safeguards we put in to make sure that when that genomic data gets other sources of data that it doesn't ever go near underwriters? You know, how do we quarantine that data that it's only used to improve patient outcomes...and never for estimating risk, you know, for the business side?* (Participant 1) Some even expressed resignation or inevitability of conflicting interests leading to misuse. *...and these are not things that I advocate nor does the entire... our company advocate at all, but...at the end of the day a company's gonna do what a company's gonna do.* (Participant 20)

4. Discussion

We conducted a qualitative analysis of interviews of 40 developers in the U.S. who were working on ML-based predictive analytics for health care. In our analysis of ML developers' perceptions of responsibility for harms of their work, we found that many of them raised issues indicating an awareness of a moral component of those harms – that is, that those harms could be caused by developers' actions (Figure 1: *Moral awareness)* and that developers or others might have responsibility to mitigate those harms. Few of these developers, however, described taking action to prevent or mitigate harms, possibly because of lack of knowledge about how to do so, or perceiving lack of agency (Figure 1: *Moral action*). However, developers also expressed uncertainty about responsibility for averting harms as an individual developer working in a company and moral conflict between personal values and those of their companies (Figure 1: *Conflict*).

One subset of developers, while recognizing harms, also displayed several forms of distancing themselves from harms or responsibility for those harms that were similar to a phenomenon described in the literature as moral disengagement. (Bandura, Barbaranelli, Caprara, & Pastorelli, 1996) Bandura *et al.* developed this construct as a cognitive mechanism to "deactivate moral self-regulatory processes and thereby help to explain why individuals often make unethical decisions without apparent guilt or self-censure." (Bandura, 1986) We do not claim that this cognitive mechanism is active in the ML developers that we interviewed, or make any claims about psychological processes in general. However, we do find similarities between the types of rationales made by ML developers and researchers in other fields that serve to minimize harm, deflect responsibility for mitigating harm, or justifying research or its products despite the recognized harms. (White, Bandura, & Bero, 2009) Statements reflecting moral disengagement could be grouped into two general types: those that indicated minimization of the risks of ML (Figure 1: *Minimizing risk*), and those that indicated minimization of the ML developer's responsibility for those risks (Figure 1: *Minimizing responsibility*).

Our findings corroborate those of others who have found that AI developers have a number of rationales for their detachment from responsibility for their work. For example, in interviews of developers of health care AI developers, Vakkuri *et al.* heard several types of explanations that ethical concerns were not relevant to their work. One was that if projects were early-stage, i.e. "just a prototype," they didn't have any responsibility attached to them. (Vakkuri et al., 2020) Gotterbarn *et al.* (Gotterbarn, 2001) and McDonald *et al.* (McDonald & Pan, 2020) also found that computer scientists and students had a narrow view of responsibility that created moral distance by being task-oriented, by deflecting blame for errors (i.e. flaws in developers' programming being framed as "computer error"), or by casting failures in software as "inevitable or normal accident" inherent in complex systems. (Nissenbaum, 1994)

However, the subset of developers who not only recognized potential harms of their work, but also expressed a sense of responsibility for preventing or mitigating them was largely not overlapping with the group who made statements indicating moral disengagement. We do not know whether there were any particular characteristics that distinguish these two different groups of ML developers, such as education, experience with working in the health care context, role in the company, or demographic characteristics such as age, gender, race or ethnicity. We will investigate this question further in a larger sample of ML developers.

The financial conflicts of interest identified by our participants could be in part due to our sample being drawn almost completely from ML developers working at companies. That said, worries over how ML-based products might be misused in health care by health insurers and health care institutions were of concern to our interviewees. ML developers in corporate settings face not only internal values conflicts or uncertainty, but conflicts between their values and goals and those of their companies.

These findings suggest possible facilitators and barriers to the development of ethical ML that could act through encouragement of moral engagement or discouragement of moral disengagement. Regulatory approaches that depend on the ability of ML developers to recognize, accept, and act on responsibility for mitigating harms might have limited success without education and regulatory guidance for ML developers about the extent of their responsibilities and how to implement them, for example through standardization of key aspects of model evaluation such as performance metrics. Facilitators could include the integration of people with deep clinical knowledge on development teams, and alignment of organizational values with those of individual developers in order to reduce values conflicts, for example, about how to avoid misuse of MLPA models. Companies could also facilitate ethical ML development by encouraging a sense of agency among developers in making design decisions with values implications. However, the conflicts of interest inherent in corporate settings and in MLPA products aimed at increasing health care efficiency pose particular challenges to mitigating their negative impacts. While our findings suggest internal actions that ML developers and companies can take to foster ethical ML developers, they also lend support to technology company arguments that regulation should come from government and not be developed themselves (Carter, 2020), and to those who question the ability of AI and data analytic companies to critically evaluate themselves. (Martin, 2022)

Table 1. Participants' Professional and Academic Characteristics

Participant Characteristics	(n=40)	%
Management levels*		
None	15	37.5%
Mid-level	9	22.5%
High-level	16	40.0%
Data interaction levels**		
Data only	15	37.5%
Data +	25	62.5%
Academic backgrounds		
Bachelors	11	27.5%
Health-related Masters	5	12.5%
Non-health-related Masters	6	15%
Health-related PhD	5	12.5%
Non-health-related PhD	9	22.5%
MD	4	10.0%
Type of organization		
Computer software and information technology - health care	29	72.5%
Computer software and information technology - general	3	7.5%
Health insurer	3	7.5%
Hospital	5	12.5%
Number of employees at organization		
å	19	47.5%
51-1,000	5	12.5%
Over 1,000	16	40.0%

*None refers to participants without managerial duties; Mid-level refers to participants with some managerial duties; High-level refers to participants with participants with extensive managerial duties
**Data only refers to participants who handle and work directly with the data in their daily work; Data + refers to participants who not only work with data but also perform other functions within their organization.

Table 2: Forms of moral disengagement identified in statements of MLPA developers

Moral disengagement type	Example
Minimizing risk	
No difference	*...it's like your financial data is out there too and somebody can way more ruin your life from, you know,*

Harms of ML are no different in health care than in other contexts	*stealing your identity than they can from like posting that so-and-so has... except for a couple of conditions, you know... like who cares what... like that's my attitude* (Participant 20)
Status quo is worse The status quo in healthcare (without ML) is worse than any hazards that ML might present	*So I mean we're expecting them to assimilate data, draw conclusions, and make projections, and when a computer does it somehow it seems more scary, but to me actually the fact that a person can just make a decision based on their gut is more scary...* (Participant 16)
Risks justified by benefits AI has risks but they are justified by benefits	*There's been all sorts of really terrible uses of machine learning that mostly penalize people that are already penalized in lots of other ways, like people of color or other kind of minorities. It's just sort of amplifying all these other bad things that are already happening....but I'm also not like a person... you know, I want to be able to do machine learning and have progress and see...machine learning helping medicine, 'cause it has so much that it can offer I think. (Participant 15)*
Not in my AI There may be hazards of AI, but they are not relevant to the type of AI that the participant works on	*I think that the problem of bias and pitfall might be more pertinent to other types of technologies, maybe like device technology. But I'm just... all my experience has been in the clinical decision support world where I really don't see a huge amount of risk.* (Participant 10)
Minimizing responsibility	
ML doesn't make decisions The healthcare provider makes the final decision, not the ML	*It totally leaves it in the clinician's hands. The clinician understands the context within which the prediction is made and they know that, you know, it's up to them to decide whether or not the patient should be treated. It's really just an indicator. It's like the dog in cartoons that points itself in an arrow, it says look this way, and so, you know, the clinician goes and has a look at the patient and they decide whether or not to treat them and how they should go about doing so.* (Participant 9)
Off-label use What other people do with produce is the problem, not the product itself	*I mean it depends on how the analytics is used and the purpose and the motives and the intention of the users. But as producers of analytics, we intend them to be used for general good I mean I would say.* (Participant 31)
Not my job I don't have the expertise or it's not my role	*I'm not like a health economist type of person, so my... the unsatisfactory answer is my work has not tried to optimize for any of that.* (Participant 17)

Regulation prevents harms Regulation is responsible for preventing harms	*... we raised that to the company and we talked about it and we sort of said okay, there's federal laws in place to prevent that from happening, so that's why, you know, we were sort of okay with that moving forward.* (Participant 26)

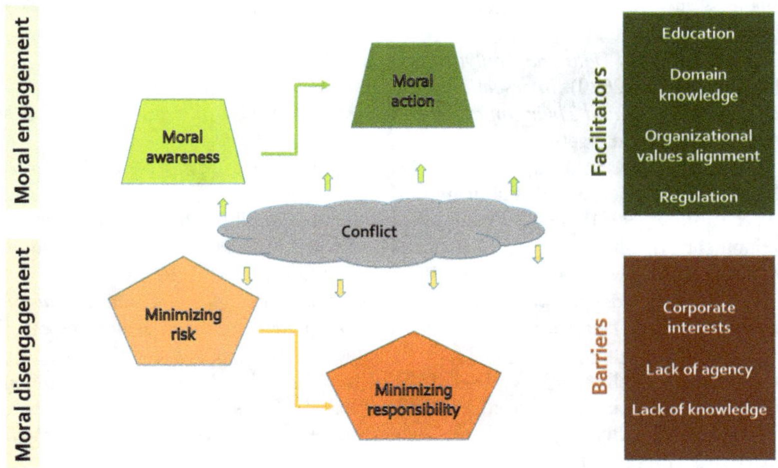

Figure 1: Facilitators and barriers to ethical ML

References

Bandura, A. (1986). *Social Foundations of Thought and Action: A Social Cognitive Theory*. Upper Saddle River, NJ: Prentice-Hall, Inc.

Bandura, A., Barbaranelli, C., Caprara, V., & Pastorelli, C. (1996). Mechanisms of Moral Disengagement in the Exercise of Moral Agency. *Journal of Personality and Social Psychology, 71*, 364-374.

Bernard, H. (2006). *Research methods in anthropology : qualitative and quantitative approaches*. New York: Altamira Press.

Carter, D. (2020). Regulation and ethics in artificial intelligence and machine learning technologies: Where are we now? Who is responsible? Can the information professional play a role? *Business Information Review, 37*, 60-68. doi:doi:10.1177/0266382120923962

Char, D., Shah, N., & Magnus, D. (2018). Implementing Machine Learning in Health Care — Addressing Ethical Challenges. *NEJM, 378*, 981–983. Retrieved from http://www.nejm.org/doi/10.1056/NEJMp1714229

Chen, I. Y., Pierson, E., Rose, S., Joshi, S., Ferryman, K., & Ghassemi, M. (2021). Ethical Machine Learning in Healthcare. *Annual Review of Biomedical Data Science, 4*(1), 123-144. doi:10.1146/annurev-biodatasci-092820-114757

Gotterbarn, D. (2001). Informatics and professional responsibility. *Sci Eng Ethics. , 7*, 221-230. doi:doi: 10.1007/s11948-001-0043-5

London, A. (2022). Artificial intelligence in medicine: Overcoming or recapitulating structural challenges to improving patient care? *Cell Reports Medicine, 3*, 2666-3791. doi:https://doi.org/10.1016/j.xcrm.2022.100622

Martin, K. (2022). *Ethics of Data and Analytics*: Taylor & Francis Group.

McDonald, N., & Pan, S. (2020). *Intersectional AI: A Study of How Information Science Students Think about Ethics and Their Impact.* Paper presented at the Proceedings of the ACM on Human-Computer Interaction.

Miles, M., Huberman, A., & Saldana, J. (2019). *Qualitative Data Analysis: A Methods Sourcebook* (4th ed.). Los Angeles: SAGE Publications.

Narvaez, D., & Rest, J. (1995). The four components of acting morally. Moral behavior and moral development: An introduction.. In L. Nucci, D. Narvaez, & T. Krettenauer (Eds.), *Handbook of moral and character education.* (pp. 385-400). Oxfordshire, UK: Routledge.

Nichol, A. (2022). *Facilitators and barriers to ethical machine learning in healthcare: A qualitative study on developer perspectives of potential harms.* Paper presented at the The 5th ELSI Congress, Virtual. https://elsicon2022.us2.pathable.com/people/Jmvd8qeFP3DKDbMph

Nichol , A., Batten, J., Halley, M., Axelrod, J., Sankar, P., & Cho, M. (2021). A Typology of Existing Machine Learning–Based Predictive Analytic Tools Focused on Reducing Costs and Improving Quality in Health Care: Systematic Search and Content Analysis. *JMIR, 23*. doi:DOI: 10.2196/26391

Nissenbaum, H. (1994). *Computing and accountability.* Paper presented at the Communications of the ACM.

Strauss, A., & Corbin, J. (1997). *Grounded Theory in Practice*. Los Angeles: SAGE Publications.

US Food & Drug Administration. (2018). *Developing a Precertification Program: A Working Model*. Retrieved from https://www.fda.gov/media/112680/download

US Food & Drug Administration. (2019). Proposed Regulatory Framework for Modifications to Artificial Intelligence/Machine Learning (AI/ML)-Based Software as a Medical Device (SaMD) - Discussion Paper and Request for Feedback. Retrieved from https://www.fda.gov/media/122535/download%0Ao

US Food & Drug Administration. (2021). *Artificial Intelligence/Machine Learning (AI/ML)-Based Software as a Medical Device (SaMD) Action Plan*. Retrieved from https://www.fda.gov/media/145022/download

Vakkuri, V., Kemell, K., Jantunen, M., & Abrahamsson, P. (2020). *"This is Just a Prototype": How Ethics Are Ignored in Software Startup-Like Environments.* Paper presented at the Agile Processes in Software Engineering and Extreme Programming: 21st International Conference on Agile Software Development, Copenhagen, Denmark.

White, J., Bandura, A., & Bero, L. (2009). Moral disengagement in the corporate world. *Account Res., 16*, 41-74. doi:doi: 10.1080/08989620802689847.

VdistCox: Vertically distributed Cox proportional hazards model with hyperparameter optimization

Ji Ae Park[1] and Yu Rang Park[1]
[1]*Department of Biomedical Systems Informatics, Yonsei University College of Medicine, 50-1 Yonsei-ro, Seodaemun-gu, Seoul, 03722, Republic of Korea*
Email: jiaepark1717@yonsei.ac.kr; yurangpark@yuhs.ac

Vertically partitioned data is distributed data in which information about a patient is distributed across multiple sites. In this study, we propose a novel algorithm (referred to as VdistCox) for the Cox proportional hazards model (Cox model), which is a widely-used survival model, in a vertically distributed setting without data sharing. VdistCox with a single hidden layer feedforward neural network through extreme learning machine can build an efficient vertically distributed Cox model. VdistCox can tune hyperparameters, including the number of hidden nodes, activation function, and regularization parameter, with one communication between the master site, which is the site set to act as the server in this study, and other sites. In addition, we explored the randomness of hidden layer input weights and biases by generating multiple random weights and biases. The experimental results indicate that VdistCox is an efficient distributed Cox model that reflects the characteristics of true centralized vertically partitioned data in the model and enables hyperparameter tuning without sharing information about a patient and additional communication between sites.

Keywords: Cox proportional hazards model; vertically partitioned data; privacy protection; hyperparameter tuning; extreme learning machine.

1. Introduction

1.1. *Characteristics of biomedical data*

Biomedical data are distributed in different locations in the form of various sources. Distributed data can be divided into horizontally or vertically partitioned data based on their distributed form. When the sites (e.g., government agencies, business establishments, or hospitals) have the same variables but different data subjects, the distributed data across the sites are known as horizontally partitioned data. On the other hand, when the sites hold disjoint sets of features for the same data subjects, the distributed data are known as vertically partitioned data. Utilizing the distributed data can increase the generalizability of research, provide insights that can prevent disease, and deliver highly customizable care to patients by considering more information about the patient. However, the confidential nature and privacy issues of patient data limit the sharing of distributed data. The data protection law in the USA, HIPAA, restricts the sharing of important data. In the European Union, the General Data Protection Regulation established a well-formulated guideline for securing the confidentiality and privacy of citizens.[1] Additionally, Canada's PIPEDA, the UK's Data Protection Act (PDA), and Russia's federal law on personal data reflect the growing global awareness of the importance of data privacy and confidentiality.[2-4] Patients are increasingly aware of the use of personal data and they are reluctant to share their data. Furthermore, owners of distributed data sources may not want to share data with other agencies, according to their institutional policies.

1.2. *Vertically distributed survival model*

Survival analysis for a time-to-event outcome (i.e., the length of time from the starting point to an event of interest, such as mortality or disease) is widely used in biomedical research. The most common model in survival analysis is the Cox proportional hazards model (Cox model). To utilize the distributed data without data sharing for privacy preservation, many studies have developed horizontally[5-9] or vertically[10,11] partitioned data-based distributed algorithms for deep learning or statistical models. The various features required for predicting a patient's prognosis do not exist in a single institution. The features have mutually exclusive characteristics in the form of vertically partitioned data. A patient's prognosis can be predicted more precisely by using information about the same patient from different institutions such as hospitals, insurance companies, and government agencies. VERTICOX[11] is the only distributed Cox model based on vertically partitioned data. VERTICOX using alternating direction method of multipliers (ADMM) has an advantage of obtaining almost the same estimated parameter as the global model. However, the algorithm deals with the standard Cox model with a linearity assumption, which limits its application in many real-world data. Because the vertically partitioned data can easily become high-dimensional data and it is difficult to confirm the interaction relationship between features distributed across sites, assuming only a simple linear relationship can be a limitation. Furthermore, ADMM requires many iterations (i.e., 2,000 and 1,500 for real data with 20 and 10 features) to obtain stable model parameters.

1.3. *Objective*

To overcome the limitation of the linearity assumption, nonparametric approaches such as neural networks can be useful alternatives. Faraggi and Simon (1995)[12] proposed an approach for modeling survival data with a simple feed-forward neural network as the basis for a nonlinear proportional hazards model. We used the optimization technique of extreme learning machine (ELM)[13] under the framework of Faraggi and Simon for the nonlinear Cox model. ELM has single hidden layer feedforward neural networks (SLFNs) that randomly choose the input weights and analytically determine the output weights. In this study, we developed a vertically distributed Cox model (referred as to VdistCox) while avoiding the transmission of patient features, which considers various functional forms in the Cox model using ELM, including hyperparameter tuning in a one-shot manner.

2. Materials and Methods

2.1. *Cox model in non-partitioned data*

In the Cox model,[14] the hazard of individual i with risk vector $\boldsymbol{x}_i$ at time t can be rewritten as the product of a baseline hazard $h_0(t)$, and a positive function of the covariates as follows:

$$h_i(t) = h_0(t)\exp(f(\boldsymbol{x}_i)), \tag{1}$$

where $f(\boldsymbol{x}_i)$ can be any function of $\boldsymbol{x}_i$, and for a standard Cox model, $f(x_i) = x_i\beta$. In Faraggi and Simon,[12] $f(x_i)$ is replaced with the output of a neural network for a nonlinear proportional hazards model rather than a linear functional form. We consider the output of the ELM as $f(x_i)$ under the framework of Faraggi and Simmon. ELM is an efficient learning algorithm for SLFNs that randomly chooses the input weights and analytically determines the output weights.[13]

2.2. *Vertically distributed Cox model*

We considered the Cox model with neural networks by replacing $f(x_i)$ in Eq. (1) with the ELM output. The proposed model (VdistCox) is communication efficient without iterative communication between the server and sites owing to the characteristics of ELM optimization.

To implement VdistCox, we set one of the sites as the master site, which plays the role of a server, to aggregate the intermediate results from the sites and derive the final model. Throughout this study, the first site was the master site. The setting of the master site does not affect the model results. VdistCox requires the following assumptions before implementation:

- There is a unique identifier for each patient (e.g., study ID) shared across institutions.
- It is not necessary to store event and time outcome information in every site. One of the sites stored the outcome should be the master party.

To illustrate VdistCox, some notations are summarized in Table 1.

Table 1. Summary of notations for VdistCox

Notation	Description
K	Number of sites
N $(= n + \tilde{n})$	Number of patients
X	$(n \times M)$ Feature matrix for model training
$\tilde{X}$	$(\tilde{n} \times M)$ Feature matrix for model validation
M	Number of features distributed across K sites
L	Number of nodes
S	Number of randomly generated input weight
$R(s)$	$((M+1) \times \mathrm{L})$ Random matrix of s-th input weight
$\beta(s)$	Output weight of s-th random input weight. L- dimensional vector
$g(.)$	Activation function
M_k	Number of features for the k-th party, k = 1, …, K
$R_k(s)$	$(M_k \times \mathrm{L})$ Random matrix of s-th input weight at k site, k = 2, …, K
X^k	$(n \times M_k)$ Feature matrix of k party for model training, k = 2, …, K
$\tilde{X}^k$	$(\tilde{n} \times M_k)$ Feature matrix of k party for model validation, k = 2, …, K

At the master site, *N* patients are randomly divided into *n* patients for model training and ñ patients for model validation, and the information is shared to the other sites. The feature matrices of the training and validation sets are denoted by

$$X^k = \begin{bmatrix} x_{1(1+\sum_{i=1}^{k-1} M_i)} & \cdots & x_{1(1+\sum_{i=1}^{k} M_i)} \\ \vdots & \ddots & \vdots \\ x_{n(1+\sum_{i=1}^{k-1} M_i)} & \cdots & x_{n(1+\sum_{i=1}^{k} M_i)} \end{bmatrix}_{n \times M_k}, \; \tilde{X}^k = \begin{bmatrix} \tilde{x}_{1(1+\sum_{i=1}^{k-1} M_i)} & \cdots & \tilde{x}_{1(1+\sum_{i=1}^{k} M_i)} \\ \vdots & \ddots & \vdots \\ \tilde{x}_{\tilde{n}(1+\sum_{i=1}^{k-1} M_i)} & \cdots & \tilde{x}_{\tilde{n}(1+\sum_{i=1}^{k} M_i)} \end{bmatrix}_{\tilde{n} \times M_k}. \quad (2)$$

X^1 and $\tilde{X}^1$ of the master are $(n \times (1 + M_1))$ matrices in which the first column of Eq. (2) is all 1. Each site randomly generates a hidden layer input weight matrix corresponding to the M_k features under a non-overlapping seed number range between sites, and the master site generates an input weight matrix including the hidden layer bias. The random matrix on the hidden layer input weights and biases is generated S times at each site. The s-*th* random matrix is denoted as

$$R_1(s) = \begin{bmatrix} b_1(s) & \dots & b_L(s) \\ r_{11}(s) & \cdots & r_{1L}(s) \\ \vdots & \ddots & \vdots \\ r_{M_1 1}(s) & \cdots & r_{M_1 L}(s) \end{bmatrix}_{(1+M_1)\times L}, R_k(s) = \begin{bmatrix} r_{(1+\sum_{i=1}^{k-1} M_i)1}(s) & \cdots & r_{(1+\sum_{i=1}^{k-1} M_i)L}(s) \\ \vdots & \ddots & \vdots \\ r_{(1+\sum_{i=1}^{k} M_i)1}(s) & \cdots & r_{(1+\sum_{i=1}^{k} M_i)L}(s) \end{bmatrix}_{M_k \times L}. \quad (3)$$

R(s), which is a centralized random matrix, is not known in reality, but it can be considered as $R(s)^T = [R_1(s)^T| \ \ ... \ \ | R_K(s)^T]$. Each k site (k = 2, ..., K) calculates $T_k(s) = X^k R_k(s)$ and $\tilde{T}_k(s) = \tilde{X}^k R_k(s)$, and sends $\{T_k(s)\}_{s=1}^S$ and $\{\tilde{T}_k(s)\}_{s=1}^S$ to the master site. The master site calculates $T(s) = \sum_{k=1}^K T_k(s)$ and $\tilde{T}(s) = \sum_{k=1}^K \tilde{T}_k(s)$. Subsequently, the master site takes any activation function on $T(s)$ and $\tilde{T}(s)$, and hidden layer output matrices, $H(s) = g(T(s))$ of size $(n \times L)$ and $\tilde{H}(s) = g(\tilde{T}(s))$ of size $(\tilde{n} \times L)$, are derived at master site. The master site estimates L output weights, $(\beta(s))^T = (\beta_1(s), \beta_2(s), \ldots, \beta_L(s))^T$, which minimizes $-LL(\boldsymbol{\beta}(\boldsymbol{s}))$ of Eq. (4) using the Newton–Raphson method.

$$-LL(\boldsymbol{\beta}(\boldsymbol{s})) = \sum_{t=1}^{T} d_t \log\left(\sum_{j\in\mathcal{R}_t} \exp\left(\sum_{l=1}^{L} \beta_l(s)\, g(x_j, b_l(s), r_l(s))\right)\right) - \sum_{t=1}^{T}\sum_{u\in\mathcal{D}_t}\left(\sum_{l=1}^{L} \beta_l(s)\, g(x_u, b_l(s), r_l(s))\right) + \lambda\|\boldsymbol{\beta}(\boldsymbol{s})\|_2^2 \quad (4)$$

Here, T denotes the number of distinct event times. At time t, $\mathcal{D}_t$ is the event set of all samples whose event occurs at time t, d_t is the number of events, and $\mathcal{R}_t$ is the risk set of all samples who caused the event or censoring after t. The negative log-partial likelihood in Eq. (4) for the estimation of the output weights includes a regularization term with tuning parameter λ. The master site computes $\hat{f}(\tilde{x}) = \tilde{H}(s)\hat{\beta}(s)$. Subsequently, the concordance index[15] of R(s), $Cindex(R(s))$, is calculated using $\hat{f}(\tilde{x})$ as a risk score. The master site selects $R(s^*)$ and $\hat{\beta}(s^*)$ as the final hidden layer input weights, biases, and output weights of VdistCox, corresponding to s with the largest $Cindex(R(s))$, where $s^* = argmax_s Cindex(R(s))$. VdistCox is exactly the same as its centralized model because $T(s)=\sum_{k=1}^K T_k(s)$ and $\tilde{T}(s)=\sum_{k=1}^K \tilde{T}_k(s)$ are the same as $XR(s)$ and $\tilde{X}R(s)$. Fig. 1 shows the overall communication process and model structure of VdistCox.

There are three hyperparameters: $g(.)$, λ, and L, in VdistCox. The activation function and the regularization parameter can be adjusted at the master site. The two hyperparameters can be explored by setting various candidate values after obtaining $T(s)$ and $\tilde{T}(s)$ at the master site. The number of hidden nodes affects the size of the random matrix R; moreover, an additional communication between the master site and other sites is required to consider various L values. A more efficient method is to generate $\{R_k(s)\}_{s=1}^S$ of size $(M_k \times L_{max})$ by setting the maximum number of nodes, L_{max}. Subsequently, $R_k(s)$ is divided into various sizes of $(M_k \times L_1)$, $(M_k \times L_2)$, ..., and $(M_k \times L_{max})$ at the master site, where $L_1 < L_2 < \ldots < L_{max}$. The number of nodes is adjusted by generating $R_k(s)$ of various sizes. Therefore, all three hyperparameters can be explored within one communication between the master site and other sites.

2.3. *Experimental Settings*

Two simulations were performed to confirm the characteristics of VdistCox in a vertically distributed setting, assuming two sites and four features. It was assumed that x_1 and x_2 are at site 1, x_3 and x_4 are at site 2, and site 1 is the master site with outcomes.

For various simulated data generations, the function of Eq. (1) was considered as follows:

- f_l (Linear): $\beta_1 x_1 + \beta_2 x_2 + \beta_3 x_3 + \beta_4 x_4$
- f_q (Quadratic + interaction): $\beta_1 {x_1}^2 + \beta_2 {x_2}^2 + \beta_3 {x_3}^2 + \beta_4 {x_4}^2 + \beta_5 x_1 x_3 + \beta_6 x_2 x_4$
- f_g (Gaussian + interaction):

$$log(5)\,exp\left(-\frac{{x_1}^2+{x_2}^2}{2(0.5)^2}\right)+log(5)\,exp\left(-\frac{{x_3}^2+{x_4}^2}{2(0.5)^2}\right)+\beta_1x_1x_2+\beta_2x_3x_4$$

We set $[0.5, 1, 0.5, 1]$ as $[\beta_1, \beta_2, \beta_3, \beta_4]$ of f_l, $[2, 1, 2, 1, 1, 1]$ as $[\beta_1, \beta_2, \beta_3, \beta_4, \beta_5, \beta_6]$ of f_q, and $[1, 1]$ as $[\beta_1, \beta_2]$ of f_g. x_1, x_2, x_3, and x_4 were randomly generated from a uniform distribution, U(-1, 1). The baseline hazard was derived from a Weibull distribution with a scale of 20 and a shape of 5. Given x_1, x_2, x_3, x_4, β's, and the baseline hazard, the event rate was set to 30%.

In the first simulation, we confirmed whether VdistCox can represent the true function by setting f_l and $f_q$or whether the interaction relationship between the vertically partitioned features can be elucidated. We manually selected the hyperparameter setting in this first simulation under several settings without a criterion for the hyperparameter optimization as follows: 10, 30, 100, and 300 for the hidden node, TanHRe, Sigmoid, ELU, Softplus, and LReLU[16] for the activation function, and 0.1, 10, 100, and 300 for the regularization parameter. (Sigmoid, 30, and 300 in the setting of f_l) and (Softplus, 30, and 0.1 in the setting of f_q) were selected as the activation functions L, and λ, respectively. The size of the simulated data was set to N = 2000, and the training and validation sets were randomly divided in an 8:2 ratio. S was set to 100.

In the second simulation, the results of VdistCox based on various hyperparameter settings were explored under the settings of f_l and f_g. As discussed in Section 2.2, to proceed with the hyperparameter tuning without additional communication, L_{max} was set to 300, and 10, 30, 100, and 300 hidden nodes were considered. TanHRe, Sigmoid, ELU, Softplus, and LReLU[16] were considered as the activation functions, and the values of 0.1, 10, 100, and 300 were considered as the regularization parameters. We explored the results of the hyperparameter settings for 4 hidden nodes×5 activation functions×4 regularization parameters = 80. The size of the second simulated data was set to N = 1500, out of which the external (N = 500) dataset was randomly extracted and then randomly divided into training (N = 800) and validation (N = 200) from the remaining N = 1000. In each function setting, S was set to 100, and the distribution of the 100 performances in the validation set under 80 hyperparameter settings was confirmed. We selected four hyperparameter settings from each of f_l and f_g, based on the following criteria among the 80 hyperparameter settings:

1. Activation function: By comparing the *Cindex*(R(s*)) values of five activation functions under L = 10, two activation functions with the largest and smallest values were selected.
2. L and λ: In the two selected activation functions, among the total L and λ combinations of 16, two combinations with the largest or smallest values of Cindex(R(s*)) were selected.

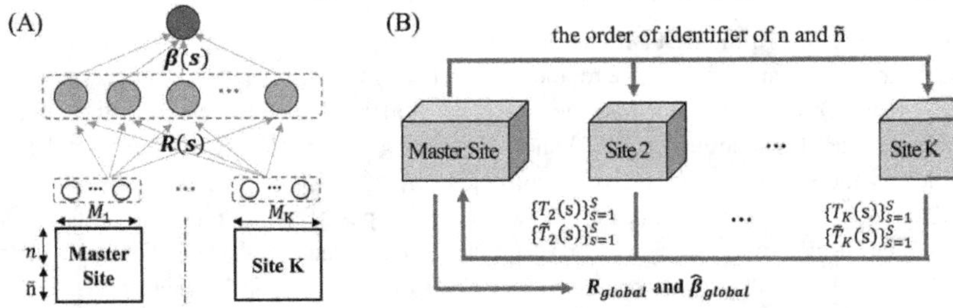

Fig. 1 Illustration of the VdistCox. (A) Model structure. (B) Process of communication.

In addition, we compared the performance of the test set between the centralized standard Cox model and the proposed model under the four hyperparameter settings selected for each function. The results were confirmed according to s^*, s^{min}, and s^{med} to examine the advantage of generating the random input matrix S times, where $s^* = argmax_s Cindex\ (\ R(\text{s})\ )$, $s^{min} = argmin_s Cindex(R(\text{s}))$, and s^{med} is s when $Cindex(R(\text{s}))$ has a median value. The centralized standard Cox model was performed with N = 1,000, combined with both training and validation sets. For the second simulation, 100 different simulated data were generated. The four hyperparameter settings based on the aforementioned two criteria were selected using the first simulated data among 100 simulated data. The 100 simulations were performed under the selected four hyperparameter settings and the results thus obtained were compared with those of the standard Cox model.

Furthermore, we confirmed the validity of VdistCox with real-data using electronic Intensive Care Unit (eICU) Collaborative Research Database.[17] We considered 27 factors included in Acute Physiology, Age, and Chronic Health Evaluation (APACHE) scores as features and the length of stay from the date of ICU admission to the date of mortality during the ICU stay as the outcome of the Cox model. We extracted 2,486 stays with all 27 features and outcomes, hospitals corresponding to the number of beds ≥500, and Caucasians; 19 hospitals were included in 2,486 stays. We randomly selected 486 stays as the test set, and divided 2,000 stays 8:2 into the training and validation sets. The comparative analysis with the standard Cox model was also performed using the eICU data, and the same 2,000 stays were used for both VdistCox and the standard Cox model. After setting the centralized eICU data with 2,000 stays and 27 features, two vertical sites were assumed. Site 1 was a master site with 14 features and outcomes, where site 2 was a site with only 13 features. For hyperparameter setting, L_{max} was set to 500, and 10, 30, 100, 300, and 500 hidden nodes were considered. As the activation functions, the five functions were used in the same manner as the simulation, and six regularization parameters of 0.1, 10, 100, 300, 500, and 1,000 were considered. Hyperparameter settings of 5 hidden nodes × 5 activation functions × 6 regularization parameters = 150 were explored.

VdistCox was implemented with R software and the source code is available from the authors upon request.

3. Results

3.1. *Simulations*

Fig. 2 shows the results of the first simulation. The contour plot shows the relationship between x_1 and x_3 when x_2 and x_4 are zero and the relationship between x_2 and x_4 when x_1 and x_3 are zero. In addition, graphs (a) to (h) confirm that the proposed model adequately describes the interaction relationship between variables under $R(s^*)$ and $\hat{\beta}(s^*)$. The graphs in (a) and (b) represent the results of $\hat{f}_l$, which is the output of VdistCox, according to x_1 when x_3 is -1 and x_3 is 1, where $f_l = 0.5x_1+0.5x_3$. Because x_1 and x_3 have no interaction, the slopes of the graphs of (a) and (b) should not change regardless of whether x3 is -1 or 1, and the results reflect this fact efficiently. In addition, (c) and (d) show the result of $\hat{f}_l$ according to x_2 when x_4 is -1 and x_4 is 1, where $f_l = x_2+x_4$, and they have a parallel shape with no change in the slope. The true slopes of (a) and (b) are smaller than those of (c) and (d), which is also reflected in the results. In the setting of $f_q = 2x_1^2 + 2x_3^2 +$

x_1x_3, the results of VdistCox represent the true functions of x1 and f_q when x_3 is -1 and x_3 is 1 (see the results of graphs (e) and (f)). Further, because the interaction of x_1 and x_3 exists, the vertices of (e) and (f) are different under the same quadratic function. In $f_q = x_2^2 + x_4^2 + x_2x_4$, when x_4 is -1 and x_4 is 1, (g) and (h) on the graph of $\hat{f}_q$ according to x_2 have different vertices under the same quadratic function form owing to the interaction of x_2 and x_4. The true coefficient of quadratic terms (e) and (f) is larger than that of (h) and (g), and the result of VdistCox efficiently reflects the true relationship, as (e) and (f) are more concave than (h) and (g).

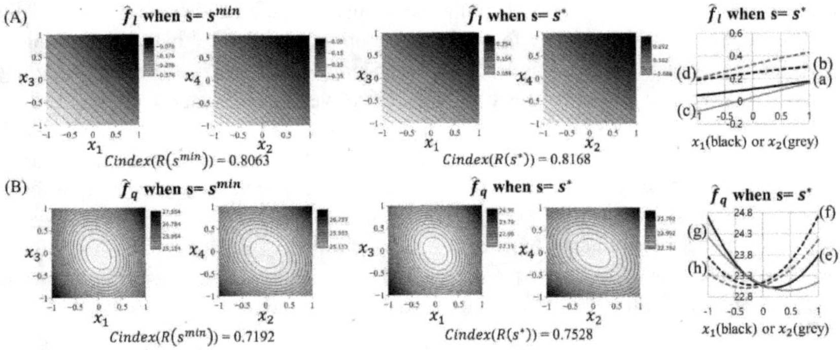

Fig. 2. Simulation results under (A) f_l and (B) f_q. Site 1 stores x_1 and x_2 and Site 2 stores x_3 and x_4. $s^* = argmax_s Cindex(R(s))$, $s^{min} = argmin_s Cindex(R(s))$, The true functions of a (black solid), b (black dashed), c (grey solid), d (grey dashed), e (black solid), f (black dashed), g (grey solid), and h (grey dashed) are $f(x) = 0.5x_1 - 0.5$, $f(x) = 0.5x_1 + 0.5$, $f(x) = x_2 - 1$, $f(x) = x_2 + 1$, $f(x) = 2x_1^2 - x_1 + 2$, $f(x) = 2x_1^2 + x_1 + 2$, $f(x) = x_2^2 - x_2 + 1$, and $f(x) = x_2^2 + x_2 + 1$, respectively.

Fig. 3 and 4 show the results of the second simulation. Fig. 3 shows the distribution of 100 Cindex(R(s))s at 80 hyperparameter settings. In the linear function setting, the performance distribution tended to increase as λ increased from 0.1 to 300. Additionally, as the number of nodes increased, the distribution of the performance did not significantly increase. Moreover, the value of Cindex(R(s^*)) was overall large in the Sigmoid among the five activation functions. However, in the nonlinear setting, as λ was small and the number of nodes increased, the performance generally increased. The LReLU had a high overall performance distribution compared to the other activation functions. The change in performance according to hyperparameter selection is larger in the nonlinear function than in the linear function. According to the two criteria of hyperparameter selection described in Section 2.3, in the linear function, Sigmoid was selected as the activation function with max(Cindex(R(s*))), and TanHRe was selected as the activation function with min(Cindex(R(s*)). The four settings of Sigmoid/L = 30/λ = 300, Sigmoid/L = 300/λ = 0.1, TanHRe/L = 10/λ = 300, and TanHRe/L = 300//λ = 0.1 were selected as the hyperparameter settings with $Cindex(R(s^*))$ values of 0.8610, 0.8287, 0.8510, and 0.8143, respectively. In the nonlinear function, LReLU was selected as the activation function with max($Cindex(R(s^*))$), and TanHRe was selected as the activation function with min($Cindex(R(s^*))$). The four settings of LReLU/L = 30/λ = 0.1, LReLU/L = 30/λ = 300, TanHRe/L = 30/λ = 0.1, and TanHRe/L = 100/λ = 300 were selected as the hyperparameter settings with $Cindex(R(s^*))$ values of 0.7405, 0.5381, 0.7033, and 0.4711.

Fig. 4 shows the distribution of $Cindex(R(s^*))$, $Cindex(R(s^{med}))$, and $Cindex(R(s^{min}))$ in the validation and test sets of 100 simulations performed under four settings selected from linear and nonlinear, respectively. In a linear setting, the standard Cox model, which can be viewed as a true model, showed a higher performance distribution than VdistCox, and the performance results of s^* and s^{med} were similar. The two hyperparameter settings of Sigmoid/L = 30/λ = 300 and TanHRe/L = 10/λ = 300, which showed similar performance in the validation set, showed similar performance in the test set, and the performance distributions s^* and s^{med} in the two settings were similar to that of the standard Cox model. The s^* of Sigmoid/L = 30/λ = 300 showed the highest performance, with an average performance of 0.7821. The average performance of the standard Cox model is 0.7860. In all settings of nonlinear function of Fig.4, s^*, s^{med}, and s^{min} showed a higher distribution of performance for the test set than the standard Cox model. The two hyperparameter settings of LReLU/L = 30/λ = 0.1 and TanHRe/L = 30/λ = 0.1, which showed similar performance in the validation set, showed similar performance in the test set, and the s^* of LReLU/L = 30/λ = 0.1 showed the highest performance with an average performance of 0.6677. In both the linear and nonlinear functions, s^* under the hyperparameter setting, which had the highest performance in the validation set, showed the highest performance in the test set on average.

3.2. *Real data*

Additionally, we explored 150 hyperparameter settings to confirm validity in real data, and four settings of ELU/L = 300/λ = 1000, ELU/L = 500/λ = 0.1, Sigmoid/L = 500/λ = 10, and Sigmoid/L = 500/λ = 0.1 were selected. As summarized in Table 2, the differences in performance in the validation and test sets between the four settings was quite large. Similar to the simulation results, the performance in the test set was also the highest at ELU/L = 300/λ = 1000, which had the highest performance in the validation set; s^{med} and s^* in this setting showed higher performance than the standard Cox model.

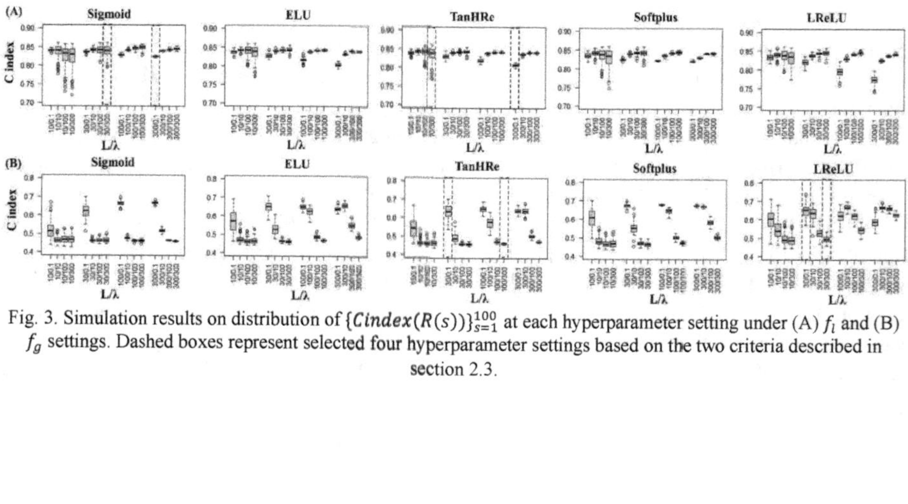

Fig. 3. Simulation results on distribution of $\{Cindex(R(s))\}_{s=1}^{100}$ at each hyperparameter setting under (A) f_l and (B) f_g settings. Dashed boxes represent selected four hyperparameter settings based on the two criteria described in section 2.3.

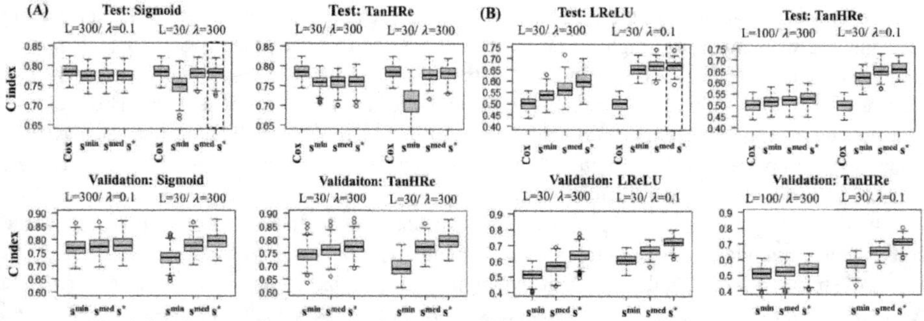

Fig. 4. Results on performances distribution in validation and test sets based on 100 simulations under the four hyperparameter settings of (A) f_l and (B) f_g. Dashed boxes represent the best results of performance among four hyperparameter settings.

Table 2. Results of performance as measured by the C-index in validation and test sets under vertical two sites setting based on eICU dataset.

VdistCox	ELU				Sigmoid			
	300/1000 (L/λ)		500/0.1 (L/λ)		500/10 (L/λ)		500/0.1 (L/λ)	
	validation	test	validation	test	validation	test	validation	test
s^{min}	0.8170	0.7149	0.4216	0.4458	0.7938	0.7162	0.2563	0.4253
s^{med}	0.8296	0.7204	0.5419	0.5086	0.8144	0.7154	0.3686	0.4686
s^*	**0.8466**	**0.7294**	0.7440	0.6017	0.8422	0.7159	0.7539	0.6502
Standard Cox model	test: 0.7160							

Bold represents the best results in the validation and the test sets in VdistCox.

4. Discussion

VdistCox shares only the value obtained by multiplying the feature value by the random value independently generated at each site in a privacy-preserving manner, and it has an efficient process that requires only one communication between the master site and other sites. Because VdistCox derives the exact same model as its centralized model without data sharing, it can provide a stable distributed model if the centralized ELM-based Cox model is valid. We confirmed the validity and characteristics of the proposed model through experiments using simulated and real data.

According to the results of the first simulation (Fig.2), VdistCox showed the real functional form between the variables, and it also reflected the interaction relationship between the vertically partitioned features.

To overcome the instability caused by the randomness, of the input weights and hidden biases, we generated the matrix of random input weights and hidden biases S times and selected the best random matrix among them. In the results of the performance of the test and validation sets of the second simulation (Fig.4), the performance of $s^*$and s^{med} was similar in the linear function setting, however it was different in the nonlinear function setting. This indicates that it is efficient to generate the R matrix multiple times in the nonlinear function setting. However, even in the nonlinear function, there was no difference in the performances of $s^*$and s^{med} depending on the hyperparameter selection (in the case of LReLU/L = 30/λ = 0.1). This means that hyperparameter selection could be a more important factor than the randomness of R. However, exploring multiple R can prevent choosing the worst random weights. The results for the performance of s^{min} were worse compared to those of s^* and s^{med} in all cases. However, in the results on real data (Fig.4), the performance on the test set of s^{min} was slightly better than that of s^* and s^{med} in Sigmoid/L = 500/λ = 10. This indicates that the selection of a random value with good performance in the validation dataset may be a selection with low generalizability in external validation. However, considering the overall results, the best performance on the test dataset was s^*.

Hyperparameter tuning can be crucial for obtaining a good trade-off between accuracy and convergence in models with neural networks; it could affect the quality of the learned model.[18] To train a distributed model under different hyperparameter settings, many computing resources are required, and the evaluation of hyperparameters is extremely expensive for a large-scale distributed dataset.[19] In the framework of VdistCox, the three hyperparameters can be explored without additional communication between the master and other sites after obtaining the T and $\tilde{T}$ matrices at the master site. The importance of hyperparameter selection was confirmed through experiments. The results of the second simulation showed a large difference in performance according to the 80 hyperparameter settings, and the importance of the hyperparameter was greater in the nonlinear function than in the linear function settings (Fig. 3). Further, we confirmed that the setting with good performance in the validation set also showed good performance in the test set (Fig.4 and Table 1). Assuming a distributed model with iterative communication, if we want to explore 80 hyperparameter settings, the distributed model will have to be run 80 times, which consumes a significant amount of computing resources. In VdistCox, a wide range of hyperparameter choices can be implemented in a one-shot manner.

Comparing the results of VdistCox and the centralized standard Cox model, in the linear function setting of the second simulation, VdistCox (Sigmoid/L = 30/λ = 300) showed a similar performance to the standard Cox model, which is a true model. In addition, in real data where the true function is unknown, the performance of VdistCox (ELU/ L = 300/ λ =1000) was higher than that of the standard Cox model, which may indicate that the true relationship between the 27 features is not linear. Vertically partitioned data combines features of various characteristics for the same patient from different sites. Therefore, compared to the data from a single site, the number of features in vertically partitioned data is more likely to become high dimensional, and the $f(x_i)$ of Eq. (1) cannot be determined in advance because we cannot distinguish which interaction exists between the numerous distributed variables. Compared to the standard Cox model based VERTICOX, the VdistCox may flexibly reflect $f(x_i)$ based on the real data characteristics in the distributed data that is difficult to share between the sites. Additionally, there is a possibility that the number of features exceeds the number of patients in vertically partitioned data in which only the number of features increases in a certain patient group (N<<M). In these data characteristics, the parameter estimation in the standard Cox model may become unstable and the accuracy of prediction may decrease. Therefore, compared to VERTICOX, which aims to accurately estimate the parameter of the standard Cox model, the VdistCox can provide a stable predictive model in high-dimensional vertically partitioned data of N<<M. Moreover, VERTICOX requires several iterations to obtain stable parameter estimates (i.e., 2,000 and 1,500 for real data with 20 and 10 features). By contrast, VdistCox requires only one communication including hyperparameter optimization.

In this study, we confirmed the characteristics and validity of our novel model, VdistCox. However, because it was performed using restricted simulated and real data, it is possible that the validity of VdistCox has not been sufficiently proven in this paper. Additionally, we have not proposed an index that can interpret the influence of features such as the hazard ratio provided by the VERTICOX. However, in the results of the first simulation, the relative influence between features from VdistCox were identified. For example, in the setting of f_l, true β_1 and β_2 were set to 0.5 and 1, respectively, and the slope of x_2 was greater than that of x_1 in (a) to (d) of Fig. 2. Furthermore, in the setting of f_q, true β_1 and β_2 were set to 2 and 1, respectively, and the concave degree of x_1 was greater than that of x_2 in (e) to (h) of Fig. 2. Explaining the influence of each feature in terms of interpretation of the model is important and further discussion in VdistCox on the interpretation is required.

5. Conclusion

The model proposed in this study, VdistCox, is communication-efficient vertically distributed Cox model by sharing once the intermediate results that are obtained by multiplying the features of each site to the input weight randomly generated at each site, while avoiding data sharing. In VdistCox using ELM, we proposed generating random input weights multiple times and a hyperparameter tuning process. In our experiments, the importance of randomness on input weights and hyperparameter selection depended on the data type (e.g., linear or nonlinear relationship between features). However, because confirming the true relationship between features in a real vertically distributed environment is difficult, considering multiple random input weights and hyperparameter tuning can be an effective means for a stable vertically distributed Cox model.

6. Acknowledgments

This work was supported by the Bio-Industrial Technology Development Program (20014841) and funded by the Ministry of Trade, Industry, and Energy (MOTIE, Korea). This research was supported by a grant of the Korea Health Technology R&D Project through the Korea Health Industry Development Institute (KHIDI), funded by the Ministry of Health & Welfare, Republic of Korea (grant number : HI19C1330).

References

1. Oya Beyan, Ananya Choudhury, Johan van Soest, Oliver Kohlbacher, Lukas Zimmermann, Holger Stenzhorn, Md. Rezaul Karim, Michel Dumontier, Stefan Decker, Luiz Olavo Bonino da Silva Santos, Andre Dekker; Distributed Analytics on Sensitive Medical Data: The Personal Health Train. Data Intelligence 2020; 2 (1-2): 96–107. doi:
2. Office of the Privacy Commissioner of Canada. The Personal Information Protection and Electronic Documents Act (PIPEDA). Available at: https://www.priv.gc.ca/en/privacy-topics/privacy-laws-in canada/the-personal-information-protection-and-electronic-documents-act-pipeda/.
3. The Data Protection Act. Available at: https://www.gov.uk/data-protection.

4. Federal Law of 27 July 2006 N 152-FZ on Personal Data. Available at: https://pd.rkn.gov.ru/authority/p146/p164/.
5. B. McMahan, E. Moore, D. Ramage, S. Hampson, and B. A. y Arcas. Communication efficient learning of deep networks from decentralized data. In A. Singh and X. J. Zhu, editors, Proceedings of the 20th International Conference on Artificial Intelligence and Statistics, AISTATS 2017, 20-22 April 2017, Fort Lauderdale, FL, USA, volume 54 of Proceedings of Machine Learning Research, pages 1273–1282. PMLR, 2017. URL http://proceedings. mlr.press/v54/mcmahan17a.html.
6. K. Bonawitz, H. Eichner, W. Grieskamp, D. Huba, A. Ingerman, V. Ivanov, C. Kiddon, J. Konecný, S. Mazzocchi, H. B. McMahan, T. V. Overveldt, D. Petrou, D. Ramage, and J. Roselander. Towards federated learning at scale: System design. CoRR, abs/1902.01046, 2019. URL http://arxiv.org/abs/1902.01046
7. Lu C, Wang S, Ji Z, Wu Yuan, Xiong Li, Jiang Xiaoqian, Ohno-Machado Lucila. WebDISCO: a web service for distributed cox model learning without patient-level data sharing. J Am Med Inform Assoc. 2015 Nov;22(6):1212–9. doi: 10.1093/jamia/ocv083.
8. Duan R. Learning from local to global-an efficient distributed algorithm for modeling time-to-event data. bioRxiv. 2021 doi: 10.1101/2020.03.04.977298.
9. PARK, Ji Ae, et al. Weight-Based Framework for Predictive Modeling of Multiple Databases With Noniterative Communication Without Data Sharing: Privacy-Protecting Analytic Method for Multi-Institutional Studies. JMIR medical informatics, 2021, 9.4: e21043.
10. S. Hardy, W. Henecka, H. Ivey-Law, R. Nock, G. Patrini, G. Smith, and B. Thorne. Private federated learning on vertically partitioned data via entity resolution and additively homomorphic encryption. CoRR, abs/1711.10677, 2017. URL http://arxiv.org/abs/1711.10677.
11. DAI, Wenrui, et al. VERTICOX: Vertically Distributed Cox Proportional Hazards Model Using the Alternating Direction Method of Multipliers. IEEE Transactions on Knowledge and Data Engineering, 2020.
12. Faraggi, D. and Simon, R. (1995). A neural network model for survival data. Statistics in medicine, 14(1):73–82.
13. Huang, G. B., Zhu, Q. Y., & Siew, C. K. (2004, July). Extreme learning machine: a new learning scheme of feedforward neural networks. In 2004 IEEE international joint conference on neural networks (IEEE Cat. No. 04CH37541) (Vol. 2, pp. 985-990). Ieee.
14. K. Dietz et al., Stat. Biol. Health Logistic Regression SelfLearn. Text., vol. 2, pp. 102–124, 2002.
15. UNO, Hajime, et al. On the C-statistics for evaluating overall adequacy of risk prediction procedures with censored survival data. Statistics in medicine, 2011, 30.10: 1105-1117.
16. RATNAWATI, Dian Eka, et al. Comparison of activation function on extreme learning machine (ELM) performance for classifying the active compound. In: AIP Conference Proceedings. AIP Publishing LLC, 2020. p. 140001.
17. Le Gall J. A New Simplified Acute Physiology Score (SAPS II) Based on a European/North American Multicenter Study. JAMA 1993 Dec 22;270(24):2957.
18. CHARLES, Zachary; KONEČNÝ, Jakub. On the outsized importance of learning rates in local update methods. arXiv preprint arXiv:2007.00878, 2020.
19. KAIROUZ, Peter, et al. Advances and open problems in federated learning. Foundations and Trends® in Machine Learning, 2021, 14.1–2: 1-210.

Algorithmic Fairness in the Roberts Court Era

Jennifer K. Wagner

School of Engineering Design, Technology, and Professional Programs; Department of Biomedical Engineering; Institute for Computational and Data Science; Bioinformatics and Genomics Program (Huck Institutes of the Life Sciences); Rock Ethics Institute, Pennsylvania State University, University Park, PA 16802 USA; and Penn State Law, University Park, PA 16802 USA
Email: jkw131@psu.edu

Scientists and policymakers alike have increasingly been interested in exploring ways to advance algorithmic fairness, recognizing not only the potential utility of algorithms in biomedical and digital health contexts but also that the unique challenges that algorithms—in a datafied culture such as the United States—pose for civil rights (including, but not limited to, privacy and nondiscrimination). In addition to the technical complexities, separation of powers issues are making the task even more daunting for policymakers—issues that might seem obscure to many scientists and technologists. While administrative agencies (such as the Federal Trade Commission) and legislators have been working to advance algorithmic fairness (in large part through comprehensive data privacy reform), recent judicial activism by the Roberts Court threaten to undermine those efforts. Scientists need to understand these legal developments so they can take appropriate action when contributing to a biomedical data ecosystem and designing, deploying, and maintaining algorithms for digital health. Here I highlight some of the recent actions taken by policymakers. I then review three recent Supreme Court cases (and foreshadow a fourth case) that illustrate the radical power grab by the Roberts Court, explaining for scientists how these drastic shifts in law will frustrate governmental approaches to algorithmic fairness and necessitate increased reliance by scientists on self-governance strategies to promote responsible and ethical practices.

Keywords: Algorithmic Fairness; Privacy; Nondiscrimination; ELSI; Law; Policy

1. Introduction

Data scientists are increasingly aware of and concerned about the ethical dimensions and societal impact of their work, as evinced by many thought-provoking ethical, legal, and social implications (ELSI) workshops,[1-3] sessions,[4] and keynotes[5-9] at the Pacific Symposium on Biocomputing and other scientific conferences. Multidisciplinary collaborations comprising biomedical data scientists, bioethicists, and other subject matter experts continue to be encouraged.[10-11] Among the major topics of concern is algorithmic fairness, for which there are numerous articulations of what precisely that entails and proper measures of it.[12] Stated simply, from a data science perspective, algorithmic fairness refers to performance parity (demonstrated through specified metrics) across different groups of people and mitigation of computational biases.[13] From a legal perspective, fairness involves the "quality of treating people equally or in a reasonable way" or "the qualities of impartiality and honesty,"[14] and information privacy is oft-used as a mechanism to prevent bias and discrimination.[e.g.,15] Fairness and privacy are conceptually distinct yet closely connected in biomedical data science and law, as limiting data that an algorithm can access, use, or disclose is viewed as a means to prevent unlawful, unfair discrimination. As worries grow regarding civil rights in a datafied culture such as the United States and as leaders call for reforms (such as an AI Bill of Rights[16-17]), it is essential that scientists and policymakers act together to advance algorithmic fairness in feasible and effective ways.

There have been considerable efforts in recent years, both within the scientific community and through public policy, to promote ethical data science.[e.g., 18] However, there has also been a recent and dramatic shift in the balance of power between the legislative, executive, and judicial branches prompting fears that the U.S. democratic "experiment" is set for failure.[19] Data scientists need to be aware of these developments and recognize the implications for their own work so that innovative alternative strategies to promote ethical and responsible data science practices can be designed, implemented, and refined. To facilitate awareness and stimulate further discussion among data scientists, I highlight some of the recent efforts taken by the Federal Trade Commission (FTC) and legislators to advance algorithmic fairness. I then offer a succinct review of three recent Supreme Court cases (*TransUnion LLC v. Ramirez*,[20] *Dobbs v. Jackson Women's Health Org.*,[21] and *West Virginia v. EPA*[22]) and foreshadow a fourth (*303 Creative LLC v. Elenis*[23]) that illustrate the Roberts Court's radical judicial activism and power grab, explaining how these shifts in law will frustrate governmental approaches to algorithmic fairness (including but not limited to fairness pursued through mandated data practices grounded in privacy principles). I conclude that the widening imbalance of powers along with instability and uncertainty of law necessitates an increased reliance by scientists on self-governance strategies to advance algorithmic fairness.

2. Recent Activity by the Federal Trade Commission to Advance Algorithmic Fairness

The FTC is responsible for preventing unfair and deceptive acts and practices in or affecting commerce, drawing its main authority from the Federal Trade Commission Act[24] and dozens of other statutes. In the absence of a specific federal statute on algorithmic fairness or comprehensive data privacy, the FTC can draw from its general authority to prevent bias and discrimination through compelling responsible data practices (such as privacy- and discrimination-aware design, reasonable bias mitigation protocols, or even diversity promoting measures) in digital health technologies. The FTC has not been using its unfairness authority to its full potential;[e.g.,25] however, the FTC's composition has shifted (with confirmations of Lina Khan as Chair and Alvaro Bedoya, a privacy law expert, as commissioner), and signs over the past two years suggest the FTC is ready to take bold steps to promote algorithmic fairness in and beyond digital health. For example, in January 2021, the FTC settled a case against Flo Health over data practices.[26] In April 2021, the FTC issued business guidance underscoring that racially biased algorithms are prohibited and warning that algorithmic performance (1) must not be exaggerated and (2) must be tested before and periodically after deployment to detect discriminatory outcomes.[27] In July 2021 the FTC announced regulatory priorities that included issues affecting the healthcare industry and technology platforms.[28] In Sept. 2021, the FTC issued a privacy and security report to Congress flagging its intention to pursue expanded remedies for unsavory data practices (such as disgorgement of ill-gotten gains) and to focus on digital platforms, including development of guidance on health-related algorithms.[29] That same month in a statement regarding the FTC health breach notification rule,[30] Commissioner Slaughter explicitly called for the FTC to "lead a market shift toward data minimalism."[31] And in March 2022, the FTC took action against a weight loss app vendor to protect children's online privacy, requiring data deletion, destruction of algorithms developed with ill-gotten data, and a hefty monetary penalty.[32]

3. Recent Legislative Activity to Advance Algorithmic Fairness

Congress also has been actively working on several pieces of legislation that would provide comprehensive data protections and advance algorithmic fairness. Among the many consumer data protection bills being debated and developed in the 117th Congress are the Consumer Data Privacy and Security Act of 2021 (S. 1494); the Setting an American Framework to Ensure Data Access, Transparency and Accountability (SAFE DATA) Act (S.2499); and the Consumer Online Privacy Rights Act (S.3195). A bipartisan bill, the American Data Privacy and Protection Act (H.R.8152), has made it farther than any other, having been reported favorably out of House Committee on Energy and Commerce on July 20, 2022—just a month after it was formally introduced.[E.g.,33] Other legislative efforts to advance algorithmic fairness include, e.g., the Algorithmic Justice and Online Platform Transparency Act (S.1896, H.R.3611); Algorithmic Accountability Act of 2022 (S.3572, H.R. 6580); Protecting Americans from Dangerous Algorithms Act (S.3029, H.R.2154); the GOOD AI Act of 2021 and 2022 (S.3035 and H.R. 7296, respectively); Promoting Digital Privacy Technologies Act (S.224, H.R. 847); Digital Accountability and Transparency to Advance Privacy Act or DATA Privacy Act (S.3065, H.R. 5807); Federal Trade Commission Technologists Act of 2021 (S.3187, H.R.4530); and Digital Platform Commission Act of 2022 (S.4201, H.R. 7858).

4. Recent Activity by the Roberts Court that Will Undermine Algorithmic Fairness

Three cases are particularly illustrative of the dramatic shift in power instigated by the Roberts Court that will frustrate approaches to advance algorithmic fairness by the FTC and Congress: *TransUnion LLC v. Ramirez*[20] (which upended Article III Standing Doctrine[34] and weakened the powers of the legislative branch), *Dobbs v. Jackson Women's Health Org.*[19] (which obliterated the Stare Decisis Doctrine[35-36] and toppled U.S. Constitution-based privacy rights at least in so far as reproductive health decisions), and *West Virginia v. EPA*[22] (which weakened the powers of both the legislative and executive branch through its invention and embrace of the Major Questions Doctrine[37] and warming interest in the Nondelegation Doctrine[38]). A fourth case worth noting is *303 Creative LLC v. Elenis*[23,39] (which the Roberts Court agreed to review and which pits nondiscrimination rights directly against Free Speech rights). Indeed, as one respected law scholar has commented, "we are in the era of the imperial Supreme Court" in that the actions are reflective not of any particular judicial philosophy but an alarming concentration of power in the Supreme Court to the detriment of all others.[40 at 2] These actions are "making America ungovernable" with respect to the most pressing policy issues of today.[18]

4.1. *TransUnion LLC v. Ramirez*

The Roberts Court decided (5-4) *TransUnion LLC v. Ramirez* on June 25, 2021, with Justice Kavanaugh authoring the majority opinion. The case involved a class action lawsuit under the Fair Credit Reporting Act (FRCA) for improper data practices, with the class consisting of 8,185 individuals falsely characterized as "potential terrorists" and "drug traffickers" on credit reports and 1,853 individuals for whom these false and misleading credit reports were distributed to third-party businesses. At trial the jury had awarded the consumers $60 million in statutory and punitive damages for multiple willful FRCA violations.[20 at 2202] In what has been described by prominent privacy law scholars as a "profound usurpation of legislative power,"[41] the Court required injury-in-fact in order to establish there has been a "concrete harm" (a prerequisite for standing to sue in federal courts). The Court basically held "no harm, no foul"[42] for violations of data and disclosure practices mandated by statute and refused to acknowledge any "concrete harm" could have been incurred by those consumers for whom an inaccurate flag in their credit report was never disclosed to a third-party. At the core of its decision, the Court acknowledged, "Congress may 'elevate to the status of legally cognizable injuries concrete, *de facto* injuries that were previously inadequate in law;"[20 at 2204-2205 (internal citations omitted)] however, the Court distorted precedent set by *Spokeo, Inc. v. Robins,*[43] tethering lawmakers' ability to create remedies only for harms with a "close historical or common-law analogue."[20 at 2204] Substituting its judgment for Congress and the jury, the Court overlooked, ignored, or discounted the diversity of privacy-related harms that exist[44] and framed the controversy as a distinction between individuals suing to ensure regulatory compliance (which is not allowed for Article III standing) and individuals suing to redress "real and actual" harms incurred personally (which is required for Article III standing).

This case will have serious repercussions for enforceable data protection laws, as dataveillance (i.e., digital data surveillance) and data injustices of today would likely have no common law analog. This includes laws that would close gaps in protections and promote responsible data practices across HIPAA (Health Insurance Portability and Accountability Act[45]) and non-HIPAA contexts alike. The Roberts Court focused on disclosure of the false information analogizing this to defamation and otherwise dismissed inaccuracies about consumers—however horrible and stigmatizing and with whatever risks they cause downstream—unless those inaccuracies were disclosed to others. In a dissenting opinion, Justice Kagan noted the ruling had transformed Article III Standing Doctrine from "a doctrine of judicial modesty to a tool of judicial aggrandizement" and lamented that Congress—not the Supreme Court—was in the better position to determine whether "something causes a harm or risk of harm in the real world."[20 (dissent at 2225)]

Federal approaches for data privacy law reform (particularly those incorporating private causes of action as a key enforcement mechanism, a feature HIPAA lacks) might be for naught even if a bill is successfully passed by Congress and signed into law given, in light of *TransUnion*, what cases may be heard by federal courts. Thus, this case complicates debates about whether federal preemption of state data protection laws would be a pro or con for consumers[46] and generates uncertainty as to whether the Roberts Court, if given the opportunity, would deem harms established by any new federal data protection statute as "concrete" to allow consumers to have their day in court if statutory violations occur. This development does not bode well for policymakers trying to use data practice measures to promote innovation and protect consumers in and out of digital health contexts.

4.2. *Dobbs v. Jackson Women's Health Org.*

The Roberts Court issued its bombshell opinion in *Dobbs v. Jackson Women's Health Org.* on June 24, 2022, with Justice Alito authoring the majority opinion. The case involved a constitutional challenge to the Mississippi Gestational Age Act, a forced birth law barring healthcare providers from providing pregnancy termination services after 15 weeks of gestation. The main holding was to uphold the law and overturn both *Roe v. Wade*[47] and *Planned Parenthood of Southeastern Pa. v. Casey.*[48] In addition to the effects of this case on the practice of medicine, news of the decision quickly prompted scholars to call attention to the far-reaching implications the case has for dataveillance enabled by digital health technologies.[*e.g.* 49-54] Such technologies are not always within regulatory reach of HIPAA.[55] But even for data situated within the HIPAA regulatory environment, there is a law enforcement exception to the Privacy Rule.[56] In light of state laws that began to take effect with the *Dobbs* decision (e.g., Texas H.B. 8, designed to evade judicial review[57-58]), increased attention needs to be given to ensuring the privacy of health data and information.[59] Recognizing the possibility that laws containing "bounty hunter" enforcement mechanisms might incentivize people to disclose protected health information under cover of the law enforcement exception to the HIPAA Privacy Rule, guidance[60] was quickly issued by the Dept. of Health and Human Services Office of Civil Rights (OCR) emphasizing the narrowness of the exception and clarifying how obligations under HIPAA interact with, and prevail over, conflicting state laws with regard to data privacy and security requirements.[61]

There is understandable concern that the exceptions to the HIPAA Privacy Rule could swallow the rule in a post-*Roe* society. Additionally, there continues to be legal uncertainty in our modern datafied culture regarding the boundaries for reasonable expectations of privacy under the Fourth Amendment. In 2018 the Roberts Court in *Carpenter v. United States*[62] declined to put an end to the Third-Party Doctrine (a categorical rule that negates an individual's expectation of privacy if information is shared with or known by third parties and allows for warrantless searches)[E.g.,63] and instead allowed for the possibility of a preserved expectation of privacy in information exposed to third parties depending upon the "deeply revealing nature" of the information; "depth, breadth, and comprehensive reach"; and "inescapable and automatic nature of its collection."[64] Health information has a more established position as sensitive and worthy of protections than other types of information; however, biomedical databases, electronic health records, and health-related information in a wide array of settings are in danger of being more readily accessed and used against individuals.[e.g.,65] While the *Carpenter* ruling was purportedly narrow (perhaps merely creating a limited exception rather than a revision to the Third-Party Doctrine[66]), we must monitor how the Roberts Court construes privacy interests in health information generally. In response to the legal uncertainties, biomedical data scientists might try data minimization and use of synthetic data; however, such efforts might unintentionally exacerbate biases in digital health algorithms.

4.3. *West Virginia v. EPA*

On June 30, 2022, the Supreme Court issued its 6-3 ruling in *West Virginia v. EPA*[20] with the majority opinion authored by Chief Justice Roberts. The case involved a challenge the Affordable Clean Energy Rule promulgated in 2015[67] to implement updated performance standards under the Clean Air Act, a 50-year-old statute.[68] The rule had never taken effect, as it had been challenged by opponents, stayed pending litigation, and repealed in 2019.[69] A review of the text and legislative history indicated that the law to stop pollution and improve air quality was intended to provide the EPA with "regulatory flexibility" to avoid rapid obsolescence attributable to unavoidable "changing circumstances and scientific developments."[22 (dissent at 2622)] Nevertheless, the Court chose to exert control rather than practice judicial restraint, substituting its own views for those of Congress and the EPA. Cunningly, the Court purported to follow precedent to reach its decision despite the fact that the "Majority Questions Doctrine" upon which it relied was not even a term used by the Supreme Court—a point noted in the dissenting opinion.[22 (dissent at 2634)] In actuality, the Major Questions Doctrine is an independent theory that sidesteps administrative law precedent (i.e., the *Chevron* Doctrine, which has persisted since 1984).[37] The gist of the Major Questions Doctrine is that in "extraordinary cases" of any notable "economic and political significance," an agency has no authority to act (including to interpret ambiguity in an agency's explicit statutory authority to act) unless Congress has explicitly empowered the agency to do so.[22 at 2608]

The case is important for data scientists because the Roberts Court has fundamentally shifted how agencies can act when implementing and enforcing statutes once they (finally) have been passed by Congress. The Court has made clear that it will second-guess (1) Congress in the breadth and specificity of statutory text used and (2) agency interpretations of statutes (not only by the EPA but any administrative agency, including, e.g., the FTC, FDA, CMS, and others). Indeed, the Court explained that "extraordinary cases"—to which the Major Questions Doctrine presumably now applies—"have arisen from all corners of the administrative state."[22 at 2608] Put simply, statutes are increasingly at risk of being struck down by the Roberts Court pursuant to the Nondelegation Doctrine if any meaningful amount of discretion is given to agencies in the interest of enabling data-informed policy and regulatory flexibility—necessary features for effective governance when involving rapidly changing science, technologies, and applications. Similarly, regulations are increasingly at risk of being struck down pursuant to the newly christened Major Questions Doctrine as exceeding the enforcement authority delegated by Congress. For algorithmic fairness in particular, policy efforts thus far have largely been based on general authority rather than explicit, specific authorization by Congress. Any laws to advance algorithmic fairness now must require specification (exhaustive enumeration) of the "major" issues that the agency is permitted or required to resolve and provide the agency with "intelligible principles" for implementation.[70]

4.4. *303 Creative LLC v. Elenis*

It would be a mistake to assume that the Roberts Court will ease off from its activist turn when the 2022-2023 session begins. Among several cases the Court has agreed to hear that could signal further trouble is *303 Creative LLC v. Elenis*.[23] At issue is the Colorado Antidiscrimination Act challenged by a graphic designer who plans to, but does not yet, offer the design of wedding websites and who does not want to offer such services for same-sex weddings. Throughout the litigation, Colorado has argued there is "nothing novel" about antidiscrimination laws that target businesses (i.e., commercial conduct)[71] and that the only speech affected is the ban on statements proposing illegal activity.[72] The Court agreed to hear the case on February 22, 2022, framing the question to be resolved as "[w]hether applying a public-accommodation law to compel an artist to speak or stay silent violates the Free Speech Clause of the First Amendment."[23]

Challenges to laws affecting commercial speech (for which the government typically has had more leeway to regulate than expressive, non-commercial speech) have traditionally been answered using the *Central Hudson* test.[73] Applying this test, a court will theoretically uphold a law restricting speech if the restriction is narrowly tailored (i.e., not more extensive than is necessary) and if the government has a "substantial" interest that is directly advanced by the restriction. This test arguably got harder for the government to overcome following *Sorrell v. IMS Health Inc.*[74] (a case in which a Vermont law imposing restrictions on the sale, disclosure, and use of pharmacy records and prescription information to detailers was struck down even though the stated intent of the law was to "protect medical privacy, including physician confidentiality, avoidance of harassment, and the integrity of the doctor-patient relationship"[74 at 2668]). There, the Supreme Court rejected the argument that the law targeted conduct and only incidentally burdened speech and instead framed the law as imposing impermissible content-based and speaker-based restrictions. According to one scholar, "[n]o commercial speech restriction has passed the *Central Hudson* test in decades, and it is now unclear whether a restriction on non-deceptive commercial speech can ever pass this test."[75]

The Roberts Court has decided a wide array of First Amendment cases,[76] earning criticism for having "turned the first amendment into a weapon" for "conservative interests."[77] While privacy law scholars have long indicated that data privacy laws are not properly envisioned within First Amendment space[78] such claims predated the provocative decision in *TransUnion. 303 Creative LLC v. Elenis* needs to be watched carefully by data scientists. Whether algorithms (or more specifically data, coding, and algorithmic outputs) can or will be considered "speech" remains an open question (although the Supreme Court in *Sorrell* suggested without deciding that "the creation and dissemination of information are speech for First Amendment purposes"[74 at 2657]). Resolving this question is left for separate in-depth discussion.[79-85] Nevertheless, one can speculate that the extent to which data minimalism and privacy-by-design practices can be lawfully required by Congress or administrative agencies (whether the FTC or FDA) might hinge, according to the Roberts Court, on whether such mandates are "compelled silence" and, similarly, the constitutionality of mandated nondiscrimination-by-design principles might hinge on viewing them as "compelled speech" as opposed to mandated conduct.[See also 86-87] Commercial speech restrictions are unlikely to pass muster if the Roberts Court applies something more than rational basis review, which is likely given the expansive protections it has extended to corporate expression over the past decade.[See 75]

The way in which the Roberts Court framed the question to be decided in *303 Creative LLC v. Elenis* suggests it is ready to expand the notion that anti-discrimination laws cannot regulate commercial speech as a public accommodation because "eliminating discriminatory bias [is] a 'decidedly fatal objective' in light of a Free Speech challenge."[88] If so, and if the Roberts Court views data or algorithms as speech, it could become all but impossible for the government to impose responsible requirements to advance algorithmic fairness (whether through data privacy or nondiscrimination mechanisms). With this in mind, and also recognizing that Section 1557 of the Affordable Care Act—the omnibus nondiscrimination provision for health activities—continues to be revised (including a proposed rulemaking announced in August 2022 that would apply to use of algorithms in clinical decision-making[89-90]), politicized, and challenged, alarm bells are properly being rung for the future of civil rights under the Roberts Court.[91-93]

5. Discussion

Given the above highlights, it seems clear that government-imposed data practice rules (e.g., regarding collection, management, processing, and disclosures) to promote algorithmic fairness and equal participation in, access to, and shared benefits and burdens of digital health and biomedical data science are going to be extremely difficult to realize in the Roberts Court era. First, such approaches might be considered as mere attempts to elevate harms that are "non-existent" or having no 1776 analog, thus leaving plaintiffs without adequate standing to have cases settled in federal courts. Second, if data and algorithmic outputs are viewed as speech, data protection laws of all sorts would be in direct tension with First Amendment protections. It seems at least plausible that privacy-by-design (although likely not nondiscrimination-by-design) measures could be considered content neutral "manner" restrictions if crafted carefully.[See 94] Third, rules to combat data biases and discrimination and advance algorithmic fairness could be considered content-based compelled speech and subjected to heightened or strict scrutiny review. With the Roberts Court taking a broad view of the First Amendment, this could spell bad news for the FTC with its more aggressive approach toward data-related policies.

With all of the legal gaps and uncertainties, now more than ever it is incumbent upon the biomedical data science community to develop and adopt self-governance strategies to advance algorithmic fairness. Contracts between individuals and entities can be used to mandate certain behaviors (including data practices and algorithmic uses), and terms of service and privacy policies should be examined and revised as appropriate. Moral clauses can address matters of ethical significance and impose duties not otherwise required by law (including performance of privacy-by design practices and due diligence to detect and remedy biases in algorithms). Feedback mechanisms are needed to incentivize responsible and deter detrimental conduct in a biomedical data ecosystem, including, e.g., mechanisms for reporting biased algorithms, removing them from further use, and correcting them. Professional societies have a role to play as well by establishing practice norms and guidance and setting enforceable codes of conduct for their members. Self-governance strategies to advance algorithmic fairness will continue to require multidisciplinary collaborations and policy-focused research, so opportunities to connect on such issues in meaningful, focused, and psychologically safe ways (e.g., new or recurring Innovation Labs[10]) should be supported and prioritized.

Acknowledgments

This work was supported in part by the NHGRI Grant No. R01HG011051. The content of this article is the author's responsibility and might not represent the views of the author's current or former funding sources, employers, clients, or any other person or entity. The author is appreciative of the constructive feedback on an early conceptualization of a portion of this work she received from colleagues during Biolawlapalooza 4.2 at Stanford Law School in May 2022.

References

1. G. Gursoy, M. Doerr, J. Wilbanks, et al. Pac. Symp. Biocomput. 2020; 25:736-738.
2. D. Petkovic, L. Kobzik, R. Ghanadan. Pac. Symp. Biocomput. 2020;25:731-735.
3. G. Gursoy, B. Malin, S.E. Brenner. Pac. Symp. Biocomput. 2022;27:417-418.
4. P. Washington, S. Yeung, B. Percha, et al. Pac. Symp. Biocomput. 2021;26:1-13.
5. R. Reich, Pac. Symp. Biocomput. 2022. https://psb.stanford.edu/previous/psb22/
6. I. Ajunwa, Pac. Symp. Biocomput. 2020. https://psb.stanford.edu/previous/psb20/
7. L. Hunter, Pac. Symp. Biocomput. 2019. https://psb.stanford.edu/previous/psb19/
8. J.K. Wagner, Pac. Symp. Biocomput. 2018. https://psb.stanford.edu/previous/psb18/
9. D. Magnus, Pac. Symp. Biocomput. 2017. https://psb.stanford.edu/previous/psb17/
10. NIH ODSS, InnovationLab: A Data Ecosystems Approach to Ethical AI for Biomedical and Behavioral Research. Mar 14-18, 2022.
11. NIH OSP. A match made in science: integrating bioethics and biomedical research. 7/20/21. Video available at https://videocast.nih.gov/watch=42402
12. S. Varma, J. Rubin. 2018. Fairness Definitions Explained. Fairware '18: IEEE/ACM Internat'l Workshop on Software Fairness, May 2018, New York, NY, USA, 1-7. https://doi.org/10.1145/3194770.3194776
13. J. Xu, Y. Xiao, W.H. Wang, et al. Algorithmic fairness in computational medicine. EBioMedicine. 2022 Sep 6;84:104250.
14. FAIRNESS, Black's Law Dictionary (11th ed. 2019)
15. J.L. Roberts, *Protecting Privacy to Prevent Discrimination*, 56 Wm. & Mary L. Rev. 2097 (2015).
16. E. Lander, A. Nelson. ICYMI: WIRED (Opinion): Americans Need a Bill of Rights for an AI-Powered World, 10/22/21, https://www.whitehouse.gov/ostp/news-updates/2021/10/22/icymi-wired-opinion-americans-need-a-bill-of-rights-for-an-ai-powered-world/
17. M. Rotenberg, S. Revanur, Opinion: Time to act now on AI Bill of Rights. The Hill. 7/19/22. https://thehill.com/opinion/technology/3566180-time-to-act-now-on-ai-bill-of-rights/
18. NIST AI Risk Management Framework, https://www.nist.gov/itl/ai-risk-management-framework
19. L. Heinzerling, The Supreme Court is Making America Ungovernable, The Atlantic, 7/29/22, https://www.theatlantic.com/ideas/archive/2022/07/supreme-court-major-questions-doctrine-congress/670618/
20. TransUnion LLC v. Ramirez, 141 S. Ct. 2190, 210 L. Ed. 2d 568 (2021)
21. Dobbs v. Jackson Women's Health Org., 142 S. Ct. 2228 (2022)
22. West Virginia v. Environmental Protection Agency, 142 S. Ct. 2587 (2022)
23. 303 Creative LLC v. Elenis, 142 S. Ct. 1106, 212 L. Ed. 2d 6 (2022)

24. Federal Trade Commission Act, 15 U.S.C. §§41-58, as amended
25. J.K. Wagner. The Federal Trade Commission and Consumer Protections for Mobile Health Apps. J Law Med Ethics. 2020 Mar;48(1_suppl):103-114.
26. FTC Finalized Order with Flo Health, a Fertility-Tracking App that Shared Sensitive Health Data with Facebook, Google, and Others, 6/22/21, https://www.ftc.gov/news-events/news/press-releases/2021/06/ftc-finalizes-order-flo-health-fertility-tracking-app-shared-sensitive-health-data-facebook-google
27. E. Jillson, Aiming for truth, fairness, and equity in your company's use of AI, 4/19/21, https://www.ftc.gov/business-guidance/blog/2021/04/aiming-truth-fairness-equity-your-companys-use-ai
28. FTC Authorizes Investigations into Key Enforcement Priorities, 7/1/21, https://www.ftc.gov/news-events/news/press-releases/2021/07/ftc-authorizes-investigations-key-enforcement-priorities
29. FTC, FTC Report to Congress on Privacy and Security, 9/13/21, https://www.ftc.gov/system/files/documents/reports/ftc-report-congress-privacy-security/report_to_congress_on_privacy_and_data_security_2021.pdf
30. Statement of the Commission On Breaches by Health Apps and Other Connected Devices, 9/15/21, https://www.ftc.gov/system/files/documents/public_statements/1596364/statement_of_the_commission_on_breaches_by_health_apps_and_other_connected_devices.pdf
31. Prepared remarks of Commissioner Rebecca Kelly Slaughter Regarding the Commission's Policy Statement on Privacy Breaches by Connected Health Apps, 9/15/21, https://www.ftc.gov/system/files/documents/public_statements/1596320/rks_remarks_on_health_breach_policy_statement_09152021.pdf
32. FTC takes action against company formerly known as Weight Watchers for Illegally Collecting Kids' Sensitive Health Data, 3/4/22, https://www.ftc.gov/news-events/news/press-releases/2022/03/ftc-takes-action-against-company-formerly-known-weight-watchers-illegally-collecting-kids-sensitive
33. J.K. Wagner, One Step Closer to Federal Data Privacy Law Reform: H.R. 8152, the American Data Privacy and Protection Act, 7/27/22. https://pbacyber.com/index.php/2022/07/27/one-step-closer-to-federal-data-privacy-law-reform-h-r-8152-the-american-data-privacy-and-protection-act-adppa/
34. STANDING, Black's Law Dictionary (11th ed. 2019).
35. STARE DECISIS, Black's Law Dictionary (11th ed. 2019).
36. B.J. Murrill, The Supreme Court's Overruling of Constitutional Precedent, CRS R45319, Sep. 24, 2018.
37. D.J. Sheffner, The Major Questions Doctrine, CRS IF12077, Apr. 6, 2022.
38. NONDELEGATION DOCTRINE, Black's Law Dictionary (11th ed. 2019).
39. 303 Creative LLC v. Elenis, https://www.scotusblog.com/case-files/cases/303-creative-llc-v-elenis/
40. M.A. Lemley, *The Imperial Supreme Court*, 7/28/22. SSRN: https://ssrn.com/abstract=4175554 or http://dx.doi.org/10.2139/ssrn.4175554
41. D. Solove, D. Keats Citron, *Standing and Privacy Harms: A Critique of TransUnion v. Ramirez*, 101 B.U.L. Rev. Online 62, 63 (2021).
42. R.J. McGahan, M. G. Lindenbaum, J. Graham, M.L. Todman, *No Harm, no Foul…*, Nat. L. Rev., 6/25/21, https://www.natlawreview.com/article/no-harm-no-foul-transunion-v-ramirez-supreme-court-holds-fed-rule-civ-p-23-does-not
43. Spokeo, Inc. v. Robins, 578 U.S. 330, 136 S. Ct. 1540 (2016)

44. D. Keats Citron, D. J. Solove, *Privacy Harms,* 102 Boston Univ. L. Rev. 793 (2022).
45. Health Information Portability and Accountability Act of 1996, Pub. L. 104-191, 110 Stat. 1936.
46. D. Solove, Further Thoughts on ADPPA, the Federal Comprehensive Privacy Bill, Jul. 30, 2022, https://teachprivacy.com/further-thoughts-on-adppa-the-federal-comprehensive-privacy-bill/
47. Roe v. Wade, 410 U.S. 113, 93 S. Ct. 705 (1973)
48. Planned Parenthood of Southeastern Pa. v. Casey, 505 U.S. 833, 112 S. Ct. 2791 (1992)
49. J.K. Wagner, A Post-Roe Future Presents Heightened Data Privacy Risks with FemTech, 6/1/22. https://pbacyber.com/index.php/2022/06/01/a-post-roe-future-presents-heightened-data-privacy-risks-with-femtech/
50. B. Corbin, The Shifting Data Privacy Landscape for Femtech & Beyond, Med Device Online, 6/29/22, https://www.meddeviceonline.com/doc/the-shifting-data-privacy-landscape-for-femtech-beyond-0001
51. D. Keats Citron, The End of Roe Means we Need a New Civil Right to Privacy, Slate, 6/27/22, https://slate.com/technology/2022/06/end-roe-civil-right-intimate-privacy-data.html
52. After the abortion ruling, digital privacy is more important than ever, Washington Post, 7/4/22, https://www.washingtonpost.com/opinions/2022/07/04/abortion-ruling-digital-privacy-important/
53. R. Torchinsky, How period tracking apps and data privacy fit into a post-Roe v. Wade climate, NPR, 6/24/22, https://www.npr.org/2022/05/10/1097482967/roe-v-wade-supreme-court-abortion-period-apps
54. A. Prince, Reproductive Health Surveillance (7/29/22). https://ssrn.com/abstract=4176557
55. E. Boodman, T. Bannow, B. Herman, C. Ross, HIPAA won't protect you if prosecutors want your reproductive health records. STAT News. 6/24/22, https://www.statnews.com/2022/06/24/hipaa-wont-protect-you-if-prosecutors-want-your-reproductive-health-records/
56. 45 CFR 164.512(f)
57. N. Totenberg, Supreme Court refuses to block Texas abortion law as legal fights move forward, NPR, 12/10/21, https://www.npr.org/2021/12/10/1053628779/supreme-court-refuse-to-block-texas-abortion-law-as-legal-fights-move-forward
58. K. Zernike, A. Liptak, Texas Supreme Court Shuts Down Final Challenge to Aborton Law, N.Y. Times, 3/11/22, https://www.nytimes.com/2022/03/11/us/texas-abortion-law.html
59. K. Spector-Bagdady, M.M. Mello. Protecting the Privacy of Reproductive Health Information After the Fall of Roe v Wade. JAMA Health Forum. 2022;3(6):e222656.
60. DHHS Office of Civil Rights (OCR) Guidance on HIPAA and Reproductive Health, 6/29/22, https://www.hhs.gov/hipaa/for-professionals/special-topics/reproductive-health/index.html
61. J.K. Wagner, Updated DHHS OCR Guidance on Health Information Privacy After Dobbs, 7/27/22, https://pbacyber.com/index.php/2022/07/27/updated-dhhs-ocr-guidance-on-health-information-privacy-after-dobbs/
62. Carpenter v. United States, 138 S. Ct. 2206, 201 L. Ed. 2d 507 (2018)
63. D. Solove, Carpenter v. United States, Cell Phone Location Records, and the Third Party Doctrine, 7/1/18, https://teachprivacy.com/carpenter-v-united-states-cell-phone-location-records-and-the-third-party-doctrine/
64. N. Ram, *Genetic privacy after Carpenter*, 105 Va. L. Rev. 1357, 1373 (2019) (citing *Carpenter* at 2223)
65. R. Knox, *Fourth Amendment Protections of Health Information After Carpenter v. United States: The Devil's in the Database*, 45 Am J L & Med 331 (2019)
66. C. Lamar, *The Third-Party Doctrine Crossroads…*, 39 Rev. Litig. 215 (2019)

67. 80 Fed. Reg. 64509-64660 (2015)
68. Clean Air Amendments of 1970, 84 Stat. 1676, 42 U.S.C. §7401 *et seq.*
69. 84 Fed. Reg. 32520-32584 (2019)
70. J.W. Hampton, Jr. & Co. v. United States, 276 U.S. 394, 409, 48 S. Ct. 348 (1928).
71. Heart of Atlanta Motel v. United States, 379 U.S. 241, 85 S. Ct. 348 (1964).
72. Respondents, Brief in Opposition, 2021 WL 5893335 (Dec. 8, 2021) at 25 and 31-33.
73. Central Hudson Gas & Elec. Corp. v. Pub. Serv. Comm'n, 447 U.S. 557, 573 (1980)
74. Sorrell v. IMS Health Inc., 564 U.S. 552, 131 S. Ct. 2653, 180 L. Ed. 2d 544 (2011)
75. J.L. Pomeranz, *United States: Protecting Commercial Speech under the First Amendment,* J Law Med & Ethics. 2022; 265-275, 268.
76. R. K. Collins, D. L. Hudson Jr., *The Roberts Court—Its First Amendment Free Expression Jurisprudence: 2005–2021*, 87 Brook. L. Rev. 5 (2021).
77. E. Segall, The Roberts Court, First Amendment Fanaticism, and the Myth of Originalism, 4/12/21, http://www.dorfonlaw.org/2021/04/the-roberts-court-first-amendment.html
78. N.M. Richards, *Reconciling Data Privacy and the First Amendment*, 52 UCLA L. Rev. 1149 (2005).
79. C.P. Guzelian, *Scientific Speech*, 93 Iowa L. Rev. 881 (2008)
80. A. Candeub, *Digital medicine, the FDA, and the First Amendment*, 49 Ga. L. Rev. 933 (2015)
81. B. Shah, *Commercial free speech constraints on data privacy statutes after* Sorrell v. IMS Health, 54 Colum. J. L. & Soc. Probs. 93 (2020)
82. S. M. Benjamin, *Algorithms and Speech*, 161 U. Pa. L. Rev. 1445 (2013)
83. J. Bambauer, *Is data speech?*, 66 Stan. L. Rev. 57 (2014)
84. J. Blackman, *What happens if data is speech?* 16 U. Pa. J. Const. L. Heightened Scrutiny 25 (2014)
85. A.M. Sears, *Algorithmic Speech and Freedom of Expression*, 53 Vand. J. Transnat'l L. 1327 (2020)
86. D.E. Ho, A. Xiang, *Affirmative algorithms? The legal grounds for fairness as awareness*. Univ. Chicago L. Rev. Online, 10/30/20, https://lawreviewblog.uchicago.edu/2020/10/30/aa-ho-xiang/
87. P. Kim, *Race-Aware Algorithms: Fairness, nondiscrimination and affirmative action*, 110 Cal. L. Rev.- (2022)
88. 303 Creative LLC v. Elenis, 6 F.4th 1160, 1178 (2021) (quoting 515 U.S. at 579 (1995)) and at 1199.
89. DHHS and CMS, NPRM: Nondiscrimination in Health Programs and Activities, Doc. No. 2022-16217, 8/4/22. Unpub. version at https://public-inspection.federalregister.gov/2022-16217.pdf
90. K. Keith, HHS Proposes Revised ACA Anti-Discrimination Rule, Health Affairs, 7/27/22. https://www.healthaffairs.org/content/forefront/hhs-proposes-revised-aca-anti-discrimination-rule
91. H. Keren, The alarming legal strategy behind a SCOTUS case that could undo decades of civil rights protections, Slate, 3/9/22. https://slate.com/news-and-politics/2022/03/supreme-court-303-creative-coordinated-anti-lgbt-legal-strategy.html
92. I. Millhiser, The supreme court will hear a big case about whether religion is a license to discriminate, Vox, 2/22/22, https://www.vox.com/2022/2/22/22945657/supreme-court-religion-lgbtq-303-creative-elenis-colorado-discrimination
93. J. Turley, Discrimination or free speech? The Hill, 2/24/22, https://thehill.com/opinion/judiciary/595642-discrimination-or-free-speech-supreme-court-decides-to-weigh-in
94. City of Austin, Texas v. Reagan Nat'l Advert. Of Austin, LLC, 142 S. Ct. 1464, 212 L. Ed. 2d 418 (2022)

Accessing clinical-grade genomic classification data through the ClinGen Data Platform*

Karen P. Dalton[1], Heidi L. Rehm[2,3], Matt W. Wright[1], Mark E. Mandell[1], Kilannin Krysiak[4], Lawrence Babb[3], Kevin Riehle[5], Tristan Nelson[6], Alex H. Wagner[7,8]

[1]Department of Biomedical Data Science, Stanford University, Stanford, CA; [2]Massachusetts General Hospital, Boston, MA; [3]Medical and Population Genetics, Broad Institute of MIT and Harvard, Cambridge, MA; [4]Department of Pathology and Immunology, Washington University School of Medicine, St. Louis, MO; [5]Baylor College of Medicine, Houston, TX; [6]Geisinger, Danville, PA; [7]Institute for Genomic Medicine, Nationwide Children's Hospital, Columbus, OH; [8]Departments of Pediatrics & Biomedical Informatics, The Ohio State University College of Medicine, Columbus, OH.

The Clinical Genome Resource (ClinGen) serves as an authoritative resource on the clinical relevance of genes and variants. In order to support our curation activities and to disseminate our findings to the community, we have developed a Data Platform of informatics resources backed by standardized data models. In this workshop we demonstrate our publicly available resources including curation interfaces, (Variant Curation Interface, CIViC), supporting infrastructure (Allele Registry, Genegraph), and data models (SEPIO, GA4GH VRS, VA).

Keywords: Clinical Genomics; ClinGen; GA4GH; Data Standards; Variant Interpretation

1. Introduction

Genome-guided precision medicine requires evaluating the clinical significance of genomic variation through the aggregation and standardized evaluation of disparate lines of functional, clinical, and observational evidence. The process by which evidence is combined and turned into a formal classification of significance is guided by professional organization or consortia-driven recommendations, such as the 2015 ACMG/AMP guidelines[1] for Mendelian disease variants, the 2017 AMP/ASCO/CAP guidelines[2] for somatic cancer variants, and the recently published 2022 ClinGen/CGC/VICC guidelines[3] for cancer variant oncogenicity. The application of these guidelines requires carefully controlled curation interfaces and expert vetting of evidence to ensure reproducible and high-quality assertions of clinical significance.

To address this need, the NIH-funded Clinical Genome Resource (ClinGen) was founded in 2013 to serve as a central authority for defining the clinical relevance of genes and variants for use in precision medicine and research. The ClinGen Data Platform represents the coordinated activities of the ClinGen data tools that drive the generation and dissemination of carefully curated, high-quality assertions of clinical relevance in public databases and precision medicine pipelines (clinicalgenome.org/working-groups/data-platform). The Data Platform enables the clinical knowledge journey: the interfaces used to curate clinical significance classifications, the frameworks for structuring and normalizing them, and the tools for exchanging and widely disseminating this clinical knowledge for use in clinical systems.

2. Workshop Topics and Presenters

2.1. Introduction - The Clinical Genome Resource

Presented by: Heidi Rehm (Broad Institute of MIT and Harvard & Massachusetts General Hospital)

This workshop describes the Clinical Genome Resource (ClinGen) and how ClinGen standardizes and supports the classification of the clinical significance of genes and variants. ClinGen activities include development of standardized frameworks for gene and variant classification, provision of the needed software structures to support this work, and crowd-sourcing the sharing of gene and variant classifications and underlying curated evidence through ClinGen's website (clinicalgenome.org), GenCC (Gene Curation Coalition) and ClinVar (NCBI supported). Conflicting classifications are resolved through interlaboratory efforts for both ClinVar and GenCC entries, and a subset of variants are reviewed and classified through the consensus-driven application of ClinGen's expert panels. This session will also examine forward-looking approaches needed to scale the classification of variants, including example patient cases with variants for use throughout each portion of the workshop. This will entail a review of evidence types used in variant classifications and discussion of how sharing this data according to harmonized data models enables more scalable approaches to variant classification.

2.2. Generating clinical-grade genomic knowledge

2.2.1. Clinical variant knowledge from Variant Curation Expert Panels

Presented by: Matt Wright, Karen Dalton, Mark Mandell (Stanford University)

The ClinGen Variant Curation Interface (VCI)[4] is a global, open-source cloud-native, variant classification platform for supporting the application of evidence-based criteria and classification of variants based on the ACMG/AMP variant classification guidelines. Publicly accessible via https://curation.clinicalgenome.org, the VCI is among a suite of tools developed by ClinGen and supports an FDA-recognized human variant curation process. It enables collaboration and peer review across ClinGen Expert Panels, and supports users in identifying, annotating, and sharing relevant evidence while making variant pathogenicity assertions. Navigation workflows support users by providing guidance to comprehensively apply the ACMG/AMP evidence criteria and document provenance for asserting variant classifications both within ClinGen expert panels and the wider genomics community.

At this part of the data journey from patient genomic data to clinically relevant interpretation of variants, data is ingested from a variety of community resources and, after complete curation, is exported to other resources within the ClinGen ecosystem and also exported with classified variants into ClinVar and the Evidence Repository. We will discuss the use of defined ontologies and data structures to produce consensus interpretations from defined methodologies at scale. The semi-structured workflow in combination with the evaluation by expert panel members moves determinations of variant pathogenicity away from the prior methods of relying on subjective judgment by a single individual toward structured review of evidence to reach expert consensus, thereby increasing the confidence in the data created.

2.2.2. Somatic cancer clinical variant knowledge from Somatic Cancer Variant Curation Expert Panels

Presented by: Kilannin Krysiak (Washington University in St. Louis), Alex Wagner (Nationwide Children's Hospital and the Ohio State University)

The crowd-sourced, public domain Clinical Interpretations of Variants in Cancer (CIViC) knowledgebase[5] is a cancer variant knowledgebase funded by the NCI Informatics Technology for Cancer Research program that collaborates closely with ClinGen and captures literature-derived evidence for the clinical assessment of genomic variants in cancers through an open evidence curation interface[6]. ClinGen Somatic Cancer Variant Curation Expert Panels (SC-VCEPs) capture evidence in CIViC using concepts from established terminologies for cancer types, therapies, histopathologies, and genes, alongside CIViC-defined structured data fields and human-readable text. The CIViC curation interface supports a rigorous evidence curation protocol[7], which is used and expanded upon by SC-VCEPs in domain-specific (e.g. tumor type and/or gene specific) curation activities. CIViC content is freely available without registration via the web interface, text downloads or API access, and its content is released under a public domain (CC0) declaration.

We will cover the fundamental data types curated in the CIViC interface, and how these apply to professional society guidelines to guide clinical interpretation of tumor variants. A hands-on exercise using Python-based Jupyter notebooks will demonstrate the use of the GraphQL API and the CIViCpy[8] SDK for accessing and applying curated content in clinical and research workflows.

2.3. Standardizing exchange and dissemination of clinical-grade genomic knowledge

2.3.1. Overview of the ClinGen Genomic Knowledge Model and the Variant Annotation framework

Presented by: Larry Babb (Broad Institute of MIT and Harvard), Alex Wagner (Nationwide Children's Hospital and the Ohio State University)

Throughout our infrastructure ClinGen has an ongoing commitment to make genomic knowledge findable, accessible, interoperable and reusable (FAIR) and has devoted consistent data engineering resources over the past 6 years to deliver on that commitment. ClinGen is an ideal platform for evolving these genomic knowledge standards with its consortium comprised of several separate software engineering teams all dedicated to an integrated ecosystem for supporting the collection and curation of evidence, the standardization of variation and other fundamental related genomic concepts, and the dissemination of fully qualified evidence-based genomic knowledge from expert groups. We will be discussing the SEPIO framework, the ClinGen Genomic Knowledge Model, and the application of the Variant Annotation framework[9] that is the foundation for the ongoing standards work being done with the Global Alliance for Genomics and Health (GA4GH)[10,11] within the Genomic Knowledge Standards working group.

We will also examine the GA4GH Genomic Knowledge statement design for representing provenance-based evidence, the assessment of that evidence based on an associated method and the final classification of the knowledge being addressed. ClinGen is leveraging this design to represent gene and variation based knowledge for Gene Validity, Dosage Sensitivity, Variant Pathogenicity and Clinical Actionability. We will walk through exercises related to Variant Pathogenicity and Therapeutic Response statements to illustrate challenges addressed by this framework and the benefits of standardized, clinical-grade, interoperable and reusable genomic knowledge content. We will then cover the application of this framework to the previously described variation curation platforms, and how it relates to downstream resources such as the Evidence Repository and LDH. A hands-on exercise will be presented for querying (and generating) compliant data with community-developed software tools.

2.3.2. Tools for variant registration and evidence association

Presented by: Kevin Riehle (Baylor College of Medicine)

This session will describe the ClinGen Allele Registry (CAR - https://reg.clinicalgenome.org)[12] which provides a canonicalization service resulting in >2.5B canonical allele identifiers (CA IDs) representing alleles that have equivalent representations across genome builds and transcripts. The Linked Data Hub (LDH: https://ldh.clinicalgenome.org), provides a structured environment that leverages excerpted data from external sources (e.g. molecular consequence, BRCA Exchange, CIViC, ClinVar, population allele frequency, etc.) with links to other core documents (e.g. variants, genes, etc.) that results in aggregation of knowledge for a given query. We will provide an overview and demonstration of the CAR and LDH as it relates to supporting curation efforts in ClinGen and how the functionality can be applied to other projects and consortia.

We will also showcase the incorporation of GA4GH-modeled ClinVar data into the LDH and how this process can be leveraged to support additional resources that maintain SEPIO and non-SEPIO structured documents. Combining the registration service (CAR) with supporting evidence (LDH) provides for downstream tool integration to support curation (e.g., Variant Curation Interface), deduplication, provenance, and other types of applications.

2.3.3. Tools for knowledge dissemination

Presented by: Tristan Nelson (Geisinger)

ClinGen has applied the models developed within the SEPIO Framework and GA4GH Variant Representation and Annotation standards to the variant assessments in ClinVar, as well as Gene Dosage and Gene Validity curations. Through our Genegraph service, we make available a form of ClinVar that represents submissions on a given variant by individual submitters (SCV), as this view of the data allows a fine-grained assessment of the professional assessments made regarding the clinical relevance of a variant, which can then be filtered based on several factors, including the purpose of the assessment and the reputation of the source. We represented the ClinGen Gene Dosage and Validity data in the same formats; demonstrating the utility and flexibility of these models in the context of diverse and highly clinically relevant datasets. We investigate some of the ways these datasets can be explored to produce clinical insights.

3. Conclusion

This workshop will introduce the methods and tools used to support the lifecycle of consuming, generating, and classifying clinical genomic knowledge. We will describe the Variant Curation

Expert Panel evaluation process for constitutional and somatic cancer variant curation, and how these data are disseminated for reuse and expert evaluation between systems through modern data normalization and community-driven data exchange standards.

4. Acknowledgments

National Human Genome Research Institute (NHGRI) awards supported AHW (R35HG011949) and KD, HR, MW, MM, LB, KR, TN (U24HG009649, U24HG006834, U24HG009650). KK is supported by the NIH National Cancer Institute award U24CA237719.

Bibliography

1. Richards, S. *et al.* Standards and guidelines for the interpretation of sequence variants: a joint consensus recommendation of the American College of Medical Genetics and Genomics and the Association for Molecular Pathology. *Genet. Med.* **17**, 405–424 (2015).
2. Li, M. M. *et al.* Standards and Guidelines for the Interpretation and Reporting of Sequence Variants in Cancer: A Joint Consensus Recommendation of the Association for Molecular Pathology, American Society of Clinical Oncology, and College of American Pathologists. *J. Mol. Diagn.* **19**, 4–23 (2017).
3. Horak, P. *et al.* Standards for the classification of pathogenicity of somatic variants in cancer (oncogenicity): Joint recommendations of Clinical Genome Resource (ClinGen), Cancer Genomics Consortium (CGC), and Variant Interpretation for Cancer Consortium (VICC). *Genet. Med.* (2022) doi:10.1016/j.gim.2022.01.001..
4. Preston, C. G. *et al.* ClinGen Variant Curation Interface: a variant classification platform for the application of evidence criteria from ACMG/AMP guidelines. *Genome Med.* **14**, 6 (2022).
5. Krysiak, K. *et al.* A community approach to the cancer-variant-interpretation bottleneck. *Nat Cancer* **3**, 522–525 (2022).
6. Griffith, M. *et al.* CIViC is a community knowledgebase for expert crowdsourcing the clinical interpretation of variants in cancer. *Nat. Genet.* **49**, 170–174 (2017).
7. Danos, A. M. *et al.* Standard operating procedure for curation and clinical interpretation of variants in cancer. *Genome Med.* **11**, 76 (2019).
8. Wagner, A. H. *et al.* CIViCpy: A Python software development and analysis toolkit for the CIViC knowledgebase. *JCO Clin. Cancer Inform.* **4**, 245–253 (2020).
9. Brush, M. H., Shefchek, K. & Haendel, M. SEPIO: A Semantic Model for the Integration and Analysis of Scientific Evidence. in *ICBO/BioCreative* (pdfs.semanticscholar.org, 2016).
10. Rehm, H. L. *et al.* GA4GH: International policies and standards for data sharing across genomic research and healthcare. *Cell Genom* **1**, 100029 (2021).
11. Wagner, A. H. *et al.* The GA4GH Variation Representation Specification: A computational framework for variation representation and federated identification. *Cell Genomics* **1**, 100027 (2021).
12. Pawliczek, P. *et al.* ClinGen Allele Registry links information about genetic variants. *Hum. Mutat.* **39**, 1690–1701 (2018).

Biomedical research in the Cloud: considerations for researchers and organizations moving to (or adding) cloud computing resources

Michelle Holko

Google, Google Public Sector
Washington, DC 20001, USA
Email: michelleholko@google.com

Nick Weber and Chris Lunt

National Institutes of Health
Bethesda, MD 20892, USA
Email: wspc@wspc.com

Steven E. Brenner

University of California, Berkeley
Berkeley, California 94720, USA
Email: brenner@compbio.berkeley.edu

As biomedical research data grow, researchers need reliable and scalable solutions for storage and compute. There is also a need to build systems that encourage and support collaboration and data sharing, to result in greater reproducibility. This has led many researchers and organizations to use cloud computing [1]. The cloud not only enables scalable, on-demand resources for storage and compute, but also collaboration and continuity during virtual work, and can provide superior security and compliance features. Moving to or adding cloud resources, however, is not trivial or without cost, and may not be the best choice in every scenario. The goal of this workshop is to explore the benefits of using the cloud in biomedical and computational research, and considerations (pros and cons) for a range of scenarios including individual researchers, collaborative research teams, consortia research programs, and large biomedical research agencies / organizations.

Keywords: cloud computing; data; bioinformatics; compute research infrastructure.

1. Background

1.1. *Growing use of the cloud in biomedical research*

For at least 30 years, biomedical research data have been growing exponentially, largely since Wally Gilbert first quantified the size of genomics data in 1990 and projected exponential growth until 2040 with a genome for everyone. NHGRI notes that "estimates predict that genomics research will generate between 2 and 40 exabytes [2] of data within the next decade [3]." Making sense from data often requires large and extensible storage and compute capacity, not only because of the sheer size of the data but also because of the complex nature of biology and systems. Additionally, data become more valuable over time, as they grow and also as we learn more about the context surrounding the data. Thus, models that encourage data stewardship and longevity have a greater chance of unlocking discovery.

Many large research organizations are moving to the cloud to handle computational biology research, including the National Institutes of Health (NIH), the National Science Foundation (NSF), the Department of Energy (DoE), the National Aeronautics and Space Administration (NASA), and many academic research institutions. NIH's Science and Technology Research Infrastructure for Discovery, Experimentation, and Sustainability (STRIDES) program is a model for enabling NIH-funded researchers to use cloud resources [4]. It provides choice to researchers by partnering with Google Cloud, Amazon Web Services (AWS), and Microsoft Azure. Through STRIDES, cloud adoption can be done at the organizational (e.g., university) and individual researcher/research lab level. NSF has also been a leader in developing tools like CloudBank for researchers to make it easier to use and track cloud computing in their research grants [5].

Biomedical research increasingly makes use of Machine Learning/Artificial Intelligence (ML/AI) research, as funding opportunities and a focus on developing public policies for ML/AI research grow [6]. These types of research efforts often require large compute and/or supercomputing, beyond what is available to many researchers, from students to principal investigators, on their own laptops. For researchers at institutions who do not have access to large on premise computation and/or supercomputers, the cloud can be a good option to enable research on larger scales. The ability to use tools for ML/AI, such as TensorFlow, can enable researchers to get the most out of their data.

1.2. *Benefits of cloud computing*

Cloud computing can also be used to increase access to compute and storage for researchers at institutions with less infrastructure or IT support. Cloud deployments are almost always more environmentally-friendly, due to both efficient use of computing resources and engineering, and site engineering that minimizes environmental impacts. Data silos are often a problem with on-premise environments, as the data on one's laptop aren't discoverable or easily shareable with collaborators. This can be overcome with cloud computing, but only if the systems are engineered to improve collaboration and data sharing. Best practices in cloud implementations and engineering are critical to avoid the need for data duplication, re-deploying systems in multiple places, and data leaks. These challenges are not inherent to cloud computing, but are often a result of the technology not being used efficiently. They are also likely signs of an evolving technology and the relevant organizations figuring out how to meaningfully incorporate cloud computing into their funding model to enable researchers.

In addition to filling an immediate need, broader adoption of the cloud into a researcher or organization's infrastructure requires a thoughtful approach and deep understanding of the technology, often in partnership with private sector colleagues. Incorporating cloud computing in an IT infrastructure means the involvement of many different teams, likely including financial, administrative, central IT, research IT, and the researchers themselves. The decision making process often happens at the level of the organization, while the needs of the individual researcher and research groups need to be accounted for in this process.

1.3. *Organizational deployments of cloud computing for research*

Beyond individual research labs, research groups, and organizations adopting cloud, there are many examples of large research consortia building databases and communities in the cloud. The *All of Us* Research Program is a good example [7]. It has developed a custom implementation of Terra, a secure, scalable, open-source, cloud-based platform for biomedical researchers to access data, run analysis tools, and collaborate [8]. The UK Biobank initially used a data download approach and has now moved to a cloud-based platform built by DNAnexus to prevent download and promote centralized data access [9]. The National Cancer Institute's (NCI's) Imaging Data Commons is also cloud-based and provides cancer images and other related data to the research community [10]. NHGRI's AnVIL platform, another implementation of Terra, for genomics provides cloud-based resources for researchers to compute directly on the platform but also allows for data download [11]. When possible, many researchers still tend to download data and compute locally versus leverage cloud computing centrally. This stifles not only collaboration, but also the potential for data reproducibility that centralized platforms with data, tools, and researcher community can offer. Another challenge is that some researchers get accustomed to one system or one cloud platform, and portability can be an issue if a system or cloud platform changes. There are tools to help with this, and many cloud providers are developing multi-cloud solutions to enable portability between and among systems, but this is another thing for researchers to consider in their cloud consideration journey. At the organizational level, the *All of Us* Research Program is committed to expanding to multi-cloud to give researchers the freedom of choice in terms of platforms and tools.

When evaluating the possibility of using cloud for research, researchers and organizational IT professionals often consider the cost, size, and age of on-premise infrastructure, familiarity with and ability to implement cloud-based systems, as well as the research-specific factors like size and persistence of data sets, frequency of use, types of analysis workflows, and bioinformatics tools and languages. The choice of which cloud(s) to use often also involves cost comparison and an evaluation of which tools are available on the various cloud platforms. Peculiarities of the academic research environment, including especially funding models, complicate the decision about whether to migrate to cloud computing. There is also an ability for organizations to create multi-cloud and hybrid solutions so that the cloud can be used to extend on-premise environments, act as a bridge to cloud computing, and/or enable choice among researchers as to which cloud platform to use. This flexibility means that there are a wide variety of options available, which can also make the decision more confusing and the path forward less clear.

2. Relevance to biocomputing

The size of data, types of data, and types of ML/AI analytic workflows that are used in biocomputing research are relevant for cloud computing, particularly as data grow and are more voluminous. As this trend towards the cloud continues, it is important to share considerations and discuss challenges together as a community. The topic is timely since not only is there a growing use of the cloud, but also growth in data and an emphasis on ML/AI research - all of which require flexible compute and the storage that the cloud can provide. NIH has addressed this topic recently in a Virtual Workshop in September 2021 on Broadening Cloud Computing Usage in Biomedical Research, MSIs, HBCUs, TCUs, etc [12].

The text string "cloud computing" search on PubMed has been growing, with 63 publications in 2021 (Figure 1). Other biomedical conferences that have covered cloud computing include the American Medical Informatics Association (AMIA) and the American Society of Human Genetics (ASHG).

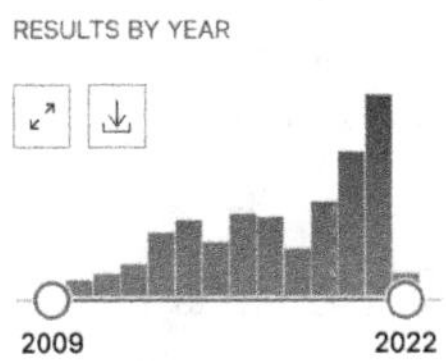

Fig. 1. Number of publications with "cloud computing" in PubMed from 2009-2021

The new policy on data sharing that will go into effect in January 2023 also means that cloud computing will be even more useful for researchers whose data don't fit neatly into one of the existing NIH primary data archives [13].

3. Workshop overview

This workshop, first and foremost, will be a balanced discussion about the pros and cons of moving to the cloud in a variety of situations, while considering different-sized labs and organizations, and for a wide range of research applications. This balanced perspective is a key feature to ensure that the discussion is an opportunity for learning and information exchange. The focus will include a range of compute options, including various public cloud providers, on-premise, hybrid and multi-cloud options.

Specific research use cases for biocomputational research in the cloud will be shared, and considerations for researchers and organizations who are evaluating the possibility of moving to the cloud, along with the range of possibilities including hybrid and multi-cloud. A discussion of the evolving technology and the relevant organizations is critical to figuring out how to meaningfully incorporate cloud computing into funding models to enable researchers.

The workshop is organized into talks and a panel discussion. The talks set the stage for the panel discussion, and cover considerations of moving to the cloud and how this went/is going. Talks include both researchers who are using the cloud, and those who are not using the cloud but have evaluated the possibility and decided against it. Session organizers also participate in talks and the panel discussion. The session includes diverse viewpoints, both from the cloud adoption perspective and the organizational type, size, and considerations perspective.

For the panel discussion, private sector researchers were invited to participate, to include the industry perspective along with larger organizations, including NIH. The panel is meant to spark discussion amongst the workshop participants. For both the talks and the panel, diversity and inclusion were goals incorporated into the final workshop organization.

References

1. Y. A. M. Qasem, R. Abdullah, Y. Y. Jusoh, R. Atan and S. Asadi, "Cloud Computing Adoption in Higher Education Institutions: A Systematic Review," in IEEE Access, vol. 7, pp. 63722-63744, 2019, doi: 10.1109/ACCESS.2019.2916234.
2. https://www.backblaze.com/blog/what-is-an-exabyte/
3. NHGRI (2021) Genomic Data Science. Accessed February 8, 2022.
4. https://datascience.nih.gov/strides
5. https://www.cloudbank.org/
6. https://www.whitehouse.gov/ostp/news-updates/2021/06/10/the-biden-administration-launches-the-national-artificial-intelligence-research-resource-task-force/
7. https://allofus.nih.gov
8. https://app.terra.bio/
9. https://www.ukbiobank.ac.uk/enable-your-research/research-analysis-platform
10. https://datacommons.cancer.gov/repository/imaging-data-commons
11. https://anvilproject.org/
12. https://datascience.nih.gov/data-ecosystem/nih-workshop-on-broadening-cloud-computing-usage-in-biomedical-research
13. https://sharing.nih.gov/data-management-and-sharing-policy/about-data-management-and-sharing-policy/data-management-and-sharing-policy-overview#after

HIGH-PERFORMANCE COMPUTING MEETS HIGH-PERFORMANCE MEDICINE

Anurag Verma
Department of Medicine, Division of Translational Medicine and Human Genetics, University of Pennsylvania, Philadelphia, Pennsylvania , USA
Email: anurag.verma@pennmedicine.upenn.edu

Jennifer Huffman
VA Boston Healthcare System, Boston, Massachusetts, USA
Email: Jennifer.Huffman2@va.gov

Ali Torkamani
Department of Integrative Structural and Computational Biology, The Scripps Research Institute, La Jolla, California, USA
Email: atorkama@scripps.edu

Ravi Madduri
Data Science and Learning Division, Argonne National Laboratory, Lemont, Illinois, USA
Email: madduri@anl.gov

1. Introduction, Background, and Motivation

Artificial intelligence (AI) is making a big impact on patient experiences, clinician workflows, researchers, and the pharmaceutical industry work in the healthcare sector. In recent decades, technological advancements across scientific and medical disciplines have led to a torrent of diverse, large-scale biomedical datasets such as health, imaging data, clinical notes, lab test results, and other 'omics data. The dropping costs of genomic sequencing coupled with advances in computing allow unprecedented opportunities to understand the effects of genetics on human disease etiologies and has resulted in the creation of population-level biobanks like the Million Veteran Program[1], UKBioBank[2], PennBioBank[3]. As a consequence, the demand for novel computational methods, computational infrastructure, and algorithm improvements to efficiently process and derive insights from these datasets, particularly where it applies to clinical translational research, has dramatically increased. In addition to handling the sheer size and quantity of biomedical data, newly developed methods must also adapt and employ state-of-the-art AI algorithms that account for the unique complexities of biomedical datasets, such as sparseness, incompleteness, and noisiness of data, data multidimensionality such as clinical measurements from electronic health records, prescription drug data, environmental exposures. Additionally, these methods have to leverage the advances in high-performance computing like GPUs, faster inter-connects, and fast-access memory to help generate the needed insights at a faster rate.

The recent explosion of high-throughput experimental techniques for generating biological 'omics datasets (e.g., genomic, transcriptomic, or metabolomic) has led to a specific set of challenges related to the integration of biomedical with multi-omics data and second to the analysis of these integrated datasets. To begin to model complex phenotypic traits, modern statistical and machine learning methods must now draw from various datasets with diverse origins, such as from analogous data across multiple model organisms or from complementary data within the same species. It leads to challenges stemming from integrating biomedical and multi-omics data, including challenges related to the identification, visualization, and reproducibility of patterns elucidated from integrated datasets.

Data-intensive computing has firmly established itself as the fourth paradigm in scientific discovery. Advances in computing have propelled discovery in many physical sciences (cosmology, high energy physics, aerospace, to name a few). The data-intensive nature of computational problems in medicine and biomedical informatics warrants the use and development of advanced computing infrastructure and software methods. In recent years, advances in computational infrastructure, methods, and algorithms enabled storage and analysis of large-scale datasets (e.g., Exascale Computing Project, Cloud Computing, ESNet)[4]. These advances have created silos of excellence, and scientific discovery propelled by computation has been driven by computationally well-endowed groups. Though distributed computing in the cloud can dramatically improve the performance of complex computational analyses by reducing runtime and local storage requirements, it is still severely limited by the availability of cloud-compatible software packages. Gaps also exist for these packages to leverage supercomputing capabilities.

To address this, we invited experts leading the development and application of artificial intelligence and cutting-edge computing approaches to drive innovation in precision medicine. We discussed current breakthroughs in which our speakers are involved and the strengths and limitations of artificial intelligence in medicine. Our workshop session focused on four major domains of AI and computing 1) AI in Healthcare 2) Genomics in medicine 4) Exascale computing to advance precision medicine.

2. Workshop Presenters

The three-hour workshop will begin with an overview presentation of the workshop followed by four presentations. The workshop will conclude with a panel discussion session, which will be moderated by Drs. Torkamani and Verma.

2.1. Workshop Speakers

2.1.1. Rick Stevens, PhD - Rick Stevens is the Associate Laboratory Director of the Computing, Environment and Life Sciences Directorate at Argonne National Laboratory, and a Professor of Computer Science at the University of Chicago, with significant responsibility in delivering on the U.S. national initiative for Exascale computing and developing the DOE initiative in Artificial Intelligence (AI) for Science. At Argonne, Rick leads the Laboratory's AI for Science initiative and currently focusing on high-performance computing systems which includes leading a significant collaboration with Intel and Cray to launch Argonne's first exascale computer, Aurora 21, which will pursue some of the farthest-reaching science and engineering breakthroughs ever achieved with supercomputing, as well as a partnership with Cerebras Systems to bring hardware on site to advance the massive deep learning experiments being pursued at Argonne for basic and applied science and medicine with supercompute-scale AI. Stevens' research spans the computational and computer sciences from high-performance computing, to the building of innovative tools and techniques for biological science and infectious disease research as well approaches to advance deep learning to accelerate cancer research. He also specializes in high-performance computing, collaborative visualization technology, and grid computing. Currently, he is the PI of the Bacterial / Viral Bioinformatics Resource Center (BV-BRC) which is developing comparative analysis tools for infectious disease research and serves a large user community; the Exascale Deep Learning and Simulation Enabled Precision Medicine for Cancer project through the Exascale Computing Project (ECP), which focuses on building a scalable deep neural network application called the CANcer Distributed Learning Environment (CANDLE); the Predictive Modeling for Pre-Clinical Screening (Pilot 1) of the DOE-NCI Joint Design of Advanced Computing Solutions for Cancer (JDACS4C) project; and the Co-design of Advanced Artificial Intelligence (AI) Systems project focused on predicting behavior of complex systems using multimodal datasets. Rick has won numerous awards for his work, including two R&D 100 Awards and an HPCwire Readers' Choice Award. Rick was elected a Fellow of the American Association for the Advancement of Science (AAAS) in 2003 and since then is a Fellow of the Institute of Electrical and Electronics Engineers (IEEE) in IEEE Computer Society, an ACM Fellow and a member of the Association for Automated Reasoning and the Association for Symbolic Logic

2.1.2. **Marylyn Ritchie, PhD** - Dr. Ritchie is a Professor of Genetics and Director of the Institute for Biomedical Informatics at the University of Pennsylvania School of Medicine. She is also Associate Director of the Penn Center for Precision Medicine, Director of the Center for Translational Bioinformatics, and Co-Director of the Penn Medicine BioBank. Dr. Ritchie is an expert in translational bioinformatics, with a focus on developing, applying, and disseminating algorithms, methods, and tools integrating electronic health records (EHR) with genomics. Dr. Ritchie has over 20 years of experience in translational bioinformatics and has authored over 375 publications. Dr. Ritchie was appointed a Fellow of the American College of Medical Informatics (ACMI) in 2020. Dr. Ritchie was elected as a member of the National Academy of Medicine in 2021; she is being recognized "for paradigm-changing research demonstrating the utility of electronic health records for identifying clinical diseases or phenotypes that can be integrated with genomic data from biobanks for genomic medicine discovery and implementation science." Dr. Ritchie holds a Ph.D. from Vanderbilt University in Statistical Genetics, an M.S. from Vanderbilt University in Applied Statistics, and a B.S. in Biology from the University of Pittsburgh at Johnstown. Dr. Ritchie is also the host of two podcasts: she co-hosts The Biomedical Informatics Roundtable podcast with Dr. Jason Moore and the solo host of The CALM Podcast: Combining Academia and Life with Marylyn.

2.1.3. **Ravi Madduri -** Ravi is a computer scientist in the Data Science and Learning division at Argonne National Laboratory and is Senior Scientist at the Center of Research Computing at the University of Chicago. He is an innovation fellow at the Polsky Center of Entrepreneurship at University of Chicago. Ravi led several successful large projects in NSF, NIH and DOE. His research interests are in building sustainable, scalable services for science, reproducible research, large-scale data management and analysis. He co-leads the MVP-CHAMPION project, which is a collaboration between VA and DOE and developed methods to perform large-scale genetic data analysis using DOE's high performance computing capabilities, including methods for generating PRS scores in Prostate Cancer, genome-wide PheWAS on Summit supercomputer. Additionally, Ravi is one of three key contributors to the National Institutes of Health $100M Cancer Biomedical Informatics Grid (caBIG), which linked 60 NIH-funded cancer centers and clinical sites engaged in cancer research. For his efforts in project management, tool development, and collaboration, Ravi received several Outstanding Achievement Awards from NIH. Ravi led the design and implementation of scientific and high-performance workflows under the caGrid toolkit. Ravi leads the Globus Genomics project (www.globusgenomics.org), which is used by thousands of researchers across the world for genomics, proteomics, and other biomedical computations on Amazon cloud and other platforms. He architected the Globus Galaxies platform that underpins Globus Genomics and several other cloud-based gateways realizing the vision of Science as a Service for creating, maintaining sustainable services for science. Ravi plays an important role in applying large-scale data analysis, deep learning to problems in biology. For his work on "Cancer Moonshot" project, he received the Department of Energy Secretary award in 2017.

2.1.4. **Jessilyn Dunn, PhD -** Dr. Dunn, is Assistant Professor in the Department of Biomedical Engineering at Duke University. She works on developing new tools and infrastructure for multi-modal biomedical data integration to drive precision/personalized methods for early detection, intervention, and prevention of disease. She leverages expertise in data science, engineering, informatics, medicine, biological sciences, and population health. Her works has direct implication by arming healthcare professionals with tools and information to detect illness and intervene early and to deliver the right treatment at the right time to the right person. Dr. Dunn received Ph.D. in Biomedical Engineering from Georgia Institute of Technology in 2015.

2.2. Panel Moderators

2.2.1. **Ali Torkmani PhD.** Dr. Torkamani is the Director of Genomics and Genome Informatics at the Scripps Research Translational Institute and Professor at The Scripps Research Institute. Dr. Torkamani's research centers on the use of genomic and informatics technologies to identify the genetic etiology and underlying mechanisms of human disease to define health risks and individualized interventions. Major focus areas include human genome interpretation, genomic discovery of novel rare diseases, comprehensive, genetically-informed machine- and deep-learning prediction of risk for common diseases, and digital communication of genetically-informed disease risk. He has authored over 100 peer-reviewed publications as well as numerous book chapters and Medscape references, and his research has been highlighted in the popular press. Dr. Torkamani's overall vision is to decipher that code in order to understand and predict interventions that restore diseased individuals to their personal health baseline.

2.2.2. **Anurag Verma PhD.** Dr. Verma is an Instructor in the Department of Medicine at the University of Pennsylvania and Associate Director of Clinical Informatics and Genomics for Penn Medicine BioBank. His research has focused on the study of the genetic basis of complex diseases using big data techniques with the main focus of studying the genetic architecture of multimorbidity, the phenotypic architecture of common genetic risk, polygenic risk scores, and phenome-wide association studies to identify the complex phenotypic and genomic interactions that lead to complex disease. He has biomedical informatics expertise in the integration of genetic data with electronic health records (EHRs) from large biobanks, with extensive experience in analyzing large biobank datasets, including Penn Medicine BioBank, Million Veteran Program, Geisinger MyCode, and eMERGE network.

2.2.3. **Jennifer Huffman PhD.** Dr. Huffman is a member of the Faculty for the Department of Medicine at Harvard Medical School and the Scientific Director for Genomics Research within the Center for Population Genomics at the VA Boston Healthcare System. She is currently an investigator with the VA Million Veteran Program. She leads research investigations into the genetic contributions to cardiovascular risk factors and coordinates and implements several infrastructure programs for the program. This has also allowed her to actively participate in several collaborations with statisticians and computer scientists to improve analyzing "big data" methods.

References

1. Gaziano, J. M. *et al.* Million Veteran Program: A mega-biobank to study genetic influences on health and disease. *J. Clin. Epidemiol.* **70**, 214–223 (2016).

2. Sudlow, C. *et al.* UK Biobank: An Open Access Resource for Identifying the Causes of a Wide Range of Complex Diseases of Middle and Old Age. *PLOS Med.* **12**, e1001779 (2015).

3. Kember, R. L. *et al.* *Polygenic Risk Scores for Cardio-renal-metabolic Diseases in the Penn Medicine Biobank.* http://biorxiv.org/lookup/doi/10.1101/759381 (2019) doi:10.1101/759381.

4. Tansley, Stewart, and Kristin Michele Tolle. The fourth paradigm: data-intensive scientific discovery. Ed. Anthony JG Hey. Vol. 1. Redmond, WA: Microsoft research, 2009.

Risk prediction: Methods, Challenges, and Opportunities

Ruowang Li
Department of Computational Biomedicine, Cedars-Sinai Medical Center, West Hollywood, California, USA
Email: ruowang.li@cshs.org

Rui Duan
Department of Biostatistics, Harvard T.H. Chan School of Public Health, Boston, Massachusetts, USA
Email: rduan@hsph.harvard.edu

Lifang He
Department of Computer Science and Engineering, Lehigh University, Bethlehem, Pennsylvania, USA
Email: lih319@lehigh.edu

Jason H. Moore
Department of Computational Biomedicine, Cedars-Sinai Medical Center, West Hollywood, California, USA
Email: jason.moore@csmc.edu

The primary efforts of disease and epidemiological research can be divided into two areas: identifying the causal mechanisms and utilizing important variables for risk prediction. The latter is generally perceived as a more obtainable goal due to the vast number of readily available tools and the faster pace of obtaining results. However, the lower barrier of entry in risk prediction means that it is easy to make predictions, yet it is incredibility more difficult to make sound predictions. As an ever-growing amount of data is being generated, developing risk prediction models and turning them into clinically actionable findings is crucial as the next step. However, there are still sizable gaps before risk prediction models can be implemented clinically. While clinicians are eager to embrace new ways to improve patients' care, they are overwhelmed by a plethora of prediction methods. Thus, the next generation of prediction models will need to shift from making simple predictions towards interpretable, equitable, explainable and ultimately, casual predictions.

Keywords: Risk Prediction; Methodology; AutoML, Explainable Artificial Intelligence, Federated Learning, Model Interpretation.

1. Introduction

The purpose of this workshop is to introduce and discuss the current and future of risk prediction in the context of disease and epidemiological research. We will discuss the pressing topics ranging from data sources to model implementation. Our speakers will discuss the most commonly used data sources, e.g., genetics, imaging, clinical, and epidemiological data, for developing the prediction models. A number of novel risk prediction methods, including automatic machine learning (AutoML), explainable artificial intelligence (XAI), and polygenic risk score, will be presented. Issues regarding how to handle the high dimensionality of the features will be discussed from the perspective of accuracy and computational scalability. Data privacy considerations during the construction and dissemination of prediction models will be addressed. Furthermore, model-based and post-hoc analysis of prediction models, including the biases and uncertainty quantification, model interpretation, and fairness and diversity of the prediction results, transferability and generalizability of the models to different populations and datasets will be thoroughly discussed. Finally, the current progress and future perspective regarding the validation and clinical implementation of the risk prediction models will be reviewed.

2. Machine learning

Recent advances in machine learning (ML) methods, combined with the rapidly increasing availability of healthcare data, forebode an avalanche of explorations of ML in medical research. Since risk prediction tasks constitute a large portion of the applications of ML in medicine, knowledge on how to develop, implement and evaluate risk prediction models, as well as interpret the results on their basis is critical for enhancing the model quality, transparency, trust and for decreasing the instances of bias. This workshop provides a roadmap to help refine and enhance understanding of risk prediction and assessment by focusing on all stages of developing and validating risk prediction models.

2.1 Automatic Machine Learning

One of the many challenges of machine learning is the selection of the method to use and the tuning of its hyperparameters. This is a challenge for both experts and beginners because there are dozens of methods and each looks at the data in a different way. It is difficult to know which method is most appropriate when using machine learning to develop risk models. Automated machine learning (AutoML) seeks to address this issue by exploring a wide range of models and hyperparameters with minimal user input. Maduchi et al. (2022) recently reviewed automated machine learning for the genetic analysis of complex traits. One of these methods, the Tree-Base Pipeline Optimization Tool (TPOT), has been applied to genomics data (Le et al. 2020) and uses expression trees to represent machine learning pipelines with operators including feature selectors, feature transformers, feature engineering algorithms, and a wide range of machine learning algorithms all available from the sci-kit learning library. Pipelines are explored and optimized using genetic programming with multi-objective optimization and cross-validation to limit overfitting. Manduchi et al. (2022) demonstrate the application of TPOT to the genetic analysis of coronary artery disease (CAD) using genome-wide association study (GWAS) data from UK Biobank. A central focus of this study was prioritizing genes based on their druggability and pharmacologic relevance to CAD. The TPOT algorithm was able to automatically identify an optimal machine learning pipeline for predicting CAD with evidence of genetic heterogeneity revealed by feature importance score methods. This study is used as an example to demonstrate the potential for AuoML to inform the development of genetic risk models for common disease.

3. Statistical modeling

Statistical modeling plays an important role in risk prediction, which has a broad application in clinical science, epidemiology, and health services. With the growing availability and variety of real-world healthcare data sources, such as claims data and electronic health records, there are emerging statistical challenges that need to be addressed for constructing more reliable and generalizable risk prediction tools. In this workshop, we discuss advanced statistical methods that address the following challenges (1) prediction models with limited and imperfect labels (2) building risk prediction models for underrepresented populations with limited data (3) combining data from multiple sources to improve the generalizability and transferability of risk prediction models. In addition to the methods, we will also discuss the theoretical insights and examples of potential real-world applications.

4. Conclusion

Our workshop puts an even focus on all stages of developing and validating risk prediction models. Rather than focusing exclusively on the methodologies, we believe by structuring a more balanced workshop theme, the speakers and the audiences will have more opportunities to exchange ideas and viewpoints. Discussion sessions would also be employed to break up the talks and to provide a venue for general dialog around themes that have evolved from the lectures.

References

1. Manduchi E, Romano JD, Moore JH. The promise of automated machine learning for the genetic analysis of complex traits. Hum Genet. 2022 Sep;141(9):1529-1544.

2. Manduchi E, Le TT, Fu W, Moore JH. Genetic Analysis of Coronary Artery Disease Using Tree-Based Automated Machine Learning Informed By Biology-Based Feature Selection. IEEE/ACM Trans Comput Biol Bioinform. 2022 May-Jun;19(3):1379-1386.

3. Le TT, Fu W, Moore JH. Scaling tree-based automated machine learning to biomedical big data with a feature set selector. Bioinformatics. 2020 Jan 1;36(1):250-256.

Single Cell Spatial Biology for Precision Cancer Medicine

Andrew J. Gentles
Department of Pathology, Stanford University
Stanford, CA 94305, USA
Email: andrewg@stanford.edu

Ajit J. Nirmal
Department of Medical Oncology, Dana-Farber Cancer Institute
Boston, MA 02215, USA
Email: AjitJ_Nirmal@dfci.harvard.edu

Laura M. Heiser
Department of Biomedical Engineering, Oregon Health & Science University
Portland, OR 97239, USA
Email: heiserl@ohsu.edu

Emma Lundberg
Department of Bioengineering, Department of Pathology, Stanford University
Stanford, CA 94305, USA
Email: emmalu@stanford.edu

Aaron M. Newman
Department of Biomedical Data Science, Stanford University
Stanford, CA 94305, USA
Email: amnewman@stanford.edu

In cancer, complex ecosystems of interacting cell types play fundamental roles in tumor development, progression, and response to therapy. However, the cellular organization, community structure, and spatially defined microenvironments of human tumors remain poorly understood. With the emergence of new technologies for high-throughput spatial profiling of complex tissue specimens, it is now possible to identify clinically significant spatial features with high granularity. In this PSB workshop, we will highlight recent advances in this area and explore how single cell spatial profiling can advance precision cancer medicine.

Keywords: Spatial biology, spatial transcriptomics, machine learning, artificial intelligence, cancer biology, precision medicine

1. Introduction, Background, and Motivation

Maps are indispensable tools for understanding and navigating our world. While the earliest maps had limited resolution, in recent decades, we have witnessed an explosion in the scale, scope, and complexity of digital mapping data. Today, large fleets of satellites perform high resolution geospatial surveys at a global scale, while smartphones and wearables provide a nearly "limitless" supply of real-time physiological data with spatial coordinates. Significant advances in spatial mapping technology have permeated other areas as well, including biology – where, for example, the IMAXT project (one of Cancer Research UK's Grand Challenges) is currently building the first 3D virtual reality map of a tumor.

Within biology in particular, technologies for mapping spatial organization are in the midst of a revolution. In 2020, *Nature Methods* highlighted "Spatially Resolved Transcriptomics" as the method of the year[1]. However, existing platforms for spatial biology are highly heterogeneous. For example, single-cell proteomic assays, such as cyclic immunofluorescence, CODEX, molecular ion beam imaging (MIBI), and imaging mass cytometry (IMC) are capable of cellular, or even sub-cellular, regional analysis but are limited to joint profiling of tens to hundreds of preselected proteins. Likewise, commercially available platforms for profiling single-cell mRNA expression in spatial dimensions, such as MERSCOPE (Vizgen) and CosMx (NanoString), are limited to preselected genes. In contrast, Visium (10x Genomics) and GeoMX (NanoString) can recover the entire transcriptome, but at lower spatial resolution. Clearly, such differences, along with the complexity of the data generated by each assay, require sophisticated analytical solutions. Moreover, while current platforms are predominantly limited to two-dimensional profiles, 3D, 4D (spatiotemporal), and even multiomic analysis capabilities are on the horizon, driving the need for increasingly powerful and scalable computational methods.

Previous PSB workshops have emphasized the importance of translational bioinformatics and precision medicine, however none have focused on the computational and analytical challenges underpinning spatial transcriptomics and proteomics. In this workshop, we will explore and highlight recent advances in this burgeoning arena, with an emphasis on cancer. As one of the major beneficiaries of spatial profiling technologies, cancer research has advanced considerably in recent years through meticulous cell atlasing and spatial profiling efforts[2-13]. For example, using MIBI to analyze 36 proteins in 41 triple negative breast cancers, Keren et al.[6] identified immune-mixed and immune-compartmentalized tumors. In the latter, the immunoregulatory protein PD1 was generally expressed on CD4 T cells, whereas in the former, PD1 was largely expressed on CD8 T cells. Moreover, compartmentalized tumors showed distinct immune structures at the tumor boundary that predicted longer survival time. These findings offer potential insights into why PD1 expression is not a reliable biomarker for response to immune checkpoint inhibition.

This workshop will cover computational aspects of multiplexed imaging, spatial transcriptomics, and platform integration (e.g., alignment of single-cell and spatial transcriptomics), with an emphasis on basic and translational cancer research. Our goal is to stimulate new ideas, foster critical debate, and form new collaborations in this exciting and challenging research area.

2. Speaker Abstracts

Atlas of clinically distinct cell states and ecosystems across human solid tumors

Andrew J. Gentles

Tumors are complex ecosystems consisting of malignant, immune, and stromal elements whose dynamic interactions drive patient survival and response to therapy. A comprehensive understanding of the diversity of cellular states within the tumor microenvironment (TME), and their patterns of co-occurrence, could provide new diagnostic tools for improved disease management and novel targets for therapeutic intervention. To address this challenge, we developed EcoTyper, a novel machine learning framework for large-scale identification of TME cell states and their co-association patterns from bulk, single-cell, and spatially resolved tumor expression data. Applied to over 6k tumor and adjacent normal samples from solid tumor types profiled by The Cancer Genome Atlas (TCGA), EcoTyper identified robust transcriptional states across 12 major cell types, including epithelial, fibroblast, endothelial, and 9 immune subsets. These states included both known and novel cellular phenotypes, nearly all of which could be validated in a compendium of scRNA-seq tumor atlases. For example, EcoTyper recapitulated the transcriptional profiles of M1 and M2 polarized macrophages, along with 7 other macrophage states. Most cell states were specific to neoplastic tissue, ubiquitous across tumor types, and significantly associated with overall survival, both in TCGA and in over 10k held-out tumor specimens. We found that specific cell states co-occur in distinct cellular communities with characteristic patterns of ligand-receptor interactions, genomic features, clinical outcomes, and spatial organization. One such ecosystem defined a normal-like state that was strongly enriched in non-malignant samples. Others delineated novel pro- and anti-tumor inflammatory environments involving specific fibroblast, endothelial, and immune cell transcriptional programs. In summary, large-scale deconvolution of cell type-specific transcriptomes across thousands of solid tumors revealed a comprehensive atlas of TME cell states and cellular ecosystems. Our results provide a high-resolution portrait of cellular heterogeneity in the TME across multiple solid tumor types, with implications for novel diagnostics and immunotherapeutic targets.

The spatial landscape of progression and immunoediting in primary melanoma at single-cell resolution

Ajit J. Nirmal

Cutaneous melanoma is a highly immunogenic malignancy, surgically curable at early stages, but life-threatening when metastatic. The spatial organization of the tumor ecosystem during early-stage melanoma is not well understood. Here we integrate high-plex imaging, 3D high-resolution microscopy, and spatially resolved micro-region transcriptomics to study immune evasion and immunoediting in primary melanoma. We collected highly multiplexed single-cell data from 70 distinct histological regions from 13 specimens (patients) selected to have multiple progression-associated histologies within a single resection. These histologies range from pre-malignant fields in which melanocytic atypia represents the first steps in cancer initiation to non-invasive (radial growth phase) and invasive (vertical growth phase) primary melanoma that eventually gives rise to disseminated disease. We find that recurrent cellular neighborhoods involving tumor, immune, and stromal cells change significantly along a progression axis involving precursor states, melanoma in situ, and primary invasive tumor. Hallmarks of immunosuppression were detectable as early as the melanoma precursor stage, and when tumors become locally invasive, a consolidated and spatially restricted environment with multiple overlapping immunosuppressive mechanisms forms along the tumor-stromal boundary. This environment is established by cytokine gradients that promote expression of MHC-II and IDO1 and by PDL1-expressing macrophages and dendritic cells engaging activated T cells. However, only a few millimeters away, T cells synapse with melanoma cells in fields of tumor regression. Thus, invasion and immunoediting can co-exist within a few millimeters of each other in a single specimen. Multiplexed single-cell imaging and micro-region mRNA profiling link morphological and molecular features of tumor evolution within and across primary cancer specimens, revealing highly localized programs of immune and tumor cell communication via paracrine cytokine signaling and direct cell-cell contact.

Systems approach to target tumor ecosystem responses for therapeutic benefit
Laura M. Heiser
Breast tumors arise and progress via processes that involve intrinsic deregulation of epithelial cells and that also alter the composition and function of associated stromal and immune cells. Together, these tumor-intrinsic and microenvironmental changes enable malignant epithelial cells in the tumor to acquire key cancer hallmarks, including proliferation, migration, immune evasion and further evolution. The resulting collection of cancer and stromal cells comprise a complex, adaptive tumor ecosystem. Dr Heiser will discuss how multiple tissue imaging was used to test the hypothesis that treatment strategies designed to simultaneously attack cancer cell state vulnerabilities and promote anti-tumor microenvironments may lead to deeper therapeutic responses in patients. To examine therapeutic responses of diverse aspects of the tumor ecosystem, they deployed a novel drug delivery microdevice that enables rapid, high-throughput assessment of the effects of multiple therapies on tumor cells and the surrounding microenvironment. When coupled with multiplex tissue imaging, this platform provides a comprehensive assessment of the state and spatial organization of the tumor ecosystem as it adapts to therapy. These studies demonstrated that many drugs designed to target malignant epithelial cells strongly impact stromal and immune cells, providing new insights into the importance of considering multiple aspects of the tumor ecosystem when designing effective therapeutic strategies. Together, this integrated experimental-computational approaches have provided insights into adaptive responses of diverse components of the tumor ecosystem that can be targeted to improve therapeutic responses.

Mapping the spatiotemporal proteome architecture of human cells
Emma Lundberg
Biological systems are functionally defined by the nature, amount, and spatial location of the totality of their proteins. We have generated an image-based map of the subcellular distribution of the human proteome, showing that there is great complexity to the subcellular organization of the cell. As much as half of all proteins localize to multiple compartments, giving rise to potential pleiotropic effects, and around 20% of the human proteome shows spatiotemporal variability. Their temporal mapping results shows that cell cycle progression explains less than half of all temporal protein variability, and that most cycling proteins are regulated post-translationally, rather than by transcriptomic cycling. This work is critically dependent on computational image analysis, and we will discuss machine learning approaches for classification of spatial subcellular patterns and how such embeddings can be used to build multi-scale models of cell architecture. We will also demonstrate the importance of spatial proteomics data for improved single cell biology and present how the freely available Human Protein Atlas database (www.proteinatlas.org) can be used as a resource for life science.

Robust alignment of single cell and spatial transcriptomes with CytoSPACE
Aaron M. Newman
Spatial transcriptomics is a powerful tool for delineating spatial gene expression in primary tissue specimens. However, commonly used platforms such as 10x Visium currently rely on bulk gene expression measurements, whereas single-cell spatial expression platforms such as Vizgen MERSCOPE have low gene recovery. To overcome these challenges, we developed CytoSPACE, a robust and efficient computational method for optimally aligning single-cell and spatial transcriptomes into a reconstructed tissue specimen at single-cell resolution. Across multiple

benchmarking experiments, CytoSPACE outperforms previous methods with respect to noise tolerance and accuracy. Using diverse examples spanning mouse brain regions, mouse kidney, and human tumors, we illustrate the ability and versatility of CytoSPACE to enable exciting new discoveries that are not obtainable from competing methods or from scRNA-seq or spatial platforms alone.

References

1 Method of the Year 2020: spatially resolved transcriptomics. *Nature Methods* **18**, 1-1, doi:10.1038/s41592-020-01042-x (2021).

2 Grunwald, B. T. *et al.* Spatially confined sub-tumor microenvironments in pancreatic cancer. *Cell* **184**, 5577-5592 e5518, doi:10.1016/j.cell.2021.09.022 (2021).

3 Hunter, M. V., Moncada, R., Weiss, J. M., Yanai, I. & White, R. M. Spatially resolved transcriptomics reveals the architecture of the tumor-microenvironment interface. *Nat Commun* **12**, 6278, doi:10.1038/s41467-021-26614-z (2021).

4 Jackson, H. W. *et al.* The single-cell pathology landscape of breast cancer. *Nature* **578**, 615-620, doi:10.1038/s41586-019-1876-x (2020).

5 Ji, A. L. *et al.* Multimodal Analysis of Composition and Spatial Architecture in Human Squamous Cell Carcinoma. *Cell* **182**, 497-514 e422, doi:10.1016/j.cell.2020.05.039 (2020).

6 Keren, L. *et al.* A Structured Tumor-Immune Microenvironment in Triple Negative Breast Cancer Revealed by Multiplexed Ion Beam Imaging. *Cell* **174**, 1373-1387 e1319, doi:10.1016/j.cell.2018.08.039 (2018).

7 Luca, B. A. *et al.* Atlas of clinically distinct cell states and ecosystems across human solid tumors. *Cell* **184**, 5482-5496 e5428, doi:10.1016/j.cell.2021.09.014 (2021).

8 Mahdessian, D. *et al.* Spatiotemporal dissection of the cell cycle with single-cell proteogenomics. *Nature* **590**, 649-654, doi:10.1038/s41586-021-03232-9 (2021).

9 Moncada, R. *et al.* Integrating microarray-based spatial transcriptomics and single-cell RNA-seq reveals tissue architecture in pancreatic ductal adenocarcinomas. *Nat Biotechnol* **38**, 333-342, doi:10.1038/s41587-019-0392-8 (2020).

10 Nirmal, A. J. *et al.* The Spatial Landscape of Progression and Immunoediting in Primary Melanoma at Single-Cell Resolution. *Cancer Discovery* **12**, 1518-1541, doi:10.1158/2159-8290.Cd-21-1357 (2022).

11 Schurch, C. M. *et al.* Coordinated Cellular Neighborhoods Orchestrate Antitumoral Immunity at the Colorectal Cancer Invasive Front. *Cell* **182**, 1341-1359 e1319, doi:10.1016/j.cell.2020.07.005 (2020).

12 Vahid, M. R. *et al.* Robust alignment of single-cell and spatial transcriptomes with CytoSPACE. *bioRxiv*, 2022.2005.2020.488356, doi:10.1101/2022.05.20.488356 (2022).

13 Wu, S. Z. *et al.* A single-cell and spatially resolved atlas of human breast cancers. *Nat Genet* **53**, 1334-1347, doi:10.1038/s41588-021-00911-1 (2021).

ERRATUM

Separating Clinical and Subclinical Depression by Big Data Informed Structural Vulnerability Index and Its impact on Cognition: ENIGMA Dot Product

Peter Kochunov PhD[1] and Yizhou Ma PhD[1]

1. Maryland Psychiatric Research Center, Department of Psychiatry, University of Maryland School of Medicine, Baltimore, MD, USA
Email: pkochunov@som.umaryland.edu and yizhou.ma@som.umaryland.edu

Kathryn S. Hatch BS[1], Si Gao MS[1], Lianne Schmaal PhD[2,3], Neda Jahanshad PhD[4], Paul M. Thompson PhD[4], Bhim M. Adhikari PhD[1], Heather Bruce MD[1], Joshua Chiappelli MD[1], Andrew Van der vaart MD, PhD[1], Eric L. Goldwaser DO, PhD[1], Aris Sotiras PhD[5], Tianzhou Ma PhD[6], Shuo Chen, PhD[1], Thomas E. Nichols PhD[7], L. Elliot Hong MD[1]

2. Centre for Youth Mental Health, The University of Melbourne, Melbourne, Australia
3. Orygen, Parkville, Australia
4. Imaging Genetics Center, Keck School of Medicine, Marina del Rey, CA, USA
5. Institute of Informatics, University of Washington, School of Medicine, St. Louis, Missouri, USA
6. Department of Epidemiology and Biostatistics, University of Maryland, College Park, MD, USA
7. Nuffield Department of Population Health of the University of Oxford, Oxford, United Kingdom.

In the above PSB article published in *Biocomputing 2022: Proceedings of the Pacific Symposium*, pp. 133-143; doi: 10.1142/9789811250477_0013 (https://www.ncbi.nlm.nih.gov/pmc/articles/PMC8719281/), the following author name is missing: *Si Gao MS*

www.ingramcontent.com/pod-product-compliance
Lightning Source LLC
LaVergne TN
LVHW010323220926
848484LV00004BB/836